Ted Smith

Mac Online!

Making the Connection

Mac Online!
Making the Connection

Carla Rose

Windcrest®/McGraw-Hill

FIRST EDITION
FIRST PRINTING

Library of Congress Cataloging-in-Publication Data

Rose, Carla.
Mac online : making the connection / by Carla Rose.
p. cm.
Includes index.
ISBN 0-8306-4254-4
1. Communications software. 2. Modems. 3. Data transmission systems. I. Title.
TK5105.9.R67 1992
044.6′165—dc20 92-24076
CIP

Acquisitions Editor: Brad Schepp
Editor: Tracey May
Book Design: Jaclyn J. Boone
Cover Design: Sandra Blair Design, Harrisburg, Pa.
Cover Illustration: Margaret Brandt, Harrisburg, Pa. WR1

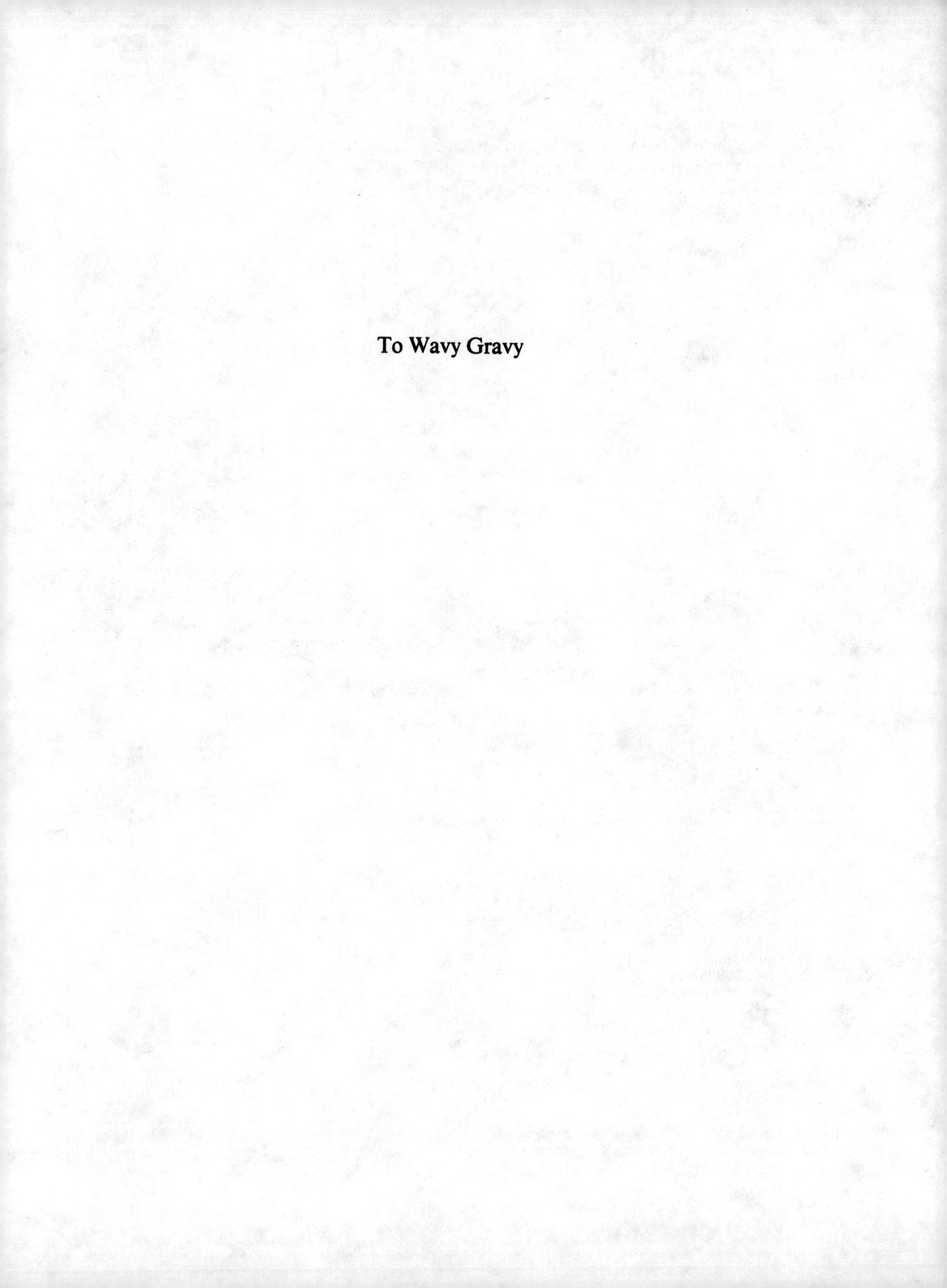

To Wavy Gravy

Contents

PART TWO

COMPARING THE SERVICES

Introduction
The world online

The following are some examples of how online services can be used. These are real people; folks who have discovered how to have more fun and get more satisfaction from their Macs by hooking up a modem and "going online."

- Danny, a high school student, looks up information about the French and Indian Wars. (America Online, *Compton's Encyclopedia*)
- Lawyer Fred is preparing a case and looks for relevant decisions. (Lexis)
- Ellen and her friends play high-stakes Texas Hold 'Em almost every night of the week. (Delphi, Poker)
- Josh writes home from college, sometimes several times a day! (MCI Mail)
- Lois, a poet, participates in a weekly critique with a half dozen other writers. (Delphi, Writer's Conference)
- Steve checks the stock market and manages his investments. (DowJones Financial Network)
- Jan does her shopping and takes two college courses for credit. (Prodigy and University of Phoenix)
- Suzi and Matt "just talk." (GEnie, LiveWire Chat Lines)

With a Mac, a telephone, and a modem to connect you, you can go online and have a world of information and entertainment at your fingertips, as well as instant communication with friends, family, and business associates from all corners of the globe. Ellen's poker buddies are in Boston, Los Angeles, and half a dozen other cities far from her home in Little Rock. Suzi, in Flagstaff, Arizona, chats with Matt in Reykjavik, Iceland. Fred, Steve, and Danny are checking various databases in Cambridge, Columbus, and Princeton.

Why go online?

Sure, you could do research at your local library, even get a group of friends to play cards around the kitchen table, but telecommunication adds another dimension to ordinary activities. It broadens your horizons and makes you a full-fledged citizen of what Buckminster Fuller was first to call the "Global Village."

On a more practical level, telecommunication is convenient. More than a dozen different commercial information services exist, and most are online 24 hours a day, every day of the year. The facts and figures you need are there when you need them, not just when the library's open. It's fast, too; you're just a phone call away from whatever you need to know. You can shop, plan a vacation or business trip, or pay your bills without leaving home. You don't have to fight traffic or look for a place to park. Sending E-mail messages means you need never play telephone tag or try to leave a coherent 30-second message on an answering machine. Most of all, it's fun. No matter what your interest, you can find people who share it, if not on one of the commercial services, then on one of the estimated 30,000 free-or-low-cost bulletin boards run by computer enthusiasts, user groups, schools, or private companies throughout the United States.

Online services have up-to-the-minute information on everything from aardvarks to zyzygy. Special interest groups cover topics as diverse as scuba diving, wine tasting, and fire fighting. Members of these groups are happy to answer your questions and talk about their topics. Online databases contain references and abstracts from thousands of periodicals and newspapers. Books in Print and the Magazine Index let online users do, in minutes, the same kind of bibliographic research that used to require hours in the library. Students can search online encyclopedias for all kinds of valuable information. Travelers can check airline schedules for convenient flights and lowest fares, order tickets, choose a hotel or condo at their destination, and even arrange for rental cars, theater tickets, and dinner reservations. In addition, travelers can read all about the city or country to which they are traveling, including its current weather. News and sports stories can reach your computer screen as quickly as they arrive at the editor's desk.

Got a problem with your Mac? There are many solutions waiting for you online. Check out your local user group's bulletin board for fast answers. Software updates are often available for downloading, and you can find people who have encountered the same problem and solved it. If not, then try the manufacturers' forums on America Online or GEnie. Over a hundred different software and hardware companies are represented online, and you can get speedy responses to your questions, as well as information on product updates and new releases.

Want to check out movie reviews, or find out how your favorite group's latest record is doing on the charts? Entertainment news is available on most online services. Would you like to play a game? You can find everything from tic-tac-toe to trivia to dozens of fantasy and role-playing games. Many of these games are played in real time against other live players, and you can chat with new friends as you compete for prizes or free online hours. You can also play games against the computer, and you can download whole libraries of games to your Mac to play as often as you like. If your head is in the stars, you can read your daily horoscope on Prodigy or GEnie, or keep track of the latest space shuttle launch courtesy of NASA.

Even though your Mac is designed to be "user-friendly," you might not think of it as a source for new friends. But when you add a modem and an online chat like Delphi's conference area or CompuServe's CB simulator, you will find yourself making friends all over the world. Conferences might be formal ones on specific topics or informal groups of old and new friends who just get together online to chat. Many couples have met first online, and gone on to meet and fall in love off line. Virtually every service boasts of marriages between members. Of course, if you'd rather fight than smooch, virtually all the services have free-wheeling debates on politics, sports, and current events. No matter what your opinion, you can find some people who agree and others who disagree. Some services invite special guests to "speak" online in a question-and-answer format. These guests might be representatives from software and computer companies, celebrities, or bestselling authors. Attending an online lecture is a fascinating way to keep in touch with the latest trends.

What else you can do by modem

Ordinarily, you use your telephone for many different purposes. You might call a friend to chat or phone the movie theater to find out what time the feature starts. Some calls are strictly business. Just as many ways exist to use your Mac and modem, too.

These days, the fax machine has become an office necessity. Haven't there been times when you've wished you could send faxes, without a fax machine, right from your desk? If you have a combination fax/modem, sending a fax directly from your Mac is as easy as printing a page of text. It's also faster and better looking, especially if you use Adobe Type Manager or System 7's TrueType, and doesn't waste paper because you don't need to print a copy to run it through a stand-alone fax machine. Some fax/modems can also receive faxes from both fax machines and other computers. Just as science fiction writers once predicted, it's now possible to send and receive documents that have never existed in anything other than electronic form.

Electronic mail, or E-mail, is another way to send a message, provided the recipient uses an E-mail service, too. It's easy, reliable, and inexpensive. If you're tired of playing long-distance telephone tag with a client or business associate in another time zone, E-mail is an easy solution. It's also a good way to keep in touch with busy friends and family members.

Interactive has long been a computer buzzword. With a modem, interactive gaming takes on a new meaning as you take on the challenge of playing against a live opponent by modem. RoboSport, BattleChess, and Armor Alley are just a few of the hottest new games you can play with your friends over the phone lines. Many games have Mac and PC versions of the same game, so you needn't confine yourself to playing only with Mac-using friends.

What this book is about

You need only three things to get started in telecommunications: hardware, software, and a telephone line. This book tells you how telecommunication works, and how to buy and use the right hardware and software. It also tells you where to go when you "go online," and how to make the most of your online time, whether you're on a pay-by-the-minute service or a free bulletin board system (BBS).

The first chapter looks inside the modem to show what makes it tick, hum, and whistle. I discuss the different kinds of modems and how to hook them up to your Mac and phone line.

Chapter 2 covers the software you need to make the hardware work. Many different kinds of terminal programs are available. I look at the most popular ones, both commercial and shareware, and give you some guidelines for choosing the best software for your needs.

Chapter 3 explains the mechanics of going online, such as setting up the parameters for communicating with another computer, dialing the call, and "logging on" to a service. I explain why you need a password and how to protect your passwords from discovery.

Chapter 4 can help you understand the structure of bulletin boards and online systems, so you can find your way around one without a road map. In this chapter, you can also learn about shortcuts for jumping from one area to another and some handy tools for viewing graphics online.

Chapter 5 unravels the secrets of E-mail systems. E-mail specialists, like MCI, and more complete services that include E-mail, like Prodigy and CompuServe, are available. There are even free mail services. Which is your best choice? I also tell you how you can send messages to many people at once, by posting your thoughts in a bulletin board or forum, and how to send instant messages to other users online.

Chapter 6 demystifies the process of sending files back and forth to other computers. After explaining the ups and downs of uploading and downloading, I talk about what kinds of files you can find online for downloading, how to shrink and expand files using data compression software, and what to do to guard against virus invasion.

In Chapter 7, you learn all about online conferences, including the special shorthand phrases and symbols, and the online rules of etiquette that separate "newbies" from old hands. You learn about "real-time" and play-by-mail games, SIGs, private and public groups, and the kinds of people you'll meet.

Chapter 8 discusses other things you can do online. I teach you some shortcuts for online research and what kinds of databases are available. This chapter also shows how to use the same airline- and hotel-booking system professional travel agents use and how to find the lowest fares. I show you where to go for all kinds of news and weather reports, stock quotations, and investment advice. Finally, go shopping online. The electronic malls are just as much fun as the real thing and a lot easier on your feet.

Chapter 9 explains how your Mac and modem can act as a fax machine to send your business and personal correspondence all over the world. I show you how to create good-looking pages, how to select the right fax/modem, and how to send a fax. I also discuss the most readable typefaces for faxing, attention-getting cover sheets, and ways to save money while faxing.

Because online services can be habit-forming and as expensive as those 900 numbers, chapter 10 looks at free services, such as user groups' bulletin board systems. I show you where to look for lists of boards in your area and special interest boards of all kinds. I also discuss starting your own BBS, such as where to get the software and how to join a network of other bulletin boards.

Chapter 11 is a guide to Remote Access. If you need a file that's in another Mac, and both have modems and remote access software, you can simply call and upload it. You can also work on shared files and update the current versions of documents on file servers or other Macs. This chapter explains how to use Apple's Remote Access or third-party programs like Farallon Timbuktu Remote. It also shows how to use a modem or local AppleTalk network for game playing and software sharing.

Part 2 of the book is a comprehensive guide to the major online services, including the pros and cons of each, the cost of joining, and how to get the most for your money every time you log on. My goal is not to rate the services, but to give you enough information about each one that you can decide for yourself which will best suit your needs. The online world is a fascinating one, full of new places to explore, new things to learn, and new friends to meet. Log on and join the fun!

1
The little box that makes it possible

Way back in kindergarten, we learned that it's polite to share. In the world of computers and modems, sharing information is not only polite, it makes your Mac a lot more useful, and it's fun. Sharing data can be accomplished in a number of ways. You can put your information on a disk and mail it to another Mac user or send printed versions of your files. Of course, depending on the postal service where you live or the whims of the various express mail companies, it might take anywhere from one to five days to get the file delivered. If you are in a hurry to get a message from one city to another, you'll reach for the telephone instead; it's much faster.

If you're in a hurry to transfer information from one computer to another, it's also much faster to use the telephone. Of course, you can't just plug the computer into the telephone and let'er rip. Telephones are designed to transmit sound in a particular way. Computers transmit their information in a different way, so you need something to translate between the two. That "something" is called a *modem*, pronounced "*moe-dem.*" *Modem* is a made-up word that stands for "modulate-demodulate." To modulate something means to change it; to demodulate it, logically enough, is to change it back again. The function of the modem is to change, or modulate, the signal that comes out of the computer before it goes into the telephone and to "unchange" it when it comes out of the phone and goes into another computer. Each computer needs to have its own modem, and both modems need to be connected to the telephone line. Figure 1-1 shows how the modem fits into the telecommunications system.

In order to understand why the modem is necessary, you should backtrack a little bit first and think about how a computer works. Do you really need to understand "why?" Possibly not. You don't need to be able to build a boat to go sailing. On the other hand, the technology isn't very complicated. If you know how a modem works, you'll be that much better equipped to choose the right modem or to figure out what's happening on those rare occasions when it *doesn't* work.

1-1 Information can flow in both directions, from your Mac to the mighty mainframe or to your office PC and back. Modems act as bridges to the phone system.

Thinking digitally

Your Mac, your friend's PC, the VAX at the office, and the huge mainframes that run CompuServe, Prodigy, and other online services all "think" in a digital format. Everything that appears on the screen, whether it's a spreadsheet, a text file, a picture of Harpo, or a game of Harpoon, is actually a string of 1s and 0s. These are more commonly called *binary digits*, or *bits*. (You probably learned the binary system back in junior high school math class, but your teacher might have called it "base two.")

Computers manipulate strings of bits, called *bytes*, in various ways, and send them back and forth over data lines to peripheral devices, such as printers, hard drives, and CD-ROMs, as well as to other computers on a local area network. Table 1-1 shows the 8-bit binary codes for the ASCII Character Set. (Actually, this chart shows only the first half of the set. The remaining 128 characters, the *Extended ASCII* Set, contain characters used for graphics.) Computers use these codes to represent text characters and formatting and control characters, like tabs, linefeeds, and acknowledgment of data received. ASCII, by the way, is pronounced "*As-key*" and stands for American Standard Code for Information Interchange.

Table 1-1 The ASCII Character Set. For characters with fewer than 8 bits, additional 0s are placed at the front of the binary "word."

Decimal	Binary	Character and/or key	Communication control character or function
1	00001	^A	SOH (Start Of Heading)
2	00010	^B	STX (Start Of Text)
3	00011	^C	ETX (End Of Text)
4	00100	^D	EOT (End Of Transmission)
5	00101	^E	ENQ (Enquiry)
6	00110	^F	ACK (Acknowledge)
7	00111	^G	BEL (Bell)
8	01000	^H	BS (Backspace)
9	01001	^I	HT (Horizontal Tab)

Table 1-1 Continued

Decimal	Binary	Character and/or key	Communication control character or function
10	01010	^J	LF (Line Feed)
11	01011	^K	VT (Vertical Tab)
12	01100	^L	FF (Form Feed)
13	01101	^M	CR (Carriage Return)
14	01110	^N	SO (Shift Out)
15	01111	^O	SI (Shift In)
16	10000	^P	DLE (Data Link Escape)
17	10001	^Q	DCI (Device Control 1)
18	10010	^R	DC2 (Device Control 2)
19	10011	^S	DC3 (Device Control 3)
20	10100	^T	DC4 (Device Control 4)
21	10101	^U	NAK (Negative Acknowledge)
22	10110	^V	SYN (Synchronous Idle)
23	10111	^W	ETB (End Transmission Block)
24	11000	^X	CAN (Cancel)
25	11001	^Y	EM (End of Medium)
26	11010	^Z	SUB (Substitute)
27	11011	^[	ESC (Escape)
28	11100	^\	FS (File Separator)
29	11101	^]	GS (Group Separator)
30	11110	^^	RS (Record Separator)
31	11111	^-	US (Unit Separator)
32	100000	space	
33	100001	!	
34	100010	"	
35	10001 1	#	
36	100100	$	
37	100101	%	
38	1001 10	&	
39	100111	'	
40	101000	(	
41	101001	)	
42	101010	*	
43	101011	+	

Table 1-1 Continued

Decimal	Binary	Character and/or key	Communication control character or function
44	101100	,	
45	101101	-	
46	101110	.	
47	101111	/	
48	110000	0	
49	110001	1	
50	1 10010	2	
51	110011	3	
52	110100	4	
53	110101	5	
54	110110	6	
55	110111	7	
56	111000	8	
57	111001	9	
58	111010	:	
59	111011	;	
60	111100	<	
61	111101	=	
62	111110	>	
63	111111	?	
64	1000000	@	
65	1000001	A	
66	1000010	B	
67	1000011	C	
68	1000100	D	
69	1000101	E	
70	1000110	F	
71	1000111	G	
72	1001000	H	
73	1001001	I	
74	1001010	J	
75	1001011	K	
76	1001100	L	
77	1001101	M	
78	1001110	N	

Table 1-1 Continued

Decimal	Binary	Character and/or key	Communication control character or function
79	1001111	O	
80	1010000	P	
81	1010001	Q	
82	1010010	R	
83	1010011	S	
84	1010100	T	
85	1010101	U	
86	1010110	V	
87	1010111	W	
88	1011000	X	
89	1011001	Y	
90	1011010	Z	
91	1011011	[	
92	1011100	\	
93	1011101	]	
94	1011110	^	
95	1011111	_	
96	1100000		
97	1 100001	a	
98	1100010	b	
99	1100011	c	
100	1100100	d	
101	1100101	e	
102	1 1001 10	f	
103	1100111	g	
104	1101000	h	
105	1101001	i	
106	1101010	j	
107	1101011	k	
108	1101100	l	
109	1101101	m	
110	1101110	n	
111	1101111	o	
112	1110000	p	
113	1110001	q	

Table 1-1 Continued

Decimal	Binary	Character and/or key	Communication control character or function
114	1110010	r	
115	1110011	s	
116	1110100	t	
117	1110101	u	
118	1110110	v	
119	1110111	w	
120	1111000	x	
121	1111001	y	
122	1111010	z	
123	1111011	{	
124	1111100	|	
125	1111101	}	
126	1111110	~	
127	1111111	DELETE	(Character delete or time delay)

The ASCII Character Set goes back to the precomputer days of teletype machines, when it was used to send news stories over a dedicated line from news syndicates like the Associated Press to your local paper, radio, or TV station. Some of the ASCII characters are clearly intended for teletype, like the ^G which rang a bell to warn news editors of a major story. This code still works. If you type Ctrl-G while you're online in a conference, you make everybody else's computer beep.

If the computer could just send its data down the phone line to another computer, you wouldn't need a modem. However, ordinary phone lines can't handle digital signals. (Later on, I talk about a new type of phone system called *ISDN*, which can.) Of course, if you had a telegraph instead of a telephone, your computer could communicate perfectly, although slowly. Morse code is inherently digital.

In the beginning were words

When Alexander Graham Bell invented the telephone, he wasn't thinking in terms of computer use. He merely wanted to transmit human speech through a wire from a microphone to a speaker. His system did this, very cleverly, by varying the amount of current that passes through the granulated carbon in the telephone's microphone. As the user speaks into the telephone mouthpiece, the carbon inside the microphone capsule is compressed. Electric current, which normally passes through the loose carbon, is slowed down by the compressed carbon, causing fluctuations in the amount of current that flows down the wires to the central exchange. There, it's amplified and sent out via another wire to be received by another telephone, where it enters a small speaker in the earpiece of the phone, energizing a magnet and making the diaphragm vibrate in the same way that the microphone did, reproducing the original sounds. Figure 1-2 illustrates this process.

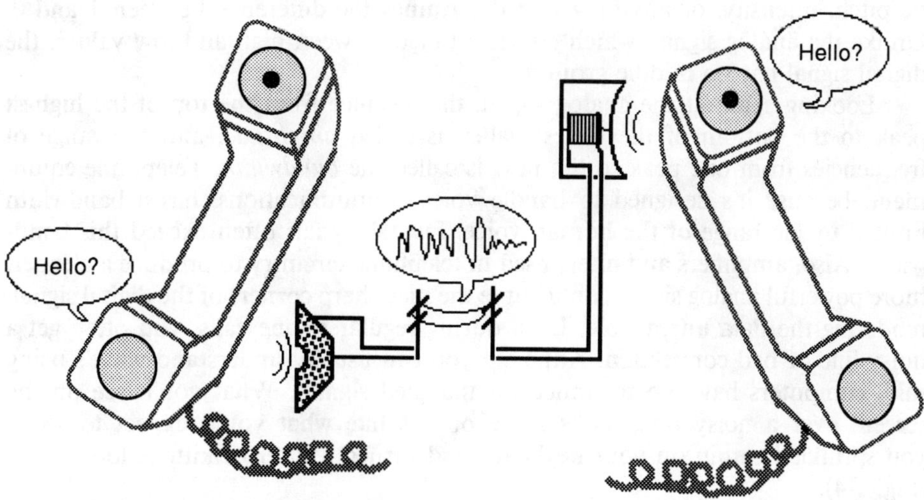

1-2 The mechanics of talking on the telephone.

Analog versus digital signals

The telephone does a fine job of handling the human voice and other analog signals. An *analog signal*, for this book's purposes, is a continuously flowing one, as opposed to a *digital signal*, which is on or off. If you were to look at an analog signal on an oscilloscope, you'd see a bunch of curvy lines, something like the ones on top in Fig. 1-3. The variations in the line represent the continuous fluctuations

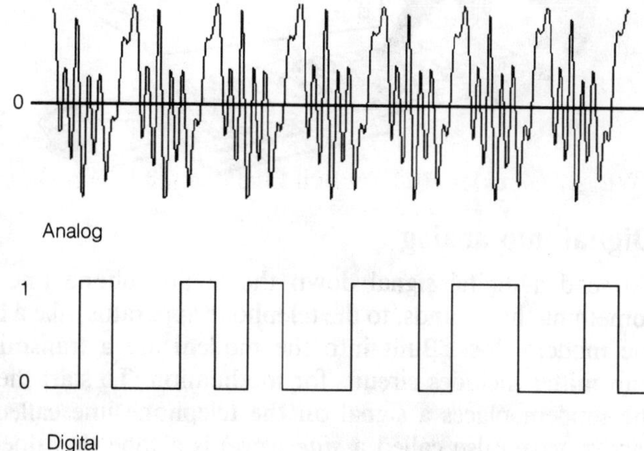

1-3 The difference between analog and digital signals.

in current that define the sound. Analog signals can be thought of as three-dimensional. They vary in pitch, intensity, and duration. Digital signals, like those shown at the bottom of the figure, are another matter. A digital signal is either on or off. It's a 1 or a 0. Period. Its wave form is square, rather than rounded. It is a two-dimensional signal, varying in duration and in one other element, which could be pitch, intensity, or anything that determines the difference between 1 and 0. Unlike the analog signal, which covers a range between high and low values, the digital signal has no middle ground.

Looking again at the analog signal, the distance from the top of the highest peak to the bottom of the lowest valley is called *amplitude*, and the range of frequencies from one peak to the next is called the *bandwidth*. Telephone equipment, because it's designed to handle voice communications, has a bandwidth limited to the range of the human voice. Digital signals often exceed this bandwidth. Also, amplifiers and filters used in telephone circuitry to produce a cleaner, more powerful analog signal could curve the nice sharp corners of the digital signal, rendering the data unreadable. Even during regular phone calls, you often get a noisy line or bad connection. Although you can usually understand what's being said, computers have no tolerance for mangled signals. What you'd see on the screen, over a noisy line, looks more or less like what you'd expect to see if you sprinkled catnip on your keyboard and turned a litter of kittens loose on it (Fig. 1-4).

1-4 Line noise looks like a kitten on the keys.

Digital into analog

To send a digital signal down the analog phone line you must convert it to something that sounds, to the telephone apparatus, like a human voice. That's what the modem does. Built into the modem are a transmitter and a receiver. The transmitter includes circuits for modulation. To start the process of sending data, the modem places a signal on the telephone line called a *carrier wave*. A pure carrier wave (also called a *sine wave*) is a tone that doesn't change frequency or strength (Fig. 1-5). It's a nice steady whistle, about in the middle of the waveband. When you add the data to the carrier wave, if you were to listen in while the modem's in use, you would hear a sort of hissing, splattering sound, like a heavy rainstorm falling on a tin roof.

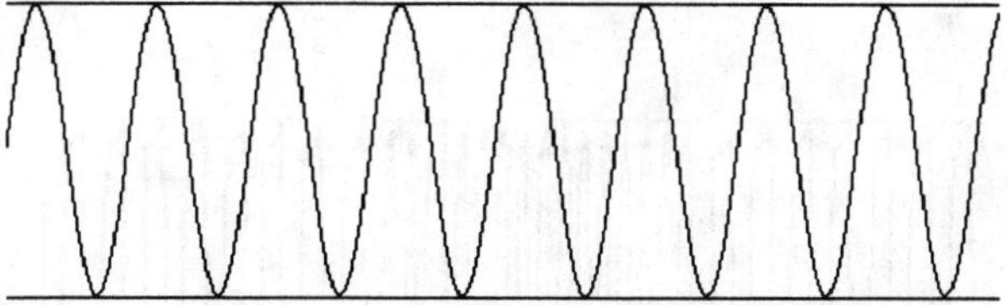

1-5 A sine wave is sometimes called a *carrier wave.*

Adding modulation

The three ways to modulate this carrier wave are through amplitude, frequency, and phase. (The typical modem is able to apply more than one of these methods.) The modem's speed, the number of bits of information it sends per second, is dependent on the kind of modulation system it's using. The simplest kind of modulation is also the slowest. As modem speed increases, so does the complexity of the modulation system, and so, alas, does the cost of the modem. Data compression schemes, present in some of the higher speed modems, compact the data so that more information is sent per byte. This means that, even though the modem may be sending data at 2400 bps, the throughput (the actual amount of data received) is effectively 9600 bps.

Amplitude modulation (Fig. 1-6) varies the height of the wave. High peaks represent 1s, and the low peaks are 0s. This system is seldom used except for very slow transmission, under 300 bits of data per second. It's not very reliable. Voltage spikes on the line and other kinds of noise or static can look just like data and confuse the computer.

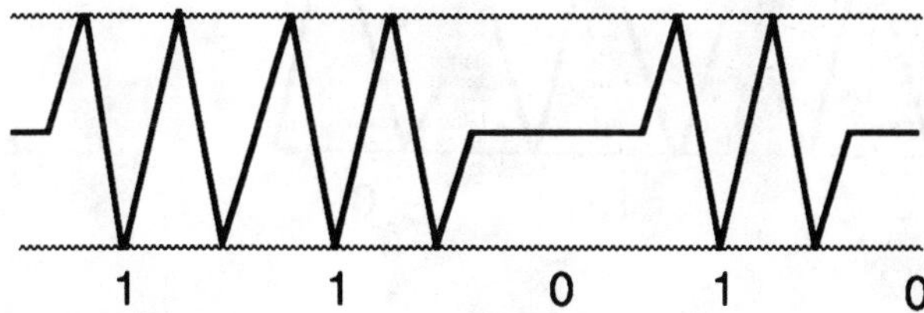

1-6 Amplitude modulation.

Frequency modulation (Fig. 1-7) uses higher and lower frequency waves to represent binary 1s and 0s. The number of waves per unit of space varies, while the height (amplitude) remains the same. Frequency modulation and a closely

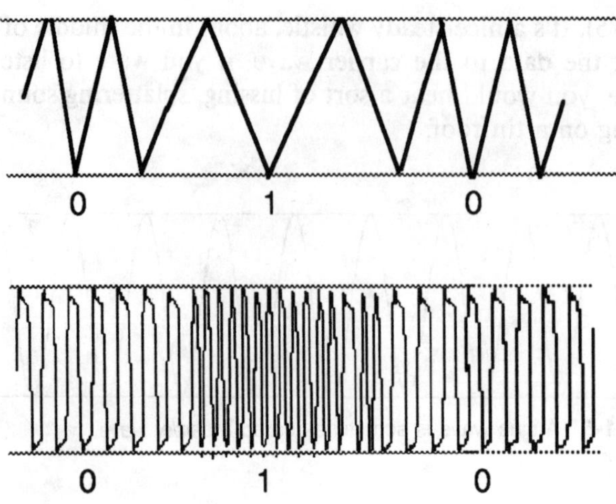

1-7 Frequency modulation and FSK.

related variation called *Frequency Shift Keying* are commonly used by low-speed (300-bits-per-second) modems.

Phase modulation (Fig. 1-8), also called *phase shift modulation*, is commonly used for relatively fast modems, those capable of transmitting 2400 bits per second. It's a little more complicated to understand. If a normal sine wave is used to represent a 1, the same wave, shifted 180° out of phase, represented the 0 bit. Shifting it out of phase simply means starting it at a different part of its cycle. In the diagram, the gray bars highlight the places where the wave has shifted phase. Phase shifts can occur at any part of the cycle.

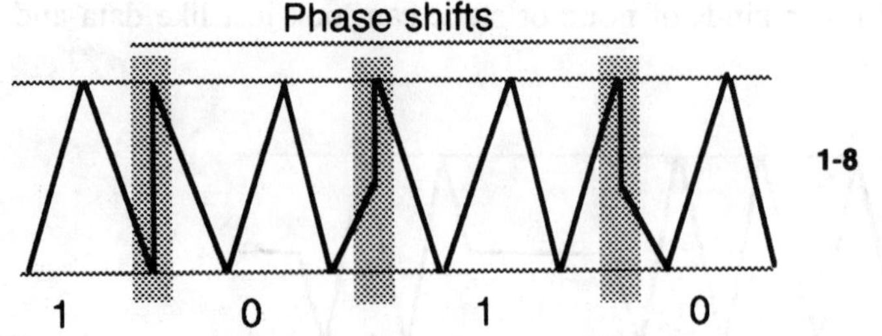

1-8 Phase shift modulation.

To send data at really high speeds, from 4800 to 19,200 bits per second or more, combinations of frequency shift and phase shift modulation are used, often with added error-correction codes to help assure that information is received correctly. These systems have exotic names like Trellis Coded Modulation and Quadrature Amplitude Modulation. They're a good deal more complicated to explain, but the point is that it's possible to move data accurately at extremely high speeds.

De-modulating the signal

When the data is received at the other end of the telephone line, it has to be re-converted to a digital signal, or de-modulated, so the other computer can understand it. When a modem receives data, it filters out the carrier wave and does, in reverse, whatever was done to modulate the digital signal. For instance, if the data had originally been converted by phase shift modulation, the receiving modem must re-shift the phase. The demodulated data, now back in digital form, goes to the computer and appears on the screen as text, or picture, or whatever was sent.

ISDN — the future of telecom

Within a few years, this whole question of changing digital data into an analog signal will be moot. A new telephone system, already available in limited areas, will be able to handle digital signals as well as it now handles analog ones. The new technology, called Integrated Services Digital Network, or ISDN for short, lets you use existing telephone lines to send digital signals, even video and audio tracks, at a very high rate of speed, with little or no loss of quality. You can even send computer data while you're talking to somebody on the same line! An ISDN line can carry three digital signals simultaneously, and two of these three channels are capable of transferring data at 64,000 bps! If you add in a data compression scheme, you could send your files at hundreds of kilobits per second! The third ISDN channel, a "slower" one at only 16,000 bps, is used for control signals, voice transmission, or as a third data channel if needed.

Instead of a modem, you make your connection through a gateway, which filters and conditions the digital signal, if needed, to match the phone company's requirements. The gateway is often built into a special ISDN phone, which looks more or less like a normal desk phone but has a DB-25 connector on the back. Right now, one modem, the Hayes Ultra 144, can connect to an ISDN network, as well as function as a "normal" high speed modem. It's priced accordingly, but as ISDN becomes more readily available, so will inexpensive gateways. It's estimated that by 1994 about half of the telephones in the US will have access to ISDN, so it will be a while yet before online services support ISDN access. If your interest in modem use is to transfer large amounts of data between your Mac and another computer, and ISDN is available in your area, it's an excellent solution. ISDN will allow you to send data at speeds of up to 57,600 bits per second or more, virtually as fast as you can send it from one computer to another on a Local Area Network.

Is yours an innie or an outie?

When you're choosing a modem for a Mac, unless it's a portable Mac, you don't really have many options. There are lots of external modems, but as of this writing,

I could find no internal modems for Macs other than the Portable and PowerBook series. If you have a PowerBook or other portable Mac, an internal modem is highly recommended. Apple even includes one in the PowerBook 170. It's one less item to carry around, it doesn't tie up the Mac's serial port, and it won't require extra cables between Mac and modem—only the phone line into the Mac. Despite these advantages, many PowerBook users prefer an external modem for several reasons. If something goes wrong with an internal modem, you'll lose the whole computer while it's being fixed. External modems can be repaired (or replaced) without sending the Mac to the repair shop. And the same external modem can be used with the PowerBook on the road and with a desktop Mac at home or in the office. Finally, external modems don't require expensive dealer installation. They can be installed by anyone who can stick a plug into a socket. If you upgrade from a Mac Plus to a Quadra, or anything in between, you can use the same modem.

Direct or coupled?

External modems used to come in two different physical types. Today, virtually all modems are "direct connect," meaning they plug into a telephone jack. The earliest modems were acoustically coupled. These had a pair of rubber cups into which the user placed the telephone handset. Sound passed from the modem into the telephone's mouthpiece, or was received from the telephone's ear piece. Since a snug fit was necessary to block out room noises, it only worked with a standard desk phone. Designer phones, cordless phones, or any other non-standard phones wouldn't fit. Acoustically coupled modems were originally developed to get around a phone company rule against connecting any non-Bell-system apparatus to a telephone line. When the Bell System broke up into smaller "baby Bells" some years ago, this rule was scrapped, enabling more efficient direct-connect modems.

What to look for when you buy a modem

Sometimes it seems as if the people who design modems go out of their way to confuse the would-be purchaser. High Speed? External? Portable? And what about faxing—send-only or send-and-receive? It's enough to make the average person begin to regret the whole notion of going online. But, if you begin at the beginning, it's actually fairly easy to figure out what you need in a modem, and which one will be your best investment.

Two factors determine the usefulness of a modem: speed and versatility. Many of today's modems also send faxes. Some can accept voice mail and store it as files on your Mac. If your Mac runs a business, faxing and voice messaging might be important to you. If you're just using your modem to play games online or to visit your user group's bulletin board system, you can save a hundred dollars or more by choosing a modem without fax capability. What about speed, though? Is a faster modem necessarily a better one?

Modem speed: bits and baud

Modem speeds are expressed in *bits per second* (*bps*) or *baud.* A *bit* is a single unit of binary information, a 1 or a 0. (A *tidbit* is a single unit of gossip, which can be transferred down a voice line at remarkable speed.) Modem speeds relate to the number of bits of data that can be transferred from one computer to another in a single second. Modem speeds can range anywhere from 300 to 57,600 bps, or even more. *Baud,* though often and incorrectly used as a synonym for bps, actually refers to the number of *changes in status per second* of the data that's traveling down the phone lines. A 300-baud modem changes status 300 times per second. At slow speeds the bps rate and baud rate are usually the same. One baud equals one bit per second, hence the confusion. But there are ways to send more than one bit per baud.

Figure 1-9 shows a piece of data being sent by phase shift modulation. Each shift is one baud. At 300 baud, there are 300 shifts per second. And if we send one bit of information per shift, that data is moving at 300 bps. If we send 4 bits per baud, we are moving data at 1200 bps, but still at 300 baud. 2400-bps modems also send four bits per baud but run at 600 baud. When you see a modem advertised as being a 2400-baud modem, you've probably encountered a copywriter who doesn't know what he or she is talking about.

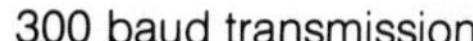

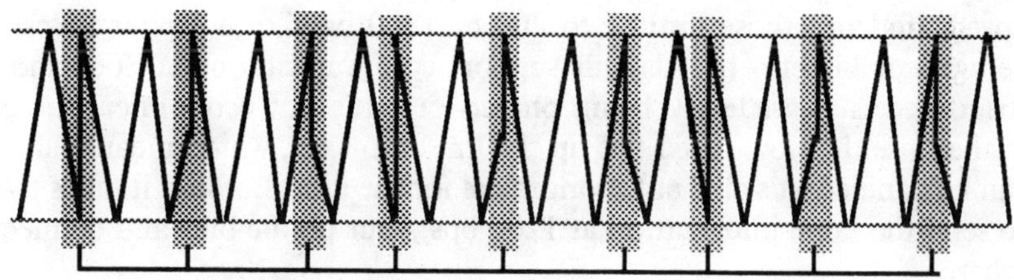

1-9 Why bps isn't baud.

What speed do I need?

Most of the modems on the market today operate at 2400 bps, and this is the single most useful speed. Bulletin boards and online services generally function at 2400 bps. Many also offer 1200-bps service for those with older, slower modems. A 2400-bps modem will also send and receive at lower speeds. This feature could be helpful if, for instance, the 2400-bps "doorway" to your favorite online service is busy, and their back-up phone number goes to their 1200-bps line. You'd still be able to get in. Or, if you have a particularly noisy line and are trying to send data to another modem, you might have better luck (in this case, fewer errors) sending it at 1200 bps, even though it will take twice as long.

Combination fax/modems typically send faxes at 9600 bps. Some receive faxes, too, and can function as 9600-bps modems. A growing number of bulletin boards and online services, including CompuServe and GEnie (in limited areas), will accommodate 9600-bps transmissions. If you're sending data back to your office while you travel, or to a client in another time zone, a pair of 9600-bps modems can soon pay for themselves in lower long distance charges.

Currently, 9600 bps is the highest acceptable speed for data communications on a voice telephone line. If you try to move data any faster over regular phone lines, you'll encounter too many errors. There is a way to send information faster, however, and that's by using a dedicated phone line, also called a leased line. These are, as the name suggests, private lines installed by and leased from the phone company to run from one computer to another. Such lines are used a great deal in business applications or wherever one computer must be in relatively constant contact with another. Your bank runs leased lines to each of its branches, and might be time-sharing on a mainframe through another leased line. Leased-line modems are far more sophisticated than those used by the average Mac owner and include features not needed by most casual modem users, such as data encryption and security codes.

What not to buy

Low-speed modems, those limited to 300 or 1200 baud, are a poor investment. Few services or bulletin boards will support communications at 300, and even 1200-baud access is gradually being phased out. It's not economical for online services because the slow speed ties up the lines too long, which means that fewer calls can be handled. It's also not economical for the user. Because it takes twice as long to send the same information at 1200 bps, your phone bills and connect fees are higher.

Other features to look for

There are, of course, other factors to consider and other features you might want in a modem. Generally speaking, it shouldn't be difficult to find a modem with the right combination of speeds and fax capability, and the chances are excellent that your modem—if it's a current model—will also have some or all of the following characteristics.

Hayes compatibility

One feature that's standard in all current modems, but might not be in an older one, is Hayes compatibility. Within the field of telecommunications, there are standards of all kinds: standards for the kind of plug and jack to use, standards for error correction, and a standard set of commands to define the actions that the modem carries out. These "action" commands are known as *Hayes commands*, after the modem manufacturer who first developed them. They're also called *AT commands* or the *Hayes Standard AT Command Set*. Any modem labeled AT compatible or Hayes compatible uses this standard set of commands. It's called the AT set because the command used to start up the modem is AT, for "attention."

Other AT commands tell the modem whether to dial with tones or pulses, to display the "result codes" (OK, RING, NO CARRIER, etc.), and to hang up when finished. (For a complete list of AT commands, see chapter 2.) Because all current telecom software uses the same commands, virtually all modem makers have adopted the Hayes command set. Unless you intend to write your own communications program, be sure that any modem you buy is Hayes or AT compatible.

Automatic dialing and answering

Auto-dial capability is a feature most users expect. It means that the modem can dial a number if told to do so, rather than requiring you to dial the phone yourself and then connect the modem. The number is dialed either by typing it from the Mac's keyboard or by using a communications program with an "auto logon" feature, which connects (logs on) to the service automatically when you click the appropriate icon or select the desired service from a menu. After the other computer answers, the modem completes the process of connecting by verifying the baud rate and other communications settings.

Auto-answer is a must if you're considering setting up your own bulletin board or if you'll be calling your home computer from the office or vice versa. It means that the modem can detect an incoming call. Putting the modem into auto answer mode tells it to answer the call after a certain number of rings (which you can set by typing a simple code) and send a wake-up signal to the communications software, which then handles the call.

Tone/pulse dialing

Switchable tone/pulse dialing is usually available but isn't really necessary unless you live in one of the few places in the U.S. that doesn't offer tone dialing. How can you tell? Old-fashioned rotary dial phones use pulse dialing. The phone company's central office knows what number you're calling by the number of clicks it counts for each digit you dial. Dialing a 1 makes one click, 4 produces four separate clicks, and so on. Tone dialing phones beep when you press the number buttons. If you can play a tune on your telephone, you have tone dialing. (Dialing 654-5666 plays "Mary Had a Little Lamb.") Even if the phone connected to the line is a rotary phone, most areas now support tone dialing, so always try it first if you're not sure. It's much faster. If nothing happens, then try pulse dialing.

Adaptive dialing lets the modem test the wire, so to speak, and decide for itself whether to use tone or pulse dialing. It would be a useful feature for a portable modem to have, but unnecessary for a fixed installation.

Built-in speaker and status lights

Most external modems are equipped with speakers, a feature that's more useful than you might initially think. The speaker lets you hear the number being dialed and the connection being made. If the line is busy or not answering, you'll hear it even before the communications program advises you. If you've dialed a wrong number and someone answers, you'll be able to pick up the phone and apologize.

If you share an office, or if your Mac and modem are located in a noisy area, look for a modem with volume control. The sounds of dialing and handshaking can be annoying to people who aren't online. There are also Hayes commands that let you set the modem speaker volume when you place the call.

If your external modem doesn't have a speaker, or if you need to keep the volume turned way down for some reason, you can tell exactly what's going on by watching the status lights. These are actually small LEDs (Light Emitting Diodes) on the front panel of the modem, which indicate what is happening inside the box at any given moment. Status lights are marked with cryptic two letter codes. You're likely to find the following:

- AA—Auto Answer: The modem has been set to receive an incoming call.
- CD—Carrier Detect: The modem detects a carrier signal from another computer and will send a signal to its computer.
- HS—High Speed: The modem is set to its high speed, generally 2400 bps.
- MR—Modem Ready: Normally on whenever it's getting power.
- OH—Off Hook: The modem is active. A call is in progress.
- RD—Receiving Data: This light flickers with every bit of data the modem receives.
- SD—Sending Data: This light flickers with every bit of data you send. It will blink every time you press a key while you're online.
- TR—Terminal Ready: This means that the Mac-to-modem connection is made. You're ready to dial out or receive a call.
- FM—Fax Mode: Modems that are capable of sending faxes will have this status light, which is on when the modem is prepared to send or receive a fax.
- VM—Voice Mode: (Only on modems capable of recording voice messages.) The modem is ready to send or receive voice mail.

One brand of modem, the Logicode Zeba, uses tiny icons on a display screen instead of the LEDs. If you have one of these, consult your owner's manual for an interpretation of the symbols.

You gotta have standards

When you go shopping for a modem, in addition to the features described above, you'll see some more cryptic designations, like the following: "V.32/V.42bis compliant with MNP 5 error correction," "Supports CCITT V.22 bis & Bell

212A/103," "9600 bps Group III SendFax capability," and "Effective throughput rates of up to 38,400 bps." The first two statements refer to the two different sets of modem standards you might encounter. These standards have been established to assure that signals put out by the modem are compatible with other modems and acceptable to phone company switching equipment.

Bell standards

In the United States, standards were originally determined by the Bell System. Bell 103 and Bell 212A are the American standards for 300 and 1200 bps communications. (The Bell System broke up before there were modems faster than 1200 bps.) The CCITT (Consultive Committee on International Telegraphy and Telephony) now determines communications standards for the rest of the world. The CCITT is part of the United Nations and is headquartered across from the UN's *Palais des Nations* in Geneva, Switzerland.

CCITT standards

Internationally, CCITT V.22 and V.21 set the standard for 300/1200 baud signals outside the U.S. CCITT V.22 bis is the standard for 2400-bps modems worldwide. V.32 and V.32 bis are the standards for higher speed transmission, in the 4800 to 14,400-bps range. CCITT also established the V.42-bis standard used for very high speed transmission. Modems are usually "downward compatible," which is to say that a modem that conforms to the V.32-bis or V.42-bis standard will also conform to V.22 and V.32 and the Bell standards. In case you're wondering, *bis*—according to my trusty Larousse—simply means "a second time," or in this case, "part two."

To make this even more confusing, a few modem manufacturers have developed their own proprietary standards. Their products may, or may not, support the CCITT or Bell standards. The only way to tell is to read the spec. sheet, read the box, and read the manual. Why does it matter? Two modems can talk to each other only if they can establish a common language, or *protocol.* If one modem sends data at 9600 using CCITT V.32 as a standard for modulation, and the other tries to demodulate it and respond using something like the US Robotics HST standard, all that will reach either computer is garbage. They'll have to fall back to a slower speed, probably 2400 bps, canceling out the advantage of buying a high speed modem. Of course, any two V.32 modems from different manufacturers will have no trouble communicating. They both speak the same language.

Things to come

Within the next two years, CCITT is expected to introduce a new standard for very high speed communication over regular (not ISDN) phone lines. Tentatively called *V.fast*, the new standard will allow speeds of 19,200 to 24,000 bps.

Some modems never make misteaks

At higher speeds, and even at 2400 bps on a noisy telephone line, errors are a problem. With data flowing so fast, one little crackle of static on the line can cause pages of garbled characters. There are two standards for error control: V.42 and V.42 bis, from the CCITT; and MNP, which stands for Microcom Networking Protocol. Just as Hayes set industry standards for commands to control the modem, Microcom set the standards for error correction and data compression. MNP software is licensed to other modem manufacturers and is used worldwide to provide error-free file transfers at very high speeds. MNP 2 to 4 are error-correction protocols. V.42 incorporates MNP-4 as well as a second error-detection scheme. Error-control protocols filter out line noise by detecting and removing the "garbage characters" it causes. Figure 1-10 shows what happens to a transfer without error correction.

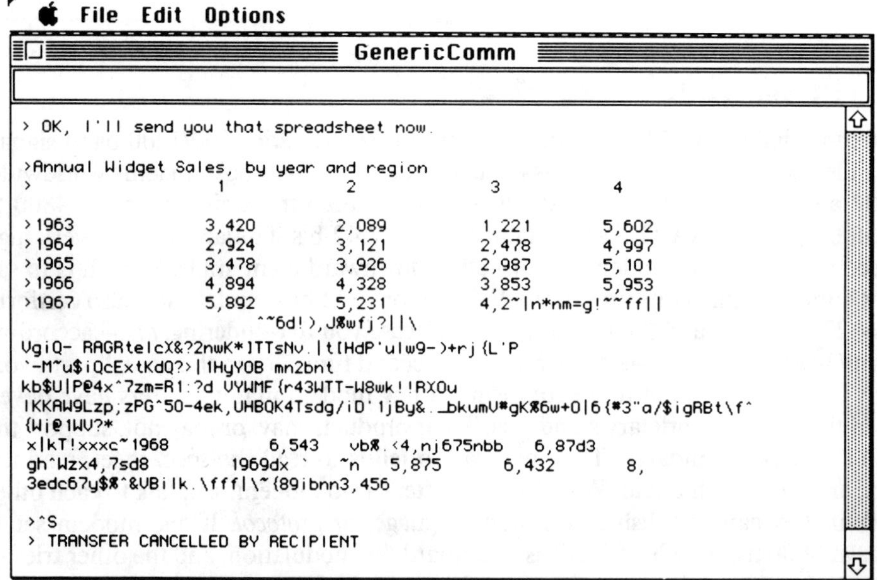

1-10 Did somebody pick up the extension?

If MNP2-4 or V.42 had been used, this would have been removed, making your spreadsheet (or whatever you were sending) look a lot cleaner. The line noise is still there, and because corrupted data must be sent over and over until it's received correctly, your throughput speed goes down accordingly.

MNP-5 and up are also data-compression protocols. MNP-5 provides a 2:1 compression. Using MNP-5 at 9600 bps give you an effective speed (or throughput) of 19,200 bps. MNP protocols and V.42 bis offer data compression at a rate as high as 4:1. Microcom's own MacModem uses MNP-9, for effective speeds of 38,400 bps over a 9600-bps line.

Is faster better?

While ultra-high-speed modems make a certain amount of sense for business use, especially when long files of data must be sent back and forth, they're just not useful to the average Mac owner. For one thing, it's difficult to find another modem with which you can communicate at that speed. Online services and BBS typically run at 1200 and 2400 bps. Some go as high as 9600, but that's still uncommon. Those that do, like CompuServe, charge extra for it, so you save little, if anything. Another reason has to do with the mechanics of file compression. How well MNP-5 compresses a file depends on the kind of file. Plain text compresses quite well, graphics less so. A file that is already compressed by a software utility such as DiskDoubler, Stuffit, or CompactPro might actually get larger if it's put through MNP-5 compression. Files that you might download from a BBS or online service are almost always compressed so they'll occupy less storage space. Using 9600 bps and MNP-5 would slow you down.

Fax standards

Fax/modems also have to conform to standards for fax transmission. Group III is the current standard and is compatible with just about every fax machine currently in use. A new standard, Group IV, is gradually being phased in, but again, it's "downward compatible" with Group III. Earlier models (Group I and II) used an analog, rather than digital, encoding system. If you were to try to send to an incompatible fax machine, you would get an error message. They simply don't speak the same language. Fortunately, it's very unusual to encounter one of these "antique" fax machines. Because they can't send to group III fax machines, and can't receive from them, almost all of them have ended up in the junk pile. (Of course, there are probably a few on the dealer's back shelf, too. If anyone offers you a "bargain" fax machine, check its group compatibility. Some bargains aren't.)

There's one other thing to look for when you read through the advertising or the manufacturer's specifications for a modem you're considering. Be sure that it's registered with the Federal Communications Commission (FCC) or if you happen to live in Canada, with the Canadian Department of Communications. All computer equipment, including modems, has to meet certain standards for radio noise emission. Essentially, this means that the device must not put out radio signals strong enough to interfere with reception of other radio signals. FCC registration also assures that your modem meets the phone company's specifications.

Mac compatibility

There are more than a dozen different brands of modem on the market. Most are compatible with the Mac. Obviously, an external modem has fewer compatibility problems than a card that must plug into the innards of your computer, though several third-party (non-Apple) companies are producing internal modem cards for the PowerBooks. As long as the modem you purchase meets the specifications described above, you should have no problems using it. Your choice, then, will depend on your needs, how much it costs, and possibly what communications software (if any) is bundled with it. Some modem manufacturers (notably Prometheus and Hayes) have developed their own communication software, while others include another third-party program, like Microphone II or White Knight. If you know which software you want to use, it might be most cost effective to buy the modem that includes it.

Making connections

You have the Mac. You have the modem. There's another thing you'll need before you can get started, namely a phone line. It's nice to have a separate line for the modem if you are going to be online for long periods of time. Otherwise, anyone calling you while you're online will get a busy signal. This might not be too terrible if you live alone, but non-modeming spouses, roommates, or other family members can get very annoyed at being deprived of telephone privileges while you play games or talk politics. They'll soon discover that they can blast you offline in a hurry by simply picking up an extension phone and clicking a few times. (Later on, I'll tell you how to get around this.)

If yours is a business Mac, you'll need an extra line so you won't miss talking to customers while you're picking up your E-mail or sending a fax. If you have a separate fax machine, your fax and modem can easily share a line. Unless you leave your Mac with its communications software in "host" mode waiting for a call, the fax machine will automatically answer its calls and print your faxes. In order to accept and switch modem calls and faxes to the appropriate machine, you'll need a *fax/modem switch*, also called a *fax line manager*. These little boxes are available at office supply stores and anywhere else fax machines and/or modems are sold. They sort out incoming calls by answering the ring and recognizing whether there's a fax-carrier signal or a modem-carrier signal on the line. If a signal is detected, the call is referred to the proper recipient; if not, it rings your phone.

Some modems, such as the DoveFax+, will act as answering machines, too. If a human caller is detected, rather than a computer or fax machine, these will play your pre-recorded message and accept one from the caller. If the caller enters a personal ID number that you provide, he or she will hear a personal message that you've recorded.

As mentioned earlier, a leased line is a particularly good idea if you are using a modem to transfer files from one location to another on a regular basis and want to use very high speeds. Leased lines are less likely to suffer from interference, and your transfers will have fewer errors.

Modular plugs

Because most Macs sit on desks, at least most of the time, there's generally a desk phone within reach. If your telephone has a modular plug, which is the little transparent one shown in Fig. 1-11, you're all set. These plugs, if you have a single-line phone, are called RJ-11 plugs, and the jacks they plug into are called RJ-11 jacks. Nearly all modems are equipped with this type of jack and plug, as are

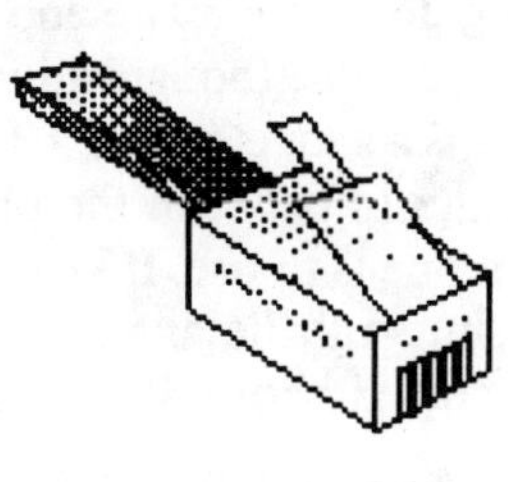

A modular plug—
RJ-11, 12, or 14

1-11 A modular RJ-type plug and jack.

virtually all single-line telephones sold in the past 10 years or so. If you have a two-line phone, the modular plug looks the same, but it's called an RJ-14. A three-line phone uses an identically shaped RJ-12. When you plug your modem into an RJ-12 or RJ-14, it will take over whichever line appears as line one.

So what's the difference between an RJ-11, an RJ-12, and an RJ-14? If you look very carefully at the "business-end" of the modular plug, you'll see little slits in the plastic and little copper wires in some, or all, of the slits. An RJ-11 uses only the innermost pair of wires (the red and green ones), but because the normal cord has four wires, all four are generally connected. The two-line RJ-14 uses red/green for line one and yellow/black for line two. (RJ-12s use a six-conductor wire and there's even an RJ-45b with 8 conductors.) Look at the manufacturer's specifications for your particular modem to be sure it will work with your RJ-11, -12, or -14 jack.

The various modular plugs are mostly cross compatible, with one important exception. If your modem accepts an RJ-12 or RJ-14 plug, don't use an RJ-11 jack that's adapted to provide power for a lighted dial telephone (such as a "Trimline" phone). These run voltage up the "spare" pair of wires, so the flashlight bulb inside the phone will shine. Modems, obviously, aren't designed for that kind of a jolt. On the other hand, if the modem only accepts an RJ-11 jack, it means there's nothing at the modem's end of the wire to make contact with the outer pair of wires and so the voltage won't go anywhere and won't do any harm.

Dis-connections

It used to be that a home would have only one telephone line coming in, and only one telephone, generally in some central spot like the front hall or the kitchen. Nowadays, it's common to find a telephone in almost every room. As a case in point, the author's house, occupied by two adults and two teenagers, has three incoming lines, nine telephones, a separate fax machine, and two modems. If the modem is sharing a "voice" line, sooner or later someone is going to try to make a call while you're online. It almost always seems to happen either in the middle of an exciting game or a minute from the end of a long download. The end result is that your modem call gets disconnected. The solution for this, thoughtfully provided by our friends at the shopping mall electronics store, is a gadget called a Teleprotector. You'll need one for each telephone. It simply plugs in between the phone and the wall jack and shuts off the other extensions when one is in use. It keeps roommates from listening in on your calls, too, and even shuts off the answering machine if you pick up while the message is playing. The cost is about $8 per protector.

A pair of jacks to open?

Some modems have a spare jack on the back into which you can plug a telephone. If yours doesn't, and you'd like to be able to use the phone when not online, pick up a *Y-adapter* (also known as a *duplex jack*) at your local phone store or electronics shop. It fits into the jack in the wall, and lets you plug in two telephone cords. When you're using your modem with a multi-line phone, if you plug the phone directly into the modem, you'll only be able to use line one. There's no way to route the other line(s) through the modem box. In this case, you really need a duplex jack.

Non-modular connectors

If you have an older phone system, you might have a different type of plug and jack, possibly with four long prongs or just a terminal block with four screws to which the phone wires are attached. Converting these to modular jacks and plugs is very easy. Conversion kits are available at phone stores, hardware stores, computer stores, and that national chain of electronics stores found in most shopping malls. Just follow the directions enclosed with the jack, and it should take no more than a minute or two to make the change. Some converters simply plug in and don't even require using tools.

Sometimes it's okay to cheat

If it's not your phone and you can't or don't want to make a permanent conversion, you can make up and carry with you a simple device with a modular jack on one end and a pair of "alligator clips" on the other. This can be clipped onto the terminal block of an old-fashioned phone or to the innards of a newer hard-wired phone. To make this "cheater cable," buy an extension cable or replacement cable at your local electronics or phone store and buy a pair of small crimp-on clips.

Cut off one plug, making the wire any length you like. Strip the cable back an inch or so, revealing the wires inside. Separate the red and green wires. (You can trim off the yellow and black ones, since you don't need them.) Peel off just enough insulation to expose about a quarter inch of the green wire. Insert it into the base of the clip and crimp it tight for a good connection. Repeat the process with the red wire. Be very careful when you strip the wires. The actual wire is very thin and will break if you pull on it. Figure 1-12 shows a finished cheater cable.

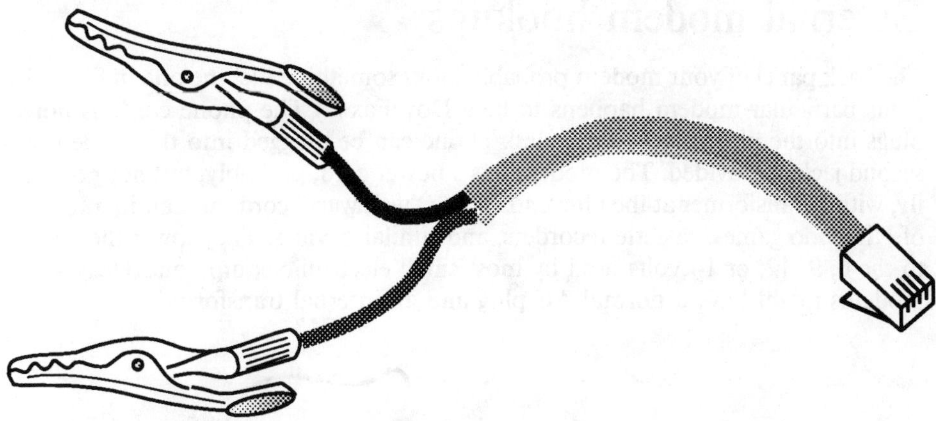

1-12 Making a cheater cord from a standard RJ-11.

To use it, you'll also need a screwdriver or a Swiss Army knife. Open up the terminal block by unscrewing its cover. You'll see four screws, like the ones shown in Fig. 1-13. Find the screws with the red and green wires and clip the red and green alligator clips onto them. Then plug in the modem and you're ready to go.

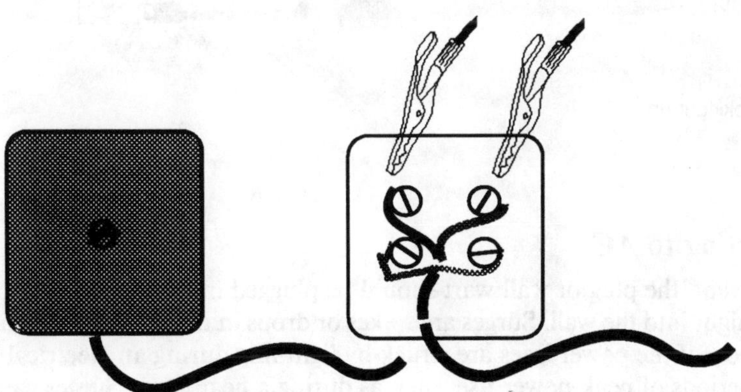

1-13 Clip red to red, green to green.

When you can't get at the terminal block, you can open up the telephone itself. To do so, unscrew the screws that hold the bottom of the instrument. Remove the plastic cover. It's usually held in by a couple of tabs and should snap out. Follow the incoming cable and find the terminals to which the red and green wires are attached. These should also be clearly marked as L1 and L2. L1 is "red," even on phones without colored wires. Clip your alligators on these, matching red to red. This should work in most situations.

External modem hookups

The back panel of your modem probably looks something like the one in Fig. 1-14. (This particular modem happens to be a DoveFax+.) The phone cord, as noted, plugs into the phone jack. Your desk phone can be plugged into the modem if a second jack is provided. The modem has a power cord, probably, but not necessarily, with a transformer at the plug end. These "wall wart" cords are familiar to users of Nintendo games, cassette recorders, and similar devices. They lower the voltage to the 6, 9, 12, or 14 volts used by most small electronic equipment. Heavy-duty modems might have a normal AC plug and an internal transformer.

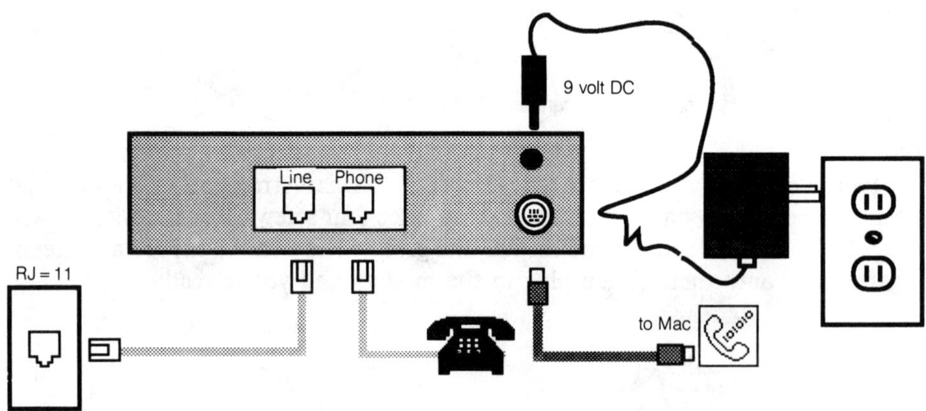

1-14 Hooking it up.

Connecting to AC

In any event, the plug or wall wart should be plugged into a surge protector rather than straight into the wall. Surges are spikes or drops in the power on the line. They come about if the power lines are struck by lightning during an electrical storm or during periods of peak power use, such as during a heat wave. Surges can damage electronic equipment, including both the modem and the Mac itself. Many surge protectors come in the form of "power strips," typically with four to six outlets. Because you probably already have one of these for your Mac, simply plug the modem into it, too. (If you don't, now is the time to get one.)

It is a particular pet peeve of mine that nobody has ever designed a power strip that takes wall warts into account. At best, you'll need to hang the end of the transformer over the edge of the power strip, a position that puts it at risk of being accidentally knocked out or kicked loose at any moment. Otherwise, it will cover up a piece of the adjacent outlet, rendering it useless. If you can tolerate additional cord clutter more easily than a wasted outlet, plug the wart into an extension cord, and plug *that* into the surge protector.

Telephone poles can get hit by lightning, too. A telephone spike protector plugs into a grounded AC outlet and accepts RJ-type modular connectors. It protects your modem, fax machine, and phone from damage due to voltage spikes on the phone line. For less than $13, it's extra insurance against trouble.

Warning

Even the best surge protector won't do you much good if the power line or phone line takes a direct hit. If you're in an area where storms are severe or where lightning has previously struck, get into the habit of unplugging your modem and Mac when the weather gets bad. Contrary to popular myth, lightning *does* strike twice. Note that you need to unplug the phone connection as well as the power. Sure, it's a nuisance, but so is a fried computer.

Connecting to the Mac

The other connector on the back of your modem goes to the computer. If you look at the back of your Macintosh, you'll see two identical ports. They may look like either of the ones shown in Fig. 1-15, depending on what model Mac you are using.

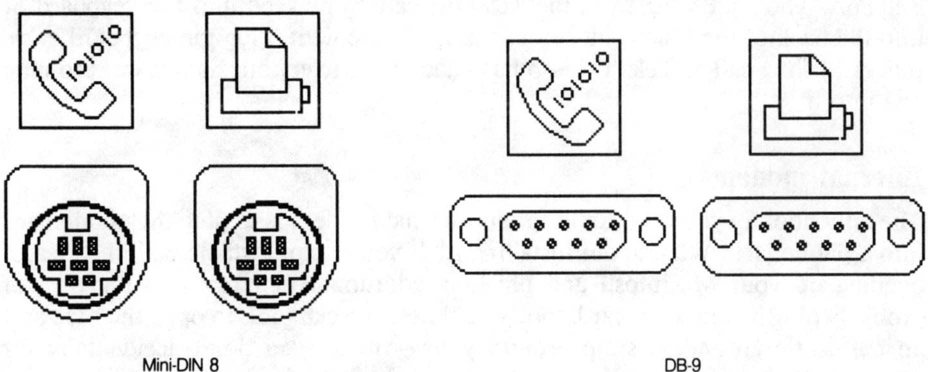

1-15 Older Macs use a DB-9, newer ones a mini-DIN-8.

If you look closely at them, you'll see that one has an icon of a printer over it, and the other an icon resembling a telephone handset. Care to guess which of these ports is the modem port? Whenever possible, use the modem port for the modem and the printer port for the printer, although they're theoretically interchangeable because both are serial ports. It's best to use the modem port for the modem because the Mac's operating system gives it priority when checking for activity. This helps guarantee that your computer won't go to sleep while you're using the modem.

Have you ever wondered about the difference between SCSI ports and serial ports? It's like this: Imagine that you have a platoon of soldiers. Each soldier carries one bit of data. If you're using a serial port, it's as if the soldiers formed a long line, one behind the other, and marched forward to drop their data bits into a bin, one by one. If the soldiers were to form ranks eight abreast, and dropped eight bits at a time into a very wide bin, they'd be illustrating a SCSI port. SCSI, by the way, stands for Small Computer System Interface and is pronounced "*skuzzy,*" not—alas—"*sexy.*"

No serial port available?

People who have two printers, or who use a video digitizer, or are on a network in addition to having a deskside printer will tend to have both serial ports tied up. There are two ways around this. One is to use a *T-switch box.* These devices let you plug in up to four different peripherals and switch back and forth between them. They also work in reverse to let four different users share one device. The other way is to use the only brand of modem that hooks up differently, the Global Village TelePort. Instead of plugging it into the modem port, you plug the TelePort into the Apple Desktop Bus, using the same type of connectors that attach your keyboard and mouse. (The TelePort's ADB plug has a built-in Y-connector, so you needn't give up your mouse, trackball, or other ADB devices.) It's a very small box, about half again as big as a pack of cigarettes, and needs no external power supply because it gets its current from the ADB. Figure 1-16 shows how to connect a TelePort. The ADB plug from the TelePort can be plugged into the keyboard or into the back of the Mac, whichever is more convenient. Plug the keyboard cable into it, as shown. The TelePort also has a jack for a telephone, if you want to plug one into it.

Internal modems

The only hookup you need to do for an internal modem is to plug the phone cord into a phone jack. What about installing it? If you're comfortable with the idea of opening up your Macintosh and plugging additional memory into it, you can probably plug in a modem card, too. You'll need special tools to open the Mac and an anti-static grounding strap around your wrist so you don't accidentally fry anything. Follow the directions carefully, and don't try it if you're not absolutely sure of what you're doing. A dead computer is a very expensive paperweight.

Multi-line phones and other odd situations

The phone line question becomes somewhat more complicated if you're using a multi-line phone, or if your desk phone is part of a PBX system, or if you're on the road and calling from a hotel phone or an airport pay phone. The chief difficulty in using a multi-line phone, other than the connector problem, is that someone is likely to pick up the line you're using. When this happens, the computer screen fills with gibberish and the modem either freezes or hangs up. If you're going to use a modem regularly at work, it's best to have a special phone line installed for it. The

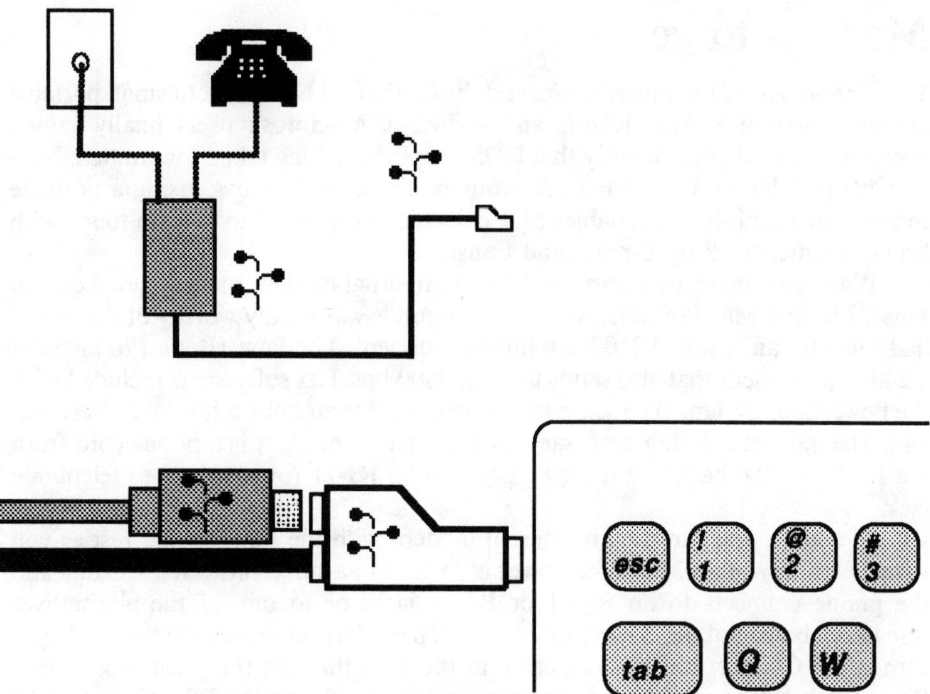

1-16 The ADB connector can plug into the keyboard, as shown, or into the back of the Mac. The cord for the keyboard or mouse then plugs into it.

cost of the installation is minor compared to the time you'll save. On the other hand, if it's just an occasional use, or if you can arrange with co-workers to stay off that line, your only problem will be finding a way to connect the modem to the phone system. One possibility is a little box that sells for about $20 at our favorite shopping mall radio and electronics store. It's called a four-line tap, and it plugs into the 1A2 (Amphenol-type) connectors that are standard in most business phone installations. It allows you to connect up to four telephones, fax machines, and/or modems to the existing system.

Offices that have an internal phone network, or PBX (Private Branch Exchange), might have another problem with modem use. Some of the more modern PBX systems are digital. Because your modem converts your digital data to an analog form, sending it over a digital phone won't work. If your office has a state-of-the-art phone system, you might either have to have an old-fashioned analog phone line installed or purchase a digital-to-analog converter. You might hear these called "A to D" or "D to A" converters. They change the modem's analog output to a signal compatible with the PBX's digital format. How can you tell if you'll need one? Look at the bottom of your telephone. If you see a label that says "Ringer Equivalent" or "REN" and a number, it's analog; and you have what some experts like to call POTS (plain old telephone service).

Modems to go

With the advent of the PowerBooks and the Outbound Notebook (a small portable computer that uses Mac ROMs and software), Macintosh users finally gained access to the kind of portability that DOS people have long taken for granted. Now that it's possible to slip a Mac into your briefcase or handbag, using a portable modem, or a built-in one, enables Mac enthusiasts on the go to keep in touch with home or office, pick up E-mail, and transfer files.

When you are using a portable Mac, an internal modem makes a good deal of sense. The first Mac Portable, which at 18 pounds was hardly worthy of the name, had a slot for an optional 2400-bps internal modem. The PowerBook 170 includes a 2400-bps modem that also sends faxes at 9600 bps. Fax software is included with the PowerBook system. The same fax/modem card is an option for the PowerBook 140. The only connection necessary for the internal modem is a phone cord from the RJ-11 on the back of the PowerBook to an RJ-11 (or alternative) telephone jack.

Of course, you can use an external modem with the PowerBook, just as you would with any other Mac. The power cord goes to a surge-protected AC line and the phone connects to an RJ-11 or RJ-14 jack, or to one of the alternatives discussed above. Put the PowerBook into Sleep mode, and make sure the modem is turned off. Connect the modem cable to the Mac through the printer port on a PowerBook 100 or to either the modem or printer port on the PB 140 or 170. (If you have a PB 100, be sure AppleTalk is inactive in the Chooser.) Turn on the modem and press any key to wake the Mac. If you also have an internal Mac modem installed, choose Control Panels from the Apple menu and open the Portable icon, as shown in Fig. 1-17. Click to choose External Modem from the Portable control panel.

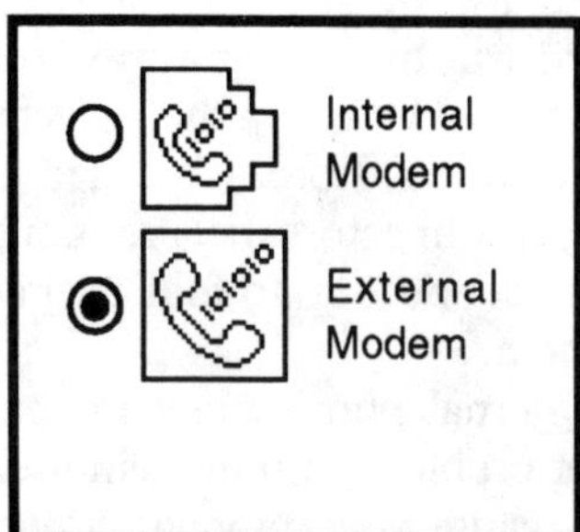

1-17 You won't see this control panel device unless there's an internal modem installed.

Modem card installation

Several third-party vendors are producing internal fax/modems for the PowerBook. Installing one of these presents an interesting problem. Apple warns that users will void their Apple warranty if they open the PowerBook themselves. Only an Apple-authorized service facility can poke into the PowerBook. When I checked with my local Apple dealer, I was told that I could expect to pay at least $50 for the modem installation. But manufacturers include installation instructions with their modem cards, and it seems like a fairly simple task. Should you try to do it yourself? Probably not, unless you're confident that nothing will go wrong with your PowerBook while it's under warranty. For what it's worth, most PowerBook problems show up right away or within the first few weeks of use.

The modem away from home

The same questions of phone line access arise on the road. Does your hotel provide an RJ-11 plug for the modem? Are you up against a digital phone system, a PBX, or a pay phone? How about when you're literally on the road? Can you call in from your cellular telephone? If there's no convenient RJ-11 plug for your modem, you might need to use an acoustic coupler or a newer alternative.

Acoustic couplers look like a pair of rubber cylinders about three inches high, joined by a piece of cable, with a telephone cord coming from one end. This cord connects the coupler to the modem. To use it, place the handset of the telephone snugly into the rubber cups. If the phone doesn't fit correctly, and it might not if it has square ends instead of rounded ones, don't even try to use the modem. Since the connection is, at best, less than ideal, you'll have more success if you send and receive at very low speeds, either 300 or 1200 bps.

Non-acoustic couplers

A better solution comes from a company called Unlimited Systems. It's a little box called KONEXX, which plugs into the handset jack on the telephone and has a standard RJ-11 jack for your modem and/or fax machine. The manufacturer claims that KONEXX also eliminates the incompatibility problems caused by PBX, digital, and hotel telephone systems. There are two KONEXX models, a simple one for modems that don't require telephone line voltage and a more advanced one that functions with those modems that need telephone line voltage and includes automatic voice/data switching. This latter feature lets you use your computer as a phone dialer or pick up and talk if your call to another modem or fax machine happens to be answered by a person instead of a computer.

Cellular phones

Using your Mac PowerBook, or any other portable modem, with a cellular telephone is possible, but you might need a special interface that fits in between the modem and the phone. Your cellular telephone dealer can provide the proper box. Read the telephone's instruction manual first, though. Some of the fancier ones have modem/fax capability built right in. Once you have the interface, there are only a couple of minor problems to deal with. The first problem occurs when you dial the call. It might not be possible to dial with your software. Instead, you might need to send the modem an off-hook command by typing ATH1 and dial the call through the cellular phone. (These commands will be explained in detail in the next chapter.)

Inevitably, cellular telephones are less reliable than hard-wired ones. You might encounter noise, signal fading, or other kinds of interference, any of which would disrupt modem communications and necessitate your re-sending the interrupted files. Of course, you should never try to go online while you're driving, for safety reasons as well as the likelihood of interruption as the signal passes from one cell to another.

Summary

Telecommunications, allowing your computer to send and receive data over telephone lines, requires the use of a modem. Modems change the computer's digital output into a signal that can be sent over the normal telephone system and change it back again, or de-modulate it, so another computer can accept it. There are several different sets of standards that apply to modems. Important ones to look for are Hayes compatibility and Bell/CCITT standards for modem speeds, data compression, and error correction. Many of the current generation of modems also have built-in fax capability, letting you send or send and receive faxes on your Mac.

Hooking up a modem isn't difficult. Most modems have four connections to be made. One cable goes to the Mac, one to the telephone jack, and one to a power supply. The fourth, plugging a telephone into the modem, is optional, but convenient. A different type of modem, the Global Village TelePort, plugs into the Apple Desktop Bus on any Mac so equipped.

PowerBooks can use either an internal or external modem. To hook up an internal modem, plug one end of the RJ-11 cable into the jack on the PowerBook and the other into a telephone jack. When proper jacks are unavailable, there are numerous alternatives, including acoustic couplers, cheater cords, and the KONEXX, an interface to PBX, hotel, and digital telephones.

2
A terminal case

Computers are not very smart. They're extremely good at adding 1s and 0s, but you need something to tell them which 1s and 0s to add and what to do with the results. That something is variously called *software, applications,* or *programs.* These words all refer to exactly the same thing: the rules for doing whatever it is you want the computer to do. (An application *is* a program, despite System 7's redundant reference to "application programs," which makes as much sense as talking about an "armchair chair" or a "sailboat yacht.") Programs exist that can do virtually anything you want done: your taxes, your biorhythms, your Great American Novel. . . . And, of course, there are telecommunication programs.

The earliest form of telecommunications was the telegraph, which used a digital code to send news and messages almost instantaneously from one place to another. A skilled telegraph operator could often send and receive at speeds up to 30 words a minute. In 1874, Emile Baudot developed a five-unit code in which every character contained five symbol elements, each being of equal duration and designated as a mark or a space according to the provisions of the code and corresponding to current on and current off, respectively. Baudot's telegraph code became the basis for the ASCII code computers use today.

As automation became part of our vocabulary, the process of sending telegraph messages was a prime candidate for new technology. Instead of tapping a key and copying the letters in pencil on a pad of paper, telegraph operators sat at *terminals,* keyboards much like a typewriter, and typed their messages. The keys struck little wheels, which turned and made electrical contact in the right patterns for the individual letters. At the far end of the wire other terminals, looking as if they were manned by ghost typists, received the electrical pulses, duplicated the keystrokes, and retyped the messages.

Early computer systems used teletype terminals to input data to the computer. Since both computer and keyboard used what was by then standardized as ASCII code, it was a logical combination. It followed, both logically and inevitably, that computer operators would soon realize that one computer could communicate with another if both could be programmed to think of themselves as teletype machines. Telecommunications, as we know it, had arrived.

Today's telecommunication software is a good deal more sophisticated than the early "dumb terminal" programs. Of course, computers themselves are a lot different. Instead of a roomful of vacuum tubes and relays, today you have a handful of microchips with a thousand times more power. Your Mac can do things that Univac's creators hardly dared to dream about. Not the least of these is the ability to talk from your keyboard to all kinds of computers in all corners of the world. But in order to do so, your Mac still has to turn itself into something resembling a teletype machine, and that's why it needs a telecommunications program. Telecom programs serve two purposes: they let the Mac communicate *with* the modem and also *through* the modem.

Talking *to* your modem

The modem, as you learned in the last chapter, is a box that translates data from the computer into a format that can be sent over the telephone lines. The modem contains a microprocessor and a ROM chip with information that tells it how to adjust its transmission speeds, how to produce the dialing sounds to place a call, how to apply the right modulation scheme and error-correction/data-compression systems, and how to handle other "housekeeping" details that your telecommunications program might ask it to do. The software must be able to tell the modem when to make a call, when to hang up, and how to do whatever is necessary in between those two steps to keep the data flowing. It does this by using the Hayes (AT) command set, and that's why it's so important for modems to be AT-compatible. Otherwise, you would need a separate modem driver to translate your commands into a language the modem could recognize. (Many telecom programs come with a set of modem drivers for specific modems, allowing users to take advantage of special features and commands the manufacturers have added.)

Hayes commands, or AT commands, are a standardized system for communicating with the modem. They're often called AT commands because they start with the letters AT for "attention." Basic commands are three-letter codes, but they might include a fourth letter or number as a modifier. For example, the command to dial a number is ATDT, meaning "Attention, Dial, using Tones." Then, you'd type the number to be dialed and hit a carriage return. Although most modems are willing to accept either caps or lower case, a few demand that you use only capital letters for your commands, something to try if you've typed atdt 555-1212 and nothing happened. Table 2-1 shows the most commonly used AT commands and their meanings.

Table 2-1 Standard AT Command Set

Command	Modifier	Example	Functions
AT		AT	ATtention, clears command buffer, "wakes up" modem. (All the commands following are preceded by the AT prefix.)
A		ATA	Use Answer mode; manually answer incoming call.

Table 2-1 Continued

Command	Modifier	Example	Functions
C		ATC	Enable/Disable carrier signal
	C0	ATC0	Disables carrier transmitter
	C1	ATC1	Enables automatic carrier on/off switching
D		ATD	Dial number following...
	DP	ATDP	Dial using pulses (rotary-type phone)
	DT	ATDT	Dial using tones (button-type phone)
	R	ATDR	Instructs modem to switch to answer mode before dialing (used to call an "originate-only" modem)
	W	ATDW	Wail for dialtone before dialing
	, (comma)	ATD,	Pause (length determined by S-register) Can be placed wherever needed, I.e.: ATDT, *70, 555, 1212
	/	ATD/	Pause .125 second before continuing
	;	ATD 555-1212;	Dial and then enter command mode. Allows you to enter password or ID for automated banking, etc.
	!	AT!	Hookflash — Hang up for .5 sec, then reconnect.
	@	AT@	Wait for silence, then dial. (Length of wait set by S register)
E		ATE	Enable/disable character echo
	E or E0	ATE0	No echo
	E1	ATE1	Echo
F		ATF	Set duplex mode
	F or F0	ATF0	Half duplex
	F1	ATF1	Full duplex
H		ATH	Hook (Acts same as picking up/putting down handset)
	H0	ATH0	Hang up
	H1	ATH1	Pick up (Off Hook)
M		ATM	Speaker on/off control
	M0	ATMO	Speaker off
	M1	ATM1	Turns speaker off when carrier is detected and CONNECT displayed on screen
	M2	ATM2	Speaker on. Carrier monitored during connection
O		ATO	Return online after setting command mode
Q		ATQ	Enable/disable result code display
	Q0	ATQ0	Enables result codes (default setting)
	Q1	ATQ1	Disables result code display
Srn		ATS0=1, etc.	Sets register (r) value to (n). S-registers determine timing of various functions, number of rings before answer, etc.
S?		ATS0?	Check current setting of parameter
V		ATV	Specify type of result codes displayed
	V0	ATV0	Numeric result codes (1,2,3)
	V1	ATV1	Verbose: codes displayed in words. (OK, RING, CONNECT)
Xn		ATXn	Enables various detection and monitoring features to show call status, speed, etc. (CONNECT 2400, etc.)

Table 2-1 Continued

Command	Modifier	Example	Functions
Z		ATZ	Restores modem's default settings.
AT&			Prefix for advanced level commands, available on some modems
Following commands do not have to be preceded by AT			
(return)			Implements the command entered
A/			Repeat last command
+++			Enter command mode (Need not be followed by return)

The truth is, though, that with many of the communications programs that are available, you'll never need to type a single one of these commands. The software automatically supports the most frequently needed commands: to *initialize* the modem—to wake it up and get its attention, to dial a number, to turn on or off the automatic answer function for incoming calls, and to disconnect the modem and hang up after a call. When you first set up your modem and communications software, you'll need to work through a pile of menus that define the ways in which you and your Mac will speak to the modem and the way you'll talk and listen through your modem. Figure 2-1 shows one of the settings dialog boxes from White

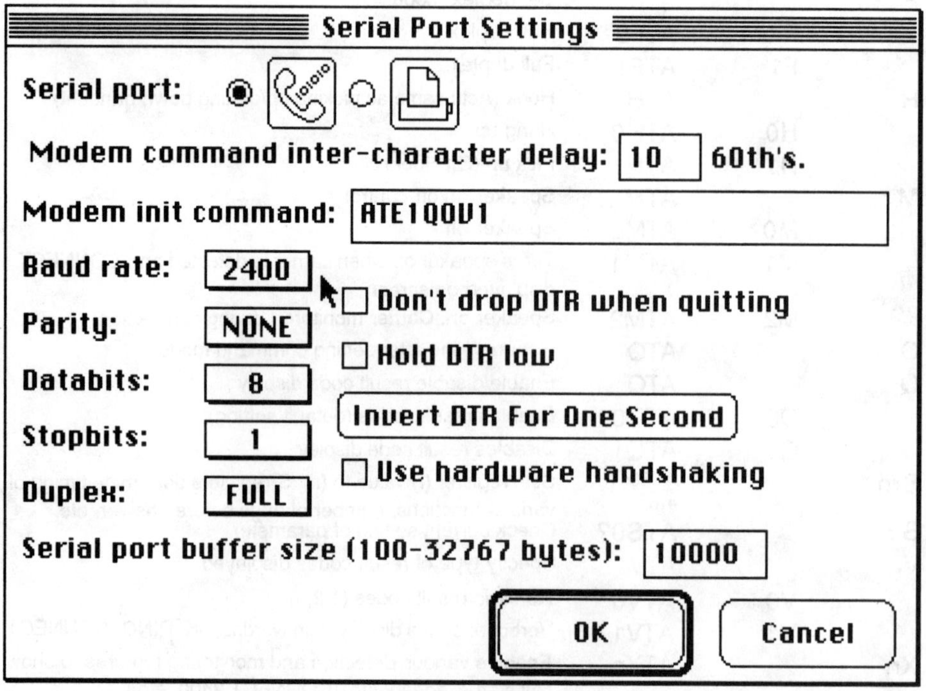

Serial Port Settings

Serial port:

Modem command inter-character delay: 10 60th's.

Modem init command: ATE1Q0V1

Baud rate: 2400

Don't drop DTR when quitting

Parity: NONE

Hold DTR low

Databits: 8

Invert DTR For One Second

Stopbits: 1

Use hardware handshaking

Duplex: FULL

Serial port buffer size (100-32767 bytes): 10000

OK Cancel

2-1 These entries show the modem which settings to use.

Knight, one of the most popular telecom programs. You'll probably spot a few familiar items.

First of all, there are the modem and printer icons, which let you tell the program which of the two serial ports it should watch for incoming data and send its outgoing data to. There's the modem initialization string ATE1Q0V1, a chain of AT commands that translates as follows: "Attention, Enable character echo, Enable result code display, Verbose display." What this means to your modem is, "Hey, wake up! When a letter is typed, show it on the screen. Show us what you're doing, like dialing and connecting . . . and spell it out in words."

DTR stands for *Data Terminal Ready*. If you quit the communications program, ordinarily (by default) the modem automatically disconnects. If you select "Don't drop DTR when quitting," your modem will stay on line. Generally speaking, though, you want it to hang up. If, for example, you have a system crash that forces you to quit the program and reboot, your phone will normally hang up at the same time. If you have selected "Don't drop DTR," the connection will be maintained, not only tying up the line but continuing to run up the bill on a cost-per-minute service. In rare instances, you might need to maintain a suppressed DTR (Hold DTR Low) or use the "Invert DTR" option to send a Flash signal. It's almost the same as using AT except that the flash lasts a full second instead of a half second. Flash is used to get the attention of a LAN or a modem-equipped PBX system. See your specific modem and software manuals for information. Your communications software also tells the modem what baud rate and settings to use. (The following chapter explains these in detail.)

Talking *with* your modem

The modem/software combination has two modes of operation: command mode, described above, talks to the modem; terminal mode talks with (or through) your modem. In terminal mode, letters you type on the keyboard go into the modem as digital signals and out to the phone line as analog signals. When you click on a button with the mouse, the program sends the appropriate code. The only exceptions to this are standard Mac menu functions such as Save, Print, Open, and so on. Virtually all telecom programs recognize the Mac operating system's command key functions for these actions.

Sending the command to dial a number takes you from offline to online. Your Mac is now a terminal, very much like the early teletype machines. There are several different kinds of terminals it can emulate. Terminal emulation defines how the program responds to certain control characters sent to it from the host system, the one it's calling. The most common of these, and the most likely to be compatible with the other systems is called *TTY* or *dumb terminal*. (TTY is a kind of shorthand for teletype.) TTY emulation has only a few commands available. Among these are clearing the screen, doing a carriage return or linefeed, backspacing, using tabs, and ringing the bell. These are the formatting commands included in the first part of the ASCII character set. A true dumb terminal can't write to disk or hold information in a screen-capture buffer. It lets you read what you're typing in, and what the other computer is responding with, and that's that. Figure 2-2 shows a dumb terminal program in use.

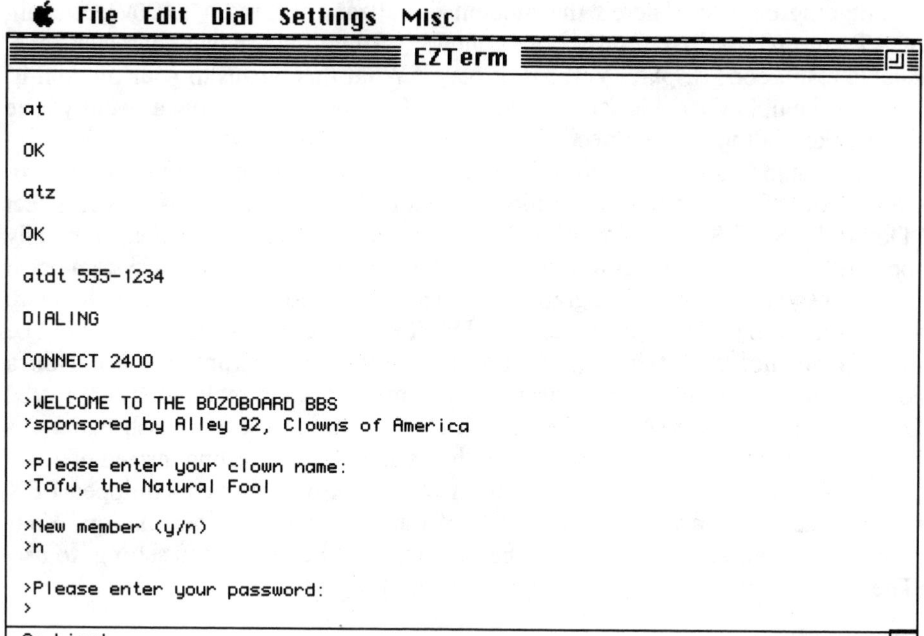

2-2 Dumb terminal.

The thing to remember about dumb terminals is that your Mac is just pretending to be one. It's not *really* dumb. So, even in TTY mode, with most of the software available today you'll be able to do quite a bit more than read and write. In fact, you'll probably discover that you're using TTY mode a lot. For one thing, it's the "lowest common denominator" for communicating with other computers. You can talk to almost any online service in TTY mode, even those that normally use a graphic interface. (The only exception is Prodigy, which uses a very different way to put its images on your screen.)

As computers began to take the place of teletype as a means of communication, computer terminals got more sophisticated. The Digital Equipment Corporation (DEC) introduced a smarter communications terminal, called the VT-52. (*VT* stands for *video terminal.*) It had more formatting options and allowed the cursor to be repositioned on the screen. It was followed by the VT-100 and VT-102, which have even more to offer. VT-100 and VT-102 are ANSI-compatible, which means they meet standards set for terminals by the American National Standards Institute. (Newer versions of software might also support VT-220 and VT-320, even more advanced DEC terminals.) VT-terminals allow for some onscreen graphics, and make it easier to enter and edit text on the screen. Some online services have

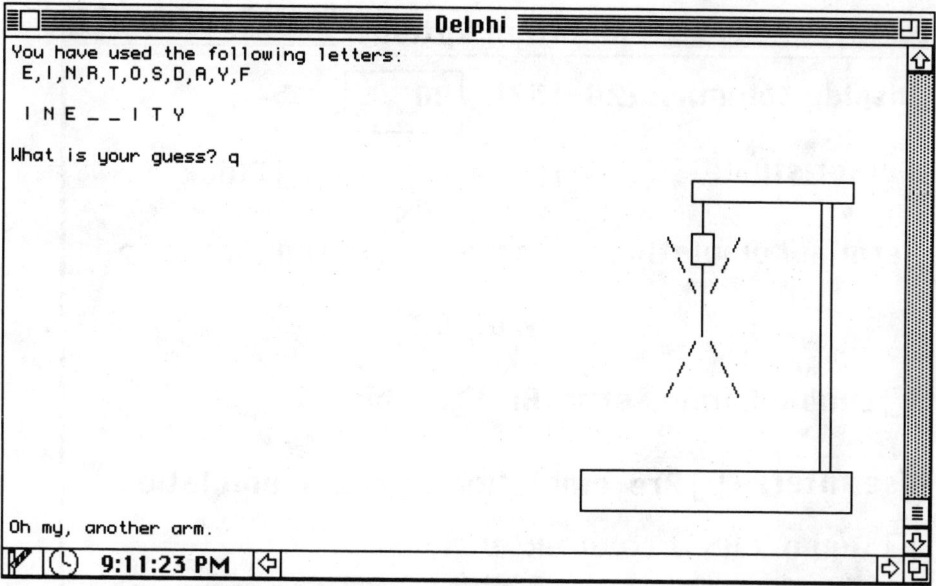

2-3 This game is offered by Delphi. Other services have similar games, some with better graphics.

special games that can only be accessed by VT terminals. Figure 2-3 shows a VT-52 game from Delphi. Note that in addition to the graphics at the side of the screen, you're entering text *above* the last line of the screen. This program has been written to send the cursor back and forth between your entry and the computer's reply and to the right of the screen to draw more of the graphic when needed.

VT or not VT? That is the question.

If you're calling, or being called by another individual computer, always use TTY emulation. When you're signing onto a new BBS or service for the first time, start with TTY and find out what kinds of terminals the host system supports. If you see something that looks like line noise mixed in with the message from the host computer, it's probably using one of the VT modes. Most host systems should be able to understand you in dumb terminal mode, though. Depending on how sophisticated the host system is, you might be asked to choose a terminal mode when you log on. TTY might also be listed as *CRT*, which stands for *Cathode Ray Tube*, a very early name for computer display screen, or it might be called *dumb* or even *other*. VT-100 and VT-102 might also be listed as ANSI. If you have a choice, VT-102 is the most desirable mode, then VT-100, VT-52, and both last and least, TTY.

If you have chosen something other than TTY, you'll have to re-set your communications program to accommodate it. Figures 2-4 and 2-5 show White Knight's Emulation Options and VT modes dialog boxes. Other telecom programs will have the same kinds of choices, though you might have to look on different menus to find them. These options let you switch from TTY to VT modes and

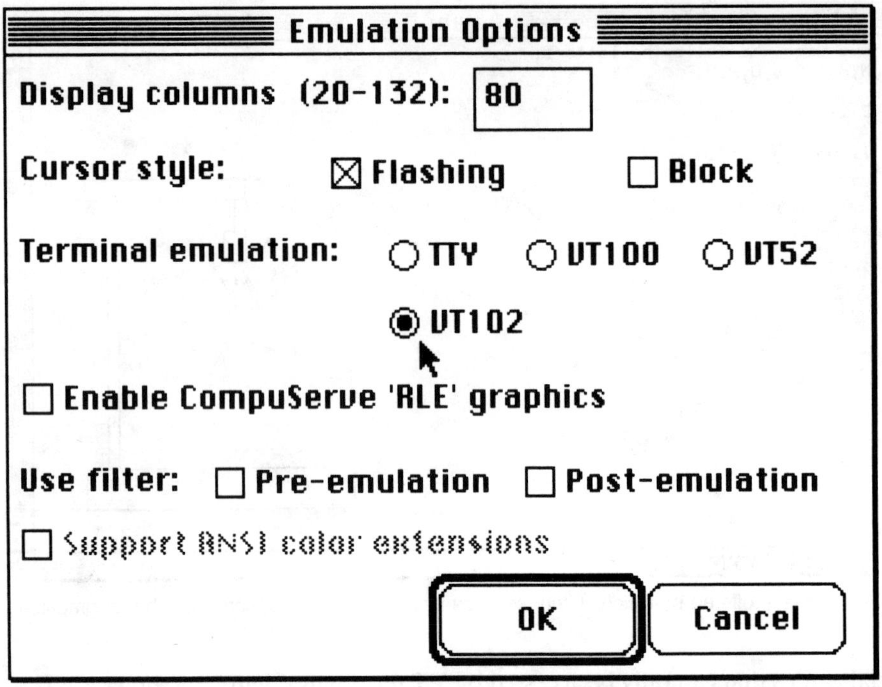

Emulation Options

Display columns (20-132): 80

Cursor style: ☒ Flashing ☐ Block

Terminal emulation: ○ TTY ○ VT100 ○ VT52 ◉ VT102

☐ Enable CompuServe 'RLE' graphics

Use filter: ☐ Pre-emulation ☐ Post-emulation

☐ Support ANSI color extensions

OK Cancel

2-4 Use this dialog box to select the type of terminal to emulate. When in doubt, choose TTY.

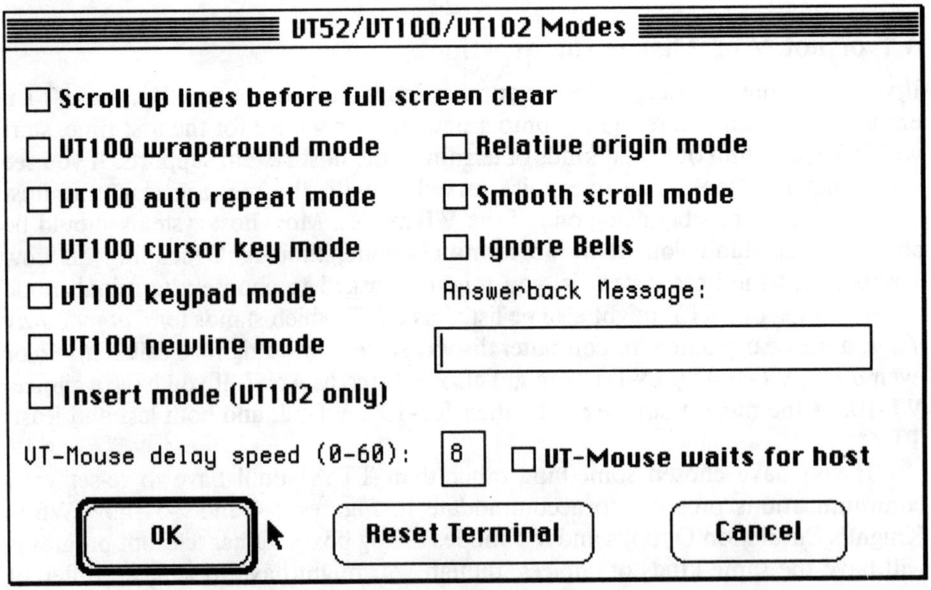

VT52/VT100/VT102 Modes

☐ Scroll up lines before full screen clear

☐ VT100 wraparound mode ☐ Relative origin mode

☐ VT100 auto repeat mode ☐ Smooth scroll mode

☐ VT100 cursor key mode ☐ Ignore Bells

☐ VT100 keypad mode Answerback Message:

☐ VT100 newline mode

☐ Insert mode (VT102 only)

VT-Mouse delay speed (0-60): 8 ☐ VT-Mouse waits for host

OK Reset Terminal Cancel

2-5 These options control how the Mac behaves in VT mode.

customize the way the program handles certain VT functions. The host computer can turn any of these functions on or off without your being aware of it. Some of the VT functions are useful. For example, wraparound mode automatically inserts a linefeed at the end of the line, letting you keep typing without using carriage returns. Auto repeat repeats characters when you hold down the key. Some other functions are less useful. In general, it's best to let the host computer define the functions it will support and not try to set them individually.

General-purpose programs

When you buy a modem, you might find a telecom program bundled with it. Hayes includes SmartCom with its modems. Prometheus MacKnowledge is included with its line of modems. Global Village gives you MicroPhone, the original version of Software Ventures' popular telecom program. Several makers include Bill Bond's excellent shareware application, FreeTerm, which, if you're just calling your local BBS or a text-based service, might be all the software you'll ever need. If your modem didn't come with a telecom program, or if you aren't happy with the one you got, a look at your favorite dealer's shelf or catalog will present you with some other options.

Telecom programs for the Mac can be defined as either menu driven or icon driven. Icon-driven programs, also known as *GUI* for *Graphical User Interface*, are more Mac-like, in *this* user's opinion. MicroPhone II, from Software Ventures, is a GUI program. Scott Watson's White Knight, published by Freesoft, is menu driven. Both programs have won all kinds of awards and both are extremely popular. There are, as you'll see, both similarities and differences.

MicroPhone II

Now in version 4, MicroPhone II is a powerful, but easy-to-learn application that comes with pre-written scripts for several services as well as all the tools you need to create your own. All a beginner needs to do to get online on is to open the appropriate file and enter the number to be called, plus name and password as shown in Fig. 2-6.

After you've made these entries, going online is as easy as pushing a button. The script tells the modem exactly what to do to set itself correctly and to place the call to the service. You'll see your user identification name or number and password entered automatically. Pushing other buttons takes you to interesting areas within the service. When you're finished, just push the Log Off button to exit the service and hang up the phone. Figure 2-7 shows some of the buttons installed in this script for GEnie.

Once you're online, communications forums in America Online, CompuServe, and GEnie can provide you with additional MicroPhone II scripts. These scripts automate the whole routine of setting communications parameters, calling and logging in, and jumping from one service area to another. All you need to do is to double click the appropriate icons. Each icon represents a different area within the service, possibly a forum, a mailbox, or a news display. When an icon is

GEnie User Profile

GEnie User ID xvy61698

Password ••••

Phone Number 8683269

Number of Tries 1

OK Cancel

2-6 Some services require a User ID. Others ask for a user name, a screen name, or a "handle."

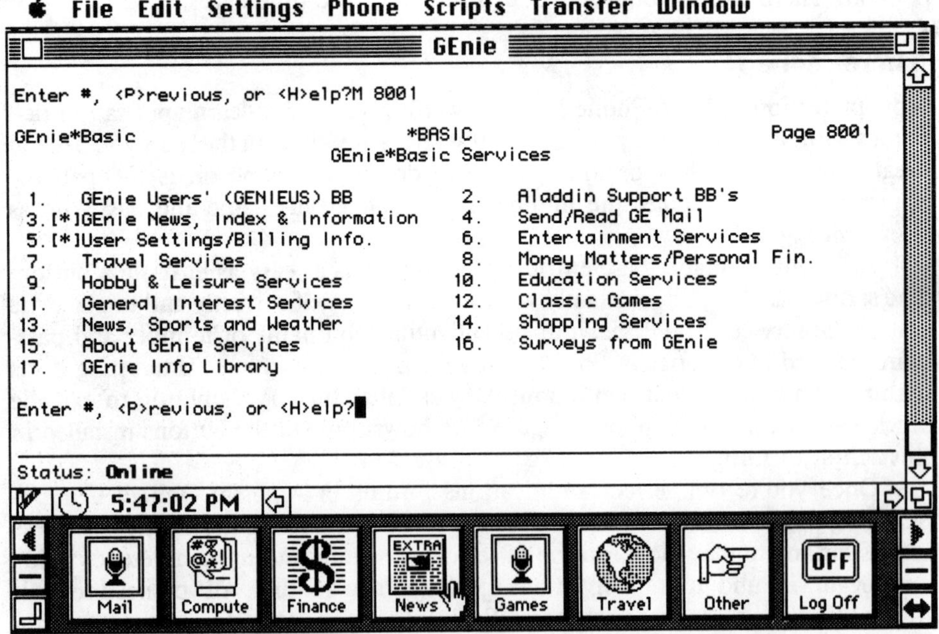

2-7 Clicking on any of these buttons enters the right code to take you to that area.

selected, the script enters the appropriate command to go to that area. The palette of icons changes within some areas. For example, when you select Mail, you'll see a set of buttons like those shown in Fig. 2-8 for creating, reading, or saving your mail.

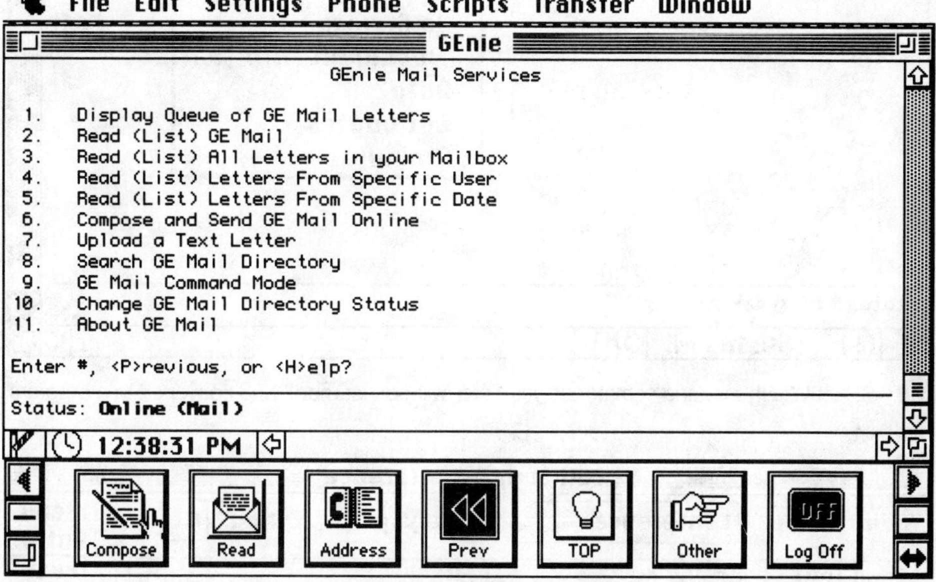

2-8 The icon bar can change to whatever assortment of choices you need to make.

Do-it-yourself scripting

MicroPhone II's manual contains instructions for creating new scripts. You might have several different scripts for a single service: one to go in quickly and check for E-mail, one to go to a specific forum area and download a file, or perhaps one that takes you to the opening menu so you can browse. Assembling scripts isn't difficult. MicroPhone II provides three different ways in which you can write a script: Watch me . . . , Script Editor, and text file entry. These are found on the Scripts menu, as shown in Fig. 2-9.

Watch me . . . is an automatic recording mode. When you use it, you'll start by assigning a name to your script, probably the name of the service or BBS you're calling, and you'll specify whether the script is invoked by a menu listing, a button, an F-key, or a Command key. Then, from within the terminal window, you'll run the online session. As you do so, the program will watch what you do and generate a script as you do it. When you're done, select End Watch Me to stop recording.

Edit Scripts . . . opens a dialog box called Script Manager. The commands in Script Manager can be used to create new scripts or to modify or copy all or parts of existing scripts. Think of the script commands (the listing in the lower left window in Fig. 2-10) as building blocks. If you stack them in the right order, you'll end up with a useful structure; but just as you wouldn't put the roof beam in the cellar, you

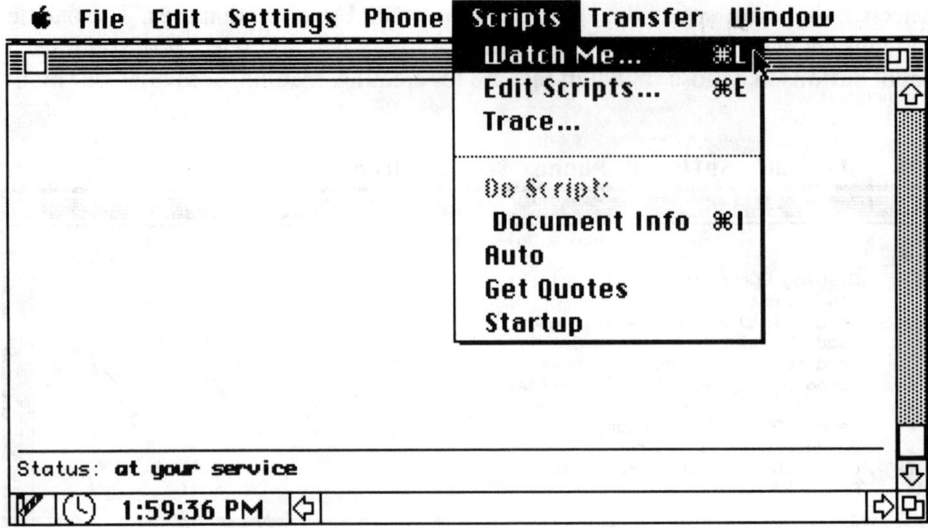

2-9 Select Watch me, and commands you enter will be "learned" and converted to a program.

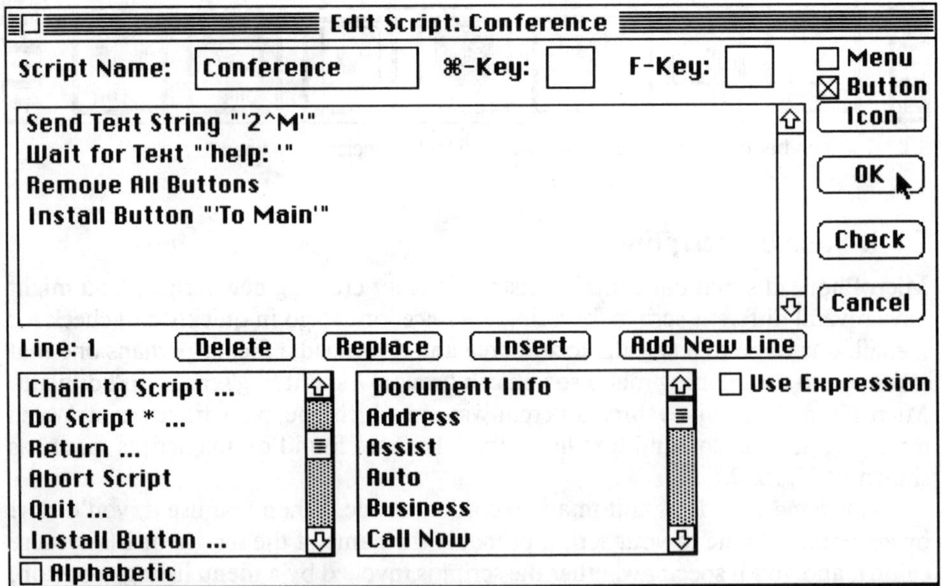

2-10 This script is activated when you click the Conference button. It takes you to Delphi's Conference area and installs a button to return you to the Main area.

have to make sure that you are using the commands in a reasonable sequence. Otherwise, you might find yourself hanging up before you get a chance to read your mail. MicroPhone II can help you "de-bug" your scripts to avoid this kind of mistake. Selecting the Trace . . . command adds a box (with a little bug, to help

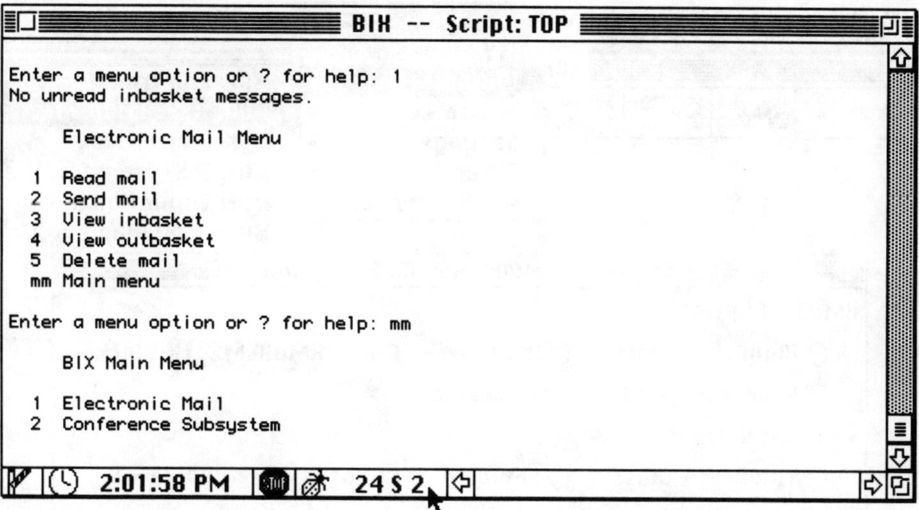

2-11 When you click on the debug box, MicroPhone II will display the contents of that line of the script.

you remember what it's doing) at the bottom of the screen (Fig. 2-11). The box lists each line of your script as it's being enacted. To read the contents of a line, place the pointer on the box and press the mouse button.

MicroPhone II supports all of the current transfer protocols. (You'll learn more about these in chapter 6.) It can also serve as a host for incoming calls. Under System 7, it displays limited balloon help. (Of course, most balloon help is limited.) Although its script editor is as powerful as any other program's, it is easy for a beginner to use, even without reading the manual.

MicroPhone, the original version of this program, has fewer features but is still a good choice for the casual user. It comes with pre-written scripts for major services, plus a generic one for BBS and for Mac-to-Mac file transfers. MicroPhone is bundled with several different brands of modem, including Global Village.

White Knight

If MicroPhone II is the ideal communications program for the computer novice, White Knight is probably the program of choice for serious users (those who think balloon help is for wimps). It supports all kinds of transfer protocols, including 3 flavors of YMODEM as well as X- and ZMODEM, Flash, and three different styles of Kermit. Unlike MicroPhone II, White Knight comes with no icons or buttons to push. Instead, it uses a system of menus, submenus, and dialog boxes like those shown in Fig. 2-12. White Knight's scripts are called *procedures* and, like Microphone's, can be assembled in a Watch Me . . . mode, by selecting Write For Me . . . from the Procedures submenu (Fig. 2-13) and then following the routine you want to turn into a repeatable procedure.

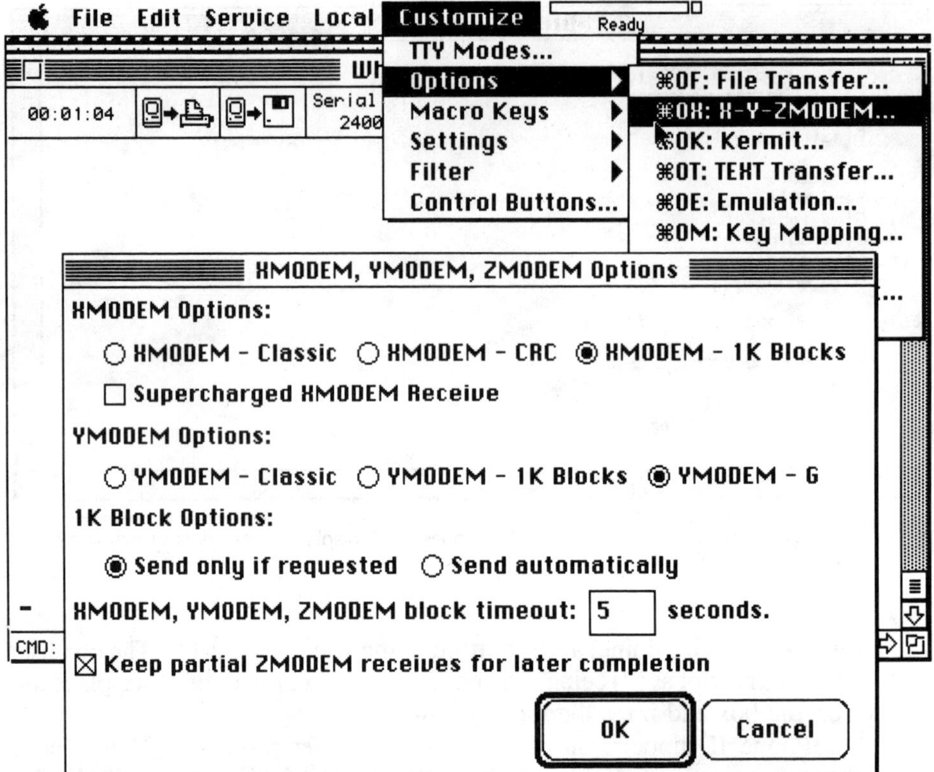

2-12 Use White Knights menus and dialog boxes to confirm settings and choose options.

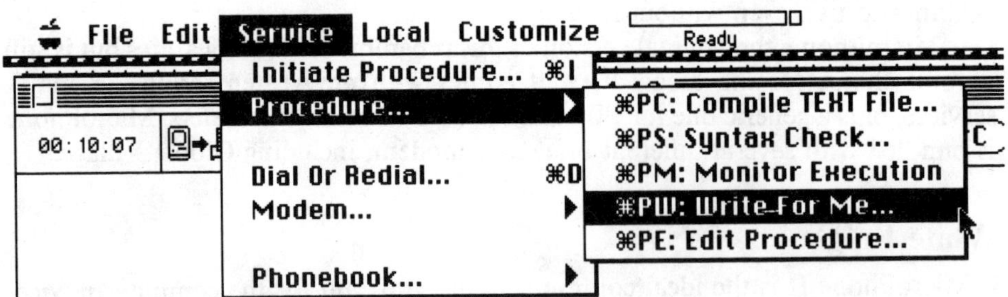

2-13 After making this choice, enter the AT commands and log in procedure in the terminal window. White Knight will turn these into a procedure.

Macros

White Knight also lets you create and use macros. A macro is a user-defined key that can do any of several useful things. It can send a string of letters (up to 240 characters) just as if you were typing them in. Macros can be used to send a command, to trigger another script, or to send a pet phrase during a conference or game. For instance, you could create a macro to enter your password for a service or to go to a specific area within the service. Macros are especially handy for those who play online games. Figure 2-14 shows the Macro Editor. This is one of a set of macros for Delphi's online Poker game. You might create a set of poker macros and another "main" macro to install them. Macros can also execute a compiled Procedure file. You could set up a macro to call MCI mail, scan your In box for waiting mail, retrieve it, and log off again.

Macros can be accessed from the status bar at the top of the terminal window or, at the user's option, from a separate macro window (Fig. 2-15). If the latter is chosen, macros can be identified with icons. White Knight doesn't come with its own set of icons, as MicroPhone II does, but it lets you "borrow" icons from other

Edit Macro Key
Set #1 Macro Key #4
Get Procedure File
Get Macro Keys File
String: /n Saratoga Slim^M
Label: change name
Invisible in Status Bar
Display as: Button
Invisible in Macro Key Window
Icon
Don't respond to mouse clicks
Double-size icon
PICT
Save
Cancel

2-14 Macros can be identified with buttons, icons, or PICT symbols you create and load in.

2-15 The Macro Key Window can show up to eight icons or buttons at a time.

applications. (HyperCard has an especially good selection.) When you choose Icon, in White Knight's Procedure Editor, you'll be asked to open another program. Doing so opens a window with that program's icons, so you can select one to identify the macro. If you have an icon editor program or ResEdit, you can also create your own custom icons to install with your White Knight macros or you can use a paint or draw program to create small PICT images.

Scott Watson and the saga of Red Ryder

White Knight is the commercially released version of a program called Red Ryder, which you can still find on user group bulletin boards and shareware collections. Red Ryder and its creator, Scott Watson, are legends in the field of Mac communications. Watson wrote the original Red Ryder program on his first 128K Mac in 1984 and released it as shareware, back when there was very little shareware available. He simply hoped and trusted that satisfied users would send him the requested fee—and they did. In fact, response was overwhelming. In the preface to the current White Knight manual, he admits to having gotten behind on cashing the checks while he wrote and released versions 2, 3, and 4. (My husband recalls waiting about six months for his check to clear.) Finally, Watson quit his job in order to devote more time to programming. Red Ryder versions through 9.4 were distributed as shareware, but version 10.0 finally went commercial, and Watson opened a company called Freesoft to distribute it.

The name Red Ryder had come, not from the radio cowboy, but from a rock 'n' roll band. Nevertheless, Watson had licensed use of the Red Ryder trademark, and when it came time to release version 11.0, the trademark was up for renewal. Wanting to keep costs down, he changed the program's name to White Knight. Now on version 11.12, the program keeps changing and improving every time Watson, or one of his customers, thinks of something else to add. Fortunately, updates are available for downloading from several sources. Watson maintains a Freesoft Roundtable on GEnie (Fig. 2-16), and White Knight users are given a free (no sign-up fee) account on that service. Sign-on instructions are provided in the White Knight manual.

One advantage to White Knight that can't be overlooked is its cost, less than half that of MicroPhone II. For your money, you get a full-featured program, with some very sophisticated scripting tools. You also get a manual that can be rather confusing, especially to the telecommunication novice.

MacKnowledge and Smartcom

Prometheus and Hayes are modem manufacturers who wrote their own telecom programs. Prometheus includes a copy of its MacKnowledge with all of its modems. Hayes ships either Smartcom or the more advanced Smartcom II, depending on the selling price of the modem. Both have similar features to those of White Knight and MicroPhone II. Smartcom uses icons and a Watch Me . . . mode called Autopilot. If you've purchased either of these brands of modem, you probably won't need additional software, unless you choose a service with a dedicated program.

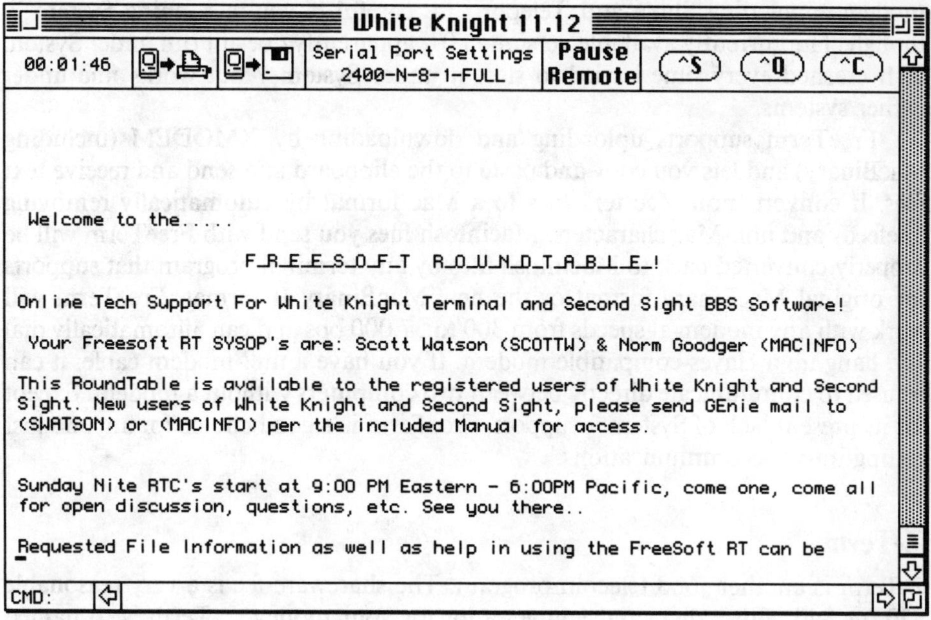

2-16 Freesoft sponsors a forum on GEnie, with bulletin boards, a library of useful White Knight procedures, and weekly live conferences.

When talk is cheap—shareware programs

Shareware authors must have taken note of Scott Watson's accomplishment in turning Red Ryder into a commercial success as White Knight. That would help explain why there are so many different shareware and freeware programs available. *Shareware*, for those who haven't experienced it previously, refers to a program that's "shared" for a small fee, rather than commercially published for a much larger fee. *Freeware* programs are, as the name suggests, free. Use them and pass them along to your friends with a clear conscience. Of course, freeware authors always appreciate a kind word if you like the program.

America Online, always a good source for Macintosh programs, has within its Mac communications library over 65 different listings for free and shareware terminal programs! Admittedly, about a dozen of these entries are for White Knight updates, but I counted at least 35 programs, some written in HyperCard, one in Japanese, some for specific purposes like getting mail and getting off again quickly, and some very good all-purpose programs.

FreeTerm

Bill Bond's FreeTerm would be a bargain even if you had to pay for it. It's a "plain vanilla" dumb terminal that's certainly adequate for calling the text-based services like Delphi, Bix, and GEnie, as well as your friendly local BBS. It has been upgraded regularly over the years and is included with a number of different modems, including Shiva and Teleport. Be careful if you're running System 7, though. The currently available version, 3.01, apparently doesn't run under System 7. It crashed every time I tried to start it under System 7 but works fine under earlier systems.

FreeTerm supports uploading and downloading by XMODEM (including MacBinary) and lets you copy and paste to the clipboard and send and receive text files. It converts non-Mac text files to a Mac format by automatically removing linefeeds and non-Mac characters. Macintosh files you send with FreeTerm will be properly converted back to Macintosh files by any terminal program that supports the original MacBinary format or the new MacBinary II format. FreeTerm will work with any modem at speeds from 300 to 57,000 bps and can automatically dial and hang up a Hayes-compatible modem. If you have a null-modem cable, it can be used to communicate directly between two computers without a modem. Except for its present lack of System 7 support, FreeTerm is a good choice for anyone just getting into telecommunications.

Z-Term

Z-Term is another good telecom program. The shareware fee is a very reasonable $30 (or $40 with a disk) and you get a lot for your money. Z-Term is so named because it can handle ZMODEM file transfers, a definite plus. ZMODEM transfers are much faster and can be "resurrected." If you lose a connection in the middle of a long download, you can resume the download right where you left it. You don't have to start from scratch, as you generally do with other download protocols. Figure 2-17 shows a ZMODEM download in process. The program keeps statistics on the relative efficiency of the transfer and tells you, to the second, how much longer it should take. Z-term also lets you use color on an LC or Mac II, so your screen can have red letters on a blue background, or black on yellow. Granted, this has limited usefulness, but the commercial programs offer it and so does Z-Term.

More important, and far more useful, is the ability to use macros. Z-Term lets you create and save sets of up to 10 macros. Figure 2-18 shows the Macro editor. Make as many sets as you like and select them from the Macros menu. They can be quickly accessed (if you know which of the set you want) by typing Command plus a number.

One drawback is that Z-Term uses a custom font, which in 9 points is extremely hard to read. In the 12-point size, which can be selected from the Terminal Preference dialog box under the Settings Menu, the type is much clearer. However, on a compact Mac, 12-point type means that your screen will hold only 68 characters across and not the full 80. You'll have to adjust screen width accordingly in any service or BBS you log onto.

Termulator

Termulator is cute. This shareware program comes from programmer Brad Quick and can be found on all the major services and BBSs. The program comes with a demo module custom designed for GEnie, shown in Fig. 2-19, as well as a fairly

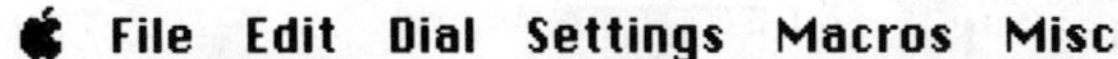

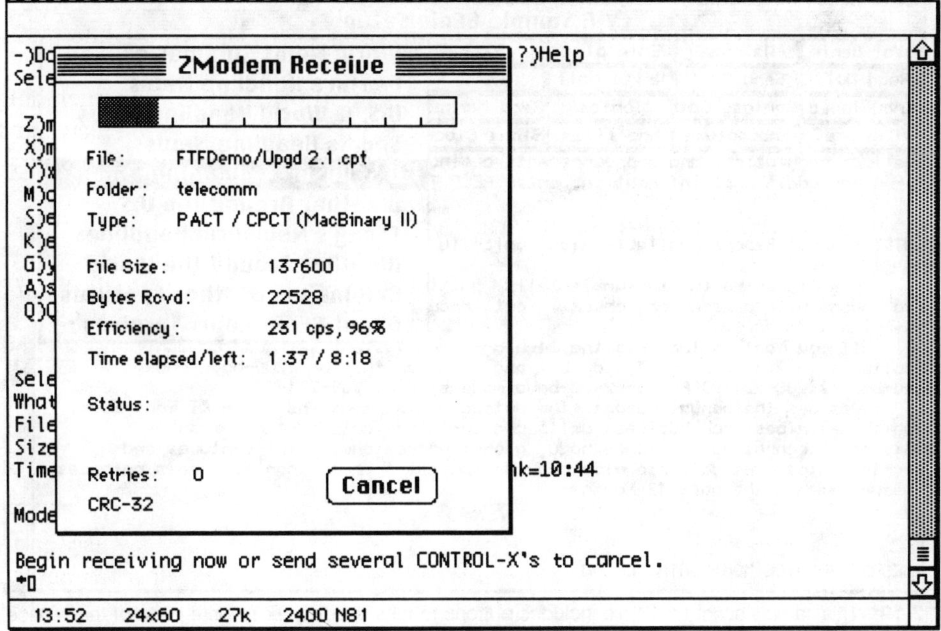

2-17 Z-Term is an excellent choice for downloading files.

Label:	Macro String:
Macro 1	go ent^M
Macro 2	TQ^M
Macro 3	enter^M
Macro 4	/send
Macro 5	/question^M
Macro 6	Oops, splat!^M
Macro 7	:-)^M
Macro 8	I hate this round!^M
Macro 9	I want my points back!!!^M
Macro 0	Yay, Tom ! (macro)^M

Set: TQ Macros — OK — Cancel

2-18 A set of Z-term macros for Delphi's Trivia Quest.

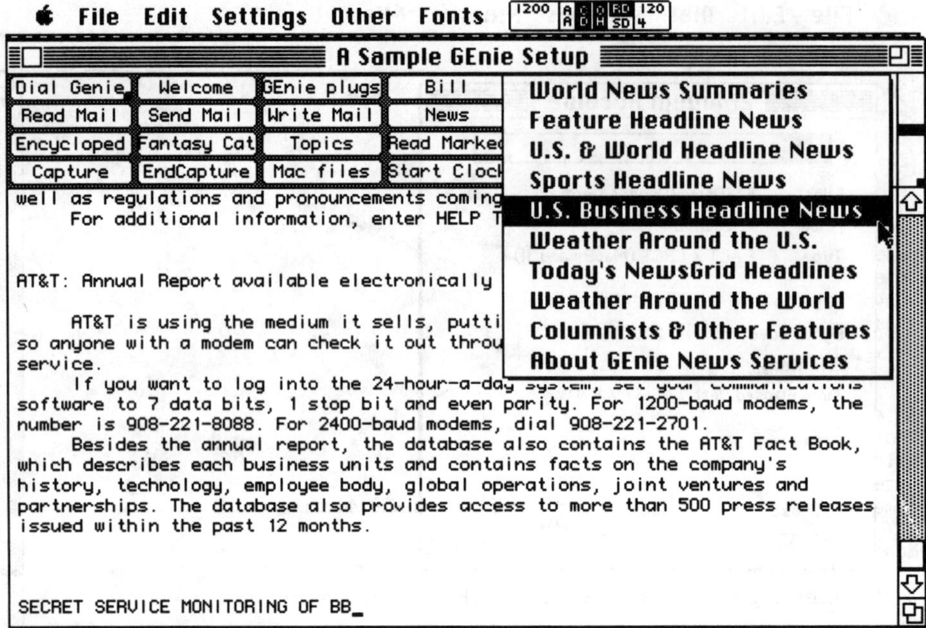

2-19 This sample script for GEnie includes buttons to take you to your favorite parts of the service, and even some sounds.

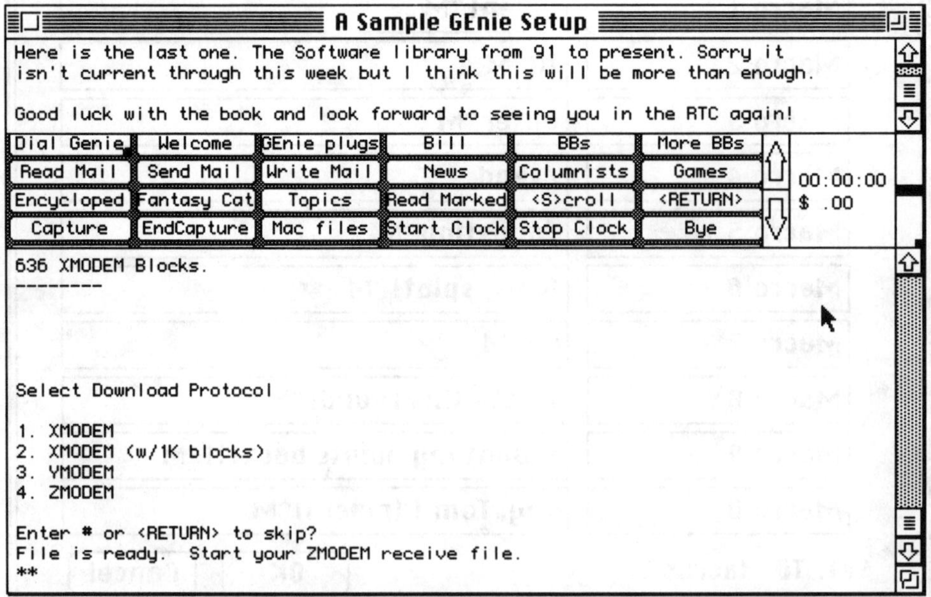

2-20 The split screen allows you to scroll back and verify the name of the file you want to download, or re-read your mail while the file is being copied.

clear instruction manual. It uses a set of programmable macro buttons to put you online and to steer you around the service. Some of these buttons lead to pop-up menus. Others simply take you where you want to go or set you up to read your mail.

The split window is one of the Termulator features that seems to make a good deal of sense (Fig. 2-20). By moving the button bar down, you can create upper and lower screens. Both display the same text. You can scroll backward in one window to read the contents, while the other window continues to show the incoming data. You can select text from one window and paste it into the other, as you might to retrieve the number or name of a file to download.

Termulator also supports the common transfer protocols, including ZMODEM and has a built-in clock timer that you can set to tell you how much money you're spending, a feature also found in White Knight. (MicroPhone II will keep time for you but won't figure the bill.) Termulator can also use sound files. The first time I tried logging off from GEnie, I was much amused to hear the Mac say "Hasta la Vista, Baby."

Dedicated software

The terminal programs previously described are fine for use with text-based services, but not all services are text based. CompuServe gives you a choice of three different ways to access its services: text, CompuServe Information Manager (CIM), and Navigator. America Online and Prodigy use their own GUI programs. These latter programs are said to be *dedicated.* You can't use them to call your local BBS or your friend's Mac. They access only their own services, but they do it in a way that's designed to be as user-friendly as possible. When you subscribe to America Online or Prodigy, you receive a copy of their program on disk, plus a manual that simply tells you how to install the program and lists what you'll find once you sign on.

America Online

America Online (AO) uses a system that combines menus and icons. It's probably the most intuitive Mac program one could imagine. When you sign on, you'll be greeted by an opening screen (Fig. 2-21) with some of the day's highlights. Clicking on any of the Highlights icons takes you directly to that area. Otherwise, the Departments button (which, like all proper Mac buttons, responds to a click or a carriage return) takes you to a window with eight different icons for everything from News, Entertainment, and Computing, to Lifestyles and Shopping. Choosing one of these takes you into that area, and gives you more options. Clicking on the mailbox sends you directly to AO's mail area. You can read your mail online or save it to read offline, download any attached files, write replies online, or send those you've already written.

The Computing area is shown in Fig. 2-22. Each folder represents a separate forum within the broad category of computing. For instance, choosing Games takes you into the Games Forum's Message, Conference and Library areas. All of America Online's forums have a similar structure.

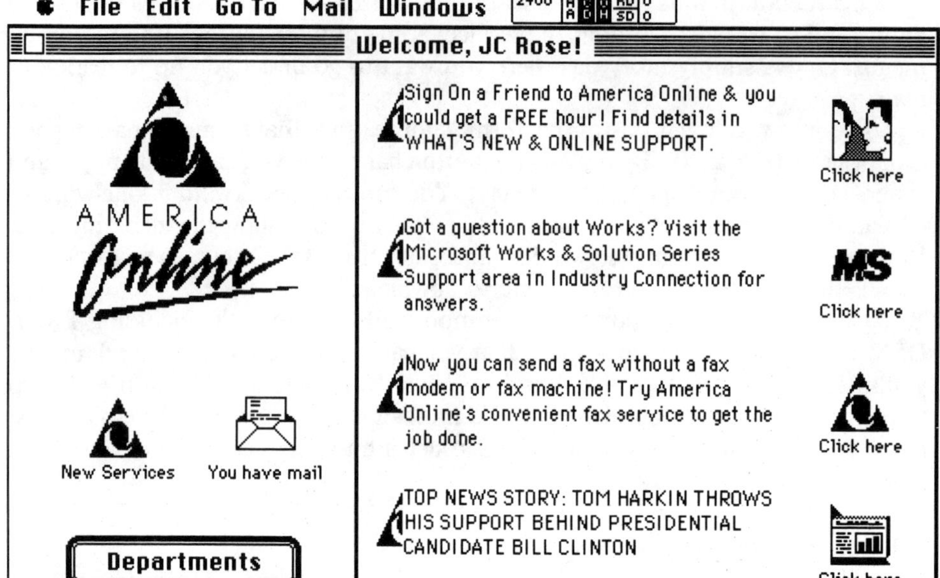

2-21 When this screen appears, a voice says, "Welcome. You've got mail!"

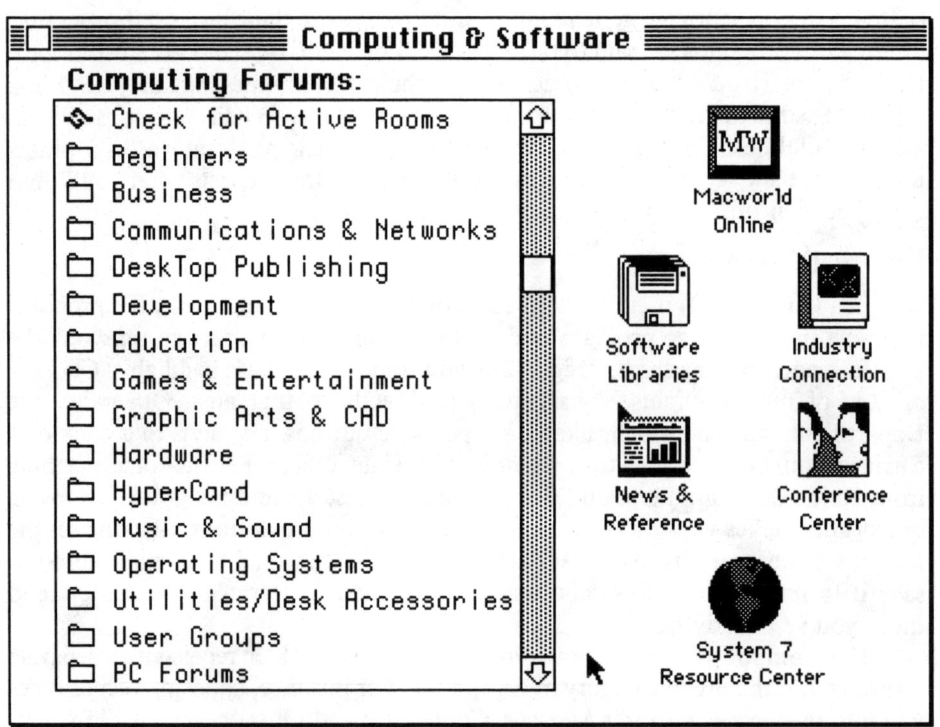

2-22 The icons at the right of the screen represent special features available within this area.

The AO software supports uploads and downloads at 1200 and 2400 bps with its own ZMODEM-style transfers. If a transfer is interrupted, you won't have to start it over again. Generally speaking, though, it's unlikely that you'll have problems. The AO system seems to be much more stable than some of the others. In two years of membership, I've only gotten disconnected once. Some other services are notorious for disconnecting (also called *bumping* or *turfing*) users.

Prodigy

Prodigy uses a very graphic interface, including bits of animation and nice bright colors (on the color Mac). Figure 2-23 shows a typical Prodigy opening screen. You can steer yourself through various Prodigy areas in any of several ways. Use the menu bar at the bottom of the screen. Enter the initial letter of the command you want to use (N for Next, J for Jump, etc.), or use Function keys on an extended keyboard or Command-key equivalents. (Prodigy supplies a chart of these in its sign-on kit.)

2-23 Prodigy welcomes you with the news and other items of interest.

Prodigy supplies not just one but two disks in its little yellow box. If you have a Mac with only one disk drive, this pretty much forces you to run the program from your hard drive, rather than from the disks, in order to avoid annoying disk swaps and to take advantage of Prodigy's printing utility. Prodigy's software takes over your system while it runs, so you won't be able to access your menu bar, DAs, most other applications, or screen savers. There are a few exceptions to this. If you have a menu bar clock, like the one on Visionary Software's First Things First program, it will remain visible, and you'll be able to access the reminder box by clicking on it. Screen savers and screen shot programs like SnapJot also remain functional.

Prodigy lets you print a copy of some, but not all, of its screens. It's not possible to print graphics screens like this weather map (Fig. 2-24), but it *will* print news articles and encyclopedia entries. The Prodigy software doesn't allow you to save anything to disk, but there are downloadable shareware utilities on other services that give you the capacity to do so. If, for instance, you are using Prodigy's encyclopedia for research, you might find it more useful to save the articles as text files rather than as hard copies.

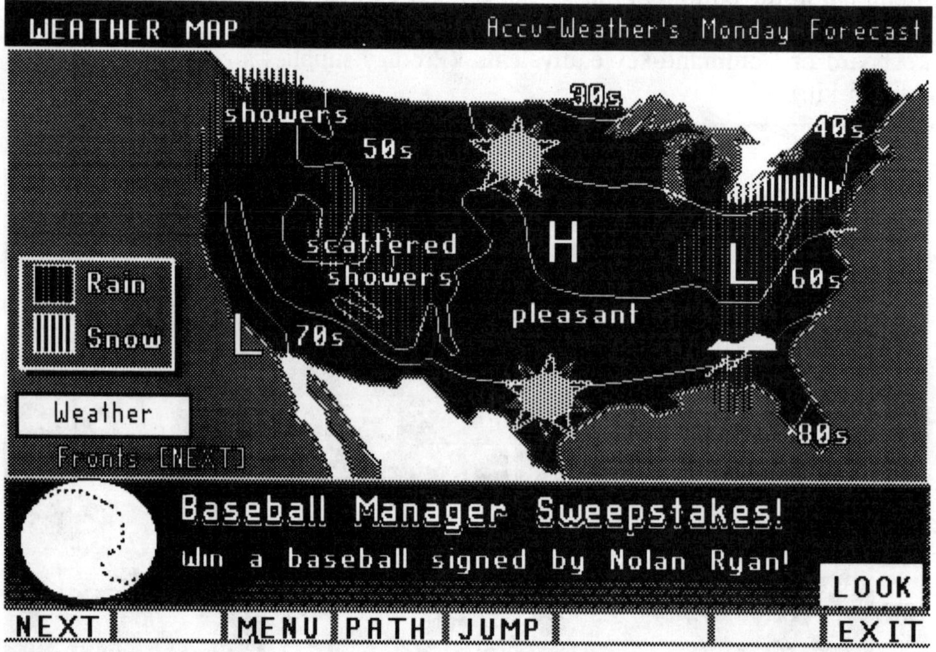

2-24 If you want to print or save a copy of the weather map, you'll need a screen-capture program.

There has been an ongoing controversy about Prodigy's software. Much of what appears on the user's screen is stored in Prodigy files on the user's hard disk. New features are added on a regular basis and thus the Prodigy program must be updated fairly often. To do so, the Prodigy service sends new program data to your computer while you're online. The new data is written onto the disk, in two files called STAGE.DAT and CACHE.DAT.

Some Prodigy service users, both PC and Mac owners, have found pieces of other files lodged within the STAGE.DAT and CACHE.DAT files. Prodigy claims this is an innocent error, caused because these files are assigned to a disk area that might have previously had other information written on it. (When something is erased from the disk, the individual bits of data aren't removed. Instead, the directory entry that shows where that data is located gets changed to show empty space so that another file can then be written over it.) Users argued that if Prodigy could write to their files, it could also read them. Prodigy spokespeople have publicly admitted the possibility but denied that the company is doing so.

However, what disturbed many users and caused a large number to cancel their Prodigy service accounts was that the information they found in the STAGE.DAT and CACHE.DAT files included data from financial programs, the text of lawyer/client memos, and in one case (reported in the Wall Street Journal on May 1, 1991) a tax lawyer found ". . . confidential tax info on most of his clients." Prodigy spokespersons have insisted that this is pure coincidence. The way operating systems work, they explain, "stray data" can appear in the files. America Online also uploads changes to its software from time to time but hasn't been the target of a similar controversy because its program is differently structured and doesn't seize empty disk space for its own use.

Cautious users, and those with confidential information on their hard disks might prefer to play it safe and either avoid using the Prodigy service altogether or always run it from a floppy disk with the hard drive safely shut down. If you're curious about the contents of the STAGE.DAT file, you can peek with a program like Norton's Fast Find, which lets you look into any file. Figure 2-25 shows a section of the author's STAGE.DAT file after running a Prodigy session. Nothing suspicious appeared.

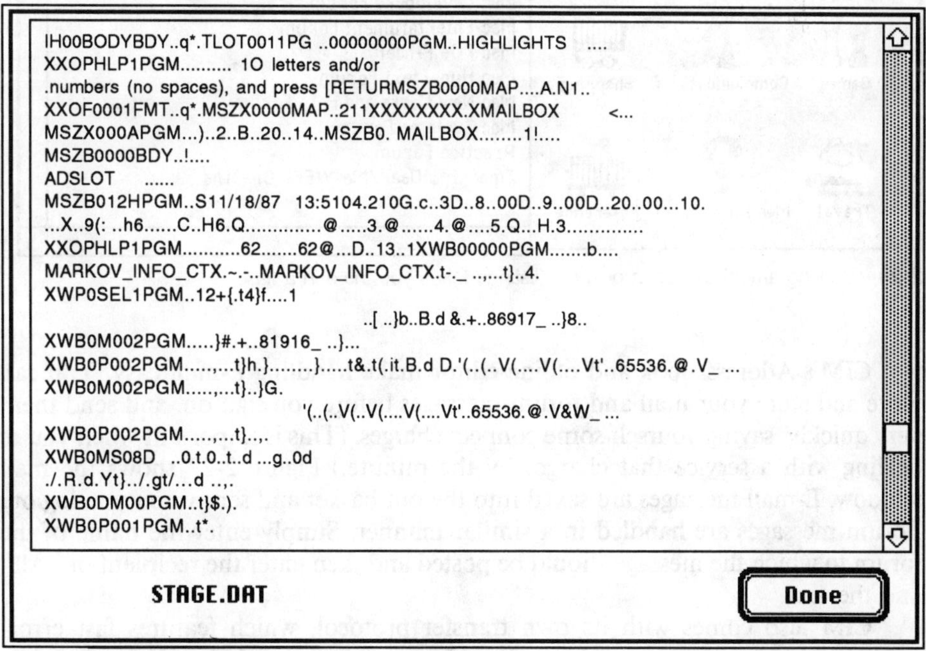

2-25 There's nothing in here to interest anyone!

CompuServe

Although it's possible to access much of CompuServe with a text-based program, using CompuServe Information Manager can make your time online easier and more efficient. CompuServe Information Manager (CIM) is a dedicated communications program with an easy-to-use graphic interface, specifically for use with the CompuServe service. It is included in the CompuServe Membership Kit, which can be purchased from the service or through computer stores and mail-order software companies. CIM features a Browse menu with icons for different areas within the service, much like America Online's "Departments," as well as a Favorite Places menu that can be customized by the user to list specific forums or areas most frequently visited. These are shown in Fig. 2-26.

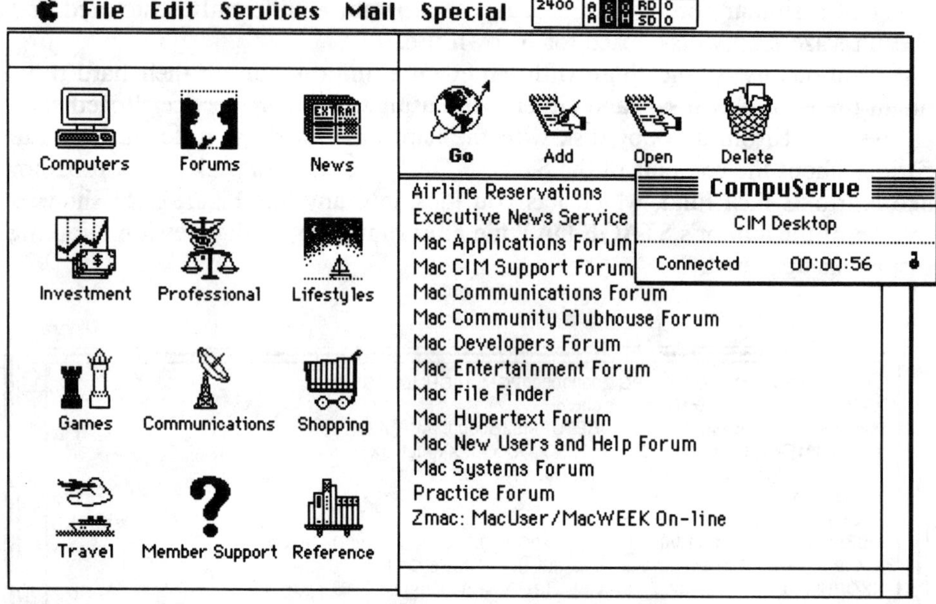

2-26 Clicking any of the icons or menu listings takes you there in a flash.

CIM's Address Book and offline editor make handling E-mail easy. You can write and store your mail and forum messages before you sign on, and send them very quickly, saving yourself some connect charges. (This is important when you're dealing with a service that charges by the minute.) Figure 2-27 shows the mail window. E-mail messages are saved into the out basket and sent when you log on. Forum messages are handled in a similar manner. Simply enter the name of the forum to which the message should be posted and then enter the recipient or "All" and the text.

CIM also comes with its own transfer protocol, which features fast error-corrected transmission using CompuServe's own B+ protocol. A 26K file took just under two minutes to transfer. The main pitfall for the novice CIM user is trying to

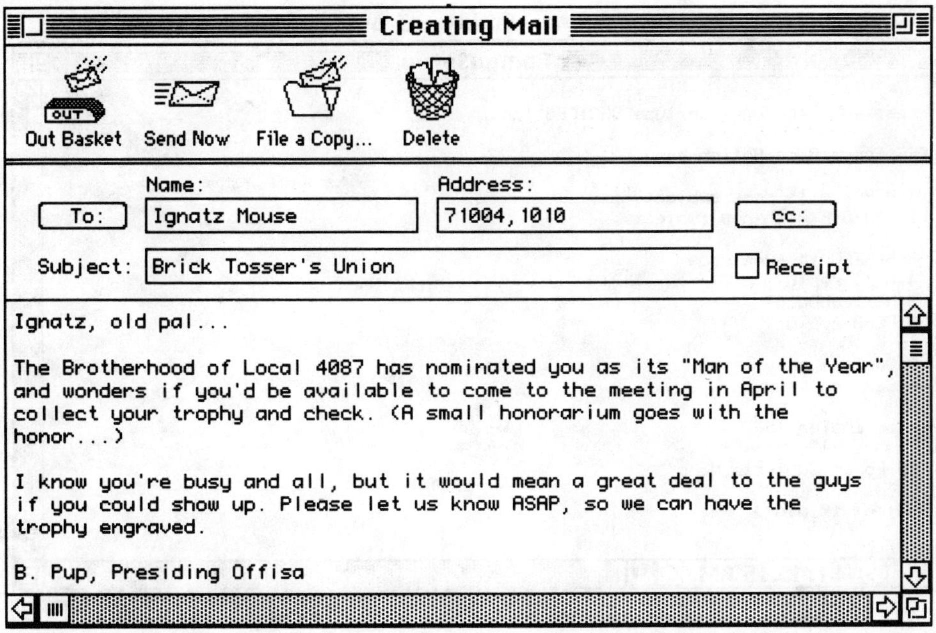

2-27 If you've written your letters offline, save them to the out basket to send them next time you log on.

figure out how to sign on. The program comes with a special Sign On file, in which the user enters ID and temporary password from the membership kit. But there's no obvious log-on command. The trick is to click on one of the Browse icons or Favorite Places listings. As soon as CIM knows where you want to go, it'll take you there.

Despite the graphic bells and whistles, parts of CompuServe remain unchanged from the clunky text-based system with which it began operations back in 1979. Requesting data from many areas places you in CIM's terminal emulation window, a dumb terminal that goes beyond merely dumb to moronic. If you succeed in locating the terminal help file by typing H or ? (but not at all prompts), you'll get the equivalent of three typewritten pages that may or may not tell you how to get back to reality again. Sometimes, Command-L (for Leave) does the trick, but in certain areas, you need to use /exit, or possible exit (no slash), or off. Which one of these you'll sign off with depends on which area you're leaving. Off gets you out of Travel. Exit leaves the Computer Library, and /Exit lets you slash your way out of the jungles of PaperChase. The ZMac area is especially hard to escape from. You'll need to type Go CIS: plus the name of the place you want to jump to. Confusing? Indeed.

If you know that you'll only need to access text areas of the service during a session, you might do well to forego CIM and just use a "normal" terminal program like MicroPhone II or White Knight. CompuServe's text menus are fairly easy to use (Fig. 2-28) and might actually get you into the area you want to visit more swiftly than getting in through CIM.

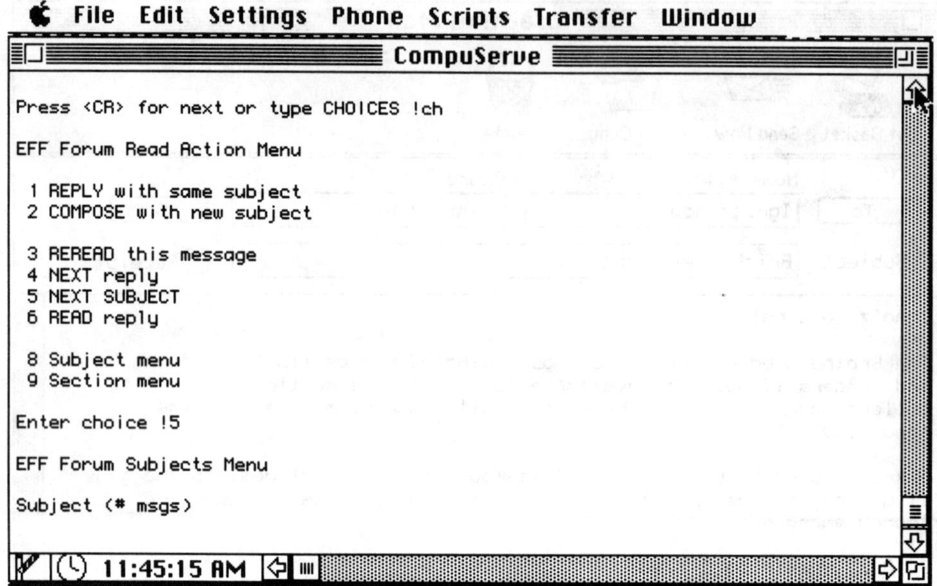

2-28 You don't always need to use CIM. Any terminal program can let you read text files.

Automated session programs

A text-based program or icon-driven program like MicroPhone II, White Knight, or CompuServe's Information Manager lets you browse through the many different areas of a large service. Unfortunately, the more time you spend online, the more you're going to have to pay. Prodigy, as of this writing, is the only online information service that charges you by the month rather than by the minute. It's possible to run up some rather outrageous bills while you're learning your way around. Automated session programs, also sometimes called *navigation programs*, can let you save money by planning your online session in advance to minimize the actual, billable connect time. They also take the worry out of going online because all the work of signing in, navigating from one area to another, and getting out again is done for you by commands buried in the program. You can just sit back and watch, go get a cup of coffee, or even set the program up to run itself while you're asleep, at work, or otherwise occupied. Because these programs will run in the background under MultiFinder or System 7, you can also use them to go online while you're doing something else with your Mac. If you're downloading files, though, your "active" program might be somewhat sluggish and your throughput efficiency is likely to be less than normal.

M-Lite

A popular PC program called Messenger-Lite (M-Lite) has just been released in a Mac version for the Delphi service. M-Lite is a terminal program that handles your mail and forum messages. If you give it a list of the forums you're interested in, it will go to each one in turn and retrieve new messages and post any that you've written. It also handles your E-mail and even purges old mail from your online files, preventing unnecessary storage charges. It will update catalogs of files in forum databases and let you download or upload using X-, Y-, or ZMODEM protocols. Best of all, you can set up your session in advance and let M-Lite log in and carry out your orders at any time you specify. If you're a toll call away from the Tymnet gateway, you can schedule your connect time at night when rates are low. M-Lite is shareware, available in the Mac library on Delphi. Messenger and Messenger Lite were originally written for use on PAN, the Musician's Network, and shareware fees go to support the PAN BBS.

Aladdin

Not available as of this writing, but promised soon is a Mac version of Aladdin, a GEnie helper that has been around for quite a while on the PC and Atari platforms. Aladdin automates mail retrieval, bulletin board posting, and software library use. When completed, it will be available for free (except the time charge for the download) in the Aladdin Round Table area on GEnie.

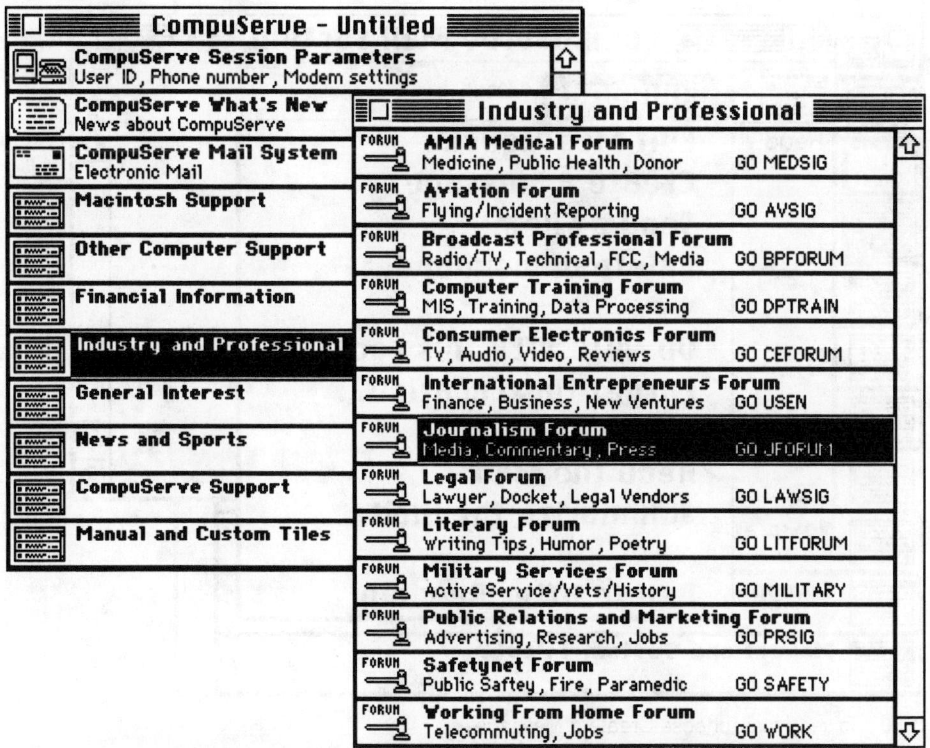

2-29 Opening one of the tiles on the left reveals a listing of forums like that on the right.

Navigator

CompuServe has created its own navigation program, aptly called Navigator. It's purchased separately from the CompuServe Membership Kit and costs less than $50 from my favorite mail order software company. Navigator lets you plan a complete online session in advance. It's not just for grabbing your E-mail, although that's certainly part of what it does. It also collects library listings, summaries of forum threads you're following, and a great deal more. Even though it sounds complicated, Navigator is the easiest to use of the session-automation programs.

To start a Navigator session, open the program to the selection window, shown on the left in Fig. 2-29. You'll see a set of boxes that Navigator calls *tiles*. The first time you log on with Navigator, you'll need to enter your user ID, modem settings, and connect phone number in the Session Parameters tile. This information will be saved from one session to the next. After that, select the tasks you want Navigator to do during the time it's online. You might want to check your mail and send messages to other members. To do so, open the Mail System tile. Commands is a pop up menu, shown in Fig. 2-30. Choose the appropriate task(s), or choose Do Not Enter . . . if you're not expecting any mail. Forget will permanently remove the location from your list of Navigator tiles.

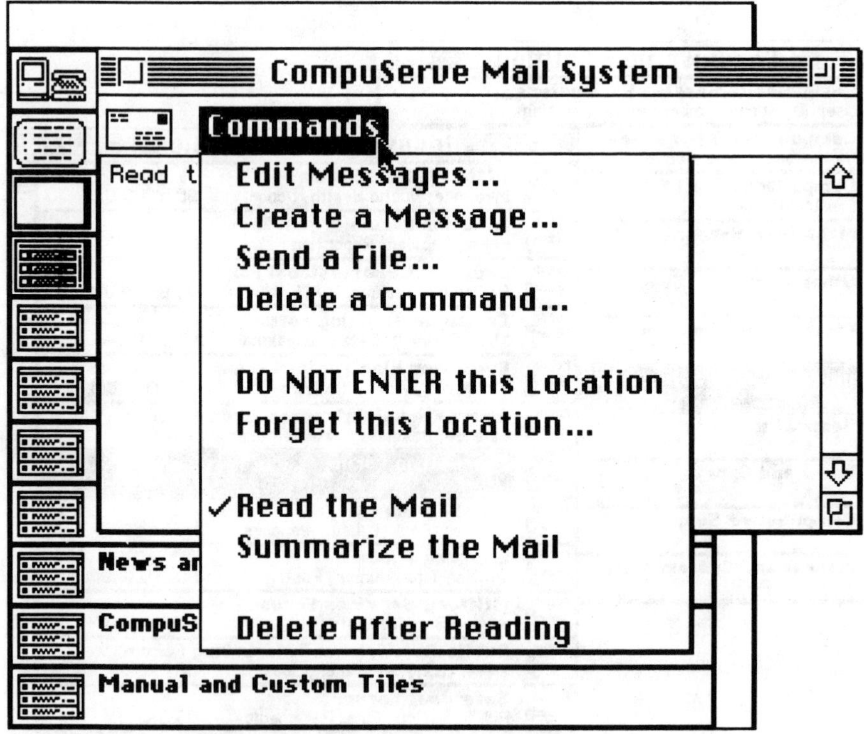

2-30 To send mail, choose Create a Message.

Continue down the list, selecting tiles and menus of interest. For example, selecting Industry and Professional gives you a listing of forums related to this category. I've selected the Literary forum, and defined some actions that are shown in the window in Fig. 2-31. Navigator will look for messages relating to fiction, non-fiction, and censorship. I've requested a list of library keywords to make my next search easier. I'll also download any files since January 1, 1992, that relate to Freedom of the Press.

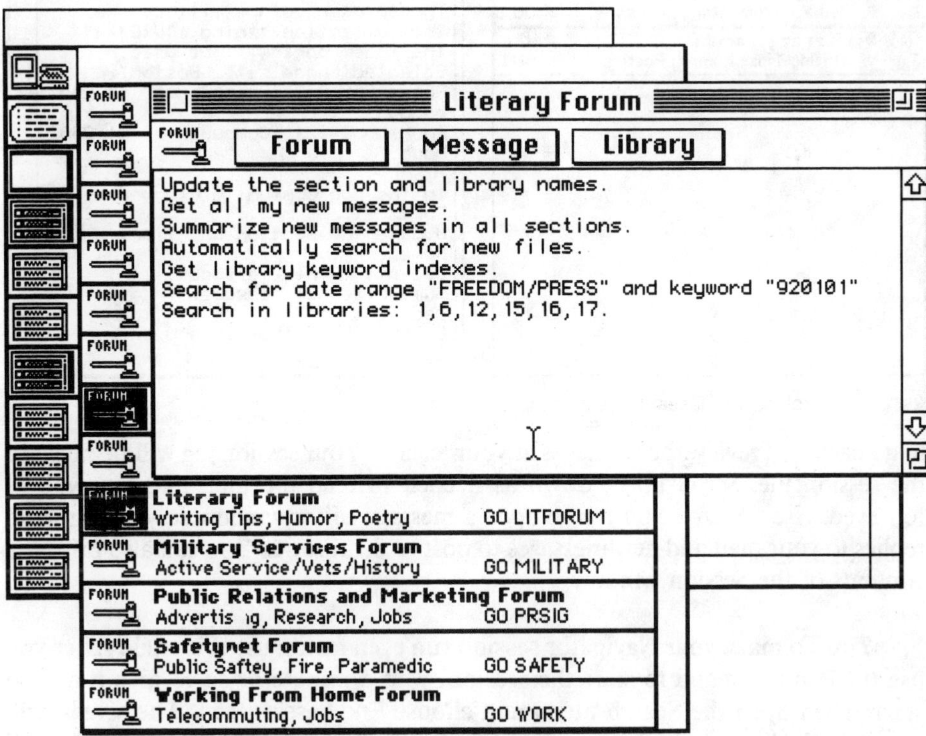

2-31 Navigator will look for messages, check for new files, and search the libraries for material of interest to us.

After I've defined the activities I want Navigator to handle in each area, I can use the Preview command to review my session script. If I've made any mistakes, or forgotten anything I intended to do, I'll be able to see the problem and fix it as I read the script (Fig. 2-32). To change any entry, all I need to do is to double click on the appropriate tile and make the changes I want. When I'm all finished, I'll save the session. I can tell it to run immediately or at a given time.

The session will be run in a window called, appropriately, Session View. Don't expect to read everything as it happens in the window. With a fast modem, the session goes so quickly that you'll never be able to read it online. After the session is finished and Navigator has disconnected from the CompuServe host, you'll be able

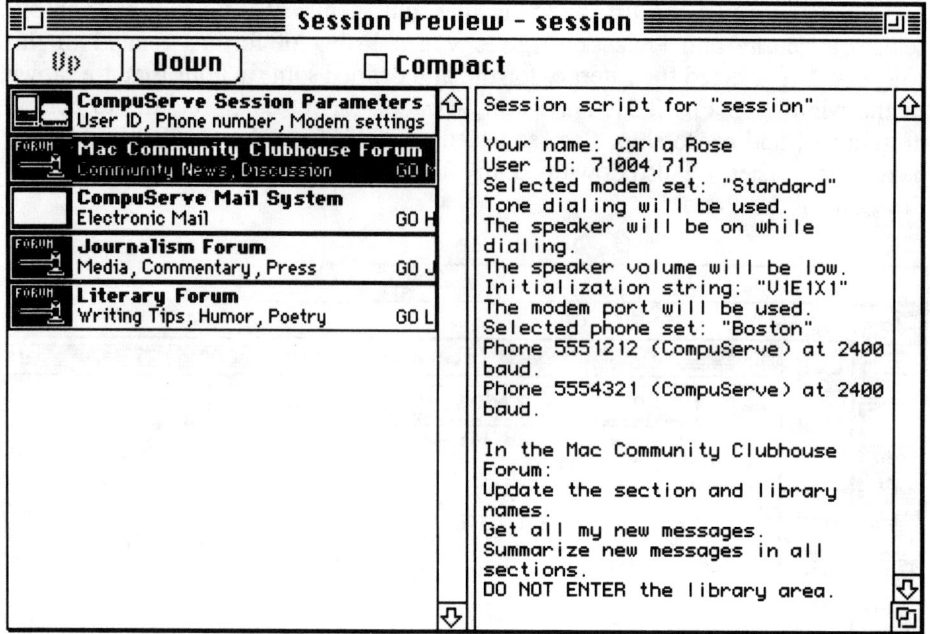

2-32 If I scroll down, I'll see the rest of the session.

to go back and review the messages at your leisure. Your session log will be saved in the session file. Scroll up or down as needed to read the mail and files you've retrieved. Use the Create button to open a message editor window so you can write replies to your mail and new messages to post to the forums. You can also print the contents of the Session window.

Tip! To make your Navigator session run even faster, use this trick. After you use the Run **command to start the session, wait a minute or so to give it a head start. Then open the Search menu and choose** Find Session Start. **The screen will return to the beginning of the session log. Data will keep on coming in, and you'll see the scroll bar indicator move to the right as the file gets longer. However, since the program doesn't have to handle the chore of typing everything to the terminal emulator window, it can handle data much more efficiently. You can also accomplish this by choosing** Stay at Session Start **from the Preferences menu.**

Navigator also lets you create and use Navigator "Face Files." CompuServe members upload animated icons of their faces, which you can download. Of course, you can add your own to the collection. When you communicate with another member whose face is in the file, you'll see his or her face along with the message. Figure 2-33 shows the author's Face File entry. Navigator blinks back and forth between the "talking" and "listening" poses to animate the face. Images are created in fat bits, as shown here, using the pointer as a pencil. You don't need to post your face, but it's fun and adds a personal touch to your automated communications.

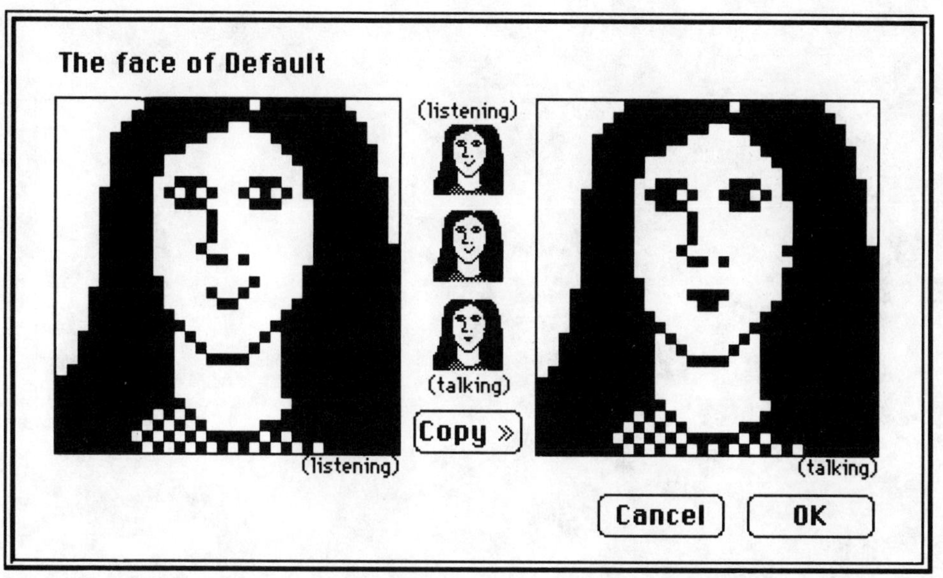

2-33 To animate the face, Navigator flashes between the "talking" and "listening" versions.

Summary

Telecommunication programs let your computer send commands to the modem and let you send messages through the modem to other computers. In order for one computer to talk to another, both must be able to send and receive ASCII code, a set of characters, punctuation, and formatting commands in binary. Telecom programs turn the computers into communication terminals that can send and receive these codes.

There are text-based terminal programs that can access any text-based service or BBS or let you talk directly to your friend's Mac or the PC in your office. There are also dedicated programs for use with a particular service. Prodigy and America Online require a dedicated program, which they provide to members. CompuServe can be reached either as text or through its Information Manager, a graphic interface that lets you use icons and menus to steer yourself to areas of interest.

Navigation programs let you plan an online session while you're offline, create mail and bulletin board notices, and list files to download or message boards to read. The session is then run as a completely automated one, saving money on connect fees. Navigation programs are specifically written for particular services.

3
Signing on

A stereotypical view of the American tourist in a foreign country has him surrounded by bewildered local citizens, repeating over and over, louder and more slowly each time, "WHERE . . . IS . . . THE . . . HOTEL?" They answer back in the local dialect, all talking at once. It's chaos. Finally, one gestures and points, and our hero trots off, only to discover he's been sent to the local hearing-aid dealer. The lesson in this is simple: you can't communicate effectively with another person if the two of you don't share a common language or if you don't follow the ground rules for talking and listening.

Similarly, your Mac can't communicate with another computer unless both agree to speak the same language. In this case, the language is one of bits and baud and parity. Before you go online, you must set your communications program to match that of the computer you'll be talking to. The two computers must agree on specific parameters for the way in which they'll send information back and forth. These are generally referred to as *communications protocols* or *serial port settings*. Typically, they are defined in a dialog box like the one in Fig. 3-1 from White Knight.

Setting the settings

Serial port

The serial port is to the Mac what your ears and mouth (or eyes and fingers) are to you. It enables two-way communication. The first setting on White Knight's list is to define which serial port the modem should communicate through. As mentioned previously, it's best to use the modem port for the modem and the printer port for the printer. Doing so prevents interruptions to your online communications when you want to print a screen capture or print from another program while your telecom program is running in the background, as it might if you're working on something else during a long download. By the way, if you're using the Global Village modem, which connects through the ADB, you'll still specify the modem port.

Serial Port Settings

Serial port:

Modem command inter-character delay: 10 60th's.

Modem init command: ATE1Q0V1

Baud rate: 2400

Parity: NONE

Databits: 8

Stopbits: 1

Duplex: FULL

Don't drop DTR when quitting

Hold DTR low

Invert DTR For One Second

Use hardware handshaking

Serial port buffer size (100-32767 bytes): 10000

OK

Cancel

3-1 The shadowed blocks indicate pop-up menus, on which you can change these settings.

Inter-character delay

If you jam letters together on a pagelikethis, it's harder for the reader to understand them. Similarly, if you jam commands together, it's harder for the modem to understand them. The Mac can send its digital information to the modem far faster than you or I could type. This setting simply tells the Mac how much of a break to insert between characters. Ten 60ths of a second isn't long, but it's enough for most modems. If yours sends error messages frequently, try increasing the time to 15 or 20. You won't notice much difference, but the modem will.

Modem init command

You won't find the modem init command setting on all telecom programs. If you intend to use "normal" modem settings, either leave the default setting ATE1Q0V1 as shown or leave the box blank and make sure that your log-on procedure includes the command ATZ to initialize the modem with its factory settings. If you want to change individual settings, for example, to turn off the modem's speaker, refer to the table of AT commands in chapter 2.

Baud rate

Once in a while, you find a mistake where you'd least expect it—a misspelled word in a *New York Times* editorial or an addition error in your favor on a bank

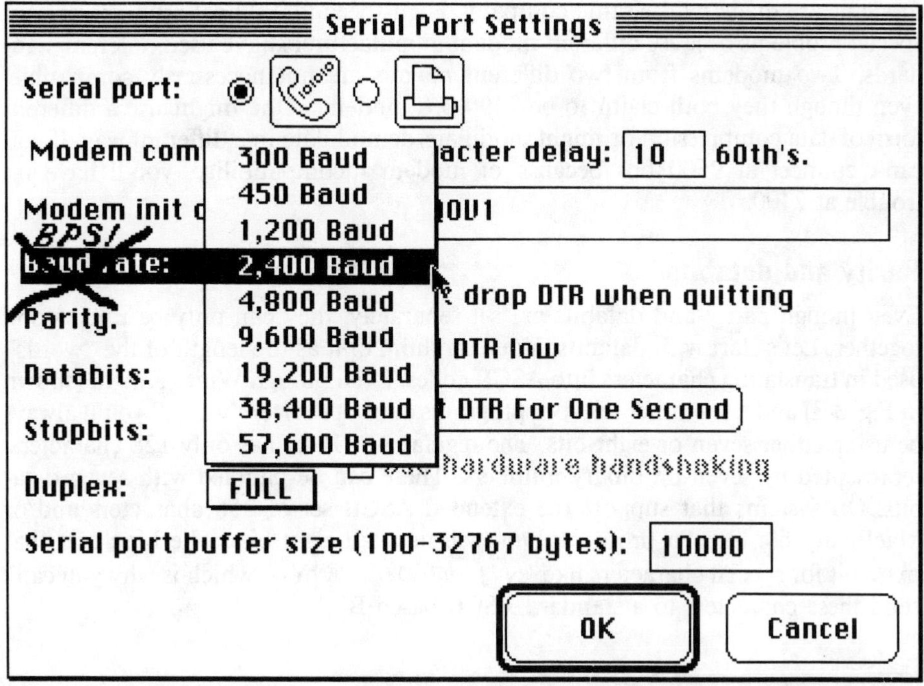

3-2 It's not baud, it's bits per second at the higher speeds. 57,600 baud is impossible!

statement. Figure 3-2 shows one of those mistakes. You know, by now, that baud is different from bps, and that what's meant here is actually the latter. But do you know what determines what rate you should select? Of course you do. It depends on the capability of your modem and that of the computer you're talking to.

A 2400-bps modem can't communicate any faster than 2400 bps. If you have a 2400-bps modem, there's no way that setting your telecom program to 57,600 bps (or even 57,600 baud) will make data flow that fast. It can't be done. It's like trying to win the Indy 500 on a bicycle. But, like the bicycle, your modem can go slower than its top speed. Your 2400-bps modem can operate at 1200, or even at 300, if necessary. Just remember, it's the slower modem that determines the speed of the communication.

To determine the correct speed setting, consider your own limits first and then those of the system you're calling. Online services and BBSs typically handle callers at 1200 and 2400 bps. (Some offer 9600 bps service at a higher cost per online minute.) If you have the choice, and your phone line tends to be relatively noise-free, choose 2400. Otherwise, set the speed to 1200 bps. Noisy phone lines can often be overcome simply by switching to a lower speed. If you have trouble connecting at 2400 bps, drop down to 1200 for better results.

If you're calling another individual, rather than a service or BBS host, you'll have to agree on modem settings before you initiate the connection. Even though you both have 9600 bps modems, it might not be your best choice, unless both modems are made by the same company. High-speed (9600 bps) modems present special problems because different modem manufacturers have used different standards. Two modems from two different makers are not necessarily compatible, even though they both claim to be 2400 bps modems. One might use a different form of data compression or might modulate/demodulate in a different way. If you can't connect at 9600 bps because of modem incompatibility, you'll have no trouble at 2400.

Parity and databits

Even though parity and databits are set separately, they can only be understood together. Let's start with databits. You can think of it as the length of the "words" used in translating characters into ASCII codes. Even though White Knight (shown in Fig. 3-3) and a few other telecom programs allow a shorter "word," you'll always be using either seven or eight bits. The regular ASCII set has only 128 characters, represented by seven-bit binary numbers. These can be handled with seven databits. On systems that support the extended ASCII set of 256 characters and/or MacBinary file transfer protocols, you will need all eight bits. The Mac uses that extra bit for special characters like: ç√ ∫~µ∂ƒ©·∆°′®†Y—which is why you can't send these characters to a standard ASCII-based BBS.

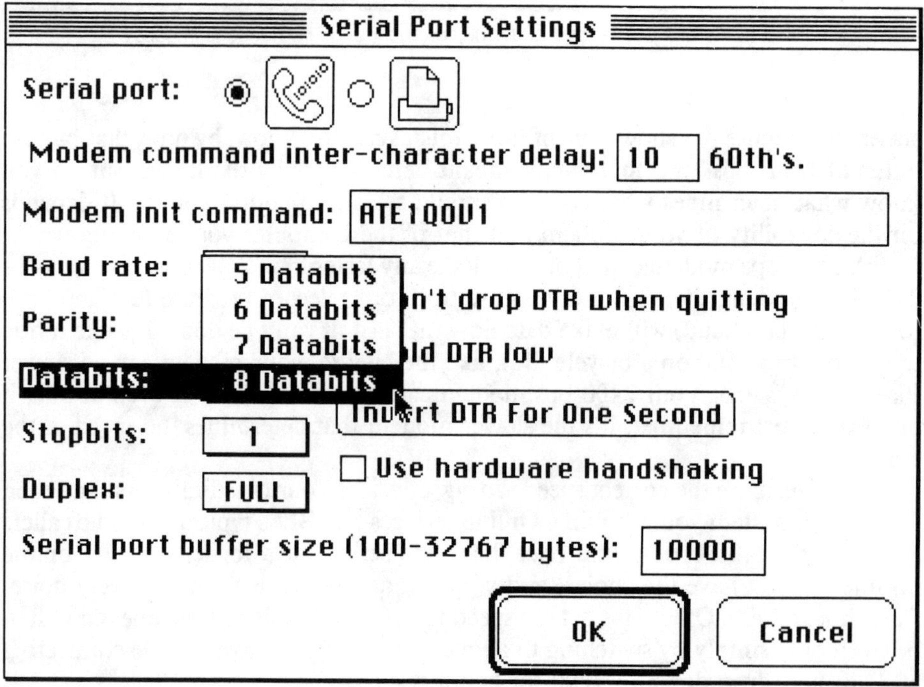

3-3 The 5 or 6 databit settings are seldom, if ever, used.

Computers normally handle bits in 8-bit words called *bytes*. If you have a 7-bit word, obviously you're a bit short. Back when computer communication was a new science and a lot more risky, it seemed wrong to waste that eighth bit, so the scientists dreamed up a system for error-checking, which they called *parity*. Parity checking adds an 8th-bit to the word. To explain it, let's look at a 7-bit ASCII character. (This one happens to be the letter Z.) It's represented by the binary digits 1011010. We add the number of 1s in the 7-bit word. There are four, and four is an even number. Parity can be either even or odd. If we've specified that parity is even, we add another 0 to make the full 8 bits add up to an even number. If parity were odd, we'd add a 1 as the parity bit to make it odd.

For every byte of data that was sent, the computer sending it would add the ones and insert the correct parity bit. The recipient made the same calculation, and if the parity bit was correct, sent back a message saying, in effect, "Okay, that adds up. Send me another." If one bit got switched around as it was being sent, a one would become a 0 or a 0 would become a 1 and the parity would be wrong. Then the computer receiving the data would ask to have that byte sent again.

This system worked fairly well, as long as only one bit got switched per byte, and it didn't happen to be the parity bit; but as you can see, there's lots of room for error. If two bits got swapped, say a 1 became a 0 and a 0 turned into a 1, the parity would be correct but the character would be quite different. As telecom got a lot more reliable and needed all 8 bits, parity checking as a form of error control got phased out. Today, most services and BBSs use 8-bit bytes and no parity checking. If you happen to encounter a system that asks you to use 7 databits, the parity will almost always be even.

Stop bits

Stop bits are the digital equivalent of spaces between words on a page. They come after the parity bit, if one is used. Otherwise, they're simply placed between bytes. The stop bit tells the computer, "Okay, that's all there is to that bit. Here comes another one." There's almost always only one stop bit, although most communications programs let you set one, two, or even one and a half. Why? Somewhere, some oddball host system might use it, just to be different. But we're willing to bet you'll never need to change the stop bit from one. Figure 3-4 shows the stop bit setting.

There are also start bits, just to make matters more confusing. A start bit is always a zero bit, but after the stop bit and before the start of the next byte.

Duplex

Duplex would be far less confusing if it were renamed something like Echoplex. It determines whether or not the computer you're talking to sends the characters you type back to you for screen display. In Full Duplex, when you type a character on

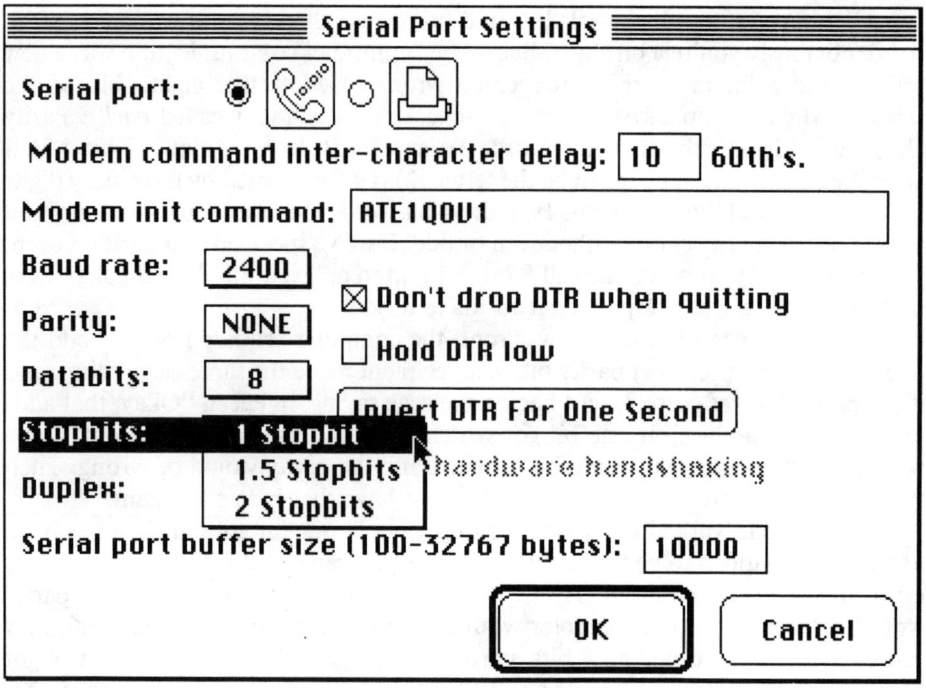

3-4 Always specify one stopbit. The other settings are hardly ever used.

your keyboard it goes immediately to the other computer, which echoes it back to yours, so you can read it on your screen. In Half Duplex, there's no echo from the other computer. Your Mac sends the character to the other computer, but then the Mac echoes the character to its own screen. Either way, the result is the same: you can see what you're typing. Full Duplex is a remote echo, and Half Duplex is a local echo. It's important for both computers to use the same duplex setting. When your computer is set to Half Duplex and the other to Full Duplex, both will be echoing characters to your screen, and you'll be seeing double (lliikkee tthhiiss). But if the other computer is set to Half Duplex, and yours to Full Duplex, you won't see anything at all when you type. Neither computer is echoing.

Most BBSs and online services operate in Full Duplex. GEnie, the notable exception, uses Half Duplex. Why? They've been around for a long time. When they wrote the software for their service, they guessed one way. Everybody else guessed another. They aren't going to change it, but if your telecom program doesn't support Half Duplex, you can still use GEnie by going to the Settings area and turning on Host Echo, as shown in Fig. 3-5. The net result will be the same as Full Duplex. Of course, you'll have to type blind until you get there, but it's not difficult.

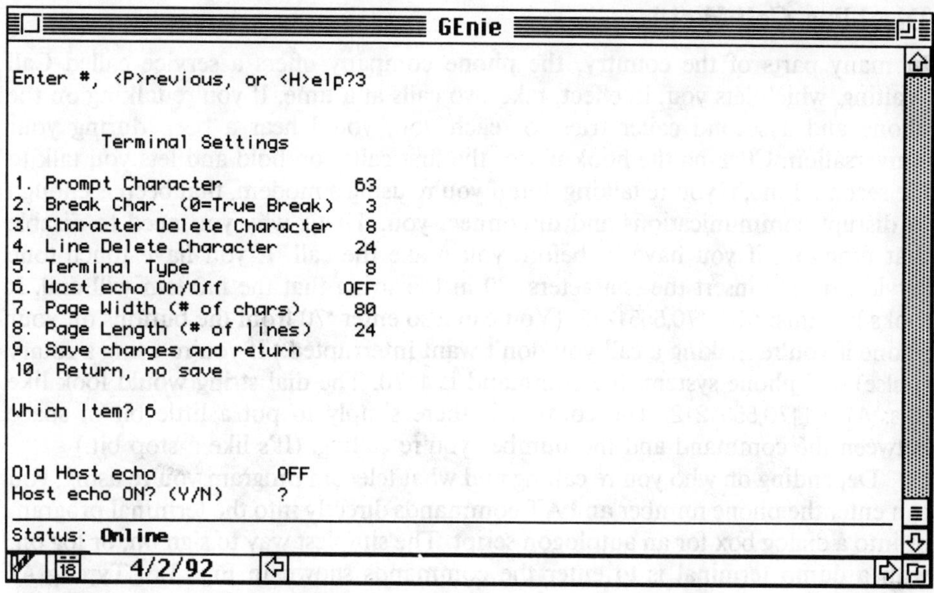

3-5 If Half Duplex isn't an option on a dumb terminal program, ask GEnie for Host echo. Type Y for yes.

The bottom line

If you're calling a service other than GEnie and you have a 2400-bps modem, start with 2400 bps, no parity, 8 databits, 1 stop bit, and Full Duplex. You'll generally see those settings reduced to shorthand form: 2400, N-8-1. GEnie, as noted, wants to use Half Duplex, but the N-8-1 is correct. Most BBSs also require N-8-1. If not, they'll tell you on their opening screens. When you log onto a new BBS using N-8-1 and get a screen full of something illegible, break the connection (by unplugging the modem from the phone line, if necessary) and reset to E-7-1. Then try again. Ninety-nine percent of the time, though, N-8-1 will be correct. If you are calling another individual, always use N-8-1, and set the speed to whatever is the highest speed both modems have in common. If there's a problem with a noisy line, fall back to a lower speed for better results.

Placing a call

You've set up the modem, set up the telecom program, and you're ready to make the call. Almost. There are still a few things to think about first. Have you taken whatever steps are necessary to assure that your call won't be interrupted? Do you have to remind your family not to pick up the phone while you're online? What about incoming calls?

Disabling Call Waiting

In many parts of the country, the phone company offers a service called Call Waiting, which lets you, in effect, take two calls at a time. If you're talking on the phone and a second caller tries to reach you, you'll hear a beep during your conversation. Clicking the hook places the first caller on hold and lets you talk to the second. Fine, if you're talking; but if you're using a modem, that beep is enough to disrupt communications and disconnect you. That's why you need to disable that function, if you have it, before you make the call. If you have touch-tone service, simply insert the characters *70 in the string that the modem will dial. It looks like this: ATDT*70,5551212. (You can also enter *70 from the buttons on your phone if you're making a call you don't want interrupted.) If you're using a rotary (pulse) dial phone system, the command is 1170. The dial string would look like this: ATDP1170,5551212. The comma is there simply to put a little bit of space between the command and the number you're calling. (It's like a stop bit.)

Depending on who you're calling and what telecom program you're using, you can enter the phone number and AT commands directly into the terminal program or into a dialog box for an autologon script. The simplest way to sign on, or log on, with a dumb terminal is to enter the commands shown in Fig. 3-6. Typing AT simply confirms that the modem is "awake." It should respond okay. ATZ sets it to its factory default settings, which are usually the correct ones for dialing out. Next, enter ATDT (if you have a tone phone) and the number to call. You'll hear the dial tone, then the appropriate set of beeps as the modem dials the number, and then

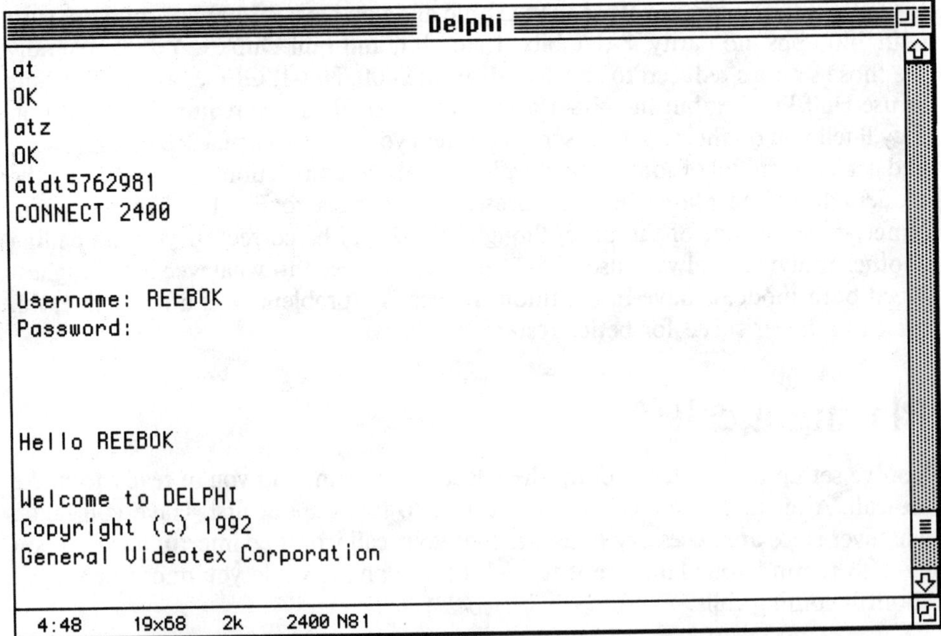

3-6 For security reasons, most services hide your password as you're typing it.

the ring signal. When the call is answered, you should hear a two-note whistle: first a low note, then a higher one. Then you'll hear a burst of "white noise," a distinctive blend of static and a sound like air escaping from a pressurized tank. These strange noises are the sounds of *handshaking*, the process whereby the two computers confirm that they're using the same speed and settings. Handshakes at different speeds sound a bit different, but the principle remains the same.

When the handshake is successful, your screen will read CONNECT and the speed. Then, you might be prompted to enter your ID and password. If nothing happens, hit the Return key once or twice. Some systems need to see a signal from you before they'll "talk." You will also need to remember to hit the Return key every time you enter a command or say something in a conference. It's as if the Return key actually "sends" whatever you've typed to the modem. (If you're calling GEnie, the procedure is slightly different. As soon as you see CONNECT, type the letter *h* three times, like this: hhh. You don't need to use the Return key. Then, GEnie will ask for your User ID.)

First-time callers

If you're calling a service for the first time, you need to follow a specific sign-on routine. Here's how it works for CompuServe. Other services will have a similar procedure. When you opened the CompuServe Information Manager package, you found a disk and a manual. You've installed the software from the disk, and (possibly) looked at the manual. In it, in the Installation and Sign-up section, there's a sticker with a temporary User ID number and temporary password. You'll need these, plus a major credit card or your checkbook. CompuServe will bill your credit card or use Electronic Funds Transfer (EFT) to debit your account for your monthly bill.

Open the Folder and double click the startup icon, shown in Fig. 3-7. You'll be

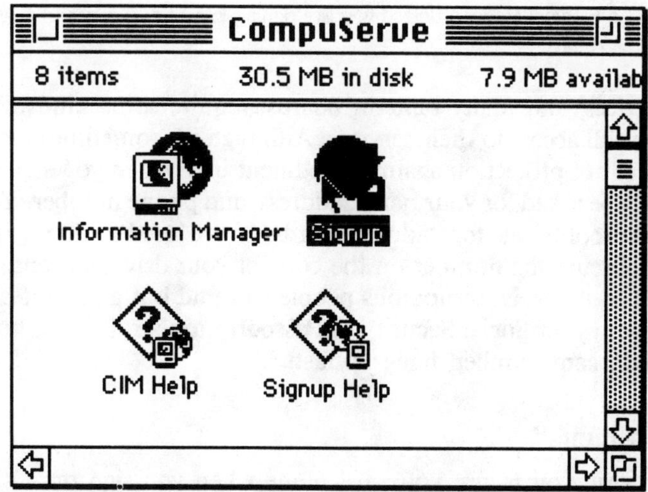

3-7 The first time you go online with CompuServe, open the Signup icon.

asked to enter the serial number and agreement number from the package. Then, follow through the screens and fill in the blanks, as shown in Fig. 3-8. When you're done, click Proceed. Eventually you'll read and agree to the rules, and then your Mac will automatically log you on, transfer the data you've entered, and complete the process by verifying your user ID number and temporary password. Within 10 days, you'll get a letter from CompuServe with a permanent password. Until then you can browse the services as much as you like using your temporary password, but you won't be able to play certain games, shop online, or contribute to forum libraries.

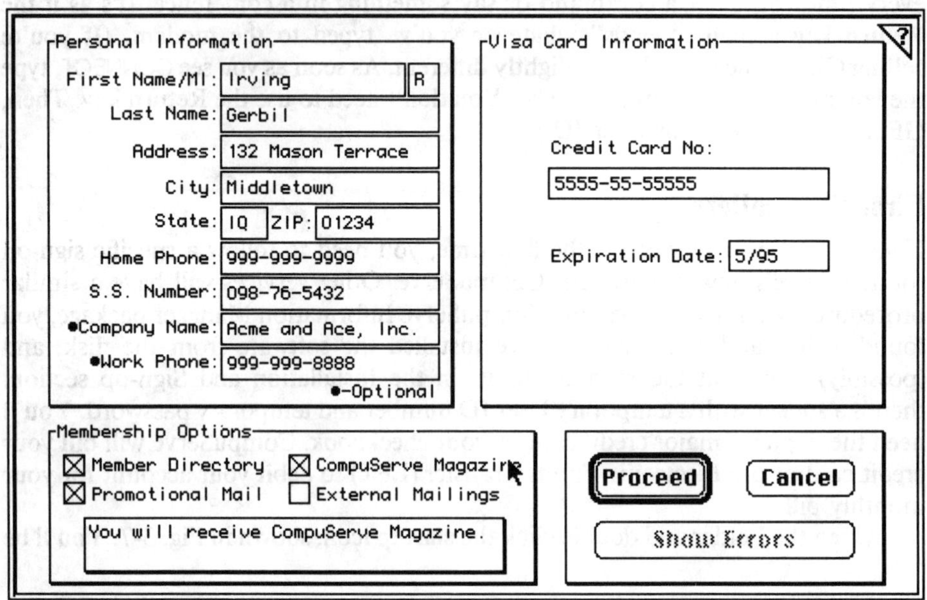

3-8 Don't choose External Mailings unless you like getting lots of catalogs and flyers.

Most services, and many bulletin boards, require some kind of verification before you get full access to their services. Although it's sometimes a nuisance, it's their only means of protection against fraudulent use. When you sign onto a BBS, you'll probably be asked for your name, address, and phone number. You might be asked to send proof of age for "adult" boards. If you need to do so, it might be a good idea to obscure the number on the copy of your driver's license or passport that you send to them. Unscrupulous people can find out a good deal about you when armed with your Social Security or Passport number. If a free bulletin board asks for a credit card number, hang up fast!

What's in a name?

Some systems ask you to use your real name when you sign on. Others let you choose a *handle* or *screen name* or nickname instead. Because your nickname is your first introduction to other members, it makes sense to choose one that says something about you. It shouldn't say the *wrong* thing, though. An outdoor-loving senior citizen we once met online was complaining about getting private messages from members inviting her to shed her clothes. When it was pointed out that her handle, NATURIST, was probably the reason, she changed to a name without a dual meaning. SNUGGLEBUNNY conveys a very different image from MetsFan, MOMOF6, or LuvMyTruck.

On some services, nicknames are generally limited to 16 characters or less and need to be all one word, but you can cheat this a little with clever spellings and punctuation. For example, a two-word name can be joined with an underline, like this: LORD_NELSON, DARTH_VADER; or just run together. Nicknames must be unique. It wouldn't do to have two users with the same name because such matters as mailboxes and billing would get confused. So you'll see handles like BOZO3 and JIM41, which might not mean there are two other Bozos or 40 more Jims on the service, only that these users have added a number to make their handles distinctive.

On services with a "chat" or "conference" area, you can usually change your handle when you enter. If you are using CompuServe Information Manager, you set up your CB Handle and Forum nickname in the Preferences box before you sign on. On Delphi, simply type /n plus your new nickname to change it. Other services have different systems.

Be careful about using names that might be considered offensive or tasteless. Aside from the comments they are likely to draw from other members, you could find yourself thrown off. Even though your right to free speech might be abridged, when you join an online service, you're agreeing to follow the management's standards of good taste. This applies not only to screen names, but also to conference titles and to anything you say or post online. (If you're on the receiving end of something you feel to be crude, insulting, or otherwise upsetting, send E-mail to the service with the details. They'll take care of it.)

Always type carefully when entering your ID and password. Many systems are "case sensitive," meaning they make a distinction between CAT and cat and Cat. Watch out for spaces and punctuation marks, too. CompuServe uses a two-word password with a period between the two words, like this: SWORD.FISH. GEnie asks you to type your User ID, a comma, and then your password, like this: XXX61616,swordfish. If you enter your password and get a message that it's incorrect, try using all caps when you retype it.

What's the password?

Remember the Marx Brothers movie in which Groucho tried to enter the door Chico was tending? The dialog went something like this:

"You can't-a-come in without da password, Boss."
"So what's the password?" asked Groucho.
"Swordfish."
"Okay, swordfish."
"Hey, Boss! You got it. Come on in."

It's not that easy to get into your online service or BBS. Some provide you with a password, others let you choose your own. But virtually all require that you use one. It provides them a certain amount of protection against hackers. It's also a safety measure for you when you're dealing with online services. Because most of those who sign up for Prodigy, CompuServe, and other commercial services use credit cards, and because you can shop online with most of these services, letting anyone use your account is just the same as handing them your wallet. It could be expensive!

You can take a number of steps to protect your passwords. First of all, when you have the opportunity to choose your own password, don't choose an obvious one. Don't, for example, use your name, nickname, or current telephone number. These are too easy to guess. Anyone trying to break into your account could easily find out the name of your spouse, child, or pet. Look for something more obscure.

Short passwords aren't a good idea, either. It takes only a few minutes to try all the possible two letter combinations. Government security procedures require the use of passwords with a minimum of eight characters. They needn't be words. Combinations of letters and characters such as %, &, \, or } will work fine. Just make sure they're in the ASCII set. Don't think you're being clever by using *password* as your password, and don't use the same password on all of your services, if you subscribe to more than one. Don't use the same password you use for your ATM card. What if the sysop (system operator) is dishonest?

Don't do as a friend of mine did. She put her passwords on little yellow stickies, all around the screen on her PC, and then had a party. A few days later one of her guests had a party of his own, with her accounts and passwords. And she's still not sure who did it.

One thing you can, and should, do is to change your passwords frequently. Another, depending on how your communications program stores its information,

Your autologon has been activated.
It will only work on this Macintosh.
To logon in the future, double click
on the icon labelled as your nickname
in your PRODIGY service folder. To
continue now, select ESC.

3-9 The icon you'll see is a generic page, in Prodigy Service Folder #1.

is not to put your password in the log-on procedure. Prodigy gives you the option of using a full auto log-on, manual log-on (entering both your password and ID every time you sign on), or a combination in which Prodigy enters your ID and you add your password. You can choose these options online by choosing Tools from the Jump menu. After you enter your password, you'll be asked to choose a nickname. Prodigy creates an icon in your service folder with that nickname. As the dialog box in Fig. 3-9 indicates, just click it to sign on.

MicroPhone II saves passwords in a separate file on the desktop. Anyone can open the file and read the password, unless you lock the file. To do so, select Passwords, under MicroPhone II's Settings menu. You'll see a dialog box like the one in Fig. 3-10. You can lock the user settings file or the log-on script, or both. For protection, you'll need to lock both. Enter a password when the programs asks for it. Be sure to keep a copy in a secure place. If you lose it, these files cannot be opened, although the program can be run.

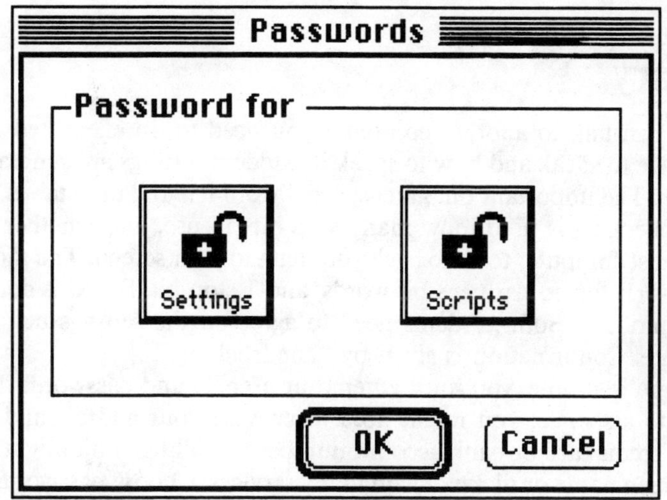

3-10 You have to lock both Settings and Scripts to keep your passwords safe.

When a password isn't enough—data encryption

It comes as no surprise to those who read detective novels or spy thrillers that telephone lines can be tapped. In fact, it's fairly easy to do so, although I won't tell you how. (If you're curious, look for Cliff Stoll's real-life thriller, *The Cuckoo's Egg.*) When you send sensitive data by modem, you run a risk, albeit a slight one, that somebody else will access it. Unless you're extremely sensitive about your Trivia Quest scores or the red hot E-mail you've been exchanging with your online romance, it's not a real problem. But for companies sending financial data, secret documents, and so on, the risk is real.

Many companies have turned to data encryption as a means of keeping private files private. There are modems that will scramble the data as it's being sent. As long as the receiving modem is the same type and has the same de-scrambler, it works beautifully. Encryption can also be done in software. One way to do it is to write, or buy, a program that uses simple substitution ciphers, just like the cryptograms on the newspaper's Puzzle Page. This system has, in fact, become the Data Encryption Standard, (DES). It's fairly simple to implement and very difficult to crack. In its simplest form, you'd simply raise each letter by 1. An A becomes a B, B becomes C, and so on. "Cat" is "Dbu." If you knew that the key was 1, it would be easy to decipher the text. But if you don't have the right key, it's gibberish.

Current DES methods use a 64-bit key, for 70 quadrillion possible ciphers! And these can be applied in different ways: to every letter, every other letter, alternating two or more different keys. The net result is an "uncrackable" code and a secure data transmission. Most of us will never need to use this kind of protection, but banks, industries, and government agencies do it every day.

Summary

Before you can talk to another computer you need to, in effect, tell the modem what language to speak and how to speak it. Modem settings are generally made in a dialog box. The important ones are: speed, "word length" in databits, whether or not parity checking is used, how many stop bits to use, and whether or not you expect the host computer to echo back your data to your screen. The most standard setting is N-8-1, for no parity, 8-bit words, and 1 stop bit. Speed is determined by the slower modem. Both modems need to agree on the settings before they can communicate. Confirmation is given by "handshaking."

Once you're online, you must enter your user ID and password. If you're just signing on to a service, you might need to provide your address and other data, including a credit card or bank account number for billing. You might be asked to choose a screen name or nickname on many services. Choose passwords that aren't likely to be guessed by someone else. It's important to guard your password to prevent unauthorized use of your account or unauthorized charges to your credit card. If the passwords are contained in a readable file, you might be able to protect the file with a password of its own.

Data encryption is a way of protecting files that must be kept secure while being sent by modem. The Data Encryption Standard, or DES, uses the principle of substitution cipher, with many possible cipher keys. It's virtually impossible to decode without the right key.

4
Getting on, online

You've signed on. Your password has been accepted. You're in. Now what? This is the moment that panic sets in for many first-time visitors to an online service or bulletin board. You might wonder what you're getting into, but most systems have so much to offer that you'll have little or no trouble finding something interesting. The problem is, unless you understand how the structure of a service or BBS works, it's easy to get "lost" online and run up large bills as you watch screen after screen of irrelevant material flash past you with no obvious way to get out. Learning your way around a system needn't mean poking into all the corners at random. There are easy ways to discover what's available, even on the largest and most complicated services.

Menus and commands

After your password has been accepted, there will be some sort of welcoming screen. If you're not a first-time caller, the screen might show the date and time of your last call and let you know whether you have mail waiting. New callers might have mail waiting, too. Many services greet you with a note telling you how to take a guided tour or where to go online to ask questions. Prodigy users get mail from the service and from many of its online merchants, too. (There's no way to block electronic junk mail, but you can delete it without reading it.)

Some services greet you with the latest news headlines, others with a listing of what's happening online in the near future. Some will try to sell you something, even as they're welcoming you aboard. Delphi's opening screen, shown in Fig. 4-1, is fairly typical. These messages are called *banners*, and they change daily. MCI Mail gives you a two-line summary of the day's top news stories every time you sign on. GEnie opens with a listing of anywhere from 10 to 15 or more special events, features, and advertisements before it goes to its main screen. BBSs frequently begin with ASCII graphics, pictures made out of typed characters, some of which are very clever. Figure 4-2 shows the opening screen for a local BBS.

After the banners roll by, you'll usually be presented with a *Main menu* and a

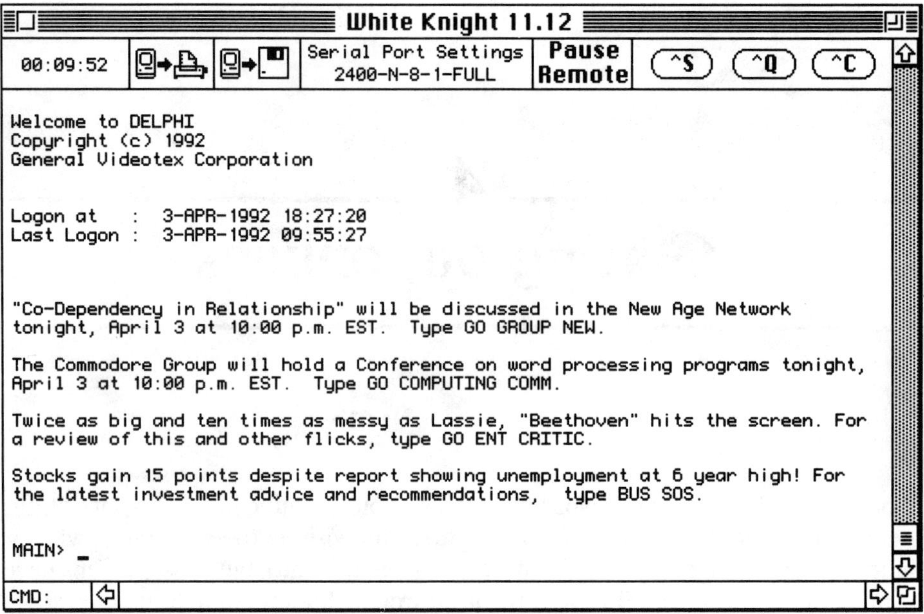

4-1 Delphi's opening screen is typical of text-based services.

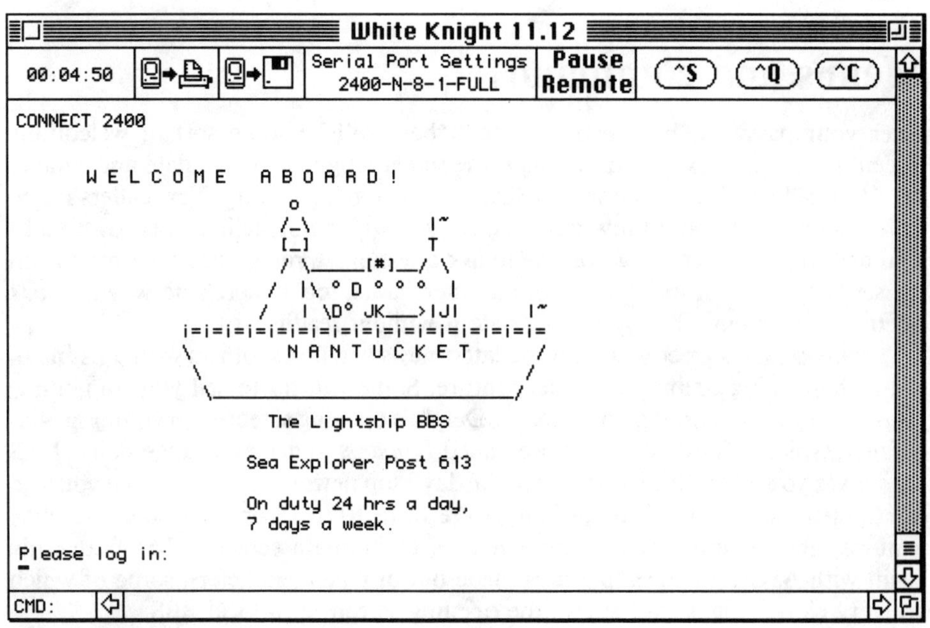

4-2 ASCII graphics can be as elaborate as you choose to make them.

prompt. The Main menu gives you a broad overview of various areas within the service. Figure 4-3 shows GEnie's main menu.

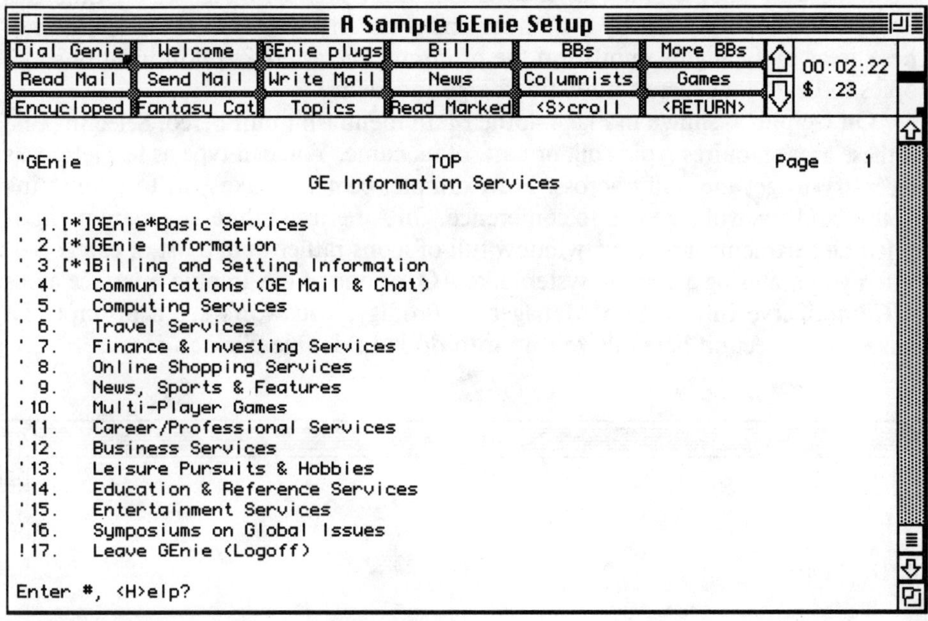

4-3 "Top" is GEnie's name for its Main menu.

Prompts

Prompts are indicators that tell you when the system is waiting for a response from you. A prompt can be any of the following characters or phrases:

- ?
- >
- !
- ACTION>
- What do you want to do now?
- Enter # or (H)elp:

Whenever you see a prompt, the service is asking you to enter some information. A prompt after a menu indicates that you need to choose something from that menu. If you don't know what to choose or how to proceed, typing a question mark or the word help generally brings you the system's help screen(s), which should tell you what you need to know.

Different systems use different kinds of prompts and want different responses from you. How you'll enter this choice depends on which service you're using and how its program is structured. Remember, when you're online you're not using your Mac. You're using the host computer. It might be a PC, another Mac, a minicomputer, or a huge mainframe. And you're using its program, which is probably not written in a Mac-like structure, so you'll have to deal with sets of commands that might be, to borrow a favorite programmer buzzword, non-intuitive. Some services are more user-friendly than others.

Let's take another look at the GEnie Main menu in Fig. 4-3. GEnie has identified its service areas by a number and a description. You can select one of these areas by typing its number at the prompt. (The asterisks [*] in front of some topics indicate that there's no extra charge for them.)

On Delphi, as shown in Fig. 4-4, the Main menu isn't numbered. Selecting one of these areas requires typing all, or part, of its name. You can type as few letters as necessary to get the point across. For example, com will take you to computing groups, and con will take you to conference. On America Online, the main menu is called Departments, and it's a window full of icons rather than a list of categories. When you are using a graphic system like AO, or one of the graphic interface areas of CompuServe Information Manager or Prodigy, you won't see a prompt. To make your selection here, all you need to do is to double click an icon.

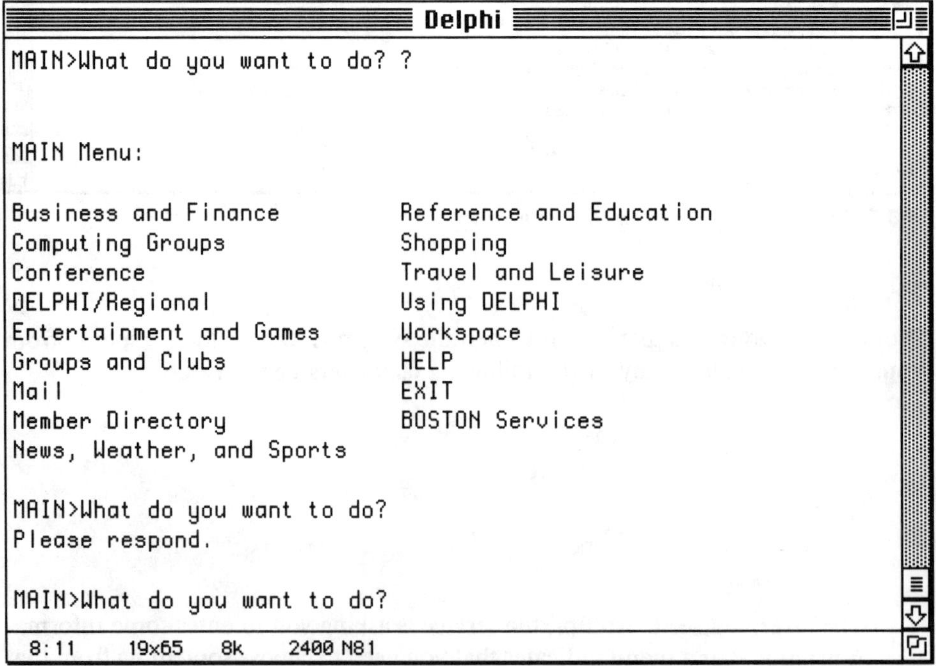

4-4 Delphi will keep on prompting you until you respond.

Going places

Many services use Go as a way to move you from one area to another. America Online has a Go To menu, shown in Fig. 4-5. No matter what part of the system

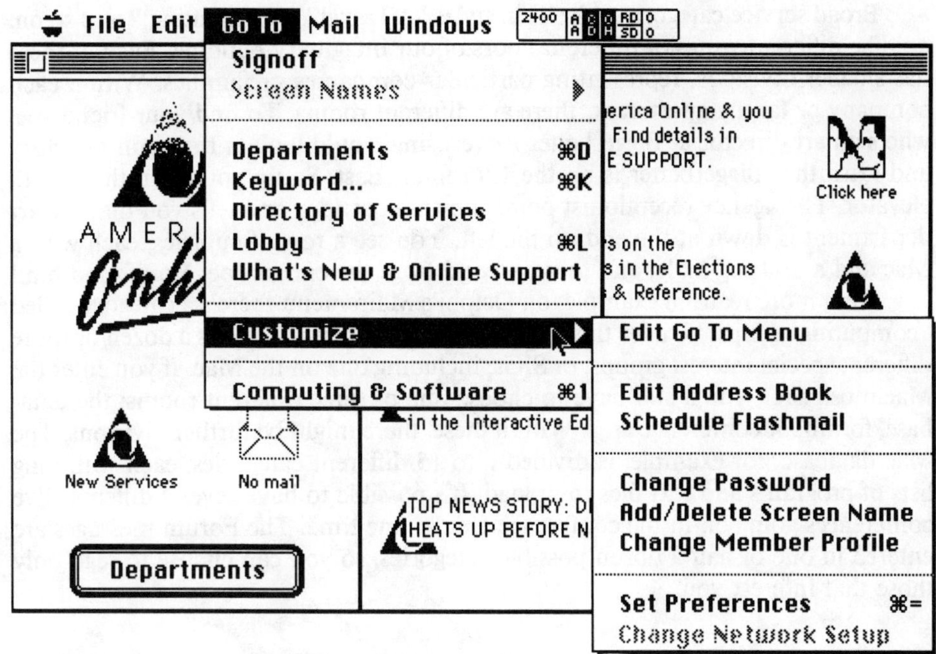

4-5 America Online's Go To menu gives you lots of shortcuts.

you're in, you can use the Go To menu to take you back to Departments (AO's Main area), to the People Connection Lobby for live conferences, or to a dialog box that lets you enter a keyword for a specific board, library, or conference room. You can also customize the Go To menu by adding entries and command keys for up to nine of your favorite AO areas. CompuServe Information Manager also uses "Go" commands. CompuServe assigns codes, which they call *navigational words,* to each area within the service. If you know the code for the area you want to transfer to, selecting Go from the Services menu, or just typing Command-G brings up a dialog box into which you can type the correct code word.

On text-based services, like Delphi, it's not necessary to type the Go command from the Main menu, but if you're in one area and want to jump to another without going back to the Main menu first, typing go and the abbreviations for the area you want to reach takes you directly there. For example, from anywhere else on Delphi, typing go gr ma for (which translates "go groups Mac forum") takes you immediately to the Macintosh users group forum.

System structure

It's all very well, you may be thinking, to know how to go from one area to another, but how can I find out what areas there are to go to? All online services, and most BBSs, are organized in pretty much the same way, and it's analogous to a large downtown building. There's a main area, sort of like the building lobby, with a directory to help you find the right apartment, company, or professional suite.

Broad service categories, like "Lifestyles," "Travel," "Computing," and so on, are like different wings or different floors of our imaginary building. Each of these has smaller divisions, representing particular companies or families. Within each company or family apartment, there are different rooms. To find your friend Joe, who's an art director at Biggerbetter Advertising, you'd look at the main directory and learn that Biggerbetter is on the 12th floor, East. So up you go in the "East" elevator. The agency receptionist points down a corridor and tells you that the art department is down at the end, to the left. You see a row of cubicles, each with a Mac and a drafting table, and there, second from the end, is Joe. You found him!

For a more realistic example, on Delphi's Main menu there's a category called "computing groups." Under this heading, there's a menu that lists a dozen or more different special interest groups, or SIGs, including one on the Mac. If you enter the Macintosh SIG, you'll still have to choose one of three different rooms: the database, forum, or conference area. Within these, there might be further divisions. The Mac database, for example, is divided into 15 different categories, each with long lists of programs and text files to upload. It's possible to have several different live conferences going on in the conference area at one time. The Forum messages are entered in one of half a dozen possible categories, so you can choose to read only those that interest you.

Forum or against 'em?

One of the things that's sure to confuse you if you use a number of different services or BBSs, is terminology. What one system means when it uses the term *forum* could be quite a bit different from what another service means by the same word. On CompuServe, forums are what Delphi calls Groups, and Delphi's forum is CIS's Messages. GEnie calls its forums RoundTables.

Within what we'll call a forum area on most services, there are usually three different sections: a library of programs and text files you can browse through and download for your own use; the conference area, a spot for members of that SIG to have real-time chats with each other; and the forum, which is a place where members post public messages to each other.

Forum bulletin boards, message boards, or whatever your service calls them, have yet another layer of structure imposed upon them. They are generally divided into categories or topics for easier reading and to help users find the specific topics in which they're interested.

Suppose we found an old coin and wanted to find out what it was. We happened to remember that our favorite online service has a coin collectors' forum. We've never investigated this forum before, but perhaps we could post a description of the strange coin and ask if anyone could identify it. Figure 4-6 shows the path we take through the system to get into the coin forum and discover that there's a topic that's exactly right for our query.

Some services list messages by topic; others in the order in which they're entered. If you don't know what you're doing, you can sometimes get stuck scrolling through several years' worth of old messages. Other services make it

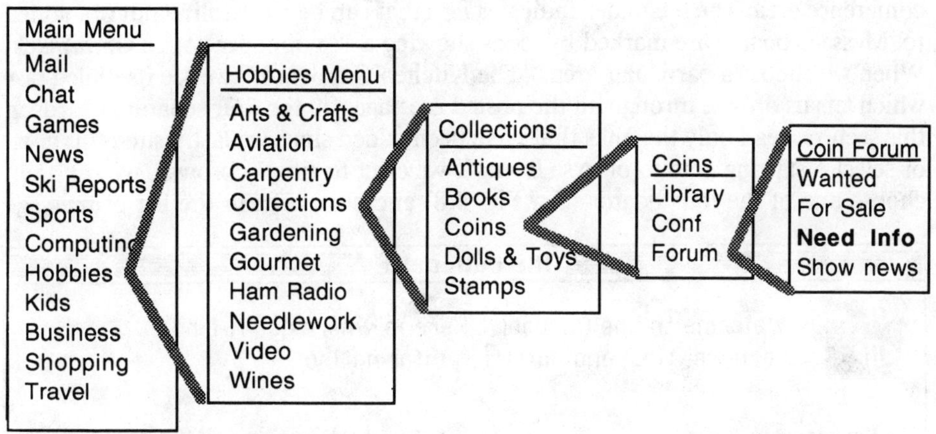

4-6 Working your way from the Main menu through the halls of submenu to the room you want.

possible to view only the topics that interest you. America Online uses a particularly effective method of handling messages.

To visit America Online's Cooking Club, we select it from the Lifestyles menu. The Cooking Club menu, shown in Fig. 4-7, lists its Library area, "The Kitchen Closet," which can also be identified by the disk icons, which tell you that there are files to copy. The icon resembling two faces identifies "The Kitchen" as a live

4-7 Choose one area of the Cooking Club to visit.

conference area. The file folder indicates files that can be read online but not added to. Message boards are marked by icons showing a slip of paper with a thumbtack. When we choose a particular area, "The Kitchen Cupboard," we see its dialog box which lets us browse through all the posted messages on the four separate boards in this section, read only the ones that have been added since we last visited this area, or select a starting date to browse from. If we elect to simply browse, we can then choose one of the four boards (*See* Fig. 4-8) and choose from the list of message

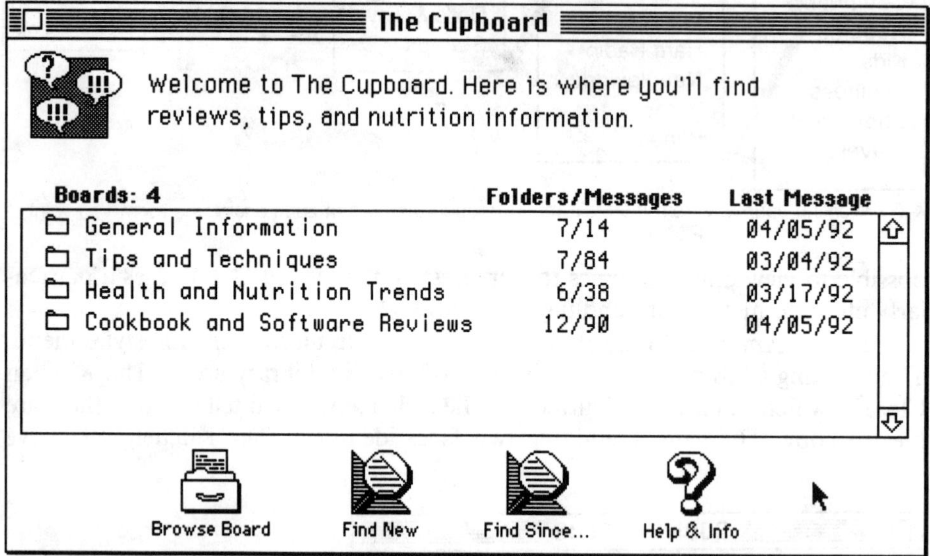

4-8 When you open the Cupboard, you'll find folders full of other folders.

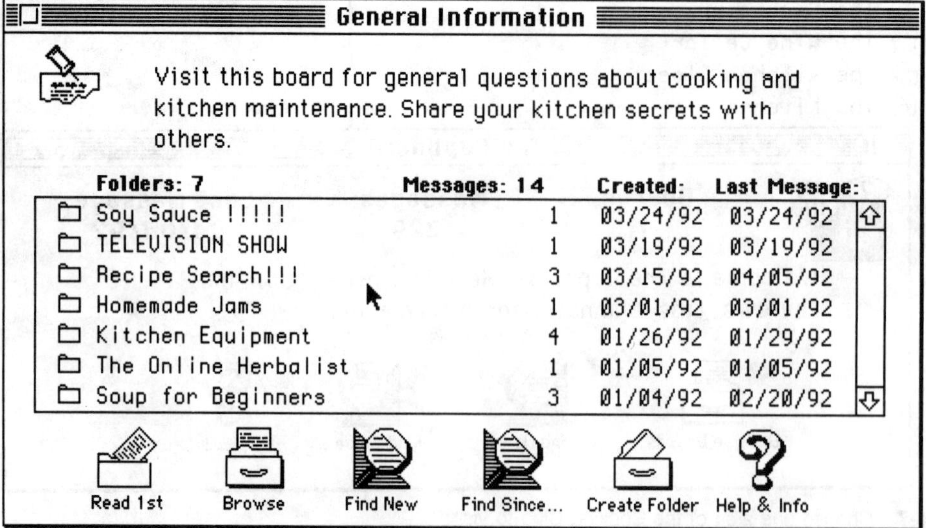

4-9 Each topic has its own folder.

topics. The numbers after the titles of the messages in Fig. 4-9 tell you how many messages are in that file. The date is the date of the most recent entry.

Prodigy handles its forums differently from the other services. Because it doesn't offer live conferences or downloadable files, its forums contain only message boards. However, it has a great many of these; so many, in fact, that messages are removed after a couple of weeks. To select a topic on Prodigy, first find the area that generally describes your interest. Prodigy calls its forums clubs. The categories are rather broad. The HomeLife Club, for example, contains messages on topics as far apart as ham radio, parenting, and genealogy (Fig. 4-10). Selecting any one of these topics leads you to lists of literally hundreds of subjects with from one to 20 or more letters. The board is updated daily.

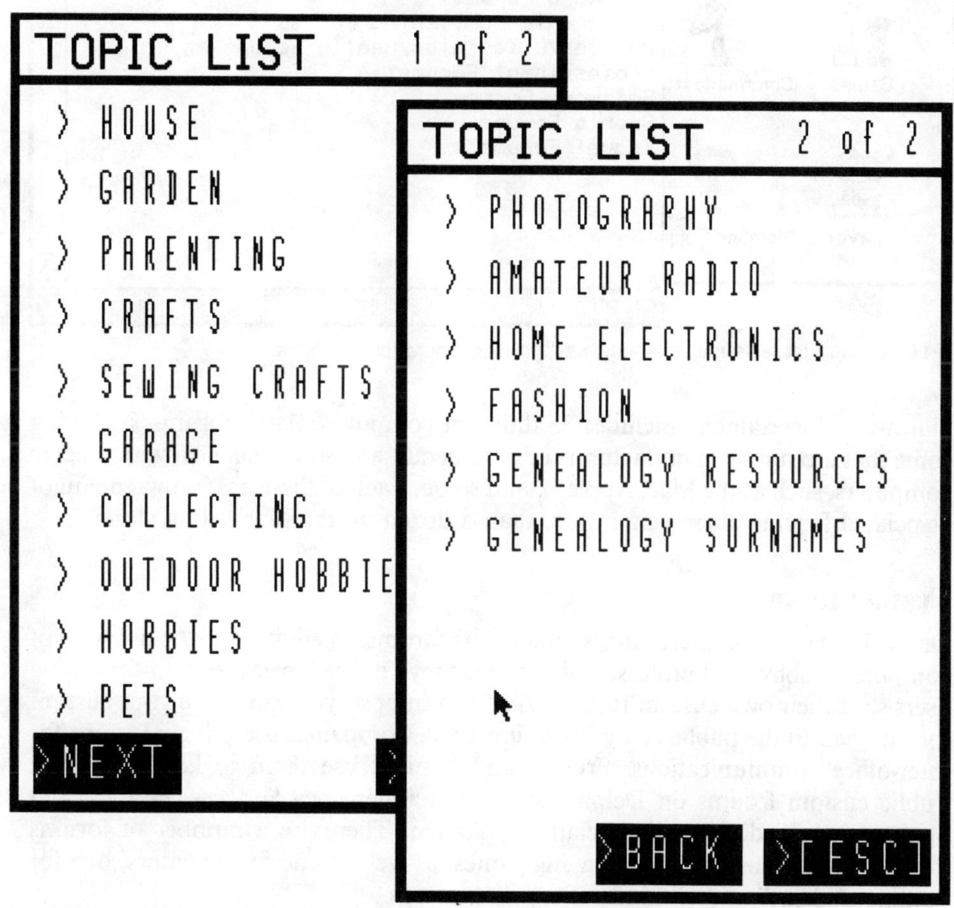

4-10 Each of these topics leads you to literally hundreds of sub-topics.

CompuServe's Main listing of forums, shown in Fig. 4-11, might not look too impressive, but each of the dozen entries leads you to a long list of separate forums.

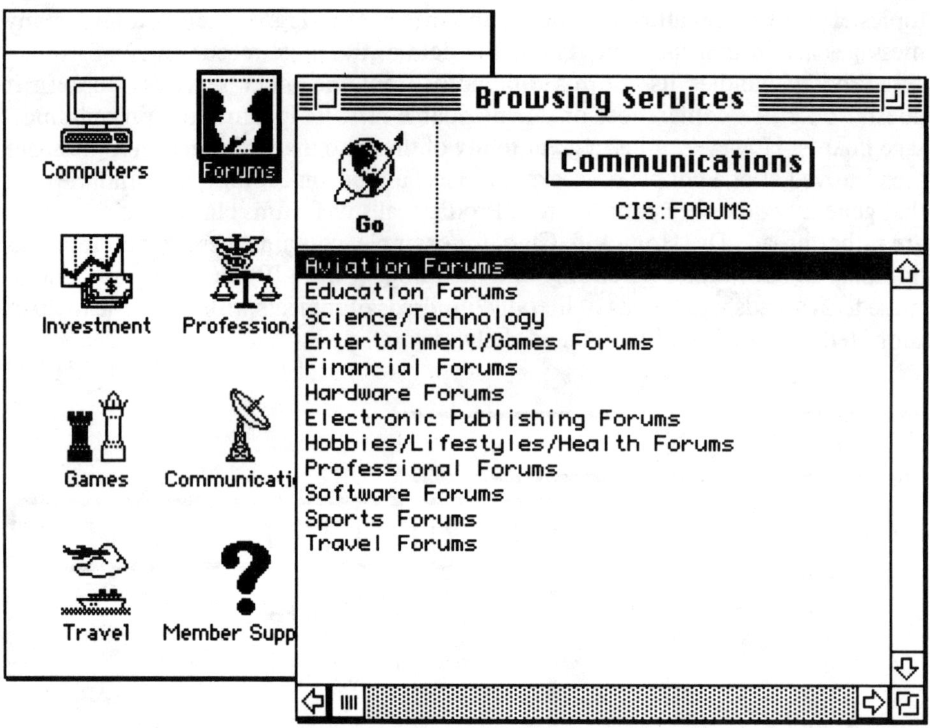

4-11 Each of these listings is a "doorway" to many more forum listings.

Hardware, for example, includes 35 different computer-related forums, including some that are run by manufacturers of peripherals, and some that deal with specific computers, such as the Mac, Apple II, and so on. Each of these has its own menu of associated forums, there being more than a dozen on the Mac listing alone.

Custom forums

Delphi has added an interesting wrinkle to its forums. In addition to the usual set of computer, hobby, and professional forums, they've developed a system for letting users start their own custom forums. As a forum host, you can make your custom forum open to the public or by invitation only. Companies use private forums for inter-office communications. Friends and families use them to keep in touch. Public custom forums on Delphi range from Emergency Services, Politics, and Sports Card Trading to Big, Beautiful Women. There are a number of forums dedicated to fantasy and role-playing games, as well as one for inventors, one for "online nudists," and all kinds of support groups.

There's a start-up charge and a monthly fee to maintain the custom forum, but these can be waived and the host can even get regular Delphi charges dropped if the forum attracts enough users. If it proves to be extremely popular, it might even be moved to the main forum area. In this case, the forum host is paid royalties by Delphi based on the number of hours the forum is in use.

Do-it-yourself forums are also featured on an interesting bulletin board and chat service called the Po!nt. The Po!nt is accessible through a gateway on CompuServe or directly. CompuServe members reach it from the Communications Menu on CIM by selecting Participate. There are hundreds of message topics, and anybody can start a new one. Participation in the Po!nt is free to CompuServe users with the Executive Option.

Non-forums

When you enter a service, you'll also find many areas that *aren't* forums: Reference sections, News and weather, Shopping services, and a great deal more. The structure of these areas is different from the forum structure, but again, if you think of them as separate rooms within an office, within a larger building, you should be able to wander from one to the next with no difficulty. Obviously, though, on the board as in real life you can't enter a room without also leaving one. Using the Go command will work in most services. Prodigy uses Jump instead of Go. If you're not sure where to go next, you can exit the area you're in and return to the Main menu, or "lobby," to take another path.

Non-forum areas have their own sets of commands, quite different from the forums. They are essentially systems within the system, or sub-systems. Examples of sub-systems include the mail system, online games, and conference areas. The commands in a sub-system are tailored to whatever you're doing there, and can involve editing messages, dealing cards and rolling dice, or entering your order for gourmet coffee, computer books, or t-shirts.

Every online service includes one or more gateways. These, as the name suggests, are a way you can access a different service. A *gateway* is a link from your "host" service to another service, called a *gateway service.* Eaasy Sabre, the airline and travel service, is a gateway service, as is Dow Jones News Retrieval. It's possible to call either of these directly, but it's also possible to enter them through most online services. Once you enter Eaasy Sabre, you must use Sabre's commands, instead of the host's. The Sabre commands will be the same, whether you're accessing it from America Online, Delphi, or CompuServe because the computer you're actually talking with is Sabre's and not the host's. Figures 4-12 and 4-13 show the same flight from Boston to Stockholm, first through Delphi's gateway, then through CompuServe's. America Online and Prodigy also connect you to Sabre, but they do it through their own "front end" programs, giving you the same information but in a more attractive format. Figure 4-14 shows the America Online gateway to Sabre.

Using commands

We've already discussed the Go command, but there are a few others you'll need to know about. These are the commands that get you help when you're lost, show you a menu or directory of files, let you look at a particular directory entry and download it, exit a menu, and most important of all, sign off the service. Com-

```
Delphi
From:  (BOS) BOSTON, MA
 To:   (STO) STOCKHOLM, SWEDEN                                 SATURDAY  JUN-13-92
------------------------------------------------------------------------------------
  Flight    Leave        Arrive    Meal Stop Aircraft OnTime  Classes of Service**
1 AA 108   BOS   750P  LHR   710A  DB    0     D10            C  Y  M  B  V  H  Q
  BA 776         910A  ARN  1240P  *     0     737            C  M  S  B  L  Q  V
2 AA 108   BOS   750P  LHR   710A  DB    0     D10            C  Y  M  B  V  H  Q
  SK 526         930A  ARN  1255P  L     0     M80            S  C  M  H  Q  B  G  V
3 LH 423   BOS   600P  FRA   700A  DB    0     D10            F  C  B  M  K
  LH3052         950A  ARN  1155A        0     320            F  C
------------------------------------------------------------------------------------
To SELECT a flight, enter the line number, or

 8  View MORE flights                          11  View all FARES
 9  CHANGE flight request                      12  Translate CODES
10  View FIRST flight display                  13  View LOWest one-way fares

** Quick Tip:  Select your flight, then choose Bargain Finder when prompted and
   EAASY SABRE will select the class of service for the lowest available fare.
>
12:35:18 PM
```

4-12 Eaasy Sabre looks the same on Delphi. . .

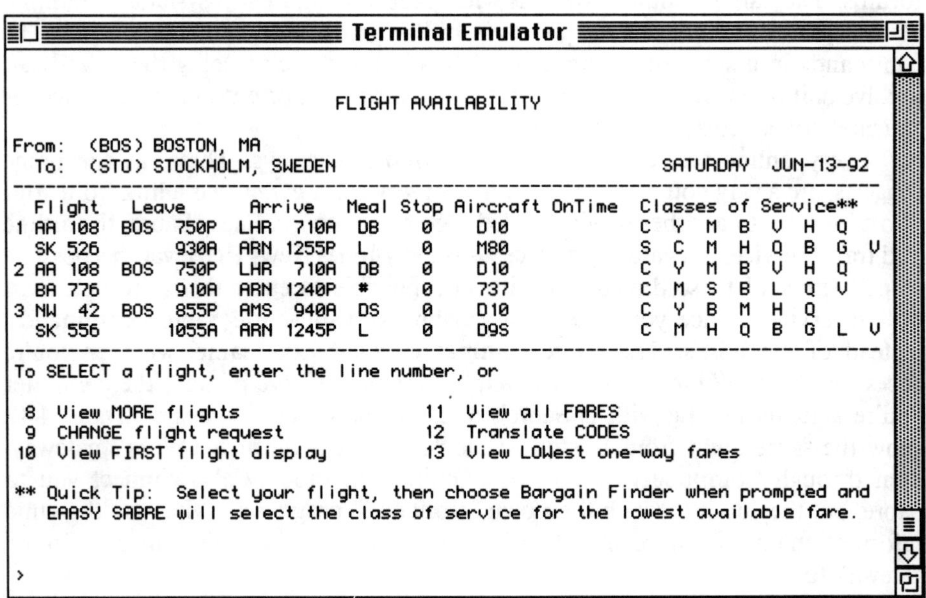

```
Terminal Emulator

                              FLIGHT AVAILABILITY

From:  (BOS) BOSTON, MA
 To:   (STO) STOCKHOLM, SWEDEN                                 SATURDAY  JUN-13-92
------------------------------------------------------------------------------------
  Flight    Leave        Arrive    Meal Stop Aircraft OnTime  Classes of Service**
1 AA 108   BOS   750P  LHR   710A  DB    0     D10            C  Y  M  B  V  H  Q
  SK 526         930A  ARN  1255P  L     0     M80            S  C  M  H  Q  B  G  V
2 AA 108   BOS   750P  LHR   710A  DB    0     D10            C  Y  M  B  V  H  Q
  BA 776         910A  ARN  1240P  *     0     737            C  M  S  B  L  Q  V
3 NW  42   BOS   855P  AMS   940A  DS    0     D10            C  Y  B  M  H  Q
  SK 556        1055A  ARN  1245P  L     0     D9S            C  M  H  Q  B  G  L  V
------------------------------------------------------------------------------------
To SELECT a flight, enter the line number, or

 8  View MORE flights                          11  View all FARES
 9  CHANGE flight request                      12  Translate CODES
10  View FIRST flight display                  13  View LOWest one-way fares

** Quick Tip:  Select your flight, then choose Bargain Finder when prompted and
   EAASY SABRE will select the class of service for the lowest available fare.

>
```

4-13 . . . as it does on CompuServe.

mands can be entered from the keyboard as words, or selected from menus or dialog boxes. GEnie lets you enter commands either by name or by menu number. A typical GEnie command menu is shown in Fig. 4-15.

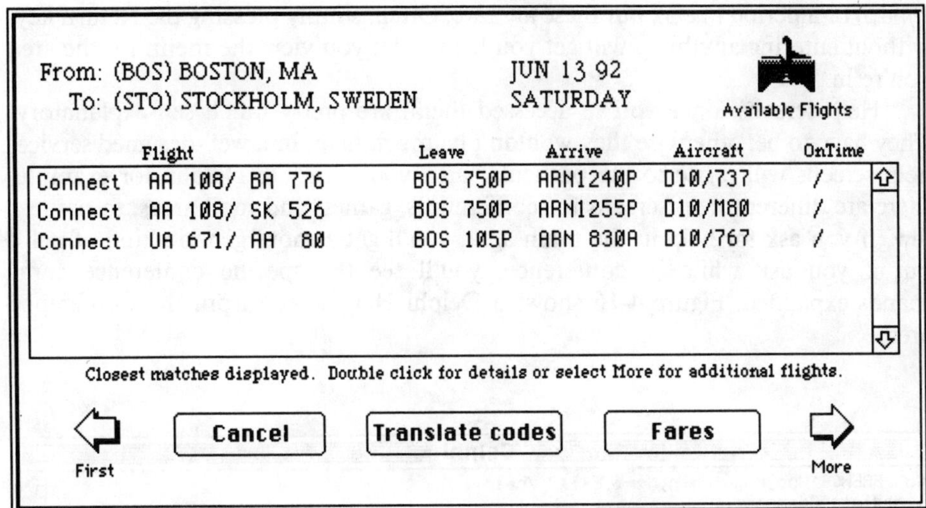

4-14 Same Sabre, same information, but a different format.

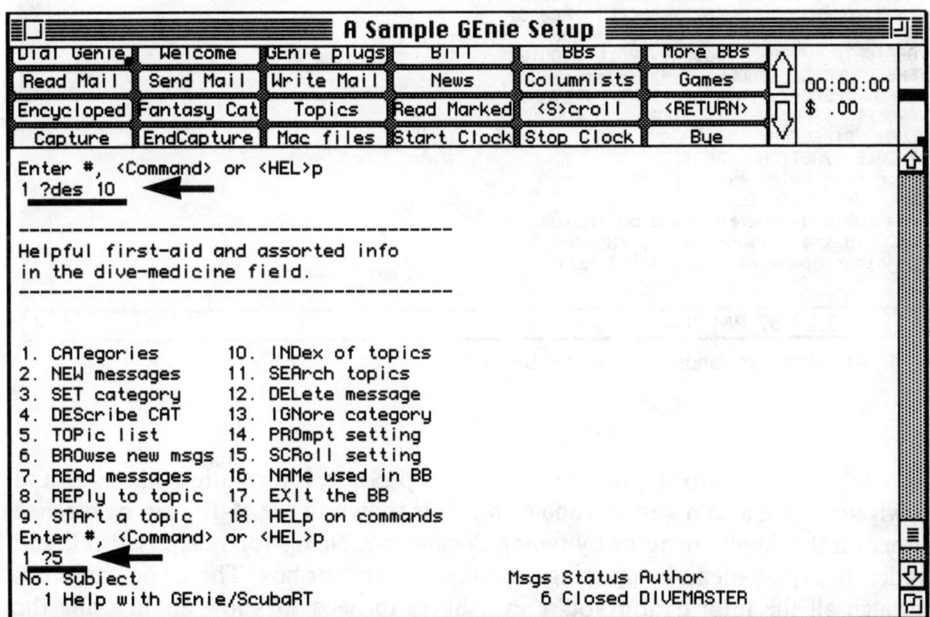

4-15 We used a word command to get the category description. We then used a number command to get the topic list.

Help

To get help, on most BBS and services, type either the word help or a question mark. If nothing happens when you do, try it again with a slash in front of it, like this: /help or /?. Some systems require that you identify all commands by placing a slash in front of them. You might find a BBS that asks you to use a double slash

(//help) or a period (.help), but these are rare. Often, simply pressing the Return key, without entering anything, will get you help or let you view the menu for the area you're in.

Help screens, once you've accessed them, are pretty much self-explanatory. They have to be; otherwise they wouldn't be much help. In a well-designed service, help screens will relate to the particular area you're in. On Delphi, for example, there are different help screens for conferences, games, and mail areas, to name a few. If you ask for help in the main area, you'll get a more generic kind of help, but if you ask while in conference, you'll see the specific conference commands explained. Figure 4-16 shows a Delphi Help screen from the Conference area.

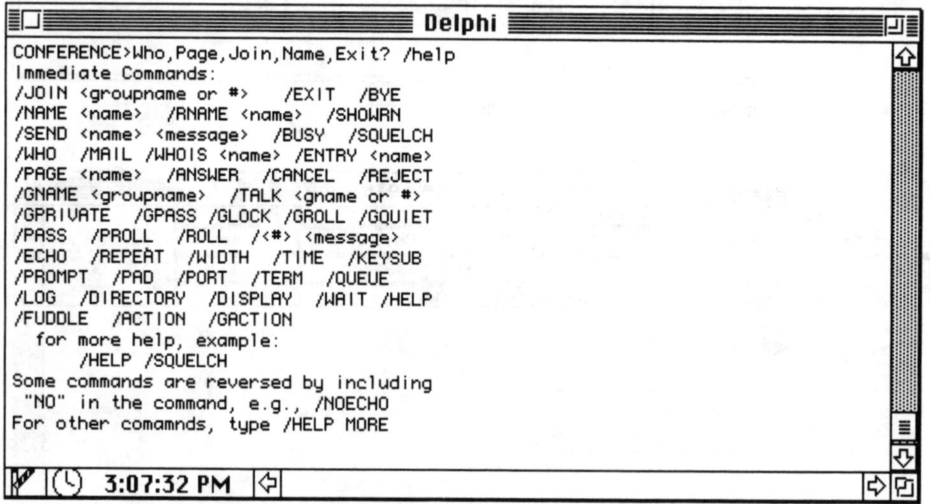

4-16 All Delphi commands are preceded by a slash.

Help is built into the programs for CompuServe Information Manager and Navigator. CIM's help screens, one of which is shown in Fig. 4-17, can be reached either on the Apple menu or by typing Command-?. Navigator's help is also found under the Apple menu by opening the About Navigator box. There you can scroll through all the information you're ever likely to need to know about using the program or print a copy of the full text by typing Command-P. Getting help online if you've entered CompuServe through a regular telecom program like MicroPhone or White Knight requires typing HELP at the ! prompt.

Prodigy help is found on its menu at the bottom of the screen, as shown in Fig. 4-18. You can also get help on other menu commands by selecting one and typing a question mark. Help is context-dependent. If you choose help while the Highlights screen is showing, you'll get information about Highlights, and how to select an item to see in detail.

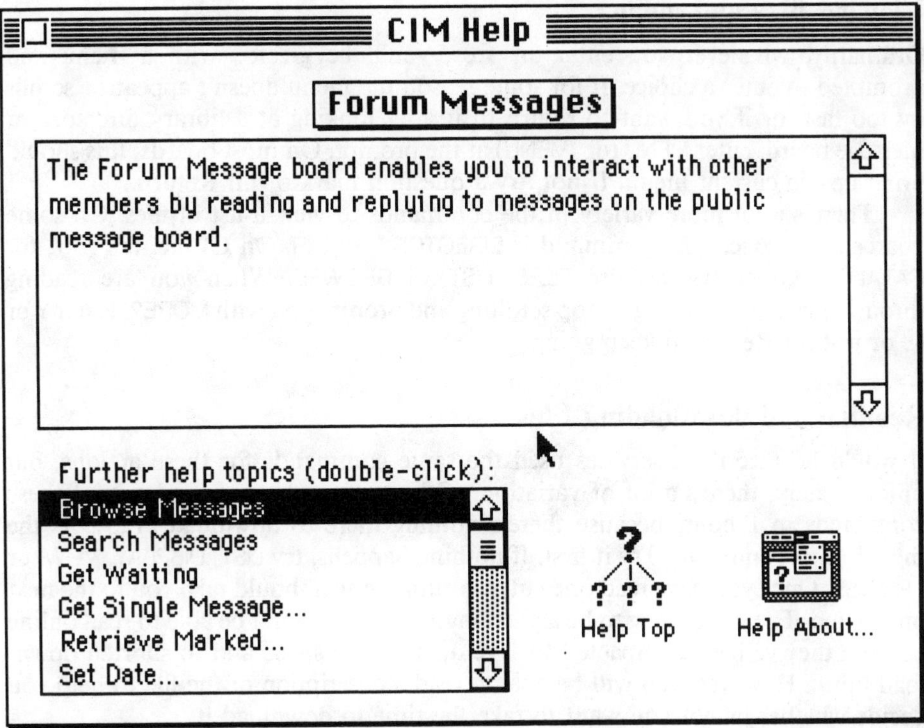

4-17 CIM Help is easy to understand.

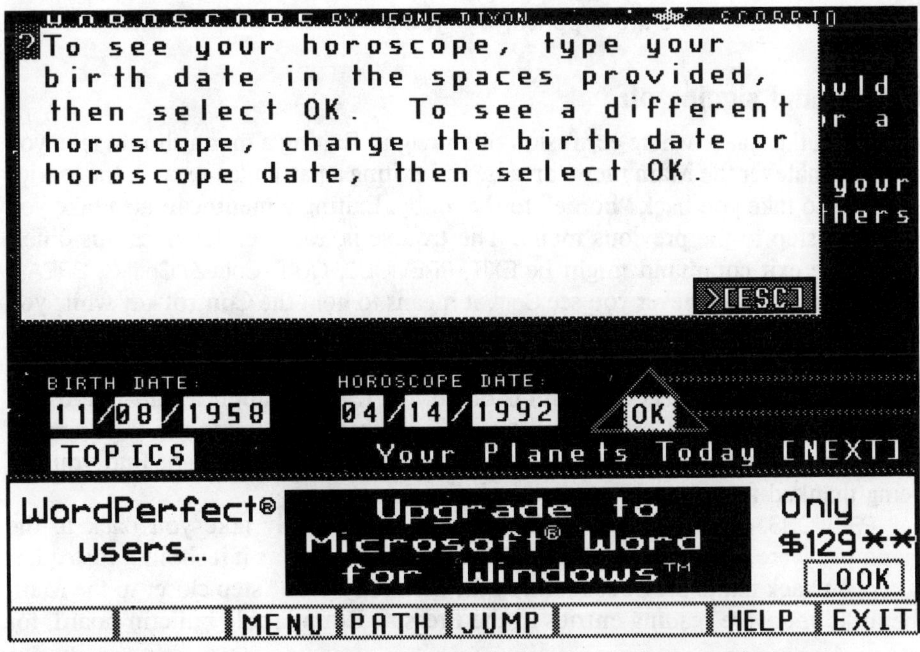

4-18 Prodigy Help is found by double clicking the Help box at the bottom of the screen.

Viewing files and menus

Ordinarily, whenever you enter an area, you'll be greeted with a menu and prompted to enter a choice. If for some reason the menu doesn't appear or scrolls by too fast, or if you want to return to it after looking at a library directory or message board, enter MENU (or /MENU) at the prompt. On most boards, this should bring up the current menu. If not, try a question mark or hit Return.

There's a lot more variety in the commands to view a list of files. On some boards and services the command is DIRECTORY, or DIR. On GEnie, it's CAT, for CATALOG. Other systems use FILES, LIST, or BROWSE. When you are reading through a list, the Mac might stop scrolling and prompt you with MORE?. Enter Y or N, or just hit Return to keep going.

Reading and downloading files

It would be nice if all services used the same commands for these actions, but unfortunately, there's a lot of variation. (Of course, you won't find any of these commands in Prodigy because there's nothing there to download.) READ is the most logical command. Try it first. If nothing happens, try LIST, DISPLAY, VIEW, or BROWSE. Once you have read one entry, hitting Return should take you to the next one in line. There are going to be a great many files you won't be able to read online because they've been compacted to save disk storage space and to shorten download times. However, you will be able to read a description of the file to help you decide whether or not you want to take the time to download it.

Downloading is also handled differently on different services. Because most support various download protocols and ask you to specify your choice, just follow their directions. If none are supplied, try typing DOWN.

Exiting and signing off

Here's another place where confusion often reigns. Exiting a menu should take you back to whatever the Main menu area is, and exiting a particular area on the service should also take you back "home" to the lobby. Exiting a menu can also take you back one step to the previous menu. The trouble is, each service does this differently. The exit command might be EXIT, PREVIOUS, QUIT, Cntrl-Z, Cntrl-C, BREAK, END, or Cntrl-Y. (Whenever you see Cntrl, it means to hold the Control key while you type the letter indicated, just as you would with the Command key for a Mac command or the Shift key to type a capital letter. Control keys are used more often on DOS-based computers. Telecom is one of the few Mac applications that uses a Control key sequence. Control keys are often indicated by typing the caret symbol Shift-6.) If you happen to type the wrong exit command, you might find yourself being thanked for using the service and disconnected.

PREVIOUS, used chiefly on GEnie, doesn't necessarily take you back to the menu you were looking at a minute ago, although it seems as if it should. Instead, it takes you back to the previous menu in the hierarchy—one step closer to the Main menu. If you were reading entries in the Freesoft RoundTable bulletin board, for example, and then exited, you'd return to the FreeSoft RoundTable menu (Fig. 4-19). From there, if you entered P (for Previous), you'd go back to the Apple/Macintosh menu, entering P again would take you to the Computing on GEnie menu, and P once more takes you all the way back to the Top, or Main menu.

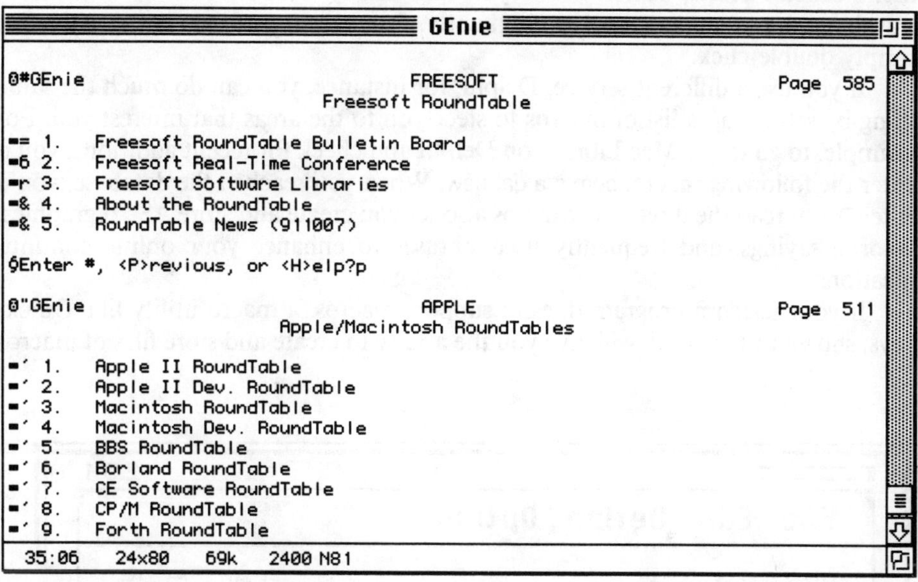

4-19 Repeatedly typing **p** will eventually take you back to the "top" screen, as will simply typing TOP.

The command for *logging off*, or exiting the service, also depends on which system you're on. Most seem to respond to BYE, although QUIT, EXIT, OFF, GOODBYE, END, and HANGUP are also used. A service that uses EXIT to get you out of a menu or forum obviously uses a different command to take you offline. Even though you could get off by unplugging the modem, it's a good idea to disconnect properly by using the appropriate command. For one thing, following the correct logoff procedure resets your modem so you can make another call or receive one. Some BBSs can be disabled if a user disconnects without logging off.

More important, some services, particularly those that charge by the minute, might not register that you've hung up until 10 minutes (or some set period) has gone by with no input, and they complete the logoff automatically. In such a case, you'd be charged as if you'd been online for that amount of time. If you have a system crash, or the service freezes up, or something unexpected happens that forces you to get out by pulling the plug, it might be a good idea to call the service's customer service number immediately and explain what happened. Generally, they'll adjust your bill accordingly. If you are going to jump right back online with the same service, though, it's probably not worth bothering to call because you'd only lose a minute or so.

Using macros

Once you've had an opportunity to explore your favorite online service a bit, you'll find that there are certain places you keep returning to. CompuServe Information Manager makes it easy for you to get there, at least on CompuServe, by providing a menu called Favorite Places, which you can modify to include the forums, news, travel, or whatever areas you visit frequently. To reach any of the places on the list, simply double click.

If you use a different service, Delphi, for instance, you can do much the same thing by setting up a list of macros to steer you to the areas that interest you. For example, to go to the Mac Library on Delphi and check for recent additions, you'd enter the following macro: com ma dat new. When you reached the database, you'd enter DIR to read the directory. Macros also let you create and store ASCII graphics, favorite sayings, and frequently used phrases to enhance your online communications.

If your telecom program doesn't support macros, a macro utility like Quickkeys, shown in Fig. 4-20, will give you the ability to create and store files of macros

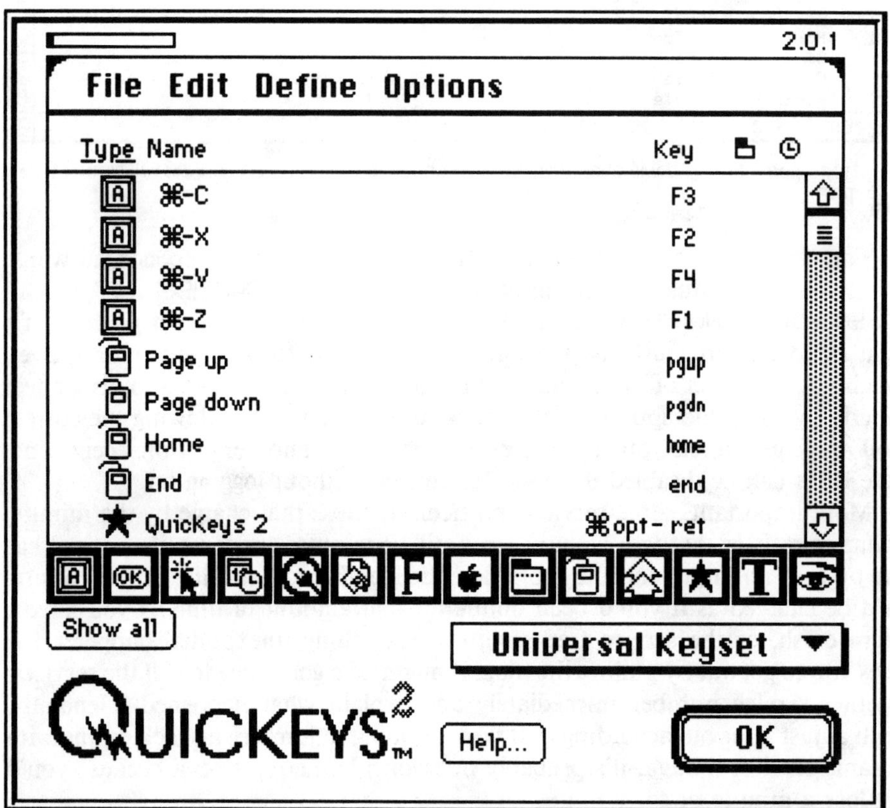

4-20 Quickkeys is accessible from the Apple menu.

for different online services as well as to make other Mac functions easier. White Knight and Z-Term are among the telecom programs that include a macro editor and can save different sets of macros for each service. Figure 4-21 shows the macro set for a local BBS.

Label:	Macro String:
Macro-1	/say Ahoy there!
Macro-2	/say Whooff, Whooff (fog horn)
Macro-3	/say Aye, Captain.
Macro-4	goto library^M
Macro-5	goto galley^M
Macro-6	goto radio room^M
Macro-7	goto wardroom^M
Macro-8	goto bridge^M
Macro-9	/say Avast, ye scurvy devils!
Macro-0	/say Land Lubber!!!

Set: Lightship set   OK   Cancel

4-21 You can save a different set of macros for each BBS you belong to.

A picture is worth a whole bunch of text

Before there were words, there were pictures. It was an ancient Chinese proverb, according to Bartlett's *Familiar Quotations*, that first claimed that "a picture is worth ten thousand words." The creators of the Macintosh saw the truth in this. One of the things that has set the Mac apart from other computers since Day One has been its ability to combine text and graphics. Instead of looking at long lists of eight-letter words ending with *.DAT* or *.EXE*, we point to icons, little pictures of the files we want to open. (With the introduction of the Windows Operating System, the PC world has finally gained this advantage, to a degree.) Our word processors let us paste in not only drawings and scanned photographs but even QuickTime movies taken from live action video or computer animation. This ability has been largely ignored in the world of online services, which must also deal with the non-Mac population. They are more or less forced to use the lowest common denominator of inter-species computer communication: ASCII text. But because we're inclined to try to communicate with both pictures and words, a variety of systems have arisen to bring graphics to the screens of not only the Mac, but less well-endowed computers, too.

The easiest and most basic of these graphics systems is the use of ASCII graphics. You can create pictures and *emoticons*, (little faces that show what you're feeling: emotion + icon) by combining a few simple keystrokes like this:

:-) Smile (Turn your head sideways if you don't see it.)
;-) Wink
:-P' Nyah, Nyah

A more complete emoticon chart is shown in chapter 7. These little bits of art add flavor and personality to online chats and correspondence, so much so that many computer users have started to incorporate them in offline letters as well.

Some ASCII pictures are quite elaborate. Some are simply funny, like the COWtoons that appear in GEnie's online magazine and crop up occasionally on other boards. Figure 4-22 shows a few of the many cows in the series. These ASCII

The cyclops that Jason and the Argonauts met had this cow

This cow lived with Dr. Doolittle

This cow belonged to Flash Gordon

This cow lived with the Little Rascals

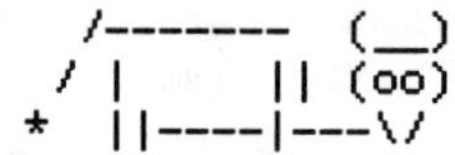

This cow belonged to the Headless Horseman

4-22 The origin of COWtoons is unclear. They first appeared on a public BBS (BitNET) several years ago.

graphics use the basic 127 character ASCII set. By using VT modes and the extended character set a lot more can be done. VT games, although graphically crude by the standards of those raised on Nintendo, are popular on some services. VT graphics games are played in the text emulation window, making them accessible to all computer users, not just Macs.

PC ANSI

A newer method for using graphic elements, available to both PC and Mac users, is called *PC ANSI mode*, or *ANSI terminal emulation*. It uses a standard set of codes for colors, as well as the extended ASCII set (128-256) of special characters, to create interesting screen displays that can be viewed by most computers. Some BBSs are using ANSI graphics to good effect. Figure 4-23 shows a screen from the Hayes Bulletin Board, run by the makers of Hayes modems. (Although we can only show it in black and white, it's very pretty on a color Mac.)

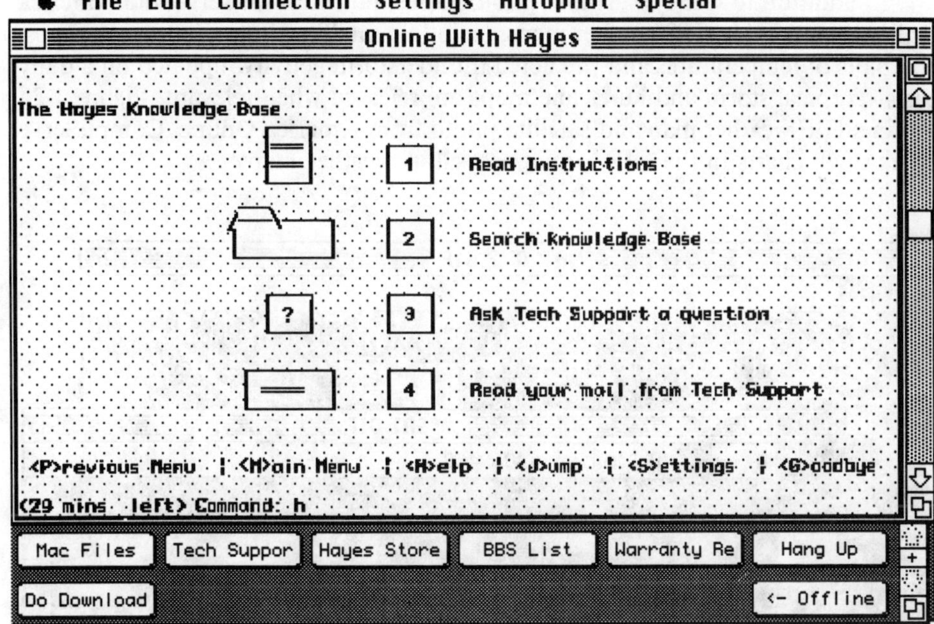

4-23 The graphics aren't remarkable, but they work just as well on a PC as a Mac.

As graphics have become more and more a part of computer use, the need for cross-platform, or cross-system, graphics became obvious. Macintosh graphics and desktop publishing programs can accept images in a variety of formats, including some not created on a Mac. PC graphics and DTP software can now handle Mac graphics, too. Scanned images can be saved in formats that are acceptable to either. What this has meant to the online user is the availability of huge libraries of compatible shareware images, contributed by PC, Mac, and even Amiga and Atari users.

GIF

The common denominator for computer graphics is a format called *GIF* (*Graphic Interchange Format*), first introduced by CompuServe in 1987. GIF files can be line art or a scanned photograph, and they can be black and white, gray scale, or color. They're stored in a compressed form for easier downloading and to occupy less disk space. Color GIF images are automatically converted to dot patterns if you're looking at them on a black and white Mac screen. GIF images cannot be seen online, except on CompuServe. CompuServe builds GIF viewing into its Navigator and CIM programs. On the other services, you have to download the GIF file and open it to see the picture. You'll also need a GIF viewer to translate the GIF back into an image. These programs are available online in graphics and utility libraries. One of the best is a shareware program called GIFConverter 2.2.8, available from America Online.

In addition to GIFs of art and photographs, both CompuServe and America Online now provide GIF weather maps, including satellite photos, jet stream maps, and plots of temperatures and predicted thunderstorm activity, updated on a daily basis. Tropical storm and hurricane maps are released when relevant. Figure 4-24 shows a GIF weather map and satellite photo from America Online. CompuServe offers stock charts in the GIF format as well as weather maps.

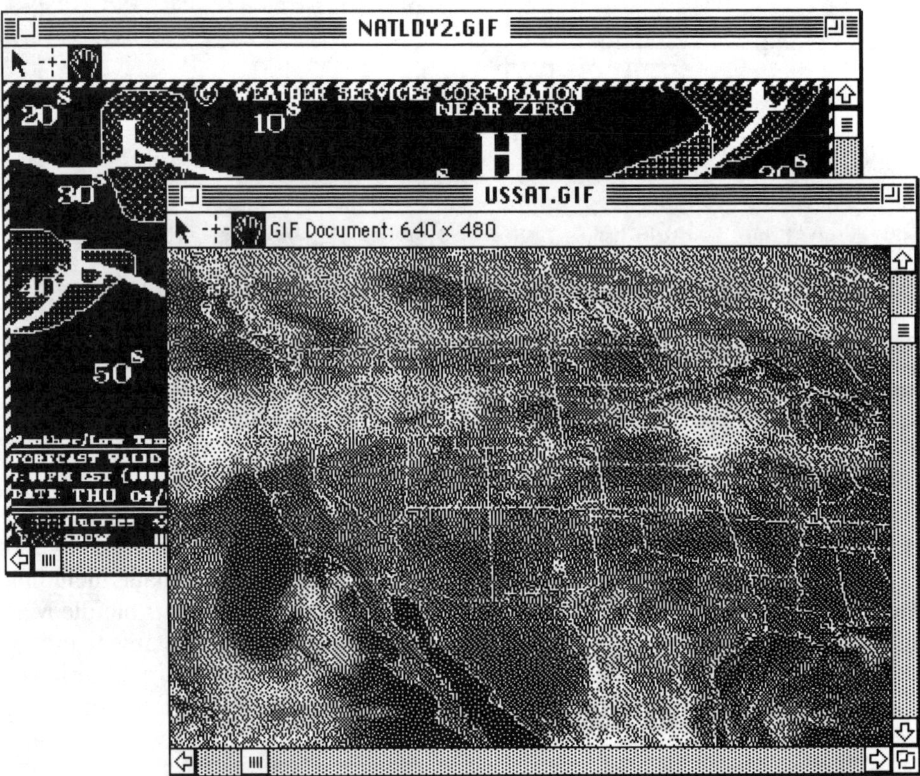

4-24 Weather watchers love these maps.

America Online also features GIF cartoons from several different artists in its Entertainment area, and GIF files of all types in its Graphics forum, including some that are emphatically *not* for family viewing. You'll find similar libraries of

GIFs on other services, as well as GIF files with portraits of service members and even their families and pets.

There's a minor problem with GIFs from America Online. Some GIF files, including the weather maps and cartoons, currently do not download with the right file type for the Mac. The solution is quite simple, however. After downloading the weather maps or other GIF images, run GIFconverter. Choose the Open command from the File menu. Open the folder where you downloaded the images. If you don't see them listed, click the Look inside all files button. The files you downloaded should appear in the box. Click the Fix file types for shown files button, to change the file types, as shown in Fig. 4-25. Then you will be able to open the files.

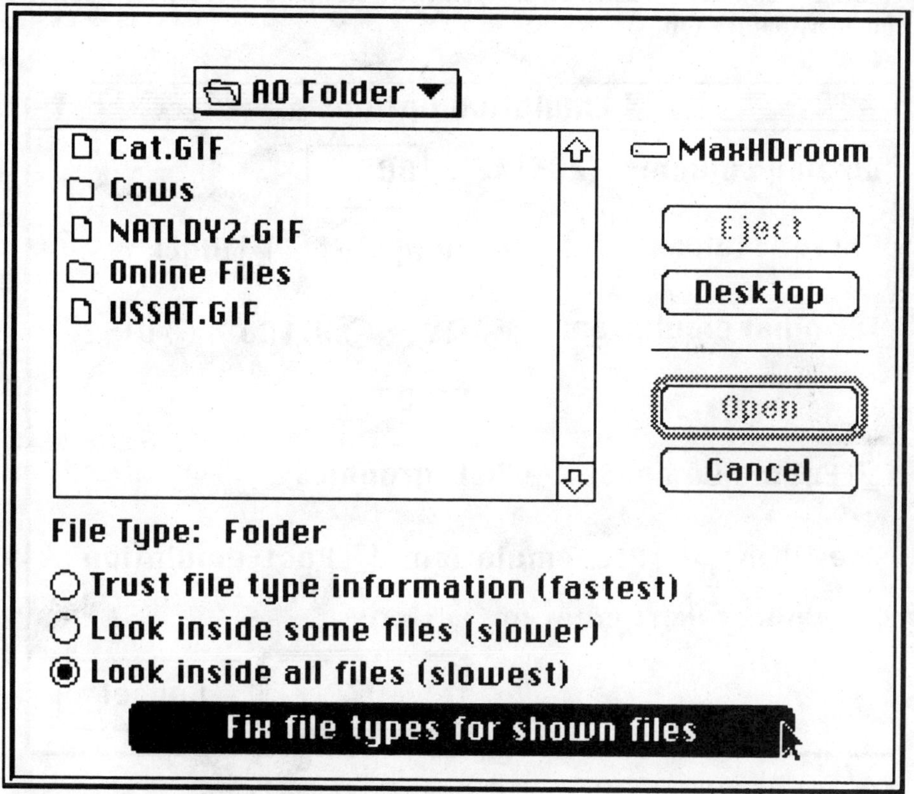

4-25 Fixing the file types makes them usable by the Mac.

RLE graphics

CompuServe also offers a second type of graphic, called *RLE* (*Run Length Encoded*) *graphics*. These aren't supported by CIM or Navigator but are available if you are using White Knight to access the service. RLE is an early graphics format, first introduced to CompuServe members in 1986. Its images are only in black and white. They can be viewed online or downloaded.

Because of a conflict in terminal emulation, you can't use VT-52 mode if you want to view an RLE graphic. Also, you must enable the Emulations Options to support them. This is done, as shown in Fig. 4-26, by checking the appropriate listing in the dialog box. RLE images are found in CompuServe's Graphics libraries. (Use RLE as a keyword to search the library.) To view a graphic while online, type CHOICES at the prompt, and select READ. You'll probably get a message from CompuServe saying something to the effect that your terminal won't support RLE graphics, and asking you if you want to go ahead anyway. Just reply Y, and watch as the RLE window appears and the graphic draws itself line by line. Figure 4-27 shows a completed RLE graphic. It's slow and in some ways obsolete technology, but it's fun.

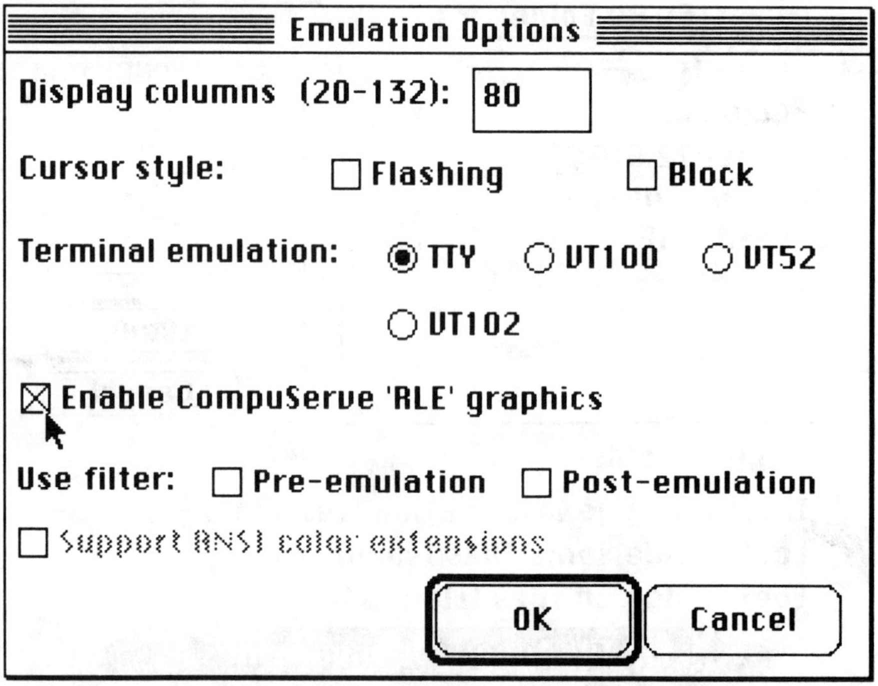

4-26 Use TTY, VT100, or 102 to view RLE graphics.

Prodigy holds the distinction of being a graphics-based service, rather than a text service. Everything it displays—mail, ads, or whatever else appears on your screen—is treated as a graphic rather than a text file. Prodigy uses a graphics description format based on the *North American Presentation Level Protocol Standard*, or *NAPLPS*. Everything on the screen is described in this format and sent to your Mac for decoding. The same decoder can interpret the software in black and white or in color, in low resolution or in high resolution, depending on what kind of monitor it's being displayed on. More important, the NAPLPS graphic descriptions

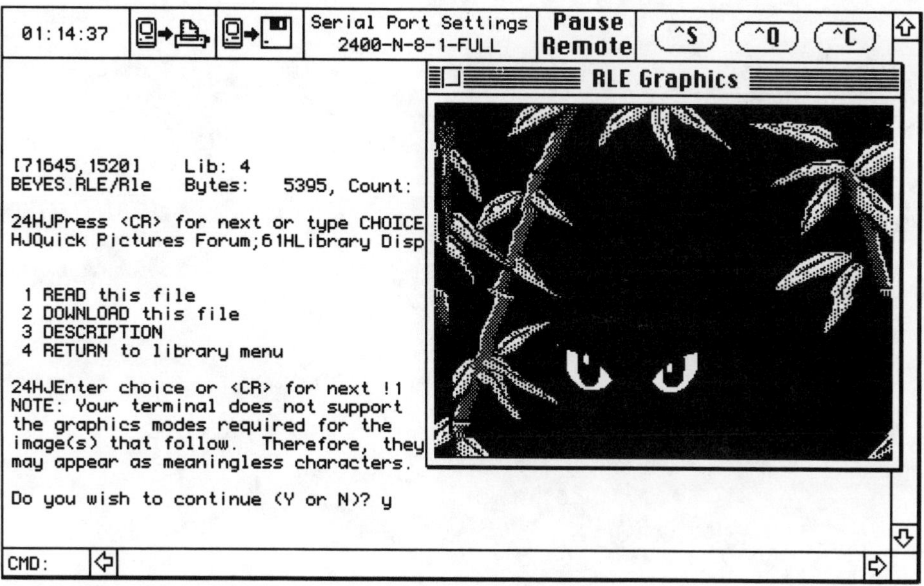

4-27 Despite the warning, it comes out just the way it's supposed to.

are the same for the Mac and the PC, so Prodigy runs on both and can send the same data to both.

Summary

To avoid getting lost online, once you log on, learn to use the system's menus and commands to navigate from one area to another. There are Main menu and submenus on virtually all systems and BBSs. They are analogous to rooms in a building or branches on a tree. Using the command Go or Go to takes you from one room to another.

On some services, a forum is a particular department, such as graphics, ham radio, or cooking. Other services call this a *SIG* (*special interest group*), a club, or a round table. A forum is the bulletin board, or message board, where members can post public messages for others to reply to and comment on. Within the department, in addition to message boards, there are libraries of files to download and a conference area where members of the group can talk with each other online in real time. Services have non-forum areas, too, including gateways to other special purpose services like EAASY SABRE for travel arrangements and Dow Jones Business News.

Commands vary from one service to the next. Help is generally available, though, by typing HELP or a question mark.

Some services feature graphics files, in the GIF format. These must be downloaded for viewing, except on CompuServe. GIF viewers are included in CIM and Navigator. CompuServe also supports an older graphic format called *RLE*, for use with text programs like White Knight. Unlike GIFs, RLE graphics are only in black and white.

5

Letters, we get letters

Which of these is more effective communication? This?

> "This is Suzy. I'm not home right now, but if you leave your name and number when you hear the. . . ."
> "Beep."
> "Uh, hi, uh . . . This is, um, Charlie, and it's . . . ah, I think it's, like, Tuesday. . . ."

Or this?

> From: BOS::CharlieB
> To: HunniBear
> CC:
> Subj: Dinner Friday?
> Beautiful Lady -
> Will you do me the honor of accompanying me to dinner at the Ritz-Carlton on Friday the 21st? It's the annual Gourmet Club bash, so the food will be *almost* as special as you, dearest Suzy. Please say yes.

Some things are best said in print, especially by those of us who freeze up when confronted with answering machines or run up huge inter-continental phone bills trying to catch up with a client on the other coast. Electronic mail, or E-mail as it's more commonly known, solves a lot of communication problems. In fact, one of the major reasons people give for subscribing to an online service is to be able to send and receive E-mail. The advantages are obvious. The "post office" is always open, and you don't need to go out in the rain to get there. Your mail is delivered immediately. You don't need a stamp or even an envelope. All you need is the recipient's electronic "address." Many systems will also give you a return receipt so you'll know when the message was read, and you can send yourself a carbon copy, too.

When you leave an E-mail message, you avoid the frustration of playing "telephone tag" with a friend or business associate who's always "in a meeting," "on the other line," or "just stepped down the hall." You don't need to rely on an answering machine tape that might not record, a receptionist who can't get your message right, or a child who says "I'll tell Daddy you called. How do you spell your name? Uh huh. B-I-L-L. Okay. How do you make a B?"

E-mailing a note to someone in a different time zone means you don't have to adjust your schedule to a working day that can be several hours out of sync. And E-mail always gets a prompt response because it's so easy to dash off a reply as soon as you've read the message.

There's another major advantage for both business and personal communication—E-mail is private. Only the sender and the recipient can read it, and if neither keeps a copy on disk or prints one, the message can never fall into the wrong hands; a definite benefit for spreadsheets and love letters alike.

Of course, there's a hitch. (With anything this convenient, there *has* to be a hitch.) Both sender and recipient have to use the same online service or bulletin board, or at least two that interconnect through a gateway.

If you need to get a message to someone who doesn't have E-mail, there are still a few possibilities. Most online services will fax your message to anyone you specify, if you don't have your own fax machine or fax/modem combination. You can even combine E-mail and "snail mail," as many online users like to call the postal service. Most services will print and send a hard copy of your message by regular mail or by overnight courier, for a fee.

E-mail systems

As you might expect, every commercial service handles E-mail. Many free bulletin boards do, too. But no two handle it in exactly the same way. Some systems keep a common "mail bag," retrieve your messages when you ask, and delete them when you've read them. Others give you an individual mail box, in which you can store your mail and re-read it if you desire, or delete any or all messages when you want. At least one service will automatically delete any message that's over a month old, whether you've read it or not. Another will store your mail indefinitely but will charge you for storage space beyond your basic allotment. Either way, it's a good idea not to get into the habit of using your mailbox as a filing cabinet. It could be either expensive or unreliable, depending on which service you happen to be using.

Speaking of charges, most online services don't charge you for E-mail sent to another member of that service. The exceptions are CompuServe and Prodigy, which let you send a certain number of messages a month for free: 60 on CIS, and 30 on Prodigy. After you have used up your "freebies," there's a charge per message for the additional ones. Prodigy wants 25 cents per message, while CompuServe asks only 15 cents. If you stop to consider that a first-class postage stamp costs more and gets the message there several days later, it's still a pretty good deal.

Internet

Suppose you want to send a message to someone who doesn't subscribe to the same service you do. If your service is Prodigy, you'll probably have to send paper mail or a fax, or even call them. But if you and the recipient belong to a user group, a local

BBS, or to CompuServe, Delphi, AO, or MCI, you have another alternative: you can send your message through a gateway to Internet. Internet is a giant network of non-commercial computer bulletin boards and commercial online services, linking MCI Mail and CompuServe with thousands of academic and research bulletin boards world-wide. Internet was formed out of the Arpanet, Bitnet, and Usenet networks, and it effectively links every major computer system in the world. If you use MCI Mail, you can reach your friends or business associates on CompuServe, your brother who works for a defense contractor, and your children in college, via the Internet gateway.

Internet is essentially a network for "serious" computer users. It connects to the online services chiefly for the convenience of its users. Even non-commerical services like the Boston Computer Society's Mac board will charge you to forward a message through their Internet gateway. But since a great many non-commercial boards are connected to Internet, which in turn is connected with MCI Mail and CompuServe, you can use the Internet route to forward messages to friends on these services without the expense of joining them yourself. Your friends might have to pay to read the messages though. CIS charges a fee of 15 cents per message for mail forwarded through Internet.

To send mail to an Internet user, you'll need his or her Internet address. It's a string of symbols and word fragments that might remind you of somebody cussing in the Sunday funnies. When sending mail from CompuServe to an Internet address, there's a set procedure to follow. At the Send to: prompt, first type a right angle bracket, and Internet, followed by a colon. Then type the user name and address, with an @ joining them, so the whole thing looks like this:

```
Send to: > INTERNET:stcody@medialab.mit.edu.
```

The first command directs the message to the Internet file, where it will be held until the next time a batch is forwarded to Internet. "stcody" is the user name for our friend Stuart Cody, and @ specifies that what follows is his *domain* in Internet terms, his specific address, Media Lab at MIT. The suffix *.edu* simply indicates that it's one of Internet's educational nodes. To send a message back to me on CompuServe he'd enter this string:

```
to: 71004.717@compuserve.com.
```

Note that the comma in the CompuServe User ID must be changed to a period to accommodate the Internet system. Without this change, Internet can't read the address. The domain is CompuServe, of course, and the suffix *.com* shows that it's a communications node.

Consult a specialist

Even though all the online services and most of the BBSs will handle E-mail for you, many people prefer to use a mail specialist for their online messaging. Just as in the medical world, mail specialists are generally better equipped to handle this particular aspect of your online life. A mail specialist like MCI can make many of your online messaging chores much less complicated.

Suppose you have a multi-page report that has to be sent to a half dozen different people in different companies. Suppose further, that one of them is in Canada, and another in Japan. And that two of them use PCs, one has a fax machine but no modem, one has a Mac and subscribes to CompuServe, one wants Telex, and one needs a hard copy. If you had to handle this yourself, it would probably take you all day. But when you use a mail specialist, all you have to do is upload the file once and specify each recipient's delivery mode. The fax, the telex, and the E-mail copies can be delivered instantly, and the hard copy (laser printed on your letterhead with your scanned signature, if you like) can go by an overnight courier or first-class mail. Even though one of your associates has CompuServe but not MCI Mail, the two services interconnect, so you can send her the file from your MCI address.

AT&T Mail, EasyLink (owned by Western Union), and SprintMail are all similar to MCI. Because these services are all primarily aimed at businesses and not individuals, they tend to use business terminology. Typically, messages are held for you in your "In Box" and those you send await delivery from your "Out Box." When you specify a recipient and delivery mode, you're creating an "envelope." Figure 5-1 shows MicroPhone II's MCI mail routine.

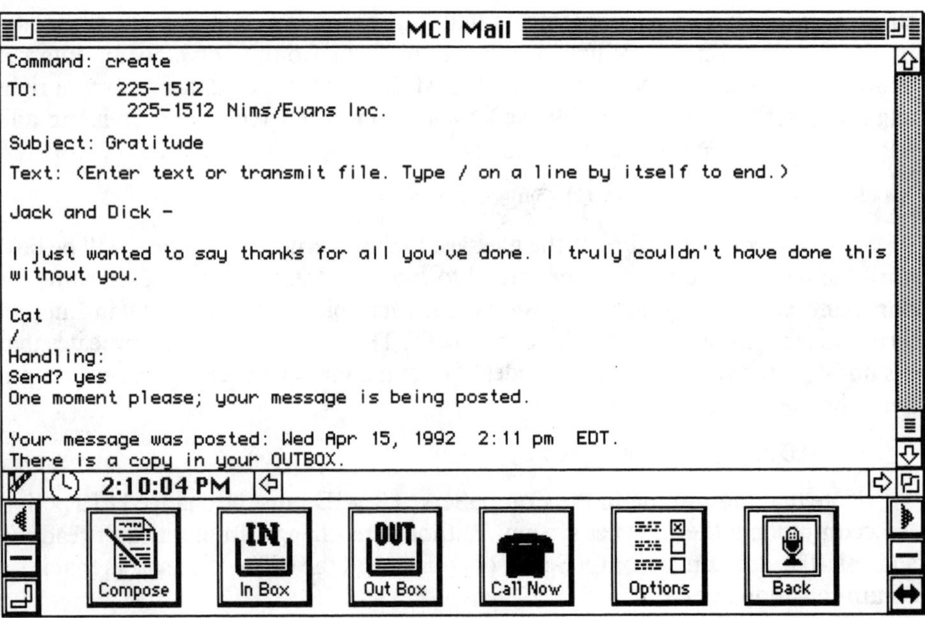

5-1 Outgoing mail is held in your Out Box until you sign on to MCI. Your In Box (on MCI's desk) holds your incoming messages until you pick them up.

DASnet

DASnet is a commercial version of Internet. It's an intersystem messaging service that works much like Internet but sets up private domains for your business or organization and links your domain to 60 others, including MCI Mail, EasyLink,

BIX, the Well, and a great many special purpose systems. It also connects with Internet and FidoNet, UUCP, and VMS Mail. It has links to countries all over the world and communicates with over 60 other networks for truly global communication. Almost any major BBS you join will have a gateway to DASnet.

Sending a message

Every service and BBS has its own mail routine. No two are quite alike, although you will find many similarities. The first step in sending a message is to know how to address it. For the sake of simplicity, we'll assume your message is to another member of the same service and that it's a text-based service. (I'll discuss GUI services next.)

When you enter the mail area of a text-based service like Delphi, GEnie, or a local BBS, you'll usually be presented with a menu of options and a prompt. To send a message, you'll need to choose CREATE, SEND, COMPOSE, or something of that sort. The system will respond by prompting you for the name of the recipient and subject of the letter, as shown in Fig. 5-2. On GEnie, you can send a carbon copy to yourself by entering your name at that prompt. On some other services, which allow multiple addressees but don't handle carbons, simply list yourself as one of the people to receive the letter.

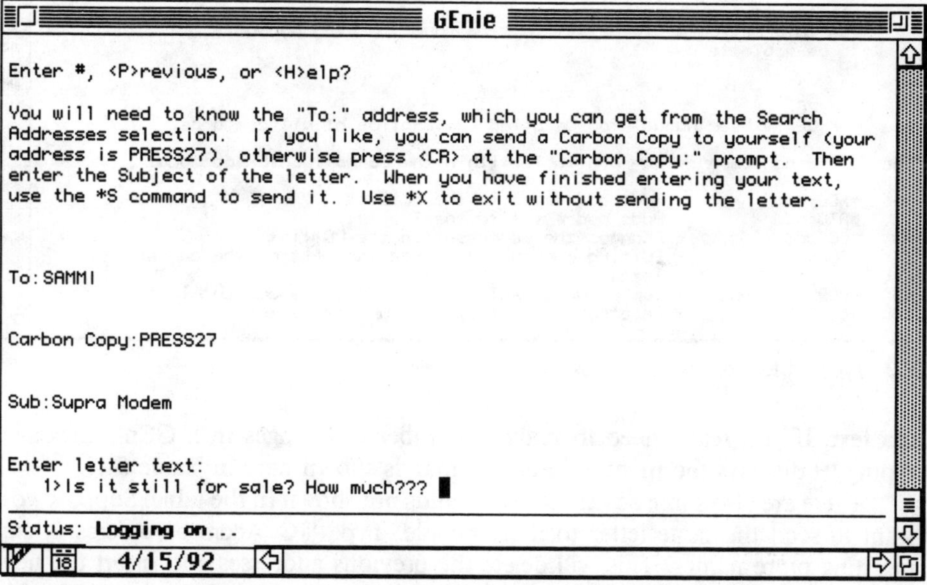

5-2 Enter the information at the prompts, then write your message. When finished, type ***S** to send it.

After you've entered the subject, you'll be prompted to write the message. Some programs include a word-wrap feature that lets you keep on typing and scrolls automatically to a new line. Others prompt you for each new line with a new line number. On GEnie, you must hit Return at the end of a line to enter it. Avoid long lines. Eighty characters is the maximum for most screens, and if you go beyond it, you're likely to end up with a garbled message. When you're done, use whatever the system's command is to send it. On GEnie, it's *S. On Delphi, it's Ctrl-Z. If you've changed your mind about sending the message, Ctrl-C cancels it on Delphi, and *X serves the same purpose on GEnie.

What if you've made a mistake, or tried to put more than 80 characters in a line? You can edit your message, although doing so is sometimes difficult. Editing a mail message online is one area that needs improvement, especially in the text-based services. Most users don't worry a great deal about spelling or punctuation in messages posted to a forum or sent to another member.

The easiest way to make a simple change that affects only one line is to replace that line. For instance, if you wanted to fix a misspelled word in line 2 of the message in Fig. 5-3, you would type *2, to be able to use it. The new text replaces the

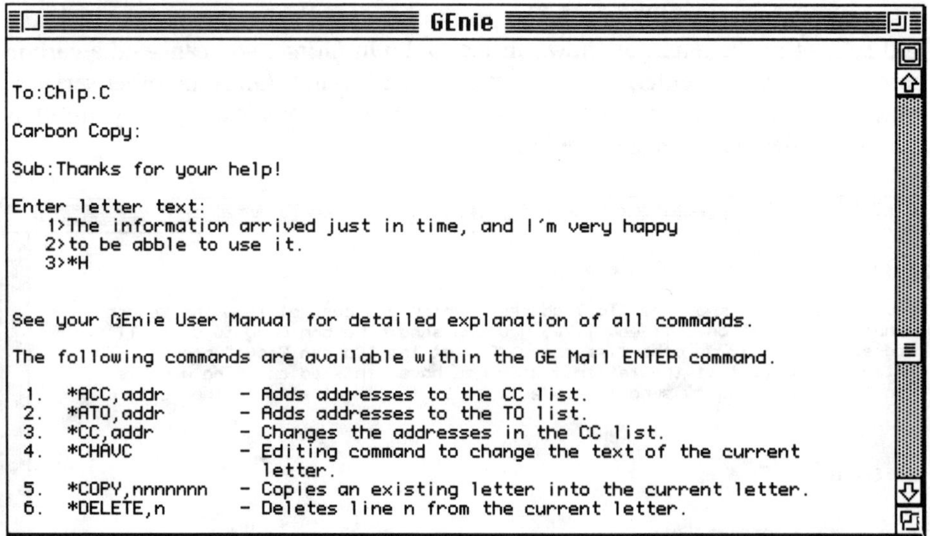

5-3 Type *H for Help in GEnie's text editor.

old text. If you really need to make a number of changes in a GEnie message, typing *H displays the menu of edit commands shown here in Table 5-1.

There are also some advanced commands not shown in the table. Suppose you want to send the same letter to more people. Type *TO, Address1, Address2, etc. inserting more names. This will delete the previous addresses and insert the new ones. *CC, Address1, etc. does the same thing for the Carbon Copy list. *ATO adds names to the original address list without removing the ones that are already there. *W (Wipeout) wipes out the current text, so you can start over, but doesn't change the addressee. *R (Resequence) renumbers the lines after you've deleted one or more, removing gaps.

Delphi Mail is handled in a similar manner. When you enter MAIL, from the Main menu, you'll have a choice of sending a fax or telex message, using translation

Table 5-1 The mail-editing commands you'll find on other services will be similar to these but may use a slash instead of a star.

The following commands are available within the GE Mail ENTER command.

1.	*ACC,addr	- Adds addresses to the CC list.
2.	*ATO,addr	- Adds addresses to the TO list.
3.	*CC,addr	- Changes the addresses in the CC list.
4.	*CHAVC	- Editing command to change the text of the current letter.
5.	*COPY,nnnnnn	- Copies an existing letter into the current letter.
6.	*DELETE,n	- Deletes line n from the current letter.
7.	*HELP	- Prints commands available to the ENTER command.
8.	*INSERT,n	- Inserts subsequent line text after line.
9.	*LIST	- Lists the current entered letter.
10.	*LNH	- Lists the current letter without header information.
11.	*LOCATE	- Editing command to locate text in the current letter.
12.	*M	- Same as *CHAVC.
13.	*NEXT	- Sends the current letter and returns user to the ENTER mode.
14.	*n,text	- Replaces line n in the current letter with text.
15.	^n	- Back up n lines in the current letter.
16.	*PASS	- Provides extra security protection to the current letter.
17.	*RESEQUENCE	- Resequences the line numbers in the current text.
18.	*SEND	- Sends the current letter and returns user to the GE Mail command level.
19.	*SUB,desc	- Changes the letter subject.
20.	*TAB,/ch/n	- Establishes a TAB character and positions.
21.	*TO,addr	- Changes the addresses in the TO list.
22.	*UPLOAD	- Accepts input from Local disk file or tape.
23.	*WIPE	- Erases the text of the current letter and returns to ENTER level.
24.	*X	- Erases the text of current letter and returns to GE Mail command level.

services, or "mail," which means E-mail. To skip the other options and go directly to E-mail, type MAIL MAIL. You can also get into the E-mail system from conference areas, workspace, or a Group database by typing /mail at any prompt. To send a message, type SEND (or just s). You'll be prompted for the user name of the recipient, and a subject. Then, type the message, remembering that Delphi wants you to press RETURN at the end of each line. Figure 5-4 shows how a Delphi message appears on the screen.

If you need to edit while you're typing, use the Delete key or Backspace key to back up and retype that line. (Use Ctrl-H if you have entered Delphi through the Tymnet gateway, which doesn't recognize the Delete key.) Delete a whole line by typing Ctrl-U or Ctrl-X. If more editing is needed, type SEND/EDIT to invoke Delphi's editing commands. Unlike GEnie, Delphi doesn't send carbon copies. You can

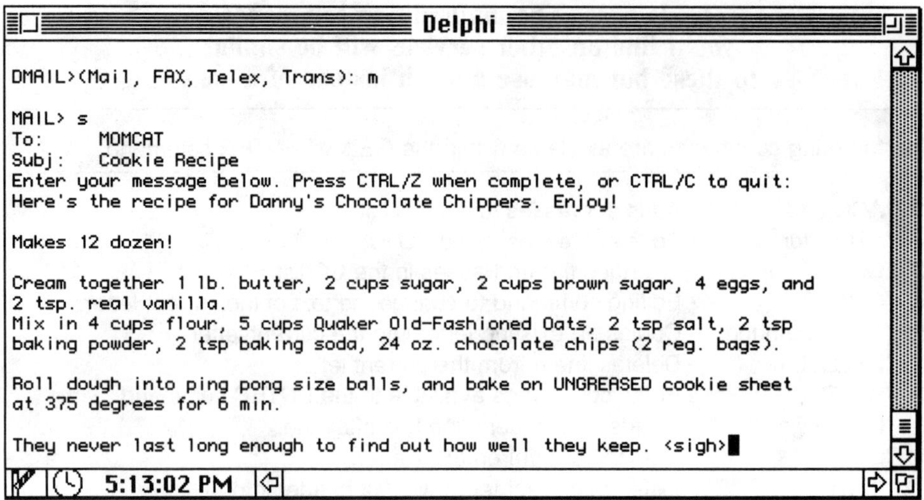

5-4 On Delphi, Ctrl-Z sends the message and Ctrl-C clears it. (Author's note: This is a recipe for one of the best cookies I've ever tasted!)

send yourself a message in either of two ways: type your name after the recipient's, like this: To: REEBOK, MOMCAT; or type SEND/SELF before you type Ctrl-Z to send the message to the recipient. If you realize you meant to send a copy of the message to someone else, you can do so, as long as you haven't left E-mail, by typing SEND/LAST. You'll be prompted to enter the user name to whom it should be sent.

Sending mail on a GUI system like America Online, Prodigy, or CIM is even easier. You'll enter your mail in a window, which serves as a buffer. Figure 5-5

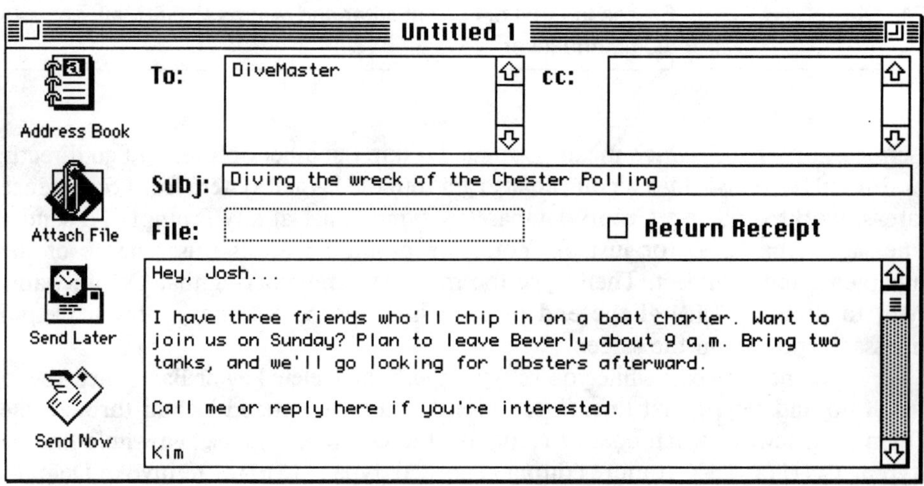

5-5 When you fill the box with text, your message will automatically scroll down.

shows an E-mail message created in America Online's mail system. Treat the text window like a word processor. Reposition the cursor to change words you've typed. Cut, copy, or paste as necessary. When you've gotten the message exactly as you want it, click the send icon. That's all you have to do. Just don't take too long polishing your message online. You could be disconnected if nothing is sent to the host computer for five minutes, or whatever you've set as a timeout period.

Prodigy limits you to six screens full of type, in their "large print" typeface. America Online also has a limit to the number of lines in one message, but since there's no limit to the number of messages you can send to other AO members, you could split your long note into several parts, and title them "Part One," "Part Two," etc.

MCI Mail and similar systems send mail to users on their own systems in much the same way described above. To send your mail from MCI to someone on a different system, if you're composing the message online, when you're asked to address the envelope, type the recipient's name followed by ems. It stands for External Mail System. Doing so brings up an EMS: prompt, as shown in Fig. 5-6. Enter the name of the service, i.e., CompuServe. At the MB: prompt, enter the recipient's mailbox or user ID number, like this: 71004,717. If you're preparing a message offline, follow the same format.

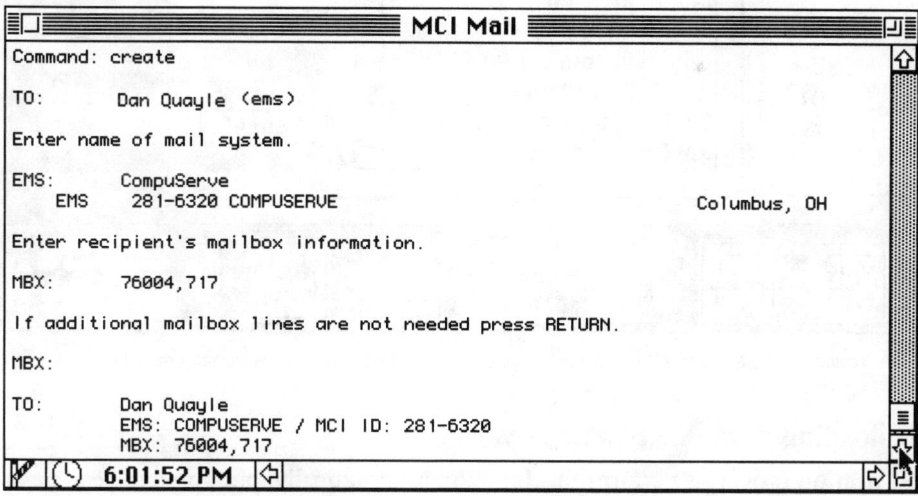

5-6 Other systems might use different prompts to send mail outside the system.

When neatness counts

One way to have good-looking messages, and to save on connect time, is to compose your mail offline. Programs like MicroPhone II and SmartCom come with mail handling sub-routines that let you compose and address your letters and save them to an outbox. Take all the time you want to polish up your metaphors and check your spelling. Then, when you log on, you can send your mail by simply clicking on the icon to scan outbox. It's fast and reliable, and because you're only online for the minute or so that it takes to connect and send them, you're not running up large bills.

Even better for the busy person, you don't need to monitor the mail as it goes out. If your telecom program permits, you can determine an appropriate time to log in and send and receive mail. It could be the middle of the night, or while you're taking a lunch break, or even while you're working on something else. Figure 5-7 shows how SmartCom's AutoPilot function lets you set a time to send and/or collect your messages.

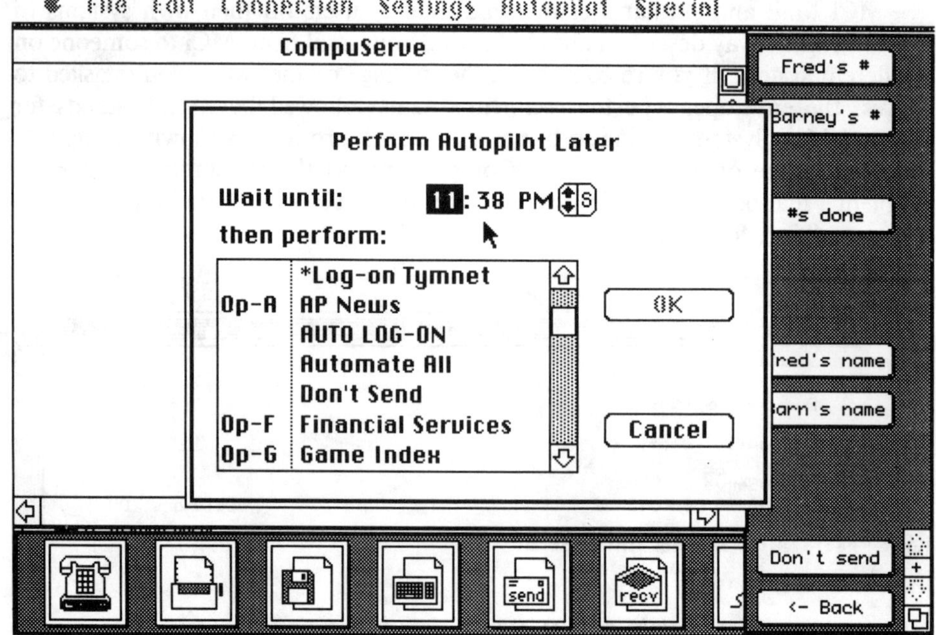

5-7 Your mail, faxes, and other online "business" can be conducted while you're asleep.

Uploading a message manually

Navigation programs perform this function automatically, but you can do it manually, too. If you write messages offline for uploading, use only alphanumeric characters and standard symbols. Don't use boldface or underlined type. Save messages as ASCII text. When you sign on, go to the mailbox and enter the recipient's online address. Then, upload your file, following whatever procedure is used by your telecom program to handle ASCII or text-only files.

E-mail to fax, telex, or printed mail

Most online services, as well as the mail specialists, have some provision for sending fax messages and Telexes, as well as hard copy delivery of messages to your correspondents who aren't at the other end of a modem or fax machine. All you have to do, generally, is to specify the type of delivery needed and the recipient's mailing address, fax, or telex numbers when you send the message.

If you don't happen to have a fax/modem or a stand-alone fax machine, sending faxes by E-mail is a good alternative. It can get expensive, though. MCI charges 80¢ for a full-page fax and an additional 30¢ for each successive half page. Skip the fancy cover sheets if you're faxing via E-mail. Your message will have the necessary information for delivery, and that's really all you need.

When the person to whom you're writing doesn't have a modem or a fax machine, your next best option is paper mail. The cost of sending a hard copy varies from service to service, but it's always a good deal more than it would cost you to send the letter yourself. The benefits are that you needn't print it and find an envelope and a stamp, and that it's mailed from the service's office in the city closest to the recipient, which means it will probably get there faster than from your hometown. Mailed messages are laser printed on a good grade of bond paper. Your message will have a header with the name of the service handling it. A sample is shown in Fig. 5-8.

This facsimile message was electronically transmitted by ***MCI Mail®***

```
May 21, 1992

Gerbil Industries, Inc.
20 Marion Street
Brookline, MA 02146

Dear Mr. Gerbil,

It has come to our attention that your account is seriously in arrears,
and we mean very seriously. You now owe approximately $4000. worth of
fresh catnip. If you do not pay up within five days, we shall be forced
to take severe punitive action.

We regret having to take this tone with a loyal customer, but business
is business. Or bidniss, as the case may be.

Yours very truly,

R.P. Katz
Katz 'n' Jammers Pub
```

5-8 A fax message on MCI's "default" letterhead.

MCI mail offers you another option. It will scan your letterhead and signature and keep these on file for use whenever you send fax or paper mail. The messages are combined electronically with the scanned images of your letterhead and autograph so your mail looks as if it came directly from you. Then they're forwarded to the service's electronic printing center closest to the recipient and sent according to your instructions—either by mail, by overnight courier, or by same-day messenger in areas where such service is available.

Some services will also let you attach a file to your E-mail letter. On America Online, you simply click on the Attach File icon, as shown in Fig. 5-9, and follow

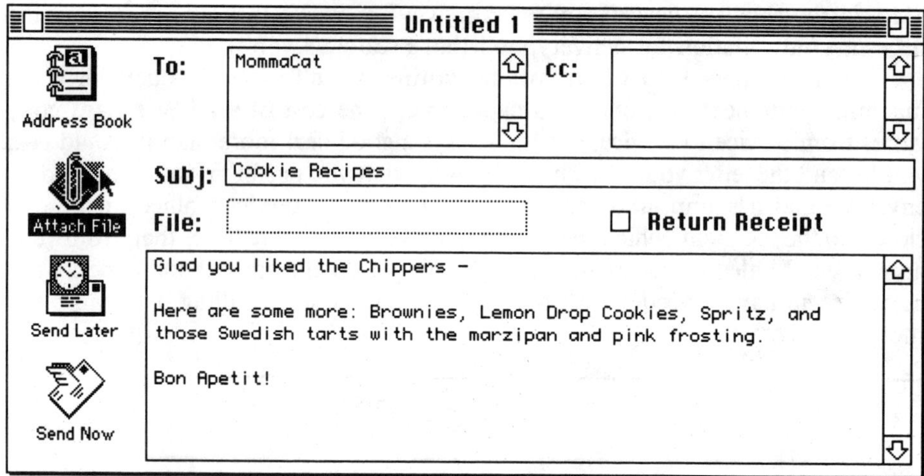

5-9 When you click the file icon, you'll be asked to locate it on the disk.

the usual procedure for uploading a file. (See chapter 6 for more information about uploading and downloading.) GEnie and CompuServe also offer this service. Remember, if you're sending a file to a non-Mac computer, it should be in ASCII text format. PC's can't open Macintosh applications.

Politically correct mail

Ever wanted to dash off an angry letter to your Congressperson or give your Senator a piece of your mind? It's a cinch if you belong to CompuServe or America Online. While anybody can fax to their legislator, AO makes it easy by providing an address book with House and Senate addresses and phone and fax numbers for the entire delegation of all 50 states. Insert the proper address and fire away! CompuServe even has a special mail rate for a "CONGRESSgram," which can be sent to the White House, too. Holiday "grams" from Santa, the Easter Bunny, and other special or seasonal promotions can also be found under the CompuServe Mail menu.

Receiving mail

Every child is told, usually in conjunction with a holiday or birthday party, that it's much better to give than to receive. Few of them fall for it. We all know it's really more fun to get. Getting mail online is usually fun, especially for the nonbusiness user. If you're simply sending memos back and forth to the home office, perhaps that's not quite so much fun, but it still beats those little pink "While You Were Out" sheets that tell you you're the loser in a game of telephone tag. America Online is many people's favorite service for getting mail because whenever they log on, if there's E-mail waiting, a cheerful voice proclaims, "Welcome. You've got mail!" He sounds so thoroughly delighted about it, you can't help but be delighted too.

When you're using AO or CompuServe Information Manager, just click the flashing mailbox icon to open your mailbox and see what's waiting in it. On Prodigy, you'll see a little blinking sign up in the right corner of the opening screen that says New Mail. Clicking it takes you to a list of waiting letters, shown in Fig. 5-10. The newest ones are at the top of the list. Those you haven't yet read are marked with a star.

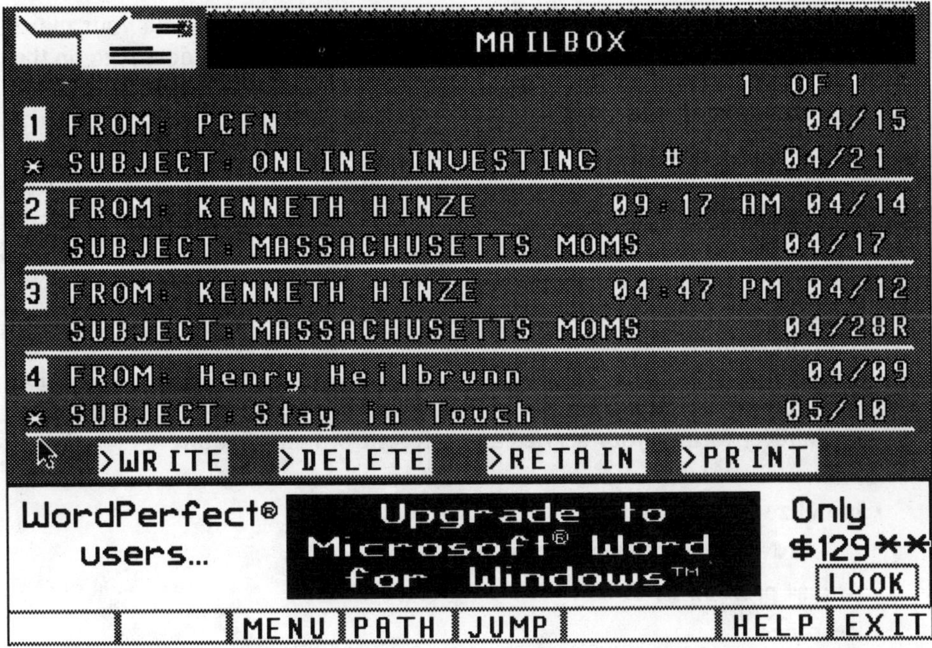

5-10 The dates at the right are the date the message was posted and the date on which it will be removed.

Junk mail

Prodigy holds the dubious distinction of having invented electronic junk mail. At least once a week, and more often around the holidays, you'll open your Prodigy mailbox, expecting missives from old and new friends, only to find ads. One of the reasons that Prodigy's rates are low is that it's supported by advertisers. Along with the little squibs that run across the bottom of the screen, advertisers can buy mass mailings to the entire Prodigy membership or to identifiable segments of it. When you first sign on with Prodigy, along with your credit card information, you're asked to enter your birth date, sex, and address. Marketing experts use these facts about you to gauge your interest in such items as DisneyWorld vacations, investments, or magazine and book club subscriptions. Whenever you fall within the target population for a particular sales pitch, you'll see "New Mail" flashing when you log in. There's really nothing you can do about it. Complaining to the sponsors won't help, as Prodigy makes your membership conditional upon your acceptance of certain terms, including their right to send you unsolicited advertising. Grin and ignore it. You can always delete messages without reading them. Besides, if the marketing people really know their stuff, you *will* be interested in whatever they're selling.

Handling mail offline

Do you stand next to your mailbox or front door mail slot to read all your mail? Probably not. Do you open the office mail as it's handed to you, or does it go on the desk until you have time to go through it? Chances are, you wait. Reading your E-mail online isn't necessary, and it certainly isn't economical. You can capture a mailbox full of letters in far less time than it takes you to read one of them. On services that charge by the minute, efficient mail handling is the key to lower monthly bills. It also leaves more time available for online fun.

The main purpose of CompuServe's Navigator is to collect mail and bulletin board messages for offline reading and response. Even if you don't use CompuServe, the principle is a good one. Any telecom program that lets you write a script can be used to create a mail retrieval system. MicroPhone II comes with a prewritten program to scan your MCI Mail In box and Out box. You can create one for any service you expect to send and receive mail on simply by entering the following steps in whatever format your service and telecom program require:

- Initialize modem and dial the service.
- At CONNECT, enter user ID and password.
- At mail prompt, go to mail box.
- Read new.
- Check for send file.
- Send contents, if found.
- Log off.

The actual programming needed to accomplish these steps is a good deal more complicated, as can be seen in Fig. 5-11. These are a few of the modules that make up MicroPhone II's MCI mail handling file. If your skills aren't up to writing a mail program, you can probably find one already written for your particular combination of software and service in one of that service's libraries or from a user group BBS. Meanwhile, you can certainly repeat the sequence manually. Just be sure there's enough of a screen buffer to catch all the mail you're likely to get.

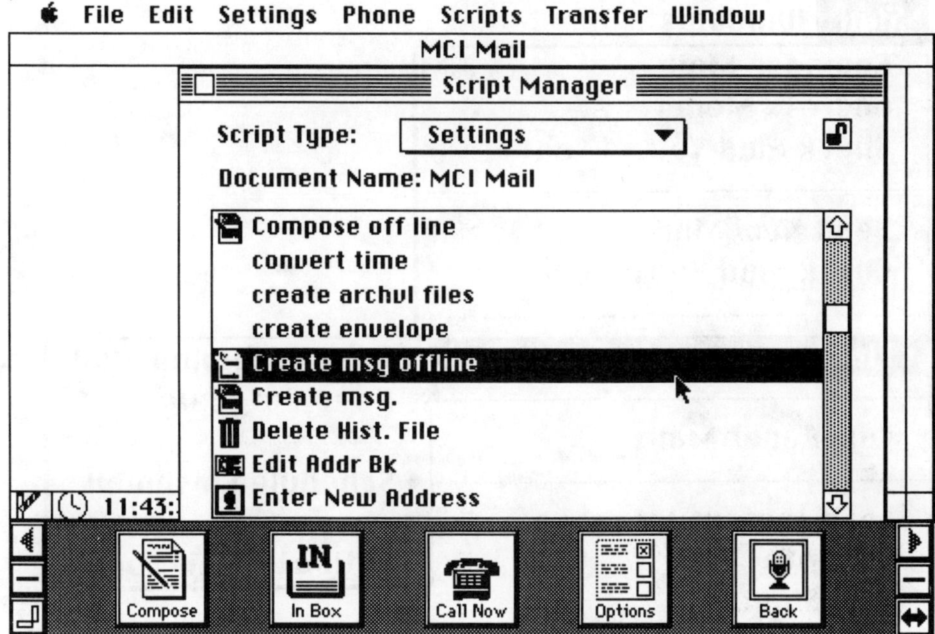

5-11 Each entry refers to a separate piece of script, for a particular function.

Flashmail

America Online has a very clever mail-retrieval system built in. It's called Flashmail, and it lets you go online on demand or at pre-specified hours to send and retrieve waiting mail. Retrieved mail is stored on your disk in your "Flashbox" and can be accessed by using the Read Incoming Mail option. Likewise, you can choose Read Outgoing Mail to review any mail you've written and designated to "Send Later" but haven't yet sent. Flashmail can be activated at any time by selecting it from the menu, as shown in Fig. 5-12. Or it can be run automatically by setting a schedule in the Flashmail Schedule box shown in Fig. 5-13. First, type in the hour on the 24-hour clock when you want to begin automatic sign on. Then choose the half hour in which you want to sign on. To choose your half hour, click in the shaded box to the right of Starting at, move the mouse to your desired time, and release it. AO assigns different starting minutes to different users to share the load more evenly across its computer system. You can also choose how many times a day and how many days a week to check mail. You can even check multiple user names. (AO allows you three different screen names per account.) Each time you activate a screen name, you will be prompted for the password for that screen name. (That way you don't have to be around to type it in when the scheduled Flashmail occurs in the middle of the night!)

The last step is to designate what you want done: post the mail you've written (and have chosen to Send Later); get your new mail and save it to the Flashbox; or download any attached files with your new mail. This last option might not be wise

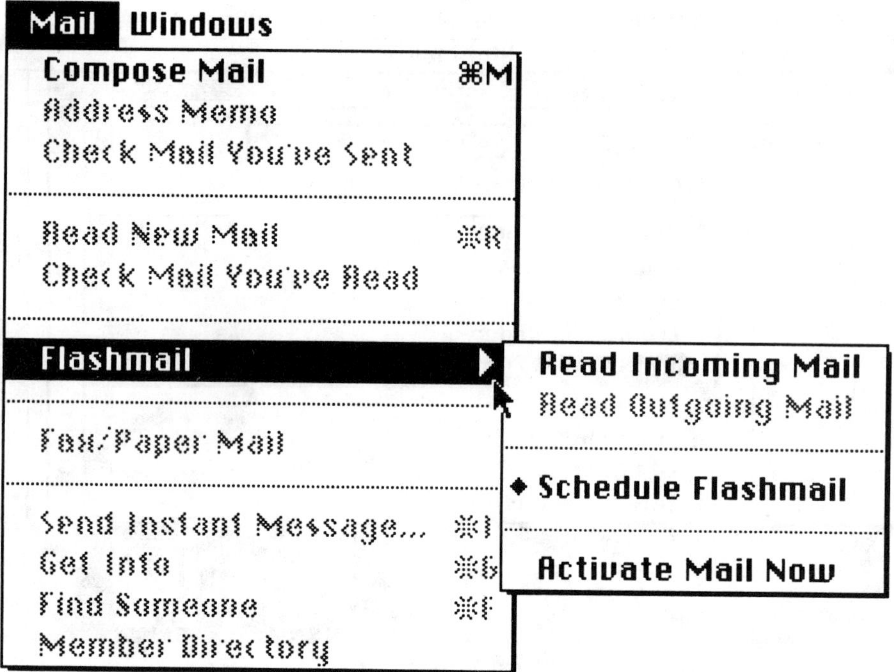

5-12 The black diamond next to Flashmail indicates that it's active. A log-on is scheduled.

Scheduled Flashmail

☒ Starting at 20 : 49 Go online... every hour

Days ☒ Sun ☒ Mon ☒ Tue ☒ Wed ☒ Thu ☒ Fri ☒ Sat

Flash Mail for ☒ JC Rose ☒ Fuzzy Puss ☒ Mommacat

Actions

☒ Post composed mail ☒ Get waiting mail ☒ Download attached files

Cancel Help OK

5-13 After you set the time to log on, be sure to click the checkbox to activate it.

if someone's apt to send you a long file. You could find yourself stuck online for an unexpectedly long time downloading unwanted data. It's better to download the letters and then go back online manually to pick up any attached files you're sure you want.

Dead letter office—purging old mail

Imagine what your desk would look like if you never threw anything away. Fortunately, your desk doesn't charge you for storage, but some services do. Others simply erase messages after a period of time, whether or not you've seen them. It's not that they want you to sign on every day to pick up the mail. They do, of course, if they charge by the minute while you're in the mail area, but most services include mail in their "basic" service package. The reason they want you to get it out of the system is a lot simpler. Mail occupies valuable disk space.

Systems such as Delphi, BIX, and various BBSs that keep your mail on file have a menu item to delete it. You can either delete individual messages or purge the whole file. On Delphi, simply type a D after scanning a message to delete it. If the method for doing so isn't clear, use the help system to learn how. Otherwise, you may well find yourself paying for E-mail people sent you months ago.

Public mail

If you want to notify everybody in the office about something, the easiest way is to post a note on the bulletin board. If you want to alert the neighborhood to keep an eye out for your lost cat, you'd post notices on telephone poles, in the Laundromat, and wherever else those who pass will see them. Online forums or bulletin boards serve that purpose, too, but they're more than just message centers or classified ads. You'll find that messages draw replies, and the replies generate more replies. So a series of postings, called a *thread*, becomes a sort of drawn out conversation among several people. Unlike life in the "real" world, it's not considered rude to barge in on a bulletin board conversation. And it's easy to participate in a dozen or more threads at a time because you can always go back and reread previous messages if you forget what's already been said on the topic. Forums tend to develop a sort of group personality. The messages on the Writer's Forum board on Delphi, for example, reflect a highly whimsical world view, while those on the Delphi computer forums, although in many cases posted by the same people, are a good deal more "nuts and bolts" oriented.

There are, as previously noted, all kinds of forums or boards on your favorite service. No matter what your interest, you can find people who share it. You can also use these boards to broaden your horizons and to learn more about topics which interest you.

Forums are friendly places, and you're always welcome to put in your two cents worth, as long as your message is in good taste and doesn't insult anyone. You'll soon discover that other forum members are eager to make you feel at home, and as soon as you've learned the ropes, you'll be helping newcomers, too.

There's not really that much to learn, either. Common sense and good manners will see you through.

The mechanics of posting messages on bulletin boards is very much like sending mail, except that you're letting everybody on the service read the message. Bulletin board messages are entered in the same way that you'd enter an E-mail message, using the same editing system. The major difference is that you write a bulletin board message in the forum area, and your command is some variation of post rather than send. Every message contains, in addition to the message itself, a date/time stamp, the name of the person who wrote it, and the name of the addressee. Your message might be a reply to a previous post, addressed to its author, or simply broadcast to All. Messages have a "subject" line and might also have a topic header. Figure 5-14 shows an example.

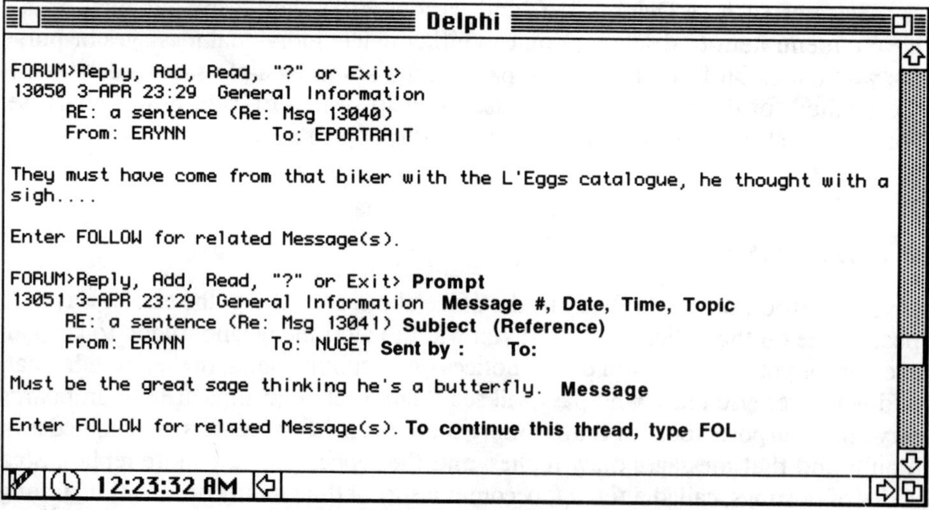

Delphi

FORUM>Reply, Add, Read, "?" or Exit>
13050 3-APR 23:29 General Information
RE: a sentence (Re: Msg 13040)
From: ERYNN To: EPORTRAIT

They must have come from that biker with the L'Eggs catalogue, he thought with a sigh....

Enter FOLLOW for related Message(s).

FORUM>Reply, Add, Read, "?" or Exit> **Prompt**
13051 3-APR 23:29 General Information **Message #, Date, Time, Topic**
RE: a sentence (Re: Msg 13041) **Subject (Reference)**
From: ERYNN To: NUGET **Sent by : To:**

Must be the great sage thinking he's a butterfly. **Message**

Enter FOLLOW for related Message(s). **To continue this thread, type FOL**

12:23:32 AM

5-14 Sample messages from the Delphi Writer's Forum.

Other users will appreciate it if your messages are posted in the right topic area and are reasonably coherent. Spelling and typing mistakes are tolerated, especially on services where editing is difficult. However, it's considered rude to type your message in CAPITAL LETTERS. That's the electronic equivalent of shouting. Avoid being vulgar, slanderous, libelous, or otherwise nasty. It will get you thrown off the service. Extraneous and irrelevant comments are a waste of time and money, yours and everyone else's. Thoughtful, informative comments are always welcome.

While it's good to be brief, just replying "yes" or "no" to a message is rude. Remember that many people are reading the board and that not all of them have seen the question you're answering. Messages, on many boards, are posted sequentially, so the person who asked the question you're answering might have done so 50 or 100 postings earlier. To make browsing easier for all concerned, refer to the question in your reply, like this: "No, I've never been to Finland, although I've traveled through Norway, Sweden, and Denmark."

Message-base organization

All forums or boards use some type of hierarchy to organize their messages. On a system like AO, Prodigy, or GEnie, it's obvious which subjects belong in which folders or categories. If there's no place where your new message seems to fit, you can start a new folder or category for it. On some BBSs and on a service like Delphi, which posts messages in the order in which they're received, assigning a category is still possible (and desirable), but it's a bit more difficult. Figure 5-15 shows the Delphi Mac forum menu and beneath it the beginnings of a posted message. To find out what topics this message could fall into, we'd type a ? at the Topic? prompt, and choose whatever seemed most appropriate. On Delphi and BIX, topics are set by the forum host or moderator. On other services, if you don't see a topic that fits your message, you can start one. To start a new topic on AO, you create a new folder, as shown in Fig. 5-16, and place your first message in it.

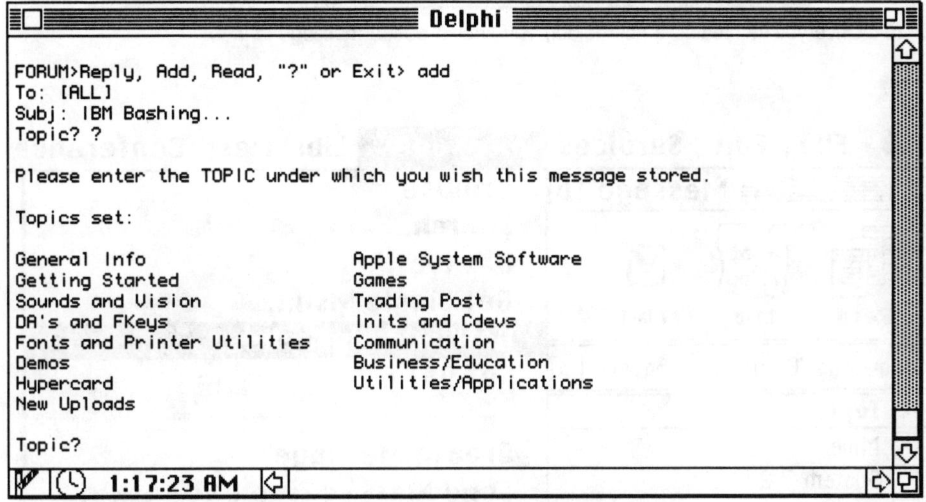

5-15 If there's no topic that seems to fit, use General Information.

Even on boards that post messages in the order received, you can follow a conversational thread. Usually the command is FOLLOW, or you'll be asked to indicate whether you want to follow the thread or read the next message in numerical order. Following threads makes for more coherent reading but can cause you to skip an occasional message or re-read the same ones if the system doesn't flag and ignore messages you've already seen. (It should, but my experience has been that it doesn't always work.)

Some message boards let you TAG or MARK a message or a thread so you can

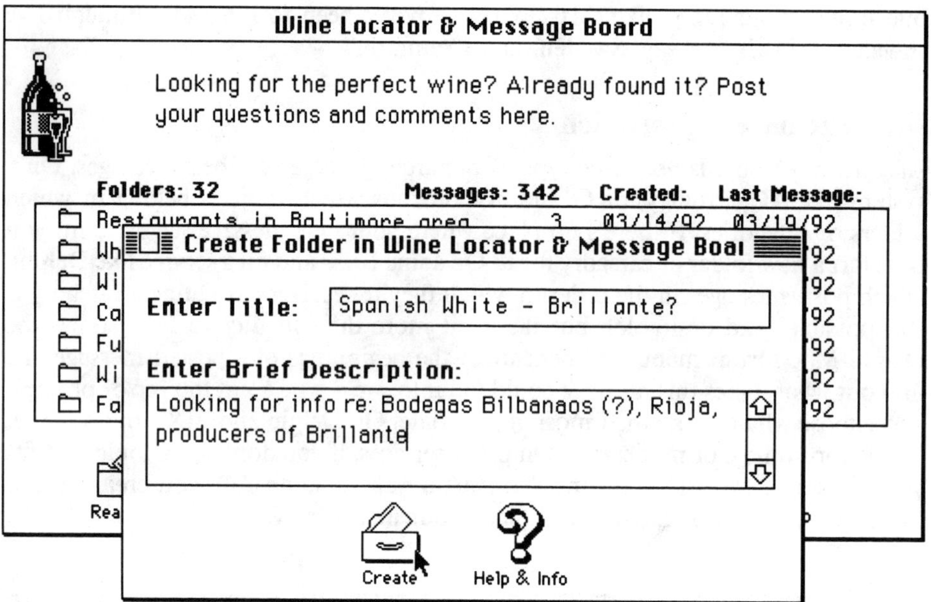

5-16 Once you've created a new folder, you should post a message in it.

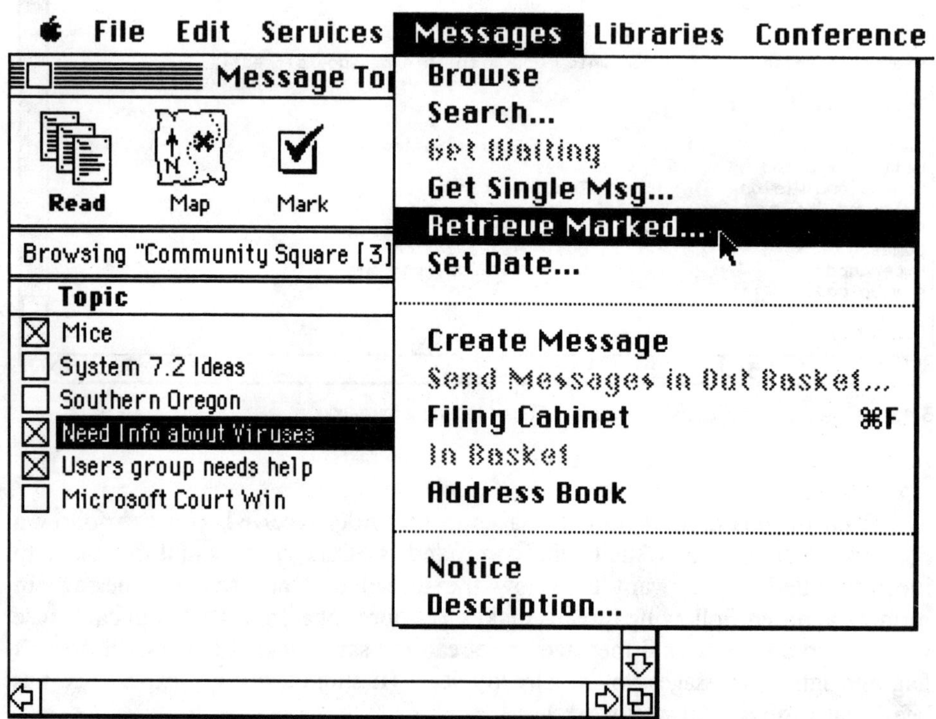

5-17 Retrieved messages will be stored in a folder in the Filing Cabinet folder.

go back and read it again or retrieve it for offline reading. Figure 5-17 shows how this works with the CompuServe Information Manager. When you enter a message base with CIM, you'll see a list of topics. Selecting any one and then clicking the Mark icon puts an X in the checkbox. After you're done scanning and marking messages to read, use the Retrieve Marked command to create a file for leisurely browsing. This file will be automatically placed in the Filing Cabinet folder inside your CIM folder. While your marked messages are being downloaded, you'll see the window in Fig. 5-18.

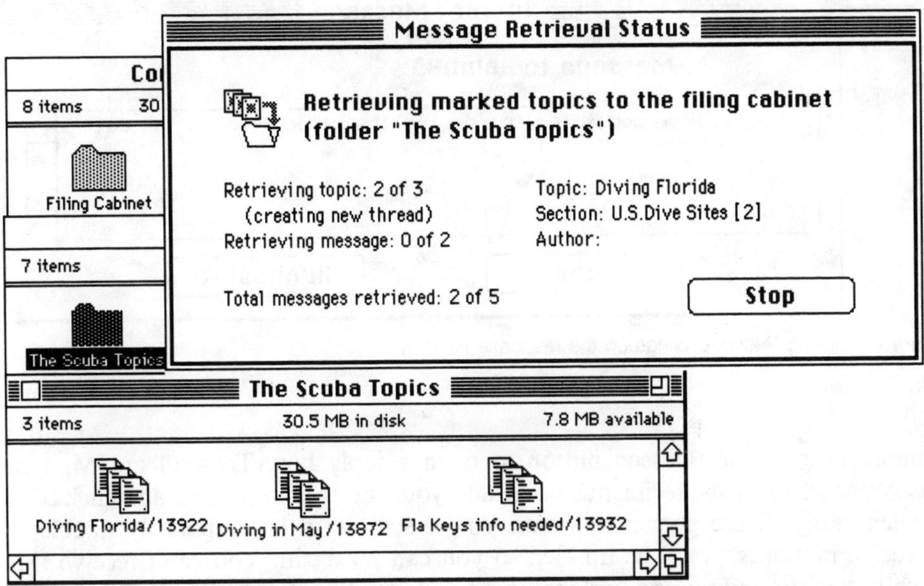

5-18 You can also choose to disconnect automatically as soon as the messages are retrieved.

Instant mail

On some services, it's possible to send an Instant Message to another member. While this is generally done in Chat or Conference mode to exchange a whispered comment without showing it to the rest of the crowd, it's also useful in other service areas. If you've just gotten mail from a friend and want to chat, rather than writing a reply, send a message that says Meet me in the conference room?

On Delphi, all you need to do, as long as you know your friend is online, is to type /zend USERNAME message. If s/he's anywhere in the system and hasn't blocked messages, the /zend command will reach him or her. There's also a /send command, which sends a message only within the forum or area you're in. You can /zend from any forum, mail or conference area but not from the Main menu or from special services like travel or news.

America Online's Instant Messages are announced with a chime and appear in a small window at the top of your screen, as shown in Fig. 5-19. To respond to a

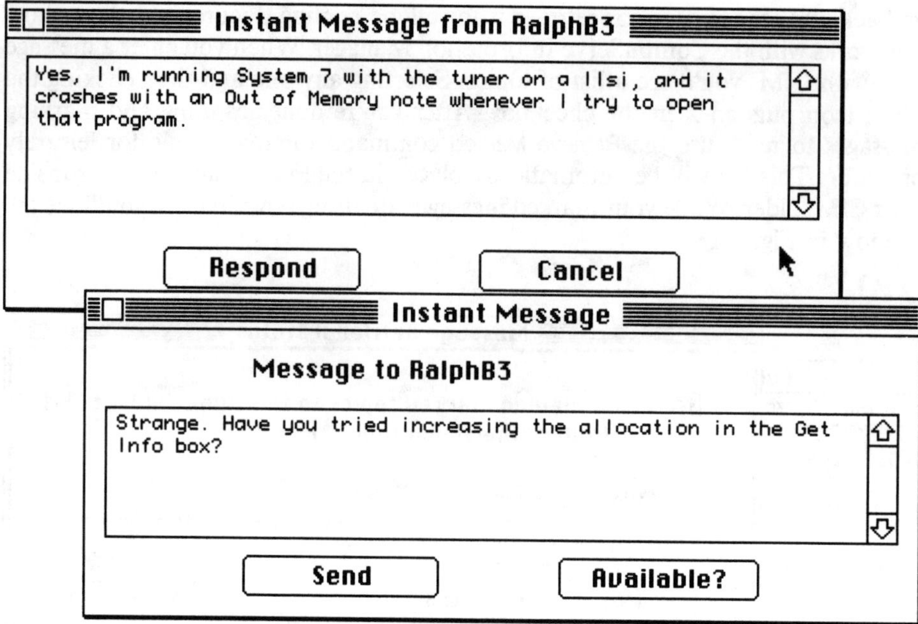

5-19 Clicking Respond brings up the response window.

message, click the Respond button to open a reply box. To send an IM, type Command-I. Enter the recipient's name and your message in the box and click Send when ready. If the person to whom you're sending it is temporarily unable to receive messages, you'll be notified so you can try again. You can't receive IMs while you're sending one, uploading or downloading a file, or using a gateway service.

Summary

For many users, electronic mail, or E-mail, is the prime reason for going online. Electronic correspondence is fast, inexpensive, and more reliable than trusting messages to answering machines, co-workers, or children. While all online services and most BBSs handle at least some E-mail, if your mailing needs are diverse, a dedicated mail specialist like MCI or SprintMail is a wise choice.

Mail can be sent as E-mail, converted into a fax or telex message, or printed and sent by U.S. Mail or overnight courier. Simply specify the desired delivery mode when you address the "envelope" or enter the name of the recipient.

Private mail and "public mail" bulletin board or forum messages are entered and edited in more or less the same way on each service, although commands to create, send, or read mail differ greatly from one service to the next. Editing a message is much easier on a GUI system because the text is entered into a buffered window and can be corrected before being uploaded. Text-based services enter incoming text one line at a time, so editing means re-accessing the message on the host computer. A better way is to compose the message offline in a word processor and enter it as ASCII text. Reading mail is also accomplished most efficiently and economically offline, especially with a navigation program or mail handling program that will quickly pick up new messages and log off. Some systems also allow you to send "instant mail" to others who are online with you.

6
A question of protocol

Suppose you've been invited to dinner at Buckingham Palace. You'd probably know that you're expected to dress a certain way, to call your hostess by a particular title, and to behave in a particular manner. It's called *protocol.* Now, suppose you're invited to a poolside barbecue at a friend's house. Again, you'd dress a certain way, behave in a particular manner, even call your host and hostess by specific titles, "Bud" and "Suzy," perhaps. It's a different protocol, but in its way just as definite.

Sending and receiving files online is also accomplished by using protocols, only in this case the purpose of the protocol is to tell your modem, rather than you, how to behave and even what to say to the host. Up to this point, you've sent data to the modem and gotten data back, one line at a time. This kind of interactive exchange is fine for logging in, browsing through bulletin boards, and even handling reasonably short mail messages. It's much too slow for handling long files. You need to be able to send and receive data in blocks instead of one line at a time in order to make the most efficient use of your time online.

The basics of file transfer

Let's begin with a few definitions. *Files* can be ASCII text, binary data, or applications, compacted or not. *Transferring* a file to another computer is a misnomer, though. You're not actually transferring that file; you're transferring a *copy* of the file. The original remains right where it was. Transfers can go in both directions: from your computer to another, and from the other computer to yours. You're said to be *downloading* when the information is coming down from the host to you; you *upload* to send a file to the host. The computers involved might be two identical Macs, a mainframe or mini at an online service or BBS, or a Mac and a PC. Any two computers can send files back and forth.

The basic steps aren't much more complicated than sending an E-mail message a word at a time. When you initiate a file transfer, you tell your Mac which file to send and how to send it. The Mac reads that file and sends it, a chunk at a time, to the modem. The modem converts the data and sends it down the phone line to the recipient's modem, which converts it back and sends it to a disk, where it's saved as a file. The major differences are that you're not entering the data as it's sent. It already exists. And the other computer isn't holding it on screen or in RAM. Files received are automatically saved. Depending on the type of transfer, the sender and receiver can check back and forth to make sure there are no errors and that the data received is the same as the data sent.

It's important to know that even though you can send files to a computer that's not a Macintosh, the other computer can't use them unless they're in a format it can read, like ASCII. It can store them and transfer them to another Mac (or back to yours), but it can't do anything with them. You can send a Mac application; for example, a game you've written, to a PC-based BBS. The file will be stored on the PC's disk as a Mac file and listed in its directory. When someone else who uses a Mac calls the board to see what's new, they'll see your game and can download it and run it with no problems, even though it's been sitting on a PC disk.

Types of files to transfer

Forums, SIGs, RoundTables—whatever your service or BBS happens to call them—usually have two or three different "rooms" within the topic area. As noted in the last chapter, one of these rooms is the bulletin board. Another, and one that's of interest to anyone in search of a bargain, is the library. Online libraries are full of interesting software that can be yours, either for free or for a reasonable fee. America Online claims to have over 30,000 Macintosh files! Other services might not have quite as many, but you'll certainly find a good selection of applications, fonts, utilities, templates for DTP, and lots of games! Mac user group BBSs also have many thousands of files online, which you can download for the cost of the phone call. Figure 6-1 shows a few of the listings from AO.

Desk Accessories

Upld	Subject	Cnt	Dnld
04/13	PhoneBook DA 2.6.3	106	04/18
04/08	Retriever LT	95	04/18
04/02	MegaCalculator	1428	04/18
03/31	Periodic Chart Desk Accessory...	71	04/14
03/27	ASCII Chart DA 4.2	82	04/14
03/24	Time Logger 2.11	248	04/18
03/22	QuickDEX II Wndw Enlrgr 1.01	82	04/18
03/11	SmartCal 2.3.4	180	04/17
03/09	PICTuresque 1.9.1	430	04/17
03/09	ResEdit 'TMPL' Data Types DA	108	04/18

Get Description | Download File | Upload File | More...

6-1 No matter what kind of software you're looking for, chances are good that somebody's written a shareware version and posted it in these libraries.

All of these programs are either *freeware* or *shareware*. Freeware, as the name suggests, is free. You can copy it, give it to your friends, upload it to other boards, do with it as you like, as long as you leave the author's name on it and upload any documentation with it. Freeware authors often request a postcard. Even if they don't, sending a card or an E-mail message is a nice gesture, especially if you really like the program or if you've found a bug.

Shareware isn't free. These files are placed there by their authors or by other users who want to pass along a really great game, good-looking type font, or useful utility. Shareware authors have chosen to distribute their programs over public BBSs and services rather than through stores. You're expected to pay whatever price the author asks, if you use the program. You're allowed a reasonable amount of time to try it out, and then you must either pay up or trash it. Shareware registration fees are generally very reasonable, and registering your program guarantees you the gratitude of the author, often expressed in concrete terms with free upgrades, source codes, or other programs he or she has written. Figure 6-2 shows some typical shareware and freeware request screens.

You might also find demo versions of commercially distributed programs.

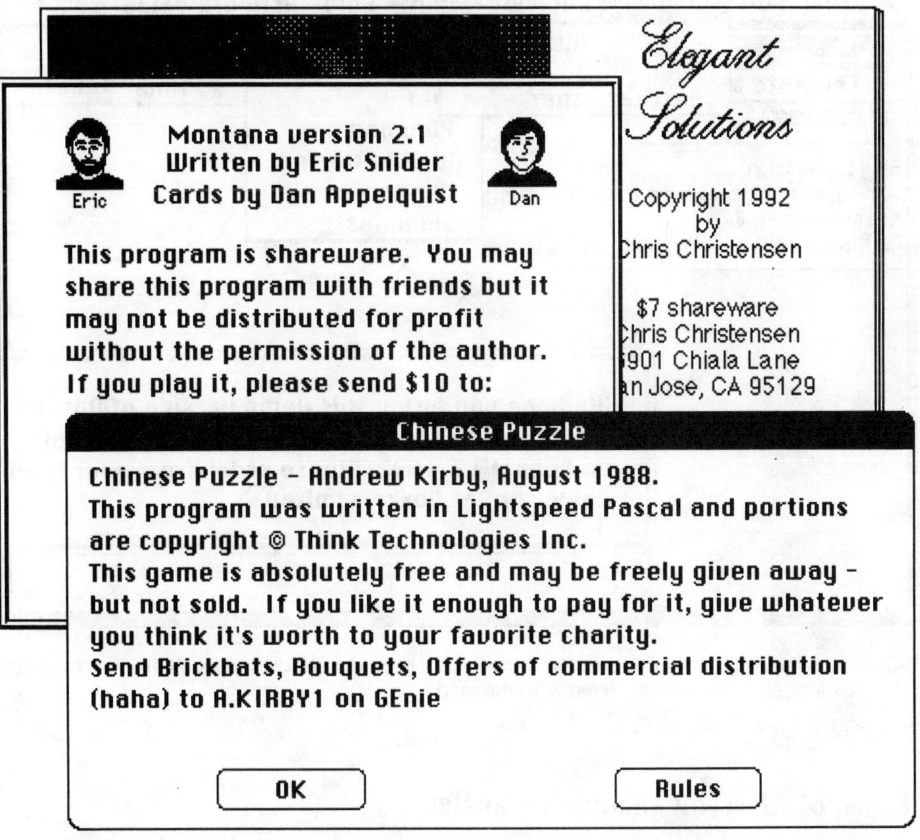

6-2 Most shareware fees are very low. Please pay them so the authors will keep on producing great shareware!

Frequently these are *hobbled* demos. You can play with them as much as you like, but some commands (usually Save and Print) are disabled. Or they might even be fully functional versions with a time limit. The program might stop working after a 10 to 30 day trial period, or it might quit after a 10-minute session. Figure 6-3 shows examples. There are also hundreds of useful text files, GIF graphics, and clip art for all occasions. There are even a number of electronic magazines that you can download. TidBITS is a Mac-oriented publication distributed through Internet and various online services. Publishers Adam and Tonya Engst put together this useful compendium of product reviews, press releases, and bug reports every other week and distribute it electronically. Home and School Mac is a monthly effort from the National Home and School MUG (Mac User Group), formerly known as the GAMER Project. An excellent source of information on the best in both shareware and commercial games and educational software, Home & School Mac is found on America Online, CompuServe, and many BBSs. (America Online is home to the Home & School MUG Forum, too.)

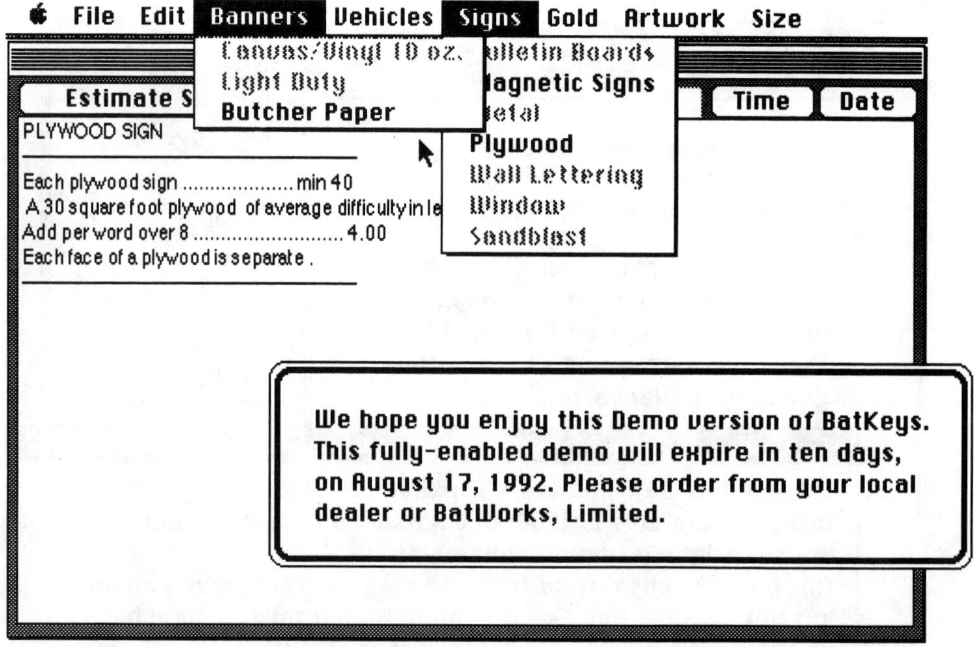

6-3 The demo sign estimating program is hobbled with many disabled menu items. The message box indicates that another demo is time limited.

Types of files you shouldn't transfer

It doesn't happen much on commercial services or on a well-run bulletin board, but occasionally a file that shouldn't have been transferred sneaks through. What kinds of files are these? There are really only two kinds to worry about. The first could get you in legal trouble. The second could crash your system.

It's legal and acceptable to share shareware. That's what it's for. But commercially published software, the kind you buy at your local computer store or by mail, is *not* shareware. When you buy a commercial program, what you are actually buying is a license to use one copy of the program on one computer at a time. Period. The program itself is protected by copyright, and there are both civil and criminal penalties for violating copyrights.

You have the right to make a back-up disk for your own use and protection. You *don't* have the right to give the program away, rent it, or distribute it, even over a local area network, without a site license. If you give a copy to your friend, you're breaking a law. If you upload it to a BBS, you *and* the operator of the bulletin board are both breaking the law. (There's legislation under discussion that would exempt BBS operators from liability for copyright violations for files their users have improperly uploaded, but it's a fairly hazy legal area and definitely one to avoid.) Obviously, anyone uploading a file illegitimately is going to be thrown off the board, at the very least, and possibly thrown in jail.

The Software Publisher's Association has also taken a firm stance against such copyright infringements. They've established a hotline for reporting software piracy and will prosecute! If you know anyone guilty of software piracy, you are urged to call the SPA's toll free line at (800) 388-7478.

Sick people = sick computers

The other item that shouldn't be uploaded, and that you need to guard against accidentally downloading, are viruses. A virus is any piece of software that attaches itself to other programs and files. Some viruses are relatively harmless; they just make your computer beep or display a (supposedly) funny message. Others can damage or delete files or even erase the entire contents of your hard disk, a decidedly unfunny message! Contrary to popular belief, not all the viruses out there are PC viruses. There are a growing number of bugs that can infect your Mac, although it used to be thought that Macs were pretty much immune from most kinds of virus. Because of the way Mac applications are written, with a resource fork and a data fork, it's harder to create a Macintosh virus. Unfortunately, the creeps who do such things have taken it as a challenge, and recent months have seen the introduction of several new Mac viruses. Because not all virus authors are skilled programmers, a virus that was intended to be essentially harmless can, through a programming error, cause possibly fatal crashes.

In addition to "true" viruses, there are two other categories of program to guard against. These are *worms* and *Trojan Horses*. Worms, unlike viruses, don't attach themselves to other programs. They can exist and multiply independently. They are spread over networks, rather than by infected disks or programs. The best example was the 1988 Internet worm, which, in just one day, crashed several thousand government and university computers using the UNIX system. The Trojan Horse, which occasioned the remark "Beware of gifts bearing Greeks," is a useful program that hides another, more malignant program inside it. The hidden program does something non-useful while the "good" program runs. A HyperCard stack called "Sexy Ladies" was one of the best-known Mac Trojan Horses. As the user watched a stack of scanned photos of scantily-clad models, the program erased his hard drive.

Staying healthy

How can you protect yourself? You can't—at least not 100% of the time. One of the most recent virus attacks came about when three infected games were uploaded to various BBSs and spread throughout the game-playing community. (The files were Obnoxious Tetris, Ten Tile Puzzle, and Tetricycle. To complicate matters, legitimate versions of at least two of these also exist.) Despite the best efforts of sysops and forum leaders, infected programs will sneak through occasionally. Your best protection is to use anti-virus software and to update it frequently. If you join a user group BBS or online service, you'll find out about new viruses and how to stop them as soon as they're discovered. You will also find this information on BitNET, Internet, Usenet, and AppleLink and in widely distributed Macintosh publications like MacWorld, MacUser, and MacWeek. Figure 6-4 shows the welcome screen from Delphi's Mac group, with the current virus warning. Because new viruses appear frequently, you will need to keep updating your anti-virus software.

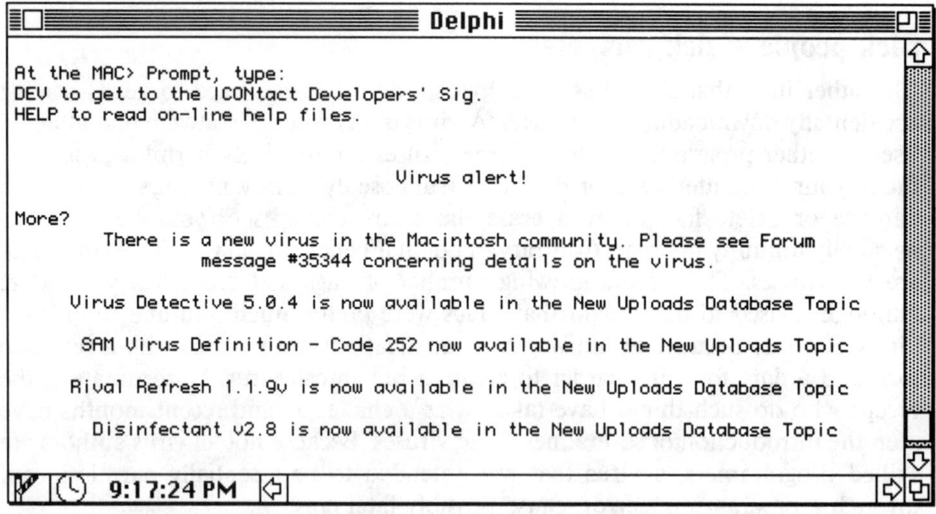

6-4 Virus warnings are one of many good reasons to join an online service.

There are several commercial anti-virus programs, including Rival, SAM, and Virex, as well as some excellent freeware programs that will help keep you virus free, as long as you use them on every new file you download and every new disk you bring into your system. One of the best free programs is Chris Johnson's GateKeeper. GateKeeper is an INIT that watches for anything that modifies your system and stops it before it can do much harm. Because there are some legitimate actions that affect your system, you need to tell GateKeeper which to allow and whether to block the others or simply to notify you and ask whether to proceed or not. This is done in the screen shown on the left in Fig. 6-5. GateKeeper keeps a log that shows system access and can give you additional information about any warnings it issues. The file selected in the right side of the figure did something illegal to change the system files. Clicking on it will bring up a dialog box describing the event in detail.

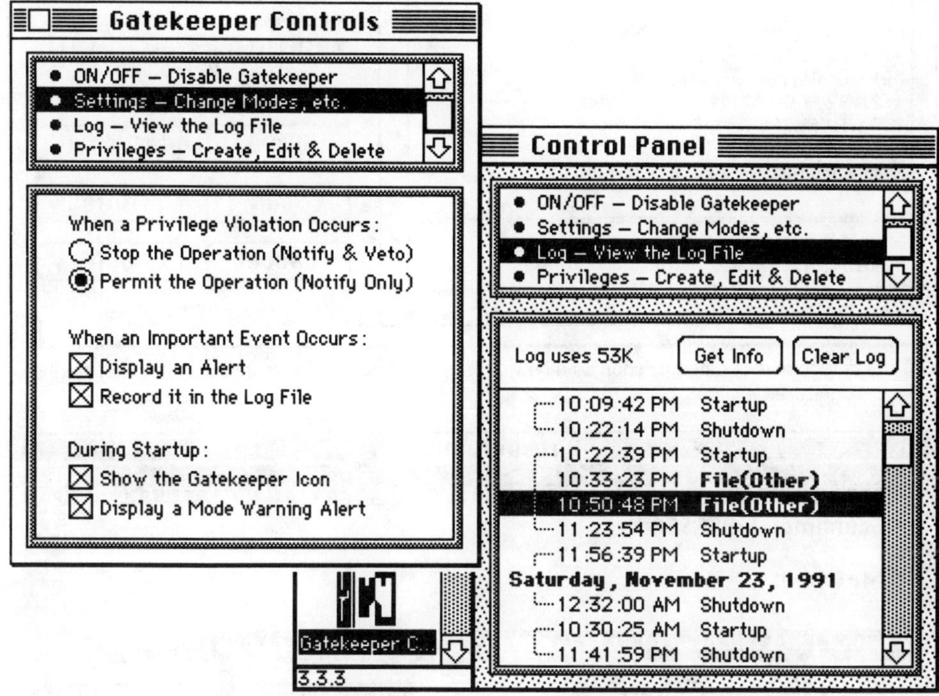

6-5 GateKeeper doesn't remove viruses. It watches the system for any unusual event and warns you. If you ask, it will prevent unusual events from happening.

Once you install it, the freeware program Disinfectant, by John Norstadt of Northwestern University, will find and remove known viruses that have already invaded your software. Figure 6-6 shows Disinfectant at work, scanning the author's disk drives for signs of infection. If any were found, clicking the Disinfect button would remove them. (It also has one of the best About screens ever written! Select About Disinfectant, under the Apple menu, and enjoy the show.) Current versions of Disinfectant come with an INIT that blocks the entry of *known* viruses. Unlike GateKeeper, it won't detect new ones, but it is a good deal easier to use. In fact, you'll never even know it's there unless it finds something.

Not freeware, but potentially worth its shareware price, is VirusDetective, also a good bet to help you avoid what its author, Jeffrey Shulman, calls "Hexually Transmitted Diseases." VirusDetective is installed as a DA. It's configurable, so

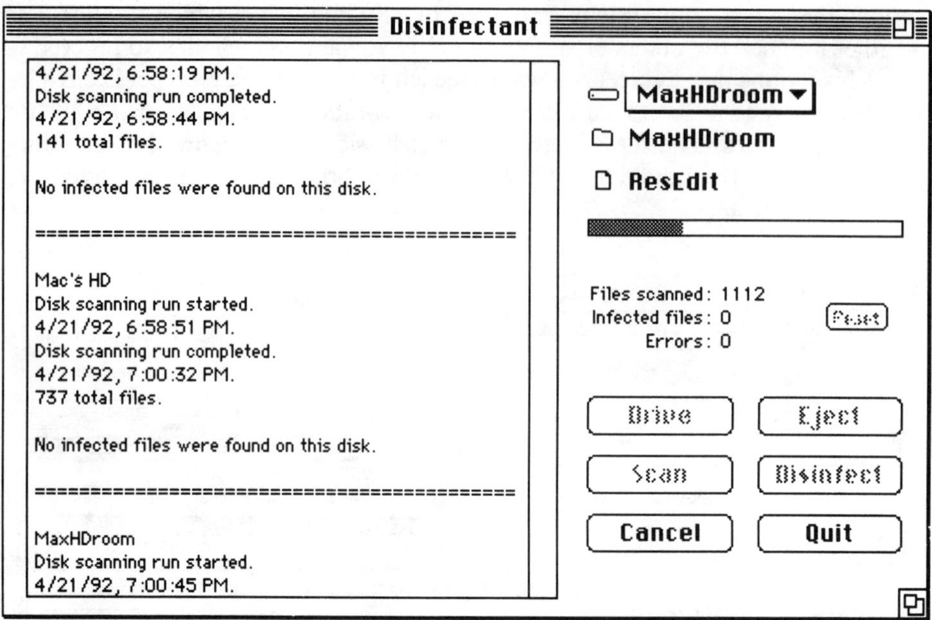

6-6 Disinfectant is updated as soon as a new virus is discovered. It looks for code it's been taught to recognize as a virus.

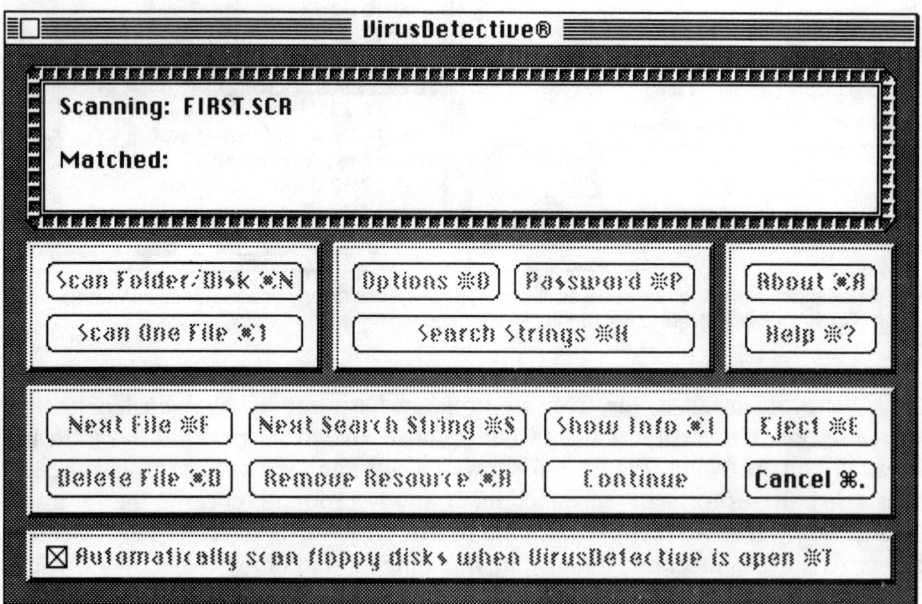

6-7 Virus Detective can scan files, folders, or disks one at a time.

you can often "teach" it a new virus, without waiting for an updated version to appear. When the WDEF virus first appeared in 1989, VirusDetective was the only anti-virus tool that could detect it.

The earliest anti-virus tool for the Mac was Vaccine, widely used and very effective when it first appeared. However, it was never updated, so it now misses more viruses than it detects. It's not recommended.

Transferring data in ASCII

Even though they're not really difficult to do, file transfers seem to be the one area that causes panic among new modem users. Perhaps they worry that sending a file means losing it. Some have a hard time understanding that the Mac *can* send information to a computer that doesn't run Mac programs. Certainly, it can be confusing, in part because there are so many options. Transfers can be made directly to another machine or via a third-party host, usually an online service's mainframe. There are two different kinds of file transfer procedures: ASCII and error-checking or error-control protocols, and at least a half dozen different varieties of the latter.

The easiest-to-understand kind of file transfer is a raw ASCII text dump. This can go from your Mac to any other kind of computer or even to a dumb terminal or telex machine. To send a file that any computer can open and read, you must first save it as ASCII text. Figure 6-8 shows how this is done in MS Word 5. Text files are

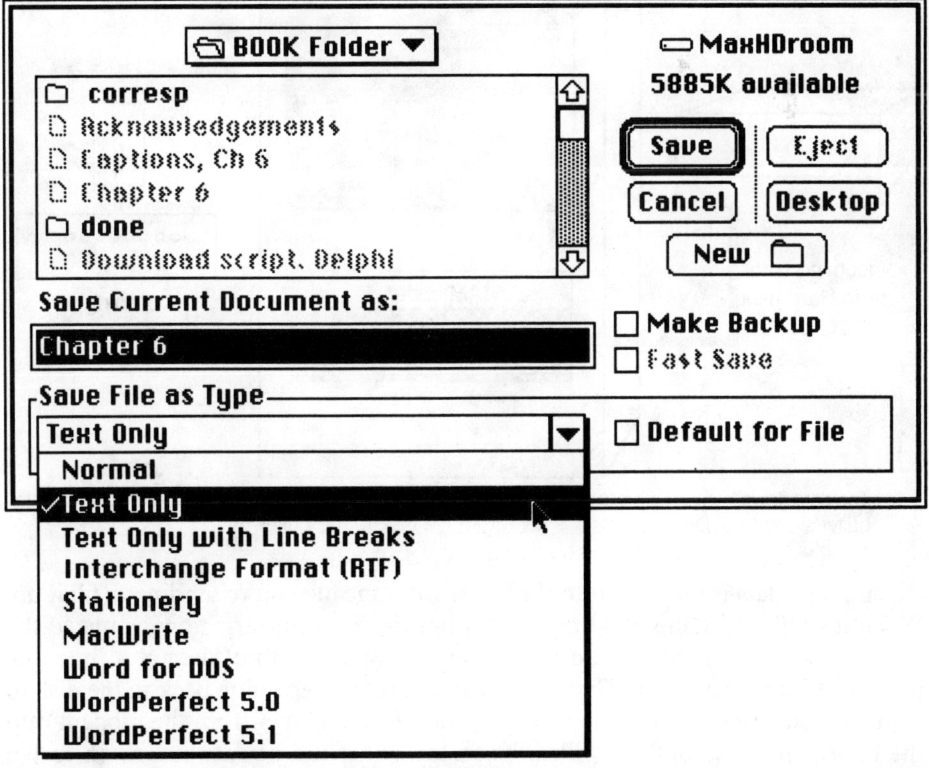

6-8 Save as "Text Only," not "Text with Line Breaks."

composed only of letters and numbers and the few control characters included in the basic 127 character ASCII set. Sending files as ASCII text works best with relatively small files and with 7-bit, rather than 8-bit, ASCII. Some systems offer an option for "stripping," or removing, the 8th bit from bytes.

Obviously, though, this only works if the file is text to begin with. MacPaint drawings, HyperCard stacks, or arcade games can't generally be saved as text, although binary files of some types can be translated into 7-bit ASCII for transmission and reconverted on receipt. It's risky, though. If a single bit is received incorrectly, the program will be useless. At least, if a text file gets slightly scrambled, you can usually guess at the missing word.

When you send an ASCII file, it's read from the computer's disk or memory and sent exactly as if you were typing it, only a great deal faster. When you receive one, it appears on your screen as if someone else were typing it to you. It scrolls past faster than you can read it on the screen and is saved to your data buffer then written to disk. A data buffer is a temporary storage area for incoming or outgoing data. It's actually a piece of RAM set aside for this purpose by the telecom program, but you can think of it as a holding tank within your Mac. The diagram in Fig. 6-9 shows how it works.

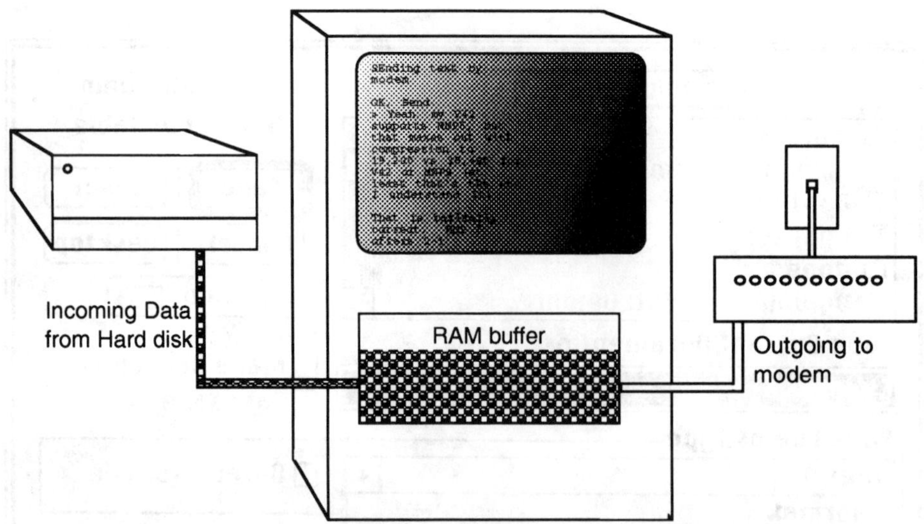

6-9 The data flows from the disk to the buffer until the buffer is full. It then goes to the modem until the buffer's empty. Then, more data is sent from the disk to the buffer.

Enough data is pumped into the buffer from the file you're sending to fill it up. When it's full, the data stops flowing in from the file and starts flowing out to the modem. Because the buffer can hold several seconds worth of data at a time, the process of sending is faster. The Mac doesn't have to keep going back to the disk to read and send each line. At the receiving end, the data flows from the modem into the buffer, until the buffer is filled. Then the buffer-full of data is written to the disk. The data flow has to stop long enough for the Mac to write the file, so a flow-control system (X-ON/X-OFF) is used to tell the sender to wait. X-OFF sends a control character to stop the data, X-ON sends a different control character to signal that it's okay to resume sending.

The mechanics of sending a text file are essentially the same in all telecom programs. Use whatever menu item or dialog box is necessary to select Send text or Send ASCII. Figure 6-10 shows the selection in MicroPhone II. You'll see a window with a list of files. Use the standard Mac methods to locate the file you want to send. In most programs, when Send Text or Send ASCII is selected, the only type of file that will show up in the window is a text file. Others will be invisible, so there's less danger of accidentally trying to send a non-text file as text. If the file you intend to send doesn't appear in the box, you haven't saved it as "text only" from your word processor.

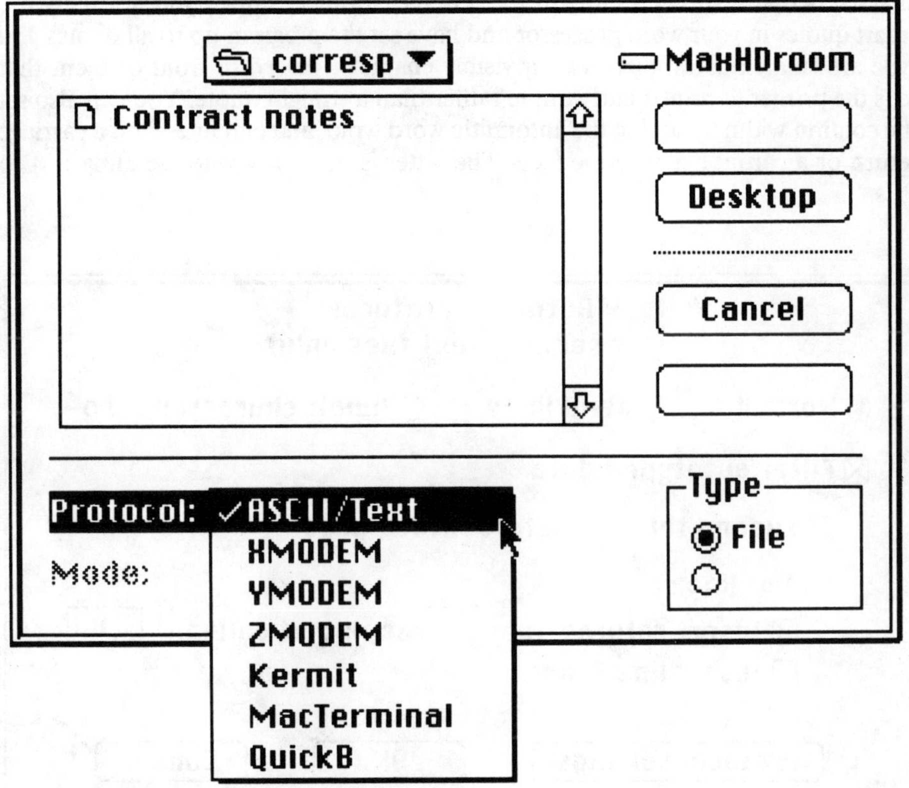

6-10 Choose ASCII from the list of protocols.

Selecting the file starts the sending process. You can usually cancel a "send" by clicking on a Cancel button. Be aware that your terminal window and keyboard might remain active during a text transfer. (It depends on the terminal program.) Any stray characters you type would then also be sent somewhere in the body of the text.

During the transfer, you may or may not see the text file going out. It depends on your Duplex mode. If you are using Half Duplex, you'll be able to watch your text flow past. If you have chosen Full Duplex, you won't see anything unless the remote machine is echoing the characters back to you. The recipient should be ready to receive the file *before* you start to send it, so that none of the text will be missed.

You can customize text sending options in many programs. Figure 6-11 shows the transfer options dialog box from SmartCom. In addition to the "normal" transfer described above, you can specify that your Mac should send text a single line at a time or should send a single character and wait for it to be echoed back before sending the next. If the recipient can't handle incoming text as fast as your Mac is sending it, you'll need to use one of these options. Otherwise, ignore them as they'll result in a very slow transfer. The filter option removes any non-ASCII text characters that might be hiding in the text file. If, for example, you normally use smart quotes in your word processor and have set the program up so all quotes you type are smart quotes, there's an invisible character placed in front of them that tells the printer to print a curly quote rather than a straight quote. You can also set the column width by setting the automatic word wrap, and end lines with a carriage return or a carriage return/line feed. The latter is necessary when sending text to PCs.

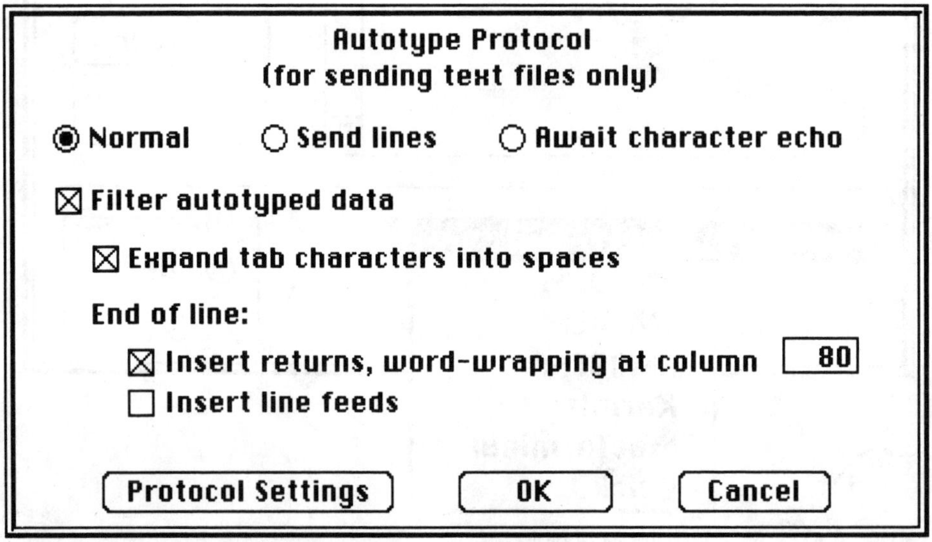

Autotype Protocol
(for sending text files only)

◉ Normal ○ Send lines ○ Await character echo

☒ Filter autotyped data

☒ Expand tab characters into spaces

End of line:

☒ Insert returns, word-wrapping at column 80

☐ Insert line feeds

Protocol Settings | OK | Cancel

6-11 Other telecom programs have a similar set of options.

Line feeds and carriage returns explained

The biggest hurdle in "inter-species communication" between Macs and non-Macs is the question of how a line of type ends. When the Mac was designed, its creators looked at the typewriter. When you reach the end of a line on a typewriter, you press Return, or if it's a non-electric typewriter, you slap a lever with your hand to simultaneously roll the paper down one line and move it into position to type the next line. So the Mac was designed to work like a typewriter. Pressing return moves you down one line and places the cursor at the start of the next. Non-Macs, on the other hand, were based on a teletype machine, which uses two different characters for a carriage return and line feed. So they expect to see two, where the Mac only uses one. This causes problems, in both directions. If you receive a text file from a PC, unless you use a filter to strip the linefeeds or ask the sender to do so, you'll end up with either an extra (empty) line between each two lines of text or a rectangle indicating an unknown character at the start of each line.

On the PC side, when you send text without the carriage return/linefeed pair, unless the recipient's software can replace them, the PC might simply choke on the file or try to print one line over the next. Most well-written telecom programs include the ability to do this, although you might have to hunt through several menus to find it. Figure 6-12 shows how it's done in MicroPhone II.

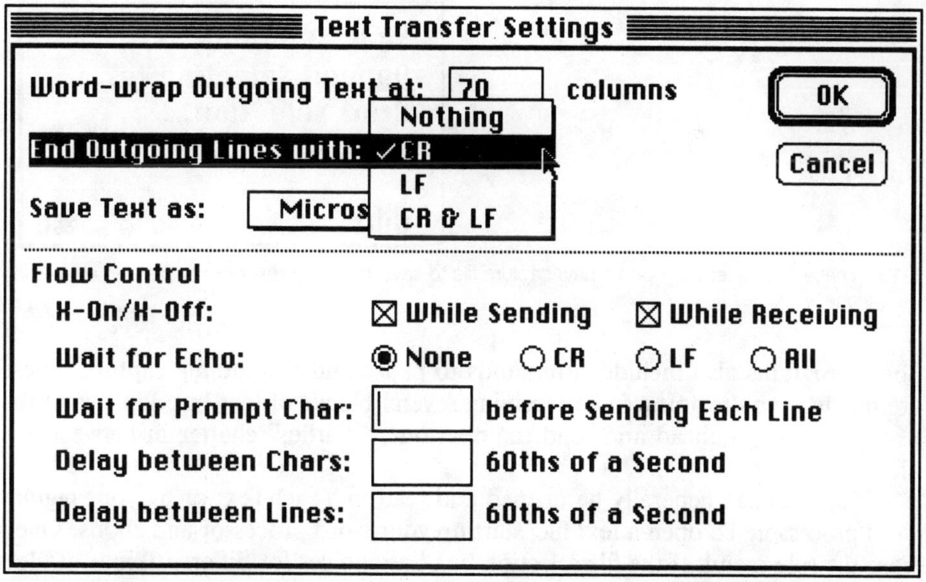

Text Transfer Settings
Word-wrap Outgoing Text at: 70 columns
OK
Nothing
End Outgoing Lines with: ✓CR
Cancel
LF
Save Text as: Micros
CR & LF
Flow Control
X-On/X-Off: ☒ While Sending ☒ While Receiving
Wait for Echo: ◉ None ○ CR ○ LF ○ All
Wait for Prompt Char: before Sending Each Line
Delay between Chars: 60ths of a Second
Delay between Lines: 60ths of a Second

6-12 Change this setting to CR & LF if you're sending text to a PC. Use CR if you're talking to a Mac.

Receiving text files

Receiving a text file is even easier than sending one. You can save it as a new file or append the incoming data to an existing file. These options are generally found as menu commands under the File menu. Figure 6-13 shows the file menus from MicroPhone II and White Knight. Once you choose to create a file or append to one, everything your modem receives will be saved into that file until you close it.

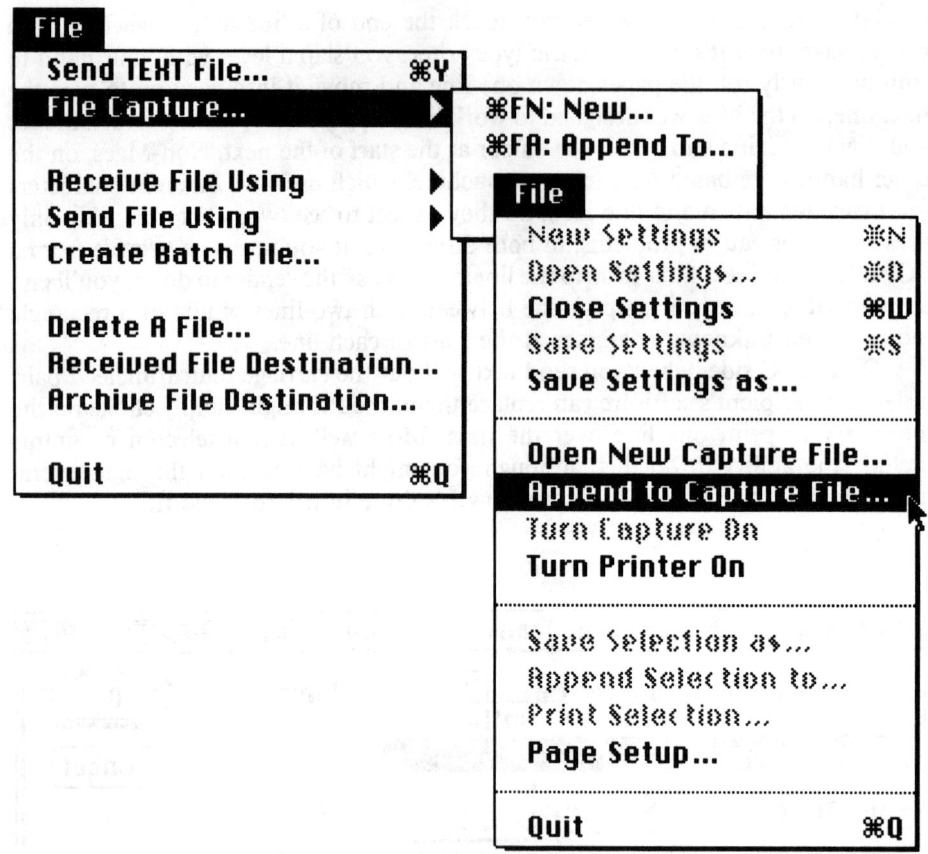

6-13 These menus let you open a new capture file to save incoming text or to append to an existing one.

Some programs also include commands to pause and resume file capture. These are handy if you're going to be receiving several blocks of text but don't want the usual, "Okay, go ahead and send the next one, Charlie," chatter in between the files.

Text files can generally be opened and read in TeachText or by your regular word processor. To open a text file, start up your word processor and choose Open from the File menu. If the file selection box has choices for different kinds of files, look for a choice that lets you open text files. Figure 6-14 shows how MS word does it. Just select the text file and open it.

If you just click on the received file, you might not be able to open it. You might encounter a dialog box like the one in Fig. 6-15. This means that the Mac has no idea what program created the file, so it doesn't know how to open it. Normally, every Mac file gets a pair of four-letter codes when it's created. One defines the file type, and the other the creator. For ASCII text files, the file type is TEXT. The file creator tells the Mac which word processor (or other program) to open in order to use that file. Both White Knight and MicroPhone let you define a file creator code

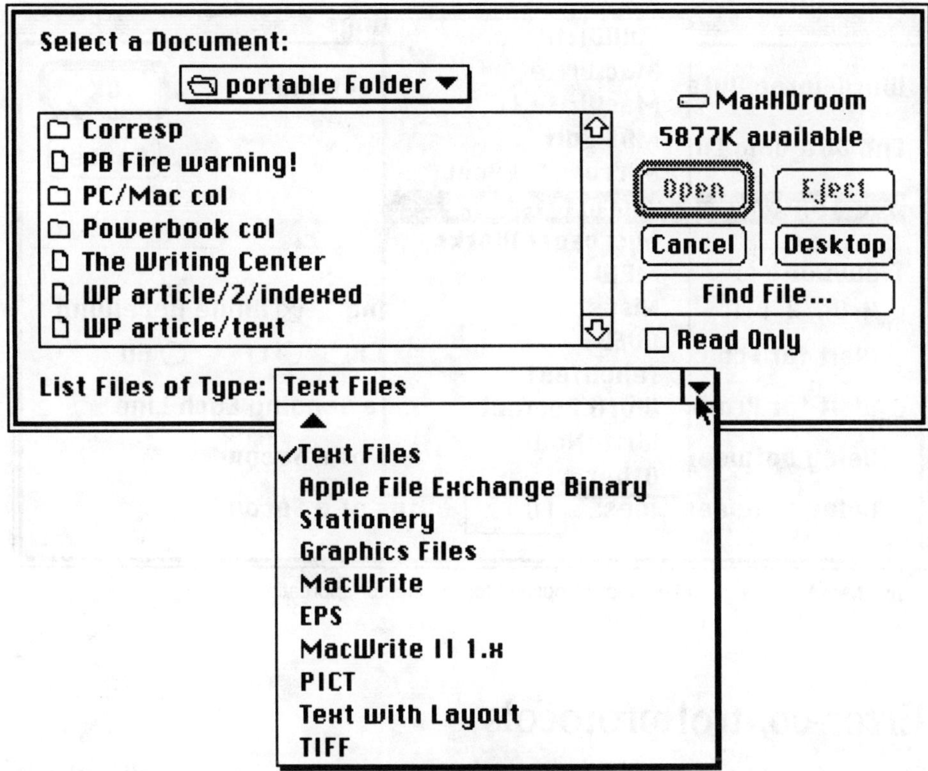

6-14 When you select Text as the file type, you'll only see files that can be opened as text files.

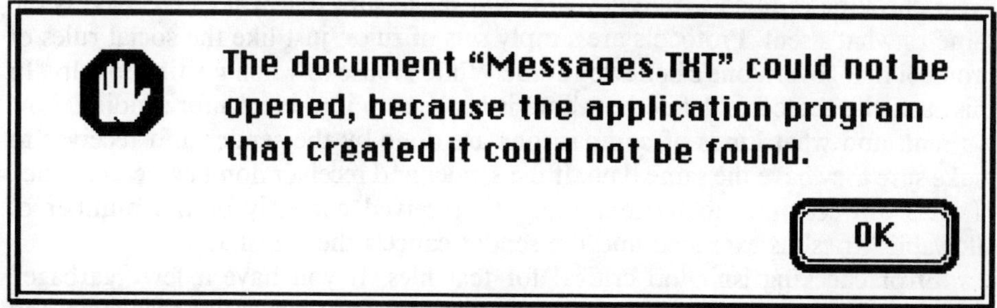

6-15 When the Mac can't find a creator, it might offer to open the program in TeachText, or it might give up.

for text files you save. This allows them to be opened in your favorite word processor without the need to convert from text and resave. Figure 6-16 shows the pop-up menu to choose a creator in MicroPhone II's Text Settings box. White Knight simply asks you to type the four-letter code for your favorite word processor into its Text File Transfer Options box.

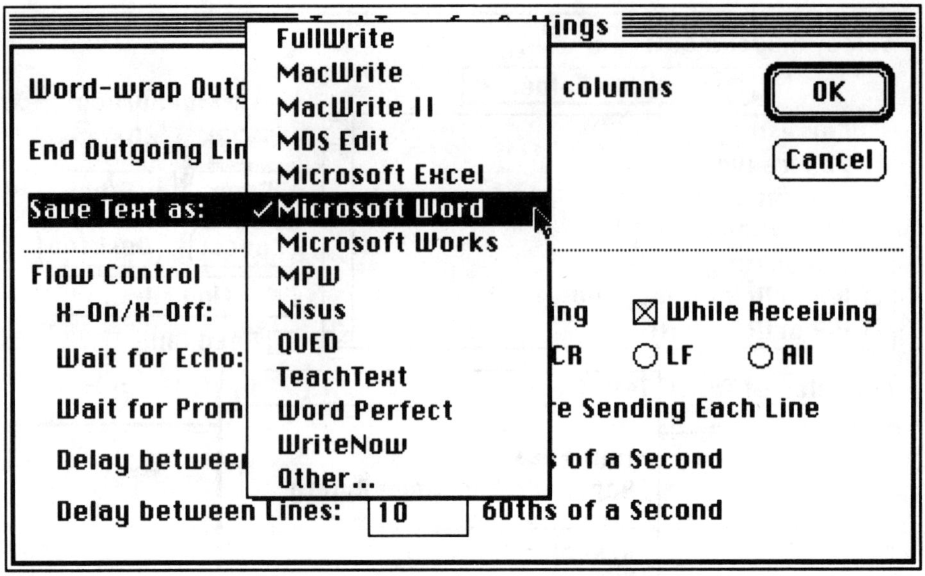

6-16 MicroPhone II gives you a lot of options for the creator application.

Error-control protocols

The chief problem with ASCII transfers is that they're not especially reliable. There's no error checking or correction, and the slightest bit of line noise or interference will dump garbage characters onto your screen and into your file. Error-checking protocols were developed to make sure that what's received is the same as what's sent. Protocols are simply sets of rules, just like the social rules of protocol that govern one's behavior at the White House or when visiting royalty. In this case, the protocols define how data is broken up into blocks for sending, how it's sent, and what kinds of comparisons are done by the sender and receiver to make sure they have the same data. If the sender and receiver don't agree, the block of data will continue to be sent until it's received correctly or the number of allowable "tries" is exceeded and the sender cancels the transfer.

Error checking isn't too critical for text files. If you have a few "garbage" characters in the middle of an inter-office menu, you can easily recognize and delete them. But if you're sending a binary data file or an application, error checking is a necessity. You'd probably never be able to identify a lost character or an added "garbage" character in the middle of a program. But the error could change the way the program ran or render it totally non-functional. Error checking is also a help when you're transferring a long text file. The longer you're online, the better the odds of line noise or other interference sneaking in. Many people routinely use one of the transfer protocols for even short blocks of text, preferring to avoid all risks.

Error-checking protocols and how they work

When you use an error-checking protocol to send a file, the data is divided into blocks, or packets, and is sent one block at a time. A block is a fixed size and can be as small as 128 bytes or as large as 1024 bytes. The sending computer reads data from the file and loads a block of data at a time into its *send buffer*. Information about the block might be added to it as a header, and then it's sent to the modem and down the wire to the other computer. At the receiving end, the header, if any, is read and acted upon and the data block is saved into the transfer file. In the time between blocks of data, the computers exchange any other "housekeeping" information they need: data receipt or error, the end of the transmission, and any other necessary control characters.

XMODEM

XMODEM is by far the most common transfer protocol. Since its creation in 1978, it has become the common denominator for all kinds of computers and telecom systems. You'll find XMODEM on practically all BBSs and online services because, even though it's not the fastest method, it's reliable and easy to use. "Classic" XMODEM uses a 128 bit data block and adds an extra bit, called a *checksum*, to each block. The checksum bit is determined by doing some fairly simple math, in a process not unlike the parity checking described in chapter 3. If the checksums don't match, the receiver sends a NAK command (Not Acknowledged) and the block is sent over and over until the checksums match. If all is well, the receiver sends ACK (Acknowledged) and the next block is sent.

Improvements made to XMODEM in recent years now let the computer use 1024K blocks for faster transmission and include a newer method of error-checking called *Cyclic Redundancy Check*, or *CRC* for short. CRC adds a second checksum bit, to increase reliability to almost 100 percent. Not all systems support XMODEM CRC or XMODEM—1K blocks, but if you find one that does, you'll save time unless you've got a particularly bad line. It takes longer to send a 1K block, so repeating badly received blocks slows things down. If there are no errors, though, the 1K blocks are much faster. Figure 6-17 shows your XMODEM options in White Knight. (Supercharged XMODEM is another variation, not yet widely supported.)

YMODEM

Classic YMODEM, an improvement on the XMODEM protocols, is also widely used. The major difference is that YMODEM allows the user to send a batch of files in a group rather than one at a time. YMODEM—1K, like its XMODEM counterpart, simply means that the data is sent in 1024-bit blocks for faster processing. YMODEM uses the CRC error-checking system. A YMODEM transfer is shown in Fig. 6-18.

YMODEM—G, which probably stands for "Good Luck, Sucker," sends the data without any error checking. It's very fast, but extremely unstable. You pay for its 98 percent efficiency with the large number of failed transfers due to just one

XMODEM, YMODEM, ZMODEM Options

XMODEM Options:

○ XMODEM - Classic ○ XMODEM - CRC ◉ XMODEM - 1K Blocks

☐ Supercharged XMODEM Receive

YMODEM Options:

○ YMODEM - Classic ○ YMODEM - 1K Blocks ◉ YMODEM - G

1K Block Options:

○ Send only if requested ◉ Send automatically

XMODEM, YMODEM, ZMODEM block timeout: 5 seconds.

☒ Keep partial ZMODEM receives for later completion

OK Cancel

6-17 If your service is working slowly, as many do when they are very busy, set the timeout for longer than 5 seconds.

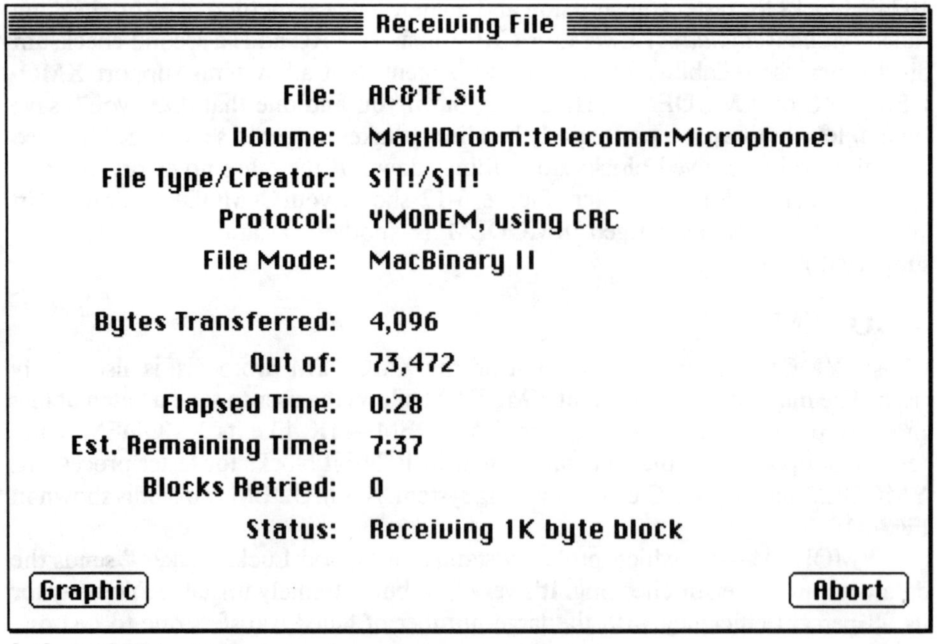

6-18 YMODEM—1K blocks is a fast, and accurate protocol.

dropped bit. It can be used with MNP error-correcting modem protocols for fast and accurate transfers or with *very* clean phone lines or direct connections.

ZMODEM

ZMODEM has elements in common with both X- and YMODEM, but it is superior to both in many ways. ZMODEM can handle files in batches and is nearly as fast as YMODEM—G, *with* error correction. ZMODEM is supported by many BBSs and most online services, and when there's a choice, it's definitely your best bet. The speed of a ZMODEM transfer comes about because it doesn't wait for an ACK message after each block. It sends data more or less continuously and watches for NAK messages. Whenever it gets one, it stops and resends that packet of data.

What makes ZMODEM preferable, though, is that it lets you resume an interrupted transfer at the point at which you left off. To do so, follow the same steps you used to start the transfer. The telecom program will search for an interrupted transfer (identifiable in the finder by a "broken" icon, as shown in Fig. 6-19) and advise the sending computer of the last block correctly received so it can begin sending again from that point. The incoming data will be appended to that file, and when the transfer is finished, the file should be complete and intact. Don't move or rename the file or the broken icon, or you won't be able to resume the transfer.

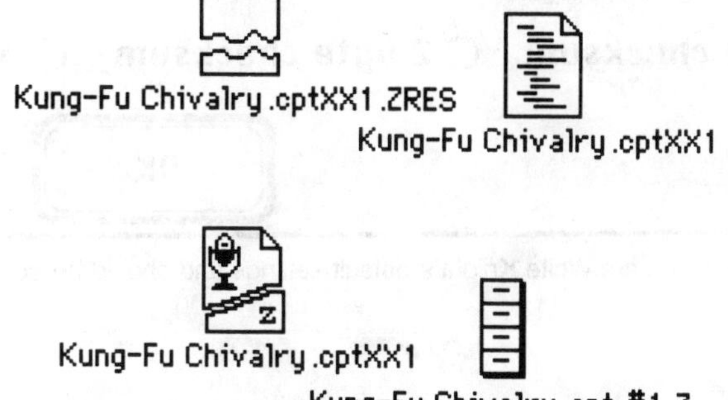

6-19 Broken icons indicate an interrupted ZMODEM transfer. Don't move them from the folder with their application icons.

Kermit

The first thing many people wonder about Kermit is the source of the name. Yes, it really was named after the famous frog. Kermit was created at Columbia University in 1981 as a means of transferring files between dissimilar computers and under widely varying conditions. Like XMODEM, Kermit transfers data in blocks, which it calls packets, and uses a checksum bit. The major difference is that Kermit uses a

7-bit data "word," while XMODEM (and Y- and ZMODEM) uses an 8-bit word. When it's necessary for Kermit to do so, it translates 8-bit words into 7-bit words and sends the leftover bit separately.

Kermit gives its users quite a few customization options, shown in the White Knight dialog box in Fig. 6-20.

Kermit Options

(•) Classic Kermit - packet size (10-94): [94]

( ) Long Packet Kermit - packet size (10-9024): [1024]

( ) Sliding Windows Kermit - window count (1-31): [31]

Treat outgoing files as: ( ) Text (•) Binary data

Packet timeout: [3] seconds.

[ ] Use line turnaround handshake character: [^Q]

Start of packet character: [^A]

End of packet character: [^M]

Error checking done with:

(•) 1 byte checksum ( ) 2 byte checksum ( ) 3 byte CRC

OK Cancel

6-20 The settings shown are White Knight's default settings and should be correct for most Kermit transfers.

All Kermit systems can handle Classic Kermit. Use the Long Packet or Sliding Windows option only if the host computer offers them.

The difference between sending text and binary data in Kermit is simple. If you're sending text, Kermit will automatically add the Linefeed characters after carriage return characters for systems that need both. When you are sending any other kind of file except ASCII text, select binary. Doing so tells the computer not to add a linefeed if it detects a carriage-return character.

Other settings, packet start and stop characters, time-outs, and turnarounds should simply be left with their default settings unless the host system administrator specifically tells you to change something. Changing values at random will almost always end up with Kermit incompatibility and no file transfer.

The MacBinary format

All digital data is binary. MacBinary refers to the way the data is filed on a Mac. The Macintosh handles its disk files in a different way from other computers. When you create a file on a PC, or any other non-Macintosh computer, you create one file, and all the data for that file goes into it. When you create a Mac file, though, you actually create two sub-files, known as *forks*. The Data fork holds the same kind of information that a data file on any other computer holds. But Macs also have a Resource fork, which holds things unique to the Mac, such as a file's icon, dialog boxes, PICT images, and other goodies. There's also a file section in the Resource fork with Finder Information, which identifies the creation date, file name, type and creator, icon number, and other information that's displayed in the Finder or Get Info box. When you receive a file from CompuServe, the dialog box lets you know which fork you're receiving, the resource fork or the data fork. CompuServe's file receive box is shown in Fig. 6-21. (There's no particular reason why you *need* this information, but it gives you something to look at while the file transfers.)

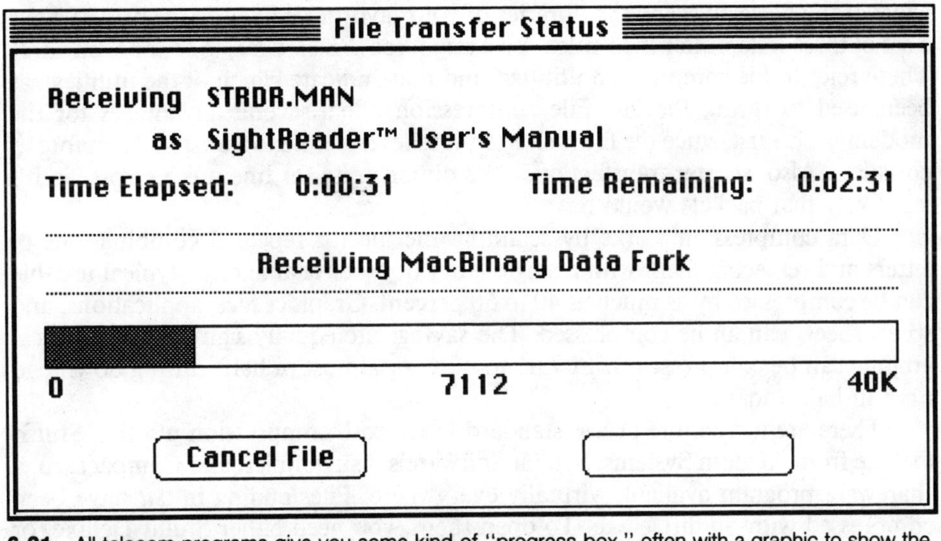

File Transfer Status

Receiving STRDR.MAN
as SightReader™ User's Manual

Time Elapsed: 0:00:31 Time Remaining: 0:02:31

Receiving MacBinary Data Fork

0 7112 40K

Cancel File

6-21 All telecom programs give you some kind of "progress box," often with a graphic to show the percentage of the file received.

MacBinary is invisible to a non-Macintosh, so you can send Mac files to a mainframe or mini host. Other Mac users can download the files you send and use them, even though the host can't read it. If the Mac receives a file that's not MacBinary, it simply saves it as text. Some non-Mac files, such as CompuServe's GIF format, can be converted to a Mac-readable file. Others can only be viewed as text.

Other protocols

In addition to the "generic" transfer protocols described previously, there are a couple of others you'll discover. CompuServe members can download from CIS using the CompuServe B + protocol, similar in many ways to ZMODEM. It uses a 512-character data block and can resume an interrupted transfer, as ZMODEM can. If you're not using CompuServe Information Manager or Navigator to handle your CIS downloads, look for a telecom program that offers the CompuServe B+ protocol. Since it's custom designed for CompuServe, it will be more efficient than even ZMODEM.

America Online members also use a resumable transfer protocol, similar to ZMODEM. AO transfers are very fast and apparently very stable. In several years of AO use, I've never had a failed transfer. AO's system is the most user-friendly of all because all you need to do is to click the appropriate button to initiate an upload or download.

Data compression—shortening transfer time

Most of the files you see in the libraries of your favorite online service or BBS have a set of three letters after their titles. You might see *.SEA*, *.CPT*, *.SIT*, or even *.ZIP*. These refer to file compression utilities, and they indicate which of the utilities has been used to shrink the file. File compression offers several advantages for the modem user. First, since the file is shorter, it takes less time to transfer. Therefore, it costs less. Also, shorter transfers offer less opportunity for line noise errors, so it's less likely that packets would have to be sent twice.

Data compression works by scanning the file for repeated combinations of letters and replacing them with a single letter or other character. A typical text file can be compressed by as much as 40 to 50 percent. Graphics files, applications, and spreadsheets can all be compressed. The savings are equally significant. A typical graphic can be compressed from 79K to 40K, or almost in half, cutting download time in half, too.

There are three more or less standard Macintosh compression utilities: StuffIt Deluxe from Aladdin Systems; Salient Software's disk doubler; and CompactPro, a shareware program available virtually everywhere. Files ending in *.sit* have been compressed with StuffitDeluxe. To open them, you need either Stuffit Deluxe, or UnStuffIt Deluxe—a freeware tool for opening stuffed files. America Online also uses and distributes StuffIt Classic under a blanket lease. Figure 6-22 shows a file being unstuffed with UnStuffIt Deluxe.

Files ending in *.cpt* have been compacted with CompactPro. Files ending in *.sea* are self-extracting files created by CompactPro or StuffIt. Double-clicking them will make them uncompress automatically, without using the application that stuffed them.

Disk Doubler can open some, but not all, StuffIt-compressed files. Disk Doubler is primarily used for compressing files to be stored on your hard disk, or archived. You might see files in a Macintosh library that end with *.zip*. These are PC files, and under some circumstances, PC text files and GIF files can be opened

6-22 It only takes a few seconds to unstuff most files.

and read on a Mac. There's a freeware program named UnZip, available in most libraries and BBSs, that will open these compressed PC files. If you go poking in dusty corners of online libraries, you might even find a program or two with the designation .PIT. These were compressed with an early utility called PackIt. GEnie has a few of these files in its library and also offers a freeware DA called UnPacker, which will open these files.

Downloading files

Now that you understand the mechanics of file transfer protocols, let's look at some actual downloads. Figure 6-23 shows how a download is requested on Delphi. To find out what files you want to download, enter the database area and type a ? to see the list of topic areas. Then, after selecting a topic, you can view its directory or list of files by typing DIR. When you spot an interesting title, stop browsing by entering N at the More? prompt. Then, type READ and the name of the file. You'll be able to read a description of the contents. If you want to download it, type D at the next prompt.

If you've previously downloaded a file using ZMODEM, you'll be able to do so automatically. Otherwise, you'll be presented with a menu of download protocols and asked to choose one. If ZMODEM is selected, nothing further need be done. The incoming file will automatically be saved with its appropriate title. If you choose another protocol, you'll be asked to save the file, and a default name will be entered for it. You can change the file name if you wish. When you click SAVE, the download will begin. You'll be notified with a beep (or whatever alert sound your Mac uses) when the file is complete.

Downloading is very easy on AO. All you need to do here is to choose the file you want to download. Click the button to see a description of it (Fig. 6-24). If you like what you see, click Download. After the usual Macintosh Save As . . . dialog box, confirms the title of the file, the download will start. AO's progress box is

```
TOPIC>Which topic? new
DBASES:New> (Dir, Read, Set, Exit) dir
Directory of All Items:

MACLOAD V1.1           PROG 17-APR DEBE
DROPPER V1.1           PROG 16-APR DEBE
SNDVOLUME              PROG 16-APR DEBE
SUPER YAHTZEE V1.0     PROG 16-APR DEBE
MACMAN V1.0.2          PROG 16-APR DEBE
PROGRESSION V1.0       PROG 16-APR DEBE
FONT CLERK V2.0        PROG 16-APR DEBE
More? n

DBASES:New> (Dir, Read, Set, Exit) read sndvol
1;1fJName: SNDVOLUME
Type: PROGRAM
Date: 16-APR-1992 02:01 by DEBE
Size: 11392   Count: 26

                          SndVolume
                     by Christopher Eliot
          A free utility for setting the speaker volume.

Keywords: SOUND, VOLUME, CONTROL, INDIVIDUAL, FILES, APPLICATIONS, UTILITY,
SYSTEM 7

ACTION> (Next, Down, Xm, List) d
Using file transfer method ZMODEM
(Use the command DOW MENU as your next download command if you want to change this,
or type a download command such as DOW 3 XMODEM for a temporary change of meth-
ods.)

ZMODEM download of file ''SNDVOLUME'' – this file will be called ''SndVolume.cpt''
on your computer (ZMODEM may modify this name to conform to your machine's require-
ments)

Type three consecutive <Control – C>'s to cancel.
ZMODEM mode
Ok, receive! (11392 bytes = 12 YMODEM blocks, 89 XMODEM blocks)
rz
**B00000000000000AL STATUS = Transfer successful.
FINAL STATUS = 1 file successfully transferred.
```

6-23 Delphi has extensive libraries of Mac utilities.

shown in Fig. 6-25. When the transfer is complete, AO's voice will report "File's done."

Uploading files

Uploading is handled in much the same way as downloading. You'll be asked to enter information about the file you're submitting. Figure 6-26 shows how CompuServe requests the information. Text-based services and BBSs ask for the same

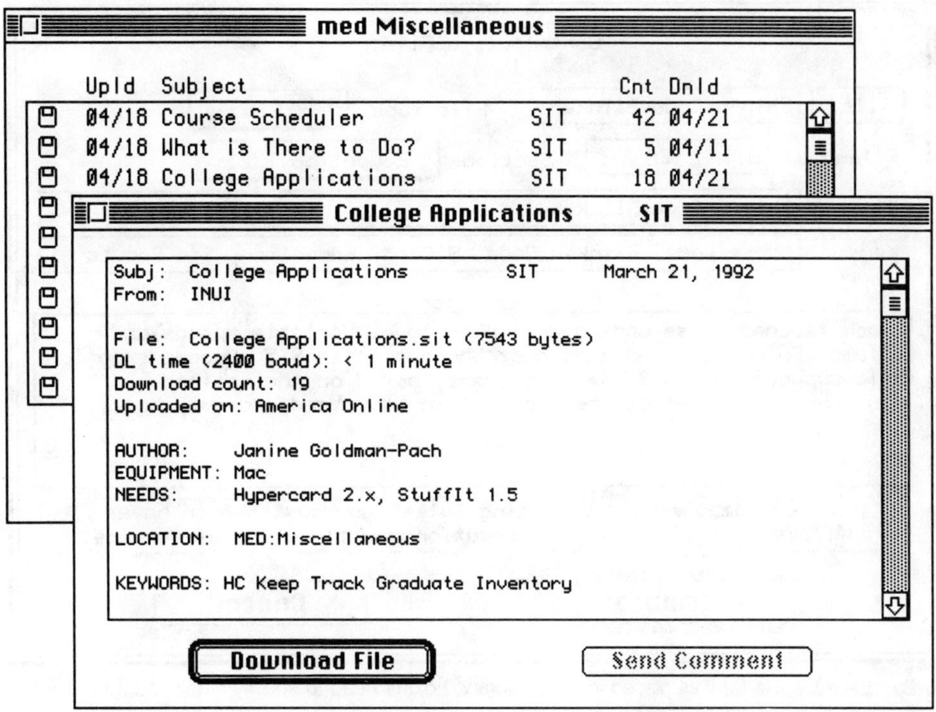

6-24 Either click the Get Description button, or double click the file name to learn more about it.

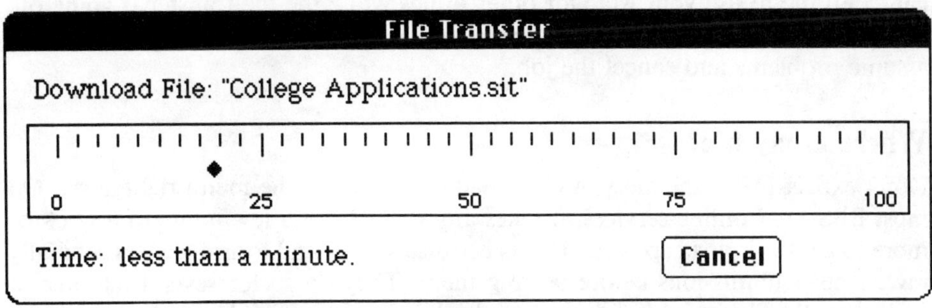

6-25 America Online's estimates of time remaining are often overly generous. This file took much less than a minute.

information, one question at a time. After you've entered the details about the file, you're ready to start the transfer. With the CompuServe Information Manager, all you need to do is click the Contribute button and wait while the file is uploaded. On other services, you might be asked to choose an upload protocol.

All telecom programs give you some sort of progress box while you're uploading or downloading. It gives you some idea of how long the transfer will take. The Apple menu remains active in all cases, and if you're using either MultiFinder or

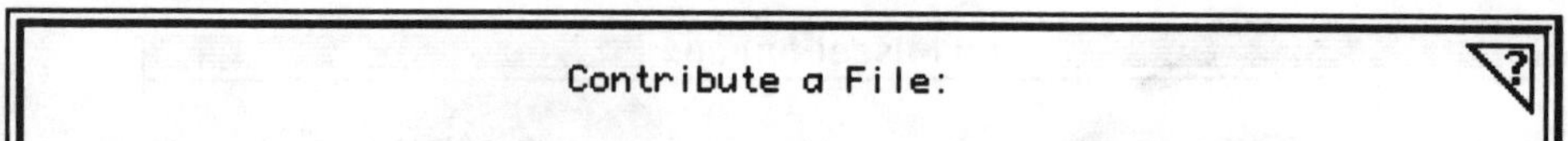

Contribute a File:

File: Ship's Code Blinker. File Type: Binary

Filename: Blink.SEA Section: Education [12]

Title: Ship's Code Blinker

Keys: Morse Code, Blinker Code, H'Card, Education, Sea Scouts

Description

Stack teaches Morse Code and Blinker code. Variable speeds and volume. Enter your own messages. Shareware fee $ 5. Proceeds go to help support Ship 613, Sea Explorers, based on the retired Lightship Nantucket at the Charlestown Navy Yard, Boston, Mass.

Under CompuServe's Operating Rules, you must own or have sufficient rights to any information you place on the Service.

Contribute Cancel

6-26 Because this file was placed in a Mac library, I didn't need to specify "Mac" as a keyword.

System 7, you can open a word processor or a game or some other application while you're transferring files. However, you need to be warned that although you can continue to use your Mac for other things while the file transfer is going on, doing so slows down the transfer, and if it takes too much time, the host might assume problems and cancel the job.

Where is my file?

Don't expect to see the file you've uploaded appear on the menu right away. On most BBSs and online services, it takes anywhere from a few hours to a week or more to get the uploads posted. This is because sysops and forum leaders generally review new submissions before posting them. They do so for several reasons: to make sure the file fits its description, to check it for viruses, and to make sure that it functions as it's supposed to. Online services are usually very careful about what gets placed in their libraries. Because users pay by the minute to download a file, they would, naturally, be upset if they discovered that they'd wasted online time copying a program that didn't open, was full of bugs, was infected with a virus, or otherwise didn't meet expectations.

Summary

File transfers can flow in two directions. You *upload* a file to another computer. You *download* from another computer to yours. Online services and bulletin boards have huge libraries of files to download and welcome your contributions. Be careful to use virus-detection software to scan all new files. Viruses can be spread through shareware. Be careful also to upload only files you have a right to. Unauthorized "sharing" is software piracy.

The simplest file transfer consists of sending ASCII text from one machine to another. All computers can read this universal language. However, text transfers are prone to errors. Because of this, most file transfers are done using error-checking protocols. The commonest are known as X-, Y-, and ZMODEM. Variations in these affect the size of the data blocks sent and how errors are detected and corrected. Two services, CompuServe and America Online, use their own proprietary transfer protocols. File compression utilities shrink the size of all kinds of files and save you time and money during transfers.

Downloading a file from a library is simple. Select the file, and the transfer protocol. (Use ZMODEM if you're given the option of doing so.) When the transfer starts, you'll see a progress box, which tells you how much more time and/or data is left. Uploads work in a similar fashion, except that you send a copy of the file instead of receiving one.

7

Can we talk?

To be honest, I've never talked to Joan Rivers, the comedian who popularized that line. But I *have* spent hours in conversation with Comedian/Composer/Renaissance Man Steve Allen, Presidential Candidate Jerry Brown, actor and magician Harry Anderson, and a host of other celebrities, as well as authors, college professors and students, and just plain people from all parts of the United States and half a dozen foreign countries. And I did it without ever leaving the comfort of my keyboard.

Chatting online is like joining a huge CB radio network. Although there are lots of channels, you're just as likely to end up in the middle of a five-way conversation as you are to find a one-on-one with somebody. It sounds confusing at first, but you'll be amazed at how easy it is once you get used to the idea of talking through your Mac. Real-time online conversations are the main reason many people join a service or BBS. Some say it's an ideal way to make new friends. Others use conferences to keep in touch with old friends and family members. Others use their online conference time to "meet" with business partners or clients. You have the convenience of a conference call, with the added benefit of an "instant" written transcript, if you desire. It's easy to "log" a conference (or any other online activity, for that matter).

It makes a certain amount of sense that online conferencing would have a great deal in common with Citizen's Band and HAM radio. In the earlier days of online activity, the same kind of people went online to chat on the few BBSs around. Like a HAM conversation, much of the talk was about equipment, only instead of bragging about the brand-new 400-meter single-sideband transceiver, with the hi-gain folded dipole antenna, the computer owner bragged about his brand new TRS-80, with 16K of RAM and cassette drive. Times, thankfully, have changed. Just as the advent of the Mac made it possible for people who weren't (and didn't want to be) "computer nerds" to use a computer, the advent of reasonably priced online information services made it possible for "the rest of us" to get into the act. And we have. At any hour of the day or night, you'll find people talking in the conference rooms on Delphi, on the CompuServe CB simulator, or GEnie's Chat Lines, on America Online's People Connection, and on the hundreds of bulletin boards that have a real-time talk area. How do you get started? Well, one way is to just plunge right in. Online chatters are a friendly group and are always willing to welcome new members and explain what's going on.

Formal conferences

If you'd rather dip a toe in the pool before you dive in, you might start by attending a "formal" conference. No, you don't need a long dress or black tie, but you *do* need to remember the rules of etiquette, just as at any formal affair. Formal conference rules are used whenever there's a guest speaker in a conference, or when there are a lot of people in the group and a specific topic or agenda to be covered. Using conference rules simple helps keep things from getting too confusing and assures that everybody who has something to say gets a chance to say it.

Formal conferences always have a *moderator*, someone who introduces the guest, if any, or the topic and keeps a list of those wanting to speak or ask a question. The moderator also reminds conference members to follow the rules and, on some services, can lock out anyone who doesn't.

The first rule to remember is not to "talk" out of turn. If you want to ask a question, simply send a question mark. If you want to make a comment, send an exclamation point. Then, wait to be called on. It's like raising your hand. (Just don't wave and shout "Oooh, oooh! Me next!")

Second, when you have the floor, keep your comments and questions brief and to the point. On those services that enter text one line at a time, use an ellipsis (. . .) if you have more than one line's worth to say. This way, the moderator will know that you're not done yet and won't call on the next person. When you *are* finished, type ga. This stands for "go ahead." The "ga" and ". . ." codes come from the old Telex codes used by teletype operators who used to chat between messages. Here's a transcript of a piece of an education conference on America Online, showing these commands in use:

AFL George: Okay, Kathy, what is it? And how will it "talk" online?

Katherin38: Would you like me to explain a project we are doing at the University? Using ISDN.

AFL George: ga

Katherin38: We have a teacher at one school, online, the class (students included) are signed online. There are as many as 10 school class rooms hooked into the same lesson . . . . . in this way schools can afford all . . .

Katherin38: kinds of special education for K-12 lets say . . . . with budget cut backs in education the way they are, we have seen lots of cut backs in areas such as art and music . . . . . I think it would be . . .

MacIdeas7 : ?

Katherin38: wonderful to see schools all over hooked up to a live program of the Boston Pops, as an example . . .

Katherin38: This kind of thing can only be done with high speed communications. Yes, Sarah!

SneezerZ : !

MacIdeas7 : Kathy, Are they able to communicate to each other, too? ga

AFL George: Using only Macs? You're next, Sneezy ;-)

Katherin38: Yes, all the schools can communicate to the core instructor to ask questions and participate in the lesson . . . . . No it can use PCs and Macs. ga

MacIdeas7 : Sounds great!

AFL George: You're next, Sneezy ;-) ga

Formal conferences needn't be stuffy, and those in individual forums usually aren't. Following the rules just makes it easier to keep the conversation on track. When you have a large group conference, like those in AO's Center Stage or CompuServe's Electronic Convention Center, which often have anywhere from 20 to 50 or more people attending, less is left to chance. Once the conference starts, "audience" chatter is turned off. You can communicate with the moderator by using AO's Ask A Question box. On CompuServe, type /Question, and you'll be told when to ask it. To find out how many more questions are ahead of yours, type /list and you'll see the waiting list. On GEnie, the procedure is similar. The RoundTable moderator can also put the group into "listen only" mode. To get the moderator's attention when you have a question or comment, type /RAI, for "raise hand." You'll get a private message telling you to prepare your question and when to send it. GEnie's RoundTables are a good place to meet celebrities. The Entertainment RT hosted a memorable evening with Steve Allen last year, and the recent session with candidate Brown attracted more than 50 participants. These meetings are usually announced in the "What's New" menus when you log in. If you see one that's especially interesting to you, it's a good idea to go to the conference or RoundTable area early. Just as in the real world, "seats" at the RoundTable can fill up. It's very frustrating to arrive late and be told, "Sorry, that group is full."

In any kind of conference, formal or otherwise, use common sense and common courtesy. Just as on the bulletin boards, make sure your comments are in good taste and suitable for public consumption, both in formal conferences and in open conversation. In a private chat, anything goes—as long as the members agree on it. Should you find that someone is making offensive remarks in a private chat or is sending them to you, there are several things you can do. The first, obviously, is to ask that it be stopped. If you're in a private chat, leave. You can squelch /sends from a particular user by typing /squ USERNAME in Delphi or /squ JOB# in GEnie. To accomplish the same thing on CompuServe, simply select Ignore from the conference menu, as shown in Fig. 7-1, and click the name of the person you don't want to hear from.

It's polite to whisper

If you want to make a private comment to another member, you can. It's done differently on different services. On Delphi, simply use the following form: /send MEMBERNAME insert your comment here. Private messages are announced by a beep (or whatever your Mac's alert sound is) and are identified by two prompt marks instead of one, as shown in Fig. 7-2. Use the Instant Message box on America Online. On CompuServe, use the Talk button, as shown in Fig. 7-3.

On GEnie, you /send to the member's job #, instead of to the user's name. Each GEnie chat member is assigned a job number as he or she enters the Chat

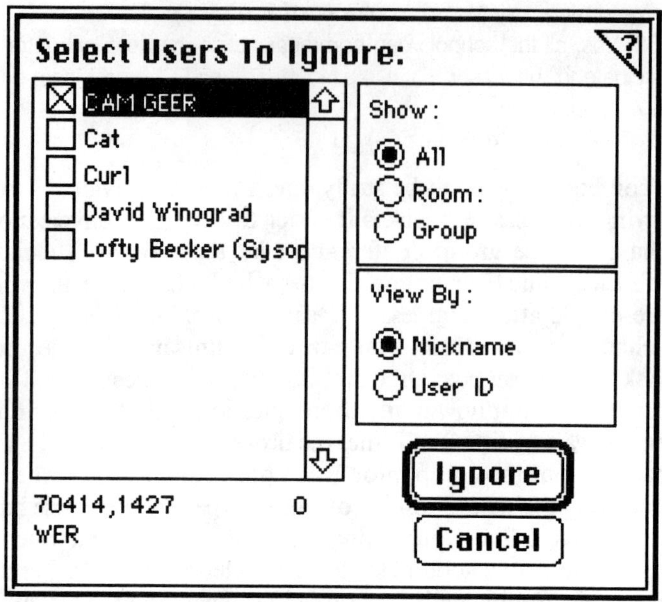

7-1 If someone's rude, wants to "hot chat" when you don't, or otherwise annoys you, just select Squelch to remove the unwanted messages from your screen.

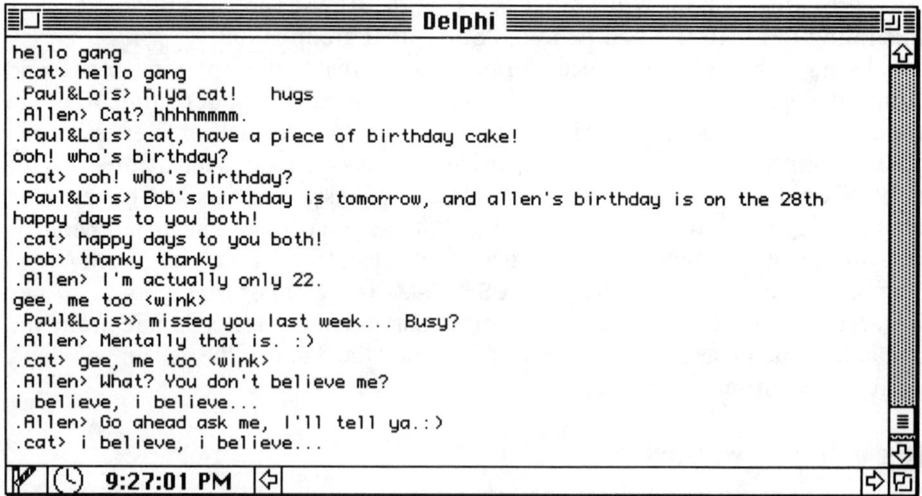

7-2 Note that all of the participants in this conference are using handles other than their regular usernames. Delphi indicates this with a period in front of the handle.

area. To get the job number of someone you want to send a message to, type /SHO HANDLE, using the "handle," or nickname, of the person about whom you want information.

7-3 When the button is clicked, a window labeled IncogNita will appear on the screen.

Informal chats

There's probably never a time when there's not someone online, looking for other people to talk to. When it's after midnight on the East Coast, it's prime time in California. West Coast nightowls often join forces with New England early birds. No matter when you sign on to any of the major services, you'll find several conversations going on. There are sometimes as many as 30 or more groups on Delphi and dozens on GEnie, AO, and CIS. BIX is less active for real-time conferencing because its cBIX area is open mostly in the evening hours.

Getting started in your first online conference is easy enough. Conference groups are identified by title, and when you enter the conference area, you'll see a list of groups. Some services list all groups, even those that are "private." Others list only the ones you can join. Delphi's Conference room, a corner of which is shown in Fig. 7-4, lists all the groups online at the time, including "published" groups from within forum areas. If, on Delphi, you try to join a private group, you'll get a message saying, "Sorry. You must be invited to join that group." CompuServe's private talks take place as "whispered" conversations within the conference room. Unlike the group conversations on public channels, private talks cannot be monitored.

That's a 10-4, good buddy

Some conferences are more like CB radio than others. On CompuServe, as on Delphi, AO, and GEnie, there are conference rooms within the forums. Talks in these areas tend to remain more or less focused on the topic at hand. Party animals

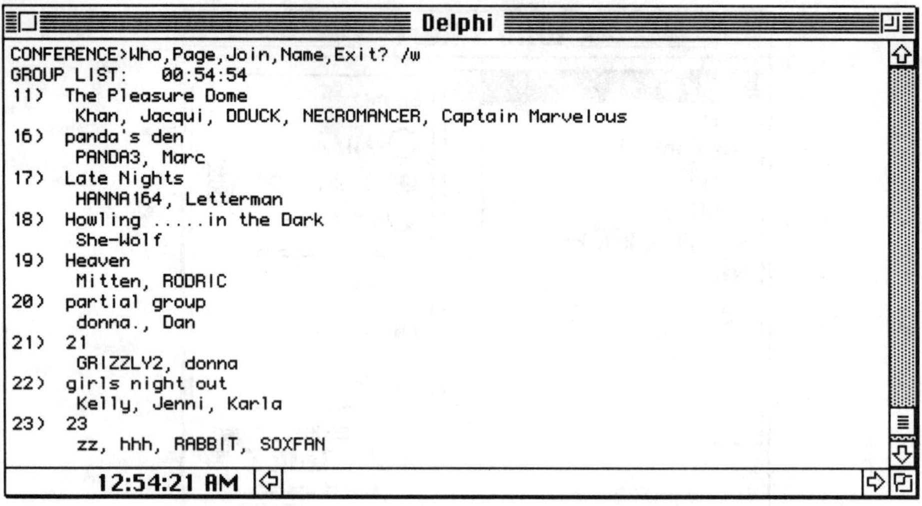

7-4 Names in capital letters are usernames, others are "handles," or aliases, used in the conference area. You can change your handle as often as you like on Delphi by typing **/N** and a new name.

and those who are interested in a more generalized conversation head for the CB Simulator or its equivalent on the other services. To understand how these areas function, I'll take a close look at a typical one.

CompuServe's CB Simulator is like a gigantic electronic cocktail party. You can drift from group to group until you find one that interests you, form your own group, talk or just listen, and even head to a quiet corner for a tête-à-tête with someone special. The CB Simulator has 36 channels on both the A and B bands. Some of these are for specific audiences (for example, Channel 1 is the Adult Channel, Channel 17 is the Teen Channel, and Channel 33 is the Alternate Lifestyles Channel). New CB-ers are encouraged to try Channel 2, the Newcomers Channel. You'll find busy channels on the A band at any time of the day. The B band tends to be much quieter during daylight but heats up in the evening with regularly scheduled trivia games and other group games, as well as groups with all kinds of interests. CompuServe Information Manager gives you a graph, shown here in Fig. 7-5, showing the members on each channel.

To reach the CB Simulator, either select it from the Services menu, type Command-G to bring up the Go box, and type CB, or double-click the Communications icon in the Browse window and select CB Simulator from the menu. These various routes are shown in Fig. 7-6. Then choose Access Band A or Access Band B and click Go. If you entered a CB handle in the CIM Preferences box, you'll use it automatically unless you decide to change it by selecting Change Handle and entering a different one. If you haven't already chosen a handle, you can do so by entering one in the box. Then, you'll see the CIM channel selector, shown in Fig. 7-7. Click on any of the channel numbers to select it. Not sure which to choose? Click the Status icon and you'll see the graph (shown in Fig. 7-5) showing which channels are busy.

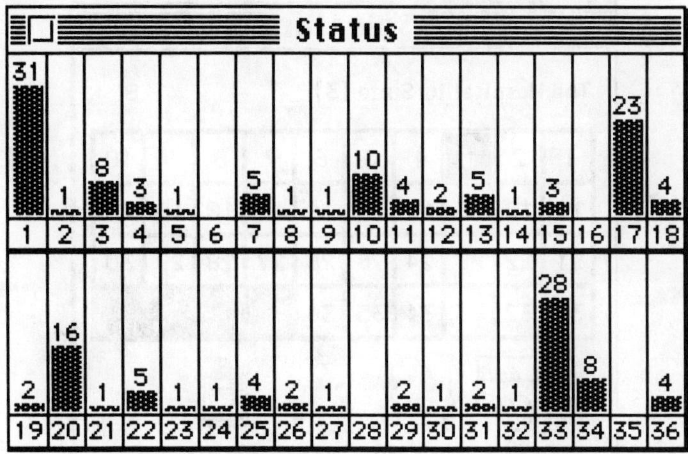

7-5 Some channels are very busy, others have only one user waiting for company.

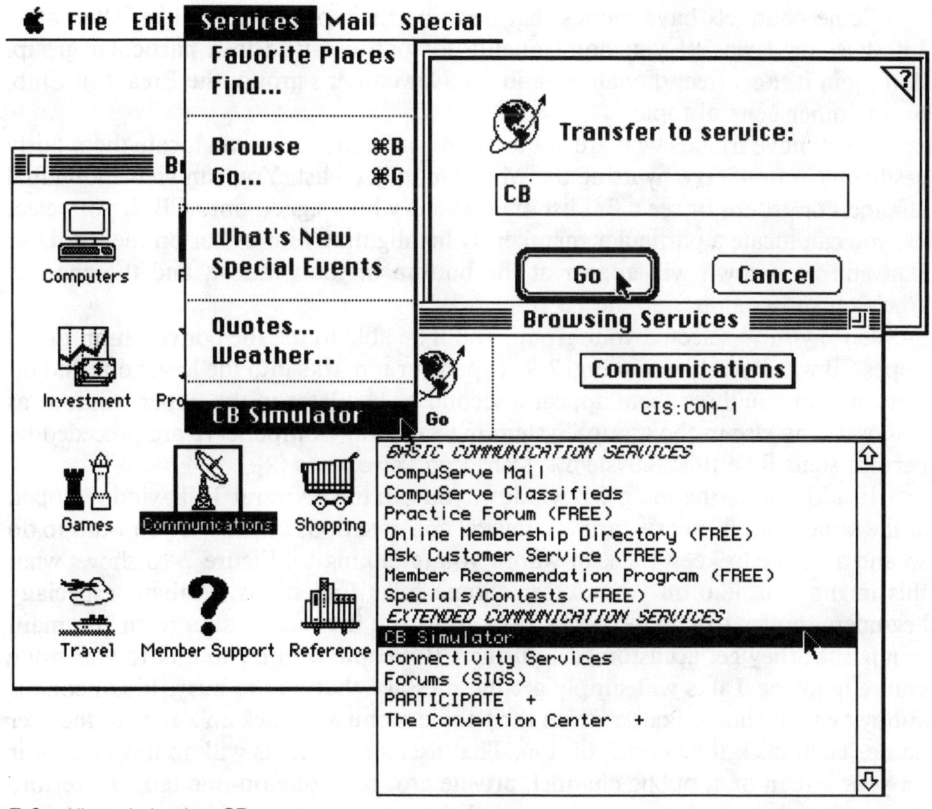

7-6 All roads lead to CB.

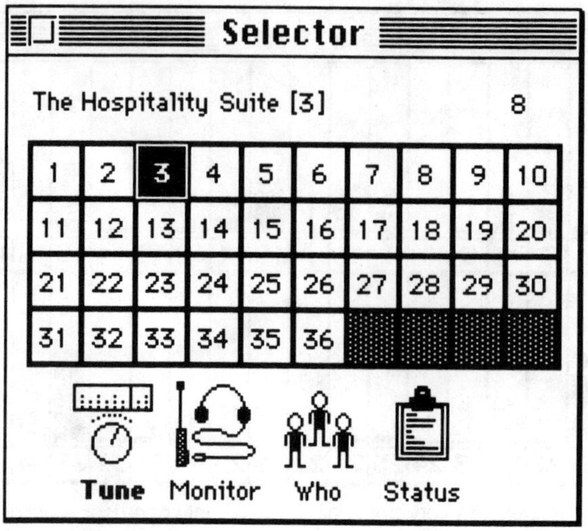

7-7 Click on any channel number to get information about it. Click the icons to see the status graph and who's on list and to monitor or join a selected channel.

Some channels have names that describe their participants, like Alternative Lifestyles or Teens. If you don't qualify for participation in a particular group, don't join it. Feel free, though, to join the Newcomer's group, the Breakfast Club, or any other general topic.

If you have friends who are apt to be in conference, you can locate them fairly easily on CompuServe by using the Who icon to get a list. You can view individual channels or groups or see a full list of everyone who's signed onto CB. If you select All, you can locate a particular member by highlighting him or her on the list. User ID# and hometown will appear at the bottom of the window, and the channel s/he's on shows alongside the ID (Fig. 7-8).

Once you've selected your group, you'll be able to see the conversation in the upper CB window, shown in Fig. 7-9. Type your remarks into the lower one and hit Return, and you'll see them appear a second or two later in the upper window, as will everyone else in the group. System messages on CompuServe are preceded by percent signs, like this: %System%: Monitoring Newcomers [2].

In addition to the main CB window, you can have several Talk windows open at the same time. You can carry on several conversations at once, if you want to do so and are able to keep track of whom you're talking to. Figure 7-10 shows what this might look like on your screen. Some folks find it easy. Others, especially beginners, prefer to choose Ignore Talks from the menu and stick with the main group until they get accustomed to using CB. People who try to talk to you while you're Ignoring Talks will simply get the message that you're busy. If someone is annoying you, choose Squelch from the People menu and click an X next to the user name. Then click the Squelch button. That user's comments will no longer appear on your screen on a public channel, private group, or one-on-one talk. To restore the squelched person's messages again, click to remove the X. You can squelch as

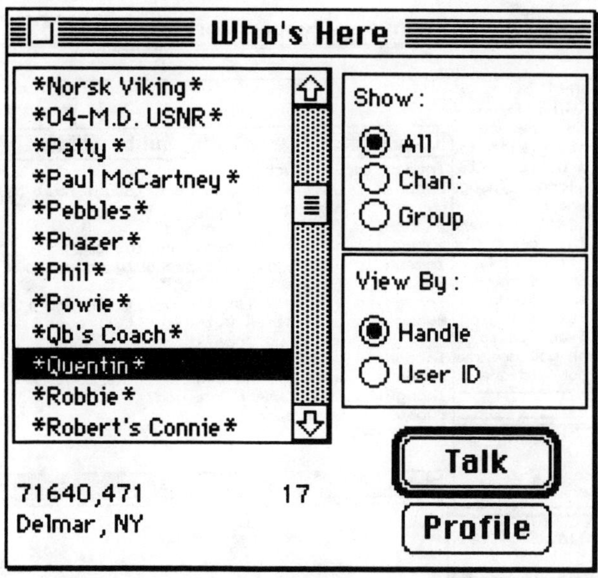

7-8 Some members like to "dress up" their handles with asterisks or other devices.

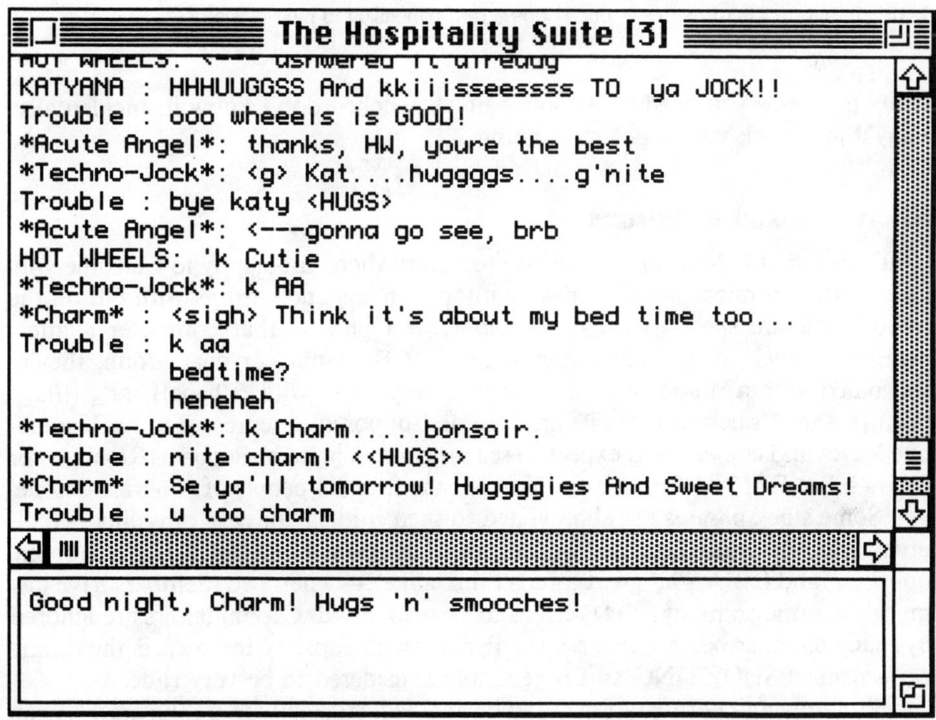

7-9 CompuServe's Hospitality Suite is Channel 3.

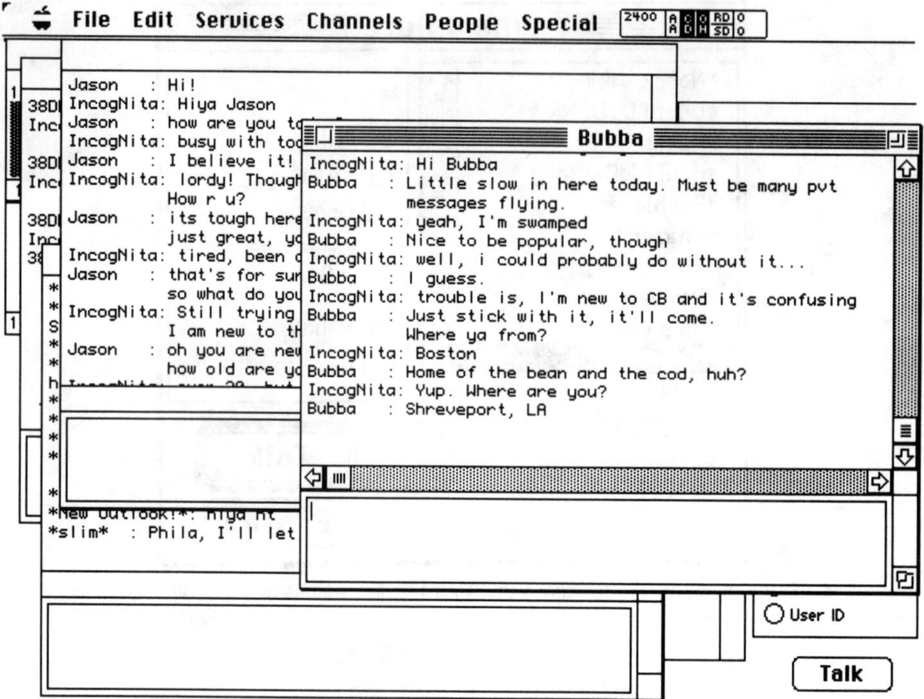

7-10 Talking to lots of people at once adds a new dimension to multi-tasking.

many people as you need to. People being squelched don't know it, incidentally. They'll just think you're not responding.

Shorthand and emoticons

You'll find that CB-ers, like people online everywhere, are happy to welcome you. Of course, you might get greetings you don't understand. Just as with CB on the radio, there are special sayings and shorthand phrases that computer chatters "speak" to each other. When friends join a CB channel or chat group, they're welcomed with a round of Hi or Hiya and very often with {{{hugs}}} or {{{{{huggers}}}}} and ***smooches***. The brackets are supposed to represent arms. If someone leaves and comes back, expect to see re-hi and Ruggies or Ruggers (Re-hugs), or just re's. See Fig. 7-11 for an example from the friendly people of America Online.

Some stock phrases are abbreviated to their initials, for ease of typing. You'll often hear (or see) BTW, for "by the way;" IMO, or IMHO, for "in my humble opinion," and GMTA, for "great minds think alike"—when two members have just made the same comment. O I C needs to be read aloud. Capital letters are ignored by many users, as being unnecessary. Typing in all caps, by the way, is the online equivalent of SHOUTING and is generally considered to be very rude.

Profanity and pornography are to be avoided, especially in public areas. Aside from being rude, it will get you thrown off some services. America Online is said to

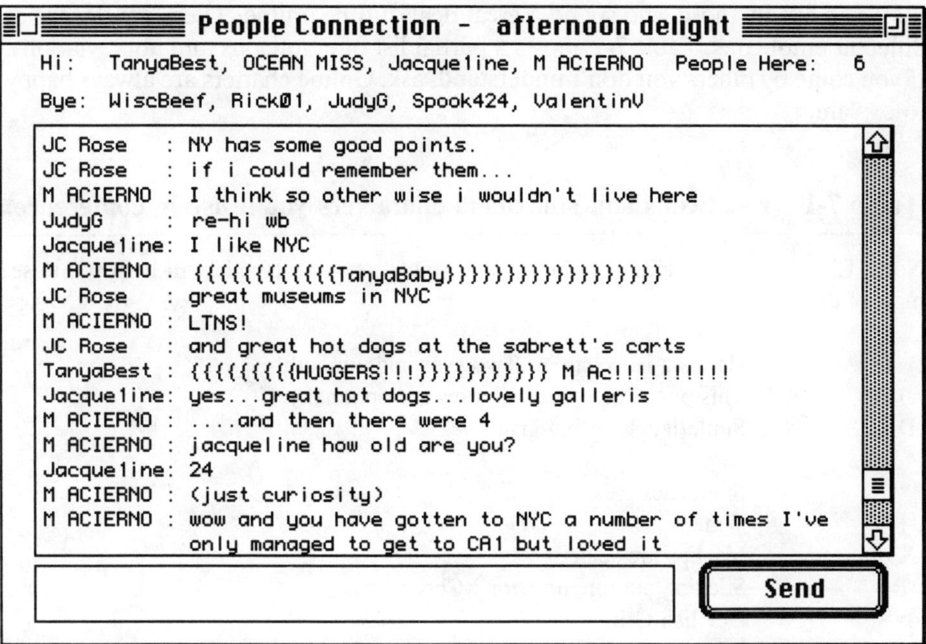

7-11 In a formal conference, unlike this one, people wouldn't be greeted as they came or left.

have anonymous helpers monitoring public conference areas in response to a number of complaints to the service about unnecessarily explicit language and user and group names. AO refers to these as Terms of Service violations, or TOSs. Other services have similar provisions for dealing with members whose public behavior is improper.

Spelling and typos are politely ignored, especially on text services such as Delphi where correcting them is difficult. Some typos even become favorite expressions, like "opps" for "oops" or "No sprots, No sports" in Delphi's Trivia game. If you come up with something you think might be incomprehensible, it's acceptable to correct just the word(s) that got mangled, as in the following exchange:

.Spook> It's been kinda clod and strimy all week.
.Cat> Huh?
.Spook> er, cold and stormy :-)

The punctuation at the end of the last line above isn't a mistake. It's an *emoticon*, a little ASCII graphic symbol that shows emotion. Tip your head to the left if you don't immediately see the smiling face. Online conversations are frequently punctuated with emoticons because the participants can't see each other and therefore can't read expressions or body language. Adding a wink or a grin to a remark can help convey the same shades of meaning as spoken dialog and takes the sting out of many exchanges that could otherwise be read as arguments. You'll also find these helpful symbols on message boards, in E-mail, and even possibly in paper mail sent out by those who spend a great deal of time online. There are dozens of different emoticons. Table 7-1 shows a partial list of emoticons and abbreviations. If you come by others you don't understand, ask. Online chatters are always happy to explain.

Table 7-1 Emoticons and shorthand characters you'll use in conference.

Note: Tilting your head to the left or turning your screen on its side will help you to see most of the shorthands.

<table>
<tr><td>:)</td><td>Here's a basic smile: Two eyes and a mouth!</td></tr>
<tr><td>:-)</td><td>This one adds a nose. (Noses are optional.)</td></tr>
<tr><td>:D</td><td>Smile/laughing/big grin</td></tr>
<tr><td>:*</td><td>Kiss</td></tr>
<tr><td>**</td><td>Smooches</td></tr>
<tr><td>;-)</td><td>Wink</td></tr>
<tr><td>:X</td><td>My lips are sealed</td></tr>
<tr><td>:-P</td><td>Sticking out tongue/Bronx Cheer</td></tr>
<tr><td>:></td><td>Devilish Grin</td></tr>
<tr><td>:I</td><td>Bored</td></tr>
<tr><td>:-#</td><td>Wears Braces</td></tr>
<tr><td>B)</td><td>Wearing My Shades</td></tr>
<tr><td>B-)></td><td>Beatnik</td></tr>
<tr><td>:-(</td><td>Frown</td></tr>
<tr><td>:-C</td><td>Really Bummed Out</td></tr>
<tr><td>:'(</td><td>Crying</td></tr>
<tr><td>:')</td><td>Tears of joy</td></tr>
<tr><td>O:)</td><td>Angel</td></tr>
<tr><td>}:></td><td>Devil</td></tr>
<tr><td>=:-O</td><td>Yikes!</td></tr>
<tr><td>:-!</td><td>Foot In Mouth</td></tr>
<tr><td>:-W</td><td>Speak With Forked Tongue</td></tr>
<tr><td>:-$</td><td>Put Your Money Where Your Mouth Is</td></tr>
<tr><td>O:-)</td><td>I'm Innocent</td></tr>
<tr><td>%-/</td><td>I'm Hungover</td></tr>
<tr><td><:-)</td><td>I'm a Dunce</td></tr>
<tr><td>C:-)</td><td>I'm An Egghead</td></tr>
<tr><td>*<:*)S</td><td>I'm a Bozo</td></tr>
<tr><td>8:-)</td><td>I'm a Little Girl</td></tr>
<tr><td>:\/</td><td>I'm a Duck</td></tr>
<tr><td>:-@</td><td>I Swear</td></tr>
<tr><td>d:-)</td><td>Baseball Fan</td></tr>
<tr><td>9:-)</td><td>I'm a Baseball Catcher</td></tr>
<tr><td>:-|</td><td>I Can Play The Harmonica</td></tr>
<tr><td>%-|</td><td>Been Working All Night</td></tr>
</table>

Table 7-1 Continued

::-)	Wears Glasses
:-{)	Has A Mustache
[:-)	Wearing A Walkman
}:-(	Bull Headed
:c)	Pig Headed
:-[	Vampire
:-&	Tongue Tied
C|:-=	Charlie Chaplin
=|:-)=	Abe Lincoln
:_(	Vincent Van Gogh
C=:-)	Chef
*<:-)	Santa Claus
:-O	Mr. Bill
:*)	Ed McMahon
#:-)	Don King
:-))	Double Chin
:-7	Smokes A Pipe
C:#	Football Player
:-)=---	Man With Tie
:-)8	Man With Bow Tie
P-)	Pirate
:-b	sticking out tongue
:-p	sticking out tongue to someone else
(^:B	Mickey Mouse (facing other way)
:-%	Tongue Tied
:-+	Tasted alum!
<oo>	Racoon
[:-)	Flattop (or Rapper)
X:)	Bow in hair / Little girl
:<>)	Pinochio
}-|	Asleep
}-O	Snoring
*:-)	Flower in hair
:-y	Smoking cigarette
{}	A hug
[])	A mug (beer or coffee)
--<---@	A Rose
akf	away from keyboard
bak	back at keyboard
bbl	be back later
brb	be right back
cul8r	See You Later

Table 7-1 Continued

gmta	Great Minds Think Alike
IMHO	In my humble opinion
LOL	Laughing Out Loud
OTF	On The Floor (laughing)
ROTF	Rolling On The Floor
ROFLMAO	Roling on Floor Laughing My A** Off
ROFLWTIME	Rolling On Floor Laughing With Tears in My Eyes
ttfn	ta-ta for now!
WB	welcome back
wtg	Way to Go

The people you meet online

A great many friendships have arisen from online meetings. Obviously, everyone online has at least one common denominator—they all use computers. Beyond that, though, there's a tremendous diversity of interests and experience. On a typical afternoon in Delphi, I've found teenagers helping each other with homework, three moms exchanging tips on raising toddlers, several couples in private chats, a group discussing the Red Sox, and a half dozen people trying for high scores in Delphi's Scramble word game. You're quite likely to encounter famous and not-so-famous writers, especially in Delphi's Science Fiction SIG and in the Writer's groups on BIX and GEnie.

There are quite a few folks online who enjoy the world of fantasy. Some of them are found in areas such as the Dragon Rampant Inn or in groups with names like Forest Glen or Planet of the Mutant Cephalopods. Dungeons and Dragons players abound online, and role-playing games attract many participants, especially on AO and GEnie. Delphi's Games forum is another good place to find others who enjoy fantasy and role-playing games, as is the Games area on CIS.

Other kinds of people, with fantasies of a somewhat different sort, can be found online in groups called Girls' Locker Room or Gay Men's Hot Tub. There is a good deal of what's known online as "hot chat" on some services, especially on CompuServe. If you don't want to participate in it, as many people do not, simply ignore invitations or squelch anyone who's a pest. If you do, a further word of warning might be in order. The news media have reported several instances of sex crimes in which the perpetrator first met the victim online. Some of these, unfortunately, involved young boys and girls as the victims. Parents need to be very careful about warning children that strangers they meet online are still strangers and should not be trusted.

Unfortunately, telecommunications can be an anonymous (and even dangerous) medium, especially on public bulletin boards where real names and addresses might not be required, or where phony ones might be entered. Commercial services that require a real name and address and/or credit card information for billing purposes might be somewhat safer in that respect, but it's still a good idea to be cautious.

A few people tend to exaggerate themselves online. Their achievements are greater, they're taller, thinner, younger, older, wealthier, or less married than in "real" life. Occasionally, you'll find someone who pretends to be *very* different than he is. The classic example of this was reported in the CompuServe magazine a year or so ago. CB Hostess CupCake provided online advice and support to "Pretty and Pregnant" for a full nine months, before learning that "P&P," being male, was neither. A second example, on another service, was the truck driver who claimed to be a teenage girl and carried on torrid online romances with several young men before admitting his gender.

On a happier note, many online friendships do go on to be offline friendships too, and more than a few end up with wedding bells. Delphi has had several weddings within the past year, and we know of at least one Delphi baby; Leo, born recently to FENWAY and PYEWACKET. AO's Romance Connection has a whole folder full of success stories called Happy Endings. Groups often plan get-togethers, pot-luck dinners, and other social events, especially when some major event like MacWorld or COMDEX or a Science Fiction Convention brings lots of people to the same area. Cupcake's CB Society column on CompuServe lists upcoming get-togethers as well as engagements and wedding and birth announcements for CIS members and their families.

Special interest groups

In addition to the main conference area or CB simulator, there are conference rooms within the forums on most services. Here, you'll find people gathering to talk about whatever the topic at hand might be. Whether it's religion, politics, scuba, or any of a hundred other topics, conversations are lively and often wide ranging. Figure 7-12 shows a brief excerpt from a conference in the Delphi Science Fiction SIG. Many SIGs have regularly scheduled weekly conferences. Some have several conferences during the week on different aspects of their topic. To give but one example of the kinds of conferences you might find, Delphi's Writers Group has a Monday night Writing Workshop, a Wednesday Poetry Conference, and a Thursday night General Discussion. Other SIGs often feature guest speakers or moderated discussions on specific topics. Once you become a member of one or more forums, you can expect to get mail from the forum leaders announcing upcoming conference events. Members can also page others into a chat in the forum conference room at any time. Most services let you find out which other forum members are online by typing a simple command like /w, or clicking on "who's here" from within the forum.

Sound effects

America Online allows you add another dimension to your online chats. AO users can punctuate their conversations with sound effects. While in a chat or conference room, you can "broadcast" sounds to other users who are in the same room. The

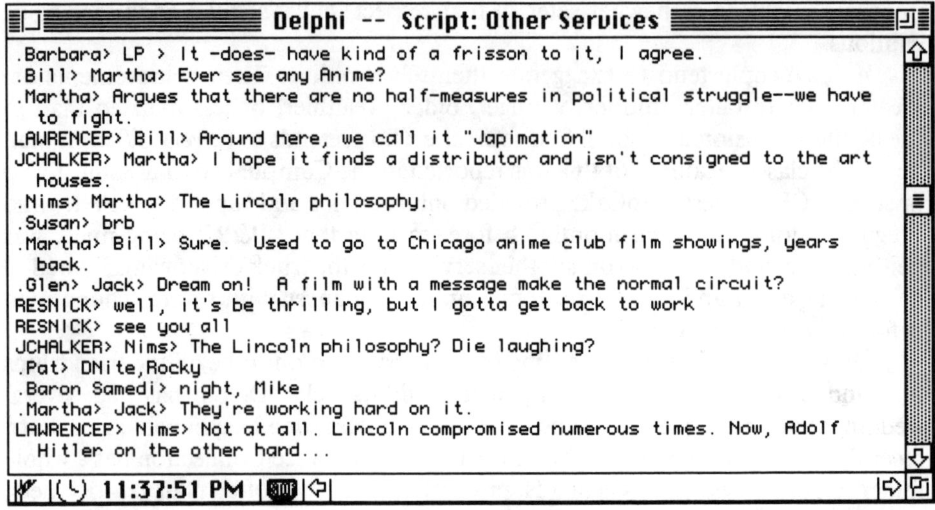

7-12 The Science Fiction SIG attracts both readers and writers of that genre. Mike RESNICK and Jack CHALKER are both well-known novelists and frequent visitors to the forum.

way this works is that the sound itself is not sent, but rather a request to play the sound is sent, because the digitized sounds themselves are typically too long to be transmitted. If a user has the requested sound available on his or her disk, it is then played. For a sound to be heard, it must reside as a named "SND" resource on the user's disk in a file visible to America Online. There are two easy ways to make "SND" resources available:

- Save all sounds to the America Online file named "Online.sounds."
- Or save your sounds in a file called "Online One," or "Online Two," or "Online Three" in the folder entitled "Online Files."

Then, they'll automatically be opened at the beginning of the session, so the "SND" resources will be available. Note that the file "Online Two" will only be opened if "Online One" is found, and "Online Three" will only be opened if both "Online One" and "Online Two" are found.

Sending a sound in a chat room is easy. Choose the "Get Sound" option from the People menu. You'll see a list of the sounds available, as shown here in Fig. 7-13. Point to the one you want to broadcast. To hear the sound first, choose "Play." If you choose "OK," the sound command will be transferred into the input box in the chat window. If you know the name of the sound you want to send, you can also type the sound command into the input field manually, such as in this example (including brackets): {S <Cuckoo>}. There can be no space between "{" and "S" but there must be a space after the "S"; be sure to end with a "}". Remember, a sound will be heard by you and other chat room members who:

- are using System version 5.0 or later.
- have a "SND" resource available with the correct name.

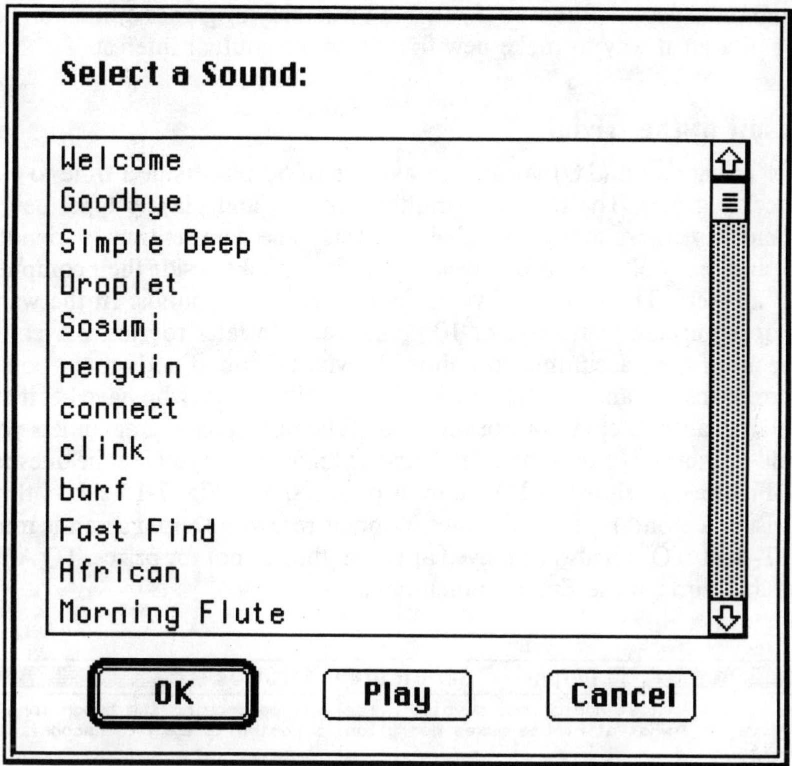

7-13 Only the sound resources (SND) currently available are shown in the box. You might have other sound files that America Online can't use.

- Have Chat Sounds enabled (in other words, they haven't chosen to use their Preferences options to disable their ability to hear chat sounds).

When you send a sound, instead of words after your name in the scrolling conversation, there will be a picture of a little loudspeaker, followed by the name of the sound. Even if other chat members don't have the sound installed, they'll know you sent one. You can find lots of interesting sound files to download in the Music and Sound Special Interest Forum. Swap your favorite sounds with your online friends, and post new ones you create in the Forum libraries for others to try out.

A time to play

Many online service users will tell you that real-time games are one of their favorite reasons for going online. Trivia fans are sure to enjoy the many different kinds of trivia games online. Poker players can always find a game. Best of all for online game addicts, some services award prizes of one or more free online hours to the winners. Others will give you a T-shirt or other goodies for winning a game. Sometimes all you get is the satisfaction of winning or the thrill of having your name and score posted. But even if you don't win, playing games online can be a lot of fun and a great way to make new friends with a mutual interest.

In pursuit of the trivial

Delphi's Trivia Quest (TQ) attracts an average of 50 players at a time to each of three weekly games. The format is multiple choice, and players type their comments and wisecracks along with their answers. The competition is friendly but intense, and many players keep a stack of reference books beside their computers to look up answers. The game is divided into six different rounds. In the warm-up round, questions are worth five or 10 points each. In later rounds, players wager some or all of their accumulated points. A pyramid round adds more points for each correct answer, and the "second life" round gives those who have bet it all and lost it all a chance to climb out of the cellar. The final question again lets you bet some, all, or none of your points. Bets must be made *before* you see the question, of course. Figure 7-14 shows a TQ game in progress, and Fig. 7-15 shows the final standings for a monthly series of games. Winners receive a Delphi ceramic mug or a Delphi T-shirt. TQ can also be played anytime, though not for prizes. TQ Anytime is accessible through the Entertainment area.

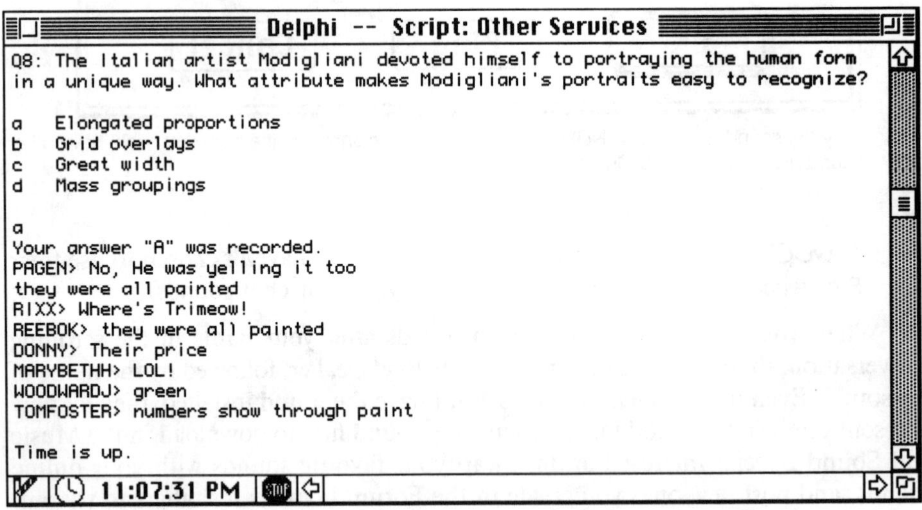

7-14 Delphi's Trivia Quest is played on Sunday, Monday, and Wednesday nights.

Other popular Delphi real-time games include Flip-it, an online version of Othello; Scramble, a word game somewhat like Boggle; and poker. All of these can be played either against the computer or against other live players. Scramble games are part of the fun in the Conference area, as well as the Entertainment area.

Scramble players vie for high scores and have made up their own rules for several variations on the basic game, which is to make as many unique words as possible from the 16 letters provided on the Scramble board. Letters need not be

Delphi

Here are the overall standings after 14 games

Player (Wins)	Gms	Pts	Player	Gms	Pts	Player	Gms	Pts
SVENSKO	13	11415	MAYBONNE	4	1600	FACEMAN	7	70
PAGEN(2)	13	9309	RITSUKO	11	1588	PKANE	7	70
TOMFOSTER(2)	12	8654	MARRIOTT	1	1482	DLWEYERS	6	60
BILLP49(1)	11	7034	ROBMERRITT	4	1320	MC_ZIGGY	6	60
JDL(1)	12	6583	ACE251	11	1300	MRGOOD	6	60
MARYBETHH	10	6044	LOUFRIESE	5	1300	ROBYNMILLER	6	60
HARRYH	13	4767	REEBOK	1	1260	2YS	5	50
HANZ(1)	5	4755	GAMERBOB	11	1220	DPBSMITH	5	50
MIKEDAL(1)	8	4539	WULFGARD	1	1210	GEATLEY	5	50
CHILLER	13	4386	JLTSKAY	10	920	JSB	5	50
JACQUID	12	4354	MNSCOTT	6	914	XQSME	5	50
SHULTZIE	10	4342	DEBE	2	892	0378	4	40
CLHEALY(1)	10	4256	SLIGHTLY	2	850	0816	4	40
LOGOT2(1)	3	3648	ECR	3	836	GIGGLES1	4	40

Press RETURN for more...

4:18:20 PM

7-15 Winners of individual games have numbers in parentheses after their names showing how many games they've won for the month. The top-ranked player won no games but finished in second place every time!

adjacent, as they must in Boggle, but can only be used with the same frequency as they appear on the board. Word score points according to their length, with longer words scoring more points. A three-letter word is worth 9 points, five letters is good for 25 points, eight letters gives you 64 points, and so on. A game is shown in Fig. 7-16.

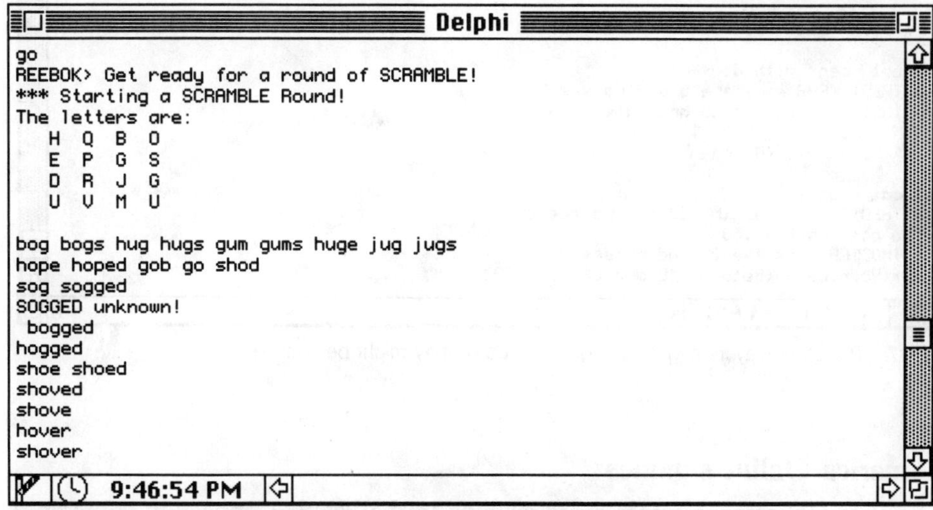

Delphi

```
go
REEBOK> Get ready for a round of SCRAMBLE!
*** Starting a SCRAMBLE Round!
The letters are:
   H  Q  B  O
   E  P  G  S
   D  R  J  G
   U  V  M  U

bog bogs hug hugs gum gums huge jug jugs
hope hoped gob go shod
sog sogged
SOGGED unknown!
 bogged
hogged
shoe shoed
shoved
shove
hover
shover
```

9:46:54 PM

7-16 Scramble can be played solitaire, as here, or by a group of people. If you're playing against opponents, you'll be told when they've already used your words.

The top scores are posted and cleared every few days. Scores close to 2,000 points are not unusual for some players who type very fast and have spent many hours in practice. Because it's hard to outscore these "experts," some Scramble players opt for their own versions of the game, in which the winner constructs the single longest word, rather than the most words or points. In another variation, players must create entire sentences out of the letters available. There's no way to score these games. They're just for fun.

Delphi's Poker parlor offers continuous play against live opponents and a cadre of poker-playing robots, all named after "Max the Vax," Delphi's original computer. Five different games are available: straight poker, 5-card and 7-card stud, draw poker, and Texas Hold 'em. Your initial bankroll is 1,000 chips, and Delphi keeps a running total of your wins and losses. Every Thursday night, there's a "live-players only" tournament, with a prize for the player furthest ahead at the end of the evening. There are several tables, each with different stakes. Novice Nook and Learner's Lair are for the beginner or timid player. Party Place and Big Bucks are for those with more confidence in their poker ability, and Sky Limits is for the high-roller. Figure 7-17 shows a hand of draw poker in progress. Betting is accomplished by simply typing in the appropriate number, or C for Check, S for See, or F for Fold. To draw new cards in 5-card stud, type the numbers of the cards to throw away, such as 5d, 4h, jc, to replace the five of Diamonds, four of Hearts, and Jack of Clubs.

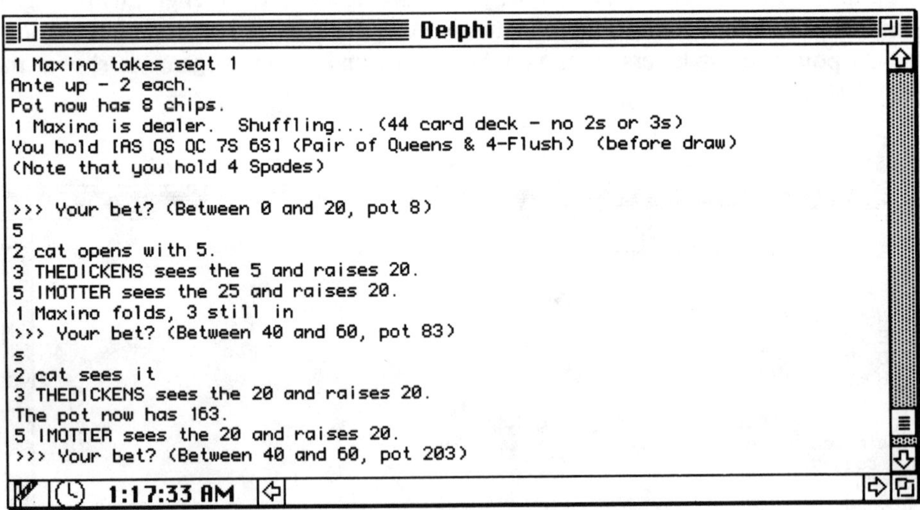

7-17 The other players might have good cards or they might be bluffing.

America Online's games

America Online runs games every evening in the People Connection conference area and several times each week in the Center Stage Auditorium. Center Stage games are more formalized than the conference area games. Audience members are chosen at random to come up on stage and play the game. Some games let the entire audience play opening rounds to determine who competes in a final round. Rules are posted in a folder in the Center Stage Area for such games as Scrambled Eggs, Lucky 7, Batter Up, MADvertising, and C'Mon Down (and Guess the Price).

Center Stage games assign each member to an interactive communications "row" upon entering Center Stage. Rows can accommodate between four and eight members. The minimum and maximum numbers are set by the emcees, depending on the event taking place. Members can "row hop" in order to chat with other members in other rows. You can also create your own row by using the Center Stage commands. You can see a listing of who's in each row by choosing it from the menu.

During Center Stage game shows, the audience can interact with the hosts on-stage on use of the Ask A Question feature. The question and comment features are also used to interact with guests at special events, allowing members to send questions or comments to the guest speakers. All input sent by either question or comment functions is received in the order sent. For that reason there might be a delay until an item you sent is received. (The Make A Comment queue isn't monitored or used for the purpose of accepting audience input at game shows.) The game show hosts cannot see text typed by members in the audience unless the stage "mikes" are turned "on" in your "row," so feel free to say what you wish to the other people in your row.

When an item is received by the game show hosts, it can't be seen by everyone in Center Stage until the hosts "broadcast" it. Items that are incomplete, irrelevant to the event, or duplicates of existing items are deleted without being broadcast. America Online's "Terms of Service" apply to all events held in the Center Stage Auditorium.

Two special functions are used only during certain types of events. The Make A Bid feature is utilized for placing bids at events such as Auctions, Baseball Card Auctions, etc. Bids will not be accepted by the system unless an event that utilizes that feature is taking place. The Polling feature is used to cast your vote at events that call for polling as part of the event. Votes cannot be cast unless the event taking place calls for polling.

Informal conference area games are hosted by AO members who volunteer to run them in return for free time online. Rules vary in these games, but game leaders are always glad to explain them or Instant Message them to you. Most games operate like the trivia game shown in Fig. 7-18. After the leader asks a question, members have about 30 seconds to shout out the correct answer. All those who manage to get it in before the "virtual" buzzer, earn a point. If only one person gets it right, s/he gets three points or more, depending on the game. While it's possible to watch what the first person types as an answer and repeat it within the allotted time, it's cheating. A game helper tallies the points after each question and announces totals at the midpoint and end of the game. To become a game host or helper and get free online time in return, start by getting thoroughly familiar with the game rules. Then ask the service for information about starting a game of your own.

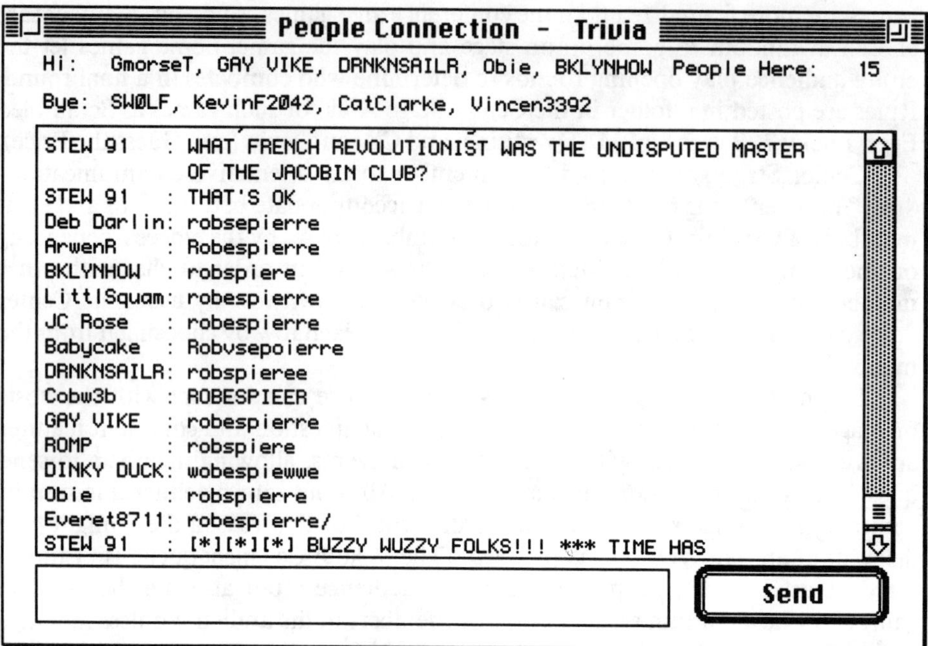

7-18 Looks like everybody knew this one.

Online trivia games are also featured on CompuServe's CB Simulator, on the B channels, and on GEnie. An interesting wrinkle on GEnie's Entertainment board lets you play scheduled trivia games against live players at terminal-equipped bars across the US. Points thus earned can be used to "purchase" merchandise prizes.

CompuServe also offers multi-player real-time games, including British Legends, a Dungeons-and-Dragons-type adventure, and Island of Kesmai, another popular adventure game, which takes you through the catacombs of Kesmai in search of adventure, treasure, and demons with which to do battle.

In addition to adventures, there are war games, simulations, including the popular Air Traffic Controller, and parlor and trivia games. There's even an online gaming lobby where members can meet and challenge each other at any of a dozen or more different commercial games, including Faces, Flight Simulator, Battle Chess, and many more, all at reduced connect time rates.

CompuServe's real-time game, You Guessed It!, is a lot of fun to play. Games begin every 15 minutes and are hosted by the effervescent Bob Illuminati. The format is like that of TV's Family Feud. Don't be surprised if the stage hands wander through, making jokes, or if the cameraman argues with the answers to the questions. It's all part of the fun, as two teams of up to five players try to guess audience responses to all sorts of questions. Winning team members earn bonus points, which add up to free online hours. The game is easy and interesting but requires a minimum of two live players. If you can't find an opponent, putting your name on the Challenge Board notifies other would-be players that you're available. Figure 7-19 shows a scene from a game of You Guessed It!. Though questions

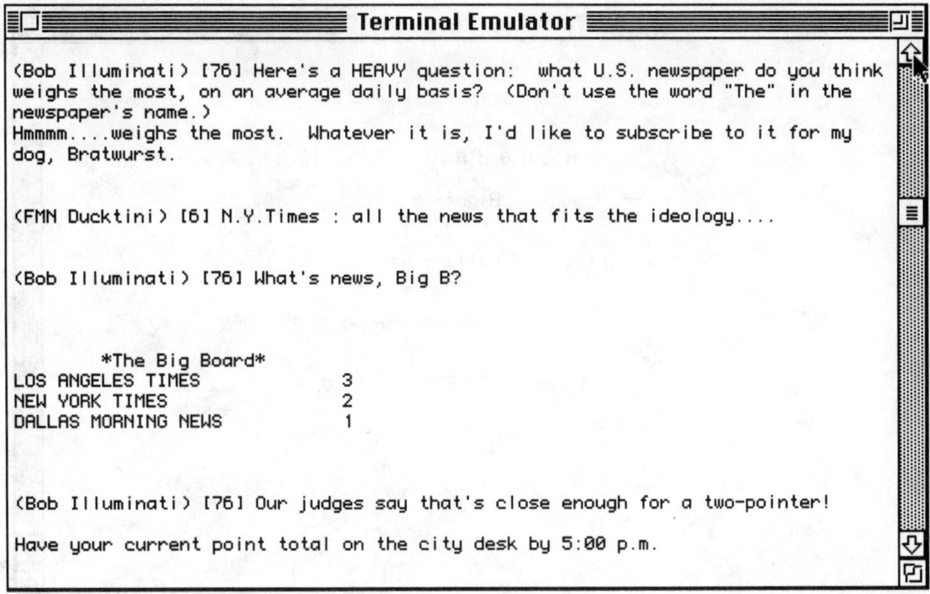

7-19 Host Bob Illuminati is known for his "virtually" awful jokes.

be repeated, the percentage of various responses changes each time, so games are never the same. You can also be in the "audience" for a game by typing /VIEW instead of /PLAY. Most of CompuServe's games are played in Terminal Emulation mode, so text gaming is preferred, while graphics are limited to the relatively unimaginative kind that can be drawn with ASCII characters. Figure 7-20 shows an example.

Prodigy games

Although Prodigy isn't an interactive service, at least in the sense that you can't interact with other people online in real time, it does have an interesting selection of games that you can play against its computer and against other players. For many users, the most exciting Prodigy game is its version of the popular sport known as fantasy-league, or rotisserie baseball. Prodigy's game, Baseball Manager, or BBM for short, carries a hefty surcharge, $119.95 for Classic BBM and $59.95 for the Lightning version, a quicker but more limited game. Figure 7-21 shows the "sports page," your daily introduction to your team's progress.

Classic BBM lets you draft your team of 28 players, set lineups, pitcher rotation, and relief pitcher priorities, and make trade and free agent deals. Figure 7-22 shows BBM's menus and your options. Your team is entered in a league against others. Every night during the 162-game baseball season, Prodigy's computers match your players against their real game performances, add up all the stats, and provide a final score for each team, plus a game summary and in-depth statistics. League standings are revised after every round of games, and your team's performance appears on the sports pages when you sign on. At the end of the

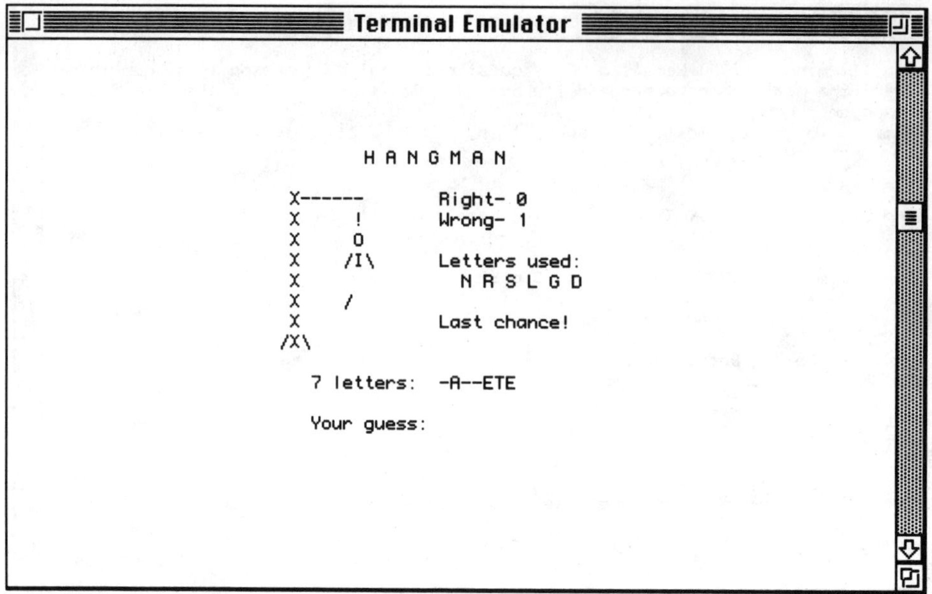

7-20 Not very exciting stuff for the Nintendo generation.

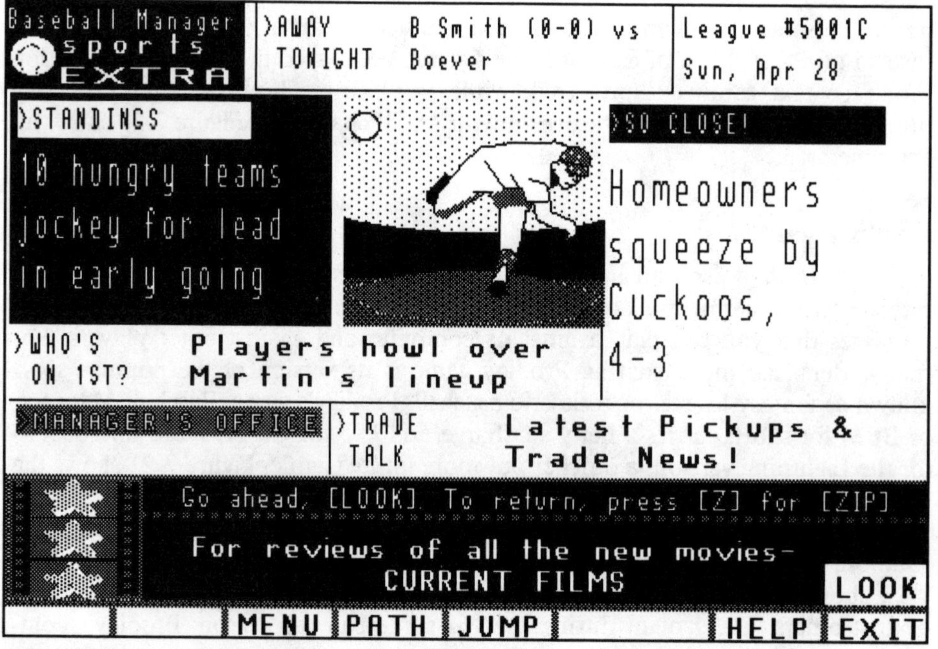

7-21 Clicking on any headline takes you to that section of the game.

7-22 You can make new decisions every day or set up your roster at the beginning of the season and see what happens.

regular season, those teams who lead their leagues will vie for first in the championship playoffs.

Lightning BBM is similar to the Classic game, but it's shorter. It uses a 54-game format. All else is the same, except that the lineup can't be changed from one game to the next. Your team always bats in the same order. To join Baseball Manager, you must sign up online. The game will be added to your monthly bill.

Prodigy also makes a point of introducing games on timely topics. The Presidential elections are at hand as this chapter is being written. Prodigy has responded with a political game called The Next President. A screen from the game is shown in Fig. 7-23. Players choose one of eight candidates to back and can advise their candidate on matters of position and strategy. A recent Movie Trivia game was tied into the Academy Awards, and other games appear around holidays or along with seasonal sports and activities.

In addition to these adult games, Prodigy's more standard game offerings include weekly episodes of detective work, tracking the kids' favorite adventuress, Carmen Sandiego. Figure 7-24 shows a scene from the game, as we track one of Carmen's henchpersons across Central America. There's also FITB (Fill In The Blanks), a Hangman-type game; Boxes, a version of Othello that can be played against the computer or by two players (both using the same computer); and Thinker, a MasterMind clone that requires you to guess four colors in correct order, out of a possible six. It's harder than it sounds. MadMaze is one of Prodigy's oldest games, but it's still popular. To play, you work your way through a maze,

7-23 Can you help your candidate win in the primaries?

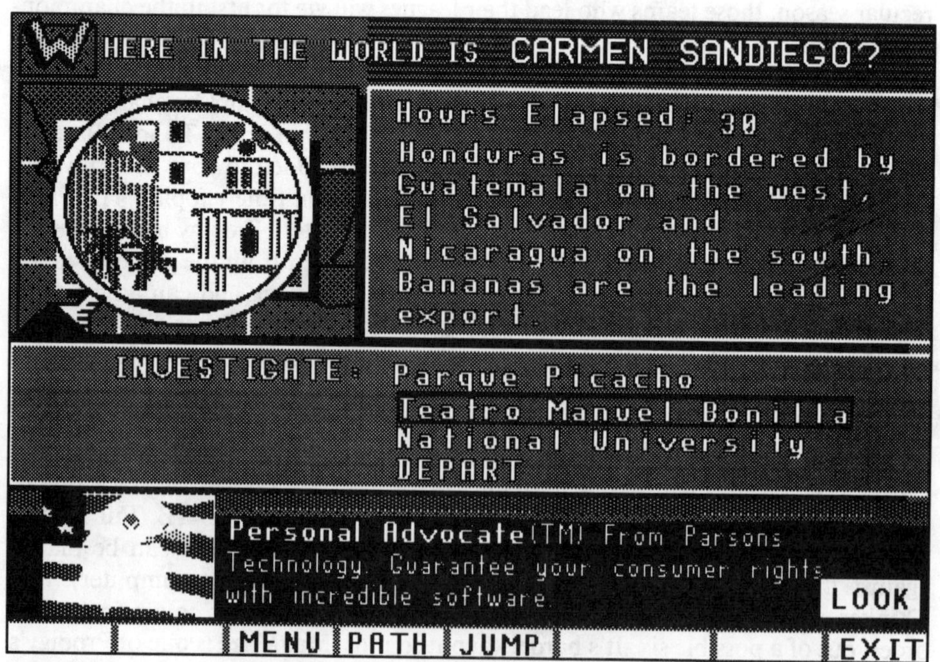

7-24 The Carmen Sandiego game has a new adventure every week.

occasionally encountering people, wizards, trolls, and the like who may or may not help you in your quest. Also popular, and very competitive, is Prodigy's Trivia challenge, called GUTS. This is trivia with a time limit. Players are given multiple choice questions, one at a time. Each question is worth an increasing number of points, but time spent looking up the answer counts against you. One wrong answer erases all the points you've earned and puts you out of the game for the rest of the week. You can, however, quit while you're ahead.

Summary

Online conferences are a good deal like CB radio. All are welcome to join in, and most chats are very informal. Formal conferences, like dinners at the State Department, use their own kind of protocol, basically rules of etiquette that assure that guest speakers don't get interrupted and questions aren't ignored. Informal chats can be public or private, but public ones must stay within the boundaries of good taste as defined by the service. Profanity and obscenity in public will get you thrown out.

Because online conversations tend to be anonymous, some people are less than truthful about themselves. There have been many success stories of couples who've met online and gone on to marry, but there are a few horror stories as well. It's wise to be careful, especially when you're meeting online acquaintances in the real world.

SIGs have online conferences on topics of interest, and you'll find these conversations more focused than the general ones in the CB or open conference area.

Real time games are another opportunity to get together online and chat with other players as you answer trivia questions, play poker, or enjoy any of the other interactive games. Prodigy's games, though not interactive, are also interesting. Baseball Manager and GUTS let you compete against other players, while other Prodigy games are based on popular board games like Othello, MasterMind, and Hangman.

8
The information machine

If you were to make a list of all the different types of information you use in the course of an average week, your list would certainly include things like the daily news, weather reports, and possibly stock quotations or other investment data. You might also find yourself listing encyclopedias, magazines, and periodical guides, and even sources like Who's Who. If you travel, you need travel guides as well as airline schedules and hotel and rental car information. If you're shopping, you need to know what's available, and you might turn to a source like Consumer Reports to find the best values. Perhaps you want to know what movie to see or what the best-selling books or records are.

Family health information is a must for many people these days. Others are more concerned with the health of their favorite soap opera characters or that of the players on the hometown team. Those in the legal profession need huge amounts of information about laws, cases, and decisions. Medical professionals need the latest research studies. Business people need all kinds of data; not just economic trends, but press releases on new products, and much more. You could get some of the information you need at the library and some from the newspaper or television. You can get *all* of it, easily and quickly, with your modem and an online service.

You've already learned about using your modem to send mail, to talk to other people, and to use the bulletin boards and libraries online. Now I'm going to discuss another way to use the modem—as an information machine. Online services have all kinds of information for you, if you know where to look.

Far away places

Planning a trip used to mean spending hours on the phone with your travel agent and getting lost in tangles of flight schedules and rate schedules. "You can fly from Cleveland to Paris, but the flight that leaves at 3 P.M. has a four-hour stopover in Gander, Newfoundland, and gets in at 6 A.M. If you take the 3:15, you'll have to change planes in Newark and Heathrow, but you won't arrive in Paris until 10 A.M.

But if you take the 4 P.M., you can save $200, provided you stay overnight in Vienna." It was enough to make you want to stay home.

Today, you can find your own flights, choose the arrival and departure times that fit your travel plans, and find the lowest fares. You can comparison-shop hotel rates and arrange for car rentals. You can even rent luxury condos in many locations. And you can find out about the places you're visiting, get questions answered, and maybe even meet some of the local people. You can do all this, and more, online. Travel agencies online provide all the services you're accustomed to getting from your local travel agent, but they offer distinct advantages. You can't call your travel agent at midnight if that's when wanderlust hits, but you *can* connect to your favorite service and check on the next flight to San Francisco, Rio, or Cancun. Tickets can be charged to your credit card and mailed to your home or office or picked up from a local travel service.

If you want to get away from it all but don't know where or how, you can browse through unique travel offerings, including themed cruises, safaris, and tours of all kinds. GEnie's "Adventure Atlas" lists trips for the intrepid, as well as for the novice traveler. Similar travel adventures are to be found on other services.

The backbone of online travel planning are two gateway services, EAASY SABRE and OAG. EAASY SABRE is the consumer version of SABRE, a ticketing and reservations service run by American Airlines. It handles reservations and ticketing for over 300 airlines, not just American. In addition, it lets you check schedules of another 600 airlines, book rooms at more than 20,000 hotel and condominium properties worldwide, and reserve rental cars virtually anywhere through 50 different companies. Tickets can be picked up at a choice of locations or mailed directly to you. EAASY SABRE is accessible through CompuServe, Delphi, GEnie, America Online, and Prodigy, as well as several other systems. There's no charge for using it beyond normal connect fees.

OAG stands for the Official Airline Guide, and it's much like EAASY SABRE, only a bit more comprehensive. It also carries a price tag, though the price varies, depending on your choice of gateway service. On CompuServe, the surcharge is $10 per hour (17¢ a minute) in the evening, and $28 per hour (47¢ per minute) during prime/daytime hours. Delphi charges more: $25.20 per evening hour (42¢ a minute) and $35.40 per prime time hour (59¢ per minute). GEnie also carries OAG as a Professional Service, at a surcharge. What you get for the money, in addition to the services described above, are easy-to-use databases full of travel news, tour listings, cruise packages, Frequent Flyer/Frequent Guest Award Program information, ski resort information and the latest ski conditions, and even more. There's also the Official Recreation Guide, Adventure Atlas, State Department Travel Advisories, and actual Arrival/Departure information for major US airports. OAG's listings cover all but one of the 415 airlines worldwide that use automated reservation systems. Listings are updated frequently, and OAG is so accurate that it sets the standard by which the Federal Aviation Administration monitors arrivals and departures. EAASY SABRE and OAG will both provide current weather, two day and extended forecasts for major cities around the world.

Using EAASY SABRE

Most people find that EAASY SABRE is sufficiently comprehensive for their travel needs. Accessing it differs, according to which online service you happen to be on, but once you're connected the interface is the same in the text-based services (GEnie and Delphi) and essentially the same in the GUI services (America Online, CIM, and Prodigy).

On most services you can use EAASY SABRE as a reference without actually "joining" it. Joining lets you make reservations, charge your tickets to a major credit card, and book hotels, cars, and other reservations online. You can join by selecting Join from the Main menu and entering your data. Figure 8-1 shows the Main menu on America Online. You'll be prompted for your name, address, and phone number and be allowed to specify your preferences for seating and meals, as shown in Fig. 8-2.

Entering your credit card number is optional when you sign up on most of the services. Only Prodigy requires it. (You can still use your EAASY SABRE account on Prodigy if you signed up on a different service and didn't enter a credit card. You just won't be able to charge tickets or guarantee hotel reservations online.) You'll also be asked to create a password to guarantee that your EAASY SABRE account can't be accessed by anyone else, even if someone manages to get online under your user name. For that reason, be sure to use a different password from the one that signs you onto the service, and as always, protect your password.

8-1 After you enter your information, you'll be asked to confirm it on this screen.

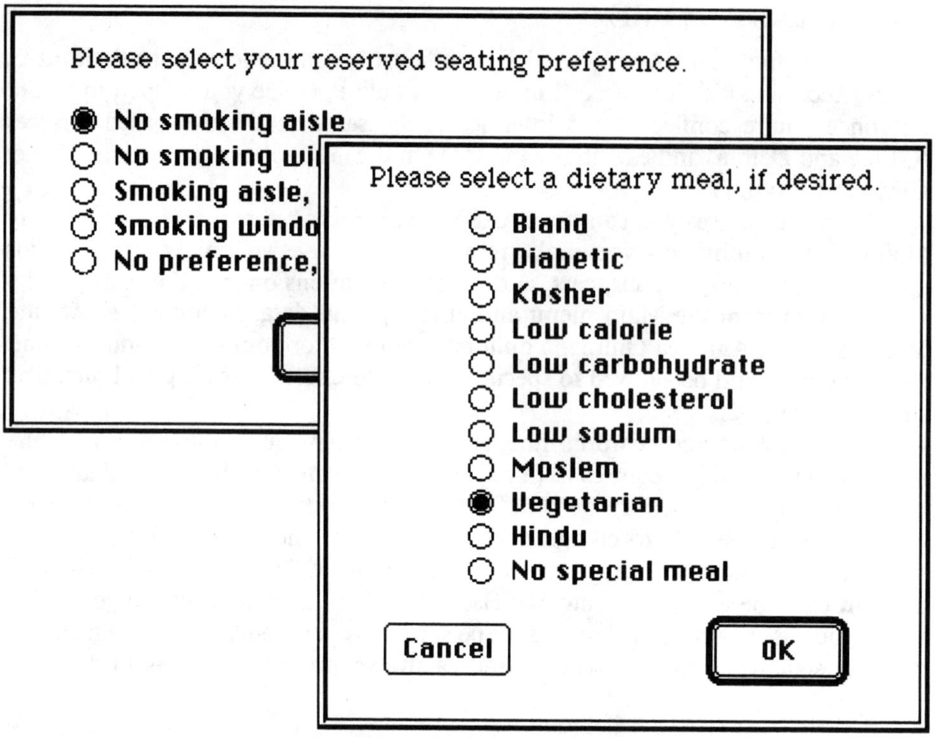

Please select your reserved seating preference.

- ◉ No smoking aisle
- ○ No smoking wi
- ○ Smoking aisle,
- ○ Smoking windo
- ○ No preference,

Please select a dietary meal, if desired.

- ○ Bland
- ○ Diabetic
- ○ Kosher
- ○ Low calorie
- ○ Low carbohydrate
- ○ Low cholesterol
- ○ Low sodium
- ○ Moslem
- ◉ Vegetarian
- ○ Hindu
- ○ No special meal

Cancel OK

8-2 Airlines are happy to accommodate your diet needs, if requested in advance.

Frequent flyer access

If you are already an AAdvantage Frequent Flyer member, you'll be sent a four-digit Personal Identification Number, enabling you to check your Frequent Flyer mileage online. This will be a different password from the one used to access EAASY SABRE. When you enter your AAdvantage number and password, be careful not to confuse *I* and *1*, or the letter *O* and the number *0*. If you enter it incorrectly three times, you'll be logged off the gateway and back to the host service. Because EAASY SABRE is a gateway service, your AAdvantage ID and password will work, no matter which online service you connect through. From time to time, you might be asked to review and agree to the EAASY SABRE terms and conditions, as shown in Fig. 8-3.

Finding a flight

To browse through the airline schedules, you need to know your departure point, destination, and the date on which you want to travel. Figure 8-4 shows how the information is entered on America Online. You can enter the cities by name or by the code, if you know it. Every airport has a unique three-letter code that is used to identify it on schedules, tickets, and even on baggage tags. Table 8-1 shows some of the more common codes. If there's more than one airport serving a particular city, you'll be asked which one you want to go to. You will also need to enter the time

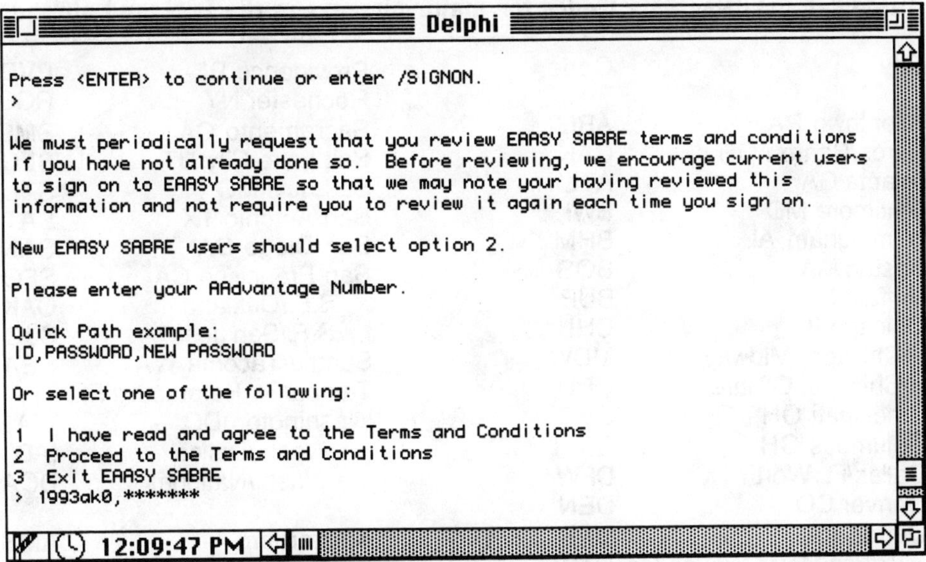

8-3 Entering your AAdvantage number is the same as agreeing to the terms, as you've already agreed to them when you applied for the number.

Schedule Request

Flight Schedule Request

Departure city: Boston
Arrival city: Stockholm

Travel date (e.g. 27NOV): June 21
Time (9AM or 3P): 9am

Preferred airline (optional): DL
Connecting city (optional):

OK

8-4 I could have entered **BOS** for Boston and **ARN** for Arlanda/Stockholm.

Table 8-1 Airline City Codes for major airports in the U.S. and abroad.

City	Code
Allentown PA	ABE
Akron/Canton OH	CAK
Atlanta GA	ATL
Baltimore MD	BWI
Birmingham AL	BHM
Boston MA	BOS
Buffalo NY	BUF
Chicago IL	CHI
Chicago, Midway	MDW
Chicago, O'Hare	ORD
Cincinnati OH	CVG
Columbus OH	CMH
Dallas/Ft. Worth TX	DFW
Denver CO	DEN
Detroit MI	DTT
Detroit/Metro Wayne Co.	DTW
Detroit MI/City	DET
Ft. Lauderdale FL	FLL
Grand Rapids MI	GRR
Gr'nsboro/Win-Salem NC	GSO
Hartford CT	BDL
Houston TX	HOU
Indianapolis IN	IND
Kansas City MO	MCI
Los Angeles CA	LAX
L.A./ Burbank	BUR
L.A./ LongBeach	LGB
L.A./ Ontario	ONT
Louisville KY	SDF
Miami FL	MIA
Milwaukee WI	MKE
Minneapolis/St. Paul MN	MSP
Nashville TN	BNA
New Orleans LA	MSY
New York NY	NYC
N.Y./ J.F. Kennedy	JFK
N.Y./ LaGuardia	LGA
N.Y./ Newark	EWR
N.Y./ Westchester Co.	HPN
Norfolk VA	ORF
Oklahoma City OK	OKC
Philadelphia PA	PHL
Phoenix AZ	PHX
Pittsburgh PA	PIT
Portland OR	PDX
Providence RI	PVD
Rochester NY	ROC
Sacramento CA	SMF
Salt Lake City UT	SLC
St. Louis MO	STL
San Antonio TX	SAT
San Diego CA	SAN
San Francisco CA	SFO
S.F./Oakland	OAK
S.F./San Jose	SJC
Seattle/Tacoma WA	SEA
Tampa/St. Petersburg FL	TPA
Washington DC	WAS
Wash./Dulles	IAD
Wash./National	DCA
Amsterdam	AMS
Athens	ATH
Brussels	BRU
Copenhagen	CPH
Dublin	DUB
Frankfurt	FRA
Geneva	GVA
Jerusalem	JRS
London/Gatwick	LGW
London/Heathrow	LHR
Madrid	MAD
Mexico City	MEX
Montreal	YMQ
Paris/Orly	ORY
Paris/DeGaulle	CDG
Rome	ROM
Stockholm/Arlanda	ARN
Tokyo	TYO
Toronto	YYZ
Vienna	VIE
Zurich	ZRH

you wish to leave. You can also choose to see only flights on a specific airline, or flights on which a particular class of service is available. To see all possible flights, enter an early morning hour. Generally, non-stop or direct flights are listed first, followed by connecting flights. All of the flights shown in Fig. 8-5 are connecting flights. Note that not all direct flights are non-stop. There might be one or more stops, but you won't need to change planes on a direct flight. Direct flights have the same flight number for all segments of the flight. On a connecting flight, you will need to change planes in the connecting city. Connecting flights are listed separately. To see more flights, select View MORE Flights. There might be many flights to your destination or only a few.

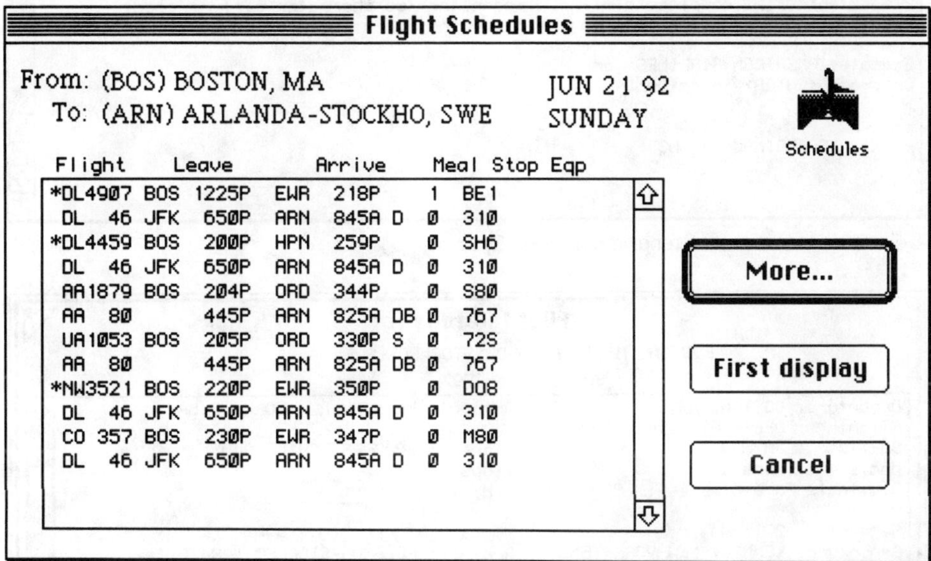

8-5 None of these combinations is desirable. Who would fly to Europe from Boston by way of Chicago?

When you're unsure what a particular airport, airline, or aircraft code means, select Translate CODES from the options and enter the code you need explained. In Fig. 8-6, you can see how to request a translation of an airline code.

For more information on a particular flight, select it. On America Online, you simply click on the desired flight. On text-based services, you might be asked to enter the line number. Figure 8-7 shows how this is done using CIM. The detail shows the type of aircraft and the fare classes available on the flight(s) you have selected. Fare classes might differ by carrier, but in general, the cryptic designations refer to the following types of service:

F = First Class
C or J = Business Class
Y = Full Fare Coach
B or M = Limited availability discounted Coach fares
Q,H,K,L,V = Limited availability restricted or excursion fares

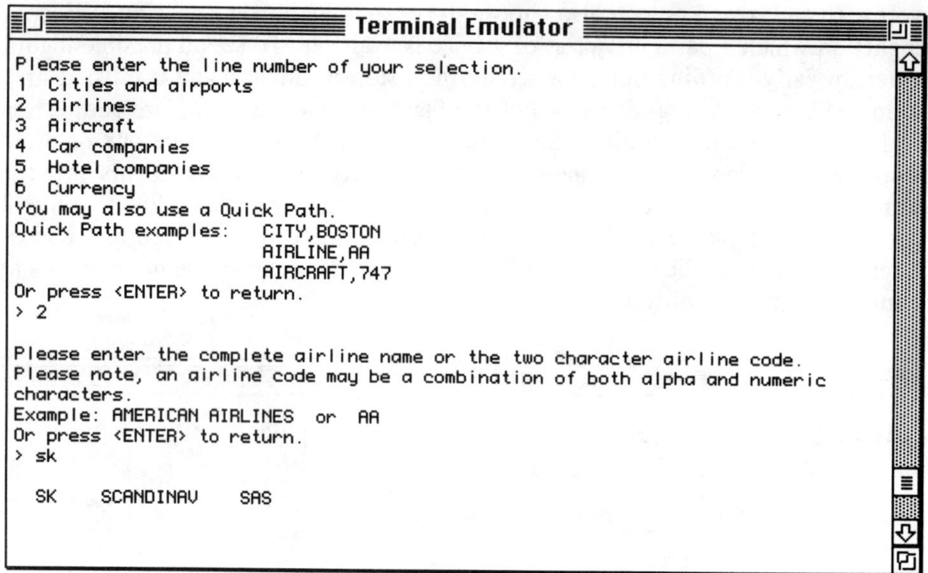

8-6 SK is the code for Scandinavian Airline Systems.

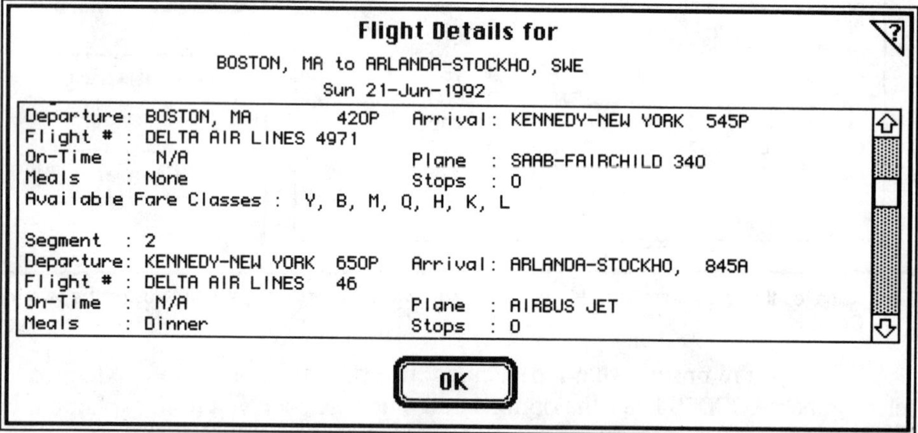

8-7 Remember that schedules reflect local time. Sweden adds six hours to eastern standard time.

Getting a fare deal

Airline pricing is almost as easy to understand as the fine print on an insurance policy or the Building Codes for Helsinki, Finland. There are all sorts of restrictions that apply to certain fares. Sometimes you have to stay over a Saturday night. For other fares, you have to travel weekdays, or weekends, or only when the moon is full—or at least that's how it seems to many befuddled tourists. The computer will find you the lowest applicable fares. On a text-based service, select View LOWest one-way fares. If you are using America Online or CIM, selecting fares will bring up the list with the lowest fares shown first, as in the example in Fig. 8-8. Simply scroll

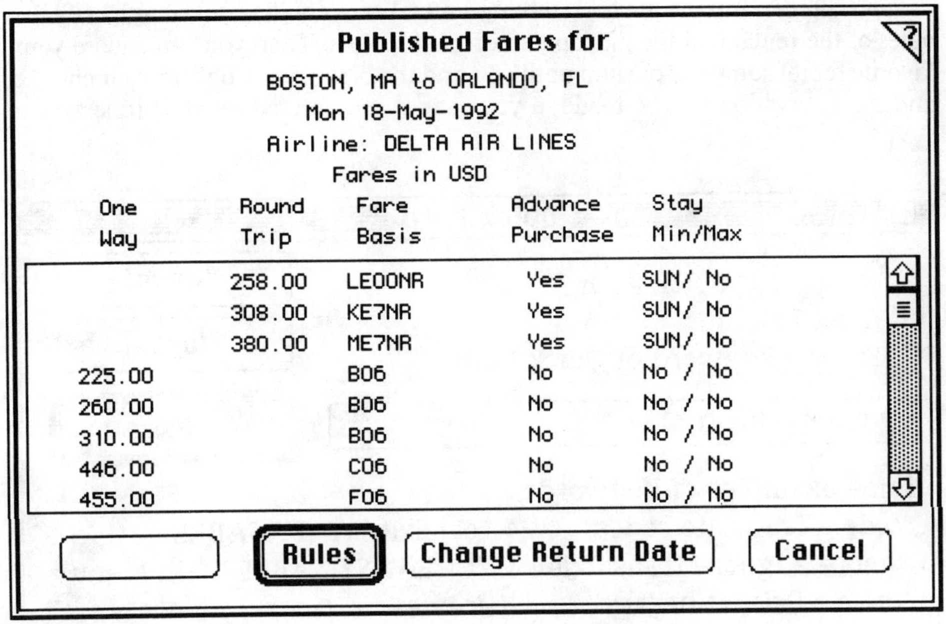

Published Fares for
BOSTON, MA to ORLANDO, FL
Mon 18-May-1992
Airline: DELTA AIR LINES
Fares in USD

One Way	Round Trip	Fare Basis	Advance Purchase	Stay Min/Max
	258.00	LEOONR	Yes	SUN/ No
	308.00	KE7NR	Yes	SUN/ No
	380.00	ME7NR	Yes	SUN/ No
225.00		B06	No	No / No
260.00		B06	No	No / No
310.00		B06	No	No / No
446.00		C06	No	No / No
455.00		F06	No	No / No

Rules | Change Return Date | Cancel

8-8 Coming home is a bargain! Only $33 more than a one-way ticket.

down to see higher classes of fares. Select Rules to determine what additional restrictions apply.

Quick paths

You can use the Quick Path option to bypass entering information one field at a time. First, enter the type of information you want, preceded by a slash. Choices are /air, /hotel and /car, to name a few. To view airline flights, enter city names or codes, date and time, and airline preference, if any, in the following format: /air,BOS,MCO,27AUG,8a,DL. Separate individual entries by commas. Capital letters aren't necessary. Figure 8-9 shows AO's QuickPath entry fields.

To make a reservation, first select your flight. You'll be asked to confirm personal information and Frequent Flyer numbers, if any, for each passenger. The reservations will be entered in the names you've specified, and you'll see your itinerary. At this time, you can choose to add more flights and car and hotel reservations, as necessary. Figure 8-10 shows the itinerary for a trip reserved on CIM.

To choose a hotel, click Add hotel or return to the menu and select Hotel Reservations. Enter the name of the city or airport closest to where you want to stay, and you'll be shown a list of hotels. Detailed information about any hotel listed is available, by selecting Detail. The Hotels listing and a portion of the detailed information are shown in Fig. 8-11. The Rates section includes any additional charges for rollaway beds, valet parking, and other extra amenities. Selecting a hotel makes your reservation and adds it to your itinerary. If you have special requests, they can be entered with the reservation information, under Remarks.

The process is the same for reserving a rental car. You'll be asked to specify the dates of the rental and the pickup and drop-off points. Then you can choose your favorite rental company or shop until you find the best price. Confirm your choices and the reservation will be made in your name and entered on your itinerary.

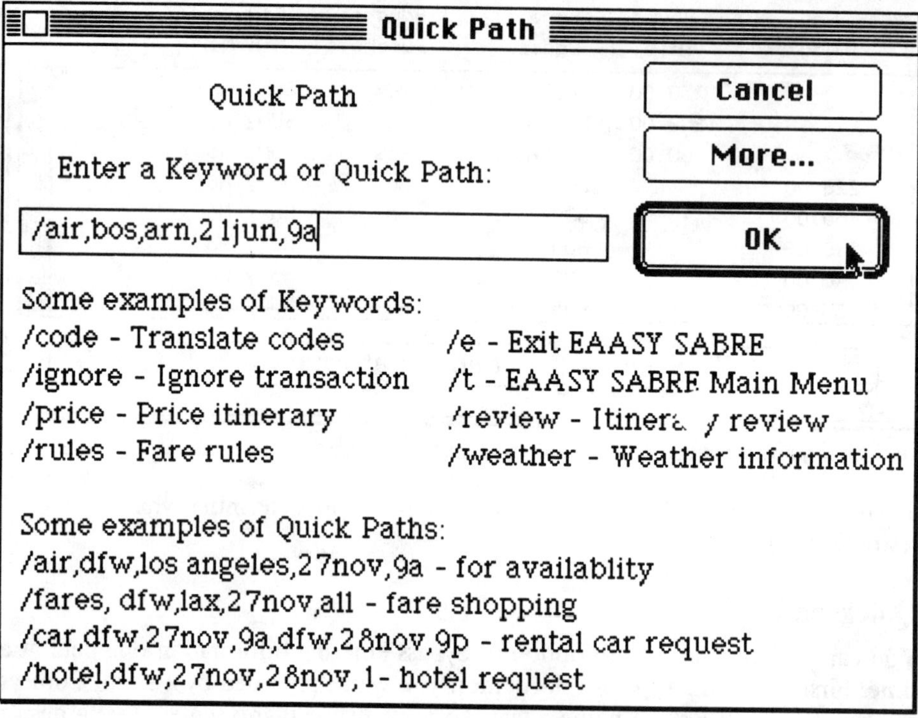

8-9 If you don't know the code, you can use Quick Path with city names, too.

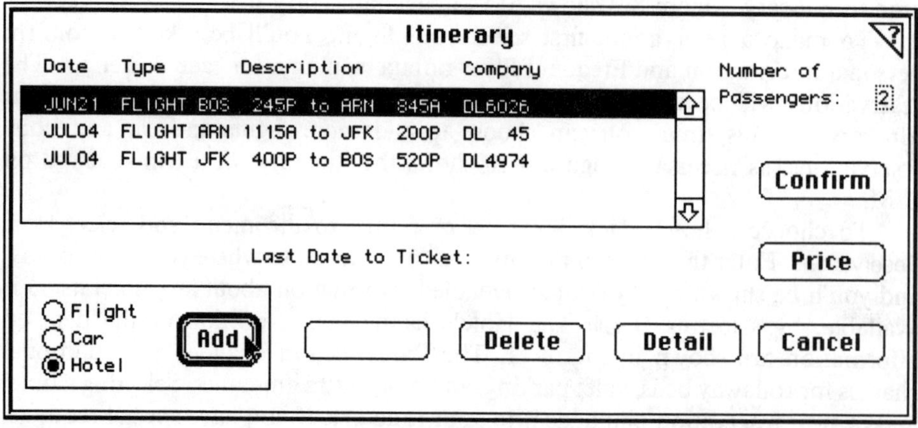

8-10 The flights are fine. Now I need to find a hotel.

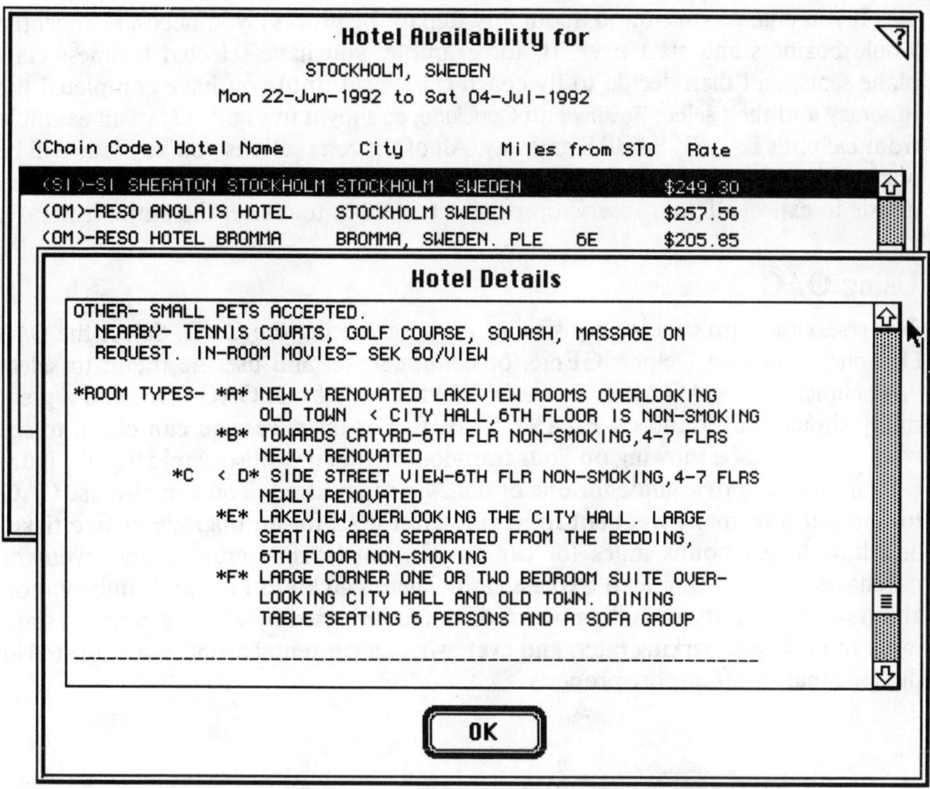

8-11 At the Requests prompt, I'll ask for a type E room on the 6th floor.

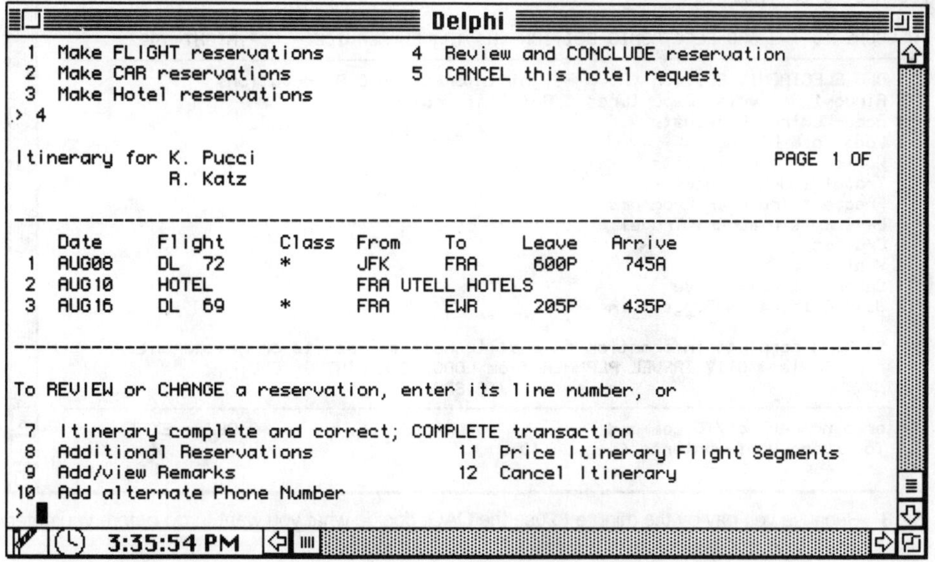

8-12 Now is the time to confirm or cancel all reservations or to change one or more.

If you change your mind about any step of the process, you needn't cancel the whole business and start over. If, for example, you have selected business class plane seats, and then decide to fly coach class, wait until you have completed the itinerary and then select Review and Conclude, as shown in Fig. 8-12, in an example from Delphi's EAASY SABRE gateway. All of the reservations you've made will be displayed, and at that point you can select any of them to change or cancel. If you decide to cancel all your reservations, select CANCEL to cancel the entire itinerary.

Using OAG

The reservation process is very similar if you are using the OAG. Select the OAG Electronic Edition on Delphi, GEnie, or CompuServe, and use the menu to select your choice. The OAG Main menu is shown in Fig. 8-13. OAG gives you a great many choices not found on EAASY SABRE. For instance, you can check to see what movie will be showing on your transcontinental or transoceanic flight. Figure 8-14 shows the movie guide for one of the 24 airlines listed. You can also use OAG to find out how many frequent flyer miles you need for an upgrade or free ticket and how to get bonus miles for car rentals, hotel visits, cruises, and even for purchases on your American Express card. There's all kinds of helpful information about major airports, including which terminals are used by which airlines, restaurants and lounges, parking rates, and even whether car rental agencies are located at the terminal or off airport property.

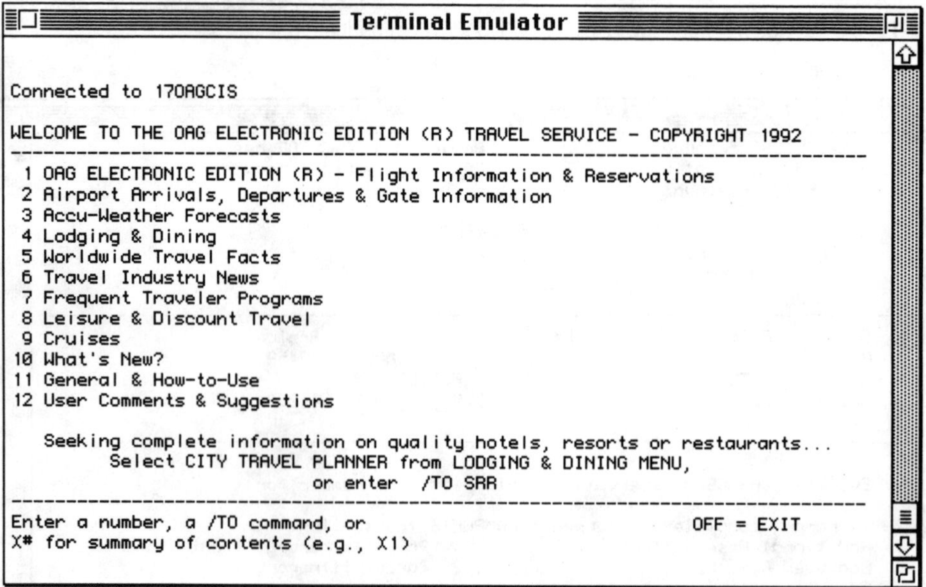

8-13 Because you pay by the minute to use the OAG, decide what you want to do before you enter.

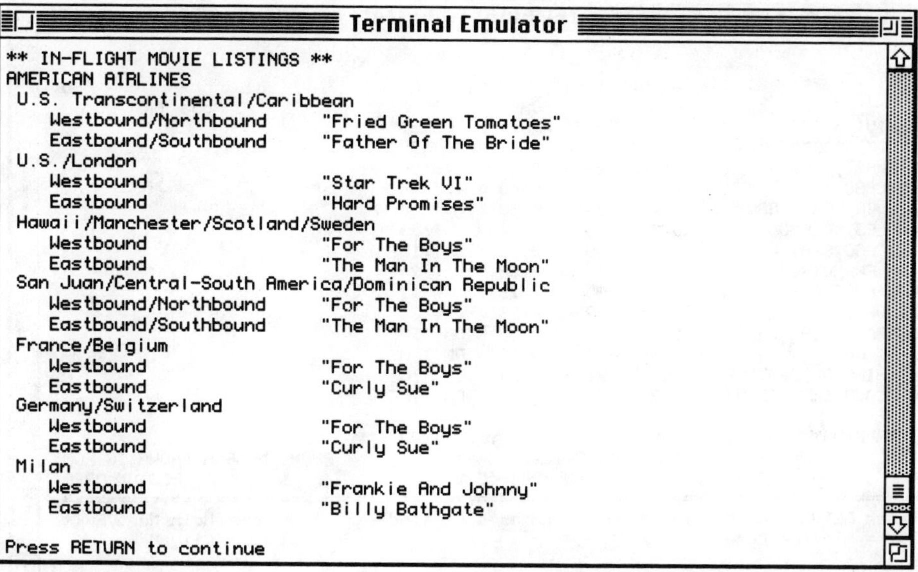

```
** IN-FLIGHT MOVIE LISTINGS **
AMERICAN AIRLINES
 U.S. Transcontinental/Caribbean
    Westbound/Northbound        "Fried Green Tomatoes"
    Eastbound/Southbound        "Father Of The Bride"
 U.S./London
    Westbound                   "Star Trek VI"
    Eastbound                   "Hard Promises"
 Hawaii/Manchester/Scotland/Sweden
    Westbound                   "For The Boys"
    Eastbound                   "The Man In The Moon"
 San Juan/Central-South America/Dominican Republic
    Westbound/Northbound        "For The Boys"
    Eastbound/Southbound        "The Man In The Moon"
 France/Belgium
    Westbound                   "For The Boys"
    Eastbound                   "Curly Sue"
 Germany/Switzerland
    Westbound                   "For The Boys"
    Eastbound                   "Curly Sue"
 Milan
    Westbound                   "Frankie And Johnny"
    Eastbound                   "Billy Bathgate"
Press RETURN to continue
```

8-14 You might not choose the flight according to what movie's showing, but it's fun to know what to expect.

Something for the folks at home

If you're heading to the airport to pick up a visitor or returning friend or family member at any of 16 major airports, use OAG to find out which gate the plane's coming into and whether or not the flight's been delayed. Figure 8-15 shows gate information for United flights arriving at Logan airport in Boston.

In the travel area on Delphi, you'll also find a good deal of other helpful information, including Metroline for information about United States cities and attractions, and Worldline, which provides all sorts of information about foreign countries, including their customs and what to see and do there. Travel forums are another good source for answers to your travel questions. Prodigy's travel club is especially good for inexperienced travelers. No matter where in the world you want to go, there are sure to be Prodigy members who've been there and can give you up-to-the-minute information on hotels, restaurants, sights to see, and sights to avoid.

Travelers' alerts

Sites to avoid are the topic for the U.S. State Department warning bulletins. If our travels are taking you toward any of the world's current or potential hot spots, check these bulletins before you leave. They'll tell you what our government is advising U.S. citizens living in the area to do and whether travel is feasible or unsafe. State Department warnings are posted on Delphi in the Travel area and on CompuServe and GEnie in the OAG section. Figure 8-16 shows an example.

```
Terminal Emulator

            United Airlines                                            ARD
                                SCHED    WILL                  Page 1 of 1
ARRIVING FROM       FLIGHT  GATE  ARRIVAL  ARRIVE
~~~~~~~~~~~~~~~~~~~~~~~~~~~~~~~~~~~~~~~~~~~~~~~~~~~

STEWART, NY           3667    27    6:00      7:00
CHICAGO                294    40    6:40 >    6:48
DENVER/SAN DIEGO       172    27    6:58 >    7:10
DULLES/ORLANDO        1476    25    7:46 >    7:36
CHICAGO/SEATTLE        114    40    8:25 >  ON TIME
SAN FRANCISCO           20    41    8:58 >    9:24
LOS ANGELES            180    25    9:23 >    9:47
DENVER/SEATTLE         354    27    9:28 >    9:33
ORLANDO/FORT LAUD.    1650    42    9:43    ON TIME
CHICAGO                678    27    9:50    ON TIME
WASHINGTON/SEATTLE      56    27   11:01    ON TIME
CHICAGO/SAN DIEGO      682    43   11:11    ON TIME

  THURSDAY        6:41 P.M.           MAY 07,1992
            Fly the Friendly Skies                    PHONE NUMBER SHOWN IS FOR
     FOR RESERVATIONS CALL 1-800-241-6522                           BOSTON AREA
=================================================================================
Press RETURN for Airline Menu, or enter a command:          MM = Main Menu/Exit
 AM = Airline Menu                                           CM = City Menu
```

8-15 If you're meeting returnees from Disney World, you'd better hurry!

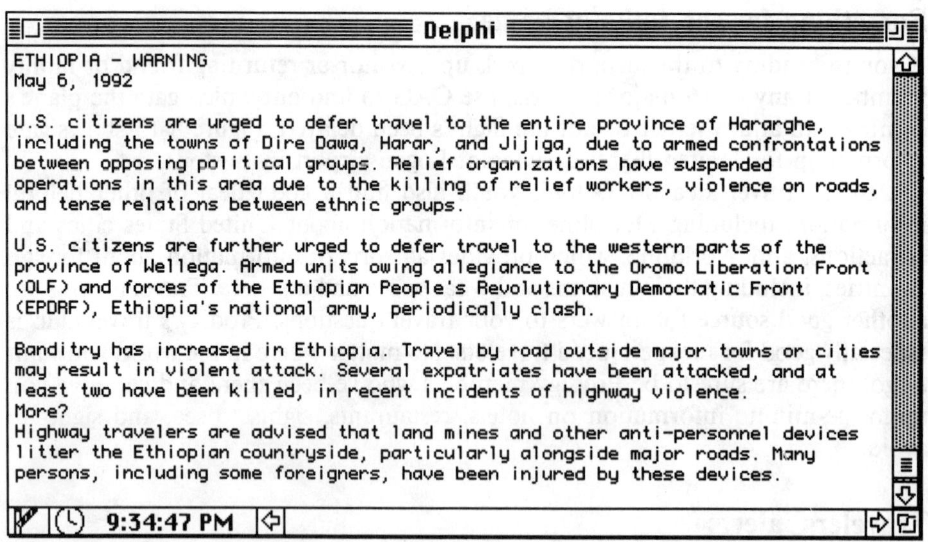

Delphi

ETHIOPIA - WARNING
May 6, 1992

U.S. citizens are urged to defer travel to the entire province of Hararghe, including the towns of Dire Dawa, Harar, and Jijiga, due to armed confrontations between opposing political groups. Relief organizations have suspended operations in this area due to the killing of relief workers, violence on roads, and tense relations between ethnic groups.

U.S. citizens are further urged to defer travel to the western parts of the province of Wellega. Armed units owing allegiance to the Oromo Liberation Front (OLF) and forces of the Ethiopian People's Revolutionary Democratic Front (EPDRF), Ethiopia's national army, periodically clash.

Banditry has increased in Ethiopia. Travel by road outside major towns or cities may result in violent attack. Several expatriates have been attacked, and at least two have been killed, in recent incidents of highway violence.
More?
Highway travelers are advised that land mines and other anti-personnel devices litter the Ethiopian countryside, particularly alongside major roads. Many persons, including some foreigners, have been injured by these devices.

9:34:47 PM

8-16 When you must travel to a trouble spot, check in frequently with the American Embassy or Consulate at your destination.

Delphi also carries health information for travelers from the Centers for Disease Control. Recent CDC bulletins have warned of Diphtheria outbreaks in Russia and Cholera in several South American countries, certainly matters of concern for anyone heading to those areas. As of this writing, America Online and Prodigy do not carry the State Department warnings.

Brush up your French?

When you head for those far away places, it's often helpful to speak at least a little bit of the local tongue. The Terra Nova section on Delphi can help, with foreign language forums that let you brush up your French, Spanish, German, Japanese (Nihongo) and even Esperanto. A German-speaking group meets regularly on Saturday mornings for conversation. Several Russian-speaking members carry on a correspondence through the forums, too. There's also a version of the Adventure text game in French, so you can play and learn at the same time. Figure 8-17 shows the game in progress. You can also find foreign language help on CompuServe's Foreign Language Education forum.

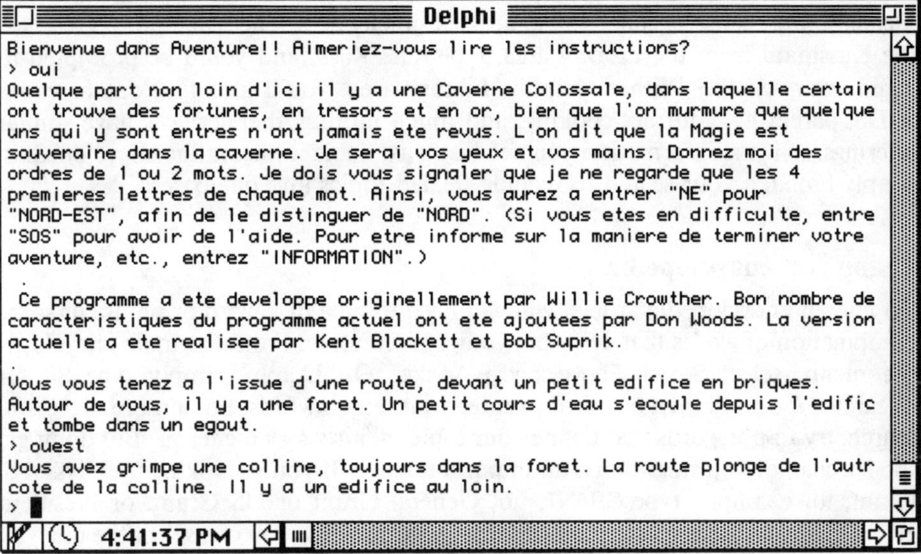

8-17 Aventure Français is good practice for a trip to France.

Online encyclopedias

Everyone ought to have access to a good encyclopedia. Students need them as a basis for research papers and as background sources for subjects as diverse as history, music, and biology. Parents need them to answer children's interminable questions, as well as to satisfy their own curiosity on thousands of different topics. People who write or do any kind of research usually start with the encyclopedia and go on from there. If you've priced a new set of encyclopedias, though, you're probably aware that they've gotten very expensive. And, with world affairs changing so rapidly, encyclopedias, like atlases, are out of date before they're even printed. Important as it is to have one at hand, it might not make sense to own one. That's why online encyclopedias are your smartest choice. They're being updated constantly to reflect changes in governments and new discoveries in the sciences almost before the dust has settled.

Each one of the major online services has some kind of encyclopedia. CompuServe and Prodigy offer the Academic American Encyclopedia, claimed to be the most up-to-date encyclopedia available anywhere. Its 33,000 articles are updated every three months, in order to keep the information as current as possible. America Online includes Compton's Encyclopedia, published by Britannica Software, Inc., a division of Encyclopedia Britannica, Inc. It features 8,784,000 words, 5,200 full-length articles, 26,023 capsule articles, and 63,503 index entries. The multimedia version of this encyclopedia took top honors at the 1991 Software Publisher's Association Awards Ceremony. Delphi and GEnie feature the Grolier Encyclopedia, also highly rated and well respected in the academic world, with over 31,000 entries.

Delphi also offers the Kussmaul Encyclopedia, an interesting, though by no means comprehensive, collection of articles, chiefly on sciences and arts. (To access the Kussmaul from the Library area, type Kuss Kuss, and you'll be prompted to begin your search.) Within Delphi's Library area, you'll also find databases on AIDS, parenting, gourmet cooking, and much more. Other services have similar offerings, so if the information you need isn't available in the online encyclopedias, simply broaden your search to include related topics and databases.

Using the encyclopedia

To find an encyclopedia article, you will need to type in a word or phrase or some combination of words that describes your desired topic. From the main encyclopedia menu, select Search Encyclopedia Articles. On Delphi, simply type SE for "Search." You will then be asked to enter your search words. For a more successful search, try to use words that define your topic in fairly specific terms. But don't get too specific, or you might miss an important entry. If you're looking up Ulysses S. Grant, for example, type GRANT, not General Grant or US Grant, or President Grant. This will take you to a list of Grants, from which you can select the one you want. If there are several menu items of interest, see them all by entering their numbers, separated by a comma, as shown in Fig. 8-18.

When you're entering search words, avoid abbreviations. If you enter NASA, you'll be told to see National Aeronautics and Space Administration, so you might as well start there. Avoid nicknames. Look for "Flag, U.S.," rather than "Old Glory." If you find no matches, try a similar word: change "power cell" to "battery."

Figure 8-19 shows how a search entry is made on AO. If you find too many matches to display, narrow your search by adding additional qualifying words: change "Drama" to "Drama and Arthur Miller." Join words and phrases with "AND" or "and." The search will find all articles with the words "drama" AND the words "Arthur Miller" in the same article.

If there are two keywords that describe your topic, you can search them both at the same time, by using "or." For example, "whale or dolphin" will find all articles with either the word "whale" *or* the word "dolphin." Use "NOT" or "not" to eliminate items you don't want. If you're looking up shrubbery, try "bush *not* George Bush."

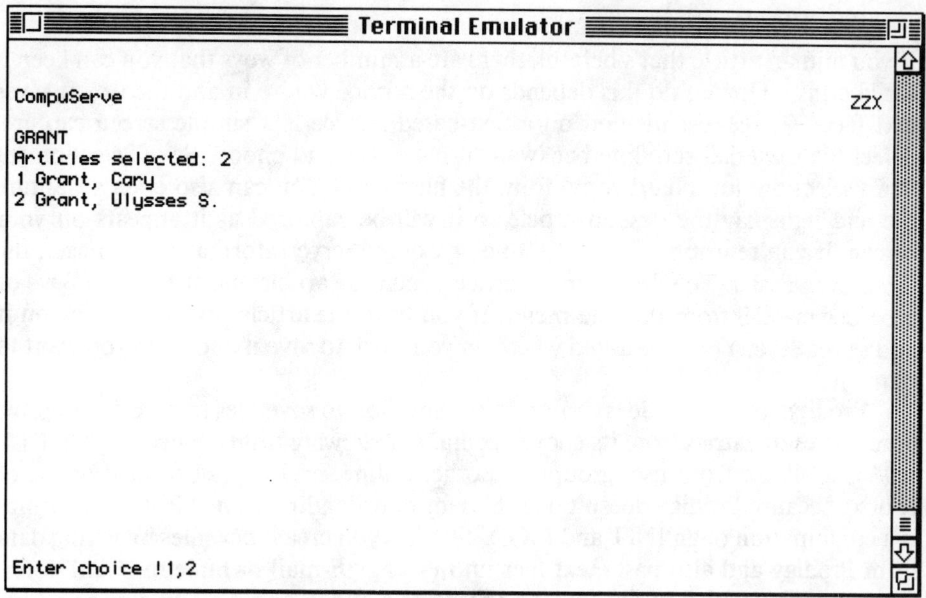

8-18 By entering both numbers, I can read about both Grants.

Search Encyclopedia Articles

Electronic Encyclopedia

Type words that describe what you are looking for, then click List Articles. For example, "war and peace." Click Help & Info for more instructions.

bush

Items 1 - 4 of 4 matching entries.

BUSH, George
BIBLIOGRAPHY FOR GEORGE BUSH
GARDEN AND GARDENING
UNITED STATES HISTORY

List Articles | More | Help & Info

8-19 If I'd entered Bush not George I'd only see the garden folder.

Saving a copy

If you find an article that's helpful, there are a number of ways that you can keep it for later use. How to do this depends on the service you're in and the way it saves text files. The easiest method on a text-based service is a simple screen capture. Select the material, scrolling backward if necessary and choose Save Selection (or Print selection, for a hard copy) from the file menu. You can also open a Capture file and redisplay the desired article so it will be captured as it appears on your screen. If you're using America Online or CompuServe Information Manager, the job is even easier. To save an entire article, open the article and then select Save or type Command-S from the File menu. If you have the article open, just click on it and select Save. You'll be asked where on your disk to save it and what you want to name it.

Prodigy, of course, doesn't normally allow you to save files to disk. It can print hard copies of entries from its encyclopedia. A shareware utility called "*P* to Disk 4.0" is available from user groups and other online services (not from Prodigy, of course, because Prodigy doesn't offer files for downloading). The *P* to Disk utility is a combination of an INIT and FKEY that lets you create new files by saving data from Prodigy and also paste text files into Prodigy E-mail or bulletin board notes. It's compatible with MultiFinder, and Systems 6 and 7, and it allows you to return to your Finder or to other applications in System 7 while Prodigy is running. All in all, it's a must for any Mac owner who is serious about using Prodigy.

Because these articles are saved in ASCII (text) format, you can open them with virtually any word processor, and from there edit them, make changes in the type size and style, copy them into other documents, or print them out from your word processing program. Of course, because all the material contained in the articles is covered by copyright, you'll need to get permission from the publisher of the encyclopedia to reproduce it. Students using encyclopedia entries in a school report need to be especially careful about rewriting the material in their own words. Many teachers belong to online services and will recognize a particular encyclopedia's "style." Use the information, but rephrase it.

Other research sources

Research begins with the encyclopedia but certainly doesn't end there. Figure 8-20 shows the references available on CompuServe, an array of information resources rivaling that of many of our public libraries. Many of these references are also available on one or more of the other services. You'll find Consumer Reports, for example, on Prodigy. America Online, though it doesn't carry Peterson's College Database, includes a similar one from the College Entrance Examination Board, as well as a forum hosted by the College Board, with a friendly advisor who answers all sorts of questions about college admission, including those concerning taking the SATs and Achievement Tests. AO users can also order study materials for these tests online, though it's not yet possible to register for the actual tests (or take them) via computer. Figure 8-21 shows how a college search is conducted on America Online. You can look up specific colleges by name or list a major or other feature as a keyword and receive a list of colleges that fit that keyword. Clicking on the name of any one of these brings up an article about it, which, like the encyclopedia articles, can be printed or saved as a text file.

Students who need help with homework can visit the tutoring center in AO. Every night of the week there are teachers online waiting to answer homework questions and to help with ideas for research projects and papers at all levels from grade school through college. Some online help sessions are scheduled for particular nights. If you want to consult an expert in a specific area, you can page one to set up an appointment. Figure 8-22 shows the Teacher Pager. Simply enter the topic and level and the times you are available. You can usually expect a response within 48 hours.

Get healthy

HealthNet, found on Delphi and CompuServe, is a comprehensive listing of articles on many aspects of health care, from Sports Medicine and First Aid to surgery, tests, and diagnostic procedures. GEnie's Pop-Med health information service is similar.

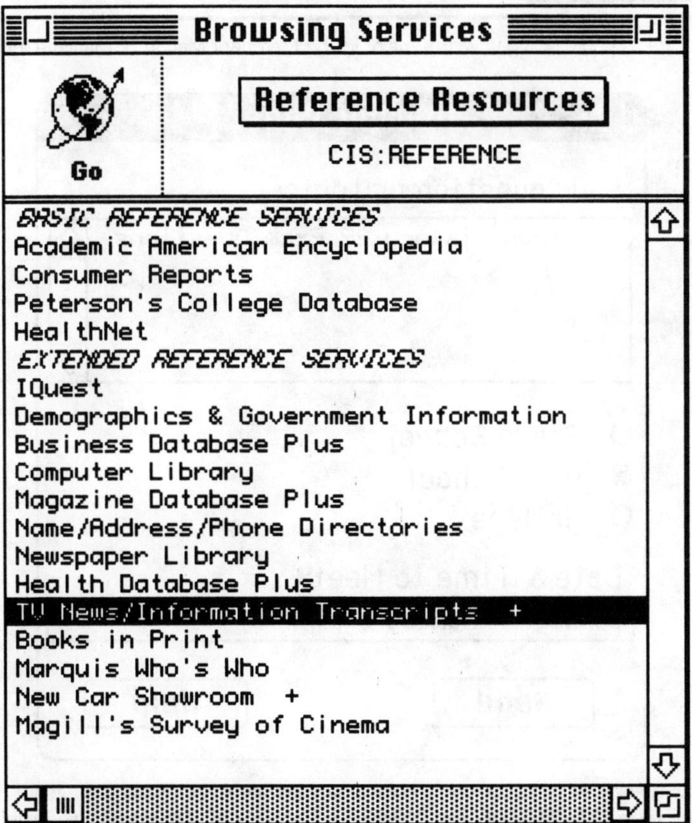

8-20 The variety of databases available online is quite amazing.

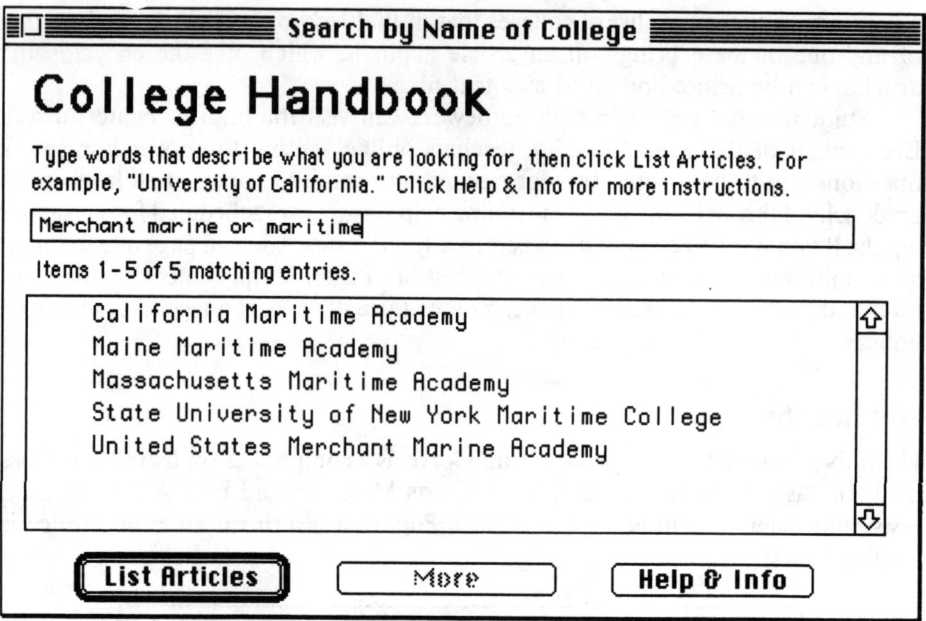

8-21 These are the only colleges with a major in the Merchant Marine or Maritime industry.

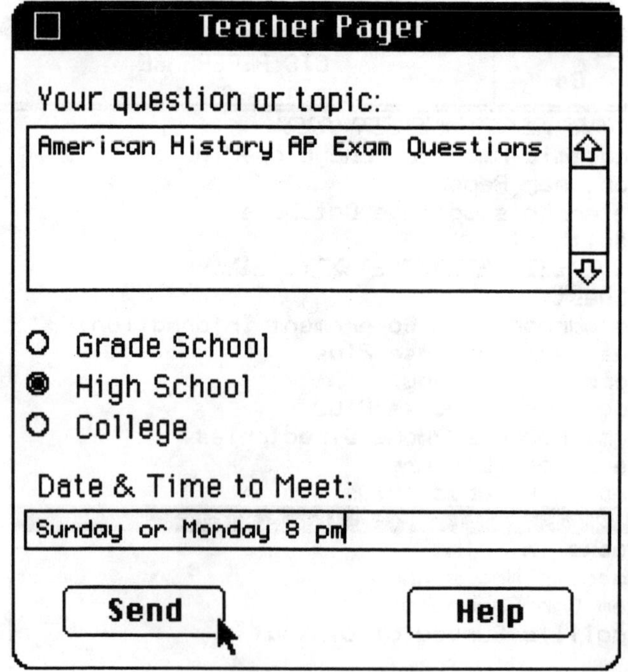

8-22 There's nothing as good for one's grades as a private tutor, unless it's a team of tutors. This request brought three history teachers to the conference room on Monday night.

CompuServe's Health Database Plus is a listing of thousands of magazine and journal articles on all kinds of medical topics. By entering a keyword, such as "von Recklinghausen's Disease," one can choose from a listing of articles containing the selected word or phrase and display, print, or capture to a text file any or all of the listed articles. There is an additional fee for this Extended Reference Service. There are also all sorts of warnings about not using medical databases as a substitute for consulting a physician. You can find additional health information in forum libraries and bulletin boards. Delphi provides gateways to two other health-related services: CAIN, the Computerized AIDS Information Network, and WIDnet, a service of the World Institute on Disabilities, for health care professionals and disability advocates. Both have libraries of helpful information as well as moderated forums.

Using database services

The online eycyclopedias and health information libraries are examples of individual databases—collections of information from a single source in database form for electronic retrieval. The Health Database Plus is one of many database services that takes information from many sources and formats it for computerized access. Other such database services provide similar collections of business news, computer industry news, financial data, medical, scientific, and technical data, human resources, data for the legal profession, and even files of TV documentary scripts and text files of over 75 major daily newspapers. Some of these database services can be accessed through an online service like CompuServe or Delphi. Others, specifically those aimed at professionals rather than the consumer market, are available on a subscription basis. Users call them directly. Connect charges vary but tend to be quite high, typically around $100 per hour during business hours and less during the evening.

Medical data

Among those data services that might be of interest to the medical profession are BRS/Colleague and BRS/After Dark. Colleague is a menu-driven system designed for physicians, providing bibliographic citations, abstracts, and full text of some articles. After Dark offers the same services but is available only nights and weekends. It can be accessed with any standard telecommunications program. Mead Data Central's MEDIS is a full text service, consisting of a collection of medical journals, drug information, the Medline library, and a special cancer library.

Legal briefings

Lawyers can choose from a number of database services, including Mead's LEXIS, with Federal and State laws, legal journals, Shephard's Citations, and the Martindale-Hubbel Law Directory; and WESTLAW, a data service from the nation's oldest and largest legal publishers, which includes full texts of federal and state cases and opinions, the U.S. Code, case law from all federal and state Appellate courts, over 400 legal periodicals, and a great deal more. Its customer service department includes a staff of experts on legal research (all JDs) who will help users formulate the appropriate search queries to locate specific points of law. Patent lawyers will appreciate ORBIT's online patent information, including the JAPIO database of Japanese patents as well as the complete U.S. Patent library.

Everybody's business news

Accountants, financial planners, business forecasters, and anyone who needs up-to-date financial information can find it online in any of a number of different sources, CORIS, from Thompson Financial Network, is a business information source that provides company profiles, abstracts of management-oriented business articles, industry and market performance data, company and industry news, complete regional, national, and international news coverage, and a great deal more. Dataquest is aimed at the high technology market. Data Star accesses over 250 databases in the fields of business, health care, chemical and biotechnological sciences, biomedicine, and general technology. Many of them are available only on Data Star. A prime focus on this service is European business information, providing data on over 90,000 UK companies and over a million in France, and even current business and economic news from Russia. NEXIS is Mead's database for the business community. Its Major Papers Library offers full text of 11 different major daily newspapers, including the *New York Times*, the *Chicago Tribune, Washington Post*, *Boston Globe*, *USA Today*, and many others. NEXIS also provides transcripts of major news programs, including the MacNeil/Lehrer NewsHour, Nightline, World News Tonight, and several more. Reading the news or catching up with a missed program can be expensive, though. Major Papers and Transcripts each cost $21 per search.

Dow Jones News/Retrieval is probably the best known news and data source for the business community. Because it comes from the same source as the Dow Jones newswire and the Wall Street Journal, its business services are unrivaled. It functions as both a database and as an online service for the business community, with MCI's electronic mail services, world news and sports coverage, shopping, travel, and more. Among other features, DJN/R provides searchable text of the Wall Street Journal's daily editions back to January, 1984, WSJ international editions, Barron's, and other business publications back to 1985, as well as the Los Angeles Times, only one day after publication. Real-time and 15-minute delayed stock quotes will be found here, as will Dow Jones Averages.

IQuest

Database services such as CompuServe's IQuest can save literally hours of time you might otherwise spend searching through individual libraries, periodical indexes, and commercial directories. IQuest is a collection of more than 850 different databases, including those of Dialog, BRS, NewsNet, and VU/TEXT. There are two different types of database entries on IQuest: citation entries and full-text entries. Full-text entries, obviously, let you retrieve and read the entire article, while citation entries simply tell you which periodical the article is in. Citation databases are useful in that they show how much current journal space is being devoted to your topic and tell you which sources to look in. They might also contain abstracts, or short summaries, of the articles.

There are several ways to initiate an IQuest search. IQuest-I guides you through a series of menus that define your topic of interest and determines which database is right for your search. Then it prompts you for words to search for in that database. If you already know the database you want to search, IQuest-II allows you to specify it and bypass the menus. If your research category is broad, or if you're trying to find every possible reference to your topic, use the SmartScan function.

When you enter search terms for IQuest, you can simplify your entry by omitting common words such as *OF, THE, FOR, AT, BY*, and *TO*. Retrieve only the most relevant articles by using words and phrases that are unique and specific. For example, *Challenger* rather than *Space Shuttle*. Ignore uppercase or lowercase letters. Example, Canada, canada, and CANada will all be treated alike. Retrieve all words that begin with the same letters by using a slash (/) as a "wild card" at the end of a word. Example: COMPUT/ will find information on COMPUTE, COMPUTERS, and COMPUTING. Just be certain that there are enough letters in front of the slash to properly narrow the field. COM/ would give you every possible keyword starting with *COM*.

As in the encyclopedia searches, qualifiers such as *and*, *or*, and *not* help define your search parameters. Indicate concepts that should be considered together by using parentheses () around groups of words that you have combined with *AND, OR*, or *NOT*. Thus, you might group (Mac and Communications) or Telecommunications.

Figure 8-23 shows the results of an IQuest SmartScan search, showing which databases have relevant materials. Typing the number of one of these will open it and provide the references, abstracts, or full-text articles indicated. If you get stuck, typing SOS brings a trained researcher online to suggest alternate keywords when you have difficulty in finding items of interest. IQuest searches are moderately expensive, and no credit is given for searches that don't pay off because you've done something wrong or entered misleading or incorrect keywords.

Using DIALOG

DIALOG can be accessed directly or through Delphi's gateway. It contains a staggering number of different databases: over 400 different bases, with 270 million references to over 100,000 publications, including the complete text of over 1,100 periodicals! Dialog searches are somewhat more complicated to manage than IQuest's and can also get very expensive. Inexperienced users might find them even more costly if they don't understand DIALOG's somewhat obscure commands. Subscribers to the DIALOG service will receive a manual. Those who use DIALOG through Delphi's gateway should be prepared for some frustration.

```
                     Terminal Emulation
  5   D&B Million Dollar Directory........2   full text   directories
      Disclosure                          0   full text   gov't reports
      Disclosure/Spectrum Ownership       0   full text   gov't reports
      Hoppenstedt German Directory        0   full text   directories
  6   ICC British Company Directory.......5   full text   directories
      KOMPASS Europe                      0   full text   directories
      KOMPASS UK                          0   full text   directories
      Media General Plus                  0   full text   corp. reports
      Moody's Corporate Profiles          0   full text   corp. reports
      S&P Corporate Descriptions          0   full text   corp. reports
  7   S&P Register - Corporate............1   full text   directories
  8   Thomas New Industrial Products......1   full text   press releases
  9   Thomas Register Online..............1   full text   directories
 10   Trinet Company Database.............2   full text   corp. reports
 11   Trinet U.S. Businesses.............27   full text   directories
      ABC Europe                          0   full text   directories
      German Buyers' Guide                0   full text   directories
      Hoppenstedt Austria                 0   full text   directories
      Hoppenstedt Benelux Database        0   full text   directories
      Who Supplies What?                  0   full text   directories
  H   Database descriptions
  M   Main Menu
SOS   Online assistance
```

8-23 The question was about U.S. companies doing business abroad.

To begin a DIALOG search, type B for BEGIN. Dialog uses Boolean logic to search its databases, meaning that the *and*, *or*, and *not* commands are recognized. The first command you must give the system is the SELECT command, or S. This tells the system that you wish to search for specific terms. Use the COMBINE, or C, command to combine the results of two keyword searches. To see the results of a search, the command is T, or TYPE. Do *not* use Print! The command PRINT or PR will produce an offline print, and if your search has yielded 4,000 entries, as it could, you could end up with a very large pile of pages and an even larger bill. To get help online, you need to use EXPLAIN, not help! Use EXPLAIN EXPLAIN to get a command list. The command to leave DIALOG is LOGOFF. Exit won't get you out.

All the news

Each service has at least one source for news, and some have several. You can get the latest headlines from USA Today, the UPI Newswire, AP online, Reuters, and Newsgrid, as well as weather, sports, stock quotations, newsclips from the computer industry, and a good deal more. Even more important, the news is there whenever you need it and in its uncut versions—straight from the same wire services that your local TV station and newspaper subscribe to. You don't have to wait for the morning newspaper or the late night TV broadcast to find out what's going on. You can read *all* the news, without having to wonder if the newspaper editor or TV news staff thinks that the story you're interested in is important enough to include.

You can even find many of the "soft news" features you'd expect in the daily paper, including editorial cartoons (available on America Online), weather maps, your daily horoscope, and columnists of all sorts. To find online news, look for a News icon or news area on a menu. If you are using CIM, just click on the stack of newspapers, as shown in Fig. 8-24, to bring up the list of News sources. If your CompuServe membership includes the Executive Service Option, you can use the Executive News service as your personal clipping service and designate up to three personal folders in which the service will place all articles that pertain to the topics you designate. This is ideal for your children's school projects as well as for tracking stories of particular concern. For each folder, you will be asked to designate up to seven different keywords. An example is shown in Fig. 8-25. Any stories containing those keywords will be placed in the folder for a period of time that you determine (up to 14 days). Keywords can be combined using symbols to replace the *and, or* and *not* limiters. Use a plus symbol to represent *and*: A+B. The vertical bar represents *or*: A|B. The minus symbol stands for *not*: A−B. Avoid using hyphenated words as keywords because the search program will read the hyphen as a minus and assume that, for example, you mean "Mason *not* Dixon Line."

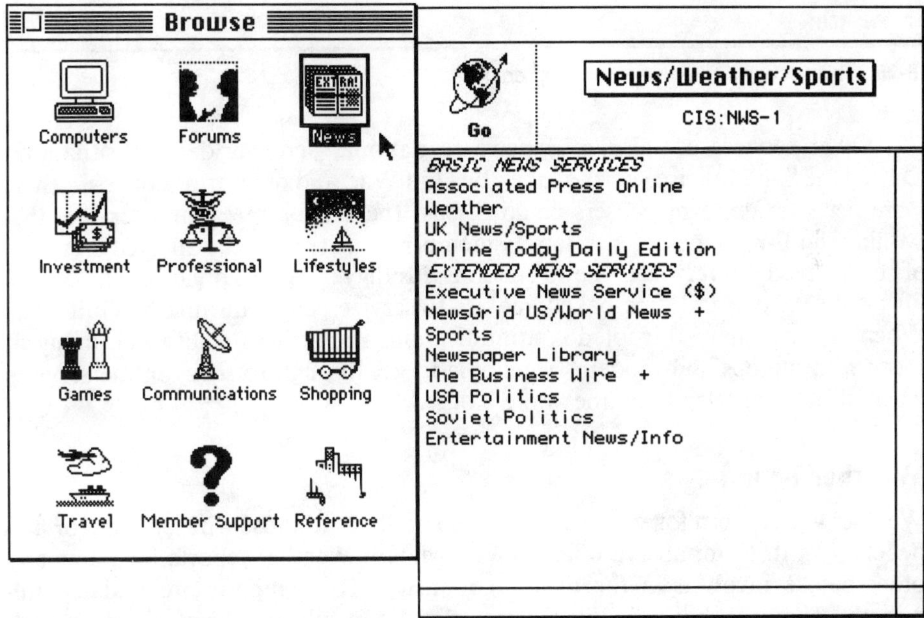

8-24 All the news that's fit to upload?

When there's a major world or national event, like the Los Angeles rioting in May 1992, the ENS creates its own folder of stories that are available to all subscribers. Stories are filed in chronological order with the newest ones "on top." ENS also lets you scan by the ticker symbol of a company in which you're interested. For example, entering aapl brings up a half dozen current stories about Apple Computer from the Reuters Financial News network.

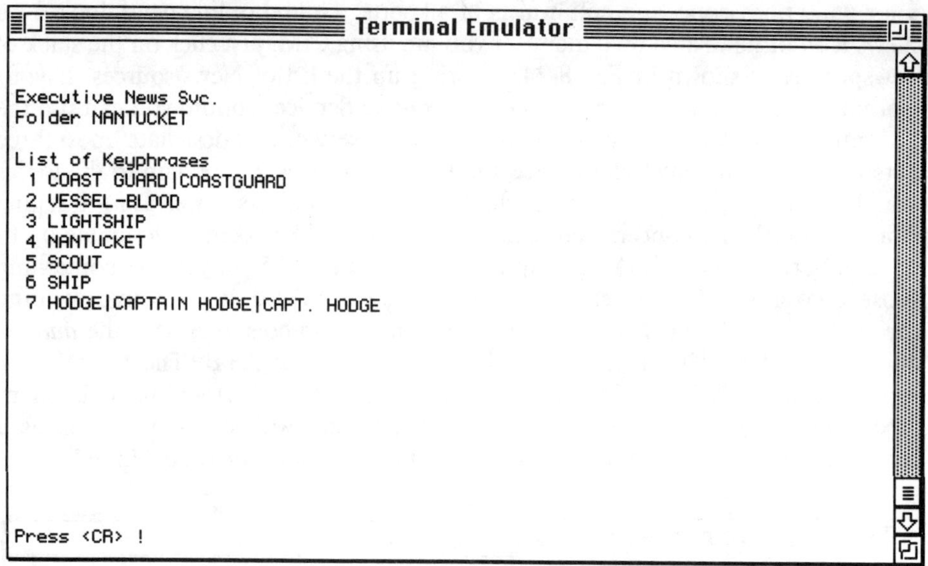

8-25 This folder will fill up when my ship comes in.

Other services are also responsive to national and world crisis situations. During the San Francisco earthquake, the Gulf War, and other times of crisis, there were news forums where users could discuss the events, messaging services that would send E-mail messages to family members or friends in the affected area, and of course, read the very latest news bulletins. Prodigy members organized a "cookie lift" and sent tons of home-baked cookies to service people during the Gulf War. When an earthquake disrupted communications in northern California, many of those with laptops and modems were able to get through to their online services when all normal telephone lines were clogged.

Weather or not

Weather is a concern for most of us, but especially so to those whose living (or life) depends on it. CompuServe offers NWS Aviation Weather reports for pilots and other people involved in the aviation industry. These reports are updated frequently. They are, however, highly specialized and full of abbreviations, making them less than helpful to the average reader. Figure 8-26 shows an Aviation weather report.

CompuServe users in coastal areas also have access to marine forecasts, emphasizing areas of concern to fishermen, shipping interests, and recreational boaters. These forecasts, provided by the National Oceanic and Atmospheric Administration, are among the most complete and accurate forecasts to be found anywhere. Prodigy, CompuServe, and America Online all provide weather maps. AO's must be downloaded and opened with a GIF viewer, but Prodigy's and CompuServe's maps can be seen online. Figure 8-27 shows a typical CompuServe weather map. On color Macs, they're in full color.

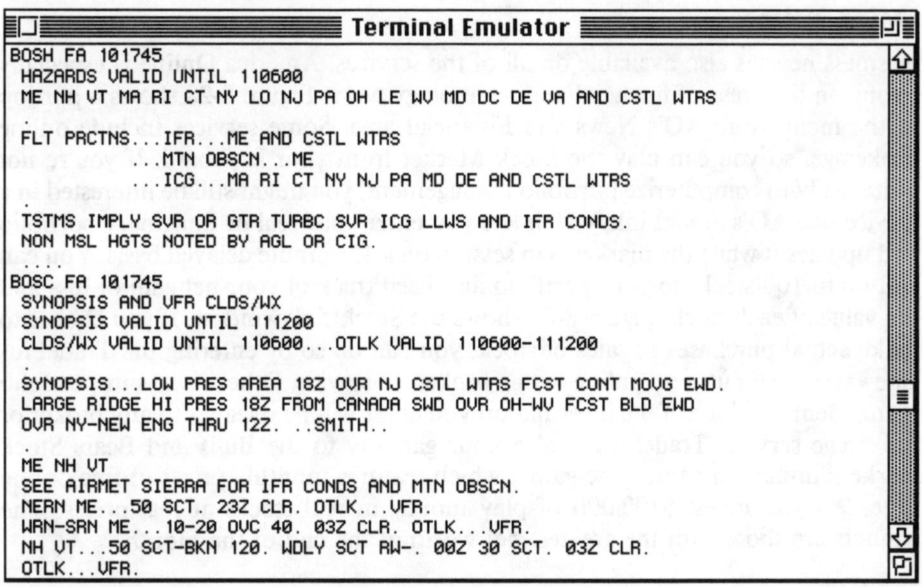

8-26 If you're a pilot, this makes sense; if not, it's rather cryptic.

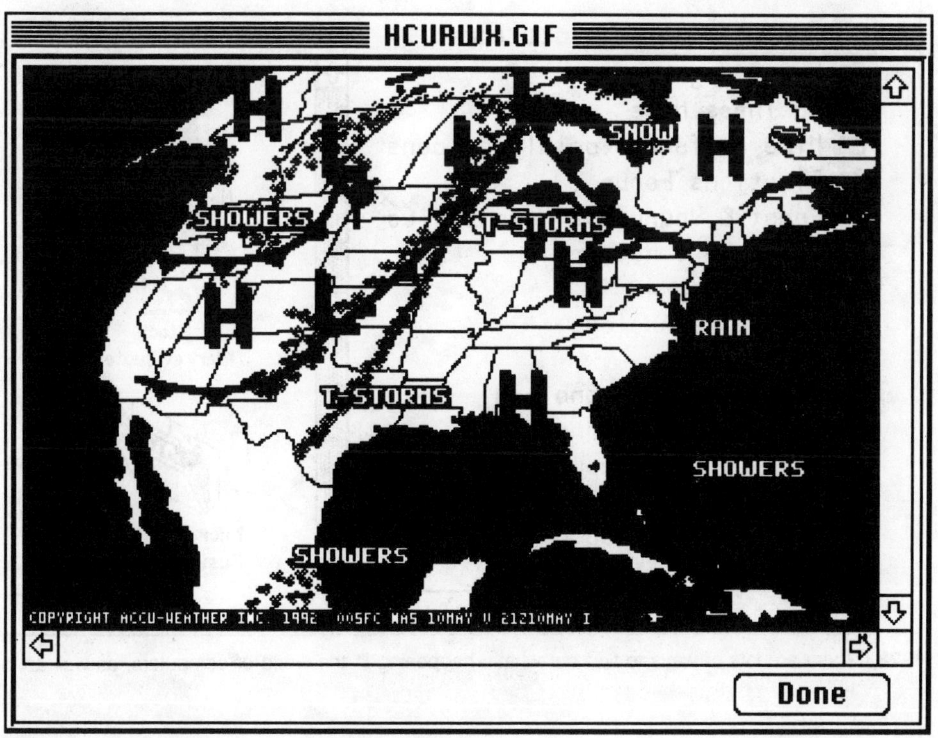

8-27 In color, these maps look like the ones on TV.

Doing business

Business news is also available on all of the services. America Online is especially strong on the areas of financial and technology news. Figure 8-28 shows a portion of the menu from AO's News and Financial area. Some services include online brokerage, so you can play the Stock Market from your keyboard. If you're not quite ready to computerize portfolio management, you might still be interested in a service like AO's StockLink, which lets you enter your real or imaginary portfolio and updates it while the market is in session on a 15-minute delayed basis. You can add up to 100 stocks to your portfolio and keep track of your net gain or loss and the value of each stock. Figure 8-29 shows the StockLink window. If you choose to make actual purchases or sales of stock, you can do so by entering the TradePlus gateway, which puts you online with a brokerage service. Otherwise, your portfolio is confidential. None of the information you enter will be released to any broker or brokerage service. TradePlus is also your gateway to the Bulls and Bears Stock market Simulation game. The game, which features monthly prizes of free online time, lets you invest $100,000 of play money in real stocks at real prices. The winners are those with the greatest net worth at the end of the month.

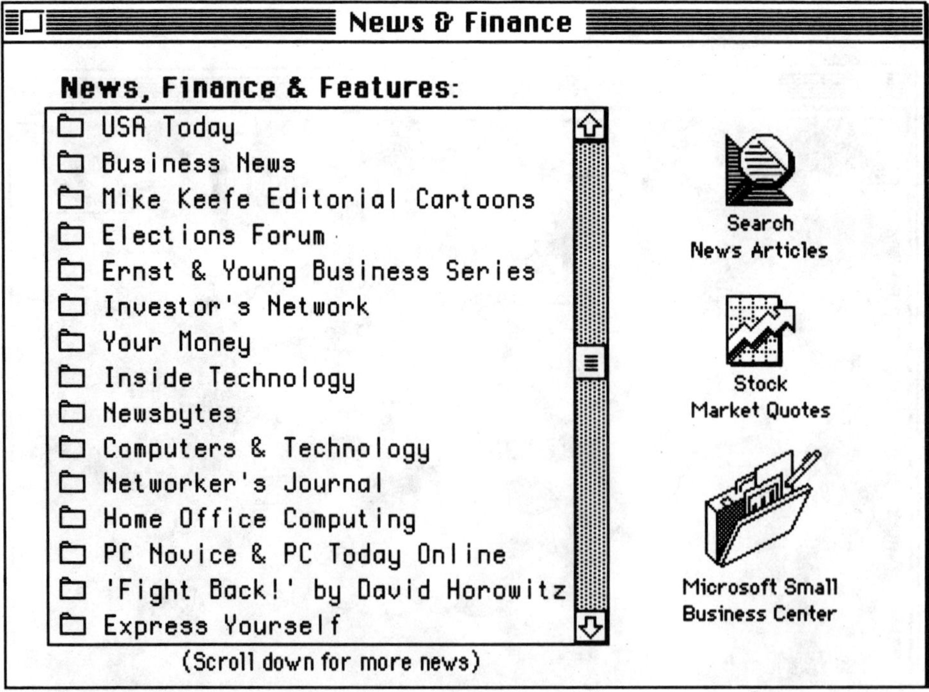

8-28 There are lots of ways to find out what's happening in the world of computers, as well as in business.

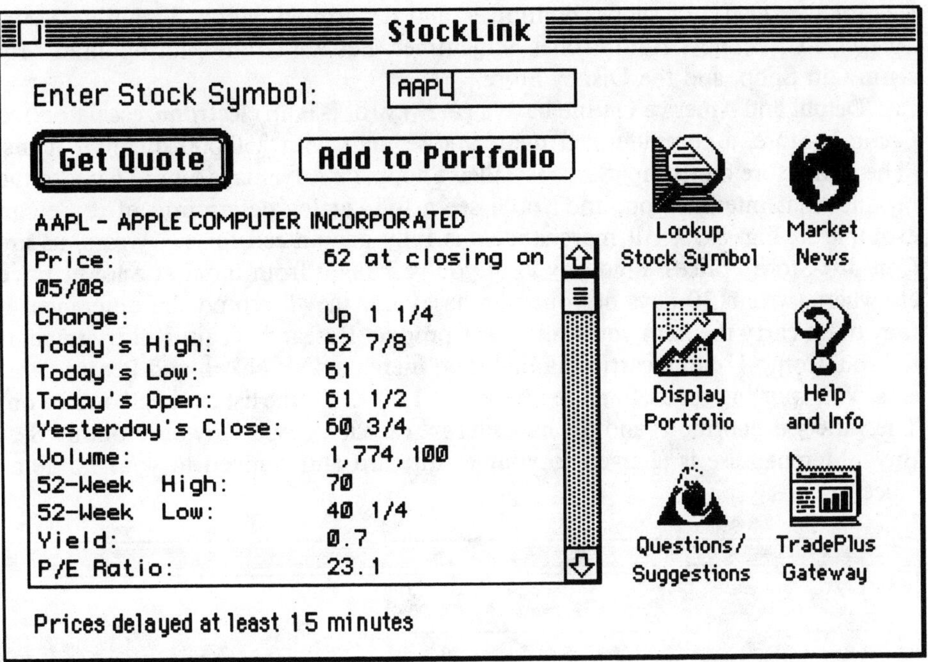

8-29 Apple had a good day.

And even more

Look online to find the latest news from the Entertainment industry, soap opera updates, the top 40 records, CDs, and tapes, and movie and TV reviews. There are recipe files, nutrition information, and wine taster's notes. You can find out from CompuServe's Books in Print if the title you're looking for is still available, then you can jump over to the electronic bookstore and order it. Need a toll-free 800 number? Look it up in the AT&T 800 Directory on CompuServe. Can't remember who played opposite Jane Fonda in *Barbarella*? You can find out by looking in Magill's Survey of Cinema. If you use a little imagination in your search, you should be able to find almost anything you might ever want to know in an online database.

Let's go shopping

Maybe shopping online isn't quite as much fun as a trip to the mall, but it's certainly convenient. You can order everything from flowers, coffee, and gourmet chocolates to exercise equipment, clothes for the entire family, and automobiles online, usually at better prices than you'd find in your hometown. Every service has some kind of online shopping. Prodigy is the champ, though. It features a whole electronic mall full of shops, boutiques, and department stores, including Sears, Spiegel, J.C. Penney, Hammacher Schlemmer, PetWorks, the Metropolitan Museum Gift Shop, and the Disney Store.

Delphi and America Online have a gateway (or is it an electronic escalator?) to Comp-U-Store, a computerized merchandise mart with 250,000 different items. (The same store on CompuServe is called Shopper's Advantage Club.) Choose the product that interests you, and you'll see a full catalog description of it. See an example in Fig. 8-30. All merchandise is fully guaranteed for two years, as are Comp-U-Store's prices. Find any item you've bought from them at a lower price elsewhere (within 30 days of your purchase) and they'll refund the difference. If they don't carry the item you want, their product Research Team will try to get it for you. Comp-U-Store carries name-brand merchandise: Nikon and Pentax cameras, Voit sporting goods, Sony, Nintendo, AT&T . . . the list could go on and on. The variety is enormous and the bargains are excellent, especially on monthly Best Buys. Merchandise is charged to your credit card and shipped to your home or office.

```
Delphi
Coffee/tea makers                          Page  2 of  3
          Model                  List $   Your $   PROGRAM
     -------------               -------  -------  --------
   7 GR                            69.95    54.39  NO
     Ttl: POUR-OMATIC COFFEE BREWER

Manufacturer: MR. COFFEE
   8 JR4                           27.95    24.38  NO

Manufacturer: PROCTOR SILEX
   9 A8004                       open       22.05  NO
  10 A8300                       open       34.89  YES
  11 A8704                       open       22.32  NO

Manufacturer: ROWENTA
  12 FK-70                         88.00    60.07  NO
     Ttl: 8 CUP

Enter HELP for instructions for
product comparisons

Enter selection(s) or <CR> for more >
4:49:49 PM
```

8-30 If you enter the number at the left, you'll get a full description of the merchandise.

CompuServe's Electronic Mall has 109 different merchants. You can order dress and casual clothing from Brooks Brothers, steaks from Omaha, books from Barnes & Noble, contact lenses, Levi's Jeans and Dockers from Sears, and a whole lot more. Although shopping online doesn't let you actually see the merchandise before you buy it, or try things on for size, you can often save enough to justify the nuisance of an occasional purchasing error. Also, online merchants have flexible return policies.

Of course, you can buy all sorts of computer equipment online, too, not just software and computer books, but everything from new modems and printers to pre-owned Macs. The Boston Computer Exchange (BoCoEx) pretty much sets the standard pricing for used computer equipment. They're a computer brokering service, matching buyers and sellers at a fair market price, less their 15 percent commission. If you have equipment to sell or are looking to buy some, this is the place! Look for BoCoEx on Delphi and in the publication MacWeek. You'll also find good deals on computer equipment and software in some of the other online shopping areas. It's always a good idea to read product reviews before you buy, so you might want to check out the MacWorld online area in AO or ZiffNet's MacWeek and MacUser on CompuServe. You can also find a lot of helpful computer information on BIX. In addition to the articles and reviews from BYTE magazine, there are many BIX Macintosh forums that tend to appeal to the more technically minded computer user and are a good source for answers to questions involving both hardware and software problems.

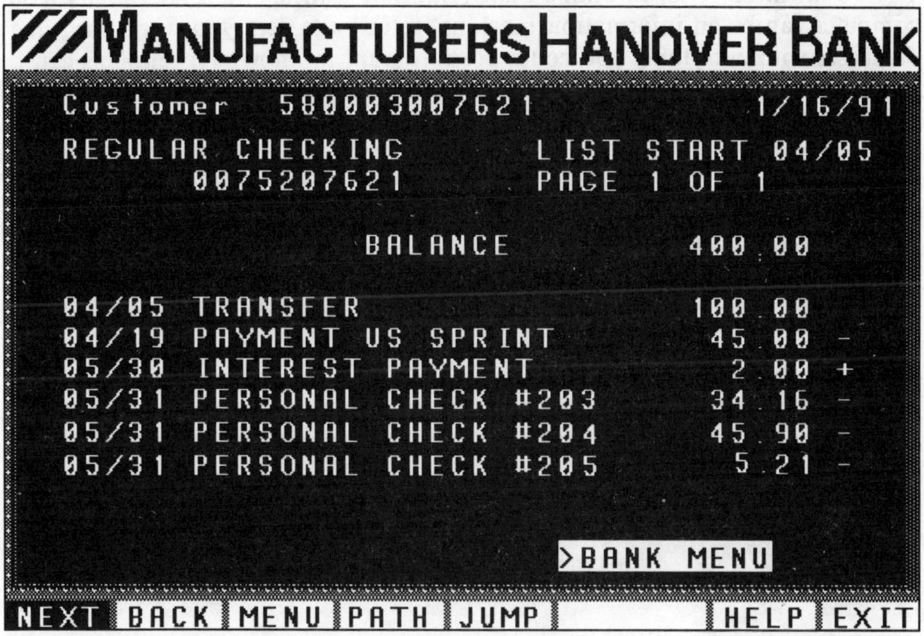

MANUFACTURERS HANOVER BANK

Customer 5800030007621 1/16/91

REGULAR CHECKING 0075207621 LIST START 04/05 PAGE 1 OF 1

BALANCE 400.00

04/05 TRANSFER 100.00
04/19 PAYMENT US SPRINT 45.00 -
05/30 INTEREST PAYMENT 2.00 +
05/31 PERSONAL CHECK #203 34.16 -
05/31 PERSONAL CHECK #204 45.90 -
05/31 PERSONAL CHECK #205 5.21 -

>BANK MENU

NEXT BACK MENU PATH JUMP HELP EXIT

8-31 One advantage to online banking is that you don't need to wait a month to see your statement.

The First National MacBank

It's easy enough to spend money online, as you've just seen. How about saving money online? The answer is, "Probably not." You can, however, pay bills online and balance your checkbook (if you have a checking account and ATM card with a participating bank). Online banking has its limits, and until they can make crisp 20s slide out of the disk drive on command, it won't be completely satisfactory, but you *can* take care of many banking chores from your keyboard. It all happens on Prodigy. (As of this writing no other service is offering online banking.)

You can choose a local bank, if any in your area are participating in Prodigy's online banking service, or open an account with Manufacturer's Hanover Trust. You will also receive an ATM card, good at thousands of Automatic Teller Machines. Once you have established a checking account, it's a fairly simple matter to sign on and pay your bills by entering the amounts, to whom they should be sent, and on what date. Figure 8-31 shows an example. If you change your mind, it's easy to stop a payment that hasn't yet been made. Just delete it. Your account is protected by a separate password, in addition to your regular Prodigy password. You can also make transfers between accounts, check your balance, and see your monthly statements online.

Summary

There's much more to do online than chat, play games, and send E-mail. Your computer can be an information machine, getting the data you want from huge databases with everything you could possibly want to know. Travel plans can be made and confirmed online, tickets purchased by credit card, and hotel rooms and rental cars confirmed. You can also find out about the places you're visiting. Online encyclopedias are updated more often than the printed ones. Databases hold huge collections of material from all sorts of periodicals, daily newspapers, and even TV scripts. Specialized databases serve the needs of the medical, legal, and business/financial professions.

You can get online news, weather, stock quotes, and even cartoons and horoscopes. In fact, you can read most of the major daily newspapers online if you wish. (They cost less in print, though.) Online portfolio management can be a game or for real, through several online brokerage services. Stock quotes lag 15 minutes behind Wall Street. Online shopping is easy and can save you money. Use buying guides like *Consumer Reports Online* to help you choose wisely. Online bill paying and banking are available only through Prodigy. They make money management easy.

9

Just the fax, Ma'am

Faxing is considered by many to be the single most useful development in office technology since the pencil. Certainly, the ability to send documents instantly from one part of the world to another has revolutionized the way business is done. It's also brought about some rather startling changes on the home front. Last night my younger son got a call from a classmate. David had forgotten to bring home his history book. Could Danny please fax him the homework? No problem—both sets of parents have home offices and fax machines. A local woman who carries on a voluminous correspondence with family members in Russia reports that the mail service, never efficient, has become increasingly unreliable. Now she faxes her mail and gets faxed answers the very next day! Restaurants and delicatessens accept faxed lunch orders, and what's delivered is much more likely to be what was ordered. By now, there are an estimated four million fax machines in use worldwide!

Two ways to fax

There are, of course, two types of fax machines: stand-alone fax machines and fax/modem combinations. Which one you buy depends on what you're likely to be sending or receiving on it. You might decide, as my family did, that you really need *both* kinds. The major difference in the two is the source of the material that can be faxed. A separate fax machine can send an image of anything that it can scan, but your Mac can only send material that it contains. If you wanted to send a cartoon from the daily paper, a page from a book, or a handwritten note, you'd need either a stand-alone fax machine or a scanner that would let you turn them into graphics or text files so they could be sent from your Macintosh.

Dedicated fax machines

A dedicated, or stand-alone, fax machine is a self-contained unit. Within it are a built-in scanner and printer, as well as the necessary electronics to convert the scanned image to a stream of 1s and 0s and to send this information over the telephone line. Most fax machines also have a telephone handset built in, so you can use one as an extension phone if necessary. When a page is scanned by a fax machine, it's translated into locations on the page, and each location is assigned either a 1 or a 0, depending on whether that particular dot is black or white. Thus, scanned images, like those on a computer screen or printed by a dot matrix printer, are said to be bit-mapped. Instead of being sent and received as text files, they are transmitted one bit at a time, until the whole page is drawn in bits.

Some fax machines have a glass plate on top, like a photocopier. They can scan and transmit an image of anything that can be placed on the glass. You can fax a drawing, a newspaper clipping, a business card, or even your hand. The drawback to this is that multi-page documents have to be set in position on the glass plate one page at a time. Someone has to stand there and switch pages until all have been sent.

Other fax machines feed documents through a set of rollers. These can feed a stack of pages without needing someone to insert each page, but they'll only accept standard 8½-x-11 paper. If you wanted to send a page from a book, a photograph, or something else in a non-standard size, you'd have to make a photocopy first. By the time the recipient got the fax of the copy, it *might* still be readable.

As a receiver of fax documents, the stand-alone machine is extremely easy to use. It waits for a call, answers, receives the data, and spits out a paper copy. No user input is required. Centralized fax machines can be used by a group of people within an office. If it has its own phone line, the fax machine can be left on, ready to receive or transmit any time of the day or night.

Faxing from the Mac

Sending a document that you've created on the Mac is simple when you use a fax/modem. You don't ever need to print a copy. You don't need to look up the recipient's number and make up a cover sheet. You don't have to carry your document to the fax machine, place the call, and send the pages one by one or make sure they feed properly into the rollers. You don't have to wait for the completion of the call to verify that the fax was received, and you don't have to keep a log showing who you called, what you sent, and when, as most businesses require. The Mac does it all for you, often while you're working on some other project or out of the office. Mac faxes can be sent late at night when long-distance rates are low.

Files to be faxed can go directly to the fax handler to be "scanned" by the software so that a bit-mapped image can be created and saved. It takes seconds, instead of minutes. The fax software creates a cover sheet for you, sends the documents, and monitors the transmission. If it's successful, the Mac notes the time and files a receipt. If the fax transmission doesn't go through, the document is sent again immediately, several times if necessary. You can set a time for the document to be faxed, and you can send the same file to a "mailing list" of people, if you wish. Your fax software includes an address book, which can contain as many names as you care to put in it.

The main advantage of sending your faxes directly is that the recipient will see the best possible quality. Faxes sent from a stand-alone machine are fuzzy, at best. Mac-generated documents, because they haven't had to go through that extra generation of printing and scanning, are much clearer, especially when you are using TrueType or a PostScript font with Adobe TypeManager.

Typical stand-alone fax machines use thermal (heat-sensitive) paper, which deteriorates over time, especially when it's exposed to bright light or heat. If you store faxes in a file cabinet near a radiator, or leave them in a beam of sunshine on your desk, it won't be long until they turn black. Faxes received on a Mac can be stored as files on a disk or printed out on plain paper, giving them an extremely long shelf life. Even more important to some users, sensitive documents sent and received on the Mac needn't be taken to a shared fax machine where others might see them. They need never exist on paper, and files can be password protected on the computer to keep them secure.

What about using both?

Although it's easier to send Mac documents from a Mac, many people prefer the convenience of a stand-alone fax machine for receiving incoming faxes. Realistically, though, cost is a factor for most of us. You can purchase a fax/modem that will send and receive for about $200 and one that adds voice messaging capability for only a little more. The least expensive fax machines start at about twice that and go up and up. A plain paper (non-thermal) fax machine will cost close to $1,000 as of this writing, more if you add optional features. In an office environment, it makes sense to have both a fax/modem and a stand-alone fax machine available. Most users will prefer to send faxes from their desks because fax handling is a background task that needn't interrupt other work, as a trip down the hall to the central fax machine invariably does. At home, a fax/modem might be adequate, especially if it's one that can receive as well as send.

The Macintosh PowerBook portables can be configured with Apple's send-only internal fax/modem or with either an internal or external third-party fax/modem that can both send and receive. If you're on the road, it's almost imperative to be able to receive faxes as well as send them. That's why so many PowerBook users balked at the Apple fax/modem, which was standard equipment when the PowerBook 170 was first released. Now you can choose from several different third-party fax/modem cards.

The mechanics of faxing

The fax side of the fax/modem uses a printer driver and functions much like a printer does. When you send a fax, it's as if you're printing it to a remote printer. The difference is that the remote printer is a group III fax machine or another computer equipped with a fax/modem capable of receiving group III faxes.

The software you need to send and receive faxes comes with the modem and is specifically designed for that particular modem. In other words, you can't use company A's fax software with company B's modem. The printer driver lets you control the various steps in sending the fax. Most fax/modems also include a DA fax manager, which lets you schedule sending faxes, bundle together several different documents going to the same address, view or print them, and create cover sheets. You can also open your fax address book from the fax manager.

All fax software works in more or less the same way, although there are individual variations in commands and in the way data is entered. We'll look at two slightly different fax systems—one from Global Village and one from Dove. If your modem and fax software come from a different maker, the principles will be the same, although dialog boxes might be slightly different.

Steps in sending a fax

To send a fax with the Global Village software, first open the document you want to fax. There are two ways to choose to send a fax. Either open Chooser from the Apple menu and double-click the fax icon or hold down the Option key and open the File menu. If you use the Option-key shortcut, instead of the usual print commands you'll see fax commands. Figure 9-1 shows the File menu from Microsoft Word, with and without the Option key pressed. When you select fax, whether you do so from the Chooser or from the File menu, a dialog box opens that lets you take care of all the details of sending the fax. When you use Chooser to select the fax software, it will stay "chosen" until you choose something else. If you use the Option-key shortcut, you're only choosing to send one fax. Afterward, the printer will be reselected and will reappear on the File menu.

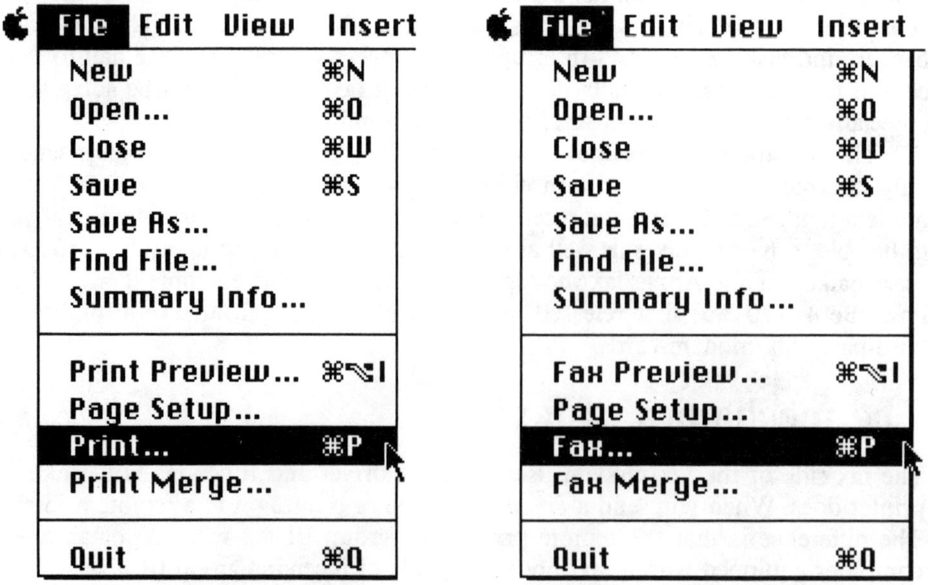

File Edit View Insert
New ⌘N
Open... ⌘O
Close ⌘W
Save ⌘S
Save As...
Find File...
Summary Info...
Print Preview... ⌘⌥I
Page Setup...
Print... ⌘P
Print Merge...
Quit ⌘Q

File Edit View Insert
New ⌘N
Open... ⌘O
Close ⌘W
Save ⌘S
Save As...
Find File...
Summary Info...
Fax Preview... ⌘⌥I
Page Setup...
Fax... ⌘P
Fax Merge...
Quit ⌘Q

9-1 The Fax commands replace the Print command on the menu whenever you select **Fax**. This lets you know whether your document will be printed or faxed.

Your first fax

If this is the first time you've tried to send a fax with this software, you'll have to go through some setup procedures. You will see a Phone setup box and then a Fax setup box. The Phone setup box is shown in Fig. 9-2. This dialog box lets you enter data that tells the modem how to dial the numbers you enter in the address book. If you must dial *9* to get an outside line, for example, it can be entered here, so you won't have to add it every time you enter a phone number. Since this usually requires waiting for the dial tone, add a comma to tell the modem to pause. Enter the long-distance prefix and local area code where you are, not the one you're calling. Select Pulse dial if the system from which you're calling doesn't use Touch Tone dialing. Select Ignore Off Hook only if the modem is attached to a multi-line push-button phone system. Select Ignore Dial Tone only if your PBX system has a non-standard dial tone.

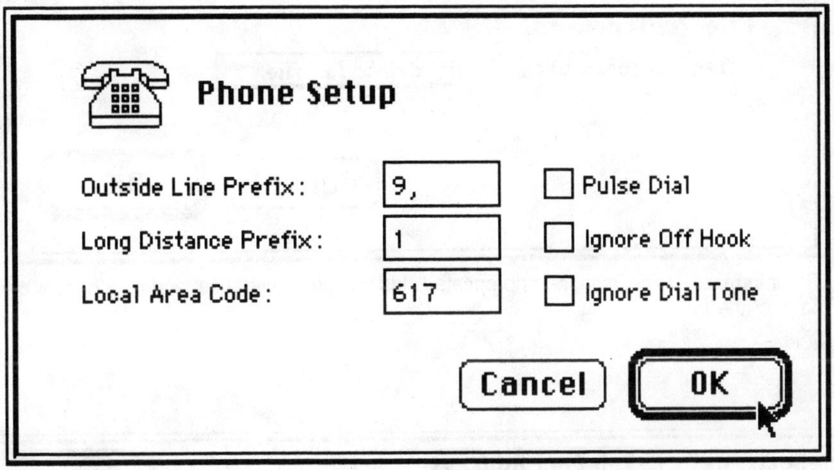

9-2 Be sure to enter your own area code in this box, not the one you're calling.

The Send Fax setup box, shown in Fig. 9-3, lets you enter your "station name," which is the name of your company, your name, or whatever designation you want to appear at the top of each faxed page. The station fax number is the number of the phone line attached to your fax/modem. Set an appropriate number of retries and time in between them, and decide what you want to do with the fax file after the fax has been sent. Your two options are to save or to delete the file. Deleting doesn't mean deleting the document that was faxed, only the fax version of it. Saving it lets you view the fax file at a later date. Because fax files require about 30K of disk space per page, you need to be aware of the free space available for storage on your disk.

The send fax dialog box

The setup boxes will appear only the first time you use the fax software. Normally, you'll see the Fax dialog box shown in Fig. 9-4. This box is the command center for

Send Fax Setup

Station (displayed at the top of each fax page sent)

Station Name: Pink Pussycat Productions

Station Fax Number: 617-555-8869

Retry Preferences (for unsuccessful fax transmissions)

Number of Retries: 3

Delay Between Retries: 10 minutes

File Preferences

After a successful fax: delete fax file

Cancel OK

9-3 This information appears in the appropriate fields on your cover sheet and as a header on each page of the fax.

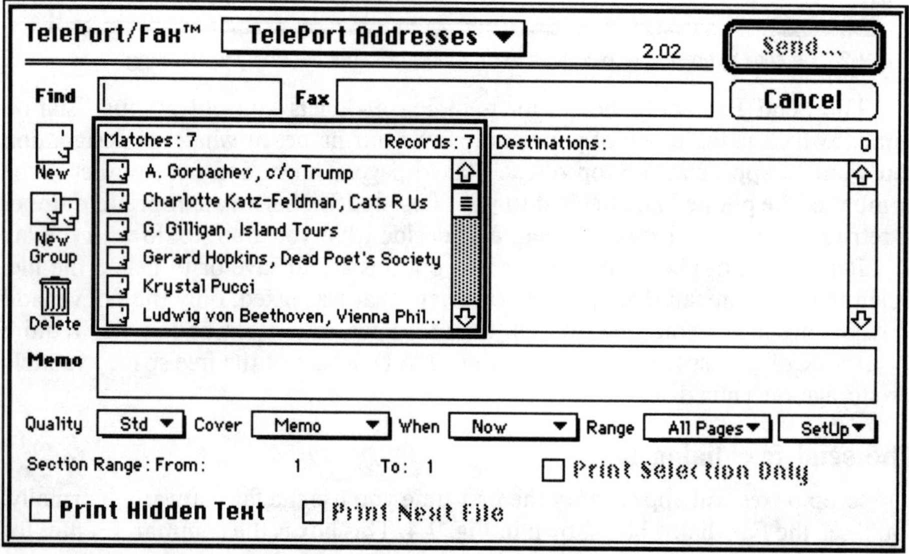

9-4 To find a name on your list, type the first few letters of the name into the **Find** box.

creating and sending faxes. It lets you open your address book and enter new names, create groups of people as a "mailing list" for your fax, delete unneeded names from the address book, and, of course, send the fax. Within this dialog box, you can also determine whether your fax is sent in standard or "high-quality" mode, when it's sent, what kind of cover page (if any) is to be prepared for it, and whether you're sending the whole document or just a few pages from it. These choices are made from the pop-up menus at the bottom of the box.

Entering a new address

To enter a new address for a fax, select the New icon and type the information into the fields as shown in Fig. 9-5. Entering an organization is optional, but you must enter a name and a fax number. Always enter an area code with the telephone number, even if it's the same as yours. You can use parentheses to separate the area code or just enter the numbers. The software compares the area code with the one you have entered in the Phone setup box, and if they are the same, doesn't dial it. After the name is entered, click OK. The name will appear in the left-hand menu. To address a fax to that person, select the name and drag it into the Destination box, as shown in Fig. 9-6.

9-5 Enter names as they should appear on the fax cover sheets.

Using a previously entered name

If the recipient's name is already in your fax address book, all you need to do is select it and drag it to the destination window. If you need to edit a name on the list, as when a phone number has changed, simply double click it to bring up the text entry box above and change the data as necessary.

When you have a long list of names in your address book, you can use the scroll bars to locate the one you're looking for or type the first few letters of the

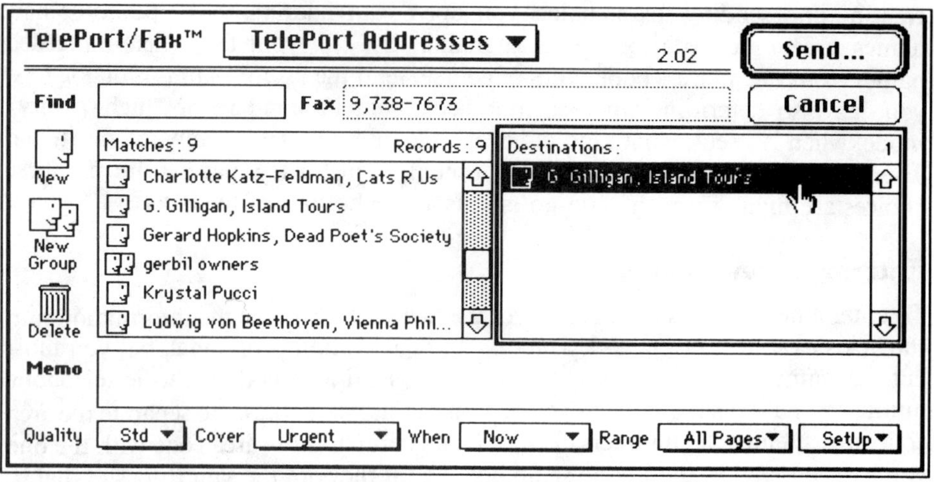

9-6 To send the same fax to several people, either create a group or drag additional names to the destination window.

name into the Find box. Only those names that contain the same combination of letters will be shown. To delete a name from the list, select it and drag it to the Delete trash can icon.

Creating a group

To send the same fax to a group of people, you must first create a group. A group can be two or more different addresses. Select the Group icon. You will see the dialog box shown in Fig. 9-7. Select the names of the people to be included in the group and drag them to the destination list. Give the group a name. Whenever you select this group, the fax will be automatically sent to all of them, with a cover sheet appropriately addressed to each.

Setting options

You have several choices to make about how and when your fax is to be sent. The first of these is quality—should the fax be sent Standard or Best quality? Standard quality uses fewer dots per inch (100 dpi) and is twice as fast as Best quality, which uses (200 dpi) and is extremely sharp. Which is more important depends on what's being sent as much as on when and where you are sending it. An ordinary memo or letter sent during the day from one side of the country to the other should probably be sent by the faster method. Artwork, an important report or spreadsheet, or anything of that nature, especially if it can be sent when long-distance rates are lowest, should be sent in the Best quality mode.

Figure 9-8 shows the menu choices for various options. The first of these is what type of cover page to use. Most fax programs come with a selection of "generic" cover pages. The information you have entered in the address book will appear in the appropriate fields on the cover page, along with your name and number as entered in the Setup dialog box. If you want to add a note to a cover page, type it into the memo box. (Later on in this chapter, I'll explain how to create custom cover sheets for your faxes and add them to this list.)

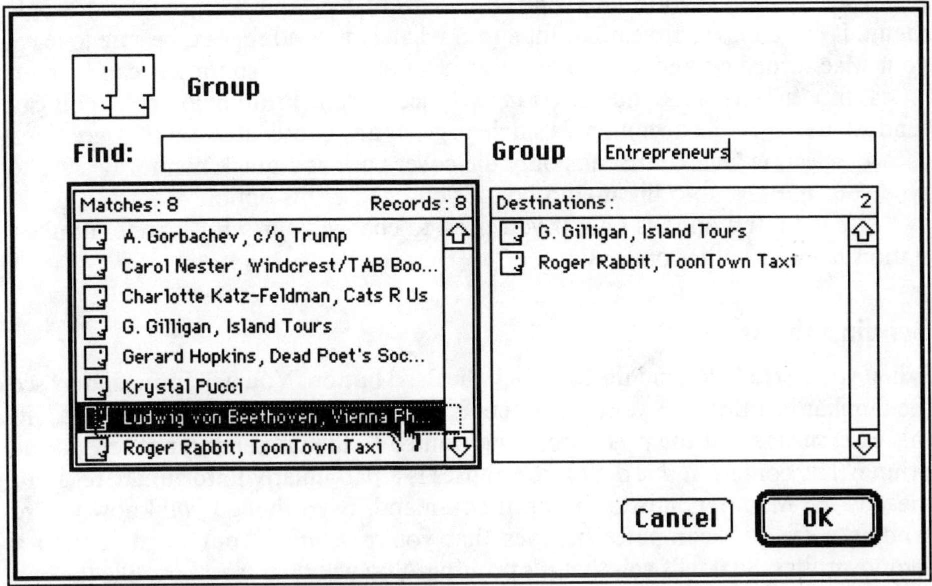

9-7 Groups can have as many members as you wish.

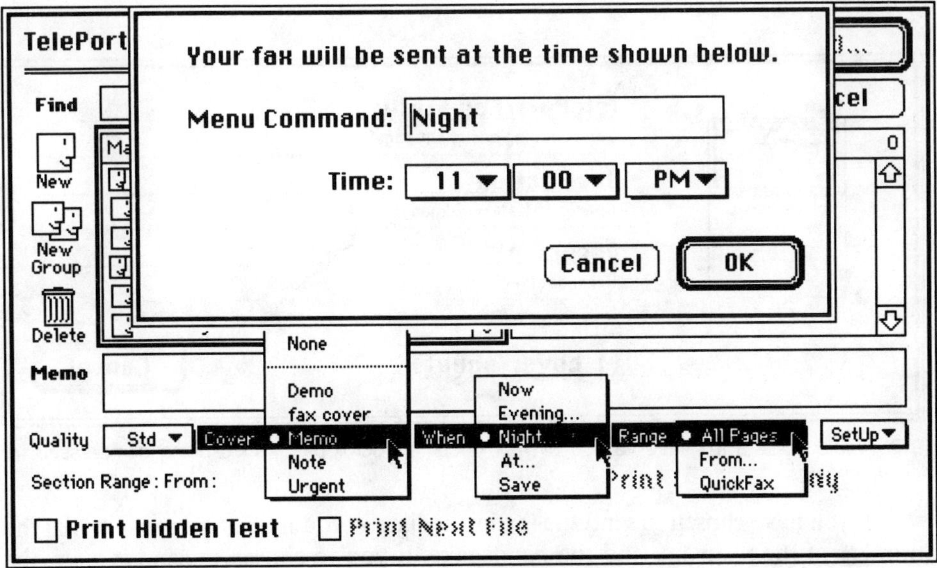

9-8 Ordinarily, you wouldn't see all these option menus at once.

The next choice you must make is when to send the fax. If you select Now, your fax will be sent immediately. Choosing Evening means that the fax will be sent after 5 P.M. local time, or whatever you determine to be an appropriate evening hour. Choosing Night means that the fax will be sent at midnight, or at whatever hours you specify. You can also set a specific time and date to send the fax, or save it in a ready-to-send form and send it later from the fax manager on the Apple menu. If you choose a time other than immediately to send the fax, be sure to leave your Mac turned on and the modem line clear at that time so the fax can be sent.

Range functions like the page range choice in your Print dialog box. You can send all the pages of a document, a single page, or any consecutive set of pages, such as 2-4. Selecting QuickFax sends only the cover page as a quick memo. Be sure to type your message into the memo box if you choose this option.

Use the setup options only if you need to change your setup phone number, station name, or other options.

Sending the fax

When you're ready to send the fax, click the Send button. You will immediately see the familiar box that says your document is being printed. Don't panic! "Print," in this case, means that the pages are being printed to the fax sender, not sent to the printer. The confusion this dialog box causes is a particularly unfortunate result of the way the Mac responds to the Print command. Even though *you* know you're sending a fax, the computer believes that you're sending your document to a remote printer. So it tells you that it's printing. You will then see a box, like the one in Fig. 9-9, that tells you that the documents you're faxing are being compressed. At this point, if you have changed your mind about sending this fax, you can click the Cancel button to stop it.

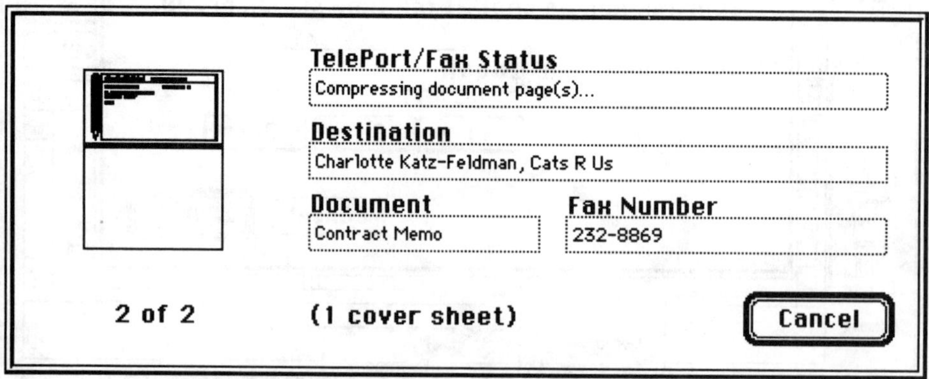

9-9 You will see a miniature version of your document scroll past as it's being compressed for sending.

If you have chosen to send the fax immediately, you'll hear the modem dial the number of the recipient, and the handshake. If you've chosen to send it later, the software will watch the clock and send the fax at the appropriate time, as long as the computer and modem are left on and the modem line isn't in use at the time.

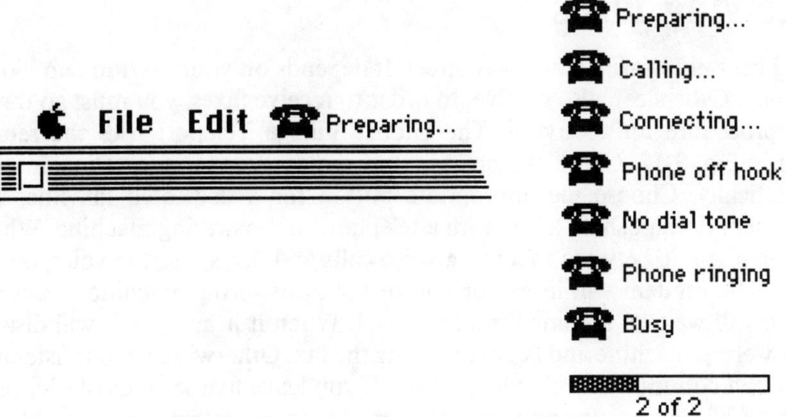

9-10 Depending on the current status of the fax, one of the symbols and messages on the right will appear on the menu bar.

The Global Village Teleport places an icon on the menu bar while the fax is being sent, which lets you track its status. Figure 9-10 shows various fax status displays you might see. The bar graph indicates what percentage of that page of fax has been sent. If you want to cancel a fax while it's being sent, click the status display and select Stop Faxing.

Sending a fax manually

Sometimes you can't send a fax automatically. You might need to send a fax manually if the recipient must turn on his or her fax machine to receive it or if there's an answering machine on the line that asks you to press a particular key on the phone if you're sending a fax. To identify fax telephone numbers that need to be dialed manually, place a bullet (•) in front of the number. (Use the key combination Option-8 to generate a bullet symbol.) To send the fax, proceed as you normally would. The computer will prepare the fax for sending. When it's ready, you'll see a dialog box like the one in Fig. 9-11, telling you to dial the number and send the fax.

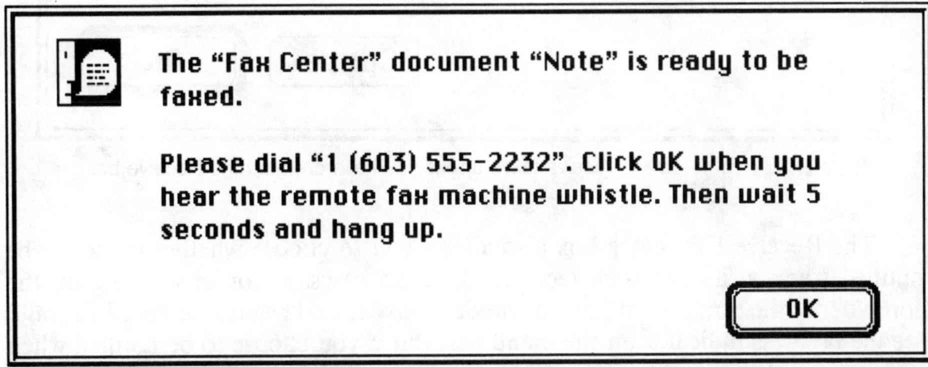

9-11 When you see this dialog box, dial the number and click when you hear the recipient's fax machine signal.

Receiving faxes

Faxing isn't necessarily a two-way street. It depends on your fax/modem. Some are send only. Others can also receive. In order to receive faxes, you must go through a setup procedure for receiving. The Global Village Teleport uses the setup box shown in Fig. 9-12. Check the box to allow the modem to receive incoming faxes automatically. Choose the appropriate button for a dedicated fax line, if your fax/modem doesn't share a line with a telephone or answering machine. When you must share a line between incoming voice calls and faxes, use the voice/fax switch setting. The modem will listen for you or your answering machine to answer the call and will wait on the line for a fax signal. When it hears one, it will disconnect the answering machine and begin receiving the fax. Otherwise, it stops listening and lets the call continue. Here's a helpful tip: If you leave five seconds of silence at the beginning of your answering machine message, callers attempting to send a fax to you will be able to do so without listening to the message.

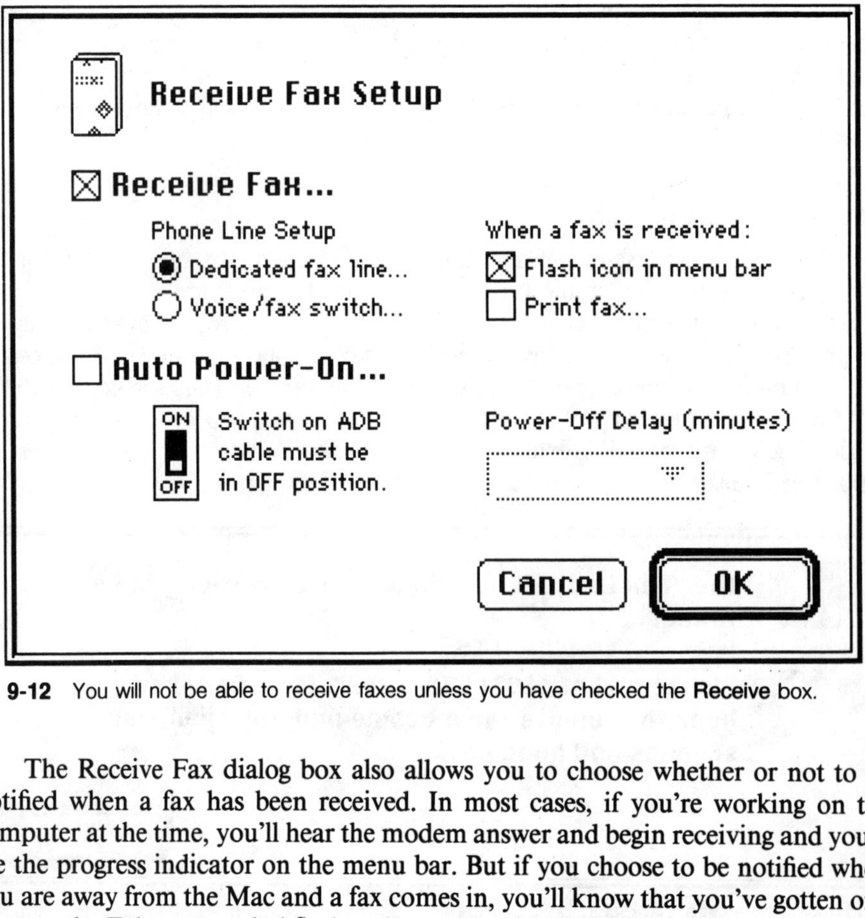

9-12 You will not be able to receive faxes unless you have checked the **Receive** box.

The Receive Fax dialog box also allows you to choose whether or not to be notified when a fax has been received. In most cases, if you're working on the computer at the time, you'll hear the modem answer and begin receiving and you'll see the progress indicator on the menu bar. But if you choose to be notified when you are away from the Mac and a fax comes in, you'll know that you've gotten one because the Teleport symbol flashes alternately with the Apple on the Apple menu.

The Auto Power-on option is not found on most modems but is available on the Global Village Teleport if you have a Mac II or PowerBook 100. It will also work with certain other Macs, notably the LC and Classic with the addition of third-party hardware. What it does is allow the Mac to turn itself on when an incoming fax is detected. It will automatically shut down again after a predetermined period of time unless you tell it to stay on. This feature is best ignored, however. There are two reasons it's not advisable. First, the computer might take a minute or more to "wake up," especially if you have a large number of INITs installed, and the incoming call will probably be disconnected before the Mac is ready to accept it. Also, this function would require that any external hard drives or other SCSI devices be left on at all times. When the Mac is turned on, it polls all of its SCSI addresses to make sure that all devices are present. If one is missing, the system will not boot. Use Auto Power-On only if you have a Mac PowerBook 100 with nothing connected to the SCSI port.

Avoiding faxes you might not want to receive

As many new fax machine owners have learned, junk mail has an electronic corollary—the junk fax. Dealers of office supplies, loan services, and employment agencies have used the fax machine as a way to solicit new customers. Even though the practice has received a good deal of adverse publicity and is currently outlawed in several states, it continues. It's a nuisance, and it can waste fax paper and tie up your phone line and fax machine or computer with messages you don't want, but what can you do?

First, don't publicize your fax number. Give it out to customers, of course, and people you trust. Don't give it to Fax directory solicitors who promise you a "free" fax listing. There's no reason to be listed in *any* directory, in fact. If you have a separate line for the fax/modem or fax machine, ask that it be unlisted.

Second, if you aren't expecting to receive any fax traffic, unplug the fax machine or modem. Most "junk fax" calls are made at night when rates are lower. Send and receive fax messages only during business hours or at predetermined times.

If you receive a "junk fax," contact the senders immediately and ask to be removed from their phone list. If they refuse, or if you get additional faxes from the same sender, contact your telephone company. Most have strict guidelines about business solicitation by telephone.

Fax status

All fax software includes some type of a fax manager window, which lets you check on the status of faxes waiting to be sent and keeps a log of faxes you've sent and received. This window is generally a DA, under the Apple menu. Figure 9-13 shows The Global Village Fax Center window. When you open this DA, you gain access to the Teleport menu. Use this window to get information about any fax that you have sent or attempted to send. You can also use this window to reschedule or re-address a scheduled fax and to view and print incoming and outgoing faxes. To

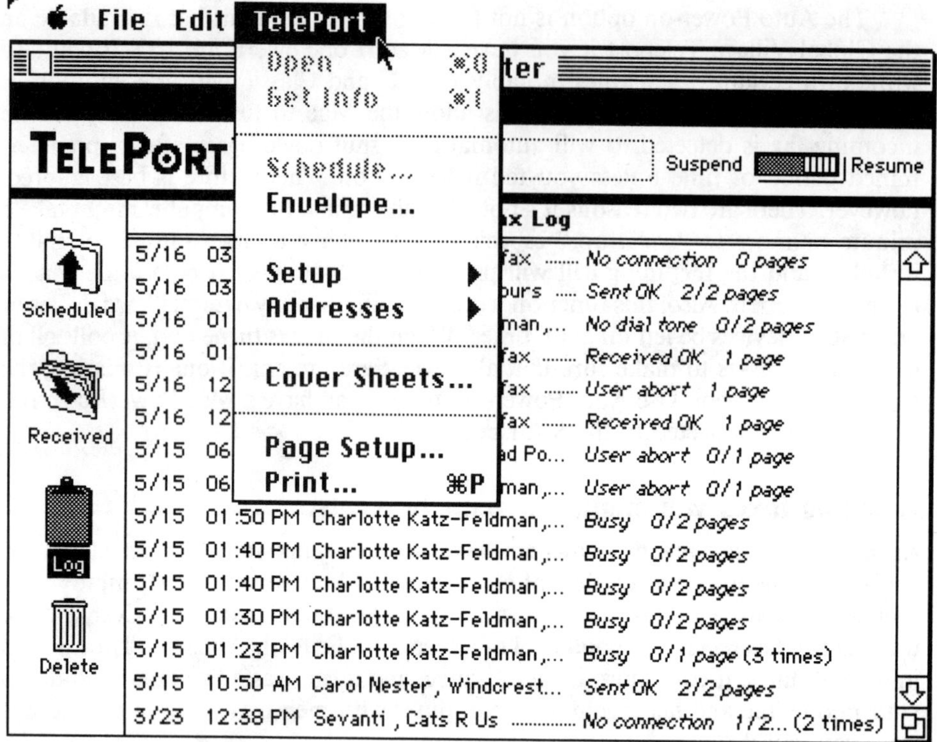

9-13 In this picture, we're looking at the fax log, a list of all faxes sent and received. The log also shows which faxes were sent unsuccessfully or canceled.

view a fax, open the appropriate folder to see the list, find the name of the fax you want to see, and double click it. Faxes you're sending will be on the Scheduled list. Faxes you've received will be on the Received list.

The fax document will open in a window like the one shown in Fig. 9-14. Tools at the bottom of the window let you zoom in on a particular area, navigate through the various pages of a document, and flip the page. Click the distant mountains to zoom out and the near mountains to zoom in. Zoom out to 33 percent to see the whole page in the window, or zoom in to 300 percent to read the fine print. Use the arrows for page up and page down and the flipped mountain to turn the page upside down. This last feature is more necessary than you might think. Faxes you receive from a fax machine will need to be flipped for on-screen viewing if they were sent upside down. They can be printed as received, though. It makes no difference which side is up on a printed fax because you can simply turn the paper around.

Creating envelopes

Suppose you have several documents to mail to the same address. You would save postage by putting them all in one envelope. Right? Of course, and you can do exactly the same thing if you have several different documents to fax. Most fax

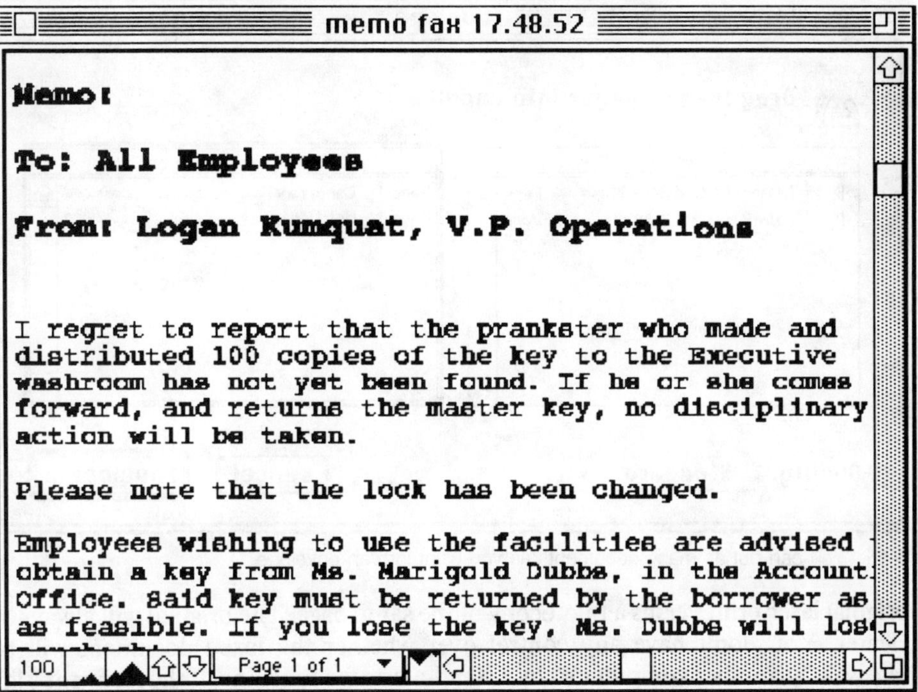
memo fax 17.48.52

Memo:

To: All Employees

From: Logan Kumquat, V.P. Operations

I regret to report that the prankster who made and distributed 100 copies of the key to the Executive washroom has not yet been found. If he or she comes forward, and returns the master key, no disciplinary action will be taken.

Please note that the lock has been changed.

Employees wishing to use the facilities are advised
obtain a key from Ms. Marigold Dubbs, in the Account
Office. Said key must be returned by the borrower as
as feasible. If you lose the key, Ms. Dubbs will los

100 Page 1 of 1

9-14 In the tool bar at the bottom of the screen, *100* refers to the current magnification percentage.

software lets you create envelopes containing different fax files or selected pages from several different documents that can be faxed together to the same recipient. Some do it automatically by checking to see whether there's more than one fax to be sent to the same phone number and automatically grouping all the faxes it finds for that number into one phone call. Others require that you create an envelope yourself and move the fax documents into it.

To do this using the Global Village Fax software, first save each document as a fax. Be sure that you haven't selected the Send Now option. If you have, the first document will be sending itself while you're setting up the next. Then choose Fax Center from the Apple menu and select Envelope from the Teleport menu. You'll see a dialog box like the one in Fig. 9-15. Select the fax files and drag them into the envelope window. Click the Envelope button to save and name the envelope. It will appear on the list as an unscheduled fax. To schedule it, drag its icon to the scheduled folder to bring up the dialog box that lets you schedule and address it. Click OK when done. The envelope of documents will be faxed whenever you've scheduled it, just as if all of the pages were physically linked.

How to have better-looking faxes

One of the advantages of sending faxes directly from your Mac is that they look better than documents sent from a dedicated fax machine because they haven't lost a generation by being scanned and re-printed. It's as if you were looking at an

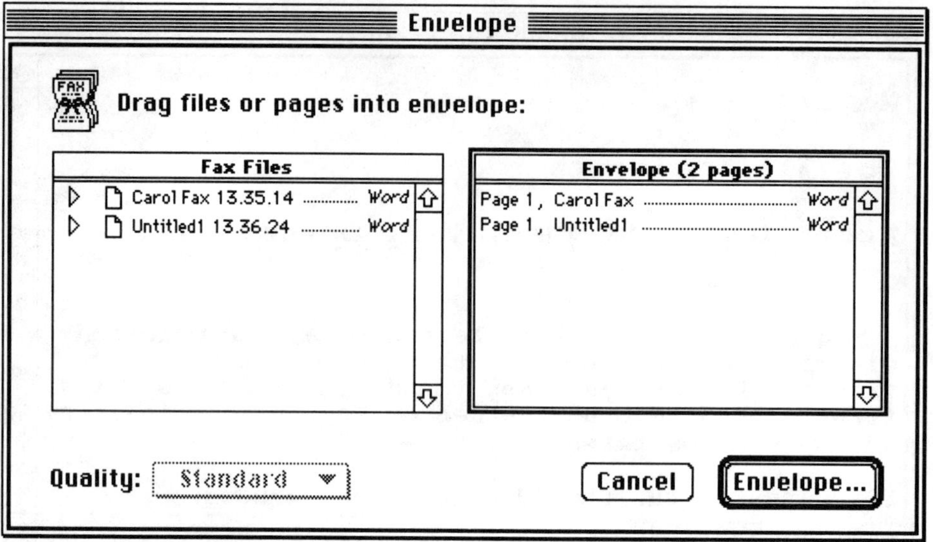

9-15 You can put as many documents as you want into an envelope.

original laser print versus a photocopy of the same page. The original will always be clearer. You don't have any control over whether the faxed document will be received by another computer or by a stand-alone fax machine. If the recipient's fax machine is misadjusted, your best efforts might be futile. Even so, there are a few steps you can (and should) take to assure that your faxed documents will be as crisp and clear as possible.

The first of these is to use legible type faces. Adobe Systems, the acknowledged type experts, commissioned a study to determine which type faces were best suited for faxing. After sending all kinds of documents over all kinds of fax machines, they determined that the four fonts shown in Fig. 9-16 were the easiest to read when faxed.

The second rule is to leave adequate amounts of white space (leading) between lines and adequate margins at the edges of pages. If you use a word processor that lets you view pages in layout form, check fax documents before you send them to make sure that the text is properly positioned on the page.

Graphics will look best if created in Draw programs rather than in Paint programs. Images saved as PICTs can be resized without distortion, and will hold

This is Helvetica.

This is Palatino.

This is New Century Schoolbook.

This is Courier.

9-16 They may not be the most interesting fonts, but they are the easiest to read.

onto their fill patterns better than Paint images. EPS drawing programs like Adobe Illustrator and Aldus Freehand can also be used to create images for faxing. Also, Paint programs use a resolution of 72 dpi (dots per inch). Fax machines and fax/modems send and receive at either 100 or 200 dpi. The difference means that some lines might develop "jaggies," that characteristic look of enlarged dots that makes your artwork appear to be assembled out of bricks. Using System 7 TrueType or Adobe TypeManager prevents this from happening to your type fonts, even at larger sizes, but jaggie Paint graphics are an unfortunate reality.

Customized cover sheets

Fax software generally comes with a couple of different "generic" fax cover sheets. They have blanks in which to enter the name of the sender and recipient, the phone numbers of both, and usually an area for a quick memo, as well as a notation about how many pages long the fax will be. These blanks, by the way, are called *fields.* When you type data, such as the name of the person to whom you are sending a fax, into a dialog box, the information is automatically entered into the appropriate field on the fax cover sheet. Each entry in the dialog boxes is keyed to a particular field on the cover sheet. If you intend to create a custom cover sheet, you must use your fax software's method of creating it to maintain the linkage between the fields on the cover sheet and the data in the dialog boxes.

Why do you need a cover sheet? If you're just sending a one page note, you might not. Sometimes, the cover sheet *is* the note. Most of the fax software we've looked at includes some kind of single page QuickFax form. There is a good reason for using one on a longer fax, though. If something goes wrong with the fax transmission, the recipient can see from the cover sheet how many pages have not been received and who to call to say, "Please try again." The problem with all of these generic forms is that they look, well, *generic.* They're not particularly interesting. You can design a better one yourself, using any graphics program that can save pages as PICT documents.

Apple's PowerBooks come with fax software that includes a separate application called Fax Cover for making up your own cover sheets. Figure 9-17 shows the fields from Apple's Fax Cover program. These fields can be renamed and resized. You can specify which to show and which to ignore. You can also add artwork to a cover sheet, as long as it's been saved as a PICT.

One way to do this is to use a Draw program, like MacDraw or SuperPaint's Draw layer. Create your fax cover sheet as a full-page document, using whatever graphics, logo, and other attributes you like. The necessary elements to be entered as fields are the date, addressee, fax number, sender, and number of pages. Be sure to leave space for these when you design your page. Remember, your own name or company name and other data can be included as part of the graphic because it won't change from one fax to the next. Fields contain only those items that will be different each time you send a fax. Figure 9-18 shows a sample fax cover. Apple's Fax Cover program incorporates the titles of the fields but doesn't let you remove unnecessary lines from a field.

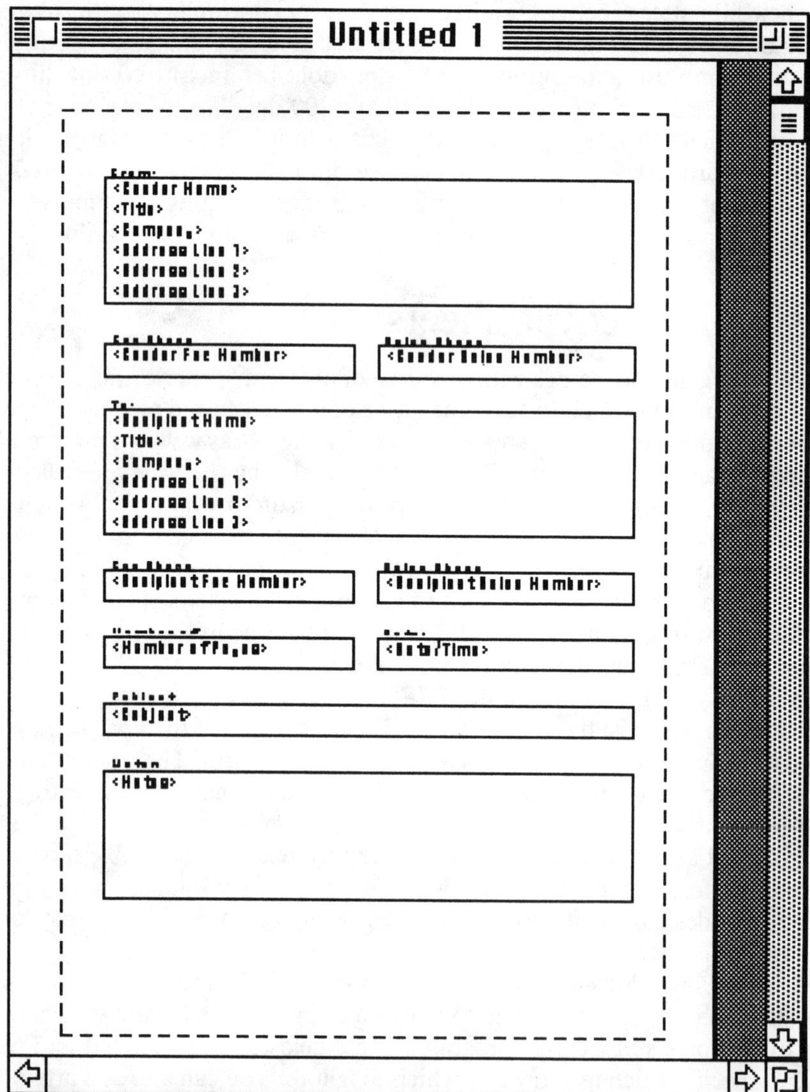

9-17 Apple's Fax Cover software uses multi-line fields.

Global Village's Fax Center also makes cover sheets from PICT files. To do so, choose Cover Sheets from the TelePort menu. You'll see a list of the cover sheets currently installed. It should look something like the one on Fig. 9-19. Choose New, and a standard Open File box will appear. Locate and select the PICT file to use as a background and click OK to open it. Drag the fields to the locations you have designated for them on the cover sheet. Change field sizes by dragging on their handles, as you would in a graphics program.

You can change the way text appears in any of these fields very easily. Double click any of the text fields to display its Field Info dialog box, as shown in Fig. 9-20. Select the font, style, and position, and click OK when you're done.

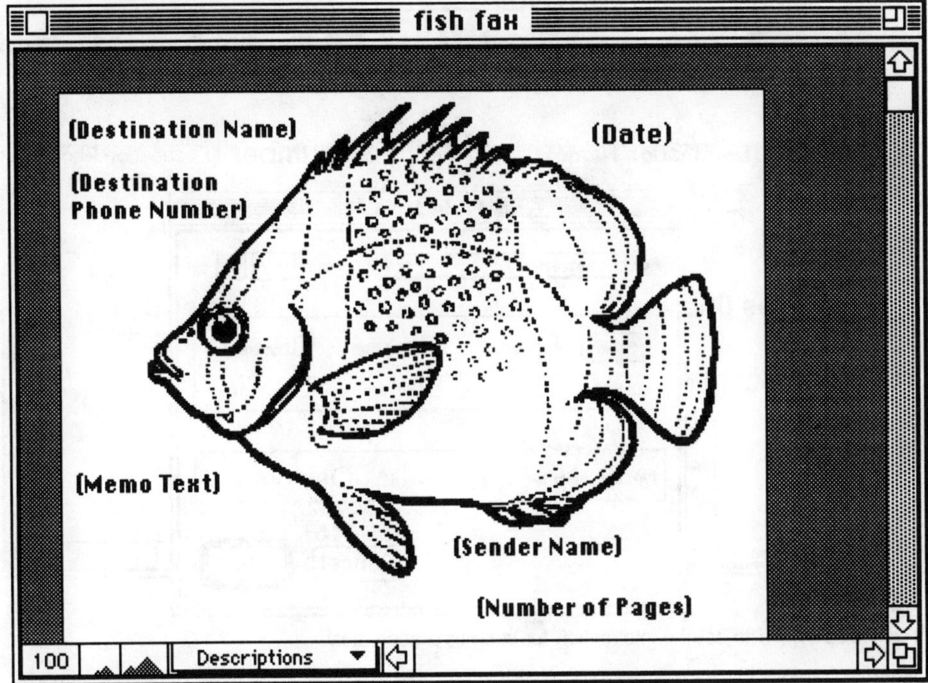

9-18 Use clip art to liven up your cover sheets.

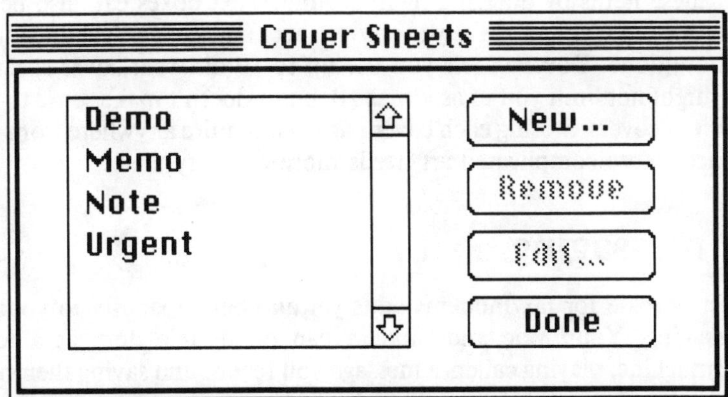

9-19 These four are the "generics" that come with the program. You can add as many as you wish.

When you're satisfied with the cover sheet, close the window by clicking in the Close box at the upper left corner. You'll be asked if you want to save the changes. If you choose Yes, the cover sheet will be added to the list of available cover sheets under the name you've given the PICT file.

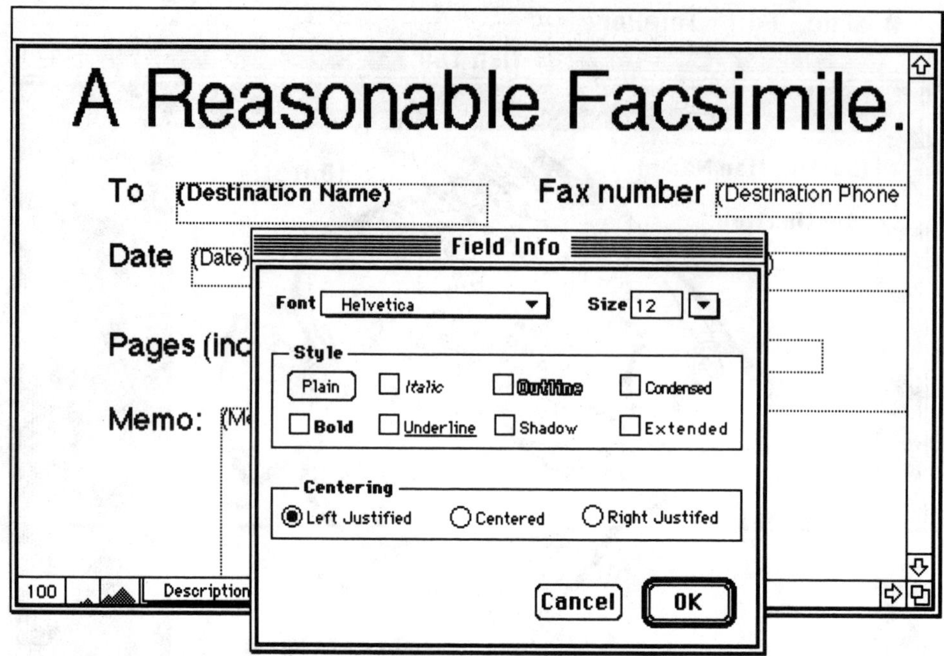

9-20 You'll need to set the information for each field separately.

Other programs, like DoveFax, have you paste graphics onto a cover sheet from the clipboard or scrapbook. You can create and paste a full-page graphic or just a logo, small picture, or piece of display type or line art. Once pasted, you can reposition these items by dragging them around. Text boxes can also be dragged into a suitable arrangement. Give your cover sheet a name and click OK to save it when you are done. DoveFax lets you use up to 10 different cover sheets. Other programs might not limit you to as few as 10, but it doesn't make sense to have too many different covers. Storing each cover page can require anywhere from 10–30K of disk space. More complicated art needs more memory.

Voice messaging

The newest wrinkle for fax/modems adds yet another capability to your Mac—voice messaging. Your Mac and modem can do double duty as a telephone answering machine, playing callers a message you record and saving their incoming messages on your hard disk for later playback. You can create different messages for different times of day or leave special messages for a particular caller. You can even create messages that need to have the caller enter a password, as well as one that allows the modem to receive a fax as well as a voice call.

DoveFax+ is typical of the fax/modems that permit voice messaging. To record an answer message for your DoveFax+, use the Recording Studio, shown in Fig. 9-21. The DoveFax+ comes with a small microphone that must be plugged

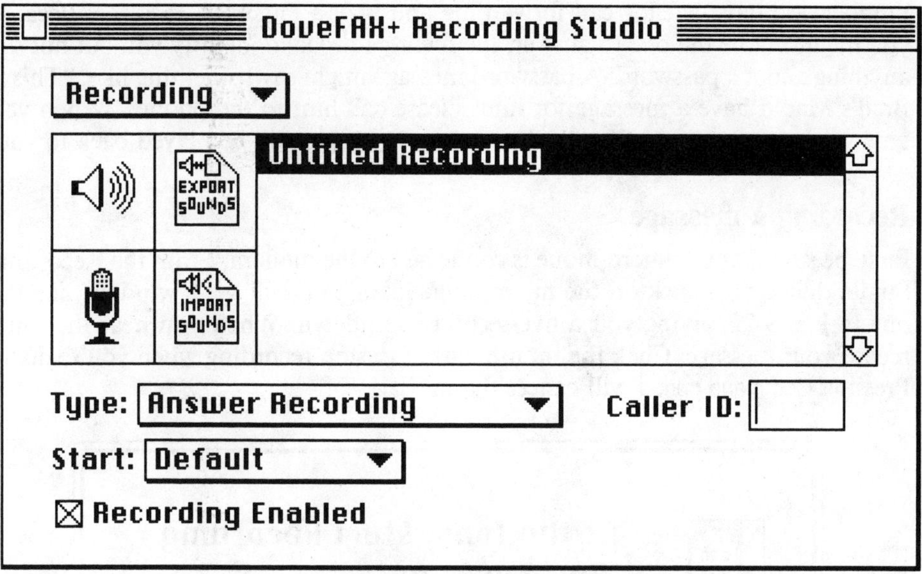

9-21 You can import sounds created in other programs by clicking the **Import** icon.

into the modem in order to record messages. (The microphones that come with the newer Macs will not work with this application.)

When you create a new message, you need to assign it a message type. Initialization messages are the first messages anyone hears when they call your Mac. Initialization messages prompt callers with user IDs to enter them. They also contain a four-second pause to allow an incoming fax to connect.

Answer messages are played to anyone who calls when the Mac answers an incoming call. You can create as many different answer messages as you want, or have disk space for, as long as one is designed as a default. You might have a special message to play from noon to one, saying that you're at lunch; another one for weekends, and perhaps a special one for the holidays. The Mac will choose the most appropriate message for the date and time, or play the default, if none of the others fits.

User messages are messages you record for specific callers. Each one has a particular caller ID attached to it. You assign ID numbers to your family, friends, or clients who might need to call in for a specific message. IDs are any combination of one to four letters or numbers that can be entered from a touch tone phone. You type the code into the appropriate box in the Recording Studio when you record the message, and the caller must enter the same code in order to hear the message played back. If, for example, you have left a message for your brother, when he calls and gets the Mac he enters his ID code. Then, the computer will play back his special message instead of the normal one.

Password messages let you enter a similar ID code from a remote phone to hear a playback of your messages. It's also possible to have the Mac forward your messages to another phone. When a message is received, the Mac will dial the number you have left for call forwarding and play a Password message. Because you might not be the one to answer, the message needs to identify you but not say anything about a password. A password message might say something like, "This is Brad's Mac. I have a message for him. Please call him to the phone." When you type your password into the telephone, your messages will be played back to you.

Recording a message

First, be sure that the microphone is connected to the modem. From the Recording Studio dialog box, click on the microphone icon. You will see a window, like the one in Fig. 9-22, giving you a five-second countdown. When you hear the tone, record your message. Click the mouse button to stop recording when you're done. Pressing Command-period will cancel the message.

9-22 You'll have five seconds to clear your throat and take a breath before you start.

Play back your message to check it by clicking on the speaker icon. If you don't like it, try again. If you're satisfied, click the Add button to add this message to the list in the window.

Use the DoveFax+ Manager, shown in Fig. 9-23, to listen to your messages. You can enter the names and ID numbers of anyone who can receive User messages in the Phone Book. (The Voice Phone Book is separate from the fax phone book.) Whenever anyone with a user ID calls, he or she is listed by name in the log. Other calls are listed as "unknown caller." If you want to call back an identified caller, click the Return Call button, and the modem will dial the call for you. Pick up the telephone handset. When you hear someone answer, click the OK button to disconnect the modem from the line and begin the conversation. You can also use the phone book to dial calls by finding the name of the person you wish to call and following the same procedure. Click Dial to start the call.

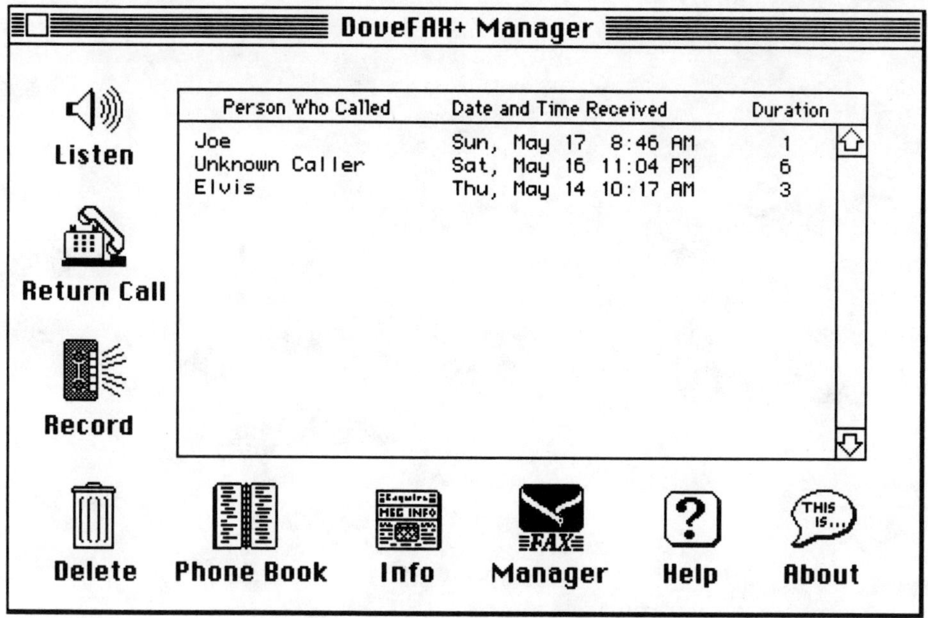

9-23 To return a call to Elvis, select his name from the caller list and click the **Return Call** icon.

Summary

These days, sending a fax is as much a part of doing business as sending a letter. With the fax/modem software available for the Mac, it's almost as easy. Stand-alone fax machines offer some advantages; fax/modem combinations have other advantages. Ideally, an office will have both types. For home use, a send-only or send and receive fax/modem is usually adequate for most needs.

Fax/modems come with special software to handle the fax function. Faxing a document is much like printing it to a remote printer. The fax/modem software uses a modified printer driver. Virtually any document that can be printed can be faxed, including graphics, spreadsheets, and scanned images. Most faxing programs include a desk accessory fax manager, which lets you monitor the progress of faxes that have been scheduled for sending and keeps a log of incoming and outgoing fax traffic.

Some fax/modems also handle Voice Messaging, an "intelligent answering machine" function that allows you to use different messages at different times of day, to record custom messages for specific callers, and to enter your own password to retrieve your forwarded messages at another location.

10
Free fun—finding a BBS (or starting your own)

Being online is fun, but it can get expensive, especially if you find yourself spending hours in the CompuServe CB simulator or downloading lots of shareware from America Online's libraries. Suppose you could enjoy the same kinds of online activities, but without the taximeter ticking away your paycheck. Sounds good? Sure it does, and that's why so many people use free bulletin boards. You can't check airline schedules for free, at least not on any of the boards I've investigated; but you can send E-mail all over the country, play games, chat, post your opinions on any topic you care to, and delve into libraries of shareware that are more comprehensive than those on most services. And you can often do it for just the cost of a local call.

Bulletin Board Systems are usually referred to as *BBSs* or *boards*. They are very different from commercial services, although some people insist on calling CompuServe or Delphi a board. It's not. There are lots of differences, aside from the cost. Services have many users at once and many lines coming in. Some bulletin boards have only one line, though large user group boards have as many as a dozen or more lines, or *nodes*. A BBS can be public or private. Many are run by user groups, both Mac and otherwise. Of course, you can sign onto an Amiga board, a PC board, or a UNIX board with your Mac. Everybody speaks ASCII. You won't be able to use shareware from a different kind of computer, of course, but you can play games with your non-Mac friends, talk, or send messages back and forth, just as if you were all using the same online service. One frequent BBS user makes the analogy that BBSs are to commercial services what shareware is to commercial programs. They're occasionally as good, usually a lot cheaper, and sometimes full of bugs—or "undocumented features."

A large number of BBSs are run by ordinary people. You don't have to be a computer hacker to start one, although in the early days of the BBS this might have been the case. Now, all you need is the appropriate software to run a BBS, and this is available either as a shareware or commercial program. People start their own bulletin boards for the same reason that many of them used to become Ham radio operators. They simply enjoy talking to others and like the feeling of using their computers to help someone else. Many also like the feeling of power that comes with being a sysop (system operator). Of course, those who get too carried away with power trips soon find that their boards aren't attracting any callers or are attracting only the ones they wish would stop calling.

You might also find some "semi-commercial" BBSs run by people who are hoping to make back some of their investment in computers, modems, and telephone lines. These boards might charge you a fee for some services or let you come in free for a few weeks and then charge you if you stay. They might be worthwhile, if they have a relatively easy interface and enough of whatever it is that you're hoping to find in a BBS to justify the cost of joining them.

What type of BBS do you want to join?

This brings up a point worth considering. What exactly *are* you hoping to find in a BBS? Some have real-time conferences. Some have lively discussions on a message board. Some have lots and lots of files to download. Some have online games. Some have several of these features. Few have all of them. If you are expecting to find everything in a BBS that you'd find in CompuServe or America Online, you're going to be disappointed. What you *will* find also depends on where you go looking. Equipment manufacturers and software dealers, especially those who make communications equipment, often have their own boards for customer support and general information. You'd certainly find a different kind of BBS user calling the Hayes Customer Support BBS than you would calling the NASA SpaceLink or the "Fred's Attic" BBS.

Who ya gonna call?

User group bulletin boards are the largest and most popular non-commercial boards. They're also one of your best sources of information on other BBSs. Some post a short list as you log off of other boards you can call. Many have full lists of BBSs in their libraries, which you can download and browse through at your leisure. You can find lists of BBSs in books like this one and in a volume called Meckler's National Directory of BBSs, which should be available in the reference area of your local library. There's even a magazine devoted to BBSs. It's called *Boardwatch*, and it's published monthly. It includes articles about computers, software, and every possible aspect of BBSing. The current subscription rate is $39 a year.

For more information, write to *Boardwatch Magazine*, 5970 South Vivian Street, Littleton, CO 80127, or call 303-973-6038 for more information. Boardwatch also runs its own BBS, the *Boardwatch* Online Information service, at 303-973-4222 (12/2400 N-8-1). Another place to look for BBS lists is in *Computer Shopper*, a monthly tabloid paper about personal computing. *Computer Shopper* is available at newsstands and computer dealers.

Your tax dollars also support a number of government bulletin boards, some of which have a great deal to offer the general public. NASA runs a BBS called SpaceLink, at the Marshall Space Flight Center in Huntsville, Alabama. It has all kinds of information about NASA, the shuttle program, and space flight in general. SpaceLink is a terrific resource for science teachers, parents, kids, and anyone else who might want to learn more about shuttle flights or life in space. The National Science Foundation's BBS has results of scientific studies, NSF data, and general information on science and technology. The Commerce department's Economic Bulletin Board has lists of other Federal BBSs, as well as interesting information about American business and industry. The FCC BBS is a public access link to the Federal Communications Commission. (The phone numbers for these and other boards mentioned in this chapter are listed in Appendix B.)

After you find a board that sounds interesting, how do you actually log on? Start by using communications settings of N-8-1. These are by far the commonest and will work with at least 95 percent of the boards you're likely to join. If you connect at the right speed but see strange characters on your screen, try again with settings of E-7-1. Most boards today will support 2400 bps, and some will also handle your call at 9600 bps, a definite advantage when the board you want to use is a long-distance call away. You might find that the BBS phone number is constantly busy. This could mean either that the board is out of order, or more likely, that it's a popular one with only one or two phone lines. Keep trying. If the board is busy in the prime evening hours, try going in early in the morning or at lunch time.

Most boards will support ASCII text from your regular telecom program, although some Mac-based boards use special software, like the TeleFinder User program. If so, when you first call the BBS using your regular telecom program, you'll be given the option of logging in or downloading the terminal software. (Download time for the TeleFinder User software averages 16 minutes using a 2400-bps modem.) When you first sign on, if you are using a regular telecom program, you'll see the connect message. Hit Return a couple of times if nothing else happens. Many boards (like many online services) wait for you to press Return a few times before they'll send anything. If you're sure you've connected, but the board doesn't respond when you press the Return key, try using the Escape key. (This is one of its few uses on a Mac.) If none of these gets a response, try Ctrl-F. This sends an ASCII character that tells the other computer you're waiting. If nothing seems to work, hang up and try again, hitting the Return key as soon as you hear the connect sound. Some modems have a very short attention span.

What happens next depends on the board. Usually you will see a Welcome to. . .message. Then, many boards ask for your name and hometown and compare them against their lists of previous callers. If no match is found, you'll then be registered as a new member. Some ask you to sign in as a new user and then complete the registration process by giving yourself a screen name and password. Figure 10-1 shows how to sign onto NASA's SpaceLink. Be sure to make a note of your screen name and password somewhere. It's a good idea to use a different password for each board you sign on to, but keeping track of them can turn into a major hassle.

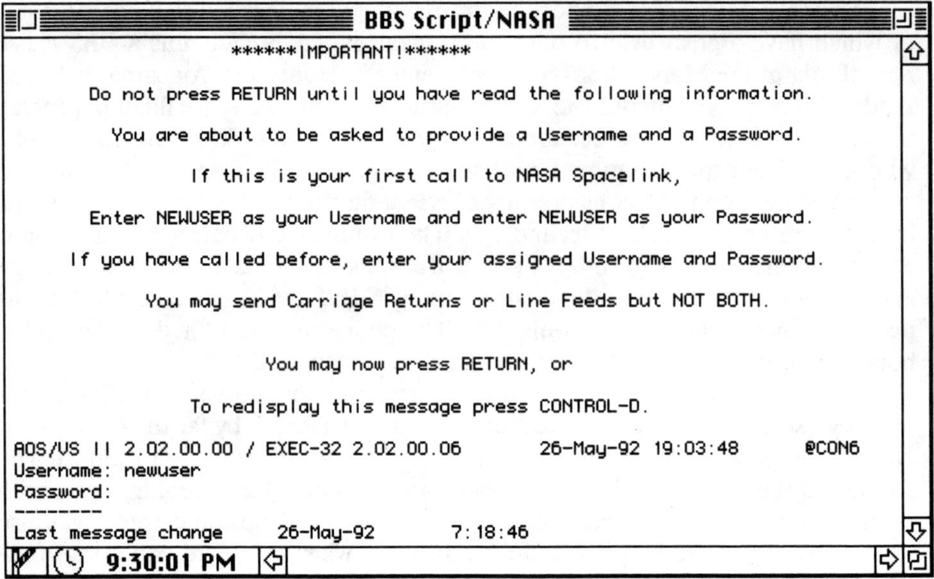

10-1 Most BBSs have definite instructions for signing on as a new user.

If you sign on and see strange codes in front of otherwise legible text, like this:

[0;36mHelp........ [1;32mNOVICE
[0;36mScrn.width.. [1;32m80
[0;36mscrn.Length. [1;32m24

you have indicated that your telecom program can accept PC-ANSI or VT-100 characters, but you haven't turned them on in the terminal preferences. As soon as you do, the strange numbers will turn into boldface initial characters.

Finding your way around a BBS is no different from finding your way around an online service. There's generally a Main menu of some kind. Figure 10-2 shows the Main menu from one of the government boards, and Fig. 10-3 shows the Main menu from a user group board. Though the content areas of the two boards are very different, the command structure is fairly similar. The FCC's board has been structured in a way that allows people who aren't too familiar with BBSs or computers to find what they're looking for. The Berklee BBS is a little bit more "computer-ish," but it's still easy for the novice user to understand. Text-based boards, like both of these, commonly use a set of one-letter or one-number commands. The following are the commands you are most likely to use:

M)essage Section Change to the Message section. When you are switched to the message section, you will see a Message menu.

F)ile Section Connect to the Files area where you will find a library of Public Domain software and a File menu.

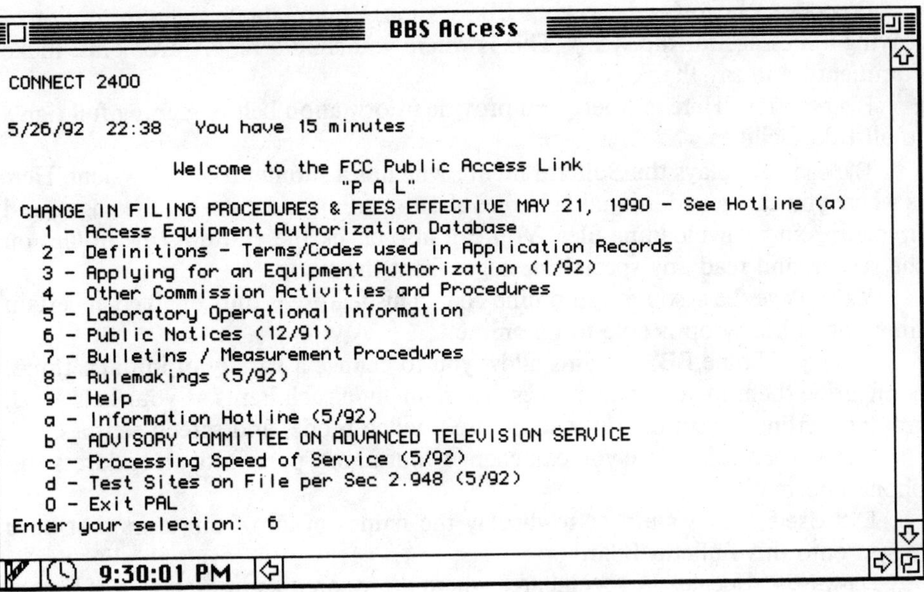

10-2 Some government boards are rather dull. Others can be fun, especially for the technical minded.

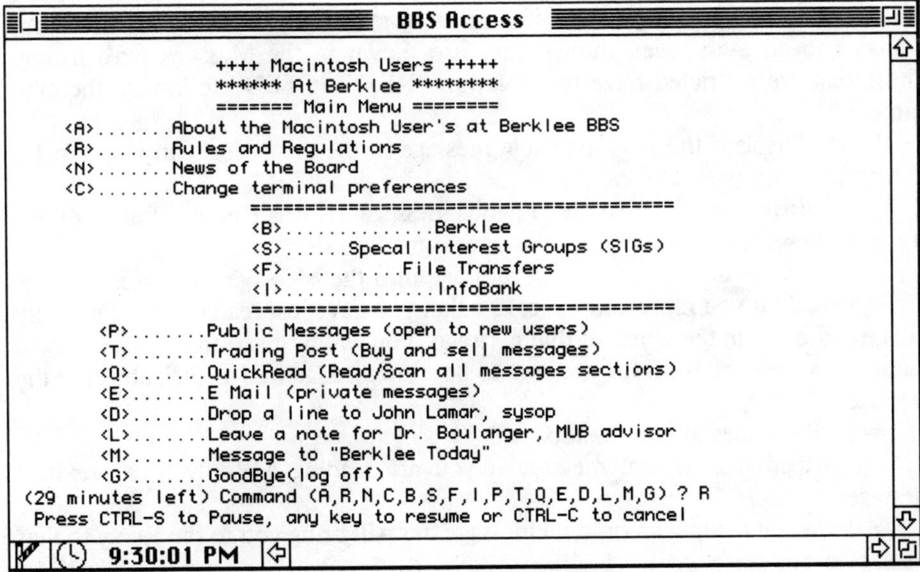

10-3 Berklee is a music school, so its board has a lot of information for the musician and some great MIDI and sound files.

G)oodbye Logoff and end your BBS session. You might be given the option of leaving a message for the sysop. This is where you should report problems, make comments, and say thank you.

R)egistration Here is where you provide information before gaining full rights to all BBS facilities.

B)ulletin Displays the Bulletin menu, which is a submenu of the system. Here is where you can get additional help files about reading and entering messages, and uploading and downloading files. You can also check the entire listing of files on the system and read any special messages from the sysop.

Y)ell Page the sysop for an online chat. This feature is only enabled at certain times when the sysop is able to be online.

C)hange Some BBS systems allow you to change a variety of initial settings, configuring them to your preferences. These include such items as your help level, graphics settings, form of editor to be used, video mode, and screen settings.

H)istory Here is where you can change your name, password, and address and phone information.

L)ist Users Allows a user to display the names of all of the users that have logged onto this Bulletin Board.

D)aily News Update A special area where the sysop puts in messages of immediate importance. Sometimes on a daily basis, and other times when the need arises.

?) This will display the Help menu for the area you're in.

Message Menu—The various commands available include:

A)rea Change Allows you to change from one message area to another. Each Bulletin Board has its unique combination of Message areas, some of which are not available to all users, even though they are shown in the Message Area listing. Those that are restricted have the notation "RESTRICTED" following the area name.

N)ext Displays the next available message in the area. You can also just hit Return to accomplish the same move.

P)rior Brings you back to the previous message. Hitting Return after reading a previous message will place you in a reverse-read mode.

E)nter Allows a user to enter a message into the Message database.

R)eply Lets you reply to the message that you have just read online. The reply will be addressed to the writer of that message. You will be given the opportunity to change to whom you want the message to be addressed, as well as the subject of the message.

=) Read messages non-stop.

−) Read the original message if you are reading a Reply to a previous message.

+) When reading an original message this will bring you to the Reply to that message if one exists.

C) Re-read the message that you have just read.

L)ist Lists the messages currently available to you within the Message area.

S)can Allows you to quickly check mail available throughout the entire Message database. Because it lists every message, it takes a very long time. *Not recommended.*

K)ill Allows you to delete messages addressed to you or messages that you have entered.

U)pload This lets you upload a formatted message using whatever transfer protocol you have previously determined that the board will accept.

J)ump Lets you go directly to the File Areas.

N)ext area Moves you to the next sequential area.

M)ain Returns a user to the Main menu.

G)oodbye Logoff and end your BBS session.

You'll find that these commands are fairly standard among the text-based boards. Some will assign different commands. For example, to sign off, you might use G for Goodbye, E or X for Exit, H for Hang-up, Q for Quit, or even D for Disconnect. Don't hang up on a board by turning off the modem or quitting the telecom program. If you do, you'll probably freeze the BBS or at least tie it up for a long time until the system realizes that you've left. Other than this, though, there's no way to damage a BBS. You can enter wrong commands, and possibly log yourself off accidentally, but you can't "break" anything. BBS systems are carefully designed to be "new user proof" as well as "hacker proof." If it were possible for someone to sign on and delete all the sysop's files, intentionally or otherwise, nobody would start a BBS.

Members have privileges

Although you don't need to join a user group to call their BBS, in many cases you'll find that members have advantages, like longer access time or access to more files and more message areas. Two of the biggest are the Boston Computer Society's BCS·MAC Board and the BMUG board run by the Berkeley Macintosh User Group. Non-members of the BCS board can read posted messages and reply to them, and download files from the "public" library area. The files that are available to the general public include the latest anti-virus software and some helpful Mac utilities. Figure 10-4 shows what's on the BCS board for a non-member.

If you are using a dedicated program like TeleFinder/User, you'll see what looks like your normal desktop, only it will suddenly sprout a whole new batch of icons and folders. Figure 10-5 shows the TeleFinder interface for one of my favorite boards, the GAMER BBS. This board has the largest collection of games and educational software available anywhere. Really! It's the home of the National Home and School Mac User Group, people who take play seriously. Game developers and shareware authors upload their latest creations here even before they reach the online services. As a non-member, you can browse through, and download, over 2,500 files from the GAMER project's library. Members of NHS MUG also gain access to the Arizona MUG's BBS in a Box collection of over 9,500

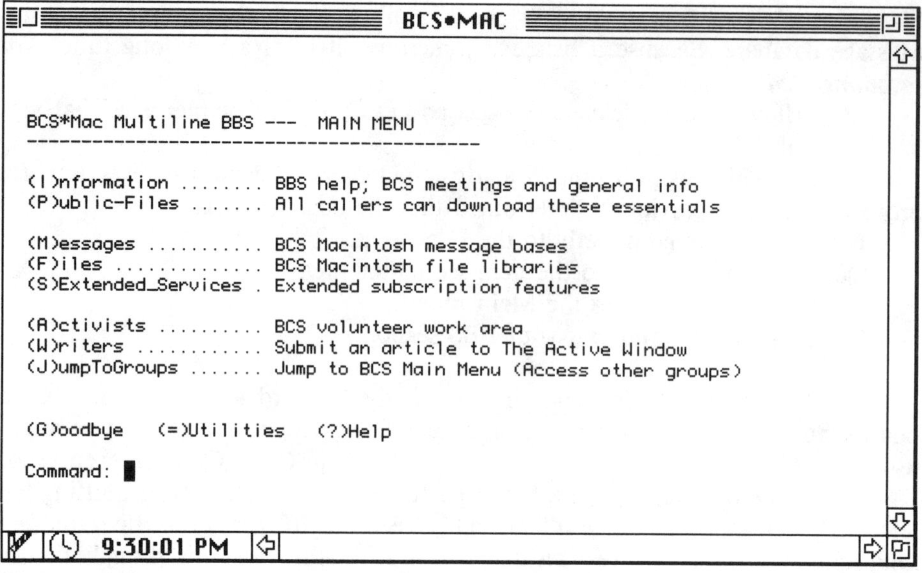

10-4 The BCS·Mac board is run by a sub-group of the Boston Computer Society, one of the largest and oldest computing groups.

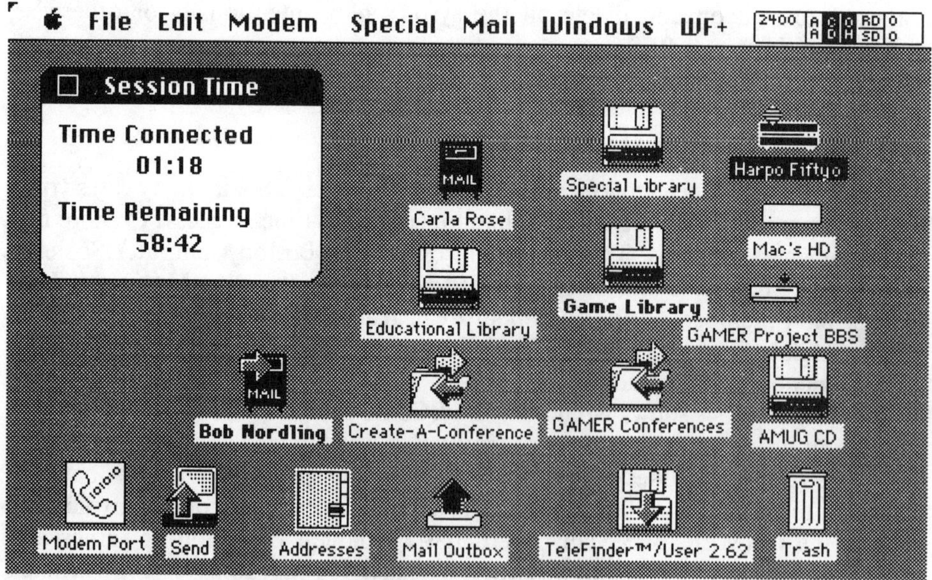

10-5 When you join this board, you get your own mailbox, too.

additional files. Figure 10-6 shows some of the categories of goodies available in the HyperCard section of the CD. If you like games, or are a parent or a teacher, these programs will delight you. The TeleFinder interface is also a delightful experience for the BBS user. It's very different from the usual text-based boards.

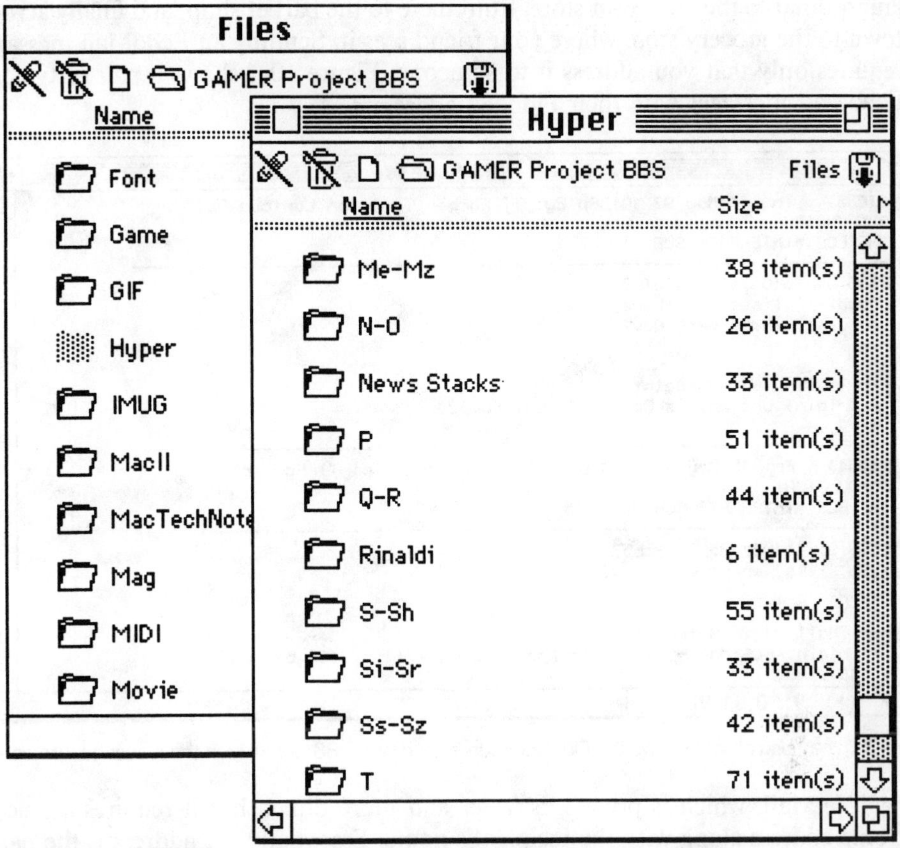

10-6 There are a tremendous number of files available on the Gamer BBS.

One of the most common text-based systems you will find online is FidoNet. Fido BBS can be identified by the dog-holding-a-disk graphic that many of them use as an opening screen, and by the often clunky system of screens you must navigate through to leave an E-mail message or read incoming mail. However, a great many users are more than willing to put up with any and all of Fido's peculiarities, simply because it's the best free mail service you'll ever find. FidoNet is a world-wide system that passes along messages from one local BBS to another and also interconnects with USENET, InterNet, and through gateways to MCI Mail and CompuServe.

FidoNet started back to 1985, by Tom Jennings and John Madill, as a quick and cheap way to send E-mail back and forth between Baltimore and San Francisco. Today there are hundreds of Fido nodes. You can send messages either through EchoMail or NetMail. EchoMail messages are public and are simply passed from one Fido node to another, through connecting hubs, until they reach a board where the recipient is a member. Then, the message is posted until the recipient picks it up. It's much like writing a message to your friend on a yellow sticky and posting it on the board in the laundromat. Someone carries it from the laundromat to the ice cream store, from there to the barber shop, and finally across town to the grocery store where your friend sees it. Sending an EchoMail message requires only that you address it to someone. Figure 10-7 shows a pair of typical EchoMail messages with their FidoNet addresses.

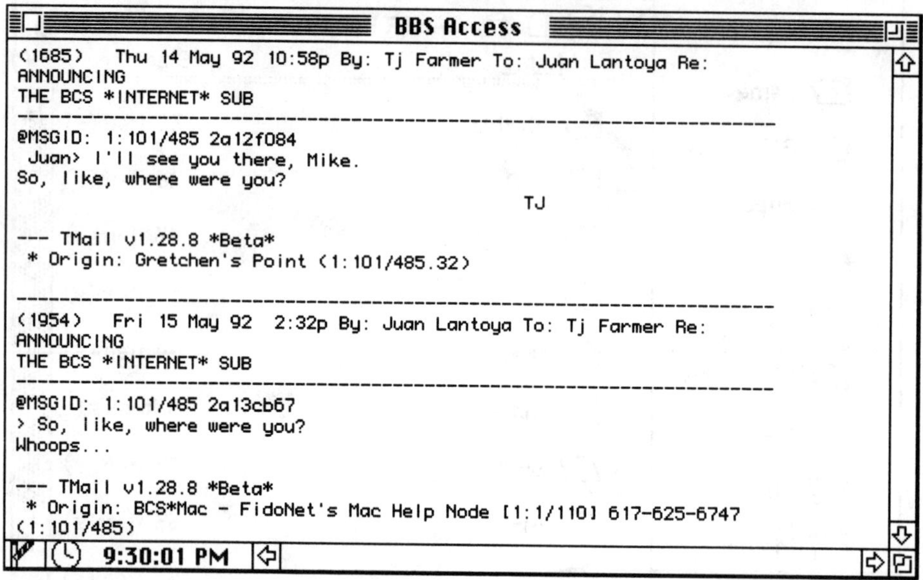

10-7 The "origin" line shows the FidoNet addresses of the BBS from which the message was sent.

NetMail, which is private, is faster and more direct, but it requires an electronic address along with the recipient's name. Essentially the address is the path the message has to follow to get from one computer to another. Tabbinet is a similar system for PCs using TBBS software. Fido systems and similar systems that relay messages are usually programmed to do so in the middle of the night and are closed to callers during that time. The BCS·MAC board, for example, handles mail from 4–6 A.M. every day.

You have 59 minutes remaining . . .

Many BBSs set a limit on the amount of connect time you are allowed per day. They do so to make sure that the board is accessible to as many people as possible because many BBSs have only one or two phone lines coming in. Sometimes you can gain additional time by uploading your shareware programs to the board. Don't upload anything you haven't created yourself, unless you have the permission of the person who did create it. And don't upload a commercial program, ever!

At least one board grants extra minutes online to those who win its slot machine or trivia games. What the time limit does mean, though, is that you have to budget your time carefully if you want to download a long file. It's possible that you might need to use the ZMODEM transfer protocol, if the board supports it, and copy the file in two separate sessions. (ZMODEM transfers can be resumed if interrupted.) If you run into problems, send a message to the sysop, asking for help. S/he can usually either give you more time for the long download or break the file into manageable pieces.

On being a good BBS user

Treat sysops with respect. They have put a lot of time and money into setting up their BBS. If you log onto a board you don't like, just log off again and try a different one. If you have problems using the board, read the bulletins and help screens for a clue as to what you're doing wrong. If the sysop of a board you use a lot is asking for contributions, send some money. After all, phone lines and modems are expensive, and if the costs of running the board become too high, it will simply be discontinued.

If you are calling a BBS for the first time, don't call in the middle of the night or early in the morning. Until you've verified the number, you can't be sure it's really a board, and otherwise normal people go a little nuts when awakened at 3 A.M. by a phone that says "Oooooo-Eeeeeee, Shhhhhhh." Obviously, if you do call a wrong number, apologize.

And now, the bad news

There are a few things you might find on BBSs that you probably won't find on commercial services. The first, and worst, of these is a computer virus. It's a lot more likely that you'd find infected files on a BBS, simply because it's much easier for the kinds of people who spread such things to get access to free boards. To protect yourself, be sure to install anti-virus software like GateKeeper, VIREX, or Disinfectant, before you start downloading any software from BBS libraries. Be especially careful about copying files from a board that doesn't verify your name and address. Bad news viruses are found most often on free boards and on those that don't require you to identify yourself.

Another bad news item found occasionally on BBSs is illegally copied software. Unauthorized, or "pirated," copies of legitimate programs, beta test versions of programs not intended for public release, and "hacked" copies of protected programs have all appeared online at one time or another. It is illegal to own or use any of these. If you find one, tell the sysop immediately so it can be removed from the board.

Other bad news comes in the form of classified ads for illegitimate services, defective merchandise, and downright scams. One of our local boards recently fell victim to a posting about an illegal "pyramid game." It was claimed that by joining the game and bringing in other members, the reader could parlay a $200 dollar "investment" into millions, in a matter of weeks. The Sysop there left the message, minus names and phone numbers, as an example of the kind of posting that would get a user banned from his board. Unfortunately, not all are so conscientious. Remember, anything that sounds too good to be true, probably is.

Starting your own BBS

Sure, you can start a BBS of your own. Should you? It takes time and money, and in many cases, all you get out of it are headaches and flames from disgruntled users who can't find the file they're looking for. Ideally, though, you get the satisfaction of providing a community service for other computer people. You get to make a lot of new friends, and you get the fun of trying out new programs that other users have uploaded to your library. Before you decide to set up a BBS, there are a lot of things you need to think about.

What type of BBS do you want to run? Having a particular focus or special interest makes your BBS appealing to those who share your enthusiasm for the topic. There are sports boards, photography boards, musician boards, and boards on practically any topic you can think of. There are boards for singles, "adult" boards, and family boards. There are boards that are open to all and boards that are limited to a select few. Will your board be Mac only or open to PC users, too? Will you have downloads, and if so, where will you get them? How about messages? Will you connect to FidoNet or another mail-sharing network? How much time will callers be allowed per day? Will you use a program that allows real-time chat, and if so, how many phone lines can you afford to add? Chat with only two phone lines isn't much fun, and chat with just one incoming line is impossible.

Can you spare the time to do it? Running a BBS ties up your computer and modem, so you won't be able to use them for your own activities. Can you locate the computer and modem away from other parts of the household? Listening to a constantly ringing phone and the sounds of a modem connecting will get annoying very quickly, especially when calls come in after midnight or at the crack of dawn.

If you have answered all these questions and are still ready to proceed, your next decision has to be about software. Among the commercial BBS programs available for the Mac are TeleFinder, FirstClass, and Second Sight. There are also a lot of shareware BBS programs, including some that access FidoNet or other mail-handling services. MacWoof is a popular FidoNet system. Second Sight, from Freesoft, is Scott Watson's commercial release of the original Red Ryder Host, one of the early Mac BBS programs. It's a text-based BBS and, like White Knight, appeals to some Mac users but completely turns off others. Both TeleFinder and FirstClass are icon-driven programs and are a great deal more "Mac-like" in their interface.

TeleFinder uses a system of icons on a reasonable facsimile of your desktop (Fig. 10-8). Disk icons and volumes of data available to the user when connected are displayed on the right side of the screen, and icons that control the software are located at the bottom of the screen. Opening any of the folders gives you a window that shows what's available in them. An example is shown in Fig. 10-9. If you double click on a specific file, you will see a regular Macintosh Get Info box, with all the details about that particular file. Downloading is simple, and TeleFinder's ZMODEM 32-bit CRC protocol is one of the fastest anywhere, making it a plus for both users and sysops. Figure 10-10 shows a TeleFinder download in process. Faster downloads mean that you can get by with fewer phone lines. TeleFinder supports both Fido and Tabbinet.

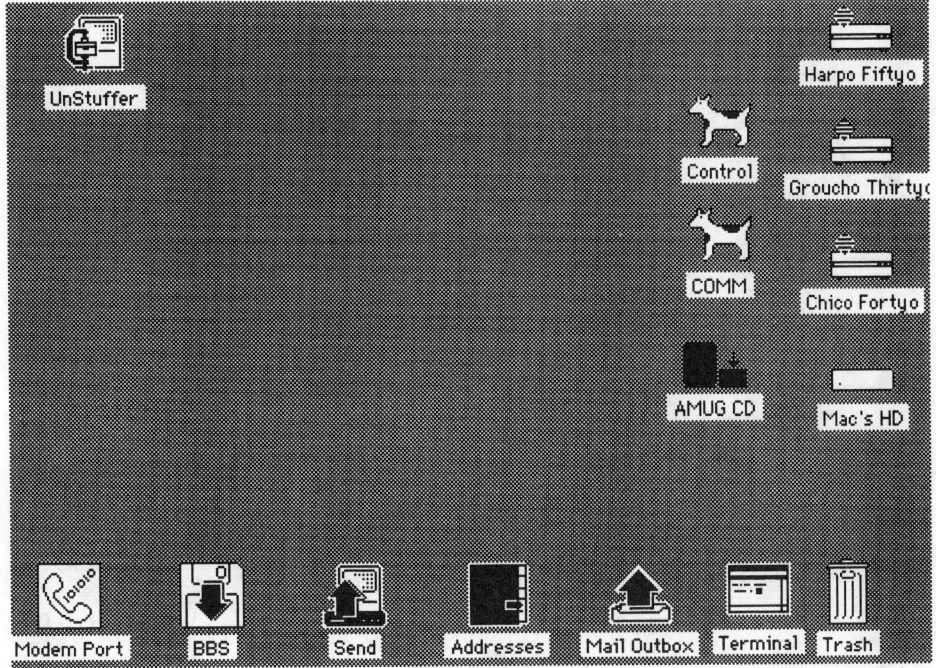

10-8 TeleFinder recreates your desktop with its own icons installed.

FirstClass uses icons, too, but in a somewhat different manner. Figure 10-11 shows a typical FirstClass desktop window. Here, the icons are customizable by the sysop, so his or her board has a distinctive "look and feel." Figure 10-12 shows the files available when you click on the Software icon.

FirstClass doesn't allow ZMODEM transfers, however, so it's not as efficient for library management as TeleFinder is. FirstClass is more user-friendly in that it supports live chat, a feature lacking in TeleFinder. The choices are clear. If you want to support multi-line real-time chat, you need FirstClass. If you'd rather maintain a library of shareware, and a mailbox system, you need TeleFinder. If you're technically oriented, and want a text-based interface, look at Second Sight, which operates much like the White Knight telecom program.

In addition to your BBS program, Mac, modem(s), and incoming phone line(s), you will need a large hard drive on which to maintain file libraries, and ideally a CD ROM player and a set of disks of shareware. BBS in a Box from the Arizona Mac User Group is an excellent series of compact disks of Macintosh programs. The material on these disks has been carefully chosen from user groups, other BBS libraries, and online services' libraries. It's virus-free and cleared for release in this form. The National Home and School MUG has also published a CD ROM disk of games and educational software, game reviews, and other goodies that would be an excellent addition to a BBS library. There are many other CD ROM collections that would also be useful additions to an online library, and most are priced at under $100.

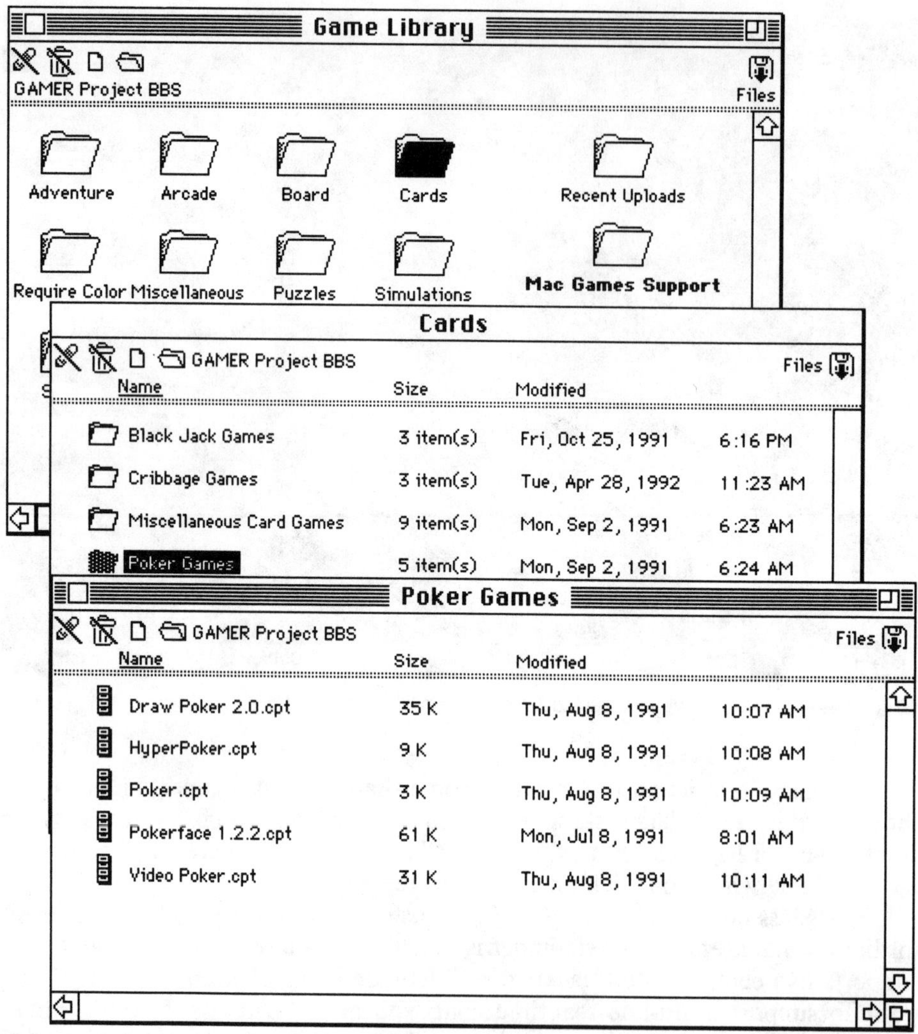

10-9 Games are broken down into well-defined categories, making it easier to find what you want.

Host mode—mini BBS

Suppose you don't want to develop a full-fledged bulletin board but just want to send files back and forth to a friend or let the people in your office work at home, downloading the data they need and uploading the finished reports, spreadsheets, or whatever. One way to accomplish this is to turn your Mac into a one-node mini-BBS by using the telecom program's host-mode settings. Host mode simply tells the computer to answer the phone and connect the caller to your telecom program. Then you can "talk" back and forth on the keyboard, or send and receive files. See your telecom manual to learn how to place your modem in host mode.

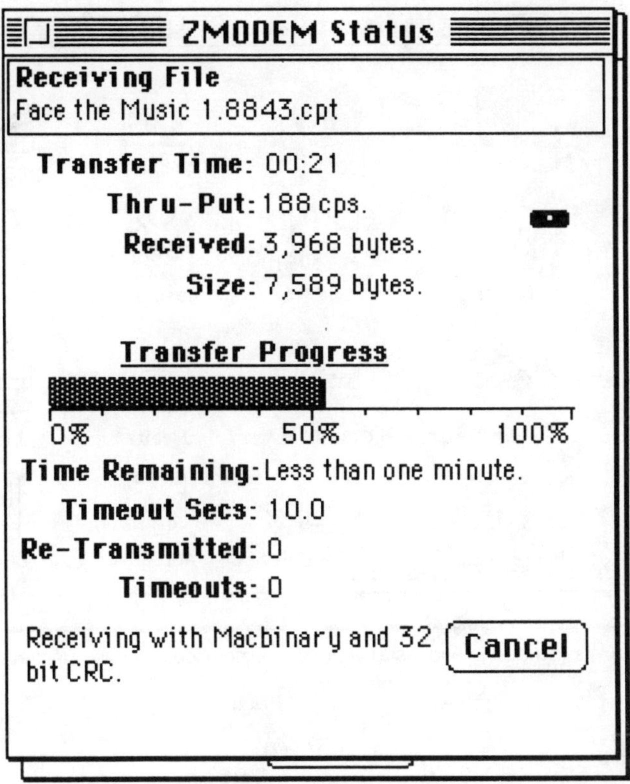

10-10 TeleFinder's download progress screen gives you a lot of information.

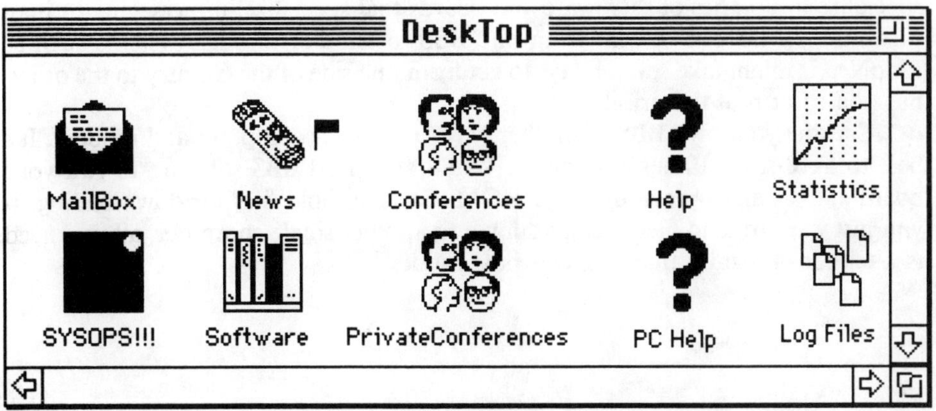

10-11 When you log on to a FirstClass board, this is more or less what you'll see.

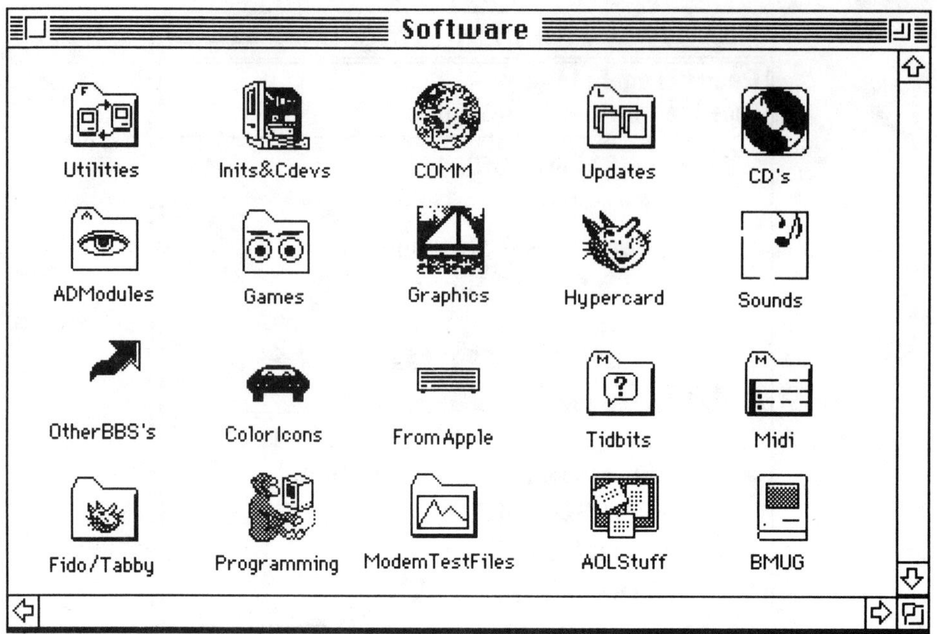

10-12 FirstClass lets you design and install your own custom icons for any files you care to include.

Summary

Bulletin Board Systems are a way to have fun online without running up huge bills. Some BBSs are run by user groups, some by equipment and software companies, and many by ordinary people who enjoy being system operators. To find a local BBS, start with your user group or your Mac dealer. Once you log onto one board, you can find lists of others. There are boards for special interests, boards that specialize in libraries of shareware and boards that specialize in messaging or mail forwarding. Mail can be sent from one BBS to another through systems such as FidoNet. It might take several days to get from one side of the country to the other, but you can't beat the price!

Starting your own BBS is another way to use your computer and modem. It's best to have several lines coming in. You'll also need BBS software to run your board and a hard drive and/or CD ROM player to hold files for downloading. If you just want to send files back and forth to another single computer, all you need is a telecom program that supports host mode.

11
Networking and remote access

People buy modems for a variety of reasons. Some like to chat online. Some like to go browsing through libraries of shareware in search of the perfect HyperCard stack or the most interesting new game. Some of us, though, use them for work—that four-letter word. Actually, for those of us who have the privilege of working at home or on the beach and phoning in our daily output, work is a lot more pleasant. Modems can make working at home a reality. If you have a Mac in the office and a Mac at home, you needn't worry about which files are on which Mac. All you need to do is use one of several remote access programs that will let the Mac you're with talk to the Mac that's far away. The newest of these is Apple's own Remote Access, included as part of System 7 with the Mac PowerBooks and available for other System 7 users from your Macintosh dealer.

Remote Access lets you retrieve any file that's on another Mac, as long as both have Remote Access installed and are connected to modems. (Of course, both Macs also have to use System 7.) But that's not quite all it can do. Remote Access also lets you enter text in a document that's stored on the remote Mac, without copying it, changing the copy, and then sending it back. You're really typing from your local keyboard into a CPU that's miles away! You can check databases by remote control or print from your home Mac to your office laser printer. You can check your office E-mail, or pick up files from other Macs on an AppleTalk network or even from PCs and file servers on an Ethernet or Token Ring! You could conceivably play a game on your home Mac, while you're 30,000 feet over Kansas communicating via cellular phone and your PowerBook. In all honesty, though, this last is not a recommended use for Remote Access, unless it's a game of chess. The system is slow—very slow. Apple admits that its PowerBook Internal Modem isn't up to the job and suggests using a 9600-bps modem for all Remote Access tasks. Even so, you need to be patient. A lot of data gets crunched through those phone lines. A complicated screen update can take quite a while.

The remote-control Macintosh

What happens when you use Remote Access? One of the two Macs is the *host* and receives the modem call. The other, or the *guest*, is the Mac who calls in. The host Mac appears on the guest's desktop as another disk. You can open it, copy from and to it, and in general treat it just as you would if it were SCSI-cabled to your Mac instead of at the other end of the phone line. You can send a file to the distant Mac's printer by selecting it in the Chooser. Similarly, if your host Mac is tied into a file server, you can access it through AppleShare. It's easy to use, and whether you're using a PowerBook or a Quadra, you can just as easily be the host or guest.

To enable the Mac to use Remote Access, it must be installed on both the host and the guest machines. Installation is done with the Apple Installer, provided on the master disk. (If you're trying to install Remote Access on a Mac Plus or SE, you will have problems. The disk provided is a 1.4 Mb disk and requires a SuperDrive.) Once you have installed it, you will need to configure your connection settings and, if you wish, enable call answering.

If you're only using it to call from your PowerBook to your home or office system, you might not want to bother with call answering. If you do choose it, it lets the Mac answer an incoming modem call and go into Remote Access host mode even if the Remote Access application isn't open. Open Remote Access from your desktop. Figure 11-1 shows its icon on the left, along with an icon for a saved connect document. When you open it you'll see the connect box, which lets you place a call to another Mac. There's also a special menu bar, with Setup and Windows, in addition to the familiar File and Edit menus.

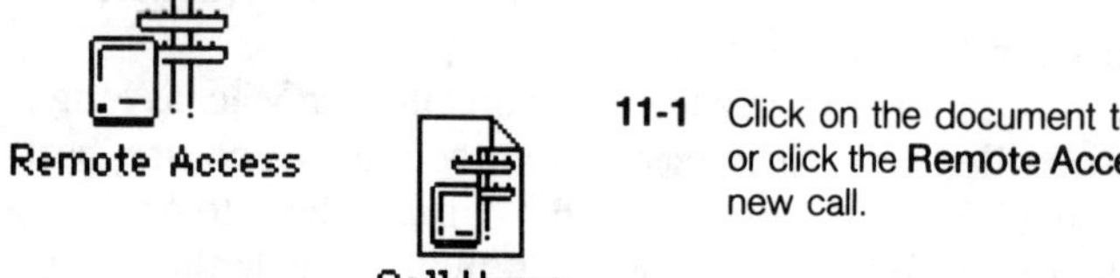

11-1 Click on the document to call that number, or click the **Remote Access** icon to set up a new call.

Select Remote Access setup from the Setup menu. You'll see a box like the one in Fig. 11-2. Begin by setting the modem port and choosing your modem from the list of those supported by Remote Access. If your modem is not on the list shown in Fig. 11-3, call the manufacturer, an authorized Apple dealer or representative, or your user group to find out if a Remote Access modem driver script is available for it. With the appropriate script, Remote Access can work with any Apple 2400-bps or Hayes-compatible modem that's 2400 bps or higher. If you understand Connection Control Languages, you might be able to write your own script. You'll need a copy of the AppleTalk Remote Access Modem Toolkit to do so. Ask your Apple dealer how to get one.

This setup box also lets you choose whether to answer incoming calls, how long to let a caller remain connected (if you want to impose a limit), and how much

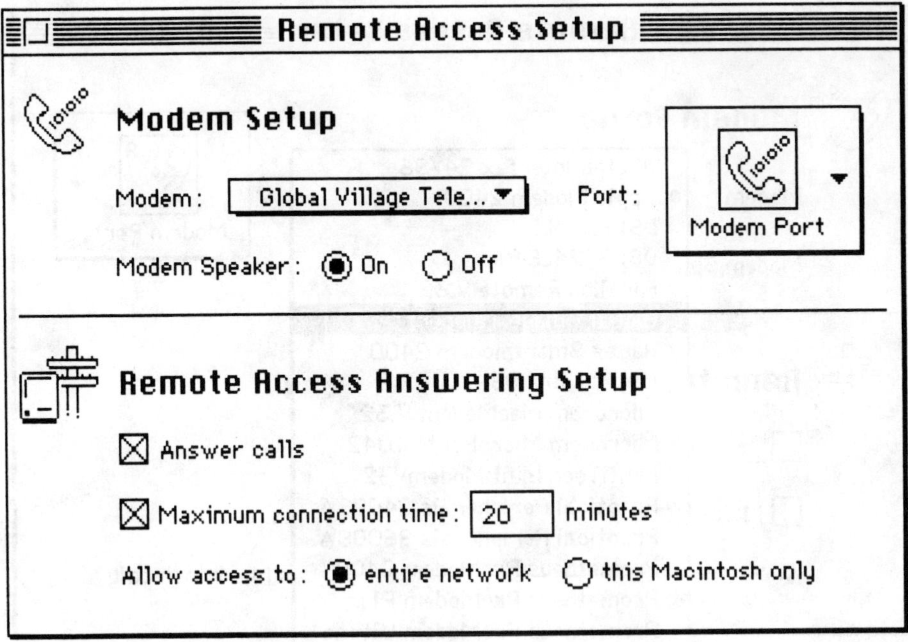

11-2 The modem set-up must be entered before you can call another Mac.

access you're granting to the caller. If your Mac is part of a network, can the caller reach the other networked Macs, too, or just yours? There might be reasons you'd want to limit access to the rest of the network. Security is a concern whenever you're letting another user into your Mac. One way to handle incoming calls is to accept only registered users and not unregistered (unidentified) guests. Users can be registered by selecting Users and Groups from the Setup menu. This opens the Users and Groups Control Panel and lets you enter the names and passwords of anyone you care to grant access to.

Calling another Mac

To place a call to another Remote-Access-equipped Mac, enter its telephone number in the connect box, as shown in Fig. 11-4. If you're a registered user of that system, enter your name and password. If you're calling as a guest, and the remote Mac accepts guest callers, you needn't enter anything but the number. Then, click the Connect button. As soon as you do so, the Status window will open. You'll hear the modem dialing the call and see the messages in the status box change. Figure 11-5 shows the series of messages you will see while a call is connecting.

Once you're connected, you can use the remote Mac just as if it were another disk attached to the one you're typing on. When you're through, click the Disconnect button (in the Status window) to break the connection and end the call.

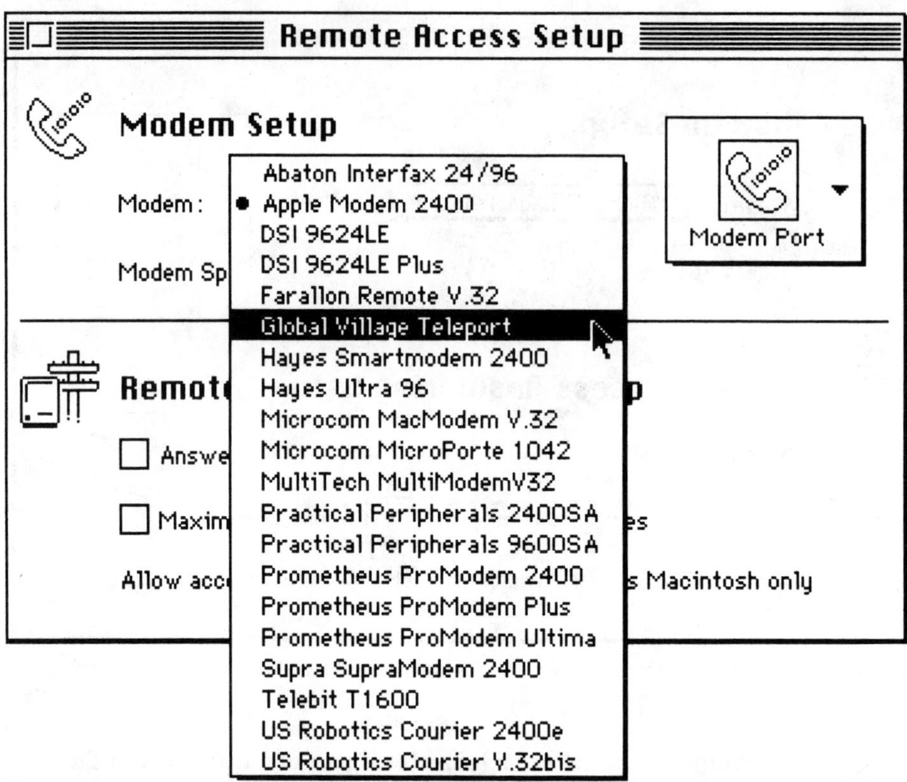

11-3 If your Hayes-compatible modem isn't on this list, call Apple or its manufacturer for the right codes.

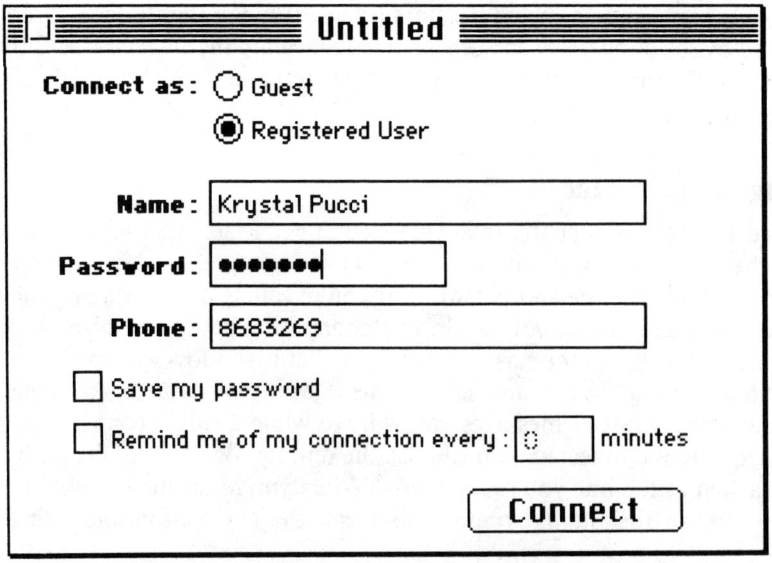

Untitled
Connect as: Guest
Registered User
Name: Krystal Pucci
Password: •••••••
Phone: 8683269
Save my password
Remind me of my connection every: 0 minutes
Connect

11-4 You needn't enter the ATDT command. The program will take care of it for you.

Sometimes, however, a connection gets broken before you're ready, perhaps due to line noise or to your having forgotten to disable Call Waiting. If this happens, you'll see a dialog box like the one in Fig. 11-6. At this point, you'll need to try to figure out what the problem might have been, correct it, and call the remote Mac again.

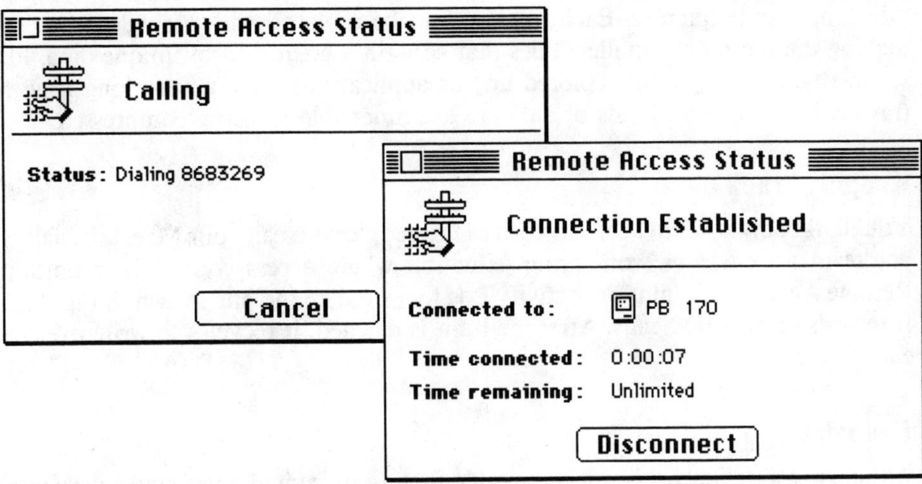

11-5 These message boxes let you follow the action.

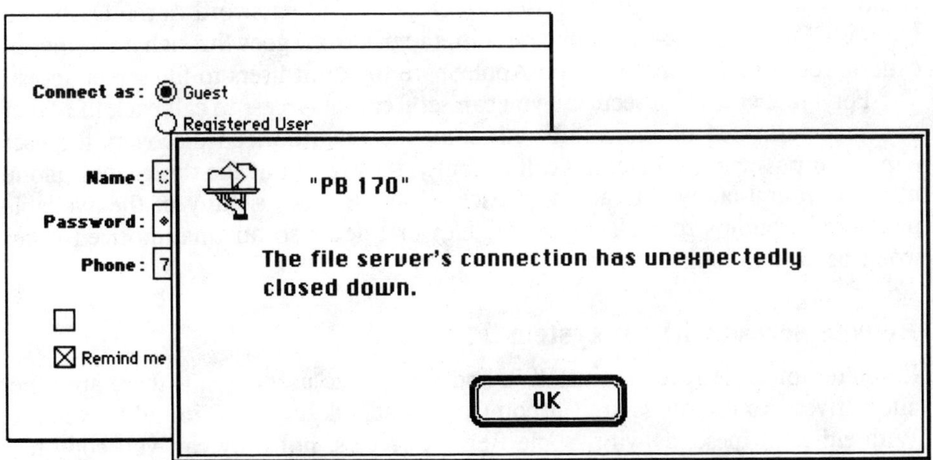

11-6 Oops, I forgot to disable call waiting.

Data compression and performance

Remote Access uses built-in protocols that compress data and check for errors. For the technically minded, these are "smart buffering," developed by Apple for data transfer optimization; MNP—the industry standard for error detection; and V.42

bis—the industry standard for data compression. If you don't really understand these terms, don't worry. All you need to know is that some kinds of files move back and forth between Macs more easily than others. Spreadsheets, text files, and files with "redundant data" can be compressed more efficiently and transferred at a much faster rate. By the way, "redundant data" isn't a put-down of your writing style. It simply means that some combinations of letters, like "ing," "tion," or "the," appear frequently. Each of these can be replaced with a single character, making the file much smaller. Files that contain a great deal of unique data, like scanned grayscale photos, colored art, or applications, take a very long time to transfer because these kinds of data are less amenable to being compressed.

Keeping track

You'll probably want to keep a record of the people who call your Mac, especially if you're in an office or work group situation where access control is important. Remote Access maintains an Activity Log for you, like the one shown in Fig. 11-7. It records up to 1,000 calls. After the limit is reached, it recycles to write over the earliest records.

Uninvited guests

Although it's unlikely, it's not impossible that an uninvited guest could determine that you have Remote Access installed, call your Mac, and raise all sorts of heck with your files. How can you prevent this? First of all, don't allow anyone to sign on without a password. Assign each user a user name and password in the Users and Groups CDEV. Whenever a call comes in, the password goes through an authentication procedure like that used on AppleShare to admit users to file server access.

For a higher level of security, you can set Remote Access to call back the caller at a predetermined phone number. If someone unauthorized discovers the user name and password, they could call in, but if they're not at the designated phone number, your Mac won't call them back. You can also use any of the available password programs to lock individual files or folders so an unauthorized caller won't be able to look at them.

Remote access without system 7

If you're not quite ready to install 7, and some Mac users aren't, there are other alternatives. Among these are Carbon Copy Mac, Okyto, and Timbuktu Remote. With either of these, as with Apple Remote Access, not only can you copy files from your remote Mac to your local Mac, and vice versa, but you can even open up an application on the remote computer and run it from the local one.

When you visit as a guest with Carbon Copy, the host Mac screen is displayed on a window on your Mac called the Guest Window. Unlike Remote Access, Carbon Copy can permit multiple guests to view the same host. Only one guest at a time can control it, however, and multiple-guest access requires a network connection rather than a modem-to-modem connection. Carbon Copy is useful for work

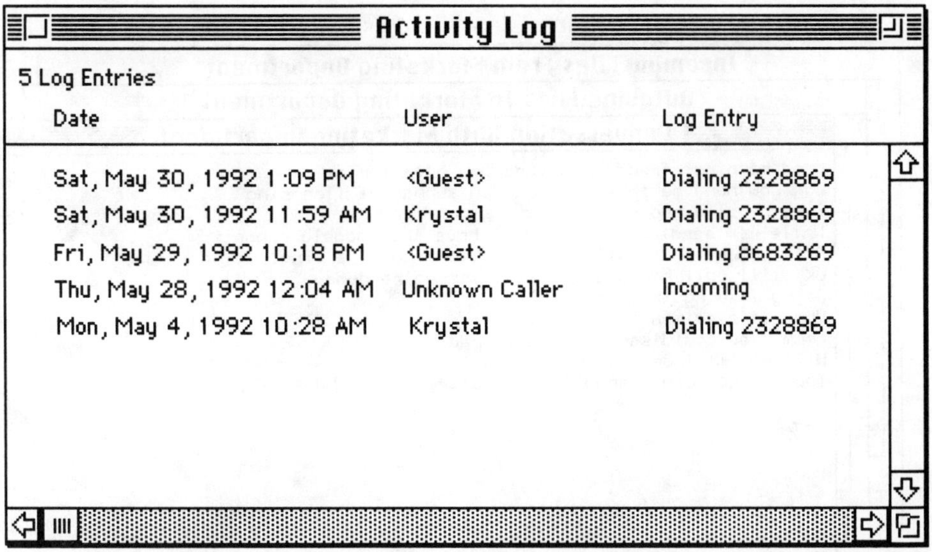

Activity Log

5 Log Entries

Date	User	Log Entry
Sat, May 30, 1992 1:09 PM	<Guest>	Dialing 2328869
Sat, May 30, 1992 11:59 AM	Krystal	Dialing 2328869
Fri, May 29, 1992 10:18 PM	<Guest>	Dialing 8683269
Thu, May 28, 1992 12:04 AM	Unknown Caller	Incoming
Mon, May 4, 1992 10:28 AM	Krystal	Dialing 2328869

11-7 If someone changes a file you didn't expect to be changed, check the date and time and you'll know who to blame.

group collaboration over a network, for training of individuals or groups either in a classroom or in remote locations, for technical support, and for remote access and file transfer. You can open and work with a file on a remote desktop, demonstrate to the host Mac's user how to accomplish a particular task, or send files in either direction in the background while both machines are doing something else.

Carbon Copy has complete security functions, including levels that let a guest merely view a host screen, control it, get files, or send files. The host can also protect its system folder from access through file transfer. It can require host user approval before performing any task specified by a guest. A callback function lets the host Mac return a call to a pre-designated number when a guest requests access, as in Apple's Remote Access program.

Okyto, pronounced "*Oh-kee-toe*," is telecommunication whiz Scott Watson's entry into the Mac-to-Mac file transfer sweepstakes. As with the other programs, both Macs must have Okyto installed and active. This program has several advantages. It works over AppleTalk and by modem. It can do more than one thing at a time. If you are sending material to an attended Mac, you can chat with the other user while files are transferring. Figure 11-8 shows Okyto's Conversation window in use. Either user can transfer files by opening the Incoming or Outgoing Files window and selecting the files to be transferred. Because you can assemble a list of files to be sent, instead of just sending one at a time, it's a good deal faster than other methods. When you add Outgoing Files, they automatically appear in a list on the other Mac as Incoming Files. Files can move in both directions at once, too, making it much more efficient for long-distance users. Figure 11-9 shows how files are selected from the remote Mac for uploading to the local one.

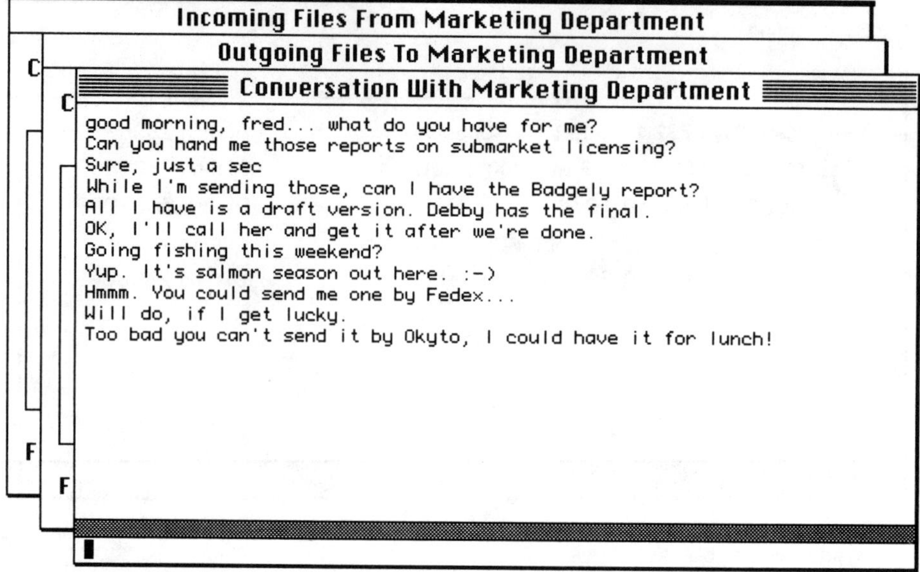

11-8 Okyto is the only remote access program that lets you talk to the other Mac as well as copy from it.

You can add password protection to screen incoming users and to determine whether they are allowed to send you files or only copy from you. You can also designate Off Limits folders for privacy. Otherwise, an incoming caller can browse through and copy literally anything on your disks. Okyto comes free with Watson's White Knight telecom program or is available separately from Freesoft, singly or in 10-packs for company use. It's the fastest and friendliest of all.

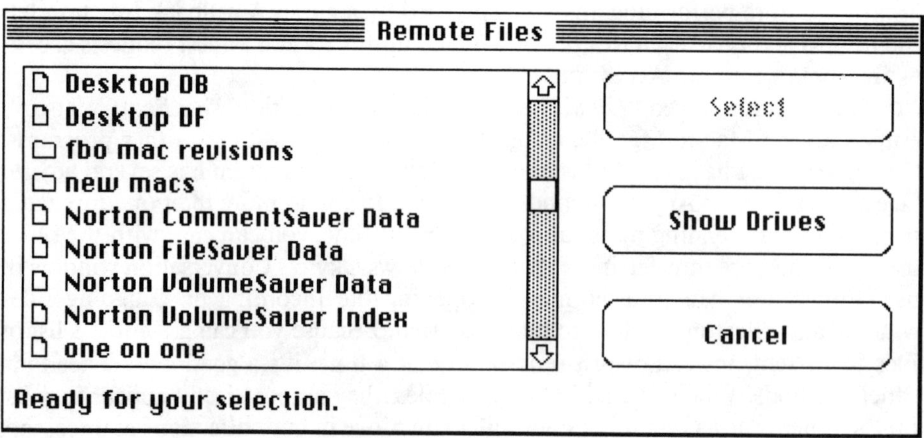

11-9 Select the files or folders you want to copy. They'll appear on your incoming list.

What if the host Mac isn't on?

The systems discussed so far all require that the host Mac and its modem be left on to receive incoming calls. Of course, it's relatively easy to call your office during the day and ask someone to turn on your desk Mac so you can call in with your PowerBook and download a needed file. But suppose you need the file on the weekend or at midnight when nobody's around to flip the switch. There's a device called a *wake-up cable* that plugs into the ADB port on your Mac II or SE. Farallon, makers of Timbuktu/Remote, include it with their Remote Access Pack, along with a V.42 bis modem. Leave your host modem set to AutoAnswer, plug in the wake-up cable, and set the software (either Carbon Copy or Timbuktu/Remote) to Host at Start-up. Before you call in from the guest Mac, set its copy of Carbon Copy or Timbuktu/Remote so that there's a delay after the connection is made. Do this by adding in the command string ATS7=120, or however many seconds you determine that it takes your host Mac to start up and load all its INITs. When you make the call, the host modem answers and sends a logic signal through the wake-up cable into the ADB, telling the host to turn itself on. The guest Mac will wait, courtesy of the Hayes S7 register string you've entered, while the host gets its act together. Then, your guest Mac will show the host in the Host window and you can do whatever you need to do with it. When you're finished, disconnecting will send a shut-down signal to the host and it will shut itself down until the next time you call it. Like Remote Access, though, these programs are slow. At anything less than 9600 bps, you won't be happy with them. Of course, if you *need* a midnight file transfer, slow is better than nothing.

Playing games by modem

File transfers by remote control and working at home on a remote Mac are all very well for working hours; but when the workday's over, it's time to play. One of the more recent trends in gaming are games that play over a modem or on an AppleTalk network. System administrators at many companies have discovered that instead of quieting down at lunch time, activity on the LAN reaches a peak. The reason—games like Spectre and Armor Alley. It seems that instead of going out to lunch, workers are brown-bagging and spending the time locked in mortal combat. In Armor Alley, which can also be played by modem, your job is to lead a convoy through the rattle of machine gun fire and the searing heat of napalm to destroy the enemy. You must fly a helicopter, man a tank, fire missiles, and dodge balloons. You have a defense budget with which to buy additional weapons, and you score points for destroying the enemy's equipment. A screen from Armor Alley is shown in Fig. 11-10. Spectre's premise is a bit different. You are at the controls of a fully armed and armored sci-fi tank. The battleground is three-dimensional, in full color on a Mac II. The animation flows so smoothly you'd think it was a movie.

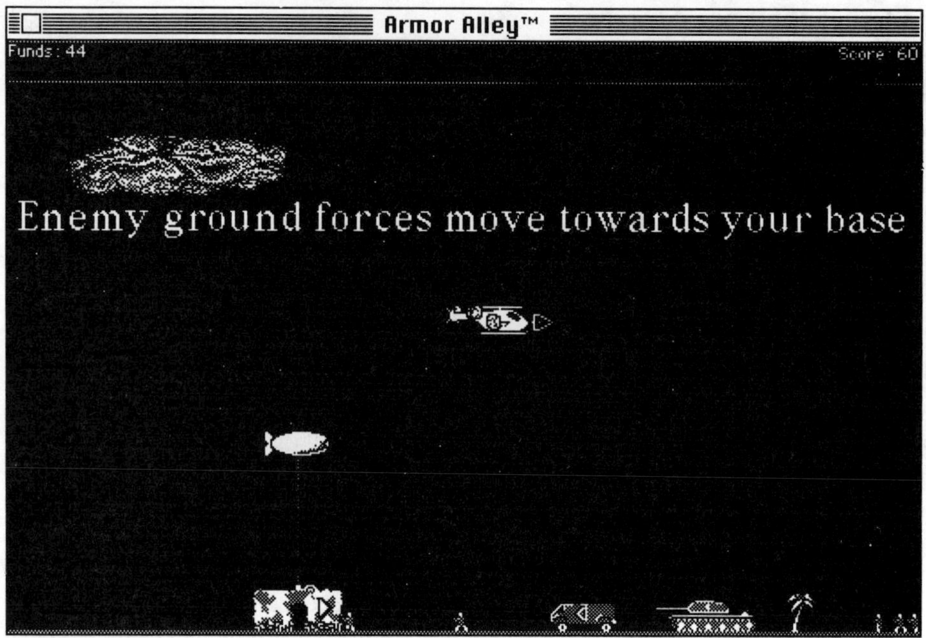

11-10 I'm flying the chopper. My opponent is driving a tank.

Those who prefer a more intellectual challenge will enjoy either of two modem-able chess games from InterPlay: Battle Chess and CheckMate, both of which have the communications program built in. When you pull down the Modem menu as shown in Fig. 11-11, you'll open a dialing box. Simply type your opponent's telephone number into the box. You don't need to type ATDT, but be sure to use the *70 command if you need to disable call waiting. Once you're connected, you set up the game with yourself as Human/White, Modem/Black. Your opponent sets Human/Black, Modem/White. (Or vice-versa, if you're willing to let him go first.) You can even send comments to each other by using the Talk window—Command-To. Figure 11-12 shows an example. Battle Chess uses clever animation and sound effects. CheckMate is a more serious chess game for more serious players.

RoboSport, from Broderbund/Maxis, is a battle between robots, a sort of Olympiad that takes place in the RoboSports arena in which two to four teams engage in deadly games of Capture the Flag, Treasure Hunt, Hostage, Baseball, and Survival. Both network and modem play are possible. The game begins with your choosing a sport and an arena, and picking the teams. Team actions are individually programmed by the players. When all is ready, the actions of the teams are turned into a movie, which is played back on the Mac screen. Players assess their damage and strategic position and program another round of moves. Play continues until a team is wiped out. Figure 11-13 shows a scene from a game of Capture the Flag.

11-11 Typing *70 before the number guarantees our game won't be rudely interrupted.

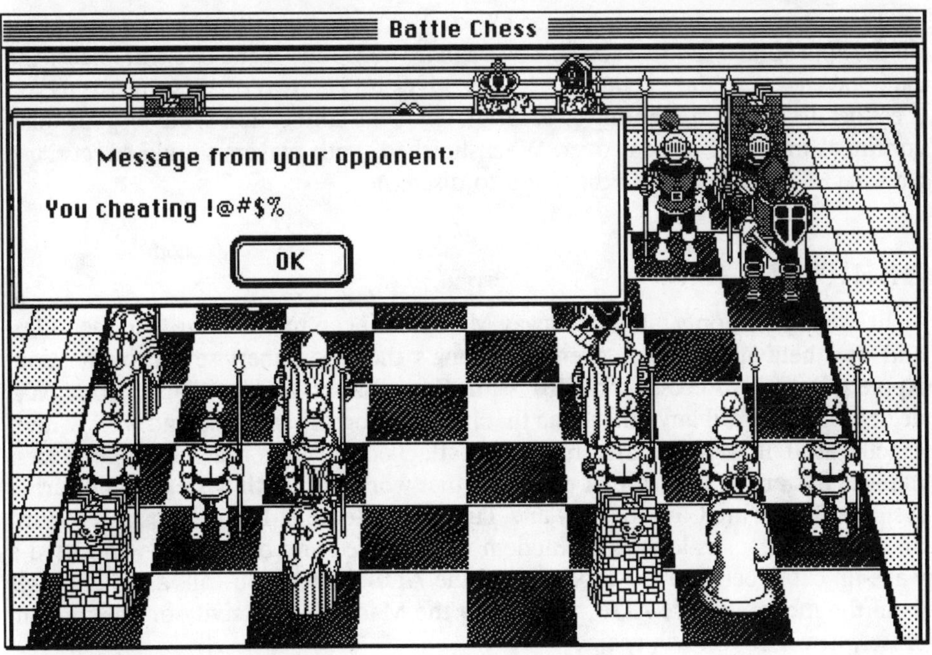

11-12 Obviously, a sore loser.

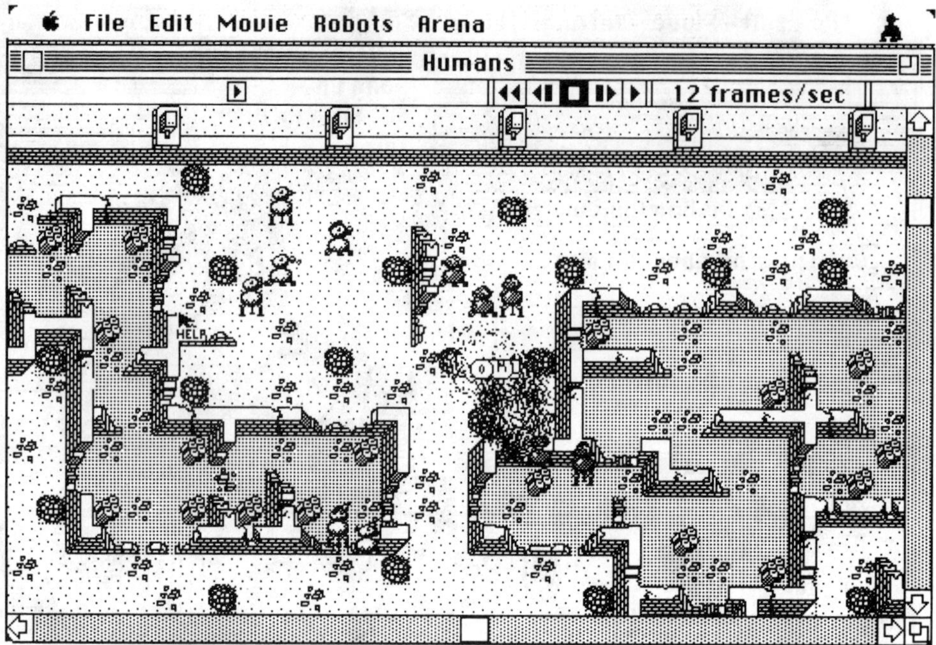

11-13 RoboSport can be highly addictive!

To play by modem, select Open Modem Link . . . from the Edit menu and set up the appropriate modem speed. The Primary computer is the one who places the call, and the Secondary is the one who receives it. The two players must agree on these details before attempting to connect. Once the connection is made, game play continues until the game is over. When finished, both players should select Close Modem Link . . . from the Edit menu to disconnect.

Summary

Your Mac cannot only talk to far away Macs, but it can read and write to their files, and use their applications, even if no one's there to supervise the connection. Apple's Remote Access, included with PowerBooks and available from Mac dealers, lets you call any other Mac that has the program installed and work with it exactly as if it were another hard disk attached to your Mac. Remote Access requires System 7. Two similar programs that work with both System 7 and earlier system versions are Carbon Copy and Timbuktu/Remote. It's also possible to turn on a distant Mac, as long as its modem is connected and on. For this you need a wake-up cable between the modem and the ADB. When you call, a signal passes from the modem to the ADB, turning on the Mac. When activity on the modem ceases, it will shut down again.

Game play by modem or AppleTalk network is also a possibility. More and more game designers are including telecom software as part of the game, and your opponent can be across town or on the other side of the world, if you don't mind paying long-distance rates. Games range from combat simulations to chess, which is, of course, the original combat simulation. Playing by modem lets you challenge live opponents and adds another dimension to gaming.

Appendix A Troubleshooting

If we begin with the premise that there are three things you need for telecomputing—hardware, software, and a telephone line—it's obvious that there are only three areas where something can go wrong. Hardware problems are usually easy to solve. Unless you've been using your modem for target practice or as a chew toy for your pet gorilla, there's not a great deal that can go wrong inside it. Modems have no moving parts to wear out. Most problems are due to lost connections. Some are caused by using incorrect settings. Some involve the host computer, and there's not much you can do except to try again. The following are the most common problems, possible causes, and suggested solutions.

Problem:

The LEDS on the modem do not light.

Solution:

There's no power reaching the modem. Check the power supply. Make sure it's plugged into a "live" outlet and the modem.

Problem:

You get an error message that says Device not present or The modem is not responding.

Solution:

- Check the cable between the computer and the modem. Make sure the connectors are firmly plugged in.
- Check to see that the modem is plugged into the modem port and that your software knows to look for it there.

Problem:

You issue a command to dial, but nothing happens.

Solution:

- Make sure the phone line is working. Plug a telephone into the jack and test it by placing a call.
- Check your software to make sure that you've correctly specified pulse or tone dialing.
- If you're calling from a system where you must dial *9* or follow some other procedure to get an outside line, be sure that your dialing routine includes the necessary elements. If your modem has dip switches, be sure that they're set correctly for dialing out. (See the modem manual for correct settings.)

Problem:

The modem dials the number but sounds extra loud as it does so. No connection is made.

Solution:

The signal is reaching the modem but not the phone line. Check the cable from the modem to the telephone jack. One end is unplugged.

Problem:

The modem hangs up when the remote system answers the call.

Solution:

- Check to be sure that the cables to the telephone line and the instrument aren't accidentally reversed. Phone plugs into the RJ-11 socket with the picture of the telephone. Cord to phone jack plugs into the other RJ-11 socket.
- Or, not enough time allowed for modem to wait for carrier. Increase modem setting Wait up to . . . seconds for carrier.

Problem:

Modem not waiting for dial tone before starting to dial.

Solution:

Dialing sequence starts before a dial tone is present. Add a comma before number to delay start of dialing.

Problem:

You can't hear the modem dialing the number, although it connects.

Solution:

You've turned the speaker off or the volume to 0. Change values in Modem settings. . . .

Problem:

The phone rings, but there's no answer.

Solution:

The service might be temporarily out of order, or you might have dialed a wrong number. Check the number and try again. If the number is correct, assume a system problem and try again in a few minutes. If the problem persists, call the service's help or information line (by voice) and report the difficulty.

Problem:

You hear a slow busy signal.

Solution:

The system has taken all the calls it can handle. All ports are in use. Hang up and try again in a few minutes.

Problem:

You hear a fast busy signal.

Solution:

The telephone company's circuits are temporarily overloaded. Hang up and try again in a few minutes.

Problem:

You hear the answering handshake from the other computer, but yours fails to respond.

Solutions:

- Check the connections. Something might have come loose after you placed the call. (Pets are notorious for unplugging modems.)
- Check the communications settings. You might be trying to communicate with a 1200-bps board at 9600 bps, or you might be using some combination other than N-8-1.
- If connections are in place and settings are correct, turn off everything and reboot the computer and modem. Then try again.
- Try a different board or service. If you can't connect anywhere, the modem might be out of order.

Problem:

You connect with the service, but you see garbage characters instead of the usual message.

Solution:

- You've connected at a different speed than your telecom program is set for. Change the setting and hit Return. It might straighten out. If not, type ATH + + + to disconnect, and try the call again at the correct speed.

- Check the number you dialed. You might have called the 1200-bps line with your modem set for 2400.
- If you're using a packet network, like Tymnet, you might need to use an identifier to tell the system your modem speed. If so, be sure you have done so.

Problem:

You've connected to the service and been prompted to enter your ID and password. When you do so, you get a message that says they're wrong.

Solution:

- You might have made a typing error. Try again.
- On many services, passwords and IDs are case sensitive. You must enter them each time exactly as you did the first time. Try all caps or all lowercase.

Problem:

You suddenly get a message that says NO CARRIER.

Solution:

- The other system has hung up without notice, or noise on the line has caused the modem to disconnect. Call Waiting is the most common source of line noise. Be sure to disable Call Waiting before going online by adding *70 to the dial string for a tone phone or 1170 for a pulse phone.
- Someone might have picked up an extension phone. The resulting noise is enough to disconnect the call.
- If you haven't entered any commands in several minutes, you might have "timed out." Most services will disconnect you if you fail to respond. Usually, they notify you first.

Problem:

The characters you're typing don't show up on your screen.

Solution:

- Your system isn't set for local character echo, and the remote system is not echoing characters back to you.
- Change the duplex mode setting on your terminal software to the opposite of what it is (i.e., Half to Full) or enable Local Character Echo in software terminal settings.

Problem:

Every time you type a character, it shows up as two on the screen, lliikkee tthhiiss.

Solution:

Your system is set to local character echo and the remote system is also echoing the character back. Disable Local Character Echo in Settings or change Duplex mode to the opposite of what it is (i.e., Full to Half).

Problem:

Incoming text is lost or seems to be missing. One or more characters from the remote system were lost.

Solution:

Occurs when large amounts of text are received from system that doesn't support Flow Control protocol or when your Flow Control (Xon/Xoff) is disabled. Make sure Flow Control is enabled.

Problem:

Characters entered from your keyboard, while online, are not always displayed correctly. Occurs without local character echo.

Solution:

Remote computer requires different parity setting. Change from No parity to Even parity. If that doesn't help, try Odd. If Odd or Even had been selected, try None.

Problem:

When sending a file, characters are not displayed correctly on your screen. Text is garbled and oddly spaced.

Solution:

The Data bits setting is incorrect. If the current setting is 7, try 8. If it's 8, try 7.

Problem:

You type a Control character, (i.e., Ctrl-Z) but nothing happens.

Solution:

Many telecom programs let you select the key that sends the control character. You can use the Control, Option, or Command key. The one selected is not the one you're using. Change the terminal preferences setting to the key you want to use for Control characters. (Typing a caret to indicate a Control character doesn't work.)

Problem:

Everything has been going along fine. Suddenly, the system appears to freeze. You enter commands, but they don't appear on your screen and the other system is not responding.

Solution:

You might have accidently typed Ctrl-S, a universal "pause" signal. It will cause the other system to stop sending to and receiving from yours. Try typing Ctrl-Q, the universal "resume" signal. If this doesn't unfreeze the system, you might have encountered either a Mac system error or a massive slowdown in the host computer. In such a case, the best thing to do is to hang up the modem, re-boot the Mac (if necessary), and try again.

Problem:

You've been chatting online with no problems when suddenly your screen fills with garbage characters and your alert signal repeatedly beeps, dings, or makes whatever its usual noise is.

Solution:

Someone has picked up an extension or something external has happened to put large bursts of noise on the phone line. If the system doesn't disconnect you, hang up by typing + + + ATH, and try again.

Problem:

You're attempting to download a file but keep getting messages that tell you that the transfer has been canceled by the sender.

Solution:

If there are too many errors, the transfer will be canceled. Errors are usually caused by noisy lines. Reinitiate the call at a lower speed. (If you've been using 2400 bps, try 1200.)

Problem:

The file you receive shows up with an incorrect name or is a plain "document."

Solution:

- The MacBinary specification might not have been used to create it. Make sure it's a Macintosh file before downloading it. Be sure that you haven't accidentally selected Disable MacBinary in the File Transfer protocol settings.
- You might be able to open the file as text or view it with a utility such as Norton's Fast Find.

Problem:

Text files received from a PC are double spaced.

Solution:

Remote system is sending line feed plus carriage return. Enable the Strip Linefeeds command in your software's Text Preferences dialog box.

Problem:

Text you send to a PC is received with overlapping lines.

Solution:

The receiver needs to see both a carriage return and a line feed at the end of each line. Select End lines with CR/LF in the Text Preferences dialog box.

Problem:

When you're receiving a text file, some of the text is missing.

Solution:

This rarely happens unless you're receiving at high speed and doing something else under System 7 or MultiFinder that uses a lot of the computer's processor capacity at the same time. An example would be assembling a newsletter in Page-Maker while you're downloading text. The processor simply can't handle everything at once. Reduce demands by closing other applications, and try again.

Problem:

Fax/modem software does not install. Startup icon has an "X" through it.

Solution:

- An error has occurred or the Mac is unable to locate the fax/modem software. Software might be improperly installed. It needs to be placed in the appropriate folders in System 7 or in the System folder if you're using System 6.0.7 or earlier. If you drag the fax software to a closed System folder, under System 7, it will sort itself into the correct files. DA fax accessories under System 6.x.x. must be installed using the Font/DA mover.
- If the software has worked previously, it might have somehow gotten renamed, moved, or damaged.

Problem:

You try to send a fax but get a message that says Fax Compression Error.

Solution:

For some reason, an error has occurred during document compression. Exit the application and try again.

Problem:

You try to send a fax, but although you hear the connection being made, the fax is not sent.

Solution:

You might have reached an incompatible fax machine. Fax/modems communicate only with Type III fax machines. Older fax machines might be incompatible.

Appendix B
Bulletin boards

Bulletin Boards are ephemeral things. Sysops shut boards down, and new ones take their place, with astonishing frequency. For this reason, I can't guarantee the accuracy of the following list. Many of the boards listed here have their own online databases of other local boards. Log onto one, and you'll get plenty of other numbers to try. Most of the boards on this list accept 2400-N-8-1. Many can also handle higher rates. A few require 1200-N-8-1. Some boards are open only limited hours each day. If at first you don't succeed, try again later.

Area Code 201:

BBS at the End of the Universe	236-7401
Big Mac BBS	531-3519
Biomedical Engineering	596-5679
CFONJ TBBS	486-2956
Digitbits	288-7269
Dragon's Cave BBS	228-4708
EEE's BBS	340-3531
Electronic Pen BBS	767-6337
Essex Computers BBS	622-5928
Finishing Technology Hotline	838-0113
Golden Apple BBS	989-0545
Jungle	805-9819
Mac Atlantic BBS	543-6950
Macintosh NJMUG BBS	666-2013
Microcosm BBS	398-1133
NJ MacLaw BBS	235-0121
NJMUG BBS	388-1676
Palace BBS	840-4463
Phantom of the Mac BBS	460-1673
Power Strip Mac BBS	348-0576

Realm of Insanity	741-5208
Right Choice	228-4589
Rock Pile	387-9232
Shadow Spawn BBS	293-7778
Silent Tower	832-6294
Target-Future	891-4950

Area Code 202:

ADA Information Database	694-0215
Ada Language System Navy	342-4568
American Inst of Bio Sci	628-2427
Automated Library Info. Exchange	707-9656
Bureau of Prisons	272-4545
Castle Anthrax	298-8151
Corps of Engineers Manpower	272-1514
DC Info Exchange	433-6639
Department of Education	626-9853
Department of the Army	355-2098
Energy Information Admin.	586-8658
Fed. Highway Administration	366-3764
Federal Deposit Ins. Corp	737-7264
General Accounting Office	275-1050
General Services Administration	535-7661
Immigration and Naturalization	786-3640
Mac OnLine	547-0435
NASA Information Center	646-6197
National Science Foundation	634-1764
Naval Observatory	653-1079
Office of Radio Active Waste Mgt	586-9359
Quick Facts	289-4112
Science Line	328-5853
Securities & Exchange Commission	272-2835
U.S. Department of Commerce	377-3870
U.S. Dept. of Justice BBS	898-0318
Veterans Administration	376-2184
World Bank	676-0920

Area Code 203:

Bit Bucket	569-8739
Country Club BBS	270-1739
Earth Network	763-3485
Elm Shore MUG BBS	458-2071
Empire BBS	226-6694
Greenwich High School Online	863-8866
Handicap News	337-1607
Hippocampus BBS	484-4621

Pretend BBS	761-1469
Sixth Sense BBS	371-7073
T.S.C.	854-9716
Web	790-6612

Area Code 204:

AdventureLine	656-2996
Headboard BBS	269-4343

Area Code 205:

ADA Net	854-5863
Connection	854-0698
Lyceum	826-9205
SmorgasBoard	745-3989
Speed of Light	262-3735

Area Code 206:

Belle	641-6892
Abraxas Information	323-7578
Beyond BBS	475-0402
Bumbershoot BBS	282-3065
Bunny Board	863-8662
Crystal Cavern	883-1383
dBBS	624-8783
Evergreen Micro Network	452-2012
Homework Hotline	859-7271
Information Station	852-7874
KTOL Radio Point BBS	459-4609
Lerxstwood Mall	232-7426
Library	641-7978
Mac Castle	630-4728
Mac Cavern	525-5194
Mac Exchange	889-9802
Mac Venture	487-2823
Mac-A-Mania Nut	242-8028
MAChine IE	329-0304
MacStuart	543-5350
MacUs Revenge	272-6343
SeaSoftNet	637-2398
Slumberland	283-6771
Uneasy Alliance	562-1223
Univ. Wash HHS	543-3719

Area Code 207:

Lyons Den	799-2374

Area Code 208:	
JJHS-BBS	455-3312
Area Code 209:	
Ellipsis BBS	575-1411
Fresno Connection	432-9778
MacStudio California	333-8143
MMUG BBS	825-8537
U.I.E. Communications	529-1141
Area Code 212:	
American Psych Exchange	662-7171
Apl Pi	753-0888
Apple Sauce	721-4122
Dorsai Diplomatic Mission	431-1944
Ellena Caverns	861-5484
Frontal Lobe	439-6126
Jeff's BBS	982-4444
LaserBoard	348-5714
Links_II Midi_Inn	877-7703
Machine	340-9666
Metro Area MUG	597-9083
NYMUG BBS	645-9484
Odyssey BBS	663-8707
Suicide Prevention	759-7033
Super 68 BBS	927-6919
Area Code 213:	
Big-Mac Attack BBS	791-7060
Dark Side of the Mac	204-2459
Digital Dungeon	820-4320
Glassell Park BBS	254-4133
Glassell Park BBS	254-4852
Kirk's BBS	376-2150
LAMG BBS	559-6227
Legendary Pirates BBS	379-2080
Mac-HACers	549-9640
MacAttack	414-2009
MachineDo	548-3546
Maclectic BBS	947-4402
Manhattan Transfer	372-4800
Nibbler's Node	936-6923
Olympus II	275-6975
Programmer's Paradise	454-7746
RADIO FREE FREZBURG	432-4139
ROME BBS	858-3037

UCLA DAIMP Drug Abuse	825-3736
Ye Olde Pawn Shoppe	273-1158

Area Code 214:

2nd Office/Mac	306-9141
Amputee Connect	238-0928
BABY BLUE	593-7365
Chrysalis	349-9397
CompuTech BBS	597-1211
HyperCap +	370-7441
Mac Shack	644-4781
MacExchange	394-9324
MACRO Mouse	739-0645
Medical Education	613-9227
Mouse Pad/Tyler Area MUG	597-6560
Optomyes	412-9660
Psychology Forum	368-5474
Southern Crossroads	556-2982

Area Code 215:

Big Board	643-7711
Bob's Mac	446-7670
Computer Paradise	657-5427
Critical Path AIDS Project	564-1090
Dragon Keep	895-2573
Electric Holt	387-4326
Garden State Macintosh	222-2743
HyperCity (™) BBS	440-7558
Illusions BBS	584-4756
Kiss of Death	293-9703
Maltese Cross	440-4439
Outer Limits BBS	638-7391
PennMUG BBS	387-8095
SATALINK	364-3324
StarLine	635-2341
The Nucleus	434-4972
Turbo-386	745-9774
Typesetters' BBS	626-4812

Area Code 216:

Appleholic's BBS	273-1340
Cleveland FreeNet	368-3888
Foot Talk	421-2548
Frayed Ends of Sanity II	943-2788
Free Net (Case Western)	368-3888
Hal's BBS	587-3435

Medina County FreeNet	723-6732
Monsterous Mac	752-4921
NEO Apple Corps	942-3389
Nerd's Nook	356-1431
Steel Valley BBS	545-0093
TARDIS BBS	671-2173
Area Code 217:	
Avalon (CUMUG)	384-3128
Champaign Urbana Macintosh Users Group	344-5204
Fire X Change	785-1526
Friendship Inn	443-1860
Information Exchange	875-7114
The Cloud Chamber	684-2081
Area Code 219:	
MacCHEG	283-4714
MCN 1	282-1054
RCN	237-0651
Area Code 301:	
Agricultural Library Forum	344-8510
Air Force Policy	735-8124
AIR Net	467-7814
BlackDog BBS	730-3264
Boys from DOS	381-2257
Bureau of Health Professionals	443-5913
Capt Peg's	570-4590
Chronic Town	681-5579
CRABBS	553-6929
Divinity II	854-3680
Dog's Dwelling	384-5847
Double Nut BBS	997-7204
FCC Public Access Link	725-1072
FDA BBS	443-7496
FireStation BBS	866-8613
Hitchhiker's BBS	992-6839
John's BBS	566-1336
Lipid Nutritional Laboratory	344-1277
MacCity BBS	599-9116
Midnight MUG	871-9637
Mouse Event	747-7820
National Space Science Data Center	268-9000
NDG Technical Forum	345-2098
National Institutes of Health	480-8400

NOAA BBS	770-0069
Nut House	764-6889
Nutrition BBS	436-5078
Oprey's Nest	989-9036
Overflow Valve	572-2360
The Idea Link	949-5764
Time Machine	477-1624
US Bureau of the Census	763-4576
Yucca's Domain BBS	869-1365

Area Code 302:

Black Bag BBS	994-3772
Dragon's Lair	738-0345

Area Code 303:

Bird Info Network	423-9775
Boulder Mac Maniacs	530-9544
Chatfield Armory BBS	972-9023
Christian Connection II BBS	352-5013
Denver Goodwill	650-7732
Dream Park	530-2571
Fort Mac	361-6965
HappyLand BBS	447-3934
MacLeisure	444-5175
MAGIC	791-8732
Mile High Mac Meet BBS	758-9195
New Age Bulletin Board	366-1106

Area Code 304:

Project Enable	766-7807

Area Code 305:

Check-In	232-0393
Fluid Power	763-7743
Ganas BBS	235-6247
Hearing Aid	653-2589
MACabre BBS	673-4083
MACATTACK! BBS	753-4605
Med Talk	749-2395
NatMAC BBS	748-7993
Sunshine Online Service	378-6828

Area Code 306:

Regina Fido (V12)	777-4493

Area Code 307:	
WYNET Wyoming Dept of Education	777-6200
Area Code 308:	
Barney's BBS	345-3845
Area Code 309:	
Genealogy BBS	692-0786
MouseCapades	755-8274
Area Code 310:	
Head Set	404-1008
LifeLine	823-6686
Manhattan Transfer	372-4800
Recovery Connect	322-2745
Steps of DC West	436-9535
Area Code 312:	
Convolutions	583-7679
Data-Mania	923-1932
Deaf Com	262-6173
Desktoppers II BBS	356-6420
Galapagos	943-3498
Growers Exchange BBS	293-0199
HyperCap +	969-7810
Inferno	752-3674
MACaritaville	766-2636
Northwestern	491-3892
Area Code 313:	
Artic BBS	588-1424
MaxMac BBS	572-9536
MCMUG MacMania BBS	278-8578
Mikie's BBS	477-9652
Area Code 314:	
Cheswick's RBBS	349-5344
COM1: Communications Center	997-1605
Control Panel	867-3939
Doc in the Box	893-6099
Mac Paradise	846-8929
Odyssey	821-4957
Show Me More Stacks BBS	997-6912
Area Code 315:	
Bird's Nest	685-3367

Digital Visions	492-8765
Enterprise BBS	682-4043
Galaxia!	695-4436
Nightshift	457-3144
Shockwave Rider	673-4894
Area Code 316:	
Xtronic Connections	793-8819
Area Code 317:	
B Line BBS	288-5569
Circle city Mac	924-2784
Falx Cerebri QBBS	290-9070
IndyServe QBBS	849-4007
MacConnections BBS	290-1762
Some Place BBS	353-9981
Area Code 318:	
CajuNet Connection	235-3207
Golddust Plantation	424-0375
Lawboard	981-3373
MAClan Host	742-8520
Swampland	239-4536
Area Code 319:	
Anesthesiology BBS	353-6528
Area Code 358:	
Bomb Shelter	084-4970
Area Code 401:	
Lands of Adventure	351-1465
Omega System Electronic BBS	785-0998
Area Code 402:	
MacNet Omaha	289-2899
Moon Base Alpha 1999	476-3886
TKG BBS	895-7419
Wind Dragon	291-8053
Area Code 403:	
Arctic Online	983-2123
Calgary Online	284-9274
Calgary's Resource . . .	277-4658
Callisto BBS (Calgary)	264-0996
M.O.U.S.E. BBS	436-4566

Mac_Xen_Link	274-4503
MacLORE BBS	284-1059
Nimbus BBS	433-7540
Student Exchange	228-9525
SunValley MicroLink	246-4504
TimeWarp Tavern II	475-1444
Area Code 404:	
Atlanta MUG BBS	447-0845
CDC Aids Info Line	377-9563
Infamous Basement BBS	354-0560
Mind Machine	431-9384
Psychology Online	390-0292
Shoe's CPU	882-5445
USS Republic	664-1075
Area Code 405:	
Cybernation	943-3178
Fort Knox Fido	843-3545
Pill Box BBS	681-5818
Plasmatic Info Exchange	624-0006
Area Code 406:	
BIKENET	549-1318
Area Code 407:	
Abacus Information Center	774-3355
C Florida Psych	645-1658
Cornucopia TBBS	645-4929
Data Exchange	297-8043
NCC-1701	380-1701
Nurses Corner	299-4762
Pharm Stat	642-6725
Pyrotechnic's	254-3655
Space Coast BBS	269-2169
Area Code 408:	
A32 User's Group	263-0299
Alcoholics Anonymous	978-9784
AllNet	736-2607
Backboard	226-3780
CPU Systems	298-1054
Crumal's Dimension	246-7854
Digikron	253-1309
File Cabinet	224-6004
FirstClassKitten	245-9209

Inferno	395-5378
Klub KAT	261-1606
Mac Happy	257-8727
Mac Outpost	245-0207
MacDaze-II	252-6801
MacScience! BBS	866-4933
MacStud	735-1160
Major League BBS	997-8591
Portal BBS	725-0561
Positive Image	270-8916
Ringworld	247-3986
Second Source (med equip)	248-3870
Shrink Tank	257-8131
South Bay Soaring Society BBS	281-4895
Sunnyvale Fido Connection	738-1119
SuperMac BBS	773-4500
Symantec BBS	973-9598
The GIF Place	297-8353
The MouseHole	738-5791
The Next Generation	432-3424

Area Code 410:

Braille Inn	893-8944
Johns Hopkins U BBS (JHUBBS)	467-7814
Whitegold!	922-7569

Area Code 412:

Behavioral Vision	247-4610
Cascade	362-2277
Endeavor Starflight	928-8452
Enigma BBS	661-5425
LaserBoard Pittsburgh	521-8646
Mac@Night	268-8974
Maltese Alien	279-7011
Mountain View Electronic Micro Mall #1	221-3564
PA BugBoard	373-2315
Pgh Computer Connection	765-0532
Pittsburgh Link	243-5465
Pittsburgh Macs	344-8504
Second Option	826-0822
The Braille Bank	655-0806
Trading Post	696-5500

Area Code 413:

Baudville	562-1870
Macintosh Only BBS!	746-3202

MacSheep BBS	283-3554
Moonrise	665-1158
Physics Forum	545-1959
Pioneer Valley PCUG1	256-1037
SpaceMet North	772-2038
SpaceMet South	592-0942

Area Code 414:

Digital Bimmers	264-6789
Forecast Office	541-9426
Milwaukee Metro Mac BBS	682-7427
PC-Express	327-5300
Racine Area Macintosh (RAM) BBS	632-3983

Area Code 415:

221BBS	329-1703
AIDS Info BBS	626-1246
Atopy	388-6187
Bay	775-2384
Berkeley Mac Users Group	849-1795
Billboard	686-4338
California State EMS	499-7891
Chemist's Comport	359-6036
Coconino County BBS	861-8290
Dimension X	574-4544
Draco Redux Apple Info System	342-3661
Dream Machine	581-3019
Embedded Systems Programming Mag	267-7674
Fog City	863-9697
Harry's BBS	824-7809
HayMUG BBS	881-2629
Inferno	490-1170
Jasmine Support BBS	285-6862
Journal of Pascal, Ada, Modula2	967-7241
Leading Technology	462-3347
Leviathan RBBS	387-5117
Mac F-X BBS	349-7322
Macademe	681-9594
MacCircles	484-4412
MACINFO BBS	795-8862
Macintosh Tribune	923-1235
MacWARP BBS	751-8396
MicroLINK	898-1696
Nwonknu HQ	365-4194
OneNet BBS	948-1349
Psychic Link BBS	849-3539

Records Department TBBS	426-0470
Sound Mind	965-1525
Stanford MUG BBS	723-7685
SuperMac BBS	962-1618
Thought Plane	932-8293
TOPS Support BBS	769-8874
TopsTalk BBS	549-5955
Twelfth Night (or, what you will)	567-0217
Zone BBS	965-3556

Area Code 416:

Apple Techlink	513-5544
Argentic	593-4025
Arkon InfoSystem	593-7460
Club Mac	462-2922
Daily Planet BBS	336-6159
Emergency Ward	499-7475
Far Jewel BBS	690-2464
InfoSource	574-1313
Land Of Oz	767-9385
LOGIC Information Systems	922-1626
Logic Now	487-9771
Magic BBS	288-1767
SoftArc	609-2250
Towne Crier	646-0263

Area Code 417:

TriStar BBS	887-3282

Area Code 418:

Bab-O-Manie	663-4312
Oasis	543-9121
SYNAPSE (Quebec Mac Club)	658-6955

Area Code 419:

College Crier	537-4110
Mac's R Us BBS	535-8722
POST Office BBS	536-8967

Area Code 501:

AHEC South Arkansas Medical	862-8711
MegaBoard	521-0547

Area Code 503:

Central Point Support BBS	690-6650
Corntown Connection	753-7250

E-CMUG	967-4250
Greyland BBS	747-6098
HP Calculator BBS	750-4448
LateNight BBS	757-8968
LinguaBase	222-9774
Outlet BBS	648-6462
PC Technics	393-0998
Rogue Valley ElectroMail	535-4692
Stax Express	228-7323
Tech-Line BBS	754-7613
Toolbox BBS	344-7387

Area Code 504:

Health Education Electronic Forum BBS	588-5743
High Concepts	391-2925
Gamer Project BBS	467-0574
New Orleans MUG BBS	837-8188
Tulane Medical Center	584-1654

Area Code 505:

Applequerque BBS	265-7357
Call BBS	891-3840
Drawing Board	525-0844
Hummingbird BBS	984-1363
Macintosh 2	678-1318
Misc Mac	898-3609

Area Code 507:

Caesar's Palace	895-8619
Medical Software	281-1989

Area Code 508:

Buzzard's Gulch BBS	759-8749
Chronic Fatigue Hotline BBS	468-6208
Cul-De-Sac B&G	429-1784
Dungeon	456-3890
Greyhawk BBS	650-1292
Macro Exchange AMIS	667-7388
Main Street U.S.A.	832-7725
Moon Mist BBS	897-9422
Mystic Tribunal	689-4493
Odyssey Part 1: Atlantis	820-1861
Odyssey Part 2: Aquarius	875-0413
Odyssey Part 3: Apocalypse	877-0768
Raceway	788-0038
Sounding Board	474-8950

SoundStage BBS	453-0392
Think Tank	655-3848

Area Code 509:

Acey BBS	966-8555
MACS BBS	924-5364

Area Code 510:

Blink Connection	276-4121
Disabled Childrens	841-5621

Area Code 512:

'02 Register BBS	250-2279
Akbar & Jeff's BBS Hut	482-9183
Annex	328-2015
Arcane Dimensions	832-1680
Atlantis	836-8777
Bull Creek BBS	343-1612
Cygnus Interstellar Info	641-2063
Diabetes Discussion	451-9737
Diner	443-3084
Foreign Design—Elite Texan	345-9469
Hellhole	474-1512
Impact Crater BBS	392-4366
M.S.I. After Hours	366-0556
Mac Exchange	658-3212
Mac Securities & Exchange Center	323-2429
Motorola Freeware BBS	891-3733
Necropolis of Dreams	472-6905
Outlandos d'Amour	288-0914
Soft World BBS	383-9898
Stomp'n Brew	993-7595
UTA School of Nursing (SON-NET)	471-7584
ZenWedgie	332-0265

Area Code 513:

Currents!	253-2476
Grand Finale	683-1686
Mac Mania BBS	561-2225
Mega-Mac	779-3722
Queen City Mac BBS	831-6079

Area Code 514:

BetaBoard I BBS	486-3454
MAC-LINK	398-9089
Mac a Mac	766-3653

MAC-LINK	935-1652
PComm	989-9450
Quebec Online	935-4257
Users Connection BBS	354-2219

Area Code 515:

Apple Corp Elite	989-4514
Cyber-Net	628-4992
Enchanted Mansion BBS	279-6769
FOG-LINE	964-7937
Micro Mack BBS	294-3977
Zoo System	279-3073

Area Code 516:

Mac's Delight	499-8471

Area Code 517:

II the MACS	655-4605
Impending Void	351-4194
Lighthouse BBS	321-0788
Wizard BBS	783-1059
Wolverine	695-9952

Area Code 518:

Mac BBS	489-2615

Area Code 519:

Wonderland Regional Macintosh BBS	672-7661

Area Code 601:

MacHaven BBS	992-9459

Area Code 602:

4th Wave / AMUG 2	947-0587
Arizona Macintosh User's Group BBS	495-1713
ARMA	246-6517
BioSPHERE	336-0744
Carpe Diem!	277-8846
EyeNet *HS*	941-3747
First DIBS	881-8720
Kitty's Sandbox	829-7522
Mactivities	722-2924
Marquis' BBS	458-8083
Medic Central BBS	553-8022
New Parents Network	326-9345
Phoenix Red Ryder Host #1	870-1810

St Joseph Hospital	235-9653
The Lion's Den	985-1861
Tiger's Den	996-0078
Tucson Apple Core (TAC)	577-6393
Tucson Chronic Fatigue	749-0040
Area Code 603:	
Apple Power BBS	424-0371
Easy Does It	228-0705
Jungle	233-1474
Recovery BBS	228-0705
Area Code 604:	
B.C. Macintosh BBS	465-0017
Carihi Secondary School BBS	923-3118
Doppler/Deep Cove BBS	277-9920
Ebenezer Christian BBS	826-6607
Hogs Hollow	948-0272
Macintosh Way BBS	574-1199
Sunshine BBS	943-1612
Area Code 605:	
Manzana BBS	665-5179
Area Code 606:	
MacCincinnati BBS	572-5375
Nurses Station	932-9597
Radio Station WFXY / Cumberland Post	248-6397
Science Spoken Here	233-5413
Area Code 607:	
Memory Alpha BBS	257-5822
Mutual Net *QNX*	533-7540
Area Code 608:	
Buyer's Review	244-0852
Caesar's Palace BBS	782-1036
Mac Line BBS	233-9487
MadMacs BBS	221-3841
Area Code 609:	
Armoury II	985-4750
Desperate BBS	737-2876
Discordia	497-0883
Funeral Home	345-8631
MIES BBS	228-1149
Stockton State College BBS	652-4914

Area Code 612:	
Bloomington BBS	888-3712
Caverns of Depth	778-1222
Conus BBS	642-4629
Creative Solutions	546-1624
Desert Oasis	636-4285
DTP Exchange	636-7580
ExchangeNET	571-7774
Glacier BBS	557-8925
Iconoclast BBS	332-4005
Mac Skyline	824-0333
MacExchange II	290-9777
Macintosh Exchange	561-2747
Nick's Nest	490-1187
Railway Post Office	377-2197
Syndicate	572-8370
System BBS	338-8844
TC MIDI BBS	588-0410
The Real American BBS	535-3196
Time Machine HBBS	427-7487
Tower Exchange BBS	420-7811
Area Code 613:	
EntrNet-Q	739-1030
Great MacHouse	562-2624
JUNGLE_electric	233-1474
MacOttawa	729-2763
Whole BIT News	521-3690
Area Code 614:	
16th Dimension BBS	864-3156
Aurora Borealis	471-5733
Beta Traders	385-3870
Second Self BBS	291-1816
Area Code 615:	
Humanities Forum	662-0371
INFO*LINK	434-2551
MacClique BBS	691-7094
Nashville Exchange	383-0727
Shadow Keep BBS	435-0446
Stepping Stones	977-7359
Zoo BBS	426-2214
Area Code 616:	
Dr. Theopolus	949-1321

MacFred's BBS	964-1594
Muon BBS	534-7149

Area Code 617:

4th Dimension BBS	494-0565
Alsys BBS	279-7054
Boston Computer Society Info Center	227-7986
Boston Computer Society Mac	625-6747
Boston Computer Society Telecomm	786-9788
Berklee College of Music	424-8318
Bionic Dog	964-8069
BOARDWALK	964-6866
Boston Gas	235-6303
Buckman's Tavern II	863-8502
Channel 1 News	354-8873
Crystal Palace	859-9478
Dog House	334-2448
Ed McGee Music BBS	374-6168
Graphics Factory	849-0347
IComm	598-5616
Mac BBS	231-2810
Mac Users at Berklee (MUB) BBS	739-2366
Mac's Diner	643-2882
MacEast	868-7987
Multinet BBS	395-6702
Newton's Corner	964-6088
NewWorld Magic	595-5627
NOW JOBS	834-4481
NPI	593-0081
On Record	324-7310
PhotoTalk	472-8612
Prism	965-7816
Reflections	593-7228
S'Ware BBS	938-3505
Stack Exchange	628-1741
Starbase BBS	264-0263
The Graphics Factory	849-0347
Tom's BBS	471-0542
Whole Wheat BBS	436-1614
WOLF'S DEN	266-6370

Area Code 618:

Emerald Keep	394-0065
Systems Support Group BBS	549-1129

Area Code 619:

Dirk Gently's Holistic Computer Agency	286-2552
Fun House	697-8714
Guardians Cavern	563-9004
Kittyhawk	371-4776
Mac INFONET	944-3646
MacConnection	259-8735
Macfanatic	574-6480
MacNERDS	758-1700
MacUG SafeHouse	272-2059
Mystic Passage	726-1591
People Net BBS	444-7006
Super Messenger	268-3636
Telemac BBS	576-1820
Telesis	280-4926
Zoo BBS	741-1962

Area Code 702:

Firefighters BBS	293-1099
Mac + BBS	293-4655
Nevada Mac—Home of A//MUG	359-4999
We the People BBS	258-0660
Western Type BBS	366-9107

Area Code 703:

Ada Info Bulletin Board	614-0215
Adult Child of Alcoholics	821-2925
Agency for International Development	875-1465
ASTEC Support BBS	338-6025
BBS THALIA	533-3938
Brewster's Barn BBS	352-1502
Bull Board	631-8772
Cluster BBS	893-3632
Craig's Place	241-5492
Culpeper Connection	825-7533
Electronic Guide	790-5934
End of the Line	720-1624
FAA	790-1740
Macintosh Network	860-1427
MainLine Mac	658-0086
Mormac BBS	709-9381
Mount Olympus	524-7312
Navy Drug and Alcohol	693-3831
Northern VA Astronomy Club	256-4777
Shadetree	231-3806

Silver Island	759-7038
U S Geological Survey	648-4168

Area Code 704:

Access BBS	255-0032

Area Code 707:

Byte out of the Apple	747-0306
K9 BBS	745-6225
MacComm Connection	795-1721
Mirror BBS	485-0987
Redwood BBS	444-9203
Sonoma Online	545-0746
WALL BBS	874-1135

Area Code 708:

Alliance Computers BBS	831-1142
Ephemeral Hedgehog	293-1886
Eye Resources Net	299-1296
FamilyNet Int'l. Echogate	887-7685
Hangar 18	655-4952
Inverse Universe	395-4914
Macinations	352-9282
MACropedia (™)	295-6926
Mad Macs	948-7008
Northwestern U BBS	491-3892
Polymorphic BBS	910-3814
Prime Time	741-1995
Sedation Exclamation!	654-2064
Shangri-La	596-3648
Spectrum MacInfo	657-1113
The Rest of Us (TRoU) BBS	291-6660
TrendTec	759-9214
Working With Works	260-9660

Area Code 713:

Brain in a Pan	480-7422
Elder Net	794-5858
Galapagos	799-9016
HAAUG Heaven BBS	664-9873
MacEndeavour	640-2533

Area Code 714:

Calif Self Help	952-2110
CMS BBS	222-6601

CMS Support BBS	259-4390
Gentle Rain BBS	593-6144
Grandpa's	952-2312
HIV/AIDS Info	248-2836
La Habra Connection	992-0716
Mac Exchange	860-1805
Macroscopic	689-8683
MacVille USA	859-5857
Mountain Air BBS	336-6080
Nymphotic Zitron	827-2018
SIGnet.Canada	858-5322
Spider Island Software BBS	730-5785
The Desktop	898-7269
Unnamed BBS	731-1039

Area Code 716:

AARDVARK Burrow	383-1635
E F X Systems	396-2699
Mac's Last Stand	248-0694
MacCursor	225-5189
MacSpence	594-1344
The Recovery Room	461-5201

Area Code 717:

Hackers Corner	597-7105
MacGallery BBS	252-3227
Mouse House BBS	285-2535

Area Code 718:

Armageddon	459-8230
Black Box	667-4470
Catholic Deaf Services	624-5817
Elm Street BBS	922-4654
Forest Hills BBS	268-1240
Laserboard	639-8826
Microvilla	237-2734
New York On-Line	852-2662
Not Even Odd	997-1189
NY NovaLink	493-4430
Wall	278-2120

Area Code 719:

Eagles' Nest	598-8413
Onion Patch BBS	570-6805
School Deaf/Blind	632-8180
Scorpion	637-1458

Area Code 800:	
Don's Dental Service	228-5124
Grateful Med Support	525-5756
Online with Hayes	874-2937
Area Code 801:	
Iomega BBS	778-4400
Mac Plus BBS	634-3655
Mainly Macintosh	374-5438
Software Tech Support Center	777-7553
Transporter	379-5239
Area Code 802:	
ACSU BBS	388-3959
CVU BBS	482-2110
Green Mountain Mac	388-9899
ShadowMacs BBS	425-2332
Area Code 803:	
Carolina Networx	788-8039
Fort Mill BBS	548-0900
Macinternational	957-6870
MacMoore	576-5710
USC College of Social Work	777-4719
Area Code 804:	
CFI BBS	422-1109
Halen's Haven	480-0506
Human Resources	624-8410
Naval Computer Telecomm	444-7841
SubZero II	978-1076
Virginia Data Exchange	723-1663
Ye Ole' World BBS	784-3771
Area Code 805:	
Farside BBS	986-1277
Fred's Place	687-1001
Gold Coast Mac	494-9221
SpacePort BBS	734-3330
Area Code 806:	
Homeboy BBS	795-6751
Area Code 808:	
Apple Grove	595-3228
Ghostcomm Tele-Services	456-8510
MacBBS	456-8498

Medic's Place	537-4140
Midnight Magic	623-1085
Restaurant	499-1101
Area Code 809:	
Caribbean Breeze	773-0195
Opus Amicus BBS (San Juan, PR)	724-0621
Area Code 813:	
Crash & Burn BBS	733-3666
ENTREvous II	542-5482
Five Points BBS	957-3349
Grapevine BBS	371-3600
Mercury OPUS	327-3556
Mystical Mire	745-2666
Area Code 814:	
Magical Mystery Tour BBS	337-2021
Sci Link	432-2476
Area Code 815:	
Castle Glen Finnain	332-3014
Primetime BBS	965-5606
TimeMachine!	962-7677
Area Code 816:	
MACapsara	356-6738
Area Code 817:	
Ation BBS	540-1142
Cleburne BBS	641-4842
Crystal Rose	547-1851
DAMUG BBS	383-3268
Obligatory Hendrix Perm	924-2922
Six Macs over Texas	346-9552
The Spectrum	428-0578
WendellNet BBS	794-5641
Area Code 818:	
Apple Bus	919-5459
BEAR'S LAIR	988-6694
CVMUG BBS	704-1365
Drawing Board	965-6241
HOUSE ATREIDES	965-7220
Ionion Polises	335-0738
Mac BBS	332-3783

Mac Lodge BBS	962-1324
Mac Valhalla	951-4445
Realm of the Darkness	792-1661
Red Dwarf	794-5843
SGVMUG BBS	444-9850

Area Code 901:

Daniel's Den	362-5313
Memphis Online	795-3453
NiteMare BBS	754-9823
USA-Net	396-7300

Area Code 902:

MENSA BBS	466-6903

Area Code 903:

Texas Connection	786-2058

Area Code 904:

Florida Archeology	488-6186
Micro Midget	994-0255
Rickards High School BBS	488-9344
Traders Tavern	434-8679

Area Code 906:

Social Work	774-8555

Area Code 907:

Alaska EMS	789-1694
Apple Diggins	333-4090
Front Page	279-9263
Graveyard	258-3912
KWHL BBS	349-8435
LOCAL Paper	225-1240
Mac BBS	272-0550
Northermost Node	452-1460
ORPHEUS	694-0963
Pentagon	349-6540
Rice Paddy in North Pole	488-9327

Area Code 908:

Castle Tabby	988-0706
Milky Way	580-0486
NJMUG BBS	388-1676
Phantasm	291-4134

Area Code 912:	
CannonBall House	477-9232
MicroLine	764-7701
Area Code 913:	
Battleship Armageddon	841-3059
Doc Talk	588-1998
Lawrence News Center	841-2752
Physical Therapy	362-5733
Area Code 914:	
Dead Deckers Society	682-0404
Hackers' Hideout	666-3360
Info-Center BBS	565-6696
Mid-Hudson Mac	562-8528
Village BBS	621-2719
Area Code 915:	
Health Professions BBS	590-9798
Pass	821-3638
Area Code 916:	
Davis MUG BBS	758-0269
DynaSoft	753-8788
hd industries BBS	446-0926
MacNexus	448-5348
NightLine-1	362-1755
Now and Zen Opus	962-1952
Phoenix Landing	966-8243
UNICOM BBS	365-5600
Area Code 918:	
Computercenter Multiuser Online	747-0250
First MidAmerica MultiAccess	250-8495
Palindrome	743-8347
TUMS BBS	234-5000
Area Code 919:	
Cynosure	929-5153
Home by the Sea	639-9728
Homestead BBS	929-0974
Mac Tonight	469-4838
Micro Message Service	779-6674
NC Central	851-8460
NC Public Safety Officer's BBS	886-8826

Part II
Comparing the Services

Each online service has some good features and some not so good ones. There's no one service that does everything well *and* is affordable. If there were, you wouldn't need this book or more than one phone number to dial with your modem. In the following pages I'll take an in-depth look at each of the major services: what's there, how to use it most efficiently, and what (approximately) you can expect to pay for it. Unfortunately, services and their prices can change overnight. Even though every effort has been made to quote accurate rates, I can't guarantee that some won't change by the time the book reaches you. Blame the services, not the author!

Another factor that enters into the rates, and because it affects many of the services can be addressed here, is the question of access. Can you call a local number and connect directly to your service, or must you use a packet-switching network? If you think packet-switching sounds like something a pickpocket might do to relieve you of your wallet, you're not far off. Packet-switching networks are data networks that relay computer data from one place to another, and using them can relieve you of quite a few bucks.

Tymnet and SprintNet are two major networks in the United States. Tymnet alone has over 1,100 nodes in the U.S. and 100 foreign countries. DataPac is the biggest in Canada, although Tymnet is also popular. Some services have their own networks and don't charge extra for these but do charge you if you use Tymnet or a similar service. Others don't have their own network but let you use Tymnet for free at certain hours. CompuServe and GEnie have their own network systems in most parts of the country that provide access to their services at no additional charge. These private packet-switching networks are also used to access other time-sharing services or private and dedicated systems.

A code in the node

When you call a packet-switching network, you are dialing into a collection of hardware called a *node*. Each of these has a phone line and a modem, plus a switch and what's called a *PAD*, or *Packet Assembly and Disassembly unit*, that makes up packets of compressed data and sends them down the line to the host computer. Because these systems use error-checking protocols as a matter of course, their data handling is going to be less prone to error than a direct connection. The PAD is also communicating with the packet-switching network's computer, which is either a mini- or a mainframe. This computer's job is to supervise the datapacket routing so your call from Boston to CompuServe will reach its computers in Columbus, Ohio, in the most efficient manner. It watches the traffic on the phone lines and might send your first data packet by way of Newark, your second through Philadelphia, and so on. And your packet might contain data from a half dozen different sources. Fortunately, it all gets sorted out again at the other end. Unless the network is exceptionally busy, you'd never know you weren't directly connected to your host. When the load is very heavy, response time can slow down, simply because there's a tremendous amount of data to handle. Ordinarily, though, it moves so fast you needn't ever think about it.

Packet-switching networks use the same telephone lines everybody else does, but because they use so many of them and for so much time, they can buy the time a lot cheaper than you or I can. If I were to call CompuServe long distance from my home near Boston, I'd run up some serious charges. Even on a Sunday night when rates are low, it's about 14¢ a minute, or about $8.40 an hour, and that's before you figure in the cost of using the service. Through Tymnet, the phone charge is $1.70 per hour, while CompuServe's own network is free on nights and weekends.

In pursuit of lower bills

Some services charge less if you happen to live close enough to call them directly. Delphi, for example, has local offices and connections in Cambridge, Massachusetts, and Kansas City, Missouri. There's no communications charge if you call their local numbers, which is fine for those in Boston or Kansas City. To reach these phones, if you're a long-distance call away, you have a choice. Use Tymnet or Sprintnet, or use a compromise service called PC Pursuit. PC Pursuit uses packet-switching network (SprintNet's) to send your phone call from your local access number to its headquarters in the city nearest your service. From there, it's a local call to your service, which costs you nothing. What do you pay? There's a flat rate for a certain number of non-prime hours per month. Star*Link is a similar service, run by Galaxy Telecom in conjunction with Tymnet.

The main reason people subscribe to PC Pursuit or Star*Link, though, is to call BBSs in other parts of the country. Because PC Pursuit has nodes in most major cities, it gets you much closer to the free or low-cost bulletin boards maintained by groups such as BMUG, NJMUG, Washington Apple Corps, and so on. If you live in Portland, Maine, the cost of a call to BMUG to download some new utilities would be prohibitive, but getting there by PC Pursuit is a bargain. To use it, you need to establish an account with them. You'll be given a local access number, plus a User ID and password. When you connect, you can direct PC Pursuit to route your call to a specific city and to dial the local BBS number on its local node.

How can you save money on connect fees? The best way is to stay off the boards or services during prime hours, usually considered to be 7 A.M. to 6 or 7 P.M. Since Tymnet, SprintNet, and even the services' own networks are busiest handling commercial traffic during these hours, they will charge you more for access, sometimes significantly more.

America Online

> AUTHOR'S NOTE: *As we went to press, America Online released new software. Version 2.0 contains several new features, including a Download Manager, which lets you select as many items as you want to download and then collect them in a batch. Some menus have changed, but the changes, like all AO features, are user-friendly.*

If the people who invented the Macintosh were to invent an online service to use with your Mac, taking full advantage of the Mac's icons and menus, the ultimate result would be America Online. And that's fairly close to how it happened. America Online started as AppleLink Personal Edition, a service for Apple II and Mac users who weren't eligible for a regular AppleLink account. (AppleLink is a private BBS run by Apple, for dealers, software developers, user groups, and Apple personnel.) It was taken over by Quantum Computer Services in 1989, renamed America Online, and given a facelift and a host of new services. Quantum also operates services for non-Macs, and within the past year has merged America Online with its popular PC-Link for the IBM user. The 150,000 or more Mac users on America Online still see the service as America Online but might occasionally encounter messages posted on a bulletin board that say "Posted on PC Link."

In spite of its now having a foot in each world, America Online continues to be one of the best sources for Macintosh shareware and help. Of course, you will also find the other facilities you'd expect any well-thought-out service to have: news, stock quotes, live conferences, online games, and forums of all kinds. But, probably due to its origins in the Apple/Mac world, you will find two areas exceptionally full of useful information. One of these is the Macintosh support area. There are forums dedicated to all kinds of Mac programs, as well as online support forums from many of the major software publishers. MacWorld Online provides libraries of product reviews, addresses and phone numbers for software publishers and hardware manufacturers, and a great deal more.

The other area that is a particular strength for America Online is the field of education. They have an incredible range of educational services, from the College Board to the National Education Association and the Association for Supervision and Curriculum Development. You can join online classes, for a small fee, in subjects that range from writing and computer programming to music theory and foreign languages. The Education area even provides live online homework help from experienced volunteer teachers every night of the week. If you think about the reasons behind this, it makes sense. One of the groups of people for whom the original AppleLink Personal was started was teachers using Apple IIs in their classrooms. So, education and computing have always been, and continue to be, an important aspect of the America Online service.

Joining America Online

Because America Online's graphic interface uses special software, you need to obtain the program disk before you can sign on. An America Online membership kit is included with many brands of modem, but if yours didn't come with one, or if it's been misplaced, they will be happy to send you a kit. Call Customer Relations at 1-800-827-6364. The kit includes one disk with all the software you need for either a color or a black and white monitor, a registration certificate with a temporary ID and password, and instructions for calling their toll-free registration number to set up your account. You'll also need a credit card or your checking account number if you intend to handle payments by letting America Online debit your account every month. (This costs an additional $2 per month, and the author does *not* recommend it.)

While you're signed on, you'll be given the local access (Tymnet or SprintNet) numbers, and your software will be sent the proper settings to match your modem to America Online's system. That's all there is to it. You will be prompted to choose a screen name and password for yourself. You can have as many as five different screen names under the same account if you wish. Some people like to use one "handle" for chatting and a different one for posting messages. It's quite acceptable to have several different personas for different online areas. Husbands and wives sharing an America Online account can each use a different screen name and send each other E-mail.

What your sign-up kit *doesn't* include is any kind of a manual or guide to what's there, beyond the most basic instructions. That shouldn't be much of a problem, though, because help is available whenever you need it. There is a fairly complete system of built-in help screens that you can open under the Apple menu or by typing Command-/. If these don't answer your questions, sign onto America Online and go immediately to the Member Support area, which is free on nights and weekends. There, you'll find a complete online guide. You'll have to read it online, though. There's no way to download it. In all honesty, you probably won't ever need to look at either the help screens or the online guide, unless you're curious about them. America Online, like all good Mac programs, is completely intuitive. If you can point to a button or a picture of what you want, America Online will take you there.

Finding your way around the screen

America Online's menus look very familiar if you've used any other Mac programs. The File and Edit menus, shown in Fig. A-1, are similar to those you'd find in any word processing application, with a few exceptions. You'll notice that the File menu gives you several Save as . . . options. You can save a duplicate of a file you've already saved by choosing Save Copy. If you want to save a section of text from a longer article, select it and use Save Selection . . .

Open Log . . . lets you keep a text file of a conversation or conference. When you open a log, you can title it or leave the default title "Log." The file will contain everything said during the conversation with the screen name of the person talking, exactly as you see it in the conference window. To suspend logging, use Suspend . . . . When you open a log, the menu command changes to Close . . . . Simply select it to close and save your log.

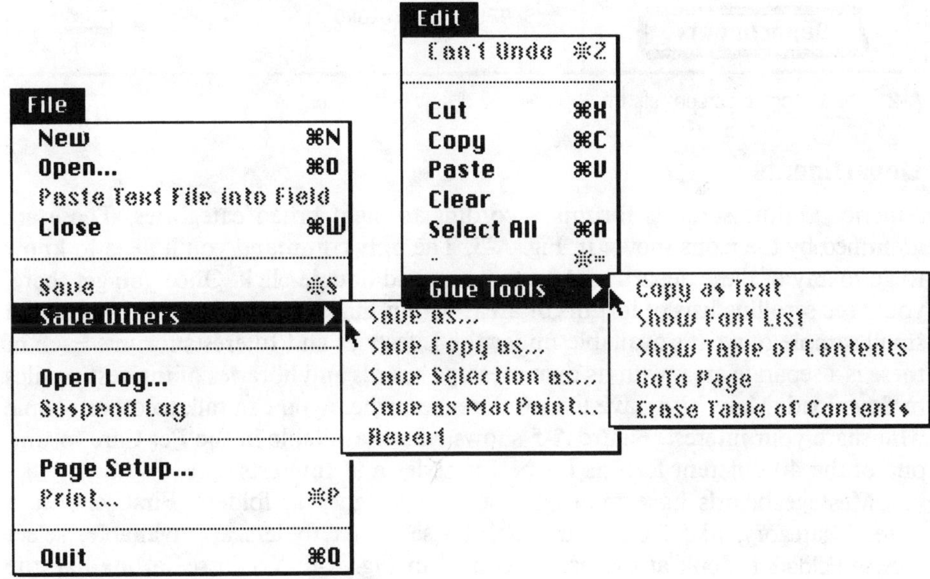

A-1 America Online's menus contain few surprises.

Going online

When you launch the program, you'll see the connect screens telling you that your Mac is dialing America Online and connecting, and then you'll be asked for your password. As soon as it's confirmed, you'll see a screen something like the one in Fig. A-2. You'll also hear a cheerful voice say "Welcome" and possibly, "You've got mail!" If you have mail waiting, click the envelope to read it. If not, choose one of the icons to take you to that day's featured items or to the top news stories. If none of these are appealing, just click the Departments button, to bring up a new set of choices.

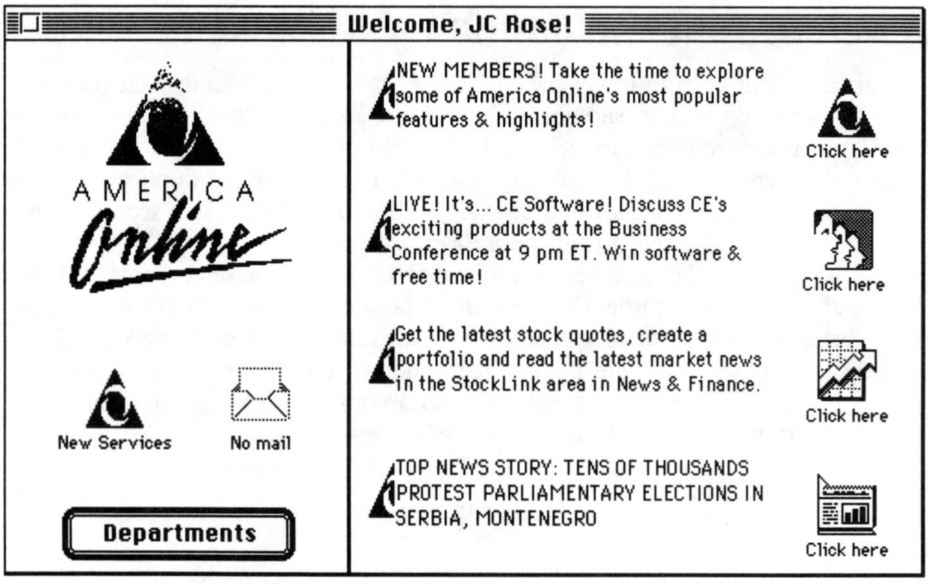

A-2 The Welcome screen lists the top news and new features online.

Departments

America Online sorts its forums according to eight broad categories. These are identified by the icons shown in Fig. A-3. The only command you'll need to know to go to any of these departments is to point and double-click. Once you get there, you'll see scrolling lists of forums or areas within that category. Figure A-4 shows a small sample of what's available under the Lifestyles and Interests forum. Each of these is a separate area, with its own message boards and libraries of interesting files to download. Many also have live conferences, where you can talk to other people who share your interest. Figure A-5 shows what's available in the Pet Care forum, one of the 40 different forums in the Lifestyles and Interests area.

Message boards have messages filed by category in folders. First, choose a general category, like Dogs and Cats. To see what folders are available, select Browse Folders to look at the list, as shown in Fig. A-6. You'll see a box like the lower one in the figure. To read the messages in a folder in sequence, click on the title of the folder to select it, and then click the icon to read the first message. An example is shown in Fig. A-7. Scroll through the following messages by using the right arrow key. To reply to a message, click the Reply icon. Type your message into the message box. You can move the cursor around to edit. Cut, copy, and paste commands work here. Messages are limited in length to about 60 lines. Although you can't create your messages offline and upload them quickly, as you can on CompuServe, you can save bulletin board messages as text files and paste them into message fields by selecting Paste Text File into Field from the File menu. (Don't try to paste a message into the Enter Subject field. It won't fit.)

A-3 Within each of these departments, you'll find many choices.

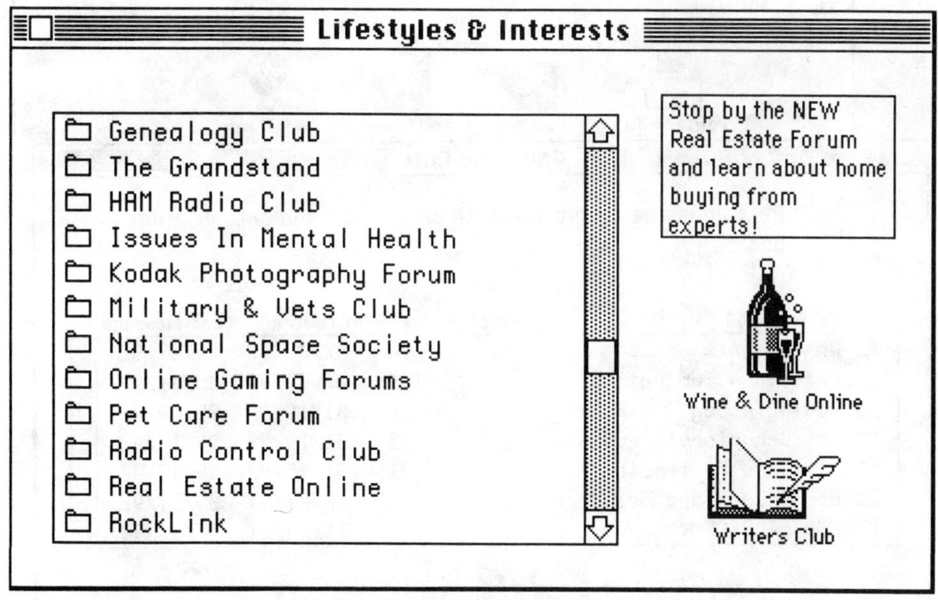

A-4 There are 40 different forums in the Lifestyles area!

Pet Care Forum

- Welcome
- General Announcements Board
- Dogs and Cats
- Horses and Farm Animals
- Reptiles and Marine Life
- Wild and Exotic Animals
- Birds
- Animals and Society
- Animal Talk Chat Room
- <<Pet Care Library>>

A-5 It's a zoo in here!

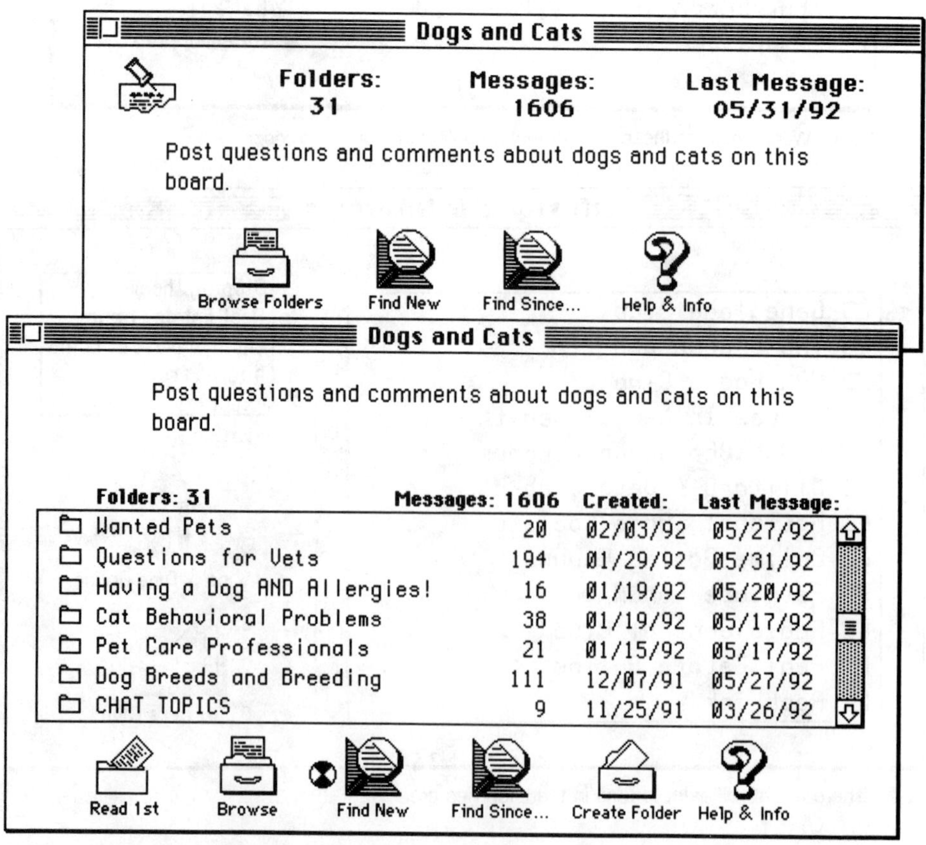

A-6 No matter what your question, someone here has an answer.

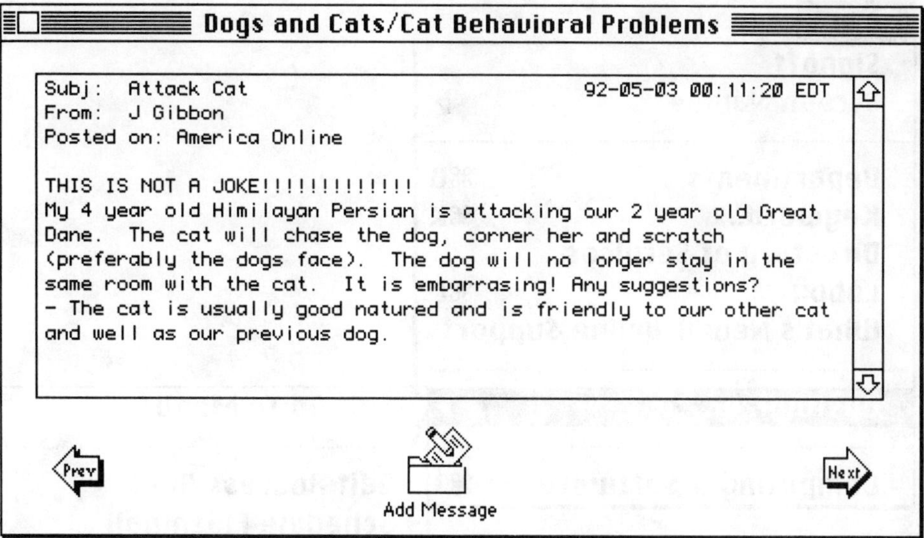

A-7 To scroll through the messages in the folder, use the arrows.

If you don't find a folder that seems appropriate for the message you want to post, you can start your own by selecting Start New Folder. You will be asked to title the folder and write a few words explaining the topic. Then, you can post the first message in that folder. Don't create a new folder unless there's none that fits your topic. When a forum becomes clogged with too many folders, the forum leaders must remove some to make room for the new ones.

Other message commands are extremely intuitive. To see only the messages that have been added since the last time you entered this forum, choose Find New. To see all the messages since a given date, choose Find Since . . . and enter a date.

Using the GoTo menu

You can return to the Departments window at any time to choose a different forum. Open the GoTo menu, shown in Fig. A-8, and choose Departments, or type Command-D to bring back the Departments window. There are other useful functions under the GoTo menu, too. You can use the Sign On command to connect if you have accidentally closed or buried the Welcome screen, with its Sign On button. After you sign on, the command on the GoTo menu changes to Signoff, and this is how you will leave America Online. Choosing Lobby or typing Command-L takes you to America Online's live chat area, a part of the People Connection.

Keywords can take you directly into a particular forum or service area without your having to work your way through several menus to get there. They are shortcuts that can save you a minute or two, and on a service that bills by the minute, every second counts! To use one, select Keyword or type Command-K and enter the keyword in the box. Table A-1 contains a list of frequently used keywords. You can also add a few of your favorite places to the GoTo menu, by choosing Edit Menu from the Customize commands.

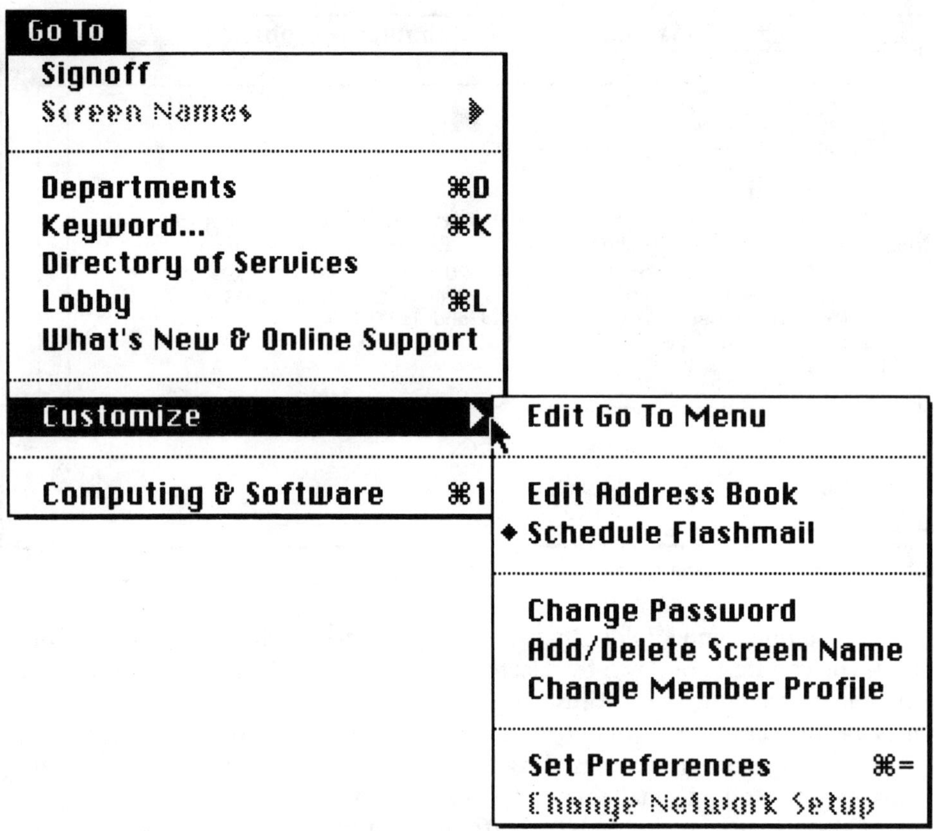

A-8 The Go To menu is the one you'll use most.

Sending E-mail

America Online's E-mail service is probably the most useful of all. Due to a recent improvement in service, you can now send mail to, and receive mail from, people on other several online services, including CompuServe, AppleLink, AT&T Mail, and MCI Mail. You can send as many messages as you want, and there's no extra charge. The America Online mail system transfers mail using Internet, which connects thousands of businesses, universities, and online services all over the world. The Internet system began in 1969 as a Defense Department computer network. Over the years it has grown to include research institutions and businesses. With America Online's mail service, you can now send mail to, and receive mail from, anyone who has an Internet address.

Entering an E-mail message is much like entering a message on a message board, except that you can create E-mail messages offline and then log on just long enough to send them and pick up any new ones. The Mail menu, shown in Fig. A-9, lets you open an E-mail message window by selecting Compose Mail, or just typing Command-M. Enter the name of the person to whom you're writing in the To: window. You can address a letter to a group of people and each one will get a copy.

Table A-1 Useful Keywords to take you directly to America Online's most interesting places.

(Note - Keyword follows description)

Tonight In The Forums: TITF
(Daily Calendar of Online Forum Activities)

Departments

ACADEMIC ASSIST. CNTR: homework
BOOK BESTSELLERS: book bestsellers, books
BUSINESS NEWS: business news
CAREER CENTER: career, careers
CLASSIFIEDS:classifieds
THE COMEDY CLUB:comedy club
COMP-U-STORE ONLINE:compustore
COLLEGE BOARD:college bd
CUSTOMER REL. HOTLINE: hotline
EAASY SABRE: eaasy sabre, sabre
ENCYCLOPEDIA: encyclopedia, aae
EXPRESS YOURSELF: express yourself, debate, opinion
HOROSCOPES: horoscopes
INDUSTRY WATCH: industry watch, career news
INT. EDUCATION SVCS: ies, courses
INVESTOR'S NETWORK: investors network, investing, investments
MARKETS: markets, dow
MASTERWORD: masterword, mw
MEMBERS' ONLINE GUIDE: online guide, manual, help
MEMBER DIRECTORY: member directory, members, directory
MENU SOFTWARE: menu
MOVIE REVIEWS: movie reviews, movies
MUSIC: music
ONLINE CAMPUS: classes
PEOPLE CONNECTION: talk
QSPACE, PLAY BY E-MAIL: quantum space, qspace
ROCKLINK: rocklink
ROMANCE CONNECTION: dating, romance
SOFTWARE: software
SPORTS: sports
SPORTSLINK: sportslink
STOCKS: stocklink, stocks, stock quotes
TEACHERS'INFO NTWRK: tin
TEACHER PAGER: teacher pager

Macintosh Forums

BUSINESS: mbs, macbusiness
COMMUNICATIONS: mcm, maccommunication
DESKTOP PUBLISHING/WP: mdp, macdesktop
DEVELOPMENT: mdv, macdevelopment
EDUCATION: med, maceducation

Table A-1 Continued

FORUM AUDITORIUM: auditoriums, forumaud
GAMES & ENTERTAINMENT: mgm, macgame
GRAPHICS & CAD: mgr, macgraphics
HARDWARE: mhw, machardware
HYPERCARD: mhc, machypercard
MUSIC & SOUND: mms, macmusic
SOFTWARE CENTER: soft, software center
USER GROUPS FORUM: ugc, ugf, user groups
UTILITIES & DAS: mut, macutilities

SIGS
Go to the following companies by selecting SPECIAL INTEREST GROUPS from the appropriate (3 letter keyword) FORUM's menu:

BERING BRIDGE PROJECT: med
BERKELEY MACINTOSH USER GROUP: ugf
BOSTON COMPUTER SOCIETY: ugf
EDUCATION CONNECTION: med
GAME DESIGNERS: mdv, mgm,
GROUPWARE: mbs, mcm, mdv
LEGAL SIG: mdp, mbs, mcm,
SCIENCE AND ENGINEERING: mbs
SERVICE BUREAU SIG: mdp
SUPERCARD: mhc
THE HELIX COLLECTION: mbs
VIRUS INFO CENTER: virus, mut
XCMD DEVELOPERS: mdv, mhc

Product Support Boards

ACTIVISION: activision
ALADDIN SYSTEMS INC: mut, stuffit
APPLIED ENGINEERING: applied engineering, ae
BEAGLE BROS: beagle bros, bb
BERKELEY SOFTWORKS: berkeley softworks, berkeley
BRODERBUND: broderbund
BYTE WORKS: byte works
CE SOFTWARE: ce software
DAVIDSON & ASSOCIATES: davidson
DOVE COMPUTER CORP.: dove
FARALLON: farallon
INFOCOM: infocom
MICROSOFT KNOWLEDGE DATABASE: microsoft
MILLIKEN: milliken
ORANGE MICRO: orange micro
SIERRA ON-LINE: sierra
SPECTRUM HOLOBYTE: spectrum holobyte, spectrum
SYMANTEC: symantec
TML SYSTEMS: tml systems, tml

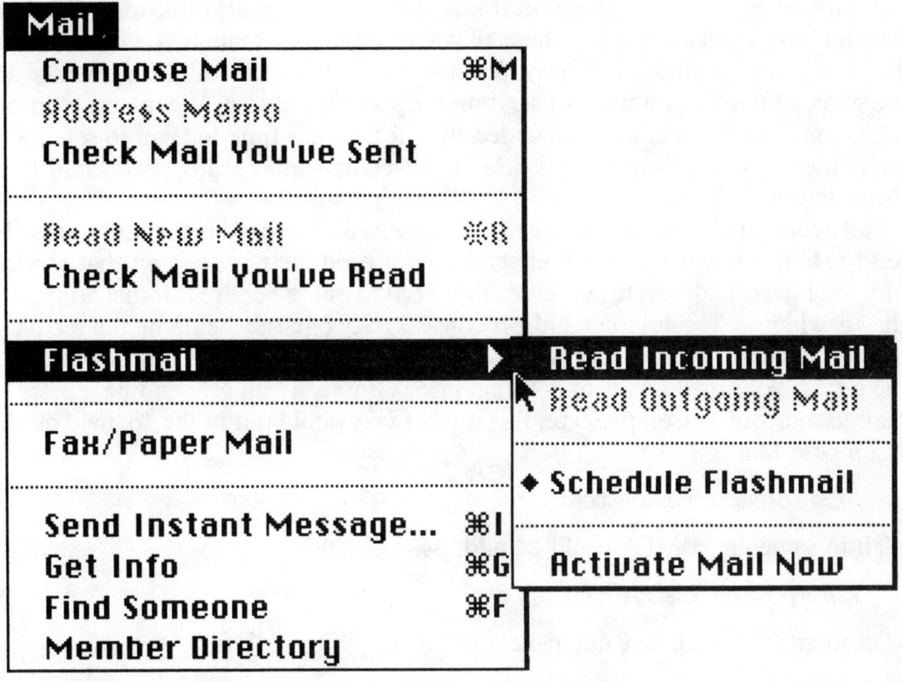

A-9 Flashmail functions somewhat like the CompuServe Navigator.

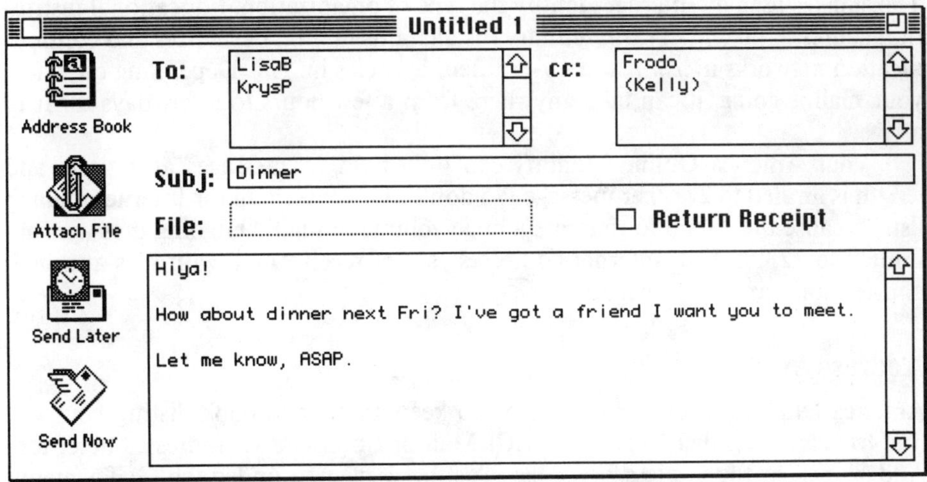

A-10 Kelly's getting a blind carbon of this message.

You can send carbon copies to others, by listing their names in the cc: window, as shown in Fig. A-10. America Online even provides a "blind" carbon copy feature. That means that you can send a copy of a memo to someone without anyone else on the distribution list knowing that person received the copy. To do this, simply insert parentheses around the name of the "blind carbon" recipient, like this: (Kelly). On the "Compose Mail" form, you can also ask for a "Return Receipt" to let you know when the mail you sent has been read. If you have a file to attach to a mail memo, that's easy. Simply click the "Attach File" icon; then locate the name of the file you want to send on the standard file list. When you send the mail, you'll see the file being uploaded. It will take less time for you to send, and your friend to receive, if you use a file-compacting utility like StuffIt or CompactPro.

To send mail to other America Online users, all you need is the user name. To send mail to someone on another service, you need their address on that service, plus the Internet address to get there. You need to put the entire Internet address in the To: window. The Internet address consists of two parts: the name the recipient uses on the other service, followed by the "@" symbol; and the Internet name of the service your mail recipient is using. For example, if you are sending a piece of mail to someone at CompuServe, this is what you would put in the To: field on the "Compose Mail" screen:

12345.678@compuserve.com

Mail to someone at MIT would be addressed like this:

krystalpucci@medialab.mit.edu

Mail to an MCI mail box might be addressed:

509-4725@mci.com

The suffixes used by Internet identify the type of organization. Educational institution addresses all end in *.edu*; military installations in *.mil*; businesses and communication networks in *.com*; and government agencies in *.gov*. Depending on where your mail is going, it can take anywhere from a few hours to a few days for it to arrive.

Your America Online Mailbox can only hold 75 messages at a time, and length is limited to 27K per message. So don't sign yourself up for Internet mailing lists, because these tend to generate a huge volume of mail. Outgoing messages are limited to 32K of text. Internet addresses cannot receive mail with files attached, and receipts can't be provided.

Address books

America Online makes it easy for you to keep an address book, listing your online friends. Keep their AT&T or MCI Mail or CompuServe addresses here, too. Add names to the address book by selecting Customize under the GoTo menu. When you want to send a message to someone who's in your address book, type Command-M to open the message window, and place the cursor in the address field. Double click the address book to open it, and select the name of the recipient. It will be entered in the address window. Type the message, and either choose to "Send Now" or "Send Later." If you are online and you opt to send your memo later, you'll be reminded that you have mail waiting to be sent before you sign off. If you are offline and you opt to send your memo later, the mail will be stored on your disk until you sign on.

To send mail right away, even if you aren't signed on, choose Activate Mail Now from the Flashmail menu. This option, available online or off, provides an easy route for immediate mail handling. Choose it to automatically send and receive mail in one quick step. Then, read your mail and any attached files offline at your leisure.

You can also use Flashmail to schedule a time for the Mac to log onto America Online and send or receive any waiting messages automatically. Choose Schedule Flashmail from the Mail menu to bring up a dialog box like the one shown in Fig. A-11. First, decide whether you want to send mail, get mail, or both, and whether you'll want to download files attached to your mail. Decide what time of day you want to handle mail and how often during the day. These items are set by popup menus. You can also choose to check mail for more than one screen name.

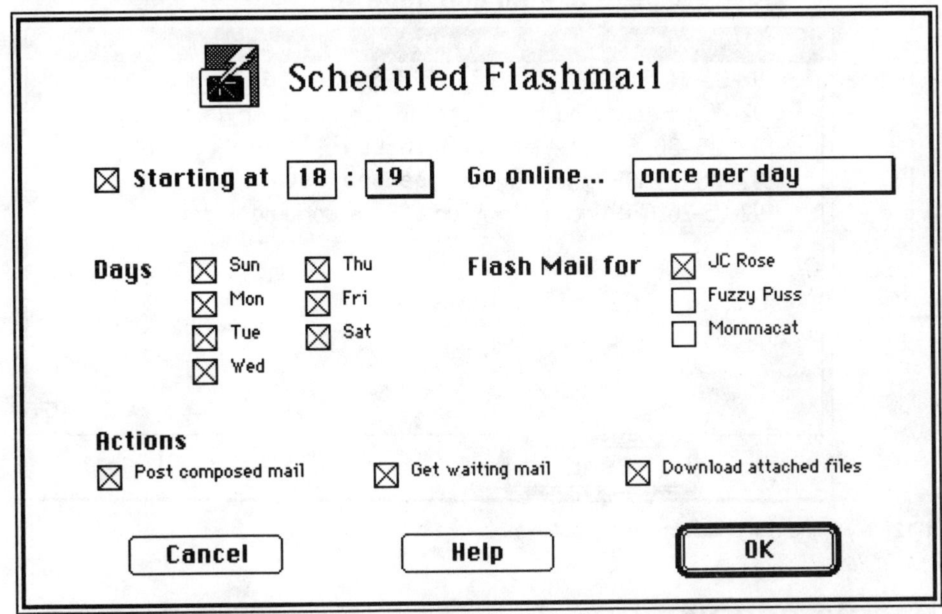

A-11 The shadowed boxes indicate pop-up menus. I could choose to go online more often if I wanted to.

You needn't be around when the mail is being sent, as long as you remember to leave the Mac and modem on and the America Online program open. Before you close the Schedule Flashmail window, you will be prompted to enter the password for each screen name you've selected so the program can sign on while you're busy elsewhere, or asleep. It is sometimes very surprising, if you've forgotten about your Flashmail schedule, to hear your Mac suddenly start to beep and then say "Welcome." If your Mac lives in your bedroom, you might not want to schedule Flashmail in the middle of the night.

Did you get my message?

Sometimes when you send E-mail to someone, you won't get a response right away. Or, you might not be sure that your Flashmail was actually posted. You can check this easily by using the Check Mail You've Sent command on the Mail menu. (You must be signed on to America Online to do this.) Check the "Status" box to see mail you've sent, and when and by whom it was read. This is shown in Fig. A-12.

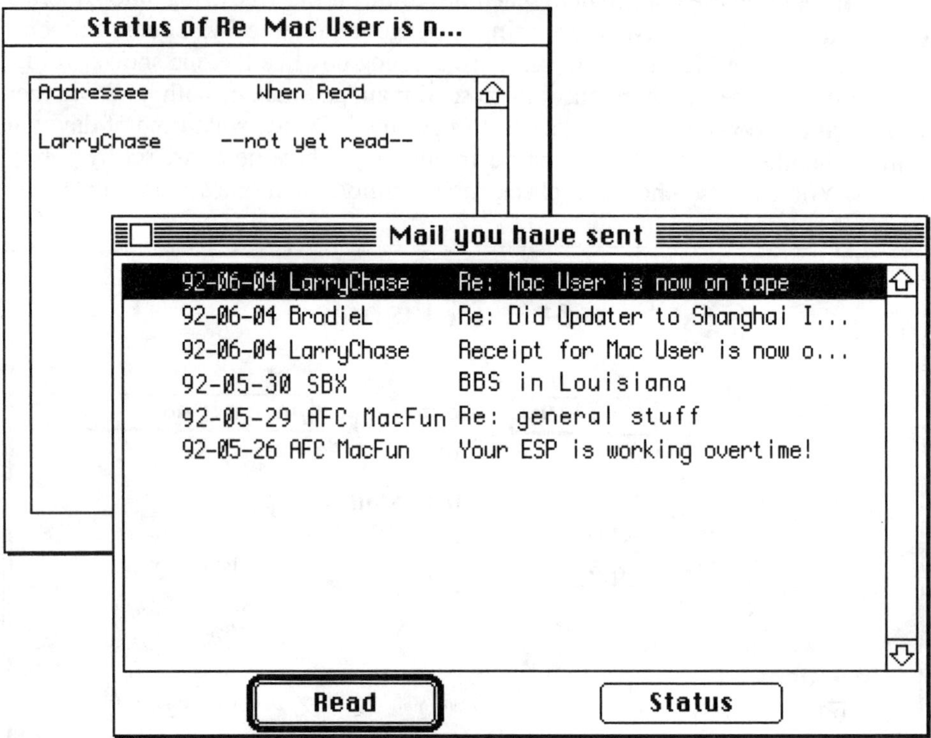

A-12 My friend Larry hasn't read my note yet.

People connection

America Online's real-time chat area is called "The People Connection." Chat groups here are in Rooms. Use the People menu to see the list of available rooms. Join a room, or create your own. During the evening, you'll usually see Trivia and other kinds of games going on in one or more of the public rooms. Feel free to join. If you don't know the rules of the game, just ask, and they'll be sent to you as a private message. Game winners get free online time as their prizes, with the first place winner getting a bit more time back than he or she spent playing the game. If you're good at games, check out the Center Stage Auditorium's game schedule. The prizes here are bigger—many more hours of free time. But the games are harder and you must be chosen from the audience to participate. Rules for Center Stage

Games are found in a folder in "The People Connection Area." During the game you can chat with other members of your row, and questions are frequently thrown out to the audience, with prizes for the best answers. Extra free hours are sometimes awarded as door prizes, too!

If you're not sure what room to join, the Lobby is always a busy spot, with lots of people coming in and out. If you're looking for a small group, look through the available Public Rooms for one with only a few people. To do so, select Go To A Public Room from the People menu. You'll bring up a list like the one in Fig. A-13.

A-13 When one Lobby is full, America Online opens another one.

You can often, but not always, guess what the chat will be about, based on the name of the room. America Online, like most services, tries to keep its screen names and room names reasonably inoffensive, but you'll still see groups here with titles like Gay Men's Bath House or Nude Hot Tub. It's considered rude to join a group you don't fit into, especially if you're doing so out of curiosity or to show them the error of their ways.

On the other hand, if someone deliberately offends you either in a chat or by a private Instant Message, copy it and send the copy with a note of the time and date of the Service. It will be dealt with. The Terms of Service define appropriate behavior in public areas, and anyone found behaving inappropriately can lose his or her membership.

Temporary annoyances can be dealt with easily by choosing Ignore from the People menu, and selecting the name of the member to ignore. Use the Highlight command to set a particular member's comments in bold face type. It makes a conversation easier to follow. The People menu is shown in Fig. A-14.

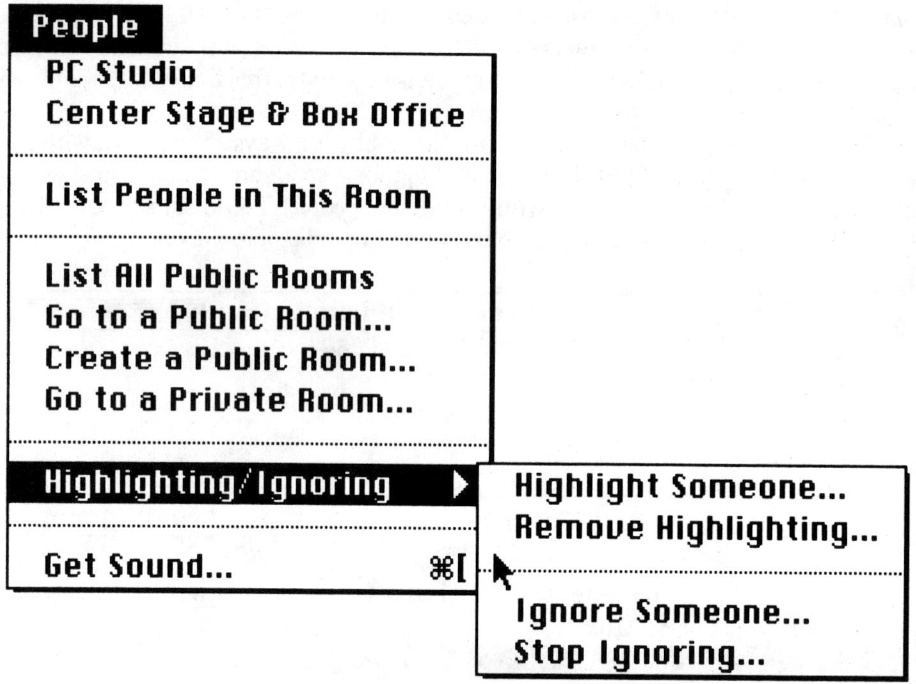

A-14 If you choose to create a public room, you'll have to give it a title.

Instant Messages can be sent from within any area, not just in Chat, since they're selected on the Mail menu. To send one, type Command-I, and type your message into the box, as shown in Fig. A-15. To find out whether the person you want to send an Instant Message to is online, enter the user name and click Available? You'll see a message like one of the two in Fig. A-16. If the person is available, enter your message in the Instant Message box and send it. When you receive an Instant Message, it will be accompanied by a chime sound.

Instant Message

Name: Pussycat

Hiya!
What's new, Pussycat?

Send Available?

A-15 You can't receive Instant Messages while you're doing a file transfer.

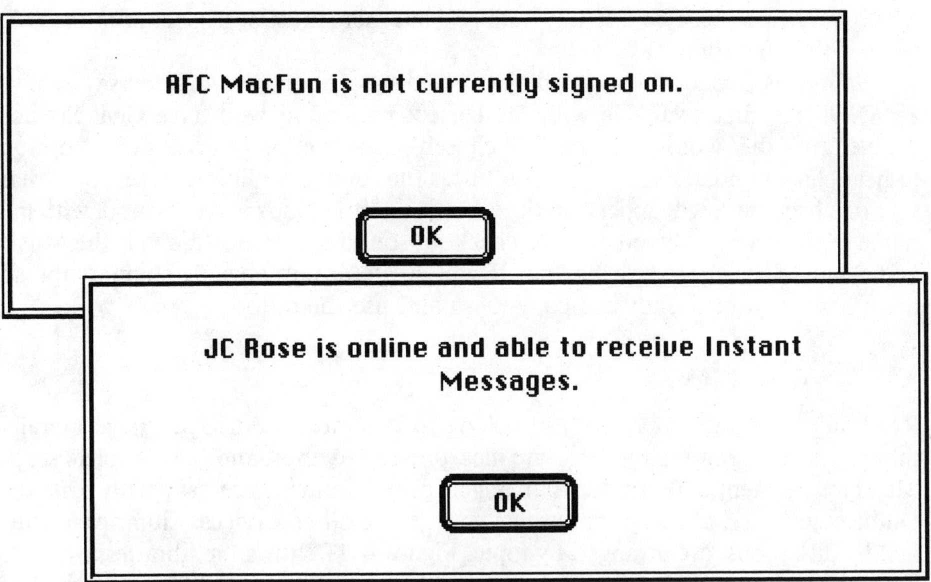

A-16 Some members love receiving IMs. Others find them annoying.

You might hear other strange sounds while you are chatting. You can even generate them yourself. Here's how they work. When you are in a chat or conference room, you can "broadcast" sounds to other users who are in the same room. The sound itself is not sent, but rather a request to play the sound is sent, because digitized sounds are usually too long to be transmitted. The name of the sound is sent, and if anyone in the chat room has this particular sound available on his or her disk, it will be played.

Sounds must reside as a named "SND" resource on the user's disk in a file visible to America Online. There are two easy ways to make "SND" resources available to America Online. Either save all sounds to the America Online file named "Online.sounds." or save our sounds in a file called "Online One," "Online Two," or "Online Three" in the folder entitled "Online Files." These files will automatically be opened by America Online at the beginning of the session, so the "SND" resources will be available. Note that the file "Online Two" will only be opened if "Online One" is found, and "Online Three" will only be opened if both "Online One" and "Online Two" are found.

How to send a sound

Making a sound in a chat room is easy. Choose the "Get Sound" option from the People menu while you are in People Connection. You will see a list of the sounds available to you. Point to the one you want to broadcast. If you choose "OK," the sound command will be transferred into the input portion of the chat room. To listen to the sound first, choose "Play." You can also type the sound command into the input field manually, as in this example (including brackets): {S <boing>}.

There can be no space between "{" and "S" but there must be a space after the "S"; be sure to end with a "}."

Sounds you send will be heard by you and other chat room members who have a "SND" resource available with the correct name and who have Chat Sounds enabled (in other words, they haven't chosen to disable their "Preferences" option to hear chat sounds). Even if you don't hear the sound, you'll know somebody has sent one because it will appear on the screen as a little loudspeaker symbol with the name of the sound. A good place to check for sound files to download is the Music and Sound Special Interest Forum. If you create any interesting sounds, upload them here so your friends can copy them and use them, too.

A trip to the library

Read any good files lately? If you belong to America Online, you have literally thousands of shareware and freeware files, program demos, and the complete set of Macintosh system software at your fingertips. Downloads are easy with America Online's software, although not as fast as on some other services. Libraries, identified by disk icons, are arranged by topic. Figure A-17 shows the libraries available in the Mac Games area. When you open a library window, you'll find that titles of individual files are listed by the date on which they were submitted, most recent first. To find out more about any file listed, either double-click it or select it and choose Description, to bring up a window like that shown in Fig. A-18. By the way, the Send Comment button lets you send a message to the Forum leader, not necessarily to the author of the file, although forum leaders do try to pass on comments to shareware authors if they're members of America Online.

After you've read about the file, you can download it by simply clicking the Download button. Measure the progress of your download by watching the ruler (Fig. A-19). Although it doesn't give you a great deal of information, you can watch the pointer bounce along, and it will tell you how much time is left. Because access to America Online is provided by Tymnet or Telenet, transfers are not prone to error and even though the system doesn't support ZMODEM, interrupted downloads are almost never a problem. If you change your mind about downloading a file, just click Cancel to abort the transfer. If you are using MultiFinder or System 7, you can go and use some other application while files are downloading. You'll know when the download is finished because you'll hear that friendly America Online voice tell you, "File's done."

Uploading is handled in a similar manner. To submit a file, choose the New Files and Free Uploading area, and click Upload. You'll see a standard Mac window to select the file you want to upload and then an upload ruler similar to the download ruler. There's no charge for uploading, but America Online forum leaders request that you use a file-compression utility, either StuffIt or a self-extracting format like CompactPro, on any file over 10K to shorten download time and to make efficient use of their storage facilities. And, obviously, anything you upload should be legitimate—either a file you've created yourself or shareware you've found on

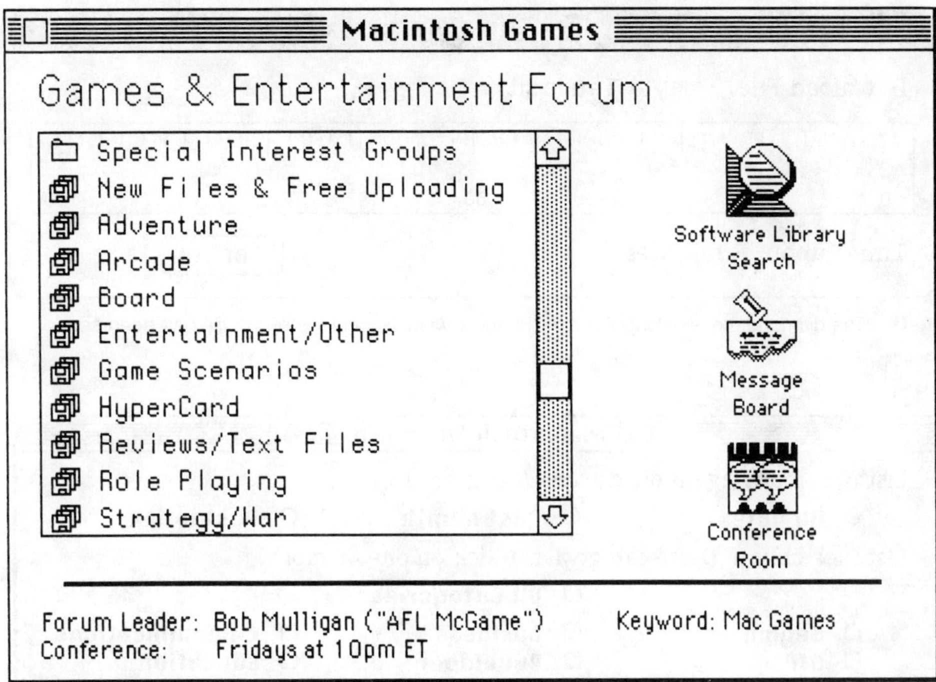

A-17 The disk icons indicate libraries. Double-click one to see what's there.

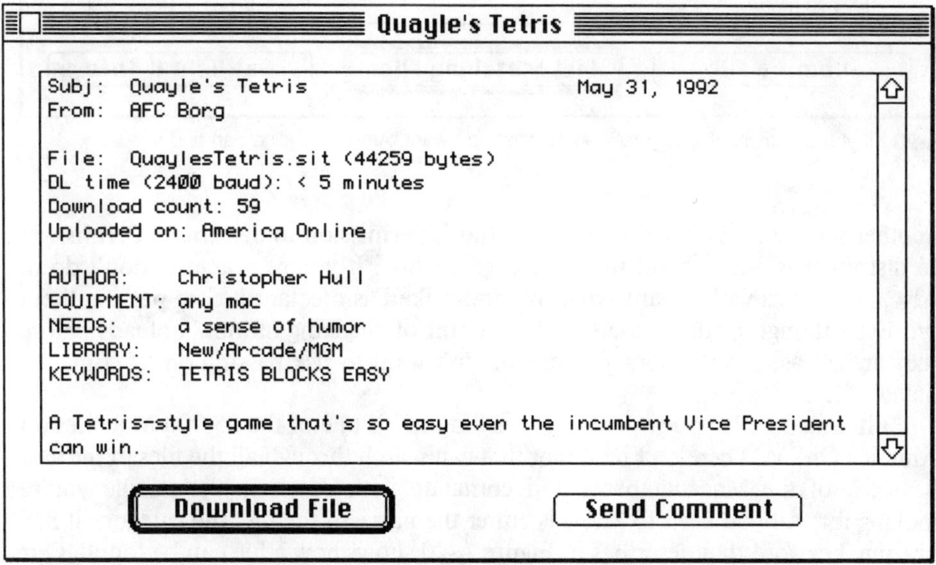

A-18 Every file has a description that includes the time it takes to download.

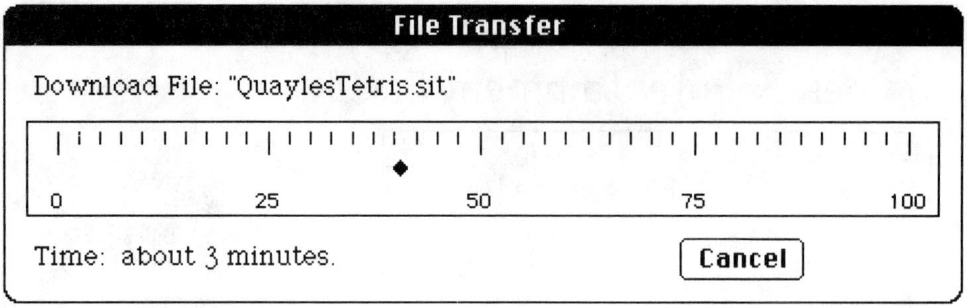

A-19 The diamond moves along the ruler to show what percentage of the file has been sent.

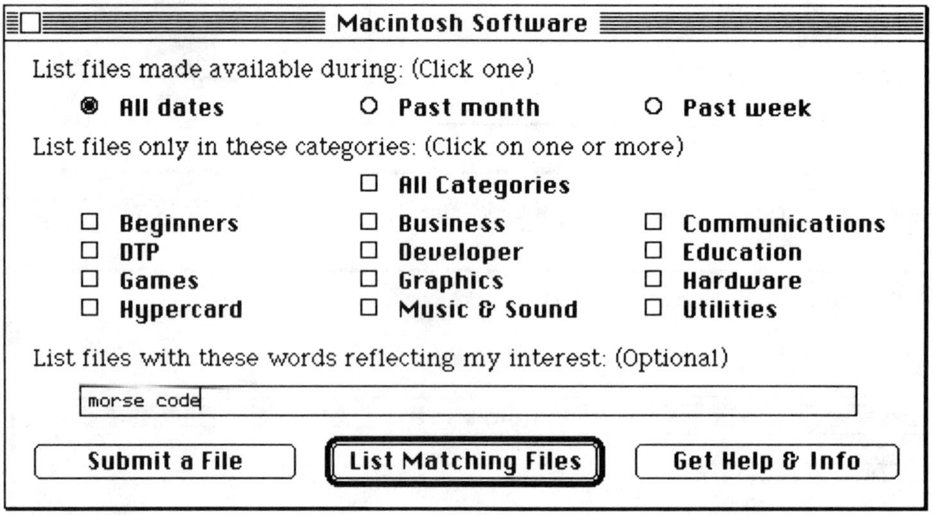

A-20 If you can think of a way to identify what you want, America Online can find it.

another service or BBS and have the author's permission to distribute. Permission to distribute is often found in the About . . . box. If you're not sure, don't do it. Also, check files with an anti-virus program like Disinfectant before passing them on. Even though forum leaders make a point of checking all new uploads before they are released to the library, you wouldn't want to risk passing on a "contaminated" file.

Finding the file you want is easy, as long as it's one of the 25,000 Mac files on America Online. There's a File finder that can search through all the files in the vast haystack of the Mac databases and come up with precisely the needle you're looking for. All you need to know is either the name of the file, the category it fits, or some keyword that describes it. Figure A-20 shows how a file can be found. Our keyword, "Morse code," brought up five different Mac Morse programs, including the one we wanted. To locate the file finder, click the icon for Software Libraries on the Computing menu, to open the window shown in Fig. A-21.

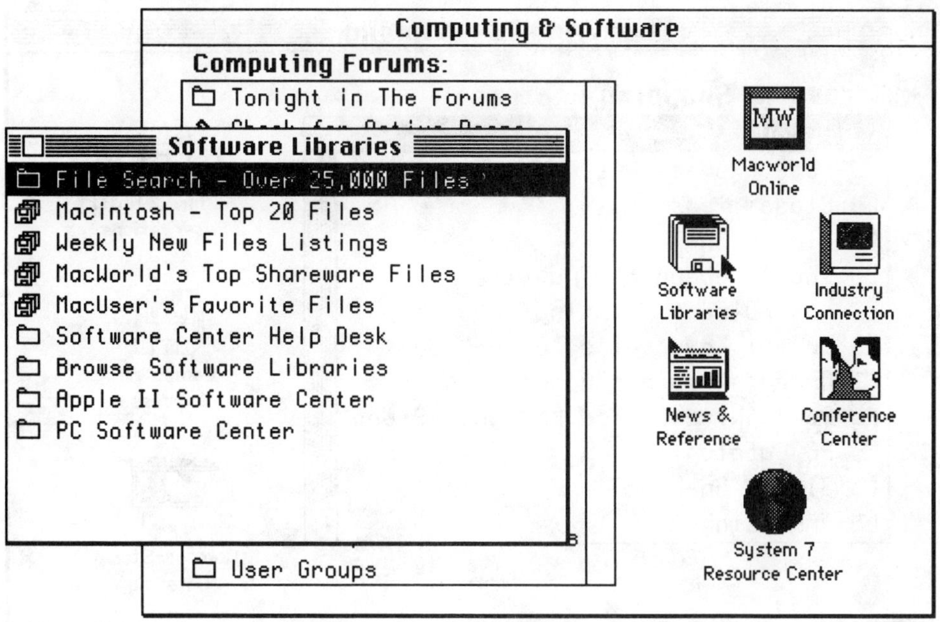

A-21 With 25,000 files for the Mac, there are bound to be some you can use.

What else is there?

Aside from the forums, there are many other areas on America Online worth investigating. Shopping is always fun, and you can order books and software, flowers, tapes and CDs, office products of all kinds, and a whole lot more on America Online. The shopping area is shown in Fig. A-22. CompuStore features appliances, sporting goods, home electronics and stereo systems, photo and video equipment, and many other categories of goods. Unlike CompuServe's version of the store, America Online's is, at least, easy to leave. Click the close box to exit the gateway. There's an Eaasy Sabre gateway so you can make all your travel plans, including air and hotel reservations and car rentals.

America Online's Eaasy Sabre gateway is by far the easiest gateway to use of any of the services. The graphic interface makes it a snap to choose flights by entering pertinent data in fields. Figure A-23 shows an example of a flight request, and Fig. A-24 shows the display of flights that fit the request.

Travelers Access gives you bargain rates on many hotels and trip packages. You can even have a custom Worldview trip planner prepared for you. This is a breakdown of what events, museum exhibits, concerts, and other interesting activities are going on in your destination while you'll be visiting. Trip planners are available for major U.S. cities and many foreign places, including the Bahamas, Mexico, and most European capitals and vacation spots. They can be created for family or couples vacations and trips, with a focus on dining and nightspots, business customs (European), and other important information.

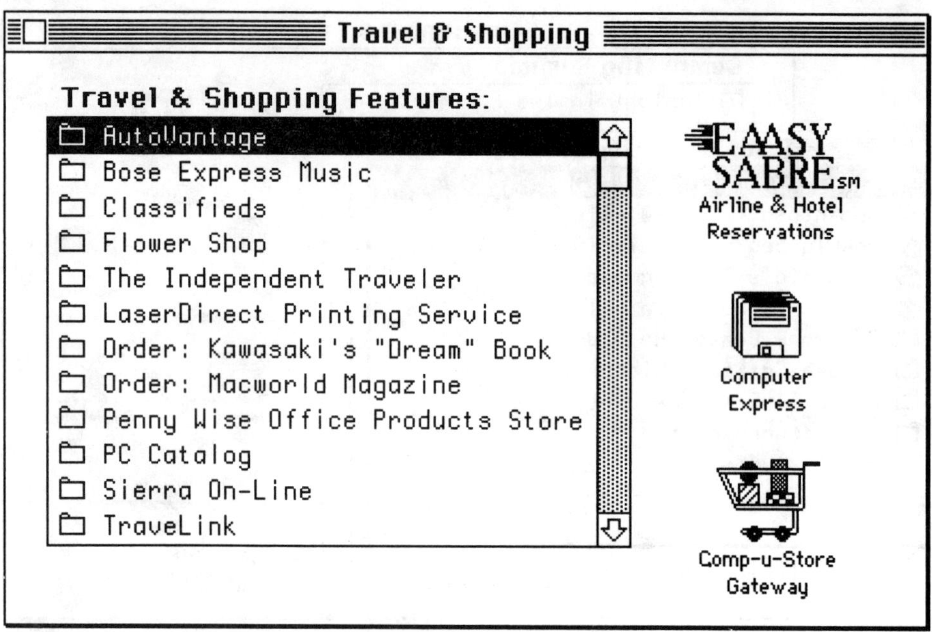

A-22 Even the PC catalog has Mac hardware and software!

Flight Availability Request

Get schedules for available flights between two cities.

From (City Name or Code): boston
To (City Name or Code): montreal

Travel Date(DDMMM): 25jul
Time of Day or Specific Flight: 4pm
(Examples: 8AM or AMERICAN 442)

Preferred Airline (Optional): dl
Connecting City (Optional):

Help | Use profile info | OK

A-23 Capital letters aren't important on Eaasy Sabre.

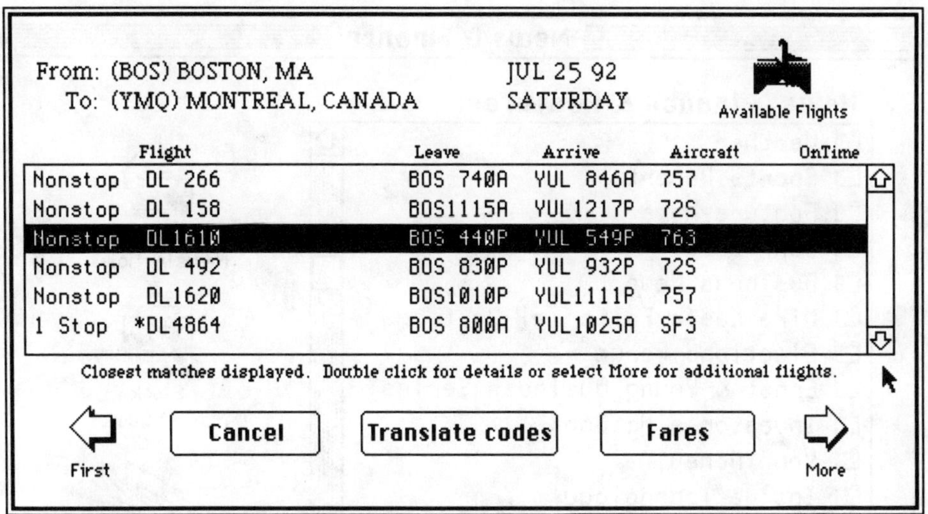

A-24 Clicking the right arrow would show us more flights.

The list of News and Features on America Online is long and varied. You'd expect to find world and national news, sports, business, and weather. But how about Editorial Cartoons, Investor's Network, Home Office Computing, Inside Technology, Book Bestsellers, and a dozen more features? You will be able to read all these and more. Figure A-25 shows a small part of the News menu. Weather on America Online features colorful maps which, unlike those on CompuServe, must be downloaded for viewing with a GIF viewer. Each map takes about a minute to download, and an excellent shareware GIF viewer is available in the weather area, as well as in the Graphics forum.

In order to see a GIF weather map, you must convert the file type to one that can be opened on the Mac. To do so, after downloading the weather maps you want to open, run the GIF converter. Choose Open from its File menu, and open the folder where you downloaded the maps. You won't see the maps right away. Click the "Look inside all files" button. The maps you downloaded should then appear in the box. Then, click the "Fix file types for shown files" button to change the file types to Mac. Then you can open the files. You can save them in any format you wish, including startup screen, EPSF, or MacPaint, and print them to any kind of printer. They'll appear as halftones on a laser printer. An example is shown in Fig. A-26.

Education and reference

As noted in the beginning of this section, education is one of America Online's traditional strong points. Teachers and parents will both find a great deal of useful information here, especially in the Parents Information Network, whose menu is shown in Fig. A-27. Teachers will certainly want to check out the NEA Online and the Teachers Information Network, a compendium of forums, databases, and ideas of all kinds. There's even an Exam Exchange. Upload your tough questions and download someone else's to try on your students.

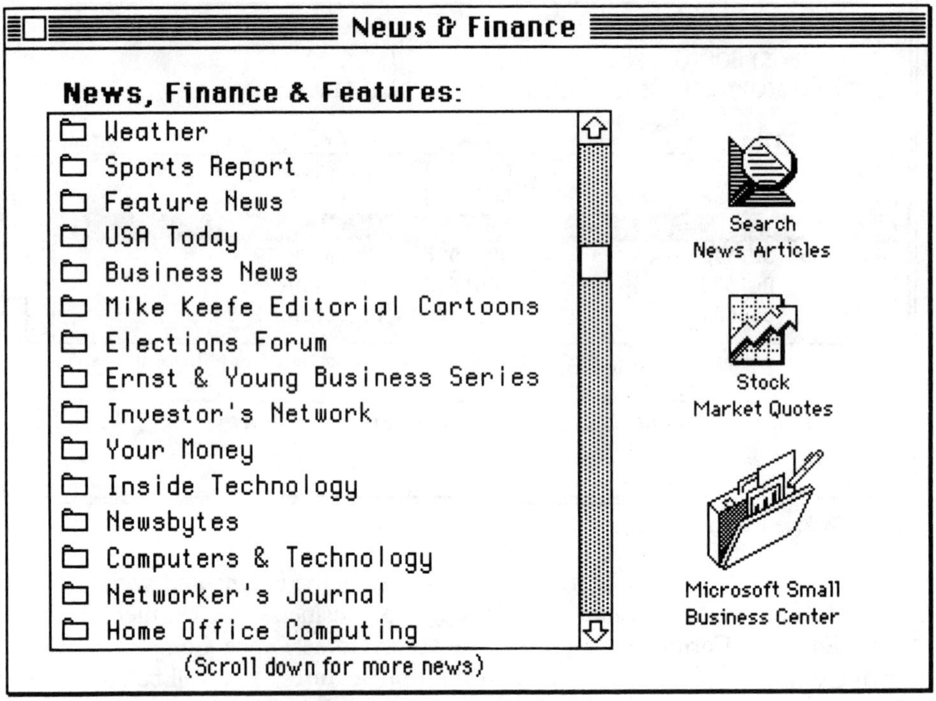

News & Finance

News, Finance & Features:

- Weather
- Sports Report
- Feature News
- USA Today
- Business News
- Mike Keefe Editorial Cartoons
- Elections Forum
- Ernst & Young Business Series
- Investor's Network
- Your Money
- Inside Technology
- Newsbytes
- Computers & Technology
- Networker's Journal
- Home Office Computing

(Scroll down for more news)

Search News Articles

Stock Market Quotes

Microsoft Small Business Center

A-25 This is just part of what's available.

Speaking of tough questions, the answers to many are here online. If you can't find what you need to know in Compton's Encyclopedia, ask a teacher for help. Look for live online homework help every night during the school year from 9–10 P.M. in the Academic Assistance Center. Or, you can make an appointment with a teacher in your field of interest by using the teacher pager shown in Fig. A-28.

The cost of online fun

If you take advantage of all there is to do online, you might expect your bills to be high. And so they will. The basic rate for America Online isn't bad. You pay $5.95 per month, with your first month's membership fee waived and one free online hour (evening or weekend) per month. But then it starts to add up. You also pay $4 per hour for every additional hour you use on evenings and weekends, and $8 per hour for daytime usage during the week. So, for example, if you sign on at noon to check the weather report for the weekend, it might take you four minutes from sign on to sign off, and it will cost you 53¢.

All areas of America Online (with the exception of the free What's New & Online Support department) are charged at the connect-time rates listed above. There's no additional rates or fees for using any area of the system, with two exceptions: the Quantum Space play-by-mail game charges per turn and per game (see keyword "qspace" for details); Fax and Paper Mail incur per-addressee charges (see keyword "fax" for details). The What's New & Online Support department is free during evening and weekend hours. Usage during the daytime on weekdays is charged at the reduced rate of $4 per hour.

The fee for your first month is waived, so the first monthly fee you'll see will be at the end of the first month. It will have the first month's time charges, and the following month's membership fee. America Online's monthly bills work on an "anniversary" basis. If you joined on the 15th of the month, your month runs from the 15th of each month at 10 A.M. to the 15th of the next month at 9:59 A.M. eastern standard time. You can see your billing date at the bottom of your current bill. Connect time is charged in one-minute increments. You are charged $4 per hour at all times. During the daytime on weekdays, you are charged an additional $4 per hour communications surcharge, for a total of $8 per hour. If you don't use your "free" hour each month, it's gone. You can't save them up and spend a whole evening online.

Members calling through access numbers in Canada, Alaska, or Hawaii incur an additional 20¢ per minute communications surcharge, no matter what time of day they call, for a total of $16.00 per hour.

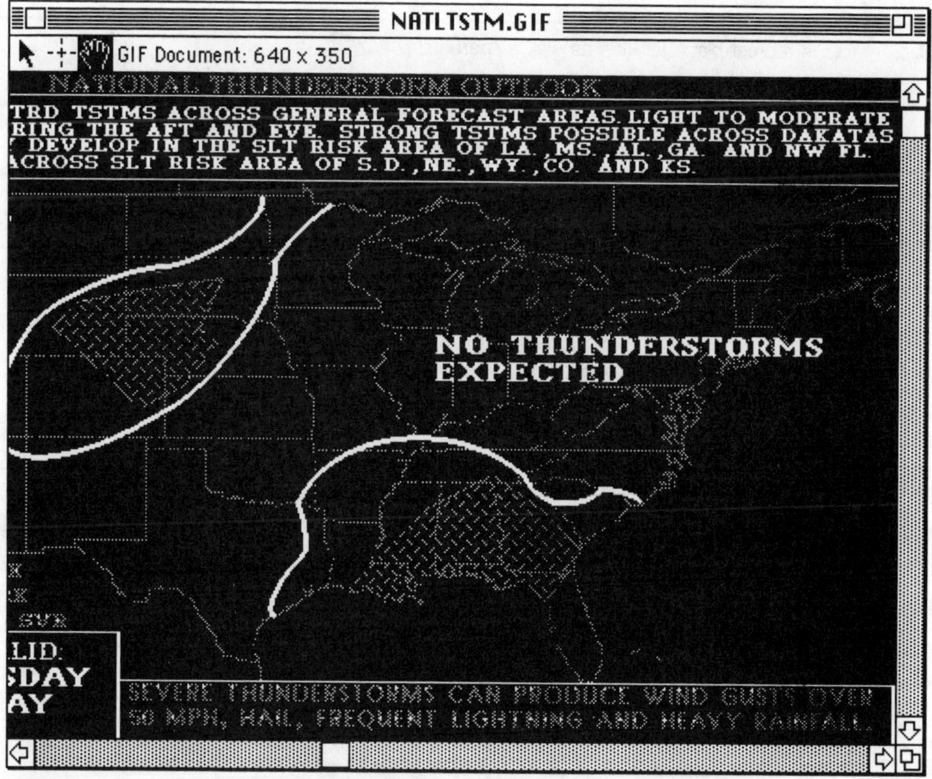

A-26 These weathermaps are much prettier in color!

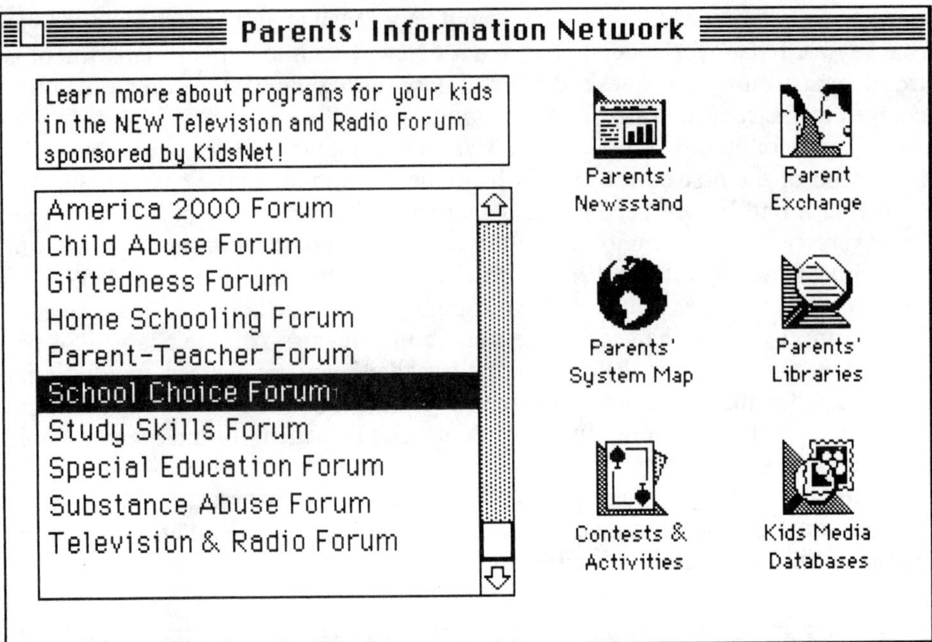

A-27 This is a great place for kids as well as parents!

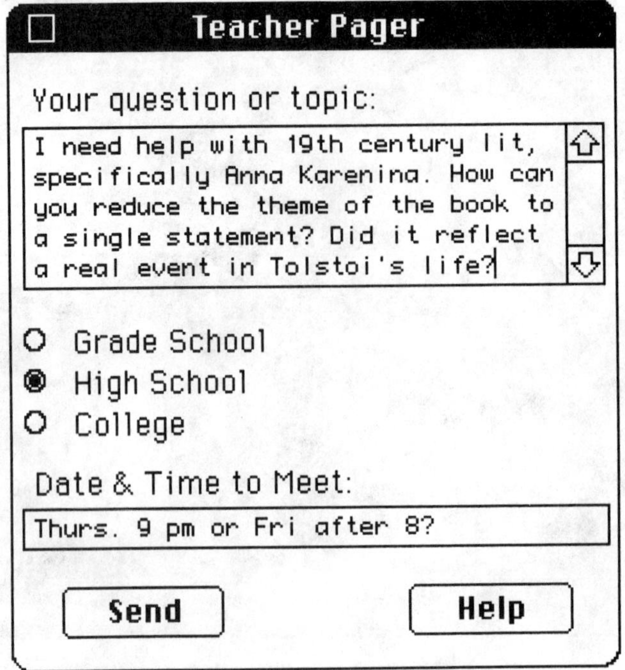

A-28 Help with your homework is available at all levels, from kindergarten through grad school.

Connect time charges are shown on your bill, separated by screen name. Any connect time charged to screen names that have since been deleted will be shown under the entry "Deleted Names." Communications surcharges for daytime usage are not separated by screen name and are shown as a separate total.

What's prime time?

Daytime weekday hours, also known as "prime time" hours, are defined as 6 A.M. to 6 P.M., Monday through Friday, your local time, excluding these five holidays: New Year's Day, Independence Day, Labor Day, Thanksgiving Day, and Christmas Day. All other hours are known as evening/weekend hours, or "non-prime time" hours. Sessions that begin during daytime weekday hours are billed at daytime weekday rates for the entire session. Sessions that begin during evening/weekend hours are billed at evening/weekend rates for the entire session.

Credited time and free time

Your free hour will be applied to your account each month on your "anniversary." *Credited time* is time won in contests or granted by Customer Relations. Credited time will carry over from month to month until it is used. Credited time and free time will be automatically applied as you use the service during evening/weekend hours; your free time is used before any credited time. Free or credited time cannot be applied toward existing charges on your bill and can only apply to usage during evening/weekend hours.

Uploads to a software library are credited back at the evening/weekend rate, regardless of what time the upload took place. These credits are cash credits and are applied back towards the time taken to upload. Thus, uploading during evening/weekend hours is free, except in Canada, Alaska, and Hawaii.

How to save money on America Online

First, don't use the service during the day. The $8 hours add up very quickly. Second, use your one free hour each month to explore and to download lists of programs you can review offline to see which ones you want copies. Many of the libraries post updated lists of their files on a regular basis. For those that don't, here's a quick way to grab descriptions of files you might want so you can read about them and decide which you want to download while the taximeter isn't running.

Use the Open Log command under the File menu to start a log when you go into an interesting library. Choose Get Description for any file you think you might want. As soon as the description box opens, click it closed and go to the next. When you've gotten the descriptions you want to see, sign off. Then, close the log, reopen it, and read the descriptions at your leisure. This trick also works with the message boards. As soon as a message appears on your screen, click the arrow to move to the next, or close the box if it's the last in line, and move to another folder. Get offline as quickly as possible. Then read your log of messages and write responses. Save each response with the title of the folder it goes into. Go back on, find the folder, click Read first, then click Add and use the Paste Text File into Field command to paste your message in the box. Be sure to put a title in the subject field first. When you're done, sign off. You can also use the log-capture system to read the news, articles in MacWorld, or anything else that appears as a text screen. The formatting might not be perfect, but all the words are there.

Don't read and write E-mail messages online. Use Flashmail instead, and be sure your Flashmail delivery is scheduled for evening time, not the middle of the day.

If you are good at games, play some of the online trivia or guessing games in the chat area or Center Stage. Winners typically get from one to five hours of free time, which, unlike your once-a-month free hour, *can* be carried over to subsequent months.

Use your free hour to explore one section of America Online at a time. Jumping around from one area to another takes time, and the meter keeps ticking as long as you're connected.

To avoid technical problems, don't start up America Online if you have another telecom program, like MicroPhone II or White Knight, open at the same time. The other program will fight with America Online to control the screen, and your sign on screens will move like frozen molasses. Also, you'll get error messages when you try to log off, and will be online much longer than you intend to be. If you have a technical problem and must disconnect the modem to get off America Online, leave a message for the service department explaining what happened and when, so you won't be charged for the time. (Be sure to leave the message after 6 P.M. so you're not charged for the time you spend posting it.)

Summary

America Online is a good service for Mac users, simply because there's so much here that's especially for us, and relatively little for the PC crowd. The software makes using the service easy to learn and extremely user-friendly. America Online's tremendous shareware collection is another plus, particularly for the new Mac owner. Downloads are a cinch, and if you do them at night or on the weekend, the price isn't prohibitive. The recent addition of Internet—MCI & AT&T Mail—CompuServe Mail makes America Online your best communications value. If you're going to subscribe to only one online service, I strongly recommend this one!

BIX

BIX is an acronym, of sorts, for *Byte Information Exchange.* This service was begun by BYTE magazine as an electronic conference system and bulletin board for its readers. Although the service is now owned by General Videotex, the parent company of Delphi, it still features BYTE magazine online and forums led by popular BYTE columnists like Jerry Pournelle. If you've ever browsed through BYTE, you'll probably realize that only a small part of it is concerned with the Macintosh. Most of the magazine is aimed at the users of those other computers—and so, alas, is most of BIX. Your subscription to BIX includes a 79-page manual called the *Menu Guide* and a 5¼″ MS-DOS floppy with the BIX simulator, a demo version of BIX that would let you learn your way around offline, if you had an MS DOS computer. There's no simulator for Mac users, and that probably suggests something about the prevailing attitudes on BIX. This is a system devised for Computer People, but certainly not for the Rest of Us.

BIX is text-based, so you'll use your regular telecom program to access it. MicroPhone II comes with a pre-written BIX script, so once you've entered your user name and password, future log ins will be fully automatic. You can easily create a similar start-up script with White Knight or your favorite telecom program. When you sign on, the first thing you see is a welcome screen and the BIX highlights listing of conferences and events. If you have been on previously and joined any conferences, you will be treated to a listing of all the new messages in any of them, a process that can take several minutes if, like me, you like to explore. Finally, you'll reach the Main menu, shown in Fig. B-1. Menu selections are made on BIX by typing the number of the menu item. The command mm at any prompt takes you back to the Main menu. p takes you to the previous menu, whatever it was.

BIX has an E-mail system, which lets you send mail to other BIX users, known as BIXen. Creating a message and sending it is fairly easy. Type the screen name of the recipient at the To: prompt. Enter the subject, and then the text of the message.

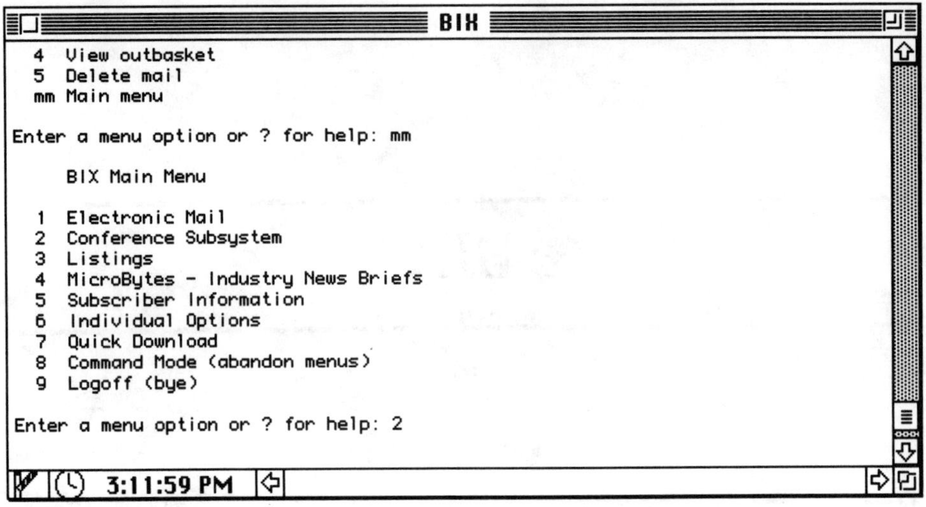

B-1 Select **Listings** to find the library, **Conference** to find almost everything else.

When you're done, go down a line, type a period and a carriage return, and you will get the Send menu. (A period on a line by itself is the BIX code for end of message.) At this time you can choose to send it, send carbons, or try to edit what you've written. Editing is not easy. To see the editing commands, choose Edit from the Send menu and type h for help.

Mostly what you'll find on BIX are conferences with many, many message boards and many, many messages. Unfortunately, BIX doesn't clean house often. Messages on some boards start in 1987, and it's very easy to get into reading a thread and find that it goes on forever. The BIX message boards are very active. As mentioned earlier, if you join any of the BIX conferences, the next time you log on, you'll see a list of all the new messages on each board in that conference. You might find that there are anywhere from a half dozen to 50 or more new messages per day on some very busy boards. BIX users like to write. In fact, many are professional writers. There's both a Journalism conference and a Writers conference, both with many boards and many users. Figure B-2 shows the Conference menu on BIX.

To find software libraries on BIX, look for the menu entry listings, and ask for Macintosh (not Mac) listings. Once you're there, you can search for a particular file by name, date, or keyword, or you can see all the files available. Figure B-3 shows the beginnings of a file search. Files are listed alphabetically and can be downloaded using whatever protocol your terminal program supports. To see descriptions of files, use Browse. Don't try to use "se" to search for a file. On BIX, it means "send," and the system will wait forever, or until you pull the plug, for the file it thinks you're about to upload.

Other than BYTE magazine and computer industry NewsBytes, you won't find any news on BIX, nor weather, nor sports, nor non-professional, non-technical forums. There's nothing here on cooking, pet care, or scuba. There's no online encyclopedia or reference service; no databases of health care topics, no travel, no

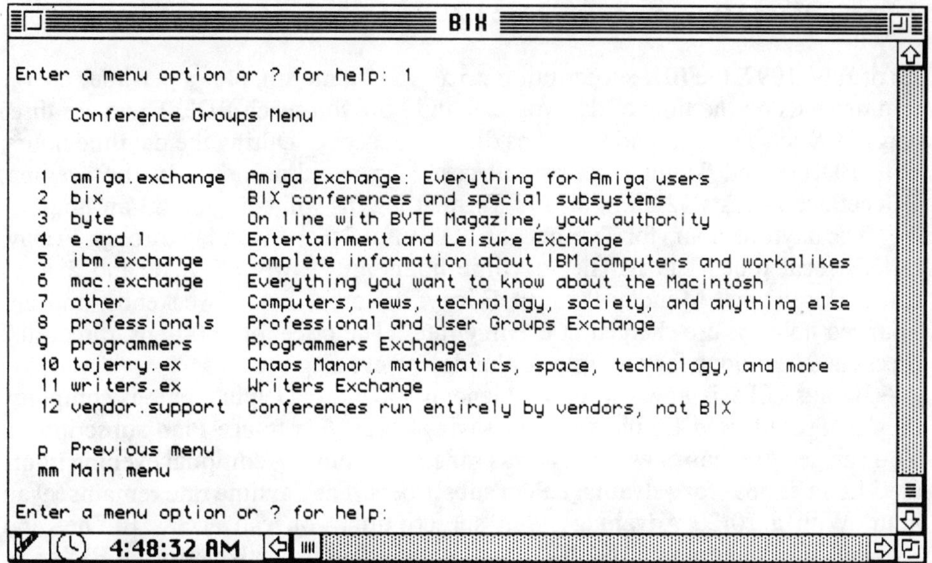

B-2 Join number 2 (bix) to find cBIX.

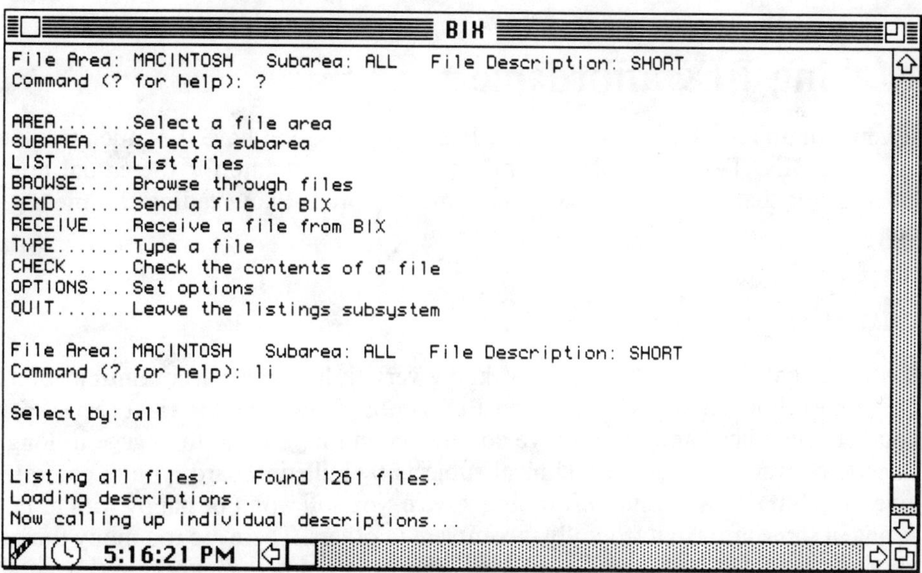

B-3 Browse will show you descriptions of the files. Do use a keyword, though. The list is fairly long.

gateway to Eaasy Sabre or anyplace else. There is "real-time" conferencing, which here is called cBIX. Access is gained by joining it from the BIX area or from another conference. Very few people ever seem to use the cBIX conference area. In the three months I used the service, I only found a live conference once, and it was very late at night.

How much does it cost?

As of July, 1992, the BIX subscription price is $13 a month, plus a per-hour charge that depends on the time of day you call and how you reach BIX. There are three ways: BIXnet, Tymnet, and 9600 bps direct-dial access. During the daytime hours, both BIXnet and Tymnet access will cost $9 per online hour. In the evening, BIXnet access costs $2 an hour and Tymnet log-ins will cost you $3 an hour.

The daytime hours for Tymnet at 6 A.M. until 7 P.M., Monday through Friday, caller's local time. The BIXnet daytime hours are between 8 A.M. and 5 P.M., caller's local time, Monday through Friday. All other hours, weekends, and announced holidays are charged at evening rates. The price for 9600-bps, direct-dial access is $4 an hour for anytime of the day or evening.

Because BIX is now owned by General Videotex, Delphi's parent company, they've also adopted Delphi's money-saving 20/20 Advantage Plan subscription. You can get 20 hours of evening access for $20 a month. Additional evening hours are $1.80 per hour for Advantage Plan subscribers. The daytime rate remains $9 an hour. With a 20/20 Advantage Plan subscription, you can access BIXnet and Tymnet interchangeably. The 20/20 Advantage Plan is available for all BIXen in the lower 48 states, regardless of whether they use BIXnet or Tymnet. It is also available to BIXnet users in Toronto.

Making BIX affordable

If you sign up for the 20/20 Advantage Plan, you shouldn't have too much trouble affording BIX. Twenty hours a month is certainly adequate for the casual user. There's not that much there to spend time on, other than reading the message boards.

Should you join BIX?

If you bought this book because you know very little about telecommunications and not a whole lot about Macs, then BIX is not going to be the right service for you. On the other hand, if you love computers and if you like to engage in long, esoteric conversations about technical subjects by bulletin board, you're going to love BIX. But if BIX is your *only* online service, you still won't be happy with it. It's strong in some areas, but woefully incomplete in others. There are too many things missing that I'd expect to be available—things like news, weather, and a good encyclopedia.

BIX has a lot going for it, if you're in the computer industry or if you're what used to be called a "hacker" before the term gained a bad reputation. It's reasonably priced, and there's a good deal of Mac software to download, if you know where to look. It's a very technically oriented service and has more to offer the PC or Amiga crowd than the typical Mac user. Personally, I vote "no."

CompuServe

CompuServe is the oldest, biggest, most comprehensive, and most expensive of the consumer-oriented online services. (A few of the specialized research services cost more.) It was one of the first computer companies to shift from time-sharing to communications services and one of the first commercial services to admit ordinary people, rather than just businesses, as members. Today, the service boasts nearly a million subscribers, and the number is growing rapidly. CompuServe's 40 mainframe computers also provide a full range of business data network services for private information transfer and credit card verification. When your card is run through the magnetic stripe reader at the restaurant, department store, or gas station, chances are that it's CompuServe who's looking up your account to find out whether your credit is still good. CompuServe's business services include InfoPlex Electronic mail, EDI Electronic Data Exchange, and a host of specialized financial and information services for business, finance, and Research and Design companies.

CompuServe offers the most flexibility in its user interfaces. You can log on in "dumb terminal" mode, using any standard telecommunication program, and access every part of CompuServe. Mac users can also use either of two customized software packages the company sells, CompuServe Information Manager (CIM) or CompuServe Navigator, to handle their CompuServe sessions with a thoroughly Mac-like icon and menu-driven program. CompuServe's front-end programs use what's called *HMI*, or *Host/Microcomputer Interface protocol*, a system developed by CompuServe to make use of your Mac's capabilities as part of a sophisticated link to the host system. This protocol is extremely stable, so your online sessions are much less likely to be disrupted by line noise and other kinds of interference. Rather than sending everything that appears on your screen as ASCII text, the HMI protocol sends data packets that tell the CIM software which screens to display and when and how to use the text blocks it receives. CompuServe also uses its own file transfer protocol, called CompuServe B+, which offers fast, error-corrected transfers.

With all these superlatives, is it the best? Possibly. When you try to be all things to all people, as CompuServe does, it's altogether too easy to end up doing none of them really well. CompuServe has more of everything than anyone else—more news services, more different kinds of forums, more channels of CB simulator—and more dissatisfied customers than any other service except Prodigy. What is it that makes people unhappy with CompuServe? For one thing, the prices are steep and illogical. It's very easy to run up huge bills without being aware of the extra charges you're adding. For another, even though many of CompuServe's services and functions have been made easy to use through the CompuServe Navigator and Information Manager programs, others still depend on terminal emulation; and terminal emulation works differently, depending on what you're doing. It's possible to get stuck in a service area and not know how to get out again without pulling the plug on your modem. This leads to frustration and eventual disenchantment with the service.

Basic commands

The most basic command of all is getting into CIM. But it's not the most obvious. To launch CIM, you double click the icon, as you would for any other Mac application. Soon you will see a welcome screen, like the one in Fig. C-1, with a rapidly spinning globe. Click the mouse to move past this screen to the Browse and favorite Places menus, shown in Fig. C-2. Choose an item from either of these or enter a Go . . . command (explained later in the section), and the program will dial the service and sign you on. (Of course, you must have entered your sign-on preferences first—the phone number to call, your ID and password, and modem settings.)

C-1 The globe spins around until you click. Then, the **Browse** and **Favorite Places** windows will open.

C-2 Click an icon or choose a favorite place to log on and go there.

To avoid getting stuck online and running up huge bills, you'll need to memorize some basic CompuServe commands and shortcut keys, and get familiar with the menu items available to you when you use CIM. Let's look at the menus first. The File and Edit menus, shown in Fig. C-3, are very much like those in any Mac application. New lets you create a document in ASCII text without having to leave CIM. This can be handy if you want to take notes or make a list of things you want to explore at a later date. You can also use it to compose messages that you can check with a grammar checker like GrammatikMac, which scans for spelling and grammar errors in ASCII text files.

Save and Save As . . . apply to ASCII files you compose while in CIM and to GIF images you view online. Save a Copy (Text) is the command you use to save a Forum message, a notice, mail, or an article you want to copy from a CIM screen. Files saved in this way are converted to ASCII text and can be opened by any word processor, Teach Text, or from within CIM. They'll have as a default title whatever the name of the window or topic of the message was. Append to File lets you add additional messages or screens to an existing File. You'll be prompted to select the text file to which to append the new material. Appended text is always added at the end of the file. Revert to Saved undoes the last changes you made to a file and takes you back to the previously saved version. Page Setup and Print work exactly as in other Mac applications. You can print any message or text screen you happen to be reading by typing Command-P.

There are three very important commands at the bottom of the File menu. Leave, Command-L, takes you out of the forum, CB simulator, game, or Mall merchant's store you are in, and back to the CompuServe desktop. You'll still be

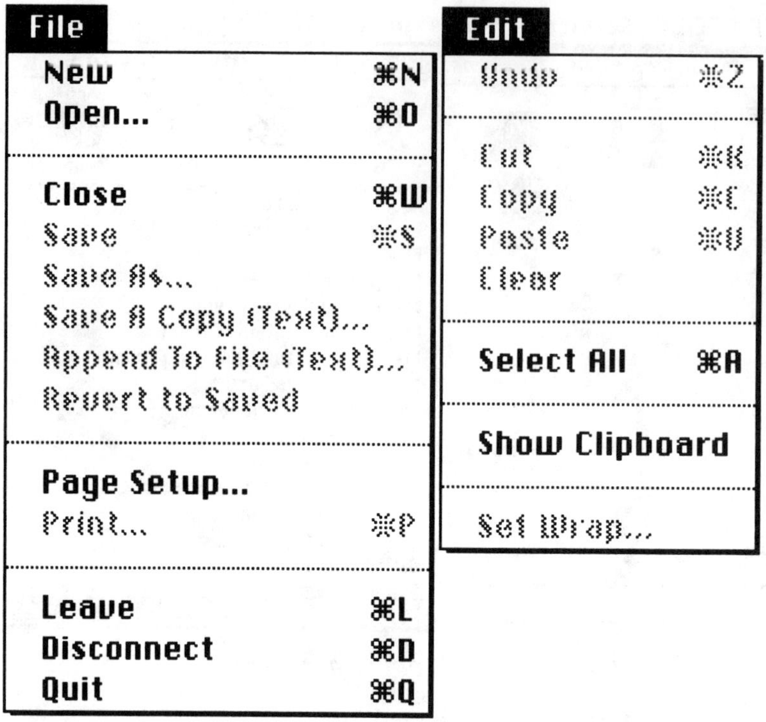

File

New ⌘N
Open... ⌘O

Close ⌘W
Save ⌘S
Save As...
Save A Copy (Text)...
Append To File (Text)...
Revert to Saved

Page Setup...
Print... ⌘P

Leave ⌘L
Disconnect ⌘D
Quit ⌘Q

Edit

Undo ⌘Z

Cut ⌘X
Copy ⌘C
Paste ⌘V
Clear

Select All ⌘A

Show Clipboard

Set Wrap...

C-3 These windows contain standard Mac commands, plus a few extras.

connected to CompuServe and be free to move on to another area. It closes the current service's window. You can generally accomplish the same thing by clicking the Close box, as in other Mac programs. Disconnect takes you offline. The session ends, but CIM remains open. Choose this option when you want to read or write a long message. It's easy enough to reconnect again, just by clicking on the area you want to go to. Quit takes you offline and out of CIM. By default, you're given the usual Mac dialog box asking if you really want to quit. (You can disable this by using the Preferences command under the Special menu.)

Edit menu commands are all standard Macintosh commands, with one addition. Set Wrap lets you specify the line length for text you enter in the mail and forum message windows. If you're sending E-mail to a Commodore 64 or other non-Mac that can only handle a 40-character screen, set wrap to 40 characters. Otherwise, leave it at 80, so that the first word that won't fit on an 80-character line is automatically moved down to the next line.

The Services menu is one of the most useful and most fun to use. It's shown in Fig. C-4. Favorite Places takes you to a list of interesting forums and services. You can customize the list with your own favorite forums, too. CIM comes with forums for Mac users installed in the Favorite Places menu, but you can delete any of them you don't visit often, and add your own. Figure C-5 shows one way of adding an entry. Select your favorite place from the menu through which you normally access

C-4 The Services menu is one you will use a great deal.

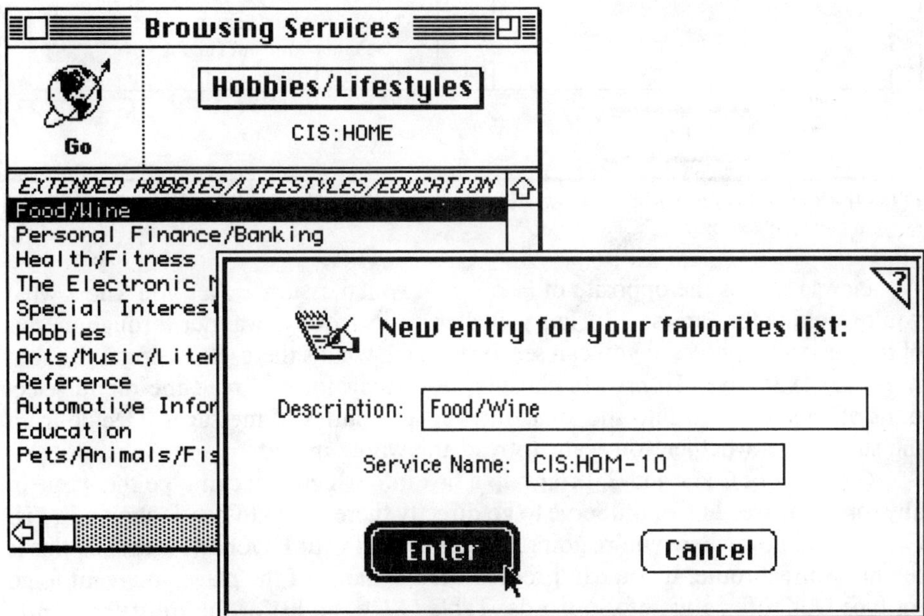

C-5 Adding your new Favorite Places is simple.

it. Food and Wine, for instance, can be found on the LifeStyles menu. Then select Add from the Favorite Places menu. When the dialog box opens, the name of your pet forum will already be entered. Just click Enter to add it. To go to any of these forums or services, select them and click the Go icon or just double click.

Find . . . helps when you're not sure what's available for a particular topic or when you know there's an area dedicated to your interest but you're not sure what it's called. As you can see in Fig. C-6, looking for "water sports" brought us to the Outdoor, Sailing, and Scuba forums, all very good guesses. Clicking the box adds it to the list of Favorite Places. Scuba is already selected because it's already on our list. Some keywords will bring up a lot of different choices. "Books" could refer you to online bookstores in the Electronic Mall, as well as to the Literary Forum. And, of course, you can add any services or forums you find to your Favorite Places menu.

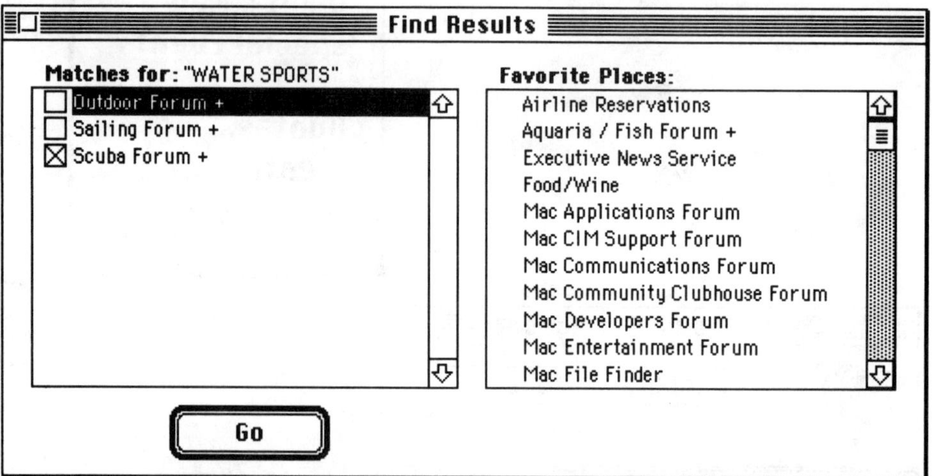

C-6 The X in the Scuba checkbox shows it's already one of my favorite places. To add Sailing, I'd put a check in its box.

Browse . . . is the opposite of Find . . . , which assumes that you know what you're looking for. Browse . . . lets you click on its icons to wander through menus of forums and services, so you can see for yourself what's there. Browsing is fun, but it can get expensive. To browse cheaply, use Navigator and read the menu selections offline. Then go into the area, and get summaries of messages. Decide from the summaries whether you want to read the whole thread.

Go . . . , or Command-G, brings up a box into which you can type the name of any forum or area in CompuServe to go directly there. The Go box is shown in Fig. C-7. If you know where you're going, but it's not on your Favorite Places list, this is the most direct route. If you can't remember the name of the place you want to go to, type QUICK for a list of Go words. Table C-1 has a list of the most frequently used Go words for Mac users.

What's New and Special Events are two different listings of news items, special promotions, and service enhancements to help you keep up to date with the latest happenings on CompuServe.

Quotes, shown in Fig. C-8, is a shortcut to the very latest Stock Market quotes for specific stocks. (Because of SEC requirements, they're delayed at least 15

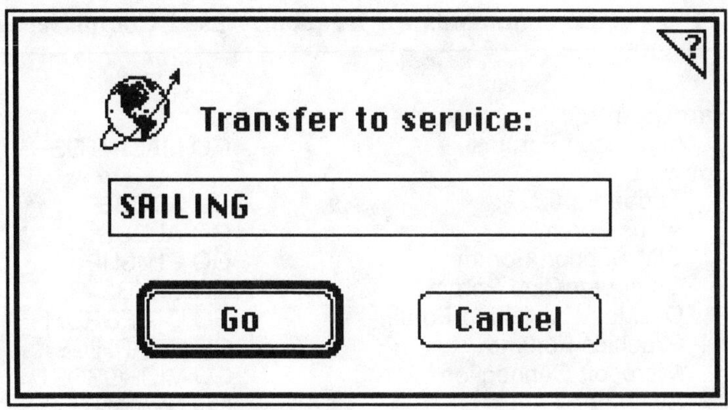

C-7 If you know where you want to go, type it here.

minutes.) To customize your list, enter the ticker symbols for stocks you want to follow. If you don't know the ticker symbol for a particular stock, use the Go command and enter LOOKUP to find it. To see the Quotes window properly, use Set Wrap from the Edit menu to set the text to wrap at 86 characters. Weather and CB Simulator, logically, take you directly to those areas.

What's there?

Describing everything that's available on CompuServe is a Herculean task. Several books have been dedicated to explaining the service, and it would take a good deal more space than is available here to include every forum, library, and gateway. If you join CompuServe, set aside some time (and money) to explore. You might be surprised at some of the things you find online. However, I can at least attempt to skim the cream from the Mac owner's point of view.

If you were to draw a diagram of CompuServe, it would resemble a pyramid, with some of the bricks overlapping. You enter the pyramid in different places, depending on whether you've chosen to use text, CIM, or Navigator. Using text mode, you enter at the tip of the pyramid, working your way through a list of choices like that shown in Fig. C-9. Both CIM and Navigator let you choose your entry point offline and go directly there, bypassing the top menu. CIM gives you both a Browse window and a second window in which you can set up a list of your favorite places to go in CompuServe. The Browse window, shown in Fig. C-10, contains icons for each of the general categories shown on the Top list. Clicking an icon takes you directly to that menu. Clicking any of those menus takes you into a forum or to another menu of choices, depending on the area you've chosen. If the Browse window disappears (and the Browse command is dimmed on the menu) while you're in a forum, and you want to get it back, here's an unofficial, but effective, way: Select Go from the Services menu, or type Command-G to bring up the Go box, and type "desktop." First, you'll see a box telling you that CIS doesn't recognize "desktop." Then, it will take you there.

Table C-1 The Go commands for frequently used CompuServe areas.

Hardware	
Macintosh Forums	GO MACINTOSH
Software	
Adobe Forum	GO ADOBE
Aldus Forum	GO ALDUS
CIM Support Forum	GO CIMSUP
Computer Club Forum	GO CLUB
Desktop Publishing Forum	GO DTPFORUM
Graphics Forums	GO GRAPHICS
Microsoft Connection	GO MICROSOFT
Symantec Forum	GO SYMANTEC
Unix Forum	GO UNIXFORUM
Electronic Publications	
CompuServe Navigator	GO NAVIGATOR
Dr. Dobb's Journal	GO DDJ FORUM
Online Today	GO TODAY
Communication	GO COMMUNICATE
CB Simulator	GO CB
CompuServe Member List	GO DIRECTORY
CompuServe Mail	GO MAIL
FAX Electronic Mail	GO FAX
Practice Forum	GO PRACTICE
Classified Ads (read only)	GO CLASSIFIEDS
International Access Numbers	GO PHONES
News, Weather, Sports	GO NEWS
Associated Press Online	GO APO
Associated Press Sports Wire	GO SPORTS
Executive News Service	GO ENS
Business Wire	GO TBW
NewsGrid	GO NEWSGRID
CompuServe Online Magazine	GO ONLINE
Weather Reports, Maps, Forecasts	GO WEATHER
UPI World News	GO ENS
News and Sports forums	
Auto Racing Forum	GO RACING
Journalism Forum	GO JFORUM
Sailing Forum	GO SAILING
Scuba Forum	GO SCUBA
Sports Forum	GO SPORTS
Travel Services	GO TRAVEL
EAASY SABRE	GO EAASYSABRE
Official Airlines Guide	GO OAG
State Department Travel Briefings	GO STATE
Travelshopper	GO PARS
Florida Forum	GO FLORIDA
Travel Forum	GO TRAVEL
Aviation Services	GO AVIATION
Shopping Services	GO SHOPPING
Classifieds (read only)	GO CLASS

Table C-1 Continued

Consumer Reports	GO CONSUMER
New Car Showroom	GO NEWCAR
Electronic Mall	GO MALL
Money Matters	GO MONEY
Stock Market Highlights	GO MARKET
Investment Brokerage Reports	GO INVTEXT
Researching a Company	GO TICKER
Security Prices and News	GO QQOTE
Standard & Poor's Company Info	GO S&P
Value Line Financial Statements	GO VLINE
Business Management & Reference	GO BUSINESS
Business Demographics	GO BUSDEM
PaperChase (MEDLINE)	GO PAPERCHASE
TRW Business credit	GO TRWREPORT
U.S. Government Publications	GO GPO
Industry and Professional Forums	
Am. Asoc. of Medical Systems	GO MEDSIG
Broadcast Professionals Forum	GO BPFORUM
Computer Consultants Forum	GO CONSULT
Consumer Electronics Forum	GO CEFORUM
Legal Forum	GO LAWSIG
Military & Veterans Services	GO VETERAN
Safetynet Forum	GO SAFETY
Working From Home Forum	GO WORK
Hobbies, Lifestyles/Education	GO HOME
Aquaria/Fish Forum	GO FISHNET
Astronomy Forum	GO SPACE
Comic Book Forum	GO COMIC
Cooks Online	GO COOKS
Geneaology Forum	GO ROOTS
Health Database Plus	GOCHL-1
MIDI/Music forum	GO MIDI
National Issues and People Forum	GO ISSUES
Pets Forum	GO PETS
Science fiction Forum	GO SCIFI
Reference and Education	
Academic American Encyclopedia	GO AAE
Books in Print	GO BOOKS
Computer Database Plus	GO COMPDB
Marquis Who's Who	GO BIOGRAPHY
TV transcripts	GO TRANSCRIPT
Phone File	GO PHONEFILE
Educators Forum	GOEDFORUM
Science & Math Ed. Forum	GO SCIENCE
Students' Forum	GO STUFO
GAMES	GO GAMES
Gamers Forum	GO GAMERS

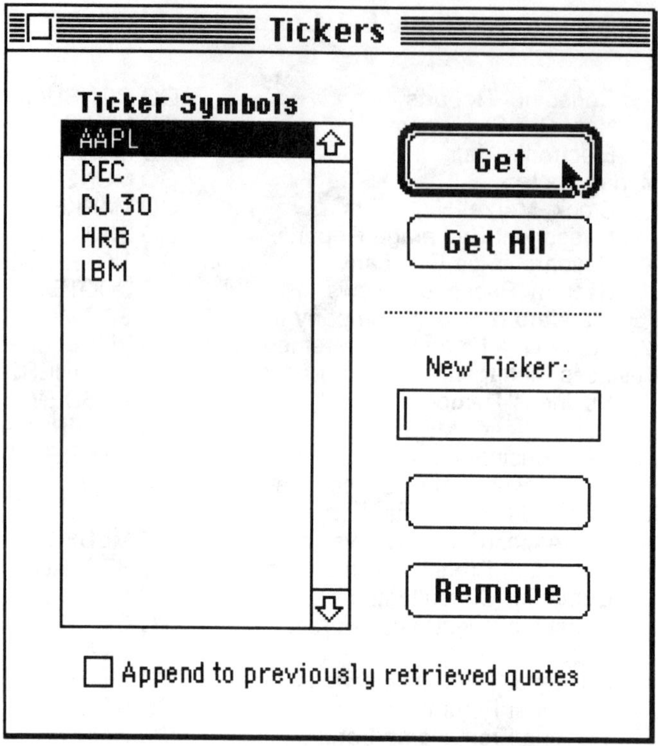

C-8 Use **Quotes** to find out how your portfolio's doing.

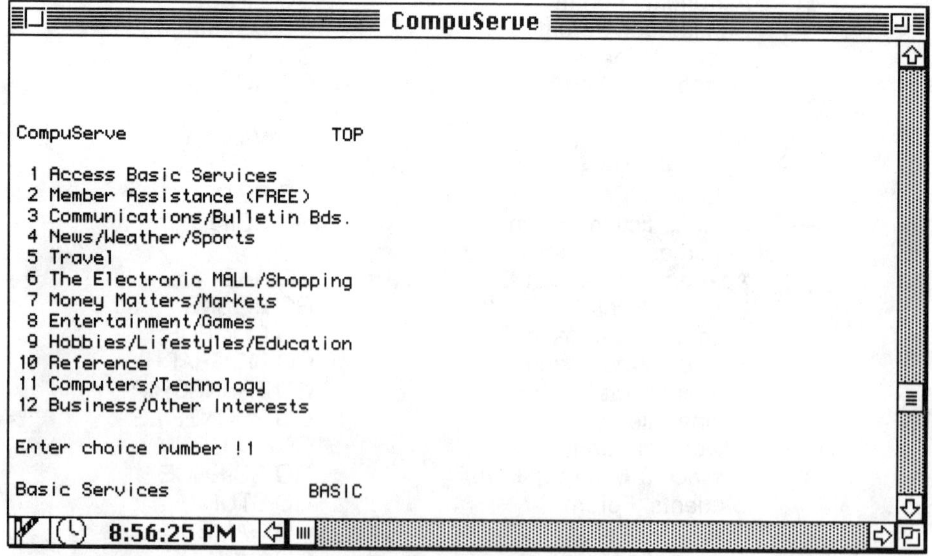

C-9 Using CompuServe with a regular telecom program is possible but more difficult for the novice. It's easy to get lost.

C-10 Selecting an icon places a box around it to show it's highlighted.

You'll find, as you explore some of these menus, that certain areas overlap. Aviation, for example, appears on the Professional menu, the LifeStyles menu, and the Travel menu. Aviation weather can be found on the Aviation menu and under Weather on the News menu, too. Mac Entertainment appears on the Computers menu and on the Games menu. These cross-referenced topics can be confusing at first, but they do actually make it easier for you to guess where online you might look for information you need. The topics are analogous to rooms in the CompuServe pyramid, with several doorways into each room. Let's take a peek into some of these rooms.

The best area to start with, for a newcomer to CIM, is the Member Support area. Its menu is shown in Fig. C-11. Here, you can learn a good deal about the service and join the Practice forum. This forum is absolutely free. You won't be billed for the time you spend here, so you can experiment as much as you like with downloading files from the Library and reading and writing messages on the Forum Bulletin Board.

In Member Support, you can also read the rules, check billing information, find another member by name or number, and browse through Online Today, CompuServe's electronic magazine. Use Member Support's Telephone Access list to find local CompuServe numbers to use when you're traveling on business or on

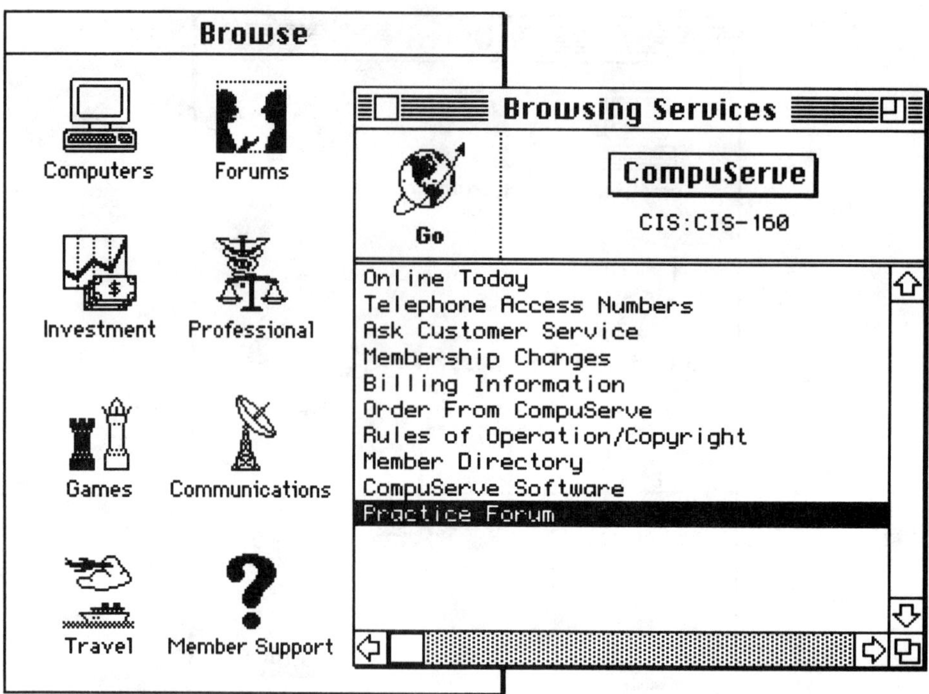

C-11 Member Support is a good place to "get the feel" of CompuServe because it's free.

vacation and need to stay in touch by modem. Member Support is one of several places online where you can get your questions about CompuServe answered. Use Feedback to ask specific questions, but be sure to check online questions and answers first to see if the answer is already there. Another source of support especially for Mac CIM users is a forum called Mac CIM Support. There are sysops to answer your questions about using CIM and to help you learn more about other areas of CompuServe as well.

Member Support is your source of help on all kinds of billing questions, and it's where you go to change your membership status if, for example, you decide to switch to the Executive Service option described later, if you want to change your password, or if you want to order CompuServe merchandise. The CompuServe store features T-shirts, mugs, posters, game maps, and a selection of user guides and reference manuals. You can also order a copy of CompuServe Navigator.

When you come to the Practice forum and any forum area, you'll start out by seeing the Forum Status window. An example is shown in Fig. C-12. If it's your first visit, you'll also be invited to join. There's no charge to join a forum. If you choose not to join, you'll still be able to browse as a visitor, but on the Who's Here list you'll be identified as visitor, rather than by name.

To read the posted messages, click the Browse Messages icon to get a list of message sections, like that shown in Fig. C-13. Select one of these and double click it or click the View Topics icon at the top of the list to see the topics within a section.

C-12 The grayed icons indicate that there are no messages waiting and no new notices.

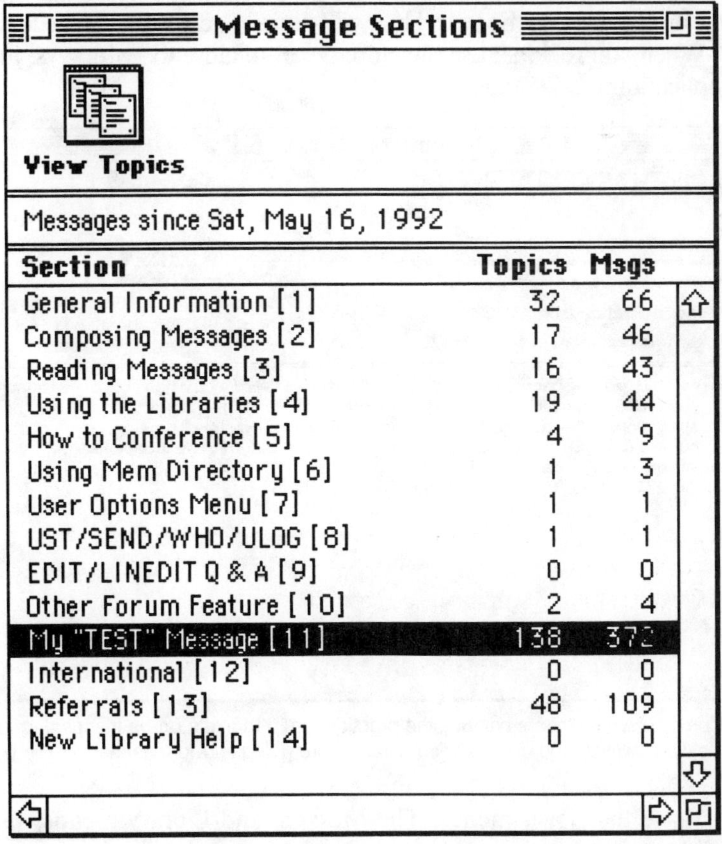

C-13 Each of these sections contains a list of topics. Each topic contains a list of individual messages.

Select a topic and double click to see the first message listed in that topic. Often, the original message is gone. CIS cleans house every few days and deletes old messages. But you can often track a thread by the replies. If you don't want to take the time (or spend the money) to read forum messages online, mark the threads that interest you and retrieve the messages as a batch before you leave the forum. They can be sent to you as text files very quickly and read at your convenience. You can even compose replies offline and log in just long enough to send them.

Figure C-14 shows a typical message in the Practice Forum. The icons at the top of the message box let you jump to another topic, read the next message in the thread, reply to the message you're reading, or file a copy of it on your disk. You can also follow messages on a map, once you've read the first in the list. Double click the Map icon, and you'll see, in convenient outline form and in chronological order, who replied to whom. There's also a small graphic representation of the map position of the message you're currently reading at the right of the box. The black message is the one you're reading. White ones above or below are in the same thread. Those off to the side are replies to a reply. Click on a white message to move to it. You can often read previous messages that have disappeared from the list by moving back up through the boxes. (They will remain accessible for at least a few more days.) When you're done, use the close boxes to close the windows, just as in any Mac application.

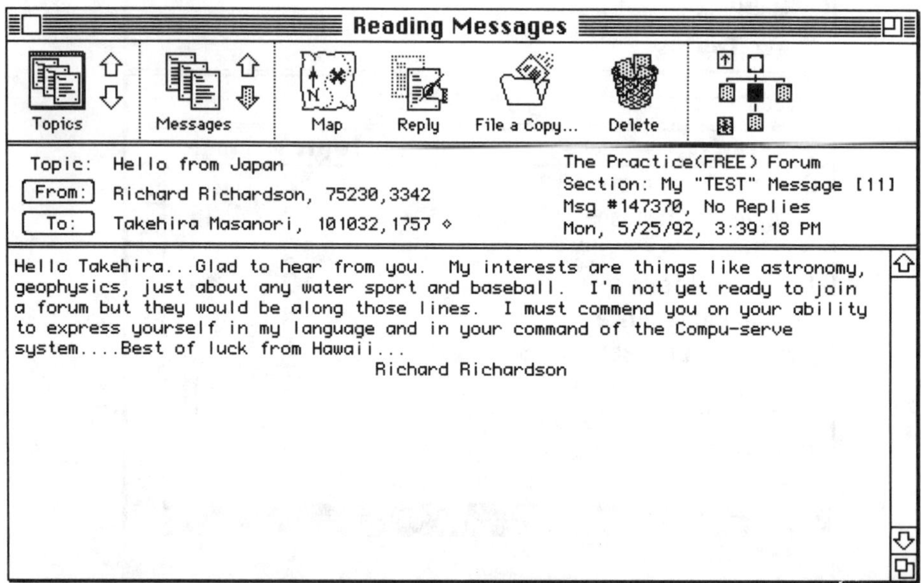

C-14 New CompuServe members can use the practice forum to make online friends and to practice their message writing and downloading skills before going into forums that charge per minute online.

Forums have their own menus. The Message and Library menus, shown in Fig. C-15, and the Conference and Forum Special menus in Fig. C-16, have many helpful commands. Suppose you wrote a message and wanted to track the replies, but you couldn't remember which topic you'd filed in under. Selecting Search from

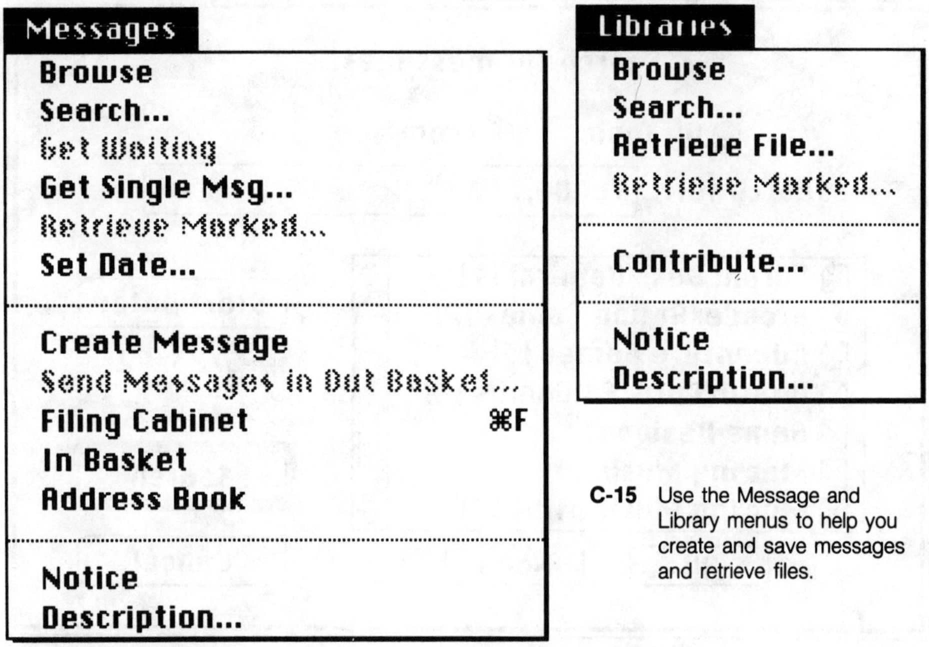

Messages

Browse
Search...
Get Waiting
Get Single Msg...
Retrieve Marked...
Set Date...

Create Message
Send Messages in Out Basket...
Filing Cabinet ⌘F
In Basket
Address Book

Notice
Description...

Libraries

Browse
Search...
Retrieve File...
Retrieve Marked...

Contribute...

Notice
Description...

C-15 Use the Message and Library menus to help you create and save messages and retrieve files.

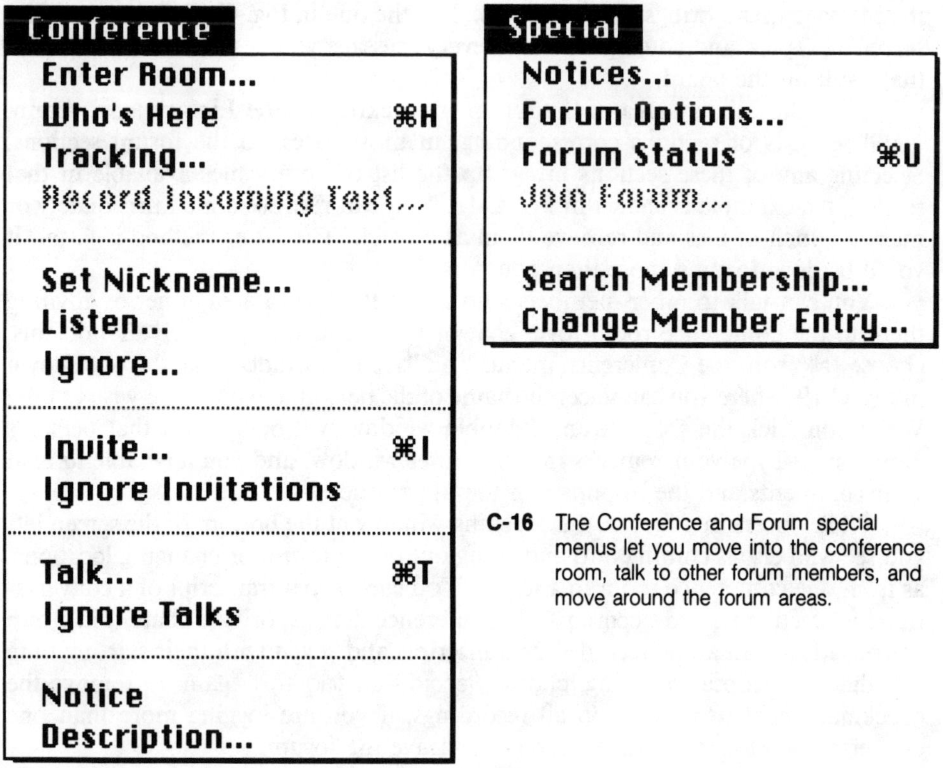

Conference

Enter Room...
Who's Here ⌘H
Tracking...
Record Incoming Text...

Set Nickname...
Listen...
Ignore...

Invite... ⌘I
Ignore Invitations

Talk... ⌘T
Ignore Talks

Notice
Description...

Special

Notices...
Forum Options...
Forum Status ⌘U
Join Forum...

Search Membership...
Change Member Entry...

C-16 The Conference and Forum special menus let you move into the conference room, talk to other forum members, and move around the forum areas.

Search for messages:

○ by Topic ◉ From ○ To

Search for: 76004,717

☒ Forum Bus./General [1]
☒ Arcade/Action Games [2]
☒ Adventure Games [3]
☒ Board/Card/Ed Games [4]
☒ Game Design [5]
☒ Mac'ing Music [6]
☒ Mac'ing Music MIDI [7]

All None

Start Date: 5/23/92

Search

Cancel

C-17 Search for messages by topic, or by the ID of either the sender or receiver.

the Message menu brings up a dialog box like the one in Fig. C-17. Enter your ID, search all topics, and you'll get a list of every message you've posted in that forum that's still on the board.

Enter the Library area of the forum by clicking on the Library icon. Again, you'll see lists of sections corresponding, in most cases, to the forum sections. Selecting any of these sections brings up the list of library files available in that section. An example is shown in Fig. C-18. You can retrieve a file immediately or mark a bunch of files and retrieve them as a batch. The latter method is faster, if you'll be downloading more than one item.

You can talk to other members who are in the forum area either by inviting them to the conference room for a chat or by just talking privately. To do this, choose Talk from the Conference menu. You'll open a window like the one shown in Fig. C-19, where you can select the name of the person to whom you wish to talk. When you click the Talk button, a double window will open, with that person's name on it. Type your remarks into the lower window, and you'll be able to read your comments and the responses in the upper one.

While you're in a forum, the Tracking window at the bottom of the screen lets you see who else is coming into and going out of the forum or changing locations, as from one conference room to another. You can keep a transcript of a conversation by selecting Record Incoming Text. Conference dialogs, private chats, and group conversations can all be recorded as transcripts and saved with their starting time and date. To stop a recording, choose Record Incoming Text again, to remove the checkmark next to it. To stop all recordings, if you are logging more than one conversation, close the active windows or leave the forum.

Library Files

Info | **Abstract** | Mark | View | Retrieve | Delete

Browsing "Arcade/Action Games [2] "

Filename	Title	Submitted	Size	Accesses
SDI11.CPT	SDI2040 1.1 - color req. Space Inva...	5/25/92	232.5K	61
AMINOI.BIN	Excellent Oids Galaxy	5/24/92	14.5K	29
TRON20.SEA	Tron, the game by P-Tech.	5/22/92	[illegible]	224
STAR.CPT	Star Stormer Demo	5/22/92	532K	40
STUNTC.BIN	StuntCopter 2.0	5/21/92	38.5K	112
SLM161.CPT	Slam Dunk! 1.61 - basketball simul...	5/19/92	198.5K	49
CAMEL.CPT	Camel - cross the desert strategy game	5/19/92	69K	112
RTCWS.CPT	RTCW's House	5/12/92	4736	36
DIAMON.SIT	Diamonds 1.6	5/12/92	407K	186
ASB112.CPT	Action-Strategy Baseball 1.12 - sim...	5/10/92	268.5K	56

C-18 To find out more about a file, double-click it or choose **Abstract** from the icons above the list.

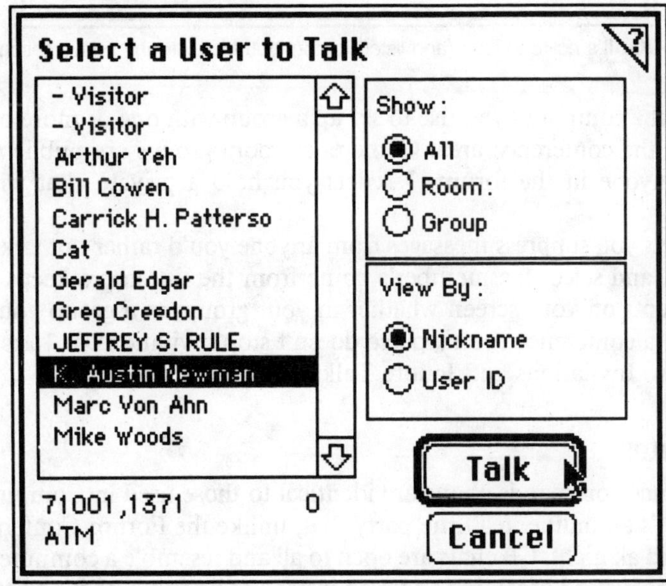

C-19 You can select **Who's Here** from the Forum Status menu to see if your friends are in the forum, then talk to them through this window.

The Listen command lets you monitor a group's conversation while you're doing something else or participating in a different conference. The group will not know you're listening, by the way. You can't reply or participate in the discussion unless you choose to enter the group, but it lets you decide whether you're interested before you join. Use the Listen window, shown in Fig. C-20, to select a group to listen to.

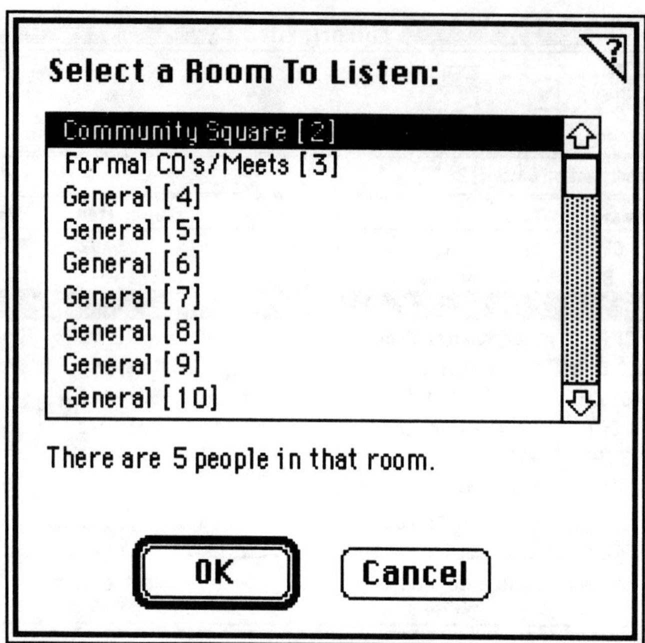

C-20 It's polite to look (and listen) before you leap into the conversation.

Invite is the command you use to set up a group with one or more other forum members in the conference area. Conference room groups are public and can be joined by anyone in the forum. Talk lets you hold a private chat with another member.

Ignore lets you suppress messages from anyone you'd rather not talk to. Simply select Ignore, and select the member's name from the list. Ignore keeps that member's comments off your screen whether in your group, in a group you are monitoring, or in a conference room. Ignore doesn't stop invitations or Talks. To do so, choose Ignore Invitations and Ignore Talks.

CB simulator

The conference commands above are identical to those used in CompuServe's CB Simulator. It's an online, realtime party that, unlike the Forum Conferences, goes on all day and all night. CB chats are open to all and resemble a computerized party line. You type instead of talking and read instead of listening, so it's a little easier to keep track of several conversations at once. There are two bands with 36 channels on each. The A band tends to attract those in the mood for a fast-paced conversation, while B-band chats are more relaxed. Some channels are reserved for certain kinds of topics. For example, Channel 1 is Adult, Channel 17 is for teens, and Channel 2 is for newcomers. There's a CB host or hostess there evenings from 6 P.M. to 2 A.M. to assist you and to answer your questions. You'll also find several channels devoted to "Alternative Lifestyles."

CB etiquette is mostly common sense. Don't choose a user name that would offend average people, and do avoid language that's profane, abusive, or offensive to anyone else. Disruptive behavior will get you kicked out. For details, consult the Guidelines for Behavior in the main CB window. Private chats are private, however. You can't be monitored unless you're on a public channel. If you offend someone, they'll usually end the chat. Similarly, if someone offends you, you can either squelch them or leave the conference.

There are several ways to access the CB Simulator. Select Go from the Services menu, and type CB in the box, choose CB Simulator from the Communications window or the Services menu. Once you arrive there, choose Access band A or B, and give yourself a nickname, or handle, if you haven't entered one in your CIM preferences. You'll see the channel selector shown in Fig. C-21. The Status icon gives you a graph showing which channels are in use. "Who," as you'd expect, tells you who else is in the CB area, or on a particular channel.

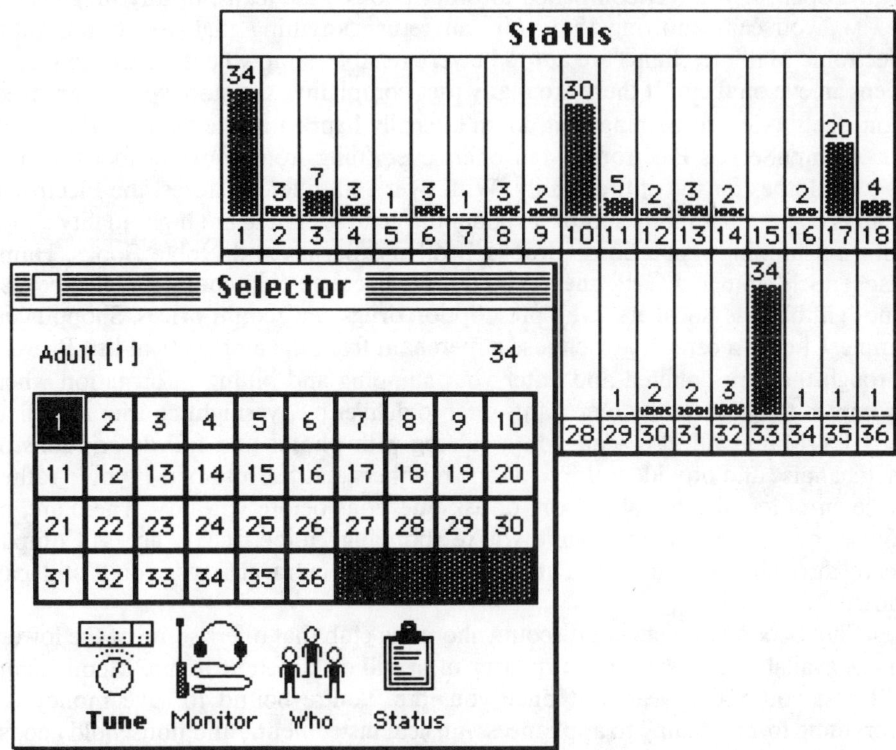

C-21 The Status Graph tells you which channels are busy. Use the Channel selector to monitor or join a channel.

By the way, you might notice that some handles have asterisks around them, like *Blondie*, *Texas Tim*, or *IncogNita*. The stars indicate that these people are members of the CB Club, and those handles are reserved for their use. If you try to enter a handle that's "decorated" like these, you'll be told it's unacceptable. CB

Club members pay a special price, which can be as low as 30¢ an hour. Of course, there's a hefty monthly sign-up fee, too. But those who are hooked on this particular service can easily spend several hours a day online, and the CB Club pricing plans help keep it affordable. That low rate doesn't apply to other areas of CompuServe, though. CB Club access is limited to the CB area, which includes both bands, plus the CB Forum and Cupcake's CB Society News, an online gossip column featuring well-known CBers.

Shopping for online bargains

Does it make sense to do your shopping online? Perhaps, if you think of it as something like ordering from catalogs. The merchandise will be charged to your credit card and delivered to your front door, making it convenient for many people who have a hard time getting out to stores. Unlike shopping malls, online stores are always open. If you feel compelled to order books, blue jeans, or anything else at 3 A.M., you can, knowing that you can return anything that you don't want. Electronic Mall merchants are apt to be very reliable, simply because CompuServe keeps an eye on them. If there are many user complaints, the store will be removed from the service, something that doesn't usually happen in the "real-world" mall.

CompuServe's Electronic Mall offers everything from gourmet foods to new cars to clothes for the entire family. With over 100 different stores, the Electronic Mall is bigger than many suburban shopping centers. These are high quality shops with outstanding reputations: Brooks Brothers, Barnes and Noble Books, Hammacher Schlemmer, J.C. Penney. You'll find chocolate chip cookies, coffee beans, fancy gift baskets, sneakers, even prescription drugs at discount prices. Shopping is simple. Choose a category or choose a merchant from the alphabetical list. Browse through the times offered and enter your shipping and billing information when prompted to do so. Many merchants offer to deliver by overnight courier as well as by UPS. Many will also send you a catalog with photos and full descriptions of merchandise and provide toll-free phone numbers and fax numbers if you'd rather place an order with a real person, or ask questions before you buy. There are, of course, no connect charges while you're shopping online. If you access CompuServe through a system like Tymnet, which adds extra charges, you'll still pay those.

Shoppers Advantage is a discount shopping club that offers some of the lowest prices available anywhere on a quarter of a million different items. Membership will cost you $30 a year, but once you join, you're bound to save money on everything from clothing to appliances, musical instruments, and household goods.

Because informed shoppers are good shoppers, CompuServe gives you online access to *Consumer Reports* Magazine. Before you buy, check to see which models are best, what brands to avoid, or what items offer a really good deal for the price. *Consumer Reports* is a widely respected publication of Consumer's Union, an independent testing organization that evaluates different categories of products every month and publishes the results.

If you are looking for real bargains, try the electronic version of a flea market or garage sale—CompuServe Classifieds. You can find almost anything you can imagine here. If you've got things you don't need, run an ad of your own and sell them. The only kinds of ads that aren't acceptable here are personals.

What's news?

CompuServe's News area keeps you up to date with the latest news, weather, and sports. Associated Press Online is a general interest newswire, with top stories updated every hour. AP Weather, National, Washington, World, Sports, and Political news are available separately. Entertainment, Business news, Wall Street reports, and the Dow Jones Averages are also yours at the click of a mouse. And that's just part of what's there.

Users of CompuServe's Executive Option have access to the Executive News Service (ENS). ENS is your own personal clipping service. If there's a topic that concerns you, you can create a folder and have copies of all the news stories that relate to your topic put in the folder. Scan the headlines, read all the stories, or select only the ones that you want to read. You can create up to three different folders at a time. Figure C-22 shows a folder I've set up with a list of keywords to locate news stories I want saved in the folder.

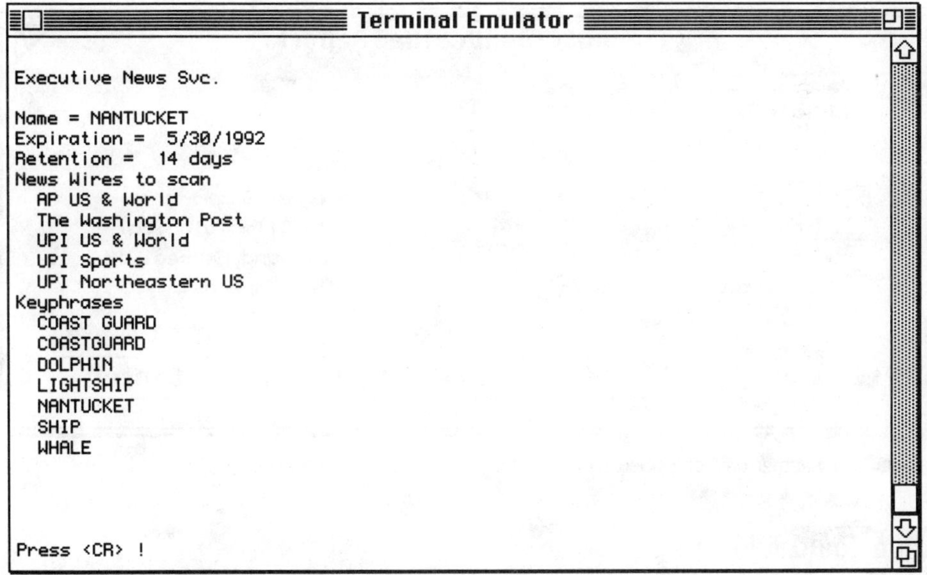

C-22 ENS scans all the papers listed and saves every story containing one or more of the keywords.

ENS creates folders on its own when there's a major news event, like a natural disaster, coup d'etat, or other world crisis. These folders are available to all ENS users. This service is also great if you have kids doing current-events projects or researching a topic for a school report. There's a surcharge for ENS and for some of the other news features, such as Soap Opera summaries and the AP Sports Wire.

International news can be found on NewsGrid. United Press International and leading press bureaus from France, Germany, Japan, China, and the Commonwealth of Independent States provide you with the latest global coverage. Search by keyword or read the U.S. or European headlines and business news.

Some news and reference services overlap. The News Library can be entered from either menu and contains full-text articles from 48 major newspapers from across the United States. Here, too, you can search a topic by keyword, plus the name of the newspaper you want to search.

There's no extra charge, however, for CompuServe's excellent weather services or for the weather maps you can view online, in full color on a color Mac. These maps are stored as GIF (Graphic Interchange Format) pictures. CIM has a special GIF decoder built in so you can look at the weather maps without the nuisance of having to download them and open them with a separate GIF viewer. Figure C-23 shows your weather options. Click the Location button and enter any place in the U.S. or any major foreign city. You can see local forecasts, extended forecasts, maps, satellite and radar views, and where available, marine weather reports, too. Figure C-24 shows some typical GIF weather maps for Europe and the eastern United States. Severe storm warnings, especially important to those who live in vulnerable areas, are posted whenever issued.

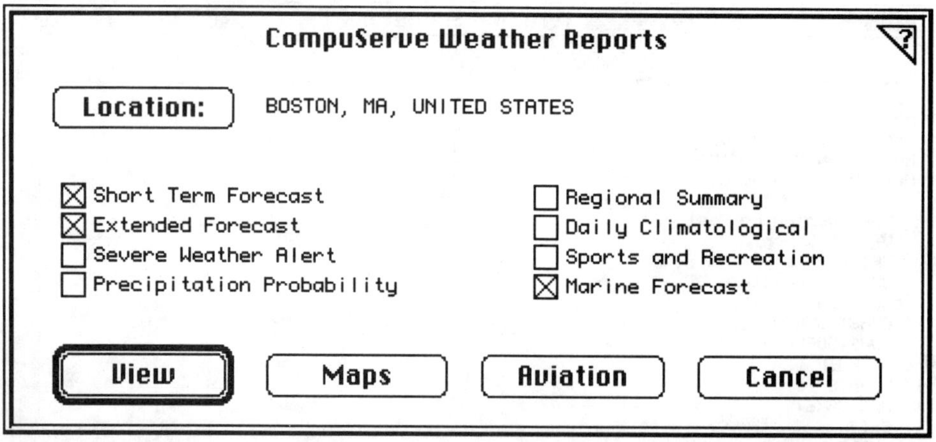

CompuServe Weather Reports
Location: BOSTON, MA, UNITED STATES
Short Term Forecast
Extended Forecast
Severe Weather Alert
Precipitation Probability
Regional Summary
Daily Climatological
Sports and Recreation
Marine Forecast
View
Maps
Aviation
Cancel

C-23 All weather on CompuServe comes from the National Weather Service.

You could look it up

The Reference Area features the Academic American Encyclopedia, published by Grolier Electronic Publishing. The encyclopedia contains over 10 million words, approximately 33,000 articles, and is updated on a quarterly basis. CompuServe doesn't add a surcharge for its encyclopedia, as some services do, making it an online bargain. Here, scanning is done alphabetically. You can enter the first few letters of a word to see a list of all the entries that begin with that combination. If you're looking for a common word, like *cat*, expect to find a great many choices. See Fig. C-25 for an example. You can narrow this down by using a # symbol after

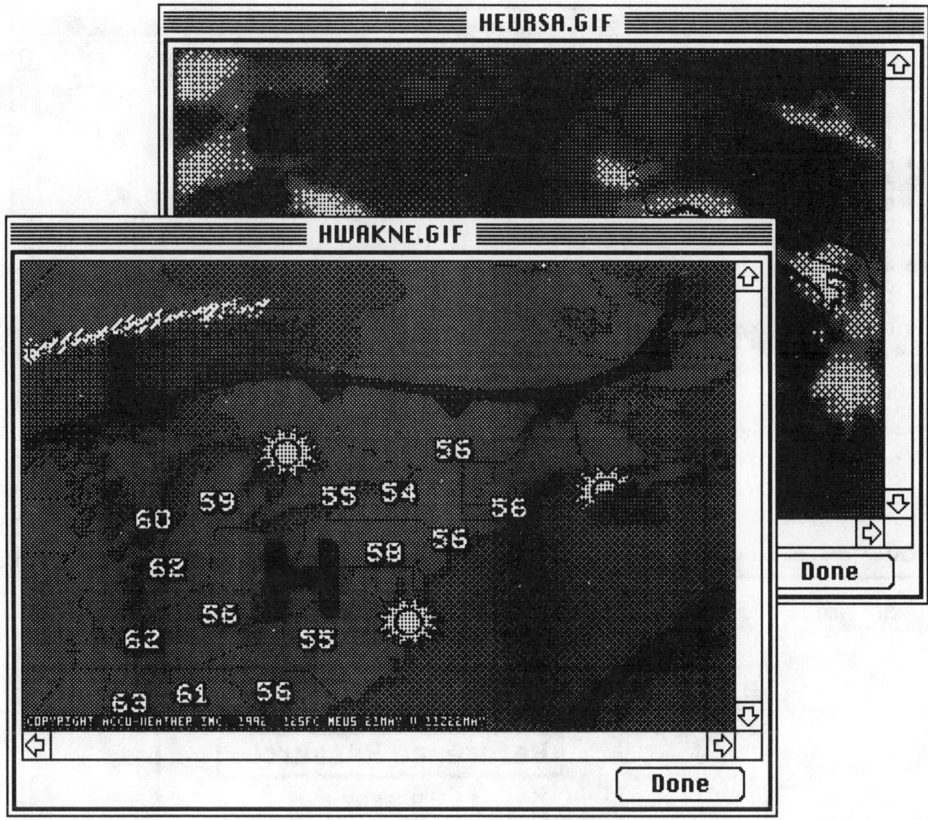

C-24 Satellite photos and weather forecast maps are available for most of the world.

the word. If we had entered cat# at the Search prompt, we'd have gone directly to the article about the cat.

Also in the reference area are databases of all kinds. Figure C-26 shows the Reference menu. You can check out that strange symptom in HealthNet, find out how good your son's chances of getting into Dear Old Ivy are in Peterson's College Database, look up magazine articles of all kinds, find all kinds of government information, including catalogs of Government Printing Office books and periodicals, and a lot more.

Time to play

CompuServe's Online games range from trivia and text adventure to realtime multi-player quiz show. Figure C-27 shows the Games menu. Some of these games require the purchase of additional game manuals or other items and some seem to be constructed primarily for IBM users. A few, like Hangman, are best ignored. Others are a lot of fun. Castle Quest takes you to a spooky castle, where you'll do battle with vampires and werewolves, and collect treasures. It's a text game, so you enter commands for actions and directions. Figure C-28 shows a game in progress.

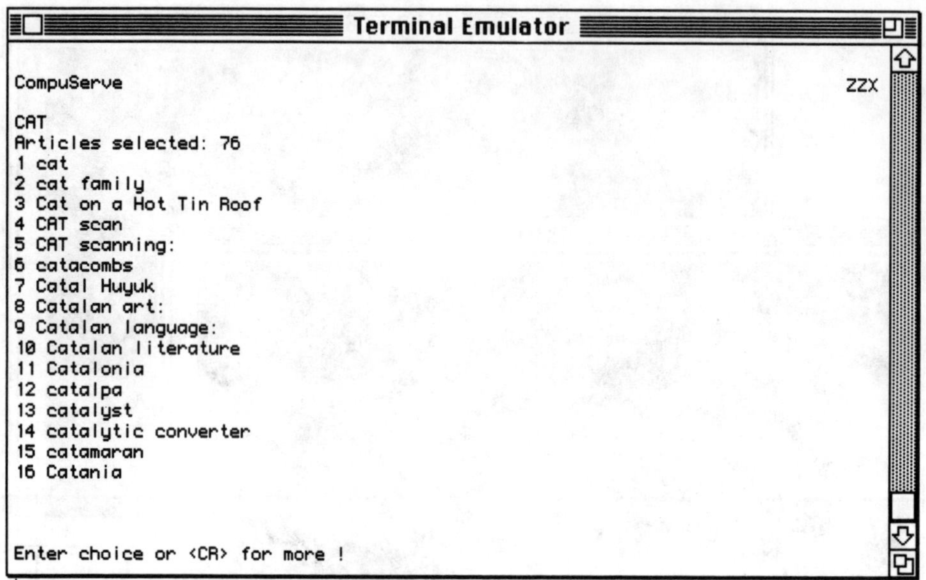

C-25 With 76 different choices, you could say CompuServe knows lots of ways to swing a cat.

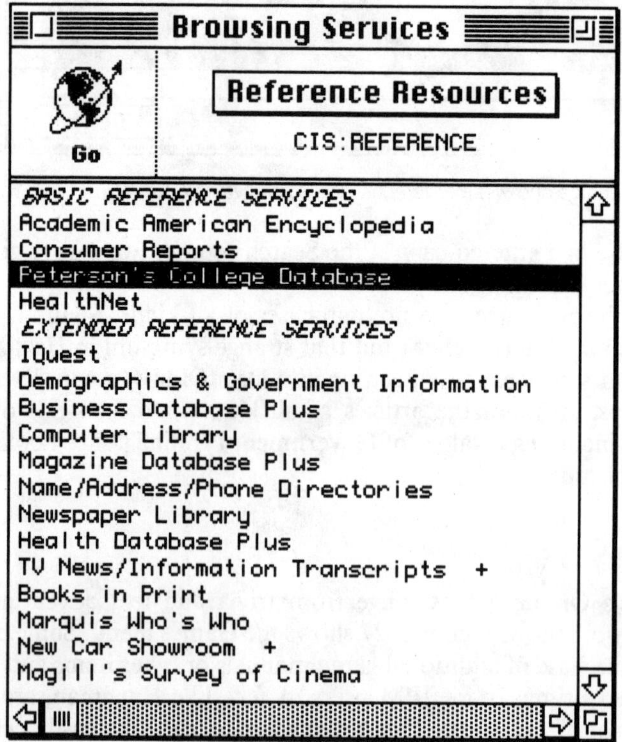

C-26 Using CompuServe's Reference section is faster than going to the library and contains almost as many resources.

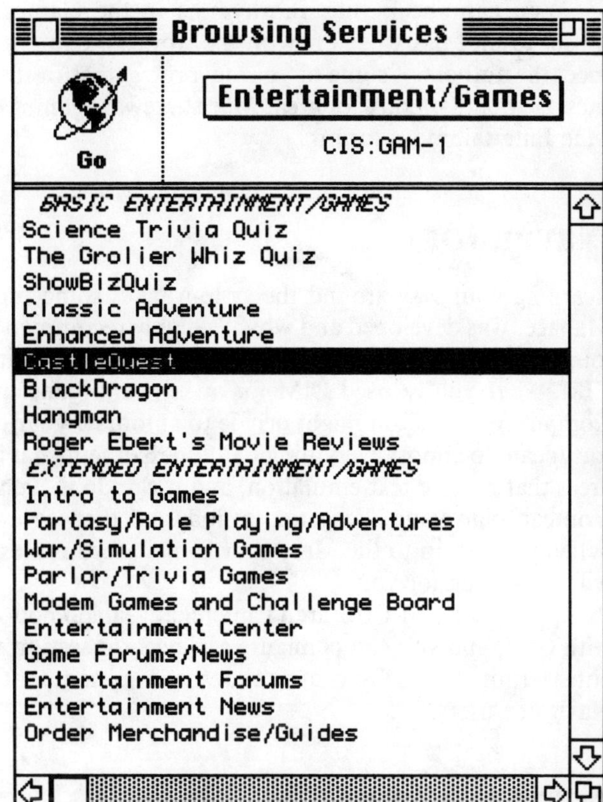

C-27 Not all of CompuServe's games are wonderful.

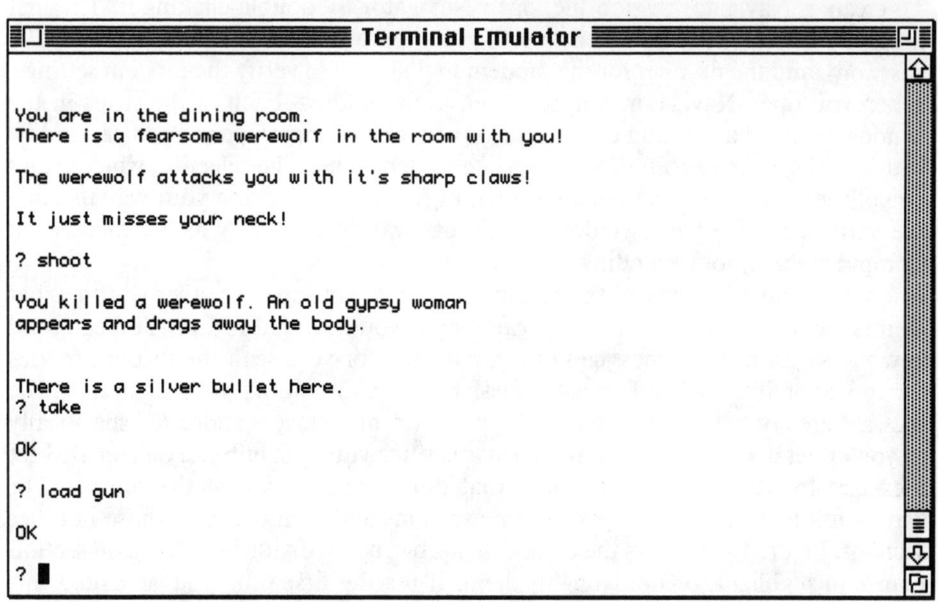

C-28 As with all text games, simple one- or two-word commands work best.

You can check your Biorhythms in the Games area and join the Games forum to find out what's new in the world of computer gaming. You might even meet the authors of some of your favorite games in the conference room or on the message boards. Look for great Mac shareware games to download and play in the Mac Entertainment forum.

Navigator

Learning your way around the system takes some time. That's why Information Manager was developed and why it's highly recommended. In fact, most Mac users join CompuServe by purchasing the Membership Kit, which includes a copy of CIM. After you've used CIM for awhile, and gone into sticker shock over your CompuServe bill, you might decide to automate your online sessions with Navigator. It can do almost everything CIM does, except chat in real time and access some areas that require text emulation, and it can do it even when you're not watching. You can plan your Navigator session, and then go away and do something else. When you return to the Mac, your E-mail, forum messages, and downloaded files will be waiting for you.

Navigator and CIM aren't interchangeable. You can do a bit of automation with CIM, and you can configure a Navigator session to stop midway and let you enter terminal mode to chat or to retrieve an item that's not otherwise available to Navigator users.

Setting up a Navigator session

To create a Navigator session file, open Navigator by double-clicking it. The first time you use it, you'll be asked to set session parameters: to enter your User ID, password, and the number for the modem to dial, and to verify the modem settings. When you open Navigator, you see a selection window. Each of the strips in the window is called a *tile*, and double clicking on any of them opens another window with choices, called *menu tiles*, that relate to that topic. The selection window and one of the menu tile windows are shown in Fig. C-29. Clicking your way through the various levels of tile windows is a great way to explore what's available on CompuServe without spending any money.

When you select any of the forum tiles listed, you open another window that defines what you will do when Navigator signs you into that forum. You can send new messages, pick up messages others have left for you, scan the forum libraries for topics of interest, and transfer files. Figure C-30 shows your choices in the message area of the forum. You can look for forum messages addressed specifically to you or get a summary of all the messages since your last entry. You can also get messages by section, ignoring those that don't interest you at the moment, or getting full text of the messages in some sections and summaries of those in other sections. Figure C-31 shows the Get Messages by Section dialog box. Click on section names to highlight, or unhighlight, them. If it's the first time you've visited this forum, Navigator might not know the names of the sections. It will get them and

CompuServe - Untitled

CompuServe Session Parameters
User ID, Phone number, Modem settings
CompuServe What's New
News about CompuServe
CompuServe Mail System
Electronic Mail
Macintosh Support
Other Computer Support
Financial Information
Industry and Professional
General Interest
News and Sports
CompuServe Support
Manual and Custom Tiles

Macintosh Support

Mac New Users and Help Forum
Guide to MAUG Forums
Mac Community Clubhouse Forum
Community News, Discussion GO MACCLUB
Mac Communications Forum
Navigator, Telecom, Fax, Lan GO MACCOMM
Macintosh System 7 Forum
Apple Macintosh System 7 GO MACSEVEN
Mac Applications Forum
Applications and Productivity GO MACAP
Mac Developers Forum
Languages, Programming GO MACDEV
Mac Systems Forum
Systems and Hardware GO MACSYS
Mac Hypertext Forum
Stack, SuperCard, Hypertalk GO MACHYPER
Mac Entertainment Forum
Games, Music, Sounds GO MACFUN
Desktop Publishing Forum
Professional DTP, Type GO DTPFORUM
Macintosh Support Forums
Software, Company Support
Zmac Information Service
MacUser, MacWEEK, Macbeat GO ZMAC

C-29 Clicking on any of these tiles will bring up another set.

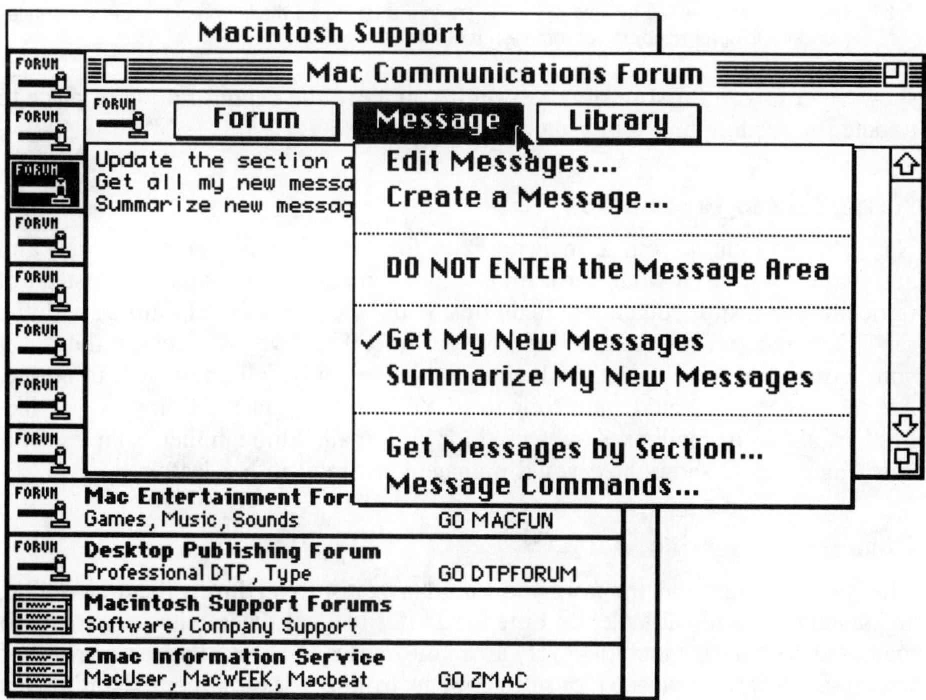

C-30 Customize the way Navigator retrieves your messages.

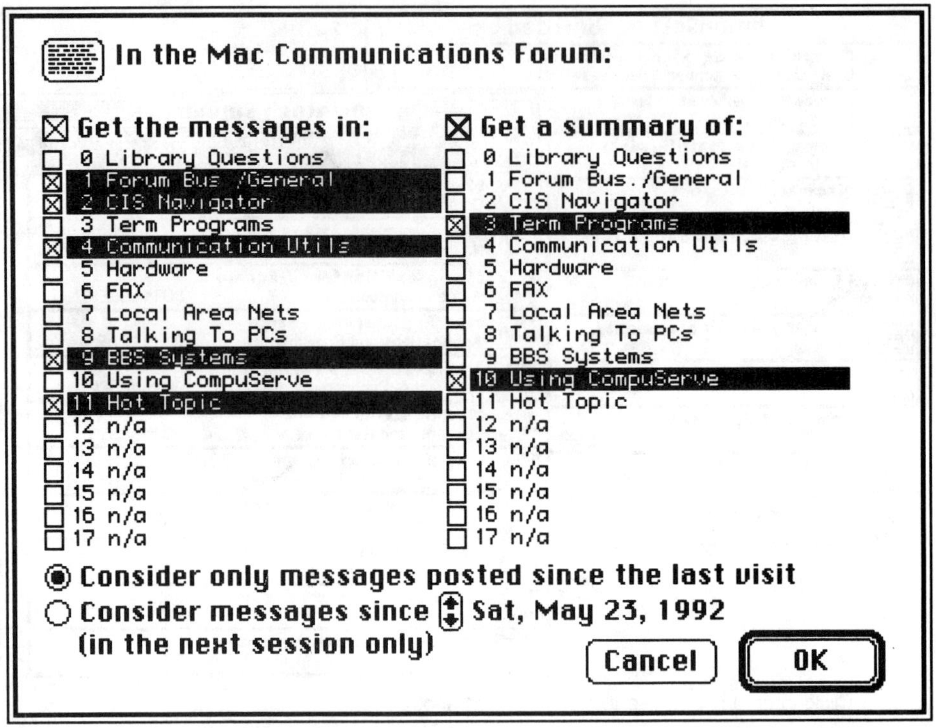

In the Mac Communications Forum:

☒ Get the messages in:
☐ 0 Library Questions
☒ 1 Forum Bus./General
☒ 2 CIS Navigator
☐ 3 Term Programs
☒ 4 Communication Utils
☐ 5 Hardware
☐ 6 FAX
☐ 7 Local Area Nets
☐ 8 Talking To PCs
☒ 9 BBS Systems
☐ 10 Using CompuServe
☒ 11 Hot Topic
☐ 12 n/a
☐ 13 n/a
☐ 14 n/a
☐ 15 n/a
☐ 16 n/a
☐ 17 n/a

☒ Get a summary of:
☐ 0 Library Questions
☐ 1 Forum Bus./General
☐ 2 CIS Navigator
☒ 3 Term Programs
☐ 4 Communication Utils
☐ 5 Hardware
☐ 6 FAX
☐ 7 Local Area Nets
☐ 8 Talking To PCs
☐ 9 BBS Systems
☒ 10 Using CompuServe
☐ 11 Hot Topic
☐ 12 n/a
☐ 13 n/a
☐ 14 n/a
☐ 15 n/a
☐ 16 n/a
☐ 17 n/a

◉ Consider only messages posted since the last visit
○ Consider messages since Sat, May 23, 1992
(in the next session only)

Cancel OK

C-31 Navigator will save the full text of messages in the topics on the left-hand list and summaries (sender, date, and subject) of those on the right.

show them to you for your next session if you leave the default setting in place to update the section and library names.

Navigating to the mailbox

Navigator will check your E-mail mailbox for incoming and outgoing mail and automatically transfer whatever it finds, unless you ask it to summarize instead of retrieving full text. If you choose to do this, you'll see a list of mail waiting, with the sender's name and subject, one message per line. Then, you can review the list at your leisure and tell Navigator which messages to get in full and which to ignore. Are there messages you'd want to ignore? Yes, there might be. CompuServe, like Prodigy, allows its mailboxes to be used for junk mail, although there's far less of it here. Figure C-32 shows how you'd manage your mail in Navigator.

Running the session

After you've assigned all the tasks you want Navigator to do during the time online, and saved the session as a file, it's time to run it. First, use the Preview command to make sure that the list includes every area you wanted to check. To see a preview of your session, type Command-P or select Preview from the session menu. You'll see a listing like the one on Fig. C-33, which you can scroll through. On the left are the

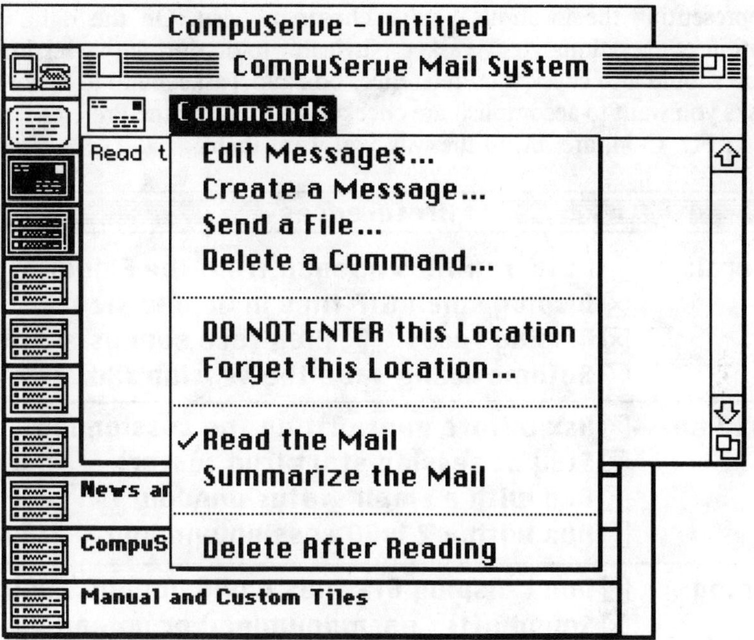

C-32 Mail messages can be retrieved or summarized.

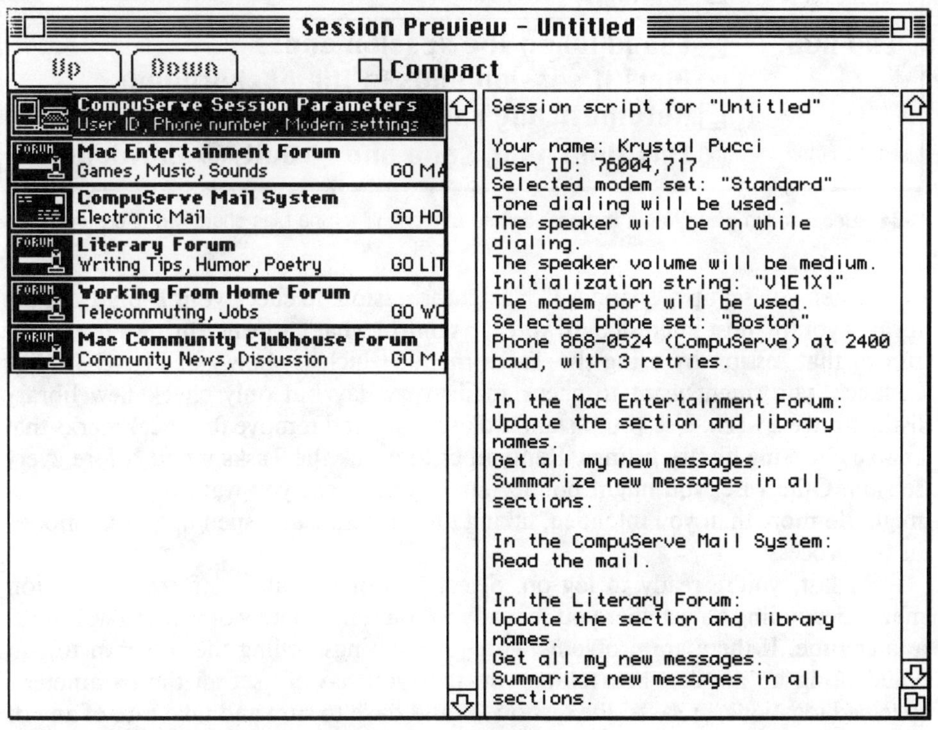

C-33 The text window lists everything I've told Navigator to do in this session.

tiles representing the locations you've chosen to visit. On the right, there's a description of everything you've asked Navigator to do during this session. At this time you should also check the Preferences box and Tasks menu to make sure that the Tasks you want to accomplish are checked off and that the Preferences settings, shown in Fig. C-34, are set up the way you want them.

Preferences	
General:	☐ Auto-run files opened from the Finder
	☒ Display small GIF files in double size
	☒ Display faces ☒ Play face sounds
	☒ Automatically save the session file
Start Run:	☒ Ask before overwriting the session log
	☒ Stay at session start (run faster)
	☒ Run with a small status window
	☐ Run with a 24x80 session window
Running:	☐ Don't display GIF files while downloading
	☒ Sound after each download or upload
	☒ Let message summaries accumulate
	☐ Don't update the high message counters
End Run:	☒ Sound when the session ends
	☒ Alert if session ends in the background
	☐ Automatically review after the session
	☒ This time only, Save and ○ Quit ◉ Shutdown

C-34 Because I'm going to run this session late at night, I'll let the Mac shutdown afterward.

When you set up a "standard" Navigator session, to check your E-mail and the forums you're most interested in, you can control what happens during a particular run of that session by using the Tasks menu, which is shown in Fig. C-35. For instance, you might want to check mail every day but only check new library listings once a week. Use your "standard" session, and remove the checkmarks that enable checking library listings. Remember to check the Tasks menu before every session. Otherwise, you might not accomplish the tasks you want to or Navigator might do more than you intended, taking longer online and spending more money in the process!

At last, you're ready to log on. Select Run or Run at . . . from the Session menu, depending on whether you're ready to run immediately or want to wait until a later time. If there are problems with your settings, telling the program to run could bring up an alert box telling you that you haven't set all the parameters, specified locations, or saved the session. You'll have to stop and take care of any of

Tasks

- Show Tasks Window ⌘K
- Do Everything ⌘E
- Just Send Responses
- Get and Send my Mail
- All but Library Listings
- ✓Send Responses
- ✓Get My Messages
- ✓Get Message Texts
- Get Message Lists
- Get Library Lists
- Download/Upload Files
- All Other Tasks

C-35 If you've told Navigator to retrieve your messages, make sure the appropriate task is checked. Otherwise, it won't be able to do as you've directed.

C-36 It's usually okay to overwrite the previous session, as long as you're through reading it.

these if they occur. Otherwise, depending on the preferences selected, you might see a warning like the one in Fig. C-36, telling you that you are about to overwrite a previous session log. The reason for this is that Navigator starts the log for its new session on top of the log of the previous one. If you haven't reviewed the previous session or if you want to save it, select Append to attach the new log to the end of the old one. Otherwise, click OK.

When the session is running, you'll see a window like the one in Fig. C-37. In it, you can see what part of the service Navigator is in and what it's doing. You can watch your session scroll past or remain at the top and let it run by itself. You can also go walk the dog, play a game, or do some other computer task and come back when you hear the signal to review the finished session. Since the session is automatically saved, you don't need to review it right away. You can come back to it whenever it's convenient.

Reviewing is done in the session view window. The main area of the window is the text area. The vertical scroll bar moves up and down the page, but the session itself is broken into a number of pages, or frames of text. Each frame might contain a single message, a thread of messages, a database file list, or other piece of the session. To move from one frame to the next, click the Prior and Next buttons under the message icon. You can also move ahead by pressing the Return key. When a message is displayed that you want to post a reply to, click the Reply button to open up a window in which you can compose your reply. The reply is automatically addressed to the sender of the message. Use Create to start a new message. Address it to anyone you like, or in a forum, you can address it to "All." You can also choose to start reviewing while the session is still running if you're especially curious about what's there. Let it go for a minute or two to get a head start, then use the "Find Session Start" command in the Search menu. From there, you can use the Next button or the Return key to move forward.

Don't be afraid to show your face

When you're reading E-mail or messages, you might notice a small talking face, like the ones shown in Fig. C-37. (You won't see faces unless you've turned on Show Faces in the Preferences dialog box.) Using faces adds a human dimension to your bulletin board and E-mail messages. Navigator lets you create and save an icon-sized picture of your own face, which you can also upload to CompuServe. These Face files are assembled into larger face files, which you can download. Navigator will show you the face of the person who wrote the message if his or her face is in your Faces file. Your own face will be shown, too, if the message is from (or to) you.

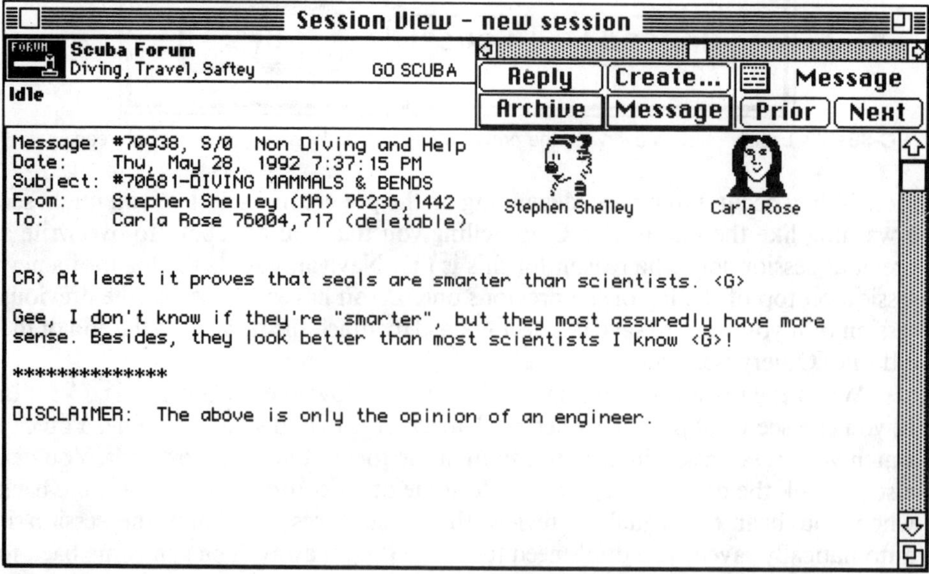

C-37 If you choose to watch the session scroll past, you can read your mail as it comes in. Otherwise, just scroll back to it, using the **Next** and **Prior** buttons.

To create a face, select Edit a Face from Navigator's Edit menu. You'll see a dialog box inviting you to select a face from the Faces folder to edit or to click New to start from scratch. When the Edit Faces window opens, you'll see two large "fatbits" areas, like those in a paint program (Fig. C-38). Click on them with your mouse to draw your face. Create two different versions of your face, one "listening" and one "talking." The three icons in the middle show the faces in actual size. The middle one shows the animated version produced by cycling the talking and listening faces. Navigator uses this effect to show that someone's "talking." Save your face with your name as its title. Put it in the Face Files folder inside the Navigator folder. Faces created in the Face Editor will be in black and white. You can ResEdit to change these to color icons, if you prefer.

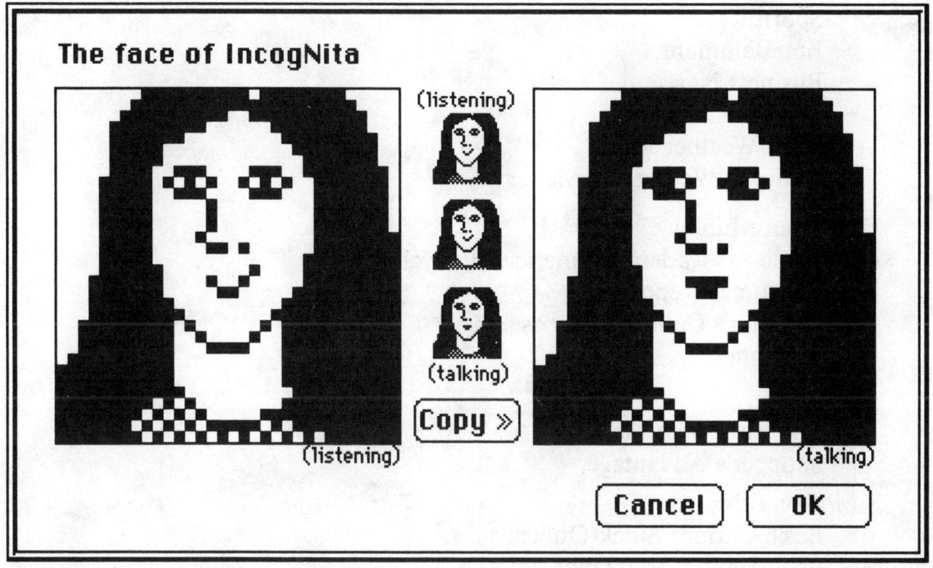

C-38 The face, modestly blushing, of the author.

Pricing structure

There are a great many things about CompuServe to love, and a few to dislike. One of its worst features is its pricing schedule. There's no convenient way to figure out how much money you're spending online because so many of CompuServe's features add on a surcharge. You can't just keep a total of how many minutes you're online and multiply by an appropriate cost per minute. Even though CIM does come with a timer, it really won't help unless you're limiting your activities to the most basic ones. You can think of the CompuServe pricing structure as something like that used by the cable TV systems. There's a basic service at a basic rate, which gets you the local channels, plus shopping services, weather and news, and an assortment of other stuff that may or may not interest you. Beyond that, you pay extra for movie and sports channels, and even more for Pay-per-view movies. On CompuServe, you'll pay one rate for basic service, an additional fee for forums and libraries, and a surcharge for "special" services.

It's tricky quoting prices in print because they are apt to change and, in fact, can change without notice. If you don't believe it, check the Rules of Operation. *Caveat Emptor*, as the Romans used to say: Let the buyer beware. That said, here are the prices as of May 31, 1992. (By the time you read this, however, service levels or costs might have changed. Check current prices in the Member services area, to be sure.)

The lowest priced level of service is called the Standard Pricing Plan. You pay $7.95 a month for CompuServe's Basic Services. Included are all of the following:

- Associated Press Online.
  - ~ Hourly News Summaries.
  - ~ Sports.
  - ~ Entertainment.
  - ~ Business News.
  - ~ Today in History.
  - ~ Accu-Weather Maps.
  - ~ National Weather Service.
- Reference Library.
  - ~ Grolier's Academic American Encyclopedia.
  - ~ Consumer Reports.
  - ~ Peterson's College Database.
  - ~ Healthnet.
- Shopping.
  - ~ The Electronic Mall.
  - ~ Shopper's Advantage.
- Money Talks.
  - ~ Basic Current Stock Quotes.
  - ~ Issue/Symbol Reference.
  - ~ Mortgage Calculator.
- Games & Entertainment.
  - ~ Science Trivia Quiz.
  - ~ The Grolier Whiz Quiz.
  - ~ ShowBizQuiz.
  - ~ CastleQuest.
  - ~ Black Dragon.
  - ~ Classic Adventure.
  - ~ Enhanced Adventure.
  - ~ Hangman.
  - ~ Ebert's Movie Reviews.
- Communications Exchange.
  - ~ CompuServe Mail.
  - ~ Classified Ads (read only).

- Member Support.
  - ~ MAC CIM Support Forum.
  - ~ Practice Forum.
  - ~ Directory of Members.
  - ~ Ask Customer Service.
- Travel and Leisure.
  - ~ Eaasy Sabre.
  - ~ Travelshopper.
  - ~ Department of State Advisories.
  - ~ Visa Advisories.

When you're using CompuServe's U.S. and Canadian networks, there are no communication (network) charges. Supplemental network charges still apply outside of the U.S. and Canada.

Services outside of the basic services area are indicated by a "+" or "$" next to the menu choice. Services marked with a "+" are charged according to the modem speed at which you've connected. These rates are listed under the Alternative Pricing Plan in the next section. "Plus" services include all of the forums. Services marked with a "$" are charged at an additional rate per hour or fraction thereof. Figure C-39 shows a typical menu with the pricing information appended.

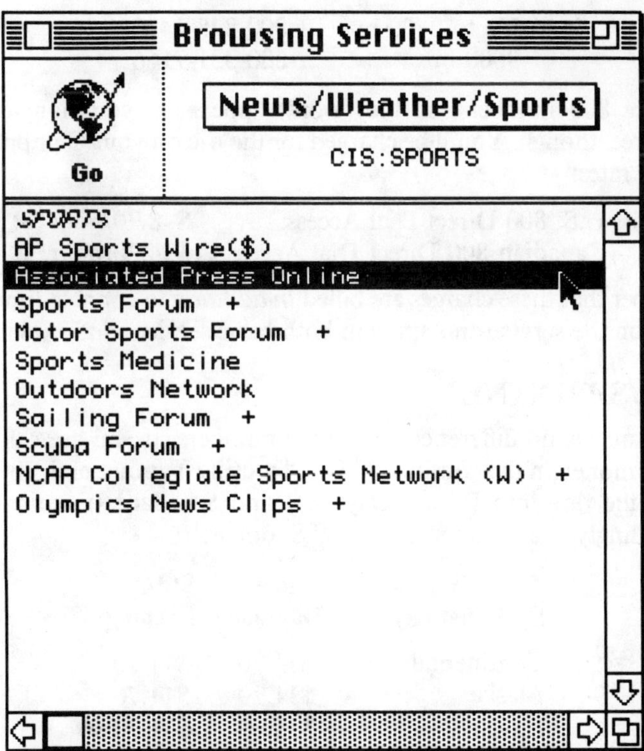

C-39 There's a surcharge for the Sports Wire. Most of the other services listed charge by the minute, except AP Online, which is a Basic service.

Alternative pricing plan

The Alternative Pricing Plan gives you many fewer options for free. In return for your $2 monthly membership support fee, you get unlimited use of the online Membership Support services, the Practice forum, Online Today, and anything else designated "Free," which includes the Shopping Mall. Everything else is considered to be an extended service and is charged at an hourly connect rate based on baud rate, plus any applicable network charges and premium surcharges. There's a one-minute minimum charge per session. The same hourly connect-time charges apply for all usage of extended services for members on the Standard Pricing Plan. The prices shown are in U.S. dollars.

300 baud.	$ 6.30/hr	$.105 per minute
1200, 2400 baud.	$12.80/hr	$.213 per minute
9600 baud.	$22.80/hr	$.38 per minute

Connect-time charges do not include network charges (DataPac, Tymnet, etc.) or premium surcharges, which are billed in addition to hourly connect time charges. Normally, anyone using CompuServe in the United States or Canada comes in on the CompuServe network, which is free, and is a local call in most areas. If you're not within a reasonable calling distance of a CompuServe local access number, there are 800-Direct-Dial-Access numbers for the U.S. and Canada:

Up to 2400 bps	1-800-848-4480
9600 bps	1-800-331-7166

These are 800 numbers, so they won't appear on your long-distance bill. They're not free, though. You'll be charged for the use on your CompuServe bill, at the following rates:

U.S. 800 Direct Dial Access:	$ 8.70/hour
Canadian 800 Direct Dial Access:	$34.70/hour

Remember that these charges are billed *in addition* to connect time charges for each session on the service and apply in both basic services and extended services.

TYMNET/SPRINTNET

Time of day makes no difference with these numbers. If you are calling at night, you can save money in the continental U.S. by using Tymnet or Sprintnet instead. Both divide the day into Prime (Daytime) and Standard (Evening) hours and charge accordingly. Rates are shown in U.S. dollars:

TYMNET (R) Sprintnet (R)	**Prime/ Daytime**	**Std/ Evening**
Continental U.S.	$11.70	$11.70
Alaska	$11.70	$11.70
Hawaii	$11.70	$11.70
Canada	$11.70	$11.70
Puerto Rico	$49.70	$49.70

Mexico	$49.70	$49.70
Israel	$49.70	$49.70
Prague	$45.70	$45.70
Moscow	$45.70	$45.70

Premium quality—premium price

Premium surcharges can mount up quickly if you develop a fondness for sports, soap opera news, or database services. Remember that all of these are charged in addition to the cost of connect time. If you want to see what kind of charges you're adding up, you can review your billing in the Member Support area. Figure C-40 shows one page from the Author's account.

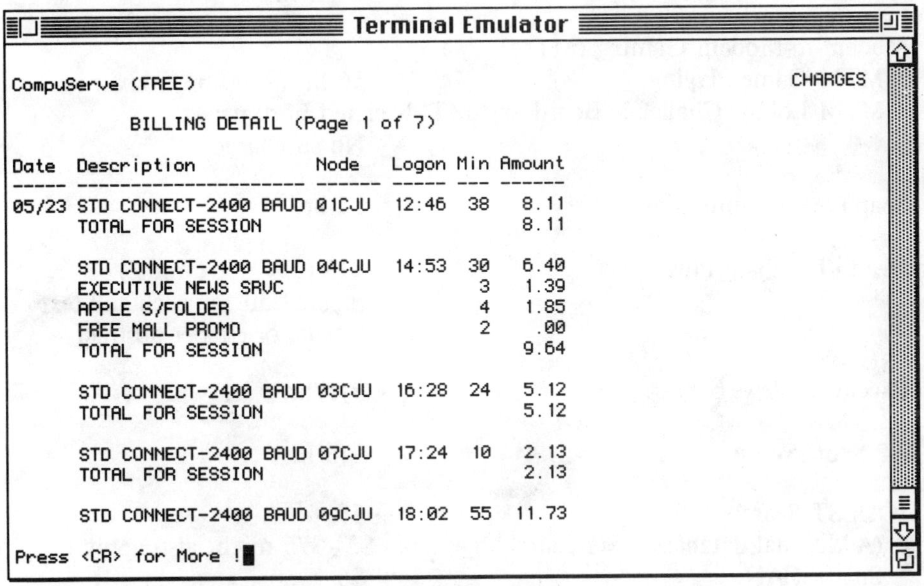

```
Terminal Emulator

CompuServe (FREE)                                              CHARGES

        BILLING DETAIL (Page 1 of 7)

Date  Description            Node   Logon Min Amount
----- ---------------------- ------ ----- --- ------
05/23 STD CONNECT-2400 BAUD 01CJU  12:46  38   8.11
      TOTAL FOR SESSION                        8.11

      STD CONNECT-2400 BAUD 04CJU  14:53  30   6.40
      EXECUTIVE NEWS SRVC                  3   1.39
      APPLE S/FOLDER                       4   1.85
      FREE MALL PROMO                      2    .00
      TOTAL FOR SESSION                        9.64

      STD CONNECT-2400 BAUD 03CJU  16:28  24   5.12
      TOTAL FOR SESSION                        5.12

      STD CONNECT-2400 BAUD 07CJU  17:24  10   2.13
      TOTAL FOR SESSION                        2.13

      STD CONNECT-2400 BAUD 09CJU  18:02  55  11.73

Press <CR> for More !
```

C-40 Notice the additional charges for ENS and the Apple News Clips Service.

Even though they are expensive, Premium services might be worth the price if they happen to offer something you need, like a particular database or news service. Not all of the services are worth the cost, in my (admittedly biased) opinion. Some can be found elsewhere for free, or for cheap, if you are willing to do some research. Here are a few of the premium services, with their surcharges:

The Neighborhood (Zip) Report	$10 per zip code
Demographic Reports—1980 Housing, 1980 Hispanic, 1980 Education, 1980 Energy, 1980 Income, Housing, Component Area	$20/report
Demographic Reports—Demographic Forecast, Income, Age by Sex, Age by Income, Housing Value by Age, Combined Income + Demographic,	

Net Worth + Disposable Income, Age 55 Plus, Year 2000, Demographic	$50/report
ACORN Target Marketing Reports—Profiles + Forecasts, Population Profile, Household Profile, Population Forecast, Household Forecast	$75/report

Dissertation Abstracts	
Search—no hits	$1
Search (retrieves up to 10 titles)	$5
Additional titles (in groups of 10)	$5
Full reference with abstract where available (selected from the titles)	$5 each
Modem-to-Modem Gaming (MTM)	
MTM Game-Playing:	$6 hr. (2400 bps maximum)
MTM Lobby, Challenge Board and MTM-related Forums:	No surcharge
Soap Opera Summaries:	$6 hr.
Health Database Plus	$15 (25¢ per minute) plus $1.50 for each full-text article, or $1 per abstract
Executive News Service	$15/hr.
AP Sports Wire	$15 hr.
IQUEST Search	$9
(Additional database search surcharges from $2–$75 might also apply.)	
SmartSCAN	$5
Abstract	$2
No hit charge	$1
Hard-copy delivery (regular service and delivery)	$18/article reprint
Hard-copy delivery (express service and delivery)	$42/article reprint
Official Airline Guide (OAG)	
During Daytime/Prime hours:	$28 hr.
During Evening/Standard hours:	$10 hr.

CB club

CB fans know it's easy to get hooked on chatting and run up huge bills. CompuServe has announced special CB Club rates for members who only wish to use the

CB areas, which include the CB forum and Cupcake's Society CB column. There's a monthly signup fee, plus a per-hour charge. And, if you aren't able to use the CompuServe network for access, you'll have to pay for Tymnet or a similar system, as mentioned above.

Two fee levels are available. Your best choice depends on how many hours you'll spend online. For a monthly signup fee of $25, you'll pay an additional $4.30 per hour online. If you choose to pay an $85 signup fee, your hourly charge will be only 30¢. The break point comes at 15 hours a month. If you spend less than 15 hours online, the $25 plus $4.30 per hour price is lower. If you spend more than a half hour a day in CB, you'll save by using the $85 plus 30 cents per-hour plan. (At exactly 15 hours, it's exactly $89.50 either way.)

Getting the most for your money

Even those who are CompuServe's biggest fans often refer to the service as CI$. It's expensive, and many of its features are available elsewhere at much lower prices. What CompuServe *does* have going for it, though, are some factors worth considering. First, the CIM software and B+ file-transfer protocol, are about the most stable telecom program you'll ever use. After all the unexpected disconnects and failed transfers I've encountered on some other services, downloading a file from CompuServe is a real pleasure. Second, there's a tremendous variety of services on CIS, more than anywhere else. If you're likely to find yourself needing information on many different topics, and in much greater depth than the encyclopedia offers, CompuServe is your best choice. No matter what you want to find out, if you can afford to spend the time and money to locate it, it's there. Businesses and professionals in many fields consider their CompuServe membership as much a necessity as their telephones and daily newspapers. And the Internal Revenue Service has no problem accepting CompuServe as a business expense, which takes some of the pain out of paying for it.

The best way to use CompuServe is to treat it as a reference service, rather than as a social occasion. Sure, you can find lots of friends online, and the forums are good for trading quips as well as more significant information, but there are other services with equally friendly users and a lot lower cost per minute. Sign up for Basic service so you can use the news and weather services and the encyclopedia as much as you want. Despite the special pricing, the CB Club is *not* a good value, unless your dearest friends are on CompuServe and on no other service. There are other services that let you chat for less.

If you intend to use the forums, invest in a copy of Navigator. It will pay for itself in shortened sessions. Try to limit your activities to one or two forums at a time. Look for the forums that have information you can't get elsewhere. Mac user groups can provide the same information and software that you'd find in CompuServe's Mac forums, and for a lot less money.

Always try to plan your session in advance, even if you're not using Navigator. If you're going to look for something specific, go directly there by using the appropriate Go command if you know it, or by using Find. When you've gotten what you've come for, get off. Use Command- D to disconnect quickly. Do as much as you can offline. Don't try to answer mail or compose forum messages while you're signed on. Mark messages, retrieve them, and disconnect. Then read the messages, compose replies, and sign on again just long enough to post them. If you plan ahead, and use your time wisely, you can keep costs to a comfortable level. When you use it carefully, CompuServe is affordable.

Delphi

Even to those of us who have been involved in telecom for a long time, it's amazing to realize that Delphi is about to celebrate its 10th anniversary. The second oldest of the consumer-oriented services, it first came online in February 1983, in response to the success shown by CompuServe in attracting the non-business computer user. Delphi's founder and head of parent company General Videotex Corporation, Wes Kussmaul, described Delphi's goal as "user-friendliness." From the beginning, Delphi has been designed in a logical manner, making it easy for the non-computer-minded to find their way around the system with as few difficulties as possible. Today, Delphi is a growing, busy, full-service board, with all the features one would expect, plus a few that are uniquely Delphic.

One thing that hasn't changed, despite 10 years of growth, is Delphi's friendliness, both in terms of its system layout and in the people you'll meet online there. Delphi users are something special. It attracts a crowd that's remarkably unconcerned about the Mac-versus-PC issues that seem to surface on other boards. These people just want to be online with their friends. It doesn't matter what kind of a computer you use. In fact, one of my favorite Delphi citizens doesn't use a computer at all, but instead a "dumb terminal" video text display screen and keyboard.

Delphi's greatest strength, according to many of its members, is its real-time activities; both conferences and interactive group games. Delphi has the simplest conference system of any of the services. It also has two encyclopedias, UPI news and weather, plus other specialized news services, forums of all kinds, and a broad range of travel options, including Eaasy Sabre and OAG gateways, plus the PARS Travel Shopper for low fares on tours and cruises.

Finding your way around

Delphi is a text-based system, so you'll use your favorite telecom program to sign on. When you first log on to Delphi, you'll see the connect signal. As soon as you see CONNECT 2400 or CONNECT 1200, hit Return two or three times. Then, you'll be prompted for your user name and password. You won't see your password being typed, but as soon as it's accepted you'll see the Welcome-to-Delphi message. There might be an announcement of an upcoming conference, contest, or other special event, and you might see a reminder that you have mail. Then, you'll see the Main menu and be asked what you want to do. Figure D-1 shows Delphi's Main menu.

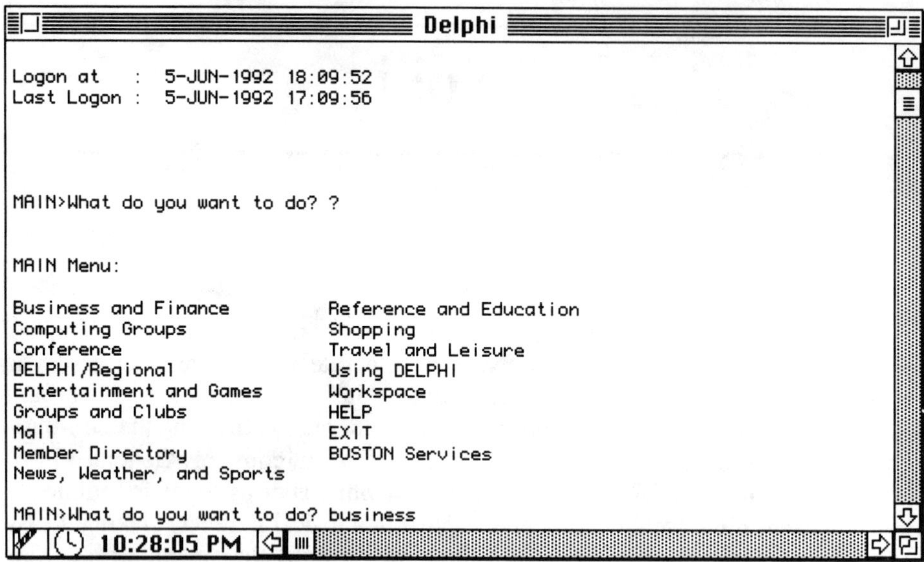

D-1 Typing a question mark will list the menu again.

Delphi is organized in an extremely logical manner. Each item on the Main menu represents a category of services. Business services are found in the Business category. News and Weather are in that category. Games are in the Entertainment area. Travel and Leisure have their own areas. The Library is your source for encyclopedias, online research services, and other databases. Groups is home to Delphi's forums, either called groups or SIGs (for Special Interest Groups). The computing groups have their own category, because there are a great many of them. In addition to the Mac group, you'll find Atari, PC, Portables, Commodore, and a great many others represented. Figure D-2 shows the list of computer SIGs on Delphi.

Commands

To select any choice of a menu, type the first few letters of its name, and hit Return. To go to the Conference area, from the Main menu, just type conf. To go to the writer's group, type gr wr. To get into the Macintosh forum, you could type comp mac for. Anything you type on Delphi must be followed by a Return, to tell the system to respond to it.

Typing a question mark at any prompt will bring up a menu of choices that are available to you within that particular area. If you've just chosen News, for example, and aren't sure what to do next, the ? will bring up the News menu. Most

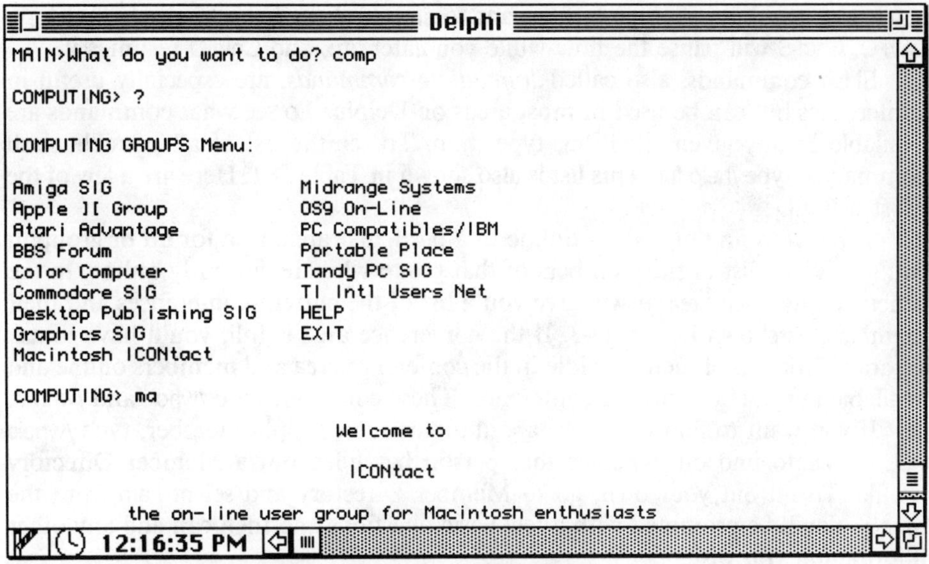

D-2 You only need to enter the first few letters of the word.

menus also include a selection called Help. Typing help will give you complete, context-sensitive help wherever you are. Special help files are available in SIG databases, with directions for transferring files, and at the SIG Main menu to tell you more about that forum. Delphi members and group managers are also glad to help you.

Key commands

Delphi uses two different kinds of commands: Control-key combinations and Slash (/) commands. Control-key combinations are mainly used when entering messages and in conferences. Control-key combinations are entered by holding down the Control key and pressing another key (using Control as if it were a Shift key). Some telecom programs let you designate the Option key or the Command key as a Control key. If you try a Control-key combination and nothing happens, try again with the Option key. Your telecom program might be set to use the Option key as a Control key. Many people prefer to use the Option key as a Control key because it's adjacent to the commonly-used "z." The combination Ctrl-Z will take you back out to the next layer of menus. If, for instance, you've been reading messages on a forum, typing Ctrl-Z will take you back to the top of the forum, so you could choose to see the data libraries or go to the forum conference area. Typing the combination again takes you out of that forum and back to the Groups menu or the Computers menu, if you've been in a computer forum. Typing it once more would take you back to the Main menu. However, it will not sign you off. To leave Delphi, use EXIT or BYE.

Ctrl-C is used to cancel an action, chiefly in sending (or actually, *not* sending) E-mail or posting messages. Control-key interrupts (Cntrl-O, S, or Q) are used to stop, pause, and resume, (respectively), output of a text file. If you've started reading a news item or library list, and you want to stop and get back to the menu, type Cntrl-O. Cntrl-S will pause the flow while you catch up, and Cntrl-Q resumes it.

Slash commands, also called *immediate commands*, are especially useful in conferences but can be used in most areas on Delphi. To see what commands are available in any given situation, type /help. To see the list of all possible slash commands, type /help full. This list is also shown in Table D-1. Here are a few of the most helpful.

Type /w to find out who's online in a particular area. In a forum or group, it will give you a list of the members of that group who are currently online. In the general conference area, it will give you a list of the current conferences and their members, as shown in Fig. D-3. If the conference area is full, you'll have to ask separately for lists of members idle in the conference area and members online and available but not currently in conference. These commands are /who i and /who a.

If you want to find out more about a particular Delphi member, type /whois USERNAME to find out whether that person has filled out a Member Directory profile. To fill out your own, go to Member Directory and select I-am from the menu. You'll be prompted with a few basic questions and then can add any other information you wish.

To get the correct time (eastern standard, or eastern daylight in summer) and to find out how long you've been online, type /T.

To get offline in a hurry, if you're in a conference or in the middle of entering a message on a forum, type /bye. If you're entering a message at the time, it will be canceled. To send the message and then log off, type /exit.

What's there to do?

Delphi has something for almost everyone in the family, with the possible exception of younger children. Older kids and teens are often found in conference after school and evenings. Many also participate in the video games, music, and science fiction forums. Between the "regular" Delphi forums and the custom forums that Delphi members have set up, there are groups for everything from aviation, art, and astronomy to role-playing games, adoption and divorce support, and even the Society for Creative Anachronism. The Groups menu is shown in Fig. D-4, and a portion of the Custom Groups directory in Fig. D-5.

To start a custom group, fill out an application in the Custom Forums area. Any Delphi member in good standing can start and be the host of a Custom forum. Custom forums can be open or closed. The host of the forum determines who's allowed to join a closed one, which might be restricted to members of a family or a group of friends. Custom forums can be used by companies as an employee BBS. If the forum is dedicated to a hobby or special interest, the host might want to open it to all Delphi members.

There is a set-up fee of $39.95 and a monthly fee of $15 to operate the forum, but the host of an "open forum" can ask to have the monthly fee waived if usage (by members other than the host) consistently exceeds 6,000 minutes per month. If forum use exceeds 9,000 minutes per month (average five hours per day), DELPHI will also pay the $20 fee for an Advantage Plan account for the host.

Table D-1 Delphi Slash commands and what they mean.

Command	Meaning
-Immediate "/" Commands (Use anywhere on Delphi):	
/BUSY	Disables conference messages
/DATE	Show date
/EXIT	Same as Control-Z
/LENGTH 24	Sets page size to 24
/NOBUSY	Re-enables conference messages
/PORT	Show terminal connection
/PROMPT	Sets prompt mode to MENU, VERBOSE, or BRIEF
/TIME	Show time
/TIMEOUT	Number of "quiet" minutes before auto log off
/WHOIS username	Shows info, if available
/WIDTH 80	Sets your terminal width to 80 columns
Immediate Conference Commands:	
/ANSWER or /ACCEPT	Accept a page
/BUSY	Unable to receive message
/CANCEL	Cancel a page
/DIRECTORY	Show directory
/ENTRY <name>	Shows date member last signed on
//EXIT or /BYE	Leave, log off
/GLOCK	No one can change group's name, password, or privacy
/GNAME <groupname>	Set group name to
/GPASS <word>	Sets group password
/GPRIVATE	No one can join this group unless invited
/GQUIET	No notice is given when people enter or leave group
/HELP	See these commands. For more help, example: /HELP /SQUELCH
/JOIN <groupname or #>	Join a group
/LOG	Save a copy of this in my workspace
/MAIL	Go to mail area
/NAME <name>	Change handle to <name>
/PAGE <name>	
//PASS <word>	Enter password to join protected group
/REJECT	Reject a page
/RNAME <name>	Show real name <user>
/SEND <name> <message>	Send a private message
/SHOWRN	Show all real names
/SQUELCH <name>	No messages from <name>
/TALK <gname or #>	Send a message to group #
/WHO	Who's here?

Some commands are reversed by including "NO" in the commands, e.g., /NOECHO

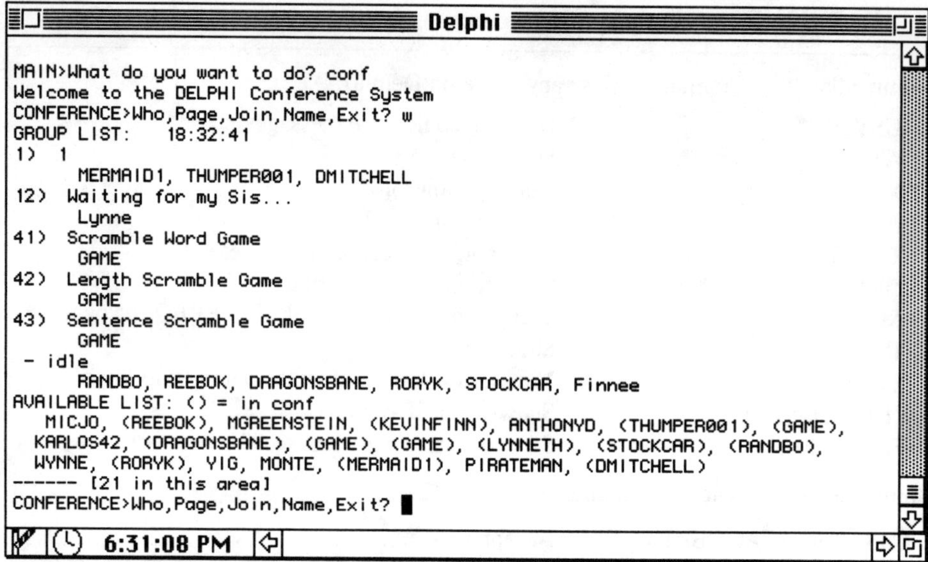

D-3 This was an exceptionally quiet evening on Delphi.

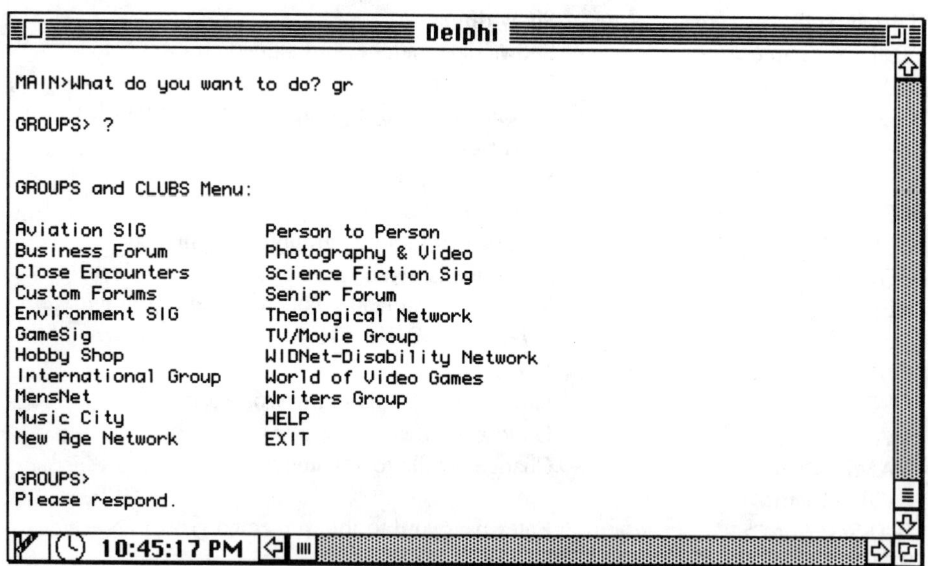

D-4 Between the regular groups and the custom groups, Delphi has something for everyone.

If the forum continues to grow significantly, the forum host can apply to expand the forum to a full-featured public special interest group on Delphi. This could include the addition of downloadable files, announcements, member directory, polls, and banner messaging. If the Custom Forum develops into a full-fledged SIG, the host might be paid royalties for it as well as receiving free online time.

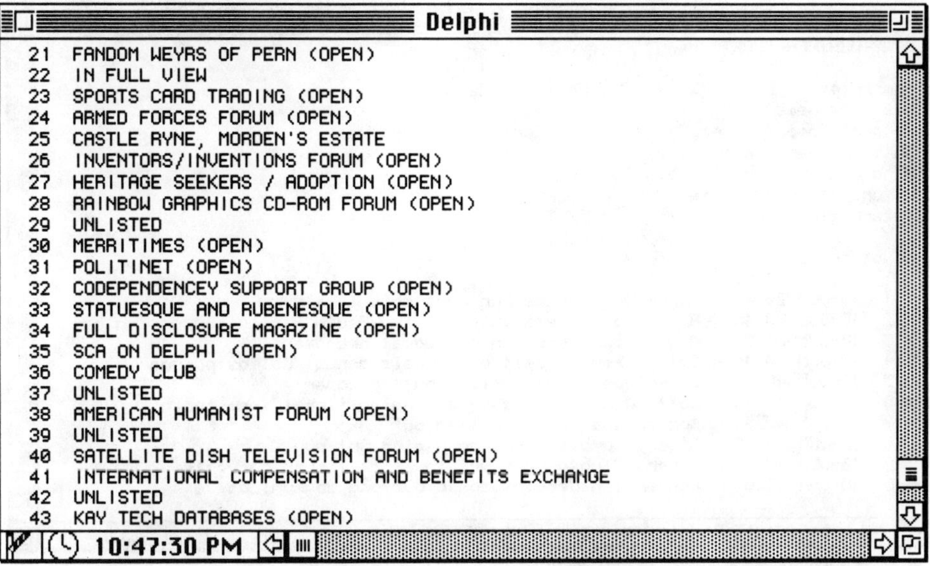

D-5 There are over 50 different Custom forums, and new ones are being added every week.

You'll find lively conversations, busy bulletin boards, and interesting databases in the HobbyShop, Science Fiction Forum, and the Writer's Group. You might also find some of your favorite authors online, especially at the SF Conference on Wednesday nights. The Macintosh Forum hosts frequent conferences with software developers and others active in the Mac community. Its shareware libraries, although not as comprehensive as America Online's, have the latest virus software, system files from Apple, and a wide variety of other materials. Also, Delphites are very good about responding to requests for files available on other services. There's usually someone in the Mac group who has access to the file you need and can upload it to the Delphi libraries.

News, sports, weather

The news area features the UPI National, International, and Human Interest newswires, as well as business news, entertainment news, sports and computer news, and summaries of hot topics from USA Today. The News menu is shown in Fig. D-6. To see the list of current news stories, type scan or just sc. Enter the numbers of stories you want to read, separated by commas.

Delphi's Accuweather forecasts are updated frequently and cover the nation on a city-by-city basis. Additional weather information can be obtained in the travel area from OAG or EAASY Sabre. Views on News is one of Delphi's busiest forums, with as many as a hundred or more messages being added each day. Delphi members have strong opinions on world and national affairs and don't hesitate to post them.

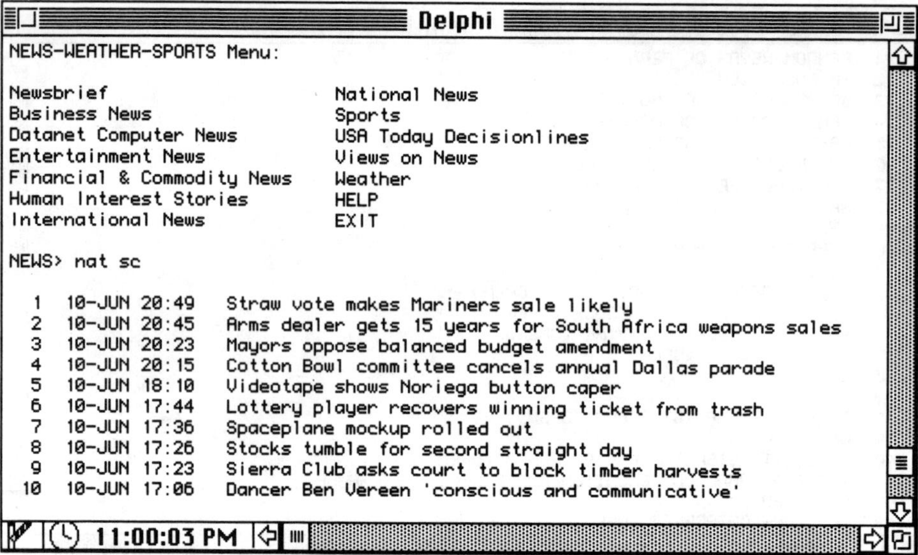

D-6 Typing **sc** for "scan" gives me a list of the current stories. To read any of these, I'd enter the number(s) of the ones I want to see, separated by commas.

Stock Market and commodity market updates are found on the Business menu, shown here in Fig. D-7, along with Press Release databases, the Trendvest portfolio analysis service, money fund reports, and a great deal more information for the business person and investor. The Business Forum is a good place to do a little networking, and its databases are full of interesting articles.

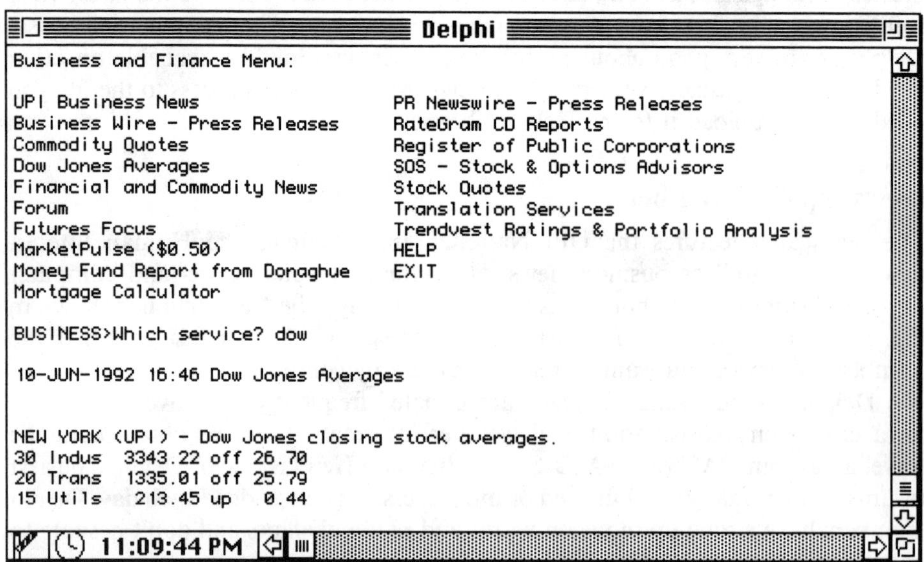

D-7 Note the extra charge for accessing MarketPulse.

Delphi's Reference menu includes two different (extra cost) services to help you find information on all kinds of topics. Delphi provides a gateway to Dialog, a database service owned by Knight-Ridder, with over two million items on file. Librarian is a separate online research service, which will respond to any question on any topic, company, product, industry, or person. Research costs depend on the scope of the search and can fall within the $275–$475 range. Information can be delivered by Delphi E-mail, or for an extra fee, hard copied and sent by U.S. Mail or Federal Express. Also in the reference area is the Grolier Encyclopedia, the same one included in CompuServe's Basic Services. There is an online guide to using the Grolier, but all you really need to know is the command "se" for search.

Delphi's own Kussmaul Encyclopedia might be a better bet if you're looking up anything in the areas of science, technology, or the arts. The Kussmaul is especially strong in the categories noted, although it's billed as a general reference work. To search the Kussmaul, first type Kuss Kuss to get into the encyclopedia, then at the enter ITEM: prompt, type the word you're looking for. The Kussmaul features an elaborate system of cross-references, so you can expect to be steered to other relevant topics as well.

Other items of interest in the Reference area, shown in Fig. D-8, include HealthNet, CAIN—The Computerized AIDS Information Network, and the On-line Gourmet, a database of recipes that I wouldn't exactly call "gourmet," but which are worth browsing through. The Schole area, sponsored by Boston University, contains a few interesting areas, including the International Exchange, which features Terra Nova, an area to encourage international understanding through conversation. Currently, a German-speaking group meets Saturday mornings.

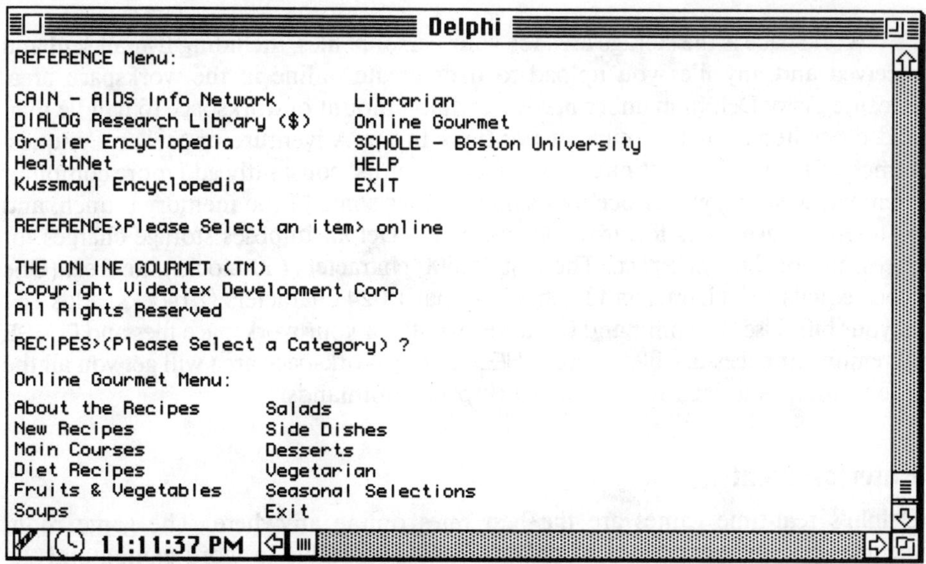

D-8 If you're not sure what to have for dinner, ask Delphi.

using Delphi is your source for billing information and where you can go to change settings, leave mail for SERVICE, and find out what's new on Delphi. The menu is shown in Fig. D-9. There's no charge for being online in this area. Of course, there's also not much to do here, other than check your bills and read about Delphi. There's no "practice" forum, or anything of that nature, but the tips on using Delpi are helpful.

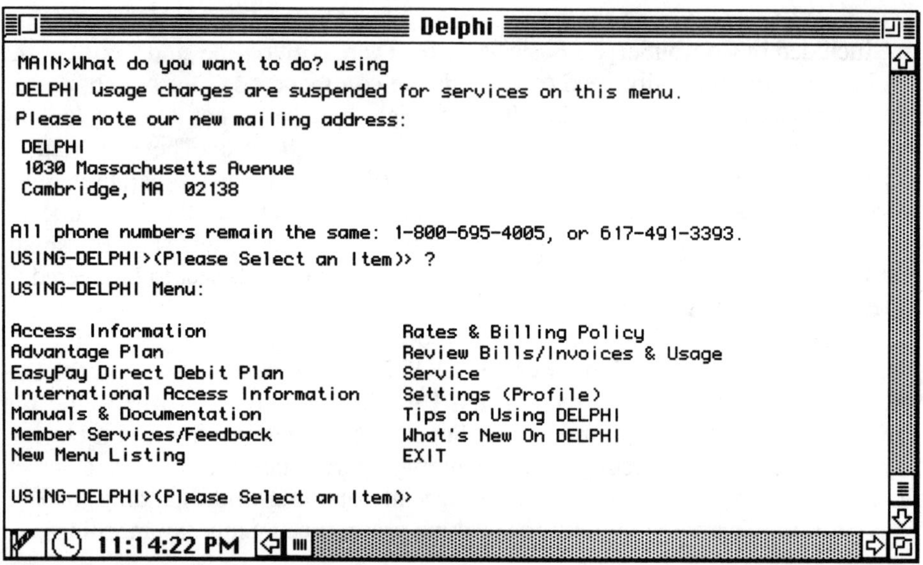

D-9 Be sure to read the information in this area. You could save both time and money.

Workspace is the storage area for your personal files, including E-mail sent and received and any files you upload to it or create online in the workspace area. Because every Delphi member needs a certain amount of workspace to handle mail and other items, such as current positions in the Adventure or Stellar Conquest games, as the service continues to grow Delphi must constantly add more computer memory. Keeping workspace files small relieves some of the memory crunch, and so to encourage users to throw out old mail, Delphi imposes storage charges for excess use of the workspace. The first 25,600 characters (50 blocks) are free. (One block equals 512 characters.) Each additional 1,024 characters (2 blocks) adds 16¢ to your bill. Use the command DIR to see what's in your workspace files and PURGE to remove unnecessary files. Typing HELP in the Workspace area will get you all the information you need to use the Workspace commands.

Entertainment

Delphi's real-time games are the best ones online anywhere. The game room includes five different kinds of poker, Flip It, Scramble (a word game), and the ever-popular Trivia Quest. Poker games are played against live opponents and/or robot poker players. When you start playing Poker, you'll have a "bank roll" of

$1,000. Depending on how well you play, you might double or triple it or blow it all. Choose from Straight Poker, 5-card or 7-card Stud, Draw Poker, or Texas Hold 'Em. Rules are available by typing help in the Poker room. Thursday evenings, there are tournaments, with live players only, no robots. Tournament scores accumulate over the month, and the overall winner gets a prize.

Prizes are also at stake in TQ, more formally known as Trivia Quest. TQ is Delphi's most popular game, with as many as 50 or more players online for each of its three weekly games. The object is to correctly answer multiple-choice questions, while keeping track of your points for betting purposes and exchanging rapid-fire one-liners with fellow players. The questions range from difficult to just plain silly, and so do the players. After you've played for a few weeks, you'll get to know all the "in jokes," and the personalities of the perennial players. As a quick guide for the newcomer, "sprots" are sports, and the cry "no sprots" means "no more #$%^&* sports questions!" Many players use macros, prepared quotes they can access with a single keystroke. Monty Python quotes are especially popular.

You can also play TQ Anytime for practice. Just type ent TQ to get there, and then ent again to enter the TQ room. If others are practicing, too, you can chat between questions, just as if it were a real game.

Scramble is played in both the entertainment area and in the conference area, where it's become such a popular game there are now three different versions of it. The basic game is to make as many different words as possible out of the 16 letters displayed on the screen within the time allotted. The players with the top 10 high scores have their names and scores posted, a distinction eagerly fought for. The scores are cleared every few days, as an incentive for new players to try it. Scramble players have worked out two variations on the original game. One is to make silly sentences out of the letters. The other is to see who can come up with the longest word. Figure D-10 shows a basic Scramble game. To start a single-player game, type go. Multi-player games start when all players have typed rd (ready).

Charges

One of the things many Delphi users appreciate is that the company is willing to send a monthly bill, rather than debiting their credit cards or checking accounts. Delphi offers two types of membership, the 10/4 Plan and the 20/20 Advantage Plan. With the 10/4 Plan, you pay $10 per month, which includes the first four hours of online time each month. Additional use is $3.96 per hour. The "advantage" in the 20/20 Advantage Plan is that your $20-per-month payment covers your first 20 hours of use each month. Additional hours, if you use more than 20, will cost you $1.80 per hour.

Of course, you might also be charged a connect fee for access during certain hours. There's no charge for using SprintNet (Telenet) weekdays from 6 P.M. to 7 A.M. or Tymnet weekdays from 7 P.M. to 6 A.M. and all day on weekends and select holidays, from the lower 48 states. There's no charge if you use PC Pursuit or direct dial either the Cambridge, Massachusetts, or Kansas City, Missouri, local Delphi offices.

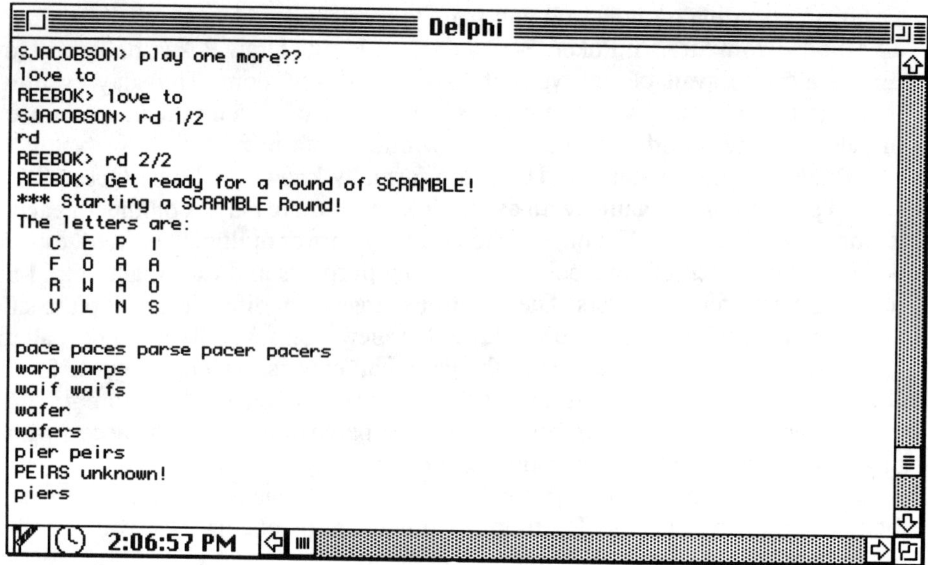

D-10 Spelling mistakes don't count in Scramble.

Otherwise, the charges can add up fast. Weekday access by either SprintNet or Tymnet will add $9 per hour. Canadians using Tymnet will pay an additional $12 per hour, while DataPac adds nearly $26 to the hourly bill.

Another way Delphi can get expensive relates to E-mail. While they don't charge for messages, there's a limit to the amount of workspace you can occupy for free. Delphi keeps your mail in a folder in the workspace area, and if you forget to delete mail you've read, it can pile up quickly and add storage fees to your bill. You'll be charged an additional 16¢ per 1,024 characters over the roughly 25,000 you're allowed for free.

Getting the most for your money

If you're planning to use Delphi quite a lot, sign up for the 20/20 plan. A dollar an hour is an excellent price for online fun, especially considering that it includes virtually all of the Delphi services. Keep track of your hours, either by noting the time as you sign off or by checking your usage records in the Using Delphi area.

If you're reading messages in a forum, read and follow only the threads that interest you. Skipping the others will save time. Use a program like Messenger-lite, available in Icon-tact, the Macintosh forum, to retrieve E-mail and forum messages. Always compose messages and replies offline. There's no point in wasting precious online minutes trying to decide what to say. Also, Delphi's message and mail-editing system is useless. If you want to have legible, properly spelled correspondence, use a word processor and set it for an 80-character line. Use a carriage return at the end of each line, as Delphi doesn't have autowrap. Save your files as text and simply paste them into the messages you address online.

Delphi is more prone to line noise than most other services. Your downloads might be interrupted. Use ZMODEM if at all possible, so an interrupted transfer can be resumed. If you are knocked offline (turfed, in Delphi parlance) during a game or while downloading a file, let the folks in Service know. Tell them what happened, when, and whether you were on Tymnet, SprintNet, or calling direct. You'll generally get a credit for a free hour if there's some record of your being abruptly terminated.

The best way to use Delphi is to concentrate on the things it's best at—conferencing and game playing, and to use another service, like America Online, as a source for shareware and research.

GEnie

GEnie, like BIX, is an acronym. GEnie stands for *General Electric Network for Information Exchange*, which is probably why everyone prefers to call it GEnie. This service came online in October 1985, and now has several hundred thousand members, from over two dozen different countries. Parent company General Electric's motto, "We bring good things to life," could well be changed to "We bring good things online." GEnie has a great many worthwhile features, and its three-tiered pricing policy makes at least some parts of it affordable to all. However, it's not free of problems.

GEnie, like Delphi and BIX, is a text-based service, so you'll use your own telecom program to sign on and explore the services. A graphical interface for Mac users, actually a version of GEnie's popular Aladdin shareware program, has been promised "real soon now" for the past two years. It's still in the works, and as of this writing, there's no telling when (or even if) it will actually appear. GEnie's management has been somewhat less than responsive when asked about Mac Aladdin. In fact, they appear to be stone-walling, particularly online in the GEnie Bulletin Boards, and now suggest that you download a HyperCard-based shareware telecom program to use instead.

Getting online

Signing on to GEnie is different from signing on to most other services. First, it requires that you set your modem to Half duplex (local echo), or else you won't see what you're typing. Second, rather than hitting Return when you see the CONNECT notice, you must immediately (within three seconds) type HHH. Then, and only then, will you be prompted for your user ID. Type it, then a comma and your password, with no spaces in between, like this: XVY61699,cats, and then press Return. Soon, you'll see a Thanks-for-Choosing-GEnie message, and then you'll be shown a screenful of "announcements," essentially what's new on GEnie, plus whatever areas or online merchants they happen to be promoting that day. Figure G-1 shows an example.

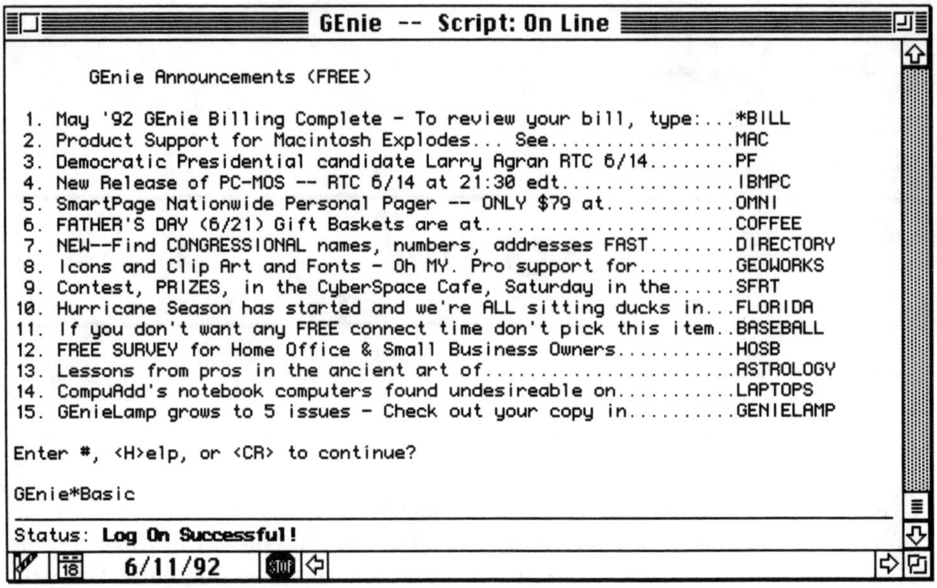

```
GEnie -- Script: On Line

     GEnie Announcements (FREE)

 1. May '92 GEnie Billing Complete - To review your bill, type:...*BILL
 2. Product Support for Macintosh Explodes... See................MAC
 3. Democratic Presidential candidate Larry Agran RTC 6/14........PF
 4. New Release of PC-MOS -- RTC 6/14 at 21:30 edt................IBMPC
 5. SmartPage Nationwide Personal Pager -- ONLY $79 at............OMNI
 6. FATHER'S DAY (6/21) Gift Baskets are at.......................COFFEE
 7. NEW--Find CONGRESSIONAL names, numbers, addresses FAST........DIRECTORY
 8. Icons and Clip Art and Fonts - Oh MY. Pro support for.........GEOWORKS
 9. Contest, PRIZES, in the CyberSpace Cafe, Saturday in the......SFRT
10. Hurricane Season has started and we're ALL sitting ducks in...FLORIDA
11. If you don't want any FREE connect time don't pick this item..BASEBALL
12. FREE SURVEY for Home Office & Small Business Owners...........HOSB
13. Lessons from pros in the ancient art of.......................ASTROLOGY
14. CompuAdd's notebook computers found undesireable on...........LAPTOPS
15. GEnieLamp grows to 5 issues - Check out your copy in..........GENIELAMP

Enter #, <H>elp, or <CR> to continue?

GEnie*Basic

Status: Log On Successful!
6/11/92
```

G-1 For more information about any of these items, type its number.

From here, pressing Return once brings up the Top menu, which lists various GEnie services. Basic Services is a good place to begin your exploration of GEnie because there's no extra charge for this area and it has a fairly comprehensive list of forums and services.

But first, if GEnie isn't displaying itself on your screen as you'd like it to, go to the Billing and Settings menu, which is item number three on the Top menu or number five on the Basic menu, and correct the settings by following the script provided. You'll be able to set line width and number of lines per screen, as well as the delete and break keys. Now you're set to go ahead and explore.

Basically, what's here?

Any menu entry with an asterisk next to it is one of GEnie's Basic services. These are included in the flat-rate fee you pay to belong to GEnie. Unlike the Value and Professional services areas, there's no extra charge for the time you're online in any of the Basic Services areas, except during prime time. Prime time on GEnie means the hours between eight in the morning and six at night on weekdays. Nights, weekends, and holidays are non-prime hours.

Basic Services gives you access to GE mail, as well as over 100 products and services during non-prime hours. Table G-1 shows a full list of GEnie's Basic Service areas. From the Basic menu, you can steer yourself around GEnie in any of several ways. Enter the menu number of the area you want to visit, or enter its keyword, or its page number from the table. Keywords for each area are displayed when you enter the area. Make a note of the ones that you are likely to use often.

Table G-1 Keywords and Page numbers for GEnie Star Basic Services.

Keyword	Page	Description
*ABLE	8011	disABLILITIES BB [*]
*ADS	8740	GEnie Classified Ads [*]
*ADVENTURE	8828	Original Adventure [*]
*ALERT	8011	Law Enforcement BB [*]
*AUTO	8009	Automotive BB [*]
*AVIATION	8009	Aviation BB [*]
*BASIC	8001	GEnie*Basic [*]
*BILL	8005	Billing Info [*]
*CALIFORNIA	8007	California! BB [*]
*CANADA	8011	Canada BB [*]
*CASTLE	8822	Castle Quest [*]
*CHESS	882	RSCARDS Basic*Chess [*]
*CINEMAN	8330	CINEMAN Movie Reviews [*]
*COLUMNISTS	8015	Columnists and Special Features [*]
*DR.JOB	8395	Dr. Job [*]
*DRAGON	8820	Black Dragon [*]
*EDUCATION	8010	Education Services [*]
*ENTERTAIN	8006	Entertainment Services [*]
*FAMILY	8011	Family BB [*]
*FCC	1175	FCC and Open Network Architecture Pricing [*]
*FLORIDA	8007	Destination Florida BB [*]
*FOOD	8009	Food & Wine BB [*]
*GAMES	8012	Classic Games [*]
*GENEALOGY	8009	Genealogy BB [*]
*GENIE	8003	GEnie News, Index & System Information [*]
*GENIEUS	8001	GEnie User's BB [*]
*GERMANY	8011	Deutschland BB [*]
*GIFTOFTIME	8080	GEnie Gift Of Time [*]
*GROLIERS	8365	Grolier's Electronic Encyclopedia [*]
*HOBBY	8009	Hobbies and Leisure Services [*]
*HOSB	8008	Home Office/Small Business BB [*]
*HOTLINE	8350	Hollywood Hotline [*]
*INDEX	8150	Index of Products & Services [*]
*INFO	8003	GEnie*Basic Services [*]
*INTEREST	8011	General Interest Services [*]
*INVEST	8008	Investors' BB [*]
*JAPAN	8011	Japan BB [*]
*JERRY	8011	Jerry Pournelle BB [*]
*JOKE	8006	TeleJoke BB [*]
*LAW	8011	Law BB [*]
*LEISURE	8009	Hobbies and Leisure Services [*]
*LIBRARY	1075	GEnie Info Library [*]
*LIVEWIRE	8020	GEnie LiveWire Magazine [*]
*LOAN	8790	Personal Loan Calculator [*]
*MAIL	8004	GE Mail [*]
*MALL	8014	GEnie Mall [*]
*MANUAL	8910	Online GEnie Manual [*]
*MEDICAL	8011	Medical BB [*]
*MIDI	8009	MIDI/WorldMusic BB [*]
*MILITARY	8011	Military BB [*]
*MONEY	8008	Money Matters & Personal Finance [*]

Table G-1 Continued

*MPGRT	8009	Multiplayer Games BB [*]
*MUSIC	8006	Music BB [*]
*NEW	8003	GEnie News & Calendar of Events [*]
*NEWS	8013	News, Sports and Weather [*]
*NOMAD	8320	The High-Tech Nomad [*]
*NPC	8011	Public Forum Non-Profit Conn. BB [*]
*ORDER	8730	GEnie Product Ordering [*]
*PET	8009	Pet-Net BB [*]
*PF	8011	Public Forum Non-Profit Conn. BB [*]
*PHOTO	8009	Photography BB [*]
*POLICY	8130	Policies and General Information [*]
*RADIO	8009	Radio & Electronics BB [*]
*RATES	8120	GEnie Rate Information [*]
*REALESTATE	8008	Home & Real Estate BB [*]
*RELIGION	8011	Religion & Ethics BB [*]
*RPI	8010	Rensselaer Polytechnic Inst. BB [*]
*SABRE	8760	American Airlines' EAASYSABRE [*]
*SAGETH	8826	Dor Sageth [*]
*SBQ	8841	ShowbizQuiz Trivia [*]
*SCUBA	8009	Scuba BB [*]
*SET	8018	User Settings [*]
*SFRT	8009	Science Fiction & Fantasy BB [*]
*SHOPPING	8014	Shopping Services [*]
*SHOWBIZ	8006	Show Biz BB [*]
*SOAPS	8280	Soap Opera Summaries [*]
*SPACE	8009	Spaceport BB [*]
*SPORTS	8009	Sports BB [*]
*SPORTSNEWS	8013	News, Sports and Weather [*]
*STALADDIN	8016	ST Aladdin Support BB [*]
*STOCK	8008	Closing Stock Quotes [*]
*STOCKS	8008	Closing Stock Quotes [*]
*TIPS	8111	System Tips and Information [*]
*TRAVEL	8007	Travel Services [*]
*WEATHER	8013	News, Sports and Weather [*]
*WRITERS	8009	Writers Ink BB [*]

Type the Keyword at the prompt, or type M (for Move to) and the page number of the area you want to visit. See Fig. G-2 for an example.

You'll find that Basic Services lets you read and post on the bulletin boards on many forums, although it doesn't give you access to their RoundTable conferences or software libraries. It's a good way to find out what's going on in a forum without having to pay extra for it. Go in from the Top menu only when you want to attend a conference or download some files from the library. Basic Services also includes the Grolier Encyclopedia, some news and weather information, sports, travel and shopping, entertainment information including movie and music reviews, and classic games. The Basic Services games area includes some of the same games you'll find on Delphi and CompuServe; notably, Adventure and Castle Quest. GEnie's real-time games, which are accessed through the Top menu, will cost extra.

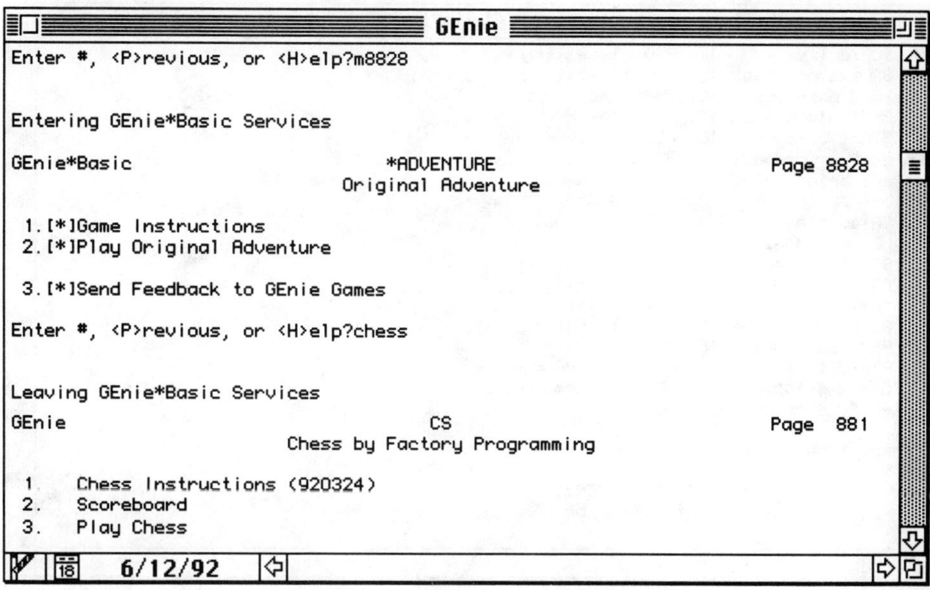

G-2 First, I typed **m8828** to go to Adventure, then I typed the keyword **Chess** to go to that area.

Bulletin boards

When you enter a bulletin board, whether through Basic Services or as part of a larger forum, you'll see a menu of commands or prompts. It's exactly the same menu in every bulletin board. See Fig. G-3 for an example. It's also one of the more frustrating aspects of life on GEnie. Whenever you're asked to choose an action from a menu, for some strange reason GEnie repeats the whole menu before it accepts whatever it was that you've told it to do. When you first enter any bulletin board, your prompts are automatically set to "full," so this entire list will present itself over and over again. To save time and reduce your frustration level, type PRO BRIEF, as I've done in Fig. G-3, to shorten the list to something manageable. Once you get thoroughly familiar with the commands, change our prompt level to "none," and all you'll see is a question mark when GEnie wants to know what you'd like it to do. Of course, you'll have to repeat this procedure in every GEnie forum or bulletin board you look at, but eventually you'll get rid of the menus.

The big top

As you begin to learn your way around GEnie, you'll find Top a very useful command. At any prompt, typing top will bring you back to GEnie's Main menu and will take you from areas that cost by the minute back into the free parts of GEnie, where you can catch your breath and figure out where you have been and where you want to go next. Menu entries on the Top menu, shown in Fig. G-4, take you to a great many more services than those on the Basic menu. Of course, you'll pay for them. Unless there's an asterisk in front of a menu item, it's not a basic

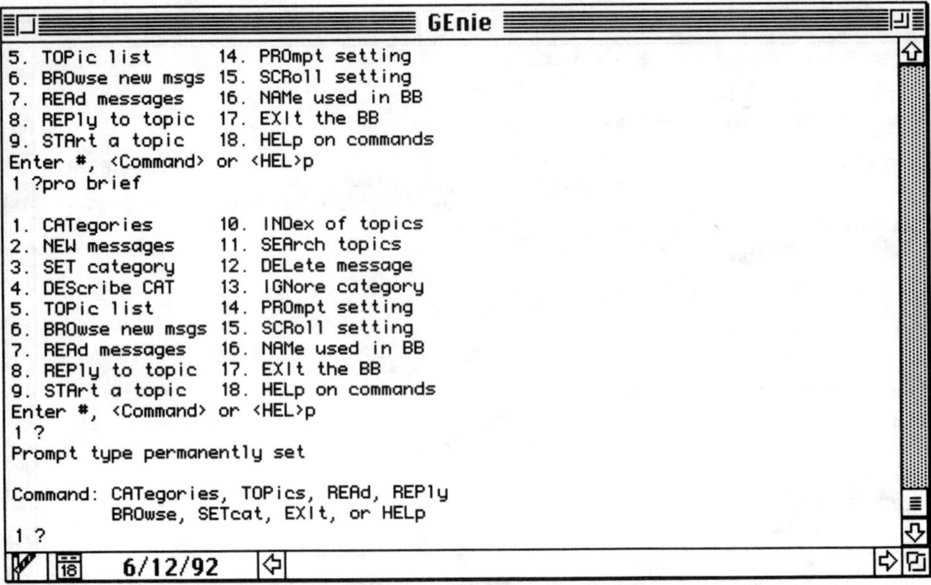

G-3 By changing the prompt, I only have to wait through two lines of type instead of 10.

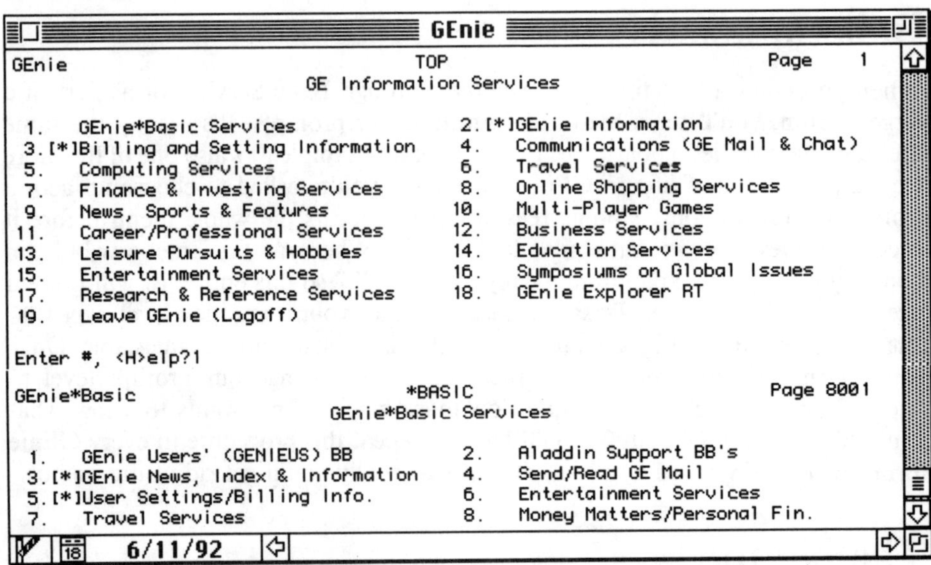

G-4 Mail is Basic, Chat is expensive.

service, which means that you're paying by the second while you're there. Some service areas also have dollar signs in front of their names. This should instantly warn you that there's a surcharge for this particular service. Figure G-5 shows an example, from the Investing area. Before you enter any of these surcharged service areas, be sure you've read the instructions and the fee schedule.

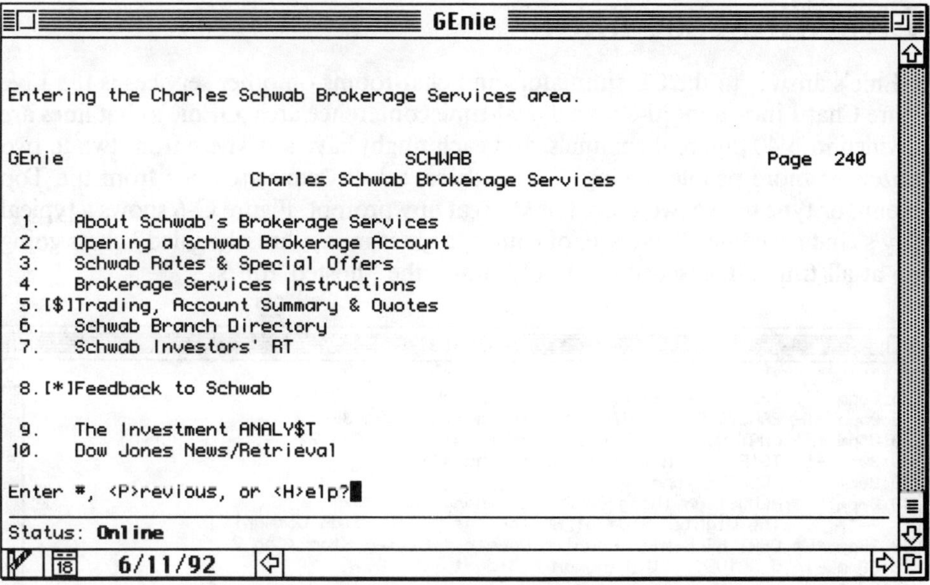

G-5 Watch out for dollar signs. They indicate premium services and extra charges.

Some Top menu areas are very useful. There's a wealth of information and a huge library of downloadable files in the Mac RoundTable. You'll also find RoundTables run by particular software publishers. Scott Watson's White Knight is supported on GEnie by the Freesoft RoundTable. All registered White Knight, Second Sight, or Okyto users can apply for membership, by sending E-mail to user name SWATSON, asking for admission to the Freesoft RoundTable. In the Mac area, you'll also be able to visit RoundTables for CE Software, Word Perfect, SuperMac, and Microsoft. Microsoft's RoundTable supports all of the many Microsoft programs for both Macs and PCs, including Word and Works.

GEnie's Top Travel menu takes you to the OAG, as well as to Eaasy Sabre. There is, as on other services that carry it, a surcharge for accessing the OAG. You will also find RoundTables dedicated to traveling in Canada, Florida, and California, as well as the Adventure Atlas and a more general Traveler's Information RoundTable. There's also an area dedicated to "Symposiums on Global Issues." The forums in this area are also available under other categories, as it includes some of those listed under travel, leisure, and professional services, too.

Other Top areas are somewhat silly. Skip the Banner Maker, unless you have a dot-matrix printer. It simply translates your words into big letters and prints them sideways on the screen. This function is more useful for the teletype user than for Mac owners, who can do a great deal more with graphics.

Soap-Opera addicts can get the latest news on their favorite shows and actors in the Entertainment area, and with no surcharge beyond the normal connect fee. Check your daily horoscope, too, and stop by the TeleJoke RoundTable for a few laughs.

Live wire chat lines

GEnie's answer to the CB simulators and chat rooms on other services is the Live Wire Chat Lines, a multi-channel, real-time conference area. GEnie's chat lines are divided into 40 different channels, and each might have anywhere from two to two dozen or more people talking. To get there, select Communications from the Top menu, or type the keyword Chat or M400 at any prompt. Figure G-6 shows a typical day's chat schedule. There are, of course, a great many "unscheduled" chats going on at all times. The schedule simply shows the "hosted" ones.

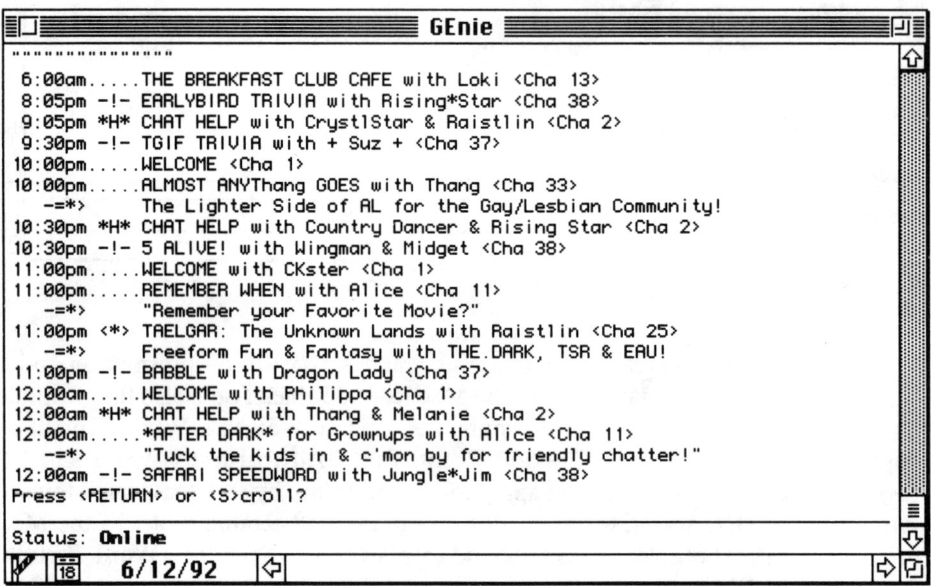

G-6 Chat hosts and game hosts are happy to answer your questions.

If you haven't already done so, you'll be asked to choose a Chat handle, or nickname. If you have one, you'll have an opportunity to change it or agree to it. Whenever you type a message, everyone will see your handle first and then your comment. The handles make it easier to keep track of who said what. Your handle can be your name or nickname, your favorite fictional character, a word that describes your profession or hobby, or anything you wish, as long as it's in good taste and not a word reserved for system use like "Sysop" or "GEnie Host."

You'll also be assigned a job number, which is GEnie's way of keeping track of who's who. Every chat member is assigned a job number as they enter the chat area. Use the job number to send private messages to other chatters or to block messages from a specific user.

When you type a comment, if someone else has just said something your words and theirs might appear to be garbled on your screen, unless your terminal program has a "chat mode" or text-buffer window. If this happens, don't worry.

GEnie is keeping track of what you type, and when you press Return it will appear on the screen as you typed it, and not garbled.

Slash commands are used in chat to move between channels, to send private messages, to change your handle, and to perform other useful functions. As with all GEnie commands, you must type at least the first three letters of the word. Some of the most commonly used commands are shown below.

/BYE—Use this to leave the Chat Lines and log off GEnie.

/CHAnnel #—Use this (with a number in place of the # symbol) to move to another Chat channel. You can change channels as often as you like.

/EXIt—Use this command to leave the chat and return to the Chat Lines menu.

/HANdle NewHandle—This command lets you change your handle while you're talking. Other users will see a message like this:

**<MOMCAT> was <FuzzyPuss>

Your handle is now <MOMCAT>

/HELp—Displays a list of Chat commands.

/MONitor #—Use this command to listen to up to four channels other than the one you're talking on. When you are monitoring, each message is preceded by the channel number of the person talking. To stop monitoring, type /XMO #.

/SENd # message—This lets you send a private message to another user. You need to know his or her job number. (*See* the /STAtus command.)

/STAtus #—Use this to see who's on a particular channel by typing the number of the channel in place of the # symbol. Type /STA * for a list of all users in the Chat area. Users are listed by handle and job number.

/SQUelch #—Use this command to turn off messages from a particular job number. /XSQ turns off the squelch function and displays messages from squelched user again.

/WHO #—This command displays the chat handle, GE Mail address, channel, and home state of a user.

Chatting on GEnie, as on other services, is a great deal of fun. It can get expensive, though, so GEnie has thoughtfully provided two kinds of Club memberships, which could save you some money if you develop a serious addiction to the Chat Lines. Of course, you'd have to spend *a lot* of time on line to justify the cost. Rather than the usual $6-per-hour non-prime rate, you could pay $30 a month for a club membership that gets you chat time at half price, or $3 per hour. This one breaks even if you spend at least 10 hours on line. Or, you could go for the other option, a flat fee of $100 per month for unlimited (non-prime) chat time.

Paying for GEnie

As noted earlier in this section, GEnie is a three-tiered service. Your basic monthly membership fee is $4.95. This gives you unlimited access, at speeds up through 2400 bps, to the basic (starred) services during non-prime hours. Non-prime time is the least expensive time to use other GEnie services, too. It runs from 6 P.M. until

8 A.M. local time, plus all day on weekends and designated holidays. The cost for prime time, 8 A.M. until 6 P.M. on weekdays is considerably higher. For other than Basic services you'll pay the following rates: At 300–2400 bps, $6 per hour for non-prime time and $18 per hour for prime time. These rates apply to the continental United States *plus* Alaska, Hawaii, and Puerto Rico. Because other services charge a great deal more for access from the latter three areas, if you happen to live in one,GEnie will be your best buy.

Access to GEnie is available at 9600 bps, too, but it costs proportionately more. You'll be charged $30 per prime hour at 9600 bps and $18 per non-prime hour. GEnie's *Basic pricing is *not* in effect when accessing at 9600 bps. You'll be charged just as much for Basic Services as for the others. Also, it's important to note that GEnie bills connect times by the second, rather than by the minute, making it even more important that you log off quickly when you're done using GEnie.

Some telephone access numbers carry an additional $2-per-hour surcharge, while others are free. Numbers with a surcharge are indicated in GEnie's phone list by a dollar sign. Figure G-7 shows some examples. Generally, if your local number carries a surcharge it will still cost you less than a long-distance call to a free access number.

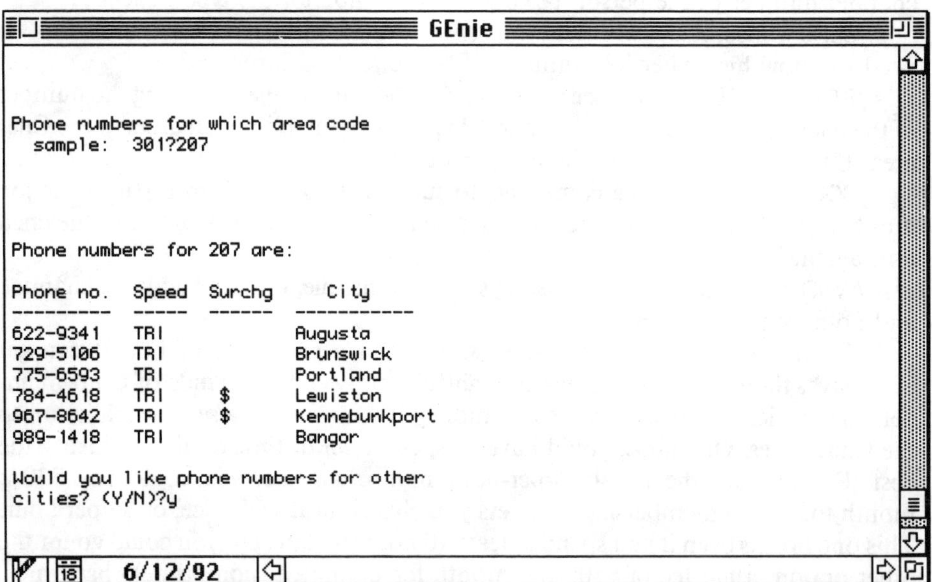

G-7 If you live between Portland and Kennebunkport, check the price of a toll call. It might be cheaper than paying the surcharge.

Premium services

A few GEnie services, sometimes called *Premium* or *Professional services*, carry additional surcharges. The Official Airline Guide (OAG) is an example of a GEnie $Professional Service. Its price of $10 per hour non-prime time and $28 per hour prime time is in addition to GEnie's normal connect-time charges, so prime time access to the OAG would actually cost you $46 per hour, or about 76¢ per minute. Network surcharges, if any, will be charged *in addition* to the standard connect charges and Professional Services pricing, so if you live in a city with a phone surcharge, your actual cost will be $48 per hour.

Dow Jones News/Retrieval is also a premium service. Connect-time fees vary, depending on specific databases accessed. Price ranges are: 45¢–$1.80 per minute non-prime time, or $2–$2.90 per minute prime time. Some News/Retrieval databases also require per-search charges or retrieval charges based upon the quantity of information. For more specific price information on Dow Jones News/Retrieval, consult the online pricing guide. GEnie QuickNews and PhotoSource also carry premium charges.

Getting the most for your money

GEnie's Basic Services are a bargain. News, weather, sports, E-mail, and the use of Eaasy Sabre and the Grolier Encyclopedia can be yours here (during non-prime hours) for about half as much as you'll pay for them anywhere else online. You can also read and post to a good variety of bulletin boards, if you choose to do so, and if you can navigate through GEnie's awkward prompts to get into them. Once you get beyond Basics, though, GEnie stops being a bargain.

One way to economize on GEnie, obviously, is to stay away during prime time. Another is to avoid the chat area, where time passes all too quickly. If you do intend to chat, join the Chat Club on the first of the month, talk every day for a month, and then decide whether you got your money's worth. If not, don't sign up again. If you are good at games, you can win free time by playing the Chat room games and the NTN Trivia games. Download the rules and study them before you start to play the game.

Unlike other services, it's less important for GEnie users to prepare E-mail and bulletin board messages offline, as these areas can be accessed as Basic services. You will find it helpful to download lists of library files, rather than browsing through them online. You can also save time downloading by entering several file numbers at once, separated by commas. GEnie will list all the files you've requested and let you specify a download protocol. ZMODEM is fastest, and most reliable. The batch of files will be downloaded with no further intervention. Obviously, if your Mac is doing other things at the same time, downloading will be slower. To save money, read a book or clean your desk while you're waiting, instead of playing Tetris or working on your novel.

Watch the opening screen for news of special events. These are frequently worth paying for. The RoundTable conferences with celebrities are a good example. For $6 an hour, you could meet Tom Clancy, Steve Allen, and many other famous and interesting people (just not *this* author).

Prodigy

If you were to combine the retailing expertise of Sears Roebuck and the user-friendliness of IBM, and try to somehow turn these into an online service, you might end up with something as well named as Prodigy. "But," you say, "Sears is in trouble, and the IBM is *not* a friendly computer." Uh huh. Now you're getting it. Prodigy is *not* a very intelligent service, especially not on a Mac.

Prodigy first came online in the fall of 1988, with the goal of eventually linking some 10 million households, with capacity for a million and a half people online simultaneously. The numbers are staggering, and although expectations have been scaled back somewhat, Prodigy today boasts over a million members and continues to add new ones at a rate that amazes even the industry experts.

What is it about Prodigy that's so appealing? Well, it's *not* the versatility, that's for sure. Prodigy simply doesn't offer the same kinds of services that CompuServe, America Online, or Delphi do. There's no live chat, for example. There are no libraries of shareware to download. There are no roundtable conferences or multi-player, real-time games.

Prodigy does have a couple of points in its favor, though. The first, and most important, is price. You pay a flat fee of $12.95 per month, less if you choose to pay in advance. For this low price, you can spend as much time as you want on Prodigy, reading and posting messages to all kinds of bulletin boards, playing games, catching up with the news, weather, and sports, making travel plans with Eaasy Sabre, reading the Grolier Encyclopedia or articles from Consumer Reports and the National Geographic, and of course, shopping for everything from computer software to children's clothes—and so can any five other members of your family or household. You can have as many as six different Prodigy addresses under the same account. You can also send up to 30 E-mail messages per month to other Prodigy members at no additional charge.

The other aspect of Prodigy that appeals to many people is its relative simplicity. You don't need to be a computer whiz to use Prodigy. Although critics refer to it as "McTelecom" and say that it is to real computer networking what the fast food burger is to real dining, there are many people who, frankly, don't want to feel challenged by their computers. They want a service that they can use easily, cheaply, and with as little thought as possible. For these folks, Prodigy is perfect. All one needs to do to navigate around the service is move the mouse to an appropriate screen area and click. Because you don't pay by the minute for Prodigy, it doesn't matter that it sometimes seems to take a while for screens to be drawn or for the system to locate and send you your mail. The truth is, Prodigy's speed has been improved a lot in the past couple of years. It's still slow by Mac standards, but if you haven't been on in a year or so, you'll be very pleasantly surprised.

Signing on to Prodigy

Prodigy uses special software and can't be run from a regular telecom program. You can purchase the Prodigy Membership Kit from computer and software dealers or direct from Prodigy. We've seen prices for the kit all the way from $9.95 (refundable) to $49.95. Many modem manufacturers include a discounted Prodigy order form with their modems. It's definitely better to get the Prodigy kit through one of these "special deals" rather than buying it at retail. If you have friends on Prodigy, ask them to see what kind of specials might be available online. Prodigy frequently has "Bring a Friend" promotions, and you might be able to save on your kit or get a free month of service.

In order to run the Prodigy software, you need at least a Mac Plus and at least a megabyte of memory. A hard disk is recommended, although Prodigy can be run from its pair of floppies. The kit includes an ID, a temporary password, and a phone directory listing access numbers for the continental U.S. and Hawaii. (If you live in Alaska, you're out of luck as far as Prodigy goes. It doesn't go that far.) After you've followed the directions for installing the software and launching the service, you'll see a screen like the one in Fig. P-1, asking for your ID and password from the kit. You'll be able to change your password once you're online, but you're stuck with the letters and numbers Prodigy has assigned you as an ID. The last letter of the ID string will be *A*, for the membership holder (the first person in the household to enroll). Subsequent members added to the account will use letters *B–F*. The first thing you might notice about Prodigy is that your Mac's menu bar has disappeared. Even though you might be using MultiFinder or System 7, once you launch Prodigy your Mac won't be able to do anything else as long as you're using the service.

The first time you sign on, it might take a long time for you to actually connect to the service and see the welcoming screen. Your Prodigy software might need to be updated by the host computer, which means that your Mac and the host have to send data back and forth about the modem. Then, you'll have to tell Prodigy who you are, where you live, and so on. Finally, you're ready to explore.

The Highlights screen is Prodigy's Main menu. A typical one is shown in Fig. P-2. You won't see this exact screen, of course, because the Highlights change every day, possibly several times a day as news stories are updated.

P-1 You must enter your ID and password before you sign on. The first time you log on to Prodigy, use the set-up box to enter your local Prodigy access numbers.

P-2 Typical Prodigy, half of these highlights are trying to sell you something.

There are several ways to communicate with Prodigy. You can use your mouse to point to an interesting item or to a command word, and double-click to activate it. You can press the Tab key until the item you want is highlighted, and press Return to select it. You can also use the arrow keys to steer yourself to the desired item and select it by pressing Return. You can type the number of the item or the first letter of a command word, such as j for Jump, and press Return. Finally, if you have an extended keyboard, you can use function keys, or you can use Command-key combinations. Table P-1 lists the common Prodigy commands with their F-key and Command-key equivalents.

Table P-1 Command-key combinations and keyboard equivalents for Prodigy commands.

Command	Type letter, +Return	Extended keyboards	Command key Equivalent:
Action	A+Return	F2	Command-2
Back	B+Return	Page Up	Command-Up arrow
Exit	E+Return		
Find	F+Return	F8	Command-8
Guide	G+Return	F5	Command-5
Help	H+Return	F1	Command-1
Index	I+Return	F7	Command-7
Jump	J+Return	F8	Command-6
Look	L+Return		
Menu	M+Return	F9	Command-9
Next	N+Return	Page Down	Command-Down arrow
Path	P+Return	F4	Command-
Review	R+Return	F10	Command-0
Tools	T+Return		
Viewpath	V+Return	F3	Command-3
Zip	Z+Return		
Escape	Escape key (Not available on Mac Plus)	Escape key	Command-W

Jump is by far the most useful of the Prodigy commands. If you know where you want to go, typing J opens the Jump box shown in Fig. P-3. Enter the JUMPword, Prodigy's term for key word, that describes what you want, and you'll be taken directly there. The Jump window also gives you access to other Prodigy functions, including the Index of JUMPwords; the Guide, which is a set of menus that lead you to related areas; and Review, which gives you a list of the last 12 places you have been on Prodigy. Next takes you to the next screen in a series or to the next page of a multi-page article or letter. Back obviously takes you in the opposite direction.

P-3 Don't start typing the JUMPword until the cursor is blinking in the field. Otherwise, Prodigy won't see it.

Look is a command the Prodigy people hope you use often. It's found in all the ads and takes you into a sales pitch. Typing Z,Return "zips" you back to wherever you were before you "looked." Tools lets you update your personal information, change credit card data, add family member accounts, change your password, and communicate with Prodigy.

What's to do?

Now that you know the commands, where can they take you? While Prodigy doesn't offer the kind of Mac support you'll find on America Online, or even Delphi, it does have a Mac area, of sorts, in its Computer Club. But since Prodigy is not a service that appeals to the technologically oriented, its computer area isn't all that busy or interesting. Where Prodigy shines, in my opinion, is in the area they call the "HomeLife Club." This area includes parenting issues, pets, home repairs, auto repairs and maintenance, and a good deal more. Because these are the kinds of things Prodigy users tend to be most interested in, the "HomeLife Club" is a lively and interesting place. Its Main menu is shown in Fig. P-4.

Prodigy has a gateway to Eaasy Sabre, as well as ties to the Condo Network for low-cost vacation rentals. Prodigy's travel forum features weekly columns and tips from professional travel writers as well as a lot of member input. Prodigy users like to travel and love to talk about where they've been, what they did, and what they liked best about it. With the number of subscribers on the service, you can generally

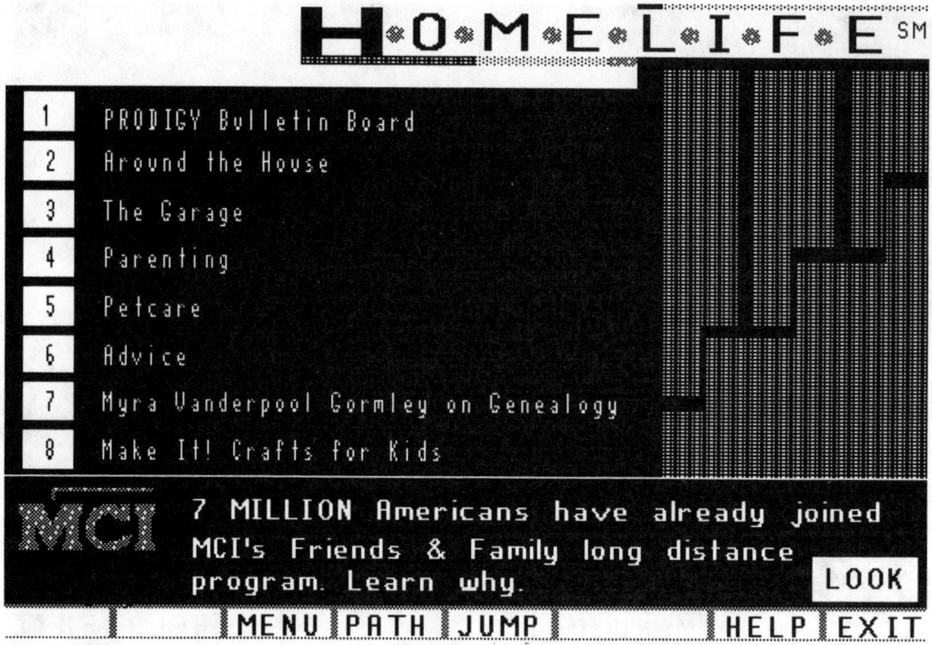

P-4 The Homelife area is one of Prodigy's most popular.

find somebody online who's just been where you're planning to go, whether it's Nome, Nairobi, or New South Wales.

Prodigy's news and weather services are adequate, though not exceptional. The weather maps are nice, especially in color, and don't need to be decoded for viewing. Figure P-5 shows a typical weather map. The news, however, is at the general level of *USA Today*, rather than the *New York Times*. News stories are brief and written simply. Only selected items are covered. You don't get to see the entire UPI newswire as you do on Delphi. There are a number of news features, of course. You'll find columnists Jack Germond and Robert Novak, science news, health news, sports, Washington gossip, and a lot more. There's also a current-events bulletin board, on which Prodigy members post their opinions on world and national affairs.

Shop 'til you drop

If you like watching the Home Shopping Channel on cable, you're going to love Prodigy. Shopping here is even easier than ordering by phone. Cruise through the ads until you see something you want. Double-click action or type a and you've bought it. What's to buy? Literally thousands of items, for you, your family, home, or office. You can shop at the Metropolitan Museum Gift Shop, the Disney Store, J.C. Penney, Sears, Spiegel, Hammacher Schlemmer, MacWarehouse, Highland, Superstore, and dozens of other shops. Merchandise will be charged to your credit card, gift-wrapped if you wish, and sent to your home or wherever you want it delivered. Power Shopping, shown in Fig. P-6, is a Prodigy area that lists special sale

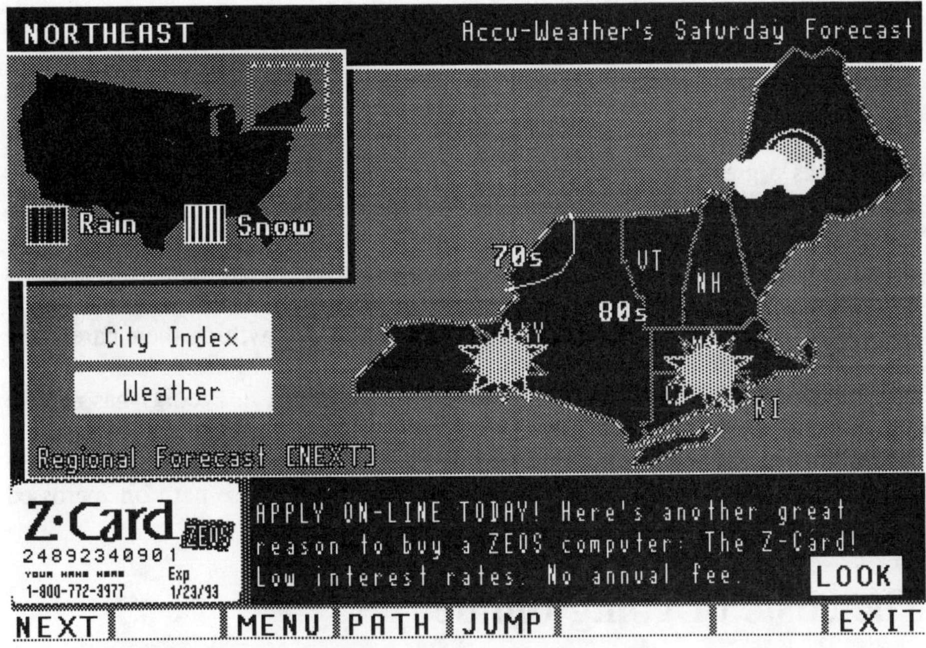

P-5 Prodigy offers national and regional maps and forecasts.

P-6 Check here for special sales and deals.

items and takes you into the Merchant Finder and Item Finder, a pair of helpful index systems that make it easier to find what you're looking for.

Kid stuff

Prodigy has a great deal to offer the younger members of the family. There are games of all kinds, from Prodigy's versions of Hangman and MasterMind, to weekly episodes of Carmen Sandiego. There's a Kids Club Bulletin Board, too. "Ask Beth" is a teenage and pre-teen advice column. Although many of Prodigy's adult users complain about Prodigy's admitted censorship of bulletin board messages, it does mean that children won't be subjected to anything their parents or Sunday School teachers wouldn't approve of. And they can't accidentally wander into the conference room where a "hot chat" is in progress. Prodigy has no live conferencing, so there's much less risk of meeting the "wrong" people online. Because E-mail costs money, it's less likely to be abused on Prodigy, too. You're not apt to be bombarded with messages from someone whose path once crossed yours, as often happens on some other services.

The costs of going online

Prodigy makes figuring out your bills a cinch. The basic charge is $12.95 per month, whether you're online 10 minutes, 10 hours a month, or 10 hours a day. If you want to pay in advance, you can cut this down to as low as $9.95 per month. Of course, you have to sign up for a full year of Prodigy at $119.40 in order to save 23 percent. Or you can sign up for a 6-month subscription for $65.70 and pay $10.95 per month, saving 15 percent.

If your household sends more than 30 E-mail messages in a month, you'll be charged a quarter apiece for the balance. Unfortunately, you can't carry over unused messages to the following month. You can check the message meter, available as an option when you select Write to send a message, to find out how many E-mail messages you have sent so far that month. Publicly posted bulletin board messages don't count as E-mail, but private replies to public messages do.

If you decide to get into the Baseball Manager game, there's an extra charge of either $119.95 or $59.95, depending on which version of the game you choose. See the sign-up information online for more details.

There's a charge of $14.95 per month for ZiffNet, a new gateway service offered by Prodigy, which lets you read computer magazines and download software. However, at this point Ziffnet is *only* for PC users. You can read the text articles online on your Mac, but the software is useless, even if you have access to a PC or to the SoftPC program for the Mac. The Mac is unable to recognize files that Ziffnet tries to send, and no downloading is actually done, although properly named (empty) files appear on your screen.

Strategic Investor, Prodigy's online investment service, will add $14.95 per month to your bill and will let you research companies and money market funds online. Worthwhile? Maybe. It features downloadable (in ASCII or Works format) spreadsheet data. If you're serious about money management, you might want to look into a service that's a bit more complete, like Dow Jones or Nexus.

Getting the most for your money

All things considered, Prodigy is not the best place to go for cheap E-mail and news. GEnie does it as well or better, as long as you're willing to stick to the Basic Services. If you do, you'll save up to eight dollars a month! Prodigy is, however, a very worthwhile service for families with kids. You can give each child his or her own Prodigy account, and let them spend as much time online as they want, playing games, posting to the Kids Club board, and even (dare I suggest) learning from the *National Geographic, Weekly Reader*, and *Nova* features. At least you can be sure they won't see material you wouldn't approve of, as they might on other services. Mostly what they'll see on Prodigy are ads.

If you're not sure about this whole business of going online, tying your computer to another one by telephone wires, try Prodigy for a month. You'll get a taste of what telecom is like, and it will whet your appetite for one of the more powerful services. And, if you cancel within the month, you can get the cost of your membership kit refunded!

Glossary

acoustic coupler (Also **acoustic modem**.) An interface with a miniature speaker and microphone. It seals with rubber cups to a telephone handset, letting you use a modem when direct connection is not possible.

analog signal Any signal that continuously varies to convey information, as does the human voice. Telephone systems are designed to carry varying volume (amplitude) and pitch (frequency).

ANSI (American National Standards Institute) Different devices that use the same "ANSI Standards" can usually be interconnected.

ANSI BBS A bulletin board and terminal standard that allows graphics, and color and screen/cursor control.

answer document A script used by a telecommunications program that controls receiving data from a remote system.

ASCII (American Standard Code for Information Interchange) Specifies digital numbers to represent 128 different English characters, numbers, punctuation marks, and control characters. Some BBSs and the Macintosh extend ASCII by an additional 128 characters.

ASCII download Transferring a file that consists of standard ASCII characters only, almost always human-readable text.

asynchronous Data transmission where the time between bits isn't critical. Start and stop bits indicate the end of one character and the start of the next.

AT commands *See* HAYES COMMANDS.

auto answer Option that lets a modem detect and answer incoming calls.

auto dial Option that lets a modem generate tones or pulses to dial a call when it receives the appropriate Hayes command.

auto logon Automatic process to call a host computer and sign on with the proper identification and password. Also, the script that controls the process.

autowrap A feature of some terminal programs and BBSs that automatically prevents words from breaking by moving them to the next line when a line gets too long.

await character echo protocol A slow way to guarantee text transmission by holding up each character until the previous character has been echoed by the remote system.

baud rate The number of times per second a digital signal makes a transition between states or is intentionally varied by changing voltage, frequency, or phase. At slow speeds, baud and bps are approximately equal, but modems faster than 300 bps usually transmit more than one bit of information for each baud.

BBS *See* BULLETIN BOARD SYSTEM.

bell The ASCII character Ctrl-G used as a prompt signal or to mark the end of a text file download. It triggers the Mac's alert signal or an actual bell on an obsolete teletype.

bell compatible Any modem that conforms to old AT&T standards for specified communications rates.

bi-synchronous A communications system that allows two computers to send and receive data at the same time.

binary Mathematical system using only two numbers: 1 and 0.

binary file A file stored in binary (rather than ASCII) format, usually containing compressed data, graphics, or applications. MacBinary format also includes system data to make a file more compatible with the Mac desktop.

bit (BInary digiT) A 1 or a 0. The smallest unit of computer information.

bits per second (bps) Measure of data bits transmitted each second on a communications channel. In other words, how quickly data can move from one computer to the other. The term *baud* is often used incorrectly for bps. Bits per second is not necessarily the same as baud, and not at all the same as characters per second.

block A group of characters, or bytes, sent as a unit. Data is sent in blocks during binary file transfers. Blocks can be 128 or 1024 (1K) bits.

board Slang for Bulletin Board System, or BBS. Also, an area online where messages are posted for public reading.

BPS *See* BITS PER SECOND.

break A signal to a remote system to temporarily interrupt communications. Can be sent by selecting Send Break from the Special menu on some programs or by typing Ctrl-Q from the keyboard.

buffer A section of computer memory reserved for temporary storage of incoming data.

bulletin board system (BBS) A communications program usually running on a PC or other small computer that allows callers to post notes or advertisements and to maintain "post office boxes" for receiving and storing electronic mail, files, and other information. Also, the "board" itself: the program, computer, modem, phone lines, and all of its files.

buttons A feature of some terminal programs that provides Mac-like on-screen controls that can be programmed by the user and activated with the click of a mouse. These are often used to type out common text strings or to initiate an Auto log-on sequence.

byte In computer processing, an 8-bit number between 0 and 255. In telecom, it is usually a single ASCII character (of 7 or 8 bits).

capture To store incoming text or other material sent from a remote system in a RAM buffer or as a file on a disk.

carrier Constant signals modified by the modem to communicate data over telephone lines.

CB simulator *See* CONFERENCE.

CCITT International Telegraph and Telephone Consultative Committee (Comitee Consultatif International Telephonique et Telegraphique). Similar to, but more international than, ANSI. They define world-wide standards for modems and fax machines.

CCITT carrier Standard carrier signals defined by the CCITT.

CCITT compatible Term used to describe modems that meet the CCITT standards for communications at speeds of 1200 bps and higher. You must have a CCITT-compatible modem to call outside the United States. These standards have been adopted by many U.S. modem makers.

character A letter, number, space, symbol, punctuation mark, or control character. Any piece of information that can be represented in one byte.

character format The characteristics of a transmitted character, including number of bits, number of stop bits, and parity.

characters per second (CPS) The number of characters transmitted per second, based on the bps (bits per second) and the length of the characters (7 or 8 bits) being sent.

chat *See* CONFERENCE.

checksum A method of verifying the integrity of data (not as good as CRC).

CIS B+ CompuServe Information Services "B Plus" file transfer protocol. This is an error-free protocol used only on the CompuServe system and supported by a few terminal programs. CompuServe also uses other standard protocols.

command An instruction that tells a program to perform a particular function. Commands can be typed or entered from a menu.

command mode An operating mode of a terminal program. Information typed on the screen or selected by the mouse controls the program, rather than being sent to another computer.

conference An interactive, real-time conversation between two or more people online. Some of these get very lively. Also called Chat or CB simulator.

connect Two computers automatically acknowledging each other's presence, establishing communication, and confirming mutual standards. Once they do this, the human operator can take over. Usually indicated by the word CONNECT appearing on the screen.

connect charges The cost of time online, usually quoted per hour but figured by the minute.

control character A non-printing character generated by pressing the Control key plus a letter key. Control characters are used by many online systems for commands. Most Mac programs let you replace the Control key with the Option key. Many boards let you type a caret (Shift-6) before the letter key for the same effect.

CPS *See* CHARACTERS PER SECOND.

cursor A blinking bar, square, or underline that prompts the user to type something or indicates where the next letter will appear on the screen.

cyclical redundancy check (CRC) Used to verify the integrity of data.

data Any kind of information.

data bits The number of bits used to make up a character.

database Any collection of related data stored on a computer. Bulletin board databases are usually organized by topic and might also be referred to as libraries. They might contain downloadable or screen-readable text, programs, data, or graphics. They frequently include search functions to help the user locate specific files or articles.

digital signal (*See* ANALOG SIGNAL.) A discontinuous signal, composed of two specific levels or values to represent 1 or 0. Many times, this is an electrical current switching on (for 1) and off (for 0).

direct connect The menu setting that allows communications between two cable-connected computers.

direct-connect modem Modem that plugs into the phone line through a jack, rather than using an acoustic coupler. Because this is less subject to noise or distortion, faster communication is possible.

display . . . with line feeds A terminal setting that adds line feeds for display and printing if the remote system does not include them in the transmitted data.

download To receive data from another computer. Might refer to a text capture or to a download using X-, Y- or ZMODEM, or KERMIT protocols.

duplex mode Setting of a communications channel to control in which direction data will flow. It can flow in either direction or in both directions virtually simultaneously.

duplex parameter Determines whether or not characters are echoed back to the sender. In Full duplex, characters received are echoed back to the sender's screen. In Half duplex, they are not.

echo Function where a host computer sends each character back to the sending computer as it is received, to confirm accuracy.

E-mail (electronic mail) Online message system for sending messages to other service or BBS users.

emulation A process that enables your Mac to respond as if it were a standardized terminal. The emulations available with most telecommunication programs are TTY, ANSI.BBS, Prestel/Videotex, and DEC VT52 or VT102.

error-correcting protocol A method to recover data lost because of line noise during a file transfer. The protocols X-, Y-, and ZMODEM, Kermit, and CIS B Plus are all error correcting.

external modem Modem circuitry and power supply packaged separately from the computer and connected to one of its serial ports.

fax modem Modem including the functions of a facsimile machine. When activated, the Print command in most programs sends a fax instead of turning on the printer. Fax modems usually receive documents as MacPaint images, which can then be printed as hardcopy by a graphics program.

file A collection of information stored on disk.

file transfer protocol A set of rules that helps two computers transfer data. Some terminal programs support two basic types of protocols: error-free and flow control.

flame Angry, or highly emotional, E-mail message or BBS posting. Flames spread: they usually generate other flames in response.

flow control A system where one computer signals another to suspend data transmission temporarily. Typically, a receiving computer has a buffer to hold incoming data while it is processed for a disk file. When the buffer gets nearly full, the receiver signals the sender to pause while it catches up.

flow control protocols Protocols that prevent the sender of a file from transmitting data faster than a receiver can process it. Includes the Normal, Send Lines, and Await Character Echo protocols.

GUI (graphic user interface) A menu- and button-driven telecomm program, designed to make a specific service easier to use and more Mac-like.

handshaking Exchange of signals to establish communications parameters.

hardware handshake A method of flow control using two control lines, usually Request to Send (RTS) and Clear to Send (CTS). Ignored by standard Mac-Modem connections.

Hayes command set Standardized instructions to control modem settings and operations, such as "dial" or "hang up." Named after Hayes Microcomputer Products, the company that formulated them. Also called *AT Commands*, from their initial letters: *ATD* means "dial;" *ATH* means "hang up." Some of the commands get very sophisticated.

Hayes compatible Modems using most or all of the AT commands, so they work like products of the Hayes company.

host System receiving the call.

host mode Program setting that prepares your modem and Mac to receive an incoming call.

ID The user name or "handle," that identifies you to a BBS or online system. Could be your real name, a nickname, or a string of random characters, depending on the system.

idle time Period of inactivity; neither system is sending or receiving data. Usually caused by a human operator taking time to think.

internal modem Circuit card that can be installed within a computer to give full modem or fax/modem capability. Macintosh internal modems are usually used only by PowerBooks.

Kermit An error-free file transfer protocol frequently found on VAX and other mini-computer host systems.

keyword The target word, or desired subject, used in a database search.

line feed A control character that causes the cursor to move to the start of the next line. Telecomm programs let you send a line feed by pressing the Return key.

line feed ASCII character 10, used by Teletypes and some computer equipment to move the paper or cursor down one line.

line noise Random static in the telephone system, interpreted by a modem as meaningful data. Can cause transmission errors l}}ke th*s.

log on, log off To establish or break connection with a bulletin board. So named because each use gets entered into a log, or electronic diary, in the system.

MacBinary A file format that allows Macintosh files to be stored on non-Macintosh computers. The MacBinary format includes a 128-byte header that contains the full Macintosh file name, the file creator and type codes, and other directory information.

macro User-defined short sequence of keystrokes and mouseclicks within a terminal program, usually activated by an on-screen button. You can set these up to type common phrases, check a mailbox, or activate full scripts.

main menu The central directory of areas and activities in a BBS, where you can select what you want to do. Most systems let you jump to the Main menu by typing "TOP."

MNP (Microcom Networking Protocol) A collection of compression and error-correction protocols designed by Microcom and followed by other modem manufacturers.

modem (MOdulate-DEModulate) An electronic device to translate digital data from a computer into analog signals that can be passed through the telephone system. It works by modulating a voice-like carrier frequency; hence, the name.

modulate To change a constant signal in step with incoming data. Other devices can read the changes and extract the data.

network The physical connection between two or more computers (i.e., an "AppleTalk network"); sometimes refers to the connection and all the computers on it.

null modem Adapter plug to connect one computer's modem cable to another's for direct data transfers without using two modems and a telephone line.

offline The state of being disconnected (electrically). Also, to prepare mail messages and other data while disconnected from a service.

online Being connected, recognized, and logged on to a service.

online service Any bulletin board or dial-up database. Usually refers to commercial services.

originate To place a call to a remote system.

packet Short burst of data on a network, identified with an address of a specific computer to use that data.

packet-switching Efficient way of transferring data on a network. All the computers are connected all the time, but they only pay attention to packets addressed to them.

parity A method of detecting errors by adding an extra bit of information that varies according to the combination of the other bits. If the parity bit and the other bits don't agree, the system knows there's an error.

password A unique code to identify a user of a service at log in, similar to a bank's ATM Personal Identification Code. Can be a word, a series of words, or a random combination of numbers and characters, depending on the service.

port (*n*) An electrical connection on a modem or computer, following a specific format that can be shared by other equipment. Macs have modem and printer ports (among others); modems have computer and telephone line ports. (*v*) To translate a program from one kind of computer to another, as in Prodigy's GUI was *ported* to the Mac.

post Instruction to a BBS to accept a message and make it available to other users, just as you'd post a piece of paper on a corkboard.

prestel A Videotex information service found in Europe. Prestel emulation is supported by some terminal programs, including Hayes SmartCom II.

prompt Sign that the host computer is waiting for a response by the user. Usually a flashing cursor or the characters *:*, >, *?*, or *!*.

prompt string Text sent by a host computer to signal a specific user response (e.g., USERNAME or PASSWORD).

protocol, file transfer A set of rules that two computers use to send a file from one to the other. Frequently includes error-correction, flow-control, and file information.

realtime Communication that takes place instantly as users type information across a service to each other.

return ASCII character number 13, used to signal the end of a string or to set the cursor to the start of the next line.

RJ-11, RJ-14 Standard modular telephone jacks. RJ-11 supports single-line phones; RJ-14 supports two-line phones (and will accept an RJ-11 plug to access the first line only).

script A set of user-defined or prewritten instructions to make a terminal program carry out predefined acts (such as log onto a service and then check for and download mail). Advanced terminal programs can have sophisticated scripting languages, with provisions for intelligent responses to a service.

send line feed with return A terminal setting that keeps new lines of data from wiping out the previous line. Might be needed by some systems because early Teletype equipment considered line feeds and carriage returns as separate commands.

send lines A protocol for transmitting data on a line-by-line, rather than continuous, basis.

SIG (special interest group) An area within a service dedicated to one particular topic (such as Macintoshes, scuba diving, or Adventure Games). Frequently includes public messages, real-time conferencing, and data libraries.

smooth scroll A terminal setting on some telecomm programs to make lines of text move smoothly on the screen (like a word processor) rather than jump a line at a time (like a typewriter). More a convenience than anything affecting data transfer.

speaker setting AT command that determines whether the modem makes audible noises on your desk just while connecting, all the time, or never.

speed and format settings Terminal program commands to determine the speed, echo, parity, and word length sent to and expected from the modem.

start bit, stop bit Used to indicate the end of one character and the start of the next.

string Any group of ASCII characters sent in a bunch and (usually) ending with a Return character. Can be text, AT commands, or instructions to the BBS.

sysop (system operator) Manager of a BBS or supervisor of an online service.

telecomm Short for Telecommunications.

telecomm program *See* TERMINAL PROGRAM.

teletype Company that manufactured, and generic name for, combination keyboard-and-printing assembly used by news organizations and early computers. Teletype terminals had no intelligence (not an indictment of that fine company) and could only send characters from their keyboards or print according to incoming instructions. Their data format was also used by early video display terminals and serves as a universal standard for text-based communications. It supports ASCII text only and no graphics.

terminal Any device that transfers data between a computer and a human. Usually includes a keyboard (but can also use a mouse, touch-screen, or voice input) and a screen (or printer).

terminal mode The operating mode in which information typed onto the screen is sent by the telecomm program to another computer (rather than interpreted internally). Also, the setting to emulate specific terminals.

terminal program, terminal software The program running on your Macintosh that transfers information between the keyboard, screen, and modem, interprets certain AT commands, and controls file uploads and downloads.

text-only download *See* ASCII DOWNLOAD.

text only file A word-processor file consisting of standard ASCII characters only: letters, numbers, and punctuation. Formatting information such as ruler width and type style is not included.

transmission speed *See* BAUD, BPS.

TTY Terminal setting that imitates a Teletype.

upload To send a file from your Mac to a host computer.

user Wetware, the human being operating a computer. In telecomm systems, the subscriber (as opposed to the sysop).

VT52/VT100/VT102 Model numbers of, and the telecomm program settings to emulate, terminals by Digital Equipment Corporation. These units can be capable of sophisticated graphics and text formatting.

XMODEM An error-free file transfer protocol used by some bulletin boards.

XON-XOFF Flow-control commands.

y connector Electrical adapter having two jacks and a single plug. In telecomm, used to wire a phone and a modem to a single phone connection. Because of handshaking requirements, cannot be used to hook two computers to a single modem.

YMODEM File transfer protocol, similar to XMODEM but allowing multiple files to be sent in a batch.

ZMODEM File transfer protocol, similar to YMODEM but more efficient and better able to cope with line noise and interruptions.

Index

A

B

C

D

E

F

G

T

V

W

X

Y

Z